ON SCOTLAND
AND THE
SCOTCH
INTELLECT

Classics of British Historical Literature

JOHN CLIVE, EDITOR

Henry Thomas Buckle

———

On Scotland
and the
Scotch Intellect

EDITED AND WITH AN INTRODUCTION BY

H. J. HANHAM

The University of Chicago Press

CHICAGO AND LONDON

ISBN:0–226–07976–7 (clothbound); 0–226–07977–5 (paperbound)
Library of Congress Catalog Card Number: 78–114958
The University of Chicago Press, Chicago 60637
The University of Chicago Press, Ltd., London
Published 1970
Printed in the United States of America

Have you read Buckle's second volume? It has interested me greatly; I do not care whether his views are right or wrong, but I should think they contained much truth. There is a noble love of advancement and truth throughout, and to my taste he is the very best writer of the English language that ever lived.

CHARLES DARWIN

Contents

Series Editor's Preface

This series of reprints has one major purpose: to put into the hands of students and other interested readers outstanding—and sometimes neglected—works dealing with British history which have either gone out of print or are obtainable only at a forbiddingly high price.

The phrase Classics of British Historical Literature requires some explanation in view of the fact that the two companion series published by the University of Chicago Press are entitled, respectively, Classic European Historians and Classic American Historians. Why, then, introduce the word *literature* into the title of this series?

One reason is obvious. History, if it is to live beyond its own generation, must be memorably written. The greatest British historians—Clarendon, Gibbon, Hume, Carlyle, Macaulay—survive today, not merely because they contributed to the cumulative historical knowledge about their subjects, but because they were masters of style and literary artists as well. And even historians of the second rank, if they deserve to survive, are able to do so only because they can still be read with pleasure. To emphasize this truth at the present time, when much eminently solid and worthy academic history suffers from being almost totally unreadable, seems worth doing.

The other reason for including the word *literature* in the title of the series has to do with its scope. To read history is to learn about the past. But if, in trying to learn about the British past, one were to restrict oneself to the reading of formal works of history, one would miss a great deal. Often a historical novel, a sociological inquiry, or an account of events and institutions couched in semifictional form teaches us just as much about the past as does the "history" that calls itself by that name. And, not infrequently, these "informal" historical works turn out to be less well known than their merit deserves. By calling this series Classics of British Historical Literature it will be possible to include such books without doing violence to the usual nomenclature.

Buckle's *History of Civilization in England* is one of those formidable Victorian books more talked about than read. Few have the patience to work their way through all of it. Some of those not dismayed by its length are put off by what they have heard about its general approach, which betokens to them an old-fashioned and misplaced confidence in establishing and making use of scientific laws of human thought and behavior. Others conclude, rashly and wrongly, that a subject such as "The Scottish Intellect in the Seventeenth and Eighteenth Centuries" is bound to be depressing as well as difficult.

Professor Hanham's introduction to this volume should lay all such fears to rest. Buckle was grappling with problems which today must still preoccupy all those students and readers of history who are concerned with the nature of the relationship between social science and history, between the social scientist and the historian. He was endowed with one of the rarest talents a historian can possess: he knew how to ask the right questions. Buckle's pages bristle with opinions, ideas, and speculations. They present a continuous display of intellectual fireworks. One may agree or disagree with his conclusions. But the spectacle itself is instructive and enjoyable.

For those particularly interested in the Victorians, Buckle remains a figure of cardinal importance. A generation ago, the late Humphry House drew attention to the way in which the *History of Civilization* brought together so many of the strands of the "advanced" thought of the early Victorian age—belief in progress, emphasis on statistics, hatred of superstition, nationalism, and interest in physical influences upon the shaping of character. Charles Dickens called Buckle "a great thinker, a great writer, and a great scholar." Many of his contemporaries shared that view. And, as Professor Hanham makes clear, these were by no means confined to the British Isles.

We may or may not agree with them in their estimate of Buckle. But there is no doubt that it is eminently worthwhile reading him in order to make up our minds where we stand. And, when we do so, we find an unexpected bonus. With its vast learning from many sources and its cosmic range of interests, his book shares one particularly endearing quality with its great Enlightenment predecessors: it is, of all things, amusing.

JOHN CLIVE

Editor's Introduction

I

Henry Thomas Buckle was a man of one book. But that one book, *The History of Civilization in England,* was one of the great books of the nineteenth century and earned Buckle instant celebrity. Translated into many languages, it remained one of the most influential of all historical works down to the First World War.

Buckle's *History* is a mere fragment of what was to be a general "philosophical history" of civilisation, not just in England, but throughout the world. Of the twenty chapters that Buckle completed, six were devoted to an exposition of his philosophy of history, seven chiefly to the history of France, one to the history of Spain, and five to Scotland. Only one chapter was devoted to England (about one-ninth of the whole). Buckle must, therefore, be read not primarily as a historian of England, but as a historical sociologist whose main interest was in the development of general historical laws.

Buckle thought of himself and was regarded by the general public as an innovator. But when the two volumes of the *History of Civilization* appeared—in 1857 and and 1861—his ideas already had something of an old-fashioned ring about them. A self-educated man, Buckle lived the life of a scholarly recluse. His world was the world of his great library. And the books in that library reflected an eighteenth-century taste in reading. For Buckle's books made him a rationalist, a deist, and anticlerical, and an enemy of enthusiasm. His historical interests were characteristic of the age of William Robertson, rather than that of

Macaulay or John Richard Green. He sought to create a "historical science" just as Adam Ferguson had tried to create a science of morals and politics. The main framework of his thought can, indeed, be traced back to Montesquieu and Adam Smith. And it is clear that Buckle thought of himself as in some sense in the same tradition as Adam Smith. He compares Adam Smith favorably to David Hume on grounds that were directly relevant to his own *History:*

> Hume, though a most accomplished reasoner, as well as a profound and fearless thinker, had not the comprehensiveness of Adam Smith, nor had he that invaluable quality of imagination without which no one can so transport himself into past ages as to realise the long and progressive movements of society, always fluctuating, yet, on the whole steadily advancing.[1]

Buckle's starting point was the necessity for making broad philosophical generalizations in history as in other branches of study. The study of history, he argued, had hitherto consisted largely in the collection of materials, not in ordering and arranging them.

> In all the other great fields of inquiry, the necessity of generalisation is universally admitted, and noble efforts are being made to rise from particular facts in order to discover the laws by which those facts are governed. So far, however, is this from being the usual course of historians, that among them a strange idea prevails that their business is merely to relate events, which they may occasionally enliven by such moral and political reflections as seem likely to be useful. According to this scheme, any author who from indolence of thought, or from natural incapacity, is unfit to deal with the highest branches of knowledge, has only to pass some years in reading a certain number of books, and then he is qualified to be an historian.[2]

The result, according to Buckle, was that history had fallen behind the physical sciences, and that there were no historians who could compare "in point of intellect" with Kepler or Newton.[3] Much speculation had been devoted to the role of chance in his-

---

1. See below, p. 278.
2. H. T. Buckle, *History of Civilization in England* (vol. 1, London, 1857; cited hereafter as *History*, 1st ed.), pp. 3–4.
3. Ibid., p. 7.

tory, which "in the external world corresponds to that of Free Will in the internal," and to the doctrine of "Necessary Connexion" and its analogue predestination.[4] But for Buckle these concepts were largely irrelevant or mistaken. His own emphasis was squarely placed on the antithesis between the action of the human mind and the action of nature.

> On the one hand, we have the human mind obeying the laws of its own existence, and, when uncontrolled by external agents, developing itself according to the conditions of its organization. On the other hand, we have what is called Nature, obeying likewise its laws; but incessantly coming into contact with the minds of men, exciting their passions, stimulating their intellect, and therefore giving to their actions a direction which they would not have taken without such disturbance. Thus we have man modifying nature, and nature modifying man; while out of this reciprocal modification all events must necessarily spring.[5]

For Buckle mind and nature are not arbitrary: each is governed by laws, and the action of each may be traced in the behavior of mankind. Men's actions may often appear to be arbitrary, or to result from the exercise of free will, but this appearance is a species of illusion. Criminals, for instance, are shown to follow discernible patterns of behavior, reflected in published crime statistics, although the decision to engage in crime is an individual decision. The same is true of suicide: though suicide seems preeminently to fall into the area of free will, suicides follow a well-charted statistical course. So do marriage rates. Clearly, in such cases, there are laws at work which govern human behavior and which may be studied apart from the study of individual thought processes.

At this point Buckle turns to an examination of the influence of nature over man. Following Montesquieu, he argues that "Man is affected by four classes of physical agents; namely, climate, food, soil, and the general aspect of nature."[6] Climate, food and soil define the general organization of society, whereas "the General Aspect of Nature produces its principal results by

4. Ibid., p. 11.
5. Ibid., pp. 18–19.
6. Buckle, *History of Civilization in England* (vol. 1, 2d ed., London, 1858; cited hereafter as *History*, 2d ed.), Table of Contents, p. vi. For Buckle editions, see below, pp. xxxvi–xxxviii.

exciting the imagination, and by suggesting those innumerable superstitions which are the great obstacles to advancing knowledge."[7] His treatment of climate, food, and soil need not detain us. The key argument concerns the General Aspect of Nature, and was summarised by Buckle in the following terms:

> Under some aspects, nature is more prominent than man; under others, man more than nature.
>
> In the former case the imagination is more stimulated than the understanding, and to this class all the earliest civilizations belong.
>
> The imagination is excited by earthquakes and volcanoes.
>
> And by danger generally.
>
> Also by an unhealthy climate making life precarious.
>
> From these causes the civilizations exterior to Europe are mainly influenced by the imagination, those in Europe by the understanding.[8]

It follows that in Europe, with which his *History* is chiefly concerned, Buckle must be concerned not with the laws of nature (which are relatively passive) but with the laws of mind. By contrast, a study of the history of India would consist primarily of a study of "the external world."[9]

At this point Buckle approaches the heart of his argument. He is committed to the notion that "mental laws" are "the ultimate basis of the history of Europe,"[10] yet he is averse to metaphysical systems. "Men of eminent abilities" have engaged in metaphysical enquiries of a psychological type for centuries, yet they seem no nearer to reconciling their differences: rather, they "are diverging from each other with a velocity which seems to be accelerated by the progress of knowledge."[11] Nor was there any hope that "by mere observation of our own minds, and even by such rude experiments as we are able to make upon them," it would be possible "to raise psychology to a science."[12] It was therefore necessary to turn away from the study of the individual mind and to study "mental phenomena . . . as they appear in the

7. *History*, 1st ed., p. 36.
8. *History*, 2d ed., p. vi.
9. *History*, 1st ed., p. 139.
10. Ibid., p. 143.
11. Ibid., p. 151.
12. Ibid., p. 151.

actions of mankind at large."[13] Mental laws must be studied in the same way as such genetical questions as why the proportion of male to female births is so constant. This question cannot meaningfully be explored by investigating individual men or women but only by studying statistical data. So too with the laws of "mental progress." They must be general laws based on general observation, not on the analysis of the individual mind.

Mental progress, according to Buckle, had conventionally been considered in two categories: moral progress and intellectual progress. Moral progress, however, was not a concept with which the thinker might make any progress, for the simple reason that "nothing to be found in the world has undergone so little change as those great dogmas of which moral systems are composed."[14] Moral truths are essentially stationary, with standards of morality ebbing and flowing toward them. By contrast, intellectual truths are constantly changing, and the world can be viewed in terms of the fact that "all the great intellectual systems" of the world "have been fundamentally different."[15] It follows that

> Since civilization is the product of moral and intellectual agencies, and since that product is constantly changing, it evidently cannot be regulated by the stationary agent; because, when surrounding circumstances are unchanged, a stationary agent can only produce a stationary effect. The only other agent is the intellectual one.[16]

Moral excellence, though "more amiable, and to most persons more attractive, than intellectual excellence," is "less productive of real good."[17] The civilization of Europe depends essentially on intellectual achievements, not on moral ones. Religious toleration and the "diminution of the warlike spirit" arise from intellectual apprehensions, not from moral imperatives. Indeed, as for moral principles: "we have incontrovertible proof that they produce not the least effect on mankind in the aggregate."[18] The history of progress should therefore consist in the study of "the progress of knowledge, and the way in which mankind has been

13. Ibid., p. 153.
14. Ibid., p. 163.
15. Ibid., p. 165.
16. Ibid., p. 165.
17. Ibid., p. 166.
18. Ibid., p. 209.

affected by the diffusion of that knowledge." As for the work of "the vast majority of historians," consisting of "the most trifling and unusable details: personal anecdotes of kings and courts; interminable relations of what was said by one minister, and what was thought by another; and, what is worse than all, long accounts of campaigns, battles, and sieges," it is "utterly useless."[19]

II

The tendency of Buckle's argument will now be clear. He was anxious to free history from the historians and to give to it a pattern of organization such as John Stuart Mill attempted to provide for the social sciences in his *System of Logic*. Indeed, Buckle and John Stuart Mill, Comte and Herbert Spencer, may be said to form a group of thinkers sharing much the same preoccupations. They wished to break the hold of superstition on the study of human affairs and to construct a science of society. Where Buckle differed from his three distinguished contemporaries was in his decision to specialize in one branch of the social sciences—history.

Buckle's links with Comte and Spencer were never close. He was never a positivist, and there is no evidence that he learned anything from Spencer (though he read him and acknowledged the fact). Reviewers were sometimes misled by associations between Buckle's terminology and Comte's into arguing that Buckle must have been a disciple of Comte. But he was not. Insofar as his work shows the influence of Comte, it is because he was a close student of John Stuart Mill, who had come to some extent under Comte's influence.

John Stuart Mill was Buckle's closest intellectual neighbor and most discerning critic. He added a whole new chapter to the new edition of his *System of Logic*,[20] which appeared after the publication of Buckle's *History,* in order to demonstrate how closely Buckle's views followed his own.

19. Ibid., p. 210.
20. John Stuart Mill, *A System of Logic, Ratiocinative and Inductive* (5th ed., London, 1862), book 6, chap. 11.

The doctrine ... that the collective series of social phenomena, in other words the course of history, is subject to general laws, which philosophy may possibly detect—has been familiar for generations to the scientific thinkers of the Continent, and has for the last quarter of a century passed out of their peculiar domain, into that of newspapers and ordinary political discussion. In our own country, however, at the time of the first publication of this Treatise, it was almost a novelty, and the prevailing habits of thought on historical subjects were the very reverse of a preparation for it. Since then a great change has taken place, and has been eminently promoted by the important work of Mr. Buckle; who, with characteristic energy, has flung down this great principle, together with many striking exemplifications of it, into the arena of popular discussion, to be fought over by a sort of combatants, in the presence of a sort of spectators, who would never even have been aware that there existed such a principle if they had been left to learn its existence from the speculations of pure science.

Mill also made himself largely responsible for collecting and publishing Buckle's posthumous works, which were nominally edited by his stepdaughter Helen Taylor.

Mill agreed with Buckle

that the intellectual element in mankind, including in that expression the nature of their beliefs, the amount of their knowledge, and the development of their intelligence, is the predominant circumstance in determining their progress.[21]

But Mill was aware that Buckle's zest for controversy had carried him onto dangerous ground. He had the good sense to see that with careful editing the *History of Civilization* could have been made a much better book. In a letter of 1860 he wrote:

The generalities of Buckle's theory are very vulnerable, and I hardly think he could have held by them if any competent person had criticised them before publication. He could have afforded to part with most of them, for the premisses are much broader than was required to support his conclusions, and it is exactly in this unnecessary margin and overplus of premisses that, as it seems to me, the error lies.[22]

21. Mill, *System of Logic*, 5th ed., 2:529.
22. *The Letters of John Stuart Mill*, ed. Hugh S. R. Elliot (London, 1910), 1:238.

What chiefly worried Mill was that Buckle had (without evidence) argued that moral standards are fixed for all time. This contradicted Mill's own view that there were possibilities for progressive improvements in the moral as well as the intellectual aspects of man's nature.[23] What most pleased Mill was Buckle's use of statistics. The idea that there were patterns in human behavior which were discernible by the use of reason had been familiar enough since Montesquieu and Adam Smith. What Buckle was able to do was to use statistics to show that there were *measurable* patterns in the past.

The modern science of social statistics had been virtually created by the great Belgian scientist Alphonse Quetelet (1796–1874).[24] His work was already well known to educated men a generation before Buckle wrote; he himself was a familiar figure in Britain, where he was one of the sponsors of the Statistical Society of London (subsequently renamed the Royal Statistical Society) and of the statistical section of the British Association for the Advancement of Science; and his best-known work, *Sur l'homme,* had been translated into English and published in Edinburgh in 1842. Quetelet's main contribution to modern thought was his demonstration, in highly dramatic form, of the regularities in human behavior, as illustrated by the statistics of births, marriage, deaths; the size of the human body; human intelligence; suicides and crimes. From these regularities he developed the concept of the "average man" (*l'homme moyen*). But Quetelet did not confine himself to the exposition of statistics. He was a man of theory as well. And in the expositions of his general ideas one sees many things that Buckle borrowed. Take, for instance, Quetelet's eloquent remarks about chance:

> Chance, that mysterious, much abused word, should be considered only a veil for our ignorance; it is a phantom which exercises the most absolute empire over the common mind, accustomed to consider events only as isolated, but which is reduced to naught before the philosopher, whose eye embraces a long series of events and whose penetration is not led astray by variations, which dis-

23. Mill, *System of Logic,* 5th ed., 2:528–30.
24. For Quetelet's work see Frank H. Hankins, *Adolphe Quetelet as Statistician,* Columbia University Studies in History, Economics and Public Law, vol. 31, no. 4 (New York, 1908).

appear when he gives himself sufficient perspective to seize the laws of nature.[25]

Or take his remarks about criminal statistics:

> Thus we pass from one year to another with the sad perspective of seeing the same crimes reproduced in the same order and calling down the same punishments in the same proportions. Sad condition of humanity! The part of prisons, of irons and of the scaffold seems fixed for it as much as the revenue of the state. We might enumerate in advance how many individuals will stain their hands in the blood of their fellows, how many will be forgers, how many will be poisoners, almost as we can enumerate in advance the births and deaths that should occur.[26]

Buckle's dramatic use of Quetelet's examples of patterns in human behavior—the revelation, for instance, that the habit of posting unaddressed letters at the chief post office in Paris followed a well-defined statistical pattern—brought Quetelet's ideas before a wider public. Indeed, Buckle's borrowings from Quetelet were largely transferred to the later editions of Mill's *Logic* and from there to a whole generation of university students.[27] Buckle, however, made little attempt to use the statistical elements in his argument in anything other than a theoretical way. It was sufficient for Buckle that he had demonstrated that there were regularities in human behavior. He did not feel called to turn statistician himself.

III

If John Stuart Mill was a discriminating and sympathetic critic of Buckle, there were many critics who were neither discriminating nor sympathetic. Buckle became something of a notorious figure—whereupon his books sold in great numbers, and he was taken up by "liberals" of all sorts throughout Europe. For a generation, indeed, no one could claim to be an educated man who had not read his Buckle.

25. Quoted by Hankins, p. 18.
26. Quoted by Hankins, p. 55.
27. Mill, *Logic* (8th ed., London, 1872), 2:532–33.

In Britain, Buckle was beating at a half-open door. Discussions of evolution and of the authenticity of the book of Genesis as a historical narrative had prepared the way. Charles Darwin, whose *Origin of Species* (1859) was published two years after Buckle's first volume and two years before his second, generously welcomed Buckle as a fellow contributor to scientific advancement.[28] The largely self-educated British middle classes found much of what Buckle had to say about constituted authority extremely congenial. And British socialists of a secularist turn of mind were inclined to see in Buckle a distinguished ally. Indeed, quite the most extravagant praise of Buckle came from the normally grudging George Bernard Shaw, writing to a Buckle admirer in 1894.

> Out of the millions of books in the world, there are very few that make any permanent mark on the minds of those who read them. If I were asked to name some nineteenth century examples, I should certainly mention Marx and Buckle among the first.
>
> As you have read both, you will have been struck by the fact that they both start from the same general view that the particular form of civilization in any place, including its laws, religion and customs, depends really on the economic conditions: that is, on its climate and on the ease or difficulty with which its food can be produced. But Marx followed this up in a direction produced by his interest in labor and his sympathy with its oppression. Buckle followed it up in a direction produced by his sympathy with freethought and its oppressions. Marx was the champion of the slave, Buckle the champion of the sceptic. The result was that in spite of their determination to be strictly "scientific" and to read everything connected with their subject so as to get at all the facts of it, you have Marx coming out as a thorough Collectivist, declaring that since the industrial organisation must be the real government, it had better be made the nominal government too, and so brought under the control of the people: whilst Buckle comes out a thorough Individualist in the old sense, declaring that "to maintain order, to prevent the strong from oppressing the weak, and to adopt certain precautions respecting the public health, are the only services which any government can render to the interests of civilisation." It is quite curious to see Buckle, who on some points sees further than Marx, yet on this industrial question

28. See epigraph, this volume, and *The Life and Letters of Charles Darwin*, ed. Sir Francis Darwin (London, 1887), 2:386.

sticking at the point of mere Manchester School free trade, which Marx left so far behind.

Naturally we too, as freethinkers, are delighted by Buckle's chapters on the history of Spain under ecclesiastical government, and of the Scotch intellect in the seventeenth century. Here he piles up his evidence just in the manner of Marx telling the story of modern Capitalism: the effect produced is one of overwhelming dislike of the whole thing, and complete conviction of its inevitable downfall. And his intense belief in the value of doubt, "the great principle of scepticism," the need of constant innovation, the unreality of mere formal or legal changes in our institutions when they are not merely the carrying out of changes in the minds of the people—all these convictions of his, hammered in as they are with just the right sort of *homely* historical examples to appeal to the man of everyday experience, are quite after my own heart. . . . I wish, by the way, that the I.L.P. and the S.D.F. would take to heart his saying that the study of history will shew, "what men seem only recently to have begun to understand, that, in politics, no certain principles having yet been discovered, the first principles of success are compromise, barter, expediency." . . .

Buckle does not strike me as a very brilliant literary artist. He explains everything very clearly and carefully, and thinks his way conscientiously down into a sentence until he has got the exact point of it; and when his feelings are deeply touched he makes an earnest and often successful attempt to be very impressive in his style. But he does not shew any of those powers by which a great artist with the pen (as distinguished from a good straightforward workman) throws all sorts of sidelights on his narrative by flashes of irony, humor, poetry, wit, tenderness and so on. It says a great deal for him that he makes you value him so highly that you take serious pains to read him carefully through in spite of the fact that he has hardly anything fascinating in his manner of writing. Marx was much more of a genius in this way. But Buckle's weaknesses are more pardonable than Marx's. For instance, both of them make a great display in their foot notes of their immense research and erudition. But the foot notes make it clear that Buckle read all his books with interest and sympathy, not quoting anything until he had taken pains to master the point of it; whereas Marx can hardly be said to have read anything except the bluebooks on which he bases his case. No doubt he turned over the leaves of a great many books and pamphlets sufficiently to make some contemptuous quotation or allusion, or to accuse the author of plagiarism; but he was evidently incapable of tolerating anybody who did not share his sensitiveness on the labor question, and simply could and would not take the trouble to make out their drift. Buckle rises above controversy much oftener than Marx—perhaps because he did not realise as keenly as Marx did the frightful conditions against which he was battling.[29]

Enthusiasm for Buckle was strongest in Russia, where he became one of the favorite authors of the nihilists. Sir Donald Mackenzie Wallace reported that "during the first year of my residence in Russia I rarely had a serious conversation without hearing Buckle's name mentioned."[30] Reflecting on the matter in later years he attributed the influence of the *History of Civilization* to the fact that it "seemed to reduce history and progress to a matter of statistics" and to lay down "the principle that progress is always in the inverse ratio of the influence of theological conceptions. This principle was regarded as of great practical importance, and the conclusion drawn from it was that rapid national progress was certain if only the influence of religion and theology could be destroyed!"[31] The Russian radical press was full of Buckle in the 1860s (the journal *Otechestvennye Zapiski* published the *History of Civilization* in serial form[32]), and there was even occasion for satirical comments about Buckle idolaters. A journalist reported a conversation with a young society lady with advanced views about the status of women, which went as follows:

> "I am reading Buckle," she told me, although I had reason to suspect that she had never read anything before in her life.
> "But you don't know any history," I observed. "What are you going to get out of him? And anyway, why read him?"
> "Goodness! Everybody nowadays reads Buckle," she objected. "There is no God you see."[33]

Buckle particularly influenced the nihilist writer Dimitry Pisarev whose works (held today in high regard in the Soviet

---

29. *Bernard Shaw: Collected Letters, 1876–1897*, ed. Dan H. Lawrence (London, 1965), pp. 456–58. Quoted by permission of The Society of Authors for the Bernard Shaw Estate.

30. Sir Donald Mackenzie Wallace, *Russia* (2 vols., London, 1877), 1:168.

31. Wallace, *Russia* (new ed., New York, 1905), p. 534.

32. N. G. Chernyshevsky, *Selected Philosophical Essays* (Moscow, 1953), p. 146.

33. Quoted in E. Lambert, *Sons against Fathers: Studies in Russian Radicalism and Revolution* (Oxford, 1965), p. 107.

Union) are filled with references to him.[34] Indeed, one of Pisarev's opponents protested that "the simple people, with undeveloped minds and ignorant of Buckle and electricity, are not less capable of feeling oppression . . . and of protesting against it than those who . . . rave about Buckle, stand high above prejudices and are acquainted with the natural sciences."[35] It is reported that Nikolay Serno-Solovevich wanted to write a universal history on the lines of Buckle.[36] And there is even one recorded case where overzeal for Buckle contributed to the undoing of a nineteen-year-old student, Isaac Hourwich.

> Under such a government as Russia then had it was practically impossible for an intelligent, thoughtful, and energetic young man to keep out of trouble long, and in the latter part of 1881 Hourwich was arrested again—this time for organizing "Self-Improvement Circles" and reading to small assemblages of boys or girls Mill's essay on "Liberty," Buckle's "History of Civilization," and Professor Ivanyúkof's "Political Economy Since the Time of Adam Smith."
>
> From an official point of view, the asking of such a question as "What is Constitutionalism?" [subject of an MS essay he wrote at Saint Petersburg] by a nineteen-year-old Jewish boy was serious and dangerous enough; but the teaching of liberty, political economy, and the history of civilization to school children by the same boy was a menace to "social order and public tranquillity" which could not possibly be tolerated. Hourwich, therefore, was sent by administrative process to western Siberia.[37]

For the most part, however, Buckle was not a man who attracted intellectual disciples. While he had predecessors in the eighteenth century and sympathizers and devotees in his own, his work did not contribute to the creation of a school or of an intellectual system. Buckle's influence was to be felt indirectly rather than directly for most of the century after his early death in 1862.

34. See Dimitry Pisarev, *Selected Philosophical, Social and Political Essays* (Moscow, 1958).

35. Quoted in Lampert, *Sons against Fathers*, p. 327.

36. Franco Venturi, *Roots of Revolution: A History of Populist and Socialist Movements in Nineteenth-Century Russia* (New York, 1960), pp. 266–67.

37. George Kennan, "How Russia Loses Good Citizens," *The Outlook*, 26 July 1913.

IV

Buckle's general theory of historical development was designed to enable him to treat of all nations and all periods of time. Had it been finished, the *History of Civilization* would have been a gigantic work. Even before the first volume had been finished, however, Buckle had come to see that he would never complete the work as he had originally envisaged it. He decided to cut down the range drastically and to aim at a history of civilization in England rather than a history of civilization throughout the world. At an important stage in his argument he therefore began to reshape his ideas and to arrange them in national rather than general terms.[38] Whereas the main tendency of his arguments was at first away from things psychological, he now began to turn his attention to the pattern of thought characteristic of individual minds in each nation. The method of analysis to be used was that suggested by the most fashionable logic textbooks of his own day, those of Mill and Whewell. Nations were to be examined in terms of their approximation to types, of which Buckle announced that he was going to consider five:

1. the laws of the accumulation of knowledge (Germany)
2. the laws of diffusion of knowledge (United States)
3. the History of the Protective Spirit (France)
4. the laws of ecclesiastical development (Spain)
5. the method of investigation that [a nation's] ablest men habitually employ (Scotland).[39]

Each nation, in other words, was to be classified in accordance with what were held to be its characteristic habits of mind.

In adopting such an approach Buckle clearly hoped to achieve two distinct things. First, he wished to move discussions about national character and development onto a higher plane than that of gossip and speculation. Quetelet had set himself as a target the organization of knowledge in terms of mathematics when, in a characteristic passage, he wrote:

38. *History*, 1st ed., pp. 210–11.
39. Ibid., pp. 222–24.

The more advanced the sciences have become, the more they have tended to enter the domain of mathematics, which is a sort of center towards which they converge. We can judge of the perfection to which a science has come by the facility, more or less great, with which it may be approached by calculation.[40]

Buckle, by contrast, set himself the task of reducing the history of nations to the study of the logical patterns established by their characteristic modes of thought.

Buckle's choice of logical forms rather than the mathematical simplicity of the social statistician, flowed naturally from the eighteenth-century cast of his thought. By inclination he was a *philosophe* rather than a social scientist. And the method of reasoning which he adopted gave him just the sort of advantages in argument which he found congenial. (There is, indeed, a parallel with Voltaire's *Lettres philosophiques* [*Lettres sur les Anglais*].) He wanted to show that ecclesiasticism was inimical to progress. By arguing not that clericalism was bad *per se,* but that the failure of the Spaniards to move boldly into the modern world and the weakness of Spanish science by comparison with Spanish literature and painting resulted from a failure of the mind, he seemed to destroy the claims of the Spanish church more effectively than any other writer. For, according to Buckle, scientific advance stems from the development of inductive methods of reasoning, and the Spanish church had so rigorously suppressed all reasoning other than deduction from unverified premises approved by ecclesiastical authority, that Spanish science had never even got off the ground. There was not in Spain even an intellectual opposition to priestly tyranny.

Scotland had a special significance for Buckle, for in Scotland alone of the European countries there had been a continuous battle in modern times between ecclesiastical obscurantism and enlightenment, yet in the end ecclesiastical obscurantism had always seemed to win. How was it, Buckle asked, that a land of great philosophers was also a land of superstition? Clearly the question worried Buckle intensely. As a result, much the most comprehensive section of the *History of Civilization* was devoted to Scotland. It was not only bigger than the rest in terms of sheer number of

40. Quoted in Hankins, p. 16.

pages (about a third of the whole); it was much the most power-fully argued.

Buckle was not, perhaps, as scrupulous about details in this part of his *History* as he should have been, but the consciousness that his own powers were failing gave an added sense of urgency to the writing. He felt himself passionately involved in the affairs of Scotland, not merely in the past, but in the present, yet his dearest wish was to turn at last to the history of England[41]— a wish that was denied him, for his health failed as soon as he had finished the Scottish chapters of the *History*.

The aspects of Scottish history to which Buckle turned his attention were ones that worried his contemporaries as much as himself. Why was there such a difference in outlook between the Scots and the English? Why was the church history of the two countries so different? Why had the Scots apparently reacted in such a different way from the French and the English to the eighteenth-century Enlightenment? Why, above all, had Scot-land produced a clerically-dominated religious revival in the first half of the nineteenth century, which had served to make Scotland unintelligible to the English, and had apparently reestablished a system of clerical tyranny?

For Buckle the answer to all these questions lay in the Scottish preference for deduction over induction. In England intellectual development had followed inductive lines—preferring inferences drawn from experience to deductions drawn from hypotheses. In Scotland the preference had been all the other way—deduc-tions drawn from theoretical propositions dominated Scottish thought and made for the tyranny of religious bigotry.

> The Scotch . . . are, in practical matters, not only industrious and provident, but singularly shrewd. This, however, in the higher departments of life, has availed them nothing; and, while there is no country which possesses a more original, inquisitive, and in-novative literature than Scotland does, so also is there no country, equally civilized, in which so much of the spirit of the Middle Ages still lingers, in which so many absurdities are still believed, and in which it would be so easy to rouse into activity the old feelings of religious intolerance.[42]

41. See below, p. 160.
42. *History*, 1st ed., pp. 226–27.

Just how deeply Buckle felt about the matter comes out toward the end of his narrative.

> In no other Protestant nation, and indeed in no Catholic nation except Spain, will a man who is known to hold unorthodox opinions find his life equally uncomfortable. . . . in no civilized country is toleration so little understood as in Scotland. Nor can any one wonder that such shall be the case who observes what is going on there. The churches are as crowded as they were in the Middle Ages, and are filled with devout and ignorant worshippers, who flock together to listen to opinions of which the Middle Ages alone were worthy. . . . And the result is that there runs through the entire country a sour and fanatical spirit, an aversion to innocent gaiety, a disposition to limit the enjoyment of others, and a love of inquiring into the opinions of others, and of interfering with them, such as is hardly anywhere else to be found.[48]

Buckle's starting point, then, was not in fact a sober inductive analysis of historical data but an instinctive repulsion against the manifestations of the evangelical movement in Scotland. In this he reflected contemporary English opinion and in turn helped to intensify it. The Disruption of the Church of Scotland on the issue of spiritual freedom in 1843 was a mystery to English observers. It smacked of priestcraft, of enthusiasm, of anti-intellectualism. Contemporary Scottish debates about the future of Scottish education were equally a closed book to most Englishmen. The Scots seemed bent on cutting themselves off from the rest of the civilized world merely out of pride in outworn traditions. And Buckle, like John Stuart Mill in his *Examination of Hamilton* (1865), seems to have determined to do what he could to prevent this self-immolation.

Nor was Buckle's book without immediate practical bearings. Coming so soon after the Scottish Universities Act of 1858 it was an important contribution to contemporary debate about the future of Scottish education. The defenders of the traditional Scottish philosophical education were already under pressure. Buckle's *History*, it has been argued, "may well have been decisive in hardening British public opinion against the claims of Scottish philosophical education, and against the institutions designed to

43. See below, pp. 393–94.

carry on its traditions."[44] Both English and Scottish conservatives already believed that Scotland should follow the example of Oxford and Cambridge and the English public schools. Now the liberals were being urged to join in condemning Scottish education, first by Buckle and then by Mill. Not that Buckle and Mill were alone in their arguments. Much of what they wrote would already have been familiar to the reader of *The Times,* which had assumed a markedly anti-Scottish tone about the time of the Disruption, and had become a permanent and intellectually distinguished critic of Scottish life and letters.

V

Buckle's account of Scottish history can be read at four separate levels. First, there is an extremely well-argued account of the history of the social structure of Scotland, centered on the question: How does one account for the social importance and power of the Scottish clergy? The answer to this question, for Buckle, lies in certain peculiarities in Scottish historical development in the Middle Ages. Geography and the proximity of hostile neighbors kept Scotland poor and held back the development of towns. As a result, there were only two great estates of the realm—the nobility and the clergy—which were inevitably rivals. At the Reformation the nobility appeared to triumph over the clergy, who were despoiled, but the clergy had the backing of the people and staged a comeback as the leaders of a popular movement. As a result the clergy became the natural leaders and spokesmen of the people and remained so even when towns began to develop. As Buckle once put it in a letter, "the real history of Scotland in the seventeenth century is to be found in the pulpit and in the ecclesiastical assemblies."[45]

The second level at which Buckle can be read is that of the gossip column and the historical debunker. Buckle managed to put together in his history a wonderful collection of historical

44. G. E. Davie, *The Democratic Intellect: Scotland and her Universities in the Nineteenth Century* (2d. ed., Edinburgh, 1964), p. 321.

45. Alfred Henry Huth, *The Life and Writtings of Henry Thomas Buckle* (New York, 1880), pp. 239–40.

anecdotes derived from older writers, which enliven his pages and enable him to make satirical comments at the expense both of the Scottish clergy and the Scottish people. Some footnotes, such as footnote 32 in chapter 1 of this edition which deals with the lack of cleanliness of the Scottish people, were obviously designed to appeal to Victorian prejudices (English travelers in the 1850s and 1860s were often much shocked by the dirt they encountered in Scotland). But the passages are always well selected and to the point. As a result, Buckle's *History* is a treasure house of anecdote.

Thirdly, there is an attempt to write the history of eighteenth century Scotland in Enlightenment terms. Francis Hutcheson becomes one of the great heroes of the Enlightenment, "every where endeavouring to break down that gloomy fabric which superstition had built up."[46] Buckle, however, is not interested in simply giving a narrative history of the Scottish Enlightenment. Much of what he writes consists of a critical analysis of the methods of argument used by four great Scottish thinkers; Hutcheson, Hume, Adam Smith, and Reid. Here his approach presents an interesting contrast with that of modern, more sociologically oriented studies, such as Gladys Bryson's *Man and Society*,[47] where the emphasis is on the empirical approach of thinkers of the Scottish Enlightenment to sociological problems. No modern scholar would accept all of Buckle's arguments on the Scottish Enlightenment, but one only needs to read Bryson and Buckle together to see how one illuminates the other. Indeed, Bryson is inclined to share Buckle's view that what saved the Scottish people from "the tyranny of their kirk" was the habit of "daily rebellion against the government," which kept alive "their energy and acuteness."[48]

Finally, there is the philosophical analysis of Scottish modes of thought, which Buckle himself regarded as his great achievement. Everywhere he writes well about Scotland, but real enthusiasm shines through this analysis. Buckle's philosophical armory is not a very formidable one. He sees that there are essentially two forms of logical argument, the deductive and the in-

---

46. See below, p. 248.
47. *Man and Society: The Scottish Inquiry of the Eighteenth Century* (Princeton, 1945; reprint, New York, 1968).
48. Ibid., p. 6.

ductive. Deductive arguments he associates with the extraction—from general premises about the nature of mankind or of God—of particular conclusions about particular events. (This is not the only meaning given to deduction in ordinary use, where it often suggests moving from a fairly narrow premise to a fairly broad conclusion, in the manner of Sherlock Holmes.) Inductive arguments Buckle associates with the collection of data and with empirical experiment on the lines suggested by Bacon. Starting from a multitude of small items of evidence, one aims by induction to erect a general theory covering all the evidence, and ultimately at a single general theory to cover all observable phenomena. Deduction, according to Buckle, proceeds from the general to the particular, induction from the particular to the general. While deduction has its uses, only induction on Baconian lines (he magnifies Bacon's contributions to science excessively) will unlock the secrets of the world. Deduction is appropriate to theology, which rests on premises incapable of inductive proof, but the world of nature and of rational man is a world to which inductive methods hold the secret.

Buckle's argument is that Scottish thinkers have all in the last resort preferred deductive to inductive methods. As a result, even the great figures of the Scottish Enlightenment committed themselves to use the same methods as the theologians, and hence restricted their own influence. Deduction for Buckle is essentially an elitist method of argument used by people claiming special knowledge. It is used by those who wish to expound the doctrines they hold to the multitude, but the nature of the method is such that it leaves the people in a state of permanent intellectual subjection. They are not encouraged to test premises, which depend in the case of theology on divine revelation and obscure texts, and in the case of philosophy on superior knowledge and intuition. Thus, according to Buckle, however democratic the Scottish people might be in social terms, their thinkers were, virtually without exception, elitists. There was, as a result, an intellectual authoritarianism about the Scots, and a preference for word spinning, which attuned their minds more readily to ecclesiastical propositions (i.e., superstition) than to the propositions of modern science.

In the last resort Buckle's analysis must be regarded as a shrewd but incomplete one. He recognized that there was a strong Cartesian strain in the Scots (and particularly in Hume), something which few others had perceived. And he recognized many of the characteristic patterns of Scottish argument. But the equipment he brought to bear in his analysis in the last resort failed him because it was inadequate for the purpose. His understanding of the scientific method, though his ideas were shared by many of his contemporaries, was slight. He failed to see the importance of intuition and deduction in the natural sciences, where the scientist moves from a hypothesis arrived at by intuition and deduction from known data to experiment and verification in order to establish both particular facts and general theories, and he placed undue weight on the merits of induction. He assumed that the authority of Newton was on his side without taking sufficiently into account the fact that Newton was as much a model for the thinkers of the Scottish Enlightenment as he was for Buckle. In short, Buckle, like so many other thinkers before and since, demonstrated that the attempt to apply concepts derived from mathematics, logic, or the natural sciences to human behavior is fraught with difficulty, and that the greatest single difficulty is the would-be social scientist's ignorance of the techniques he wishes to apply.

VI

Buckle's contemporaries were for the most part impressed by the extent of his reading and excited by his arguments. But they were reluctant to accept either his methods or his conclusions. The youthful Lord Acton condemned him for taking his main lines of argument from others, for displaying less learning and originality than Gobineau (the celebrated French writer who first began the modern study of racial characteristics), and for having less scholarship than a number of German historians.[49] Most churchmen found Buckle's markedly anti-Christian bias extremely unpalatable, and were prepared to go to astonishing lengths in

49. Lord Acton, *Essays in the Liberal Interpretation of History: Selected Papers*, ed. William H. McNeill (Chicago, 1967), pp. 22–40. (An essay by Richard Simpson, also concerned with Buckle, is included in that selection, pp. 3–21.)

misrepresenting his arguments in order to demonstrate their unacceptability.[50]

In Scotland, Presbyterians of every denomination were unalterably hostile. Those outside the ranks of organised Presbyterianism (particularly Catholics) were more favorably disposed. Alexander Russel, editor of *The Scotsman,* is said to have been enthusiastic[51]—as was perhaps natural in the Whig editor of a journal opposed to ecclesiasticism of all sorts. Buckle himself was very pleased to receive a letter from a Glasgow tavern keeper saying that every word Buckle had written about the Scottish character was true, and that he would have written as Buckle had done, had he ever learned to write books.[52] Furthermore, scholarly support for Buckle's account of Scottish history came from an eminent Scottish historian, John Hill Burton, writing anonymously in *The Scotsman.*[53] Burton accepted Buckle's account of the main outlines of Scottish history, but rejected some details.

The pattern that obtained in Scotland in 1862 has on the whole been since maintained. Buckle was widely read down to 1914 by men of an anticlerical and libertarian cast of mind, and was championed by the able Scottish secularist thinker John Mackinnon Robertson, who produced a new edition of the *History.* But good Presbyterians were hostile, and historians took very little notice of him. Today, Buckle's *History* is not included in the bibliographies of Scottish history in use in Scotland, and it is all but forgotten that such a large proportion of Buckle's work was ever devoted to Scotland. The only Scottish writer in recent years to give Buckle even passing attention is the distinguished writer on the history of ideas, George Elder Davie.

Now that Presbyterian prejudice has dimmed in Scotland it should be possible for Scots to read Buckle with pleasure and profit. He is an entertaining writer who appeals to a wide range of readers. There are good anecdotes and broad outlines for the general reader; ideas to be explored (some of them good, some

50. John Mackinnon Robertson, *Buckle and his Critics: a Study in Sociology* (London, 1895) and G. A. Wells, "The Critics of Buckle," *Past and Present*, no. 9 (April 1956), pp. 75–89, summarize the critical response to Buckle.

51. Huth, *Buckle*, p. 420.

52. Ibid., p. 337.

53. For a summary of his views see Robertson, *Buckle and his Critics*, pp. 253–55.

not so good) for the scholar. Above all Buckle stands for organizing historical narrative in terms of ideas rather than sequences of events. Scottish historians have in the past been prone to eschew ideas as dangerous distractions from the main job of getting the facts right. Now that Scottish history is in a relatively flourishing state there is perhaps room again for men of ideas.

For the twentieth century, Buckle is an important historical phenomenon. Almost single-handed he succeeded in reviving the eighteenth-century discussion of the laws of human society, which had lapsed at the time of the French Revolution. John Mackinnon Robertson was essentially right (though his terminology was somewhat unfortunate) when he wrote of Buckle's position that

> he was really proposing, albeit only broadly and not in systematic detail, to begin the reduction of all human affairs to the principle of natural law. Now, though attempts of this kind had been made in antiquity alongside of attempts at a valid physical science, and although famous writers, as Vico and Montesquieu, had done something to reduce the phenomena of societies to natural law, at a time when even chemistry and geology were far from being scientifically grasped, the mere complexity of the problem, and its specially close contact with religious prejudice, have kept it in its pre-scientific condition for the mass of educated people down till our own day. There was, indeed, a remarkable movement of sociological science in Scotland and Germany last century, following on the great and diverse stimuli of Montesquieu and Rousseau. Hume's sociological essays are among his best. Ferguson at points expressly resisted the *a priori* method of Rousseau, which was in part followed by Montesquieu and D'Alembert; Millar and Dunbar applied Ferguson's methods in some detail, and arrived at some solid results; Monboddo is admitted to have anticipated much of the method of the later anthropology; and even Kames, writing his "Sketches of the History of Man" with haste in his old age, helps to the same end. In Herder's "Ideas on the Philosophy of the History of Mankind," again, we have one of the classics of sociology, an eloquent and ingenious effort, on theistic lines, towards a cosmical view of human development. But the reaction after the French Revolution seems to have arrested this as well as other movements of critical and scientific thought for two generations. Herder's book was well translated into English in the year 1799, and a second edition was called for in 1801; but the impulse went no further, and the translation was

never reprinted. It seemed as if the forward-looking people of that time were crushed out by the triumph of the animal instincts of strife and reaction. Buckle was thus, as it were, resuscitating a buried movement and reviving a forgotten interest.[54]

It was not Buckle's fault that his *History* flashed like a meteor across the firmament and disappeared. He was working in an environment where his views were likely to be more popular than respectable, and academic opinion was sure to be dead against him. Yet no one can read Buckle without recognizing that he was a thinker of real imagination and grasp. Like Lord Acton, his ambition was to write a history of liberty; like Lord Acton, he failed to complete it, but his actual achievement was no less impressive than Acton's, and on many counts very much more impressive. The Catholic Acton and the Deist Buckle should be read together.

A Note on Buckle's Work and the Present Text

Henry Thomas Buckle (1821–62) was the only son of a London shipowner, Thomas Henry Buckle. A sickly child, he managed to avoid formal education and spent but a short time in his father's firm. After the death of his father in 1840, he devoted himself entirely to travel and to scholarship. His life after 1842 centered on the great library he amassed in London. The first volume of *The History of Civilization in England,* which Buckle described as a "general introduction," appeared in 1857 and made an enormous stir. A second edition with a much more extensive table of contents was issued in 1858. The only other volume to be completed was published in 1861. Subsequent editions of the *History* were usually divided into three volumes, the first containing Buckle's general propositions about History, the second his account of France and Spain, and the third his history of Scotland. After Buckle's death in Damascus in 1862 his unpublished papers were collected by John Stuart Mill and by his stepdaughter Helen Taylor. They were published by Helen Taylor in 1872, in three volumes, as *The Miscellaneous and Posthumous Works of Henry Thomas Buckle.*

54. Robertson, *Buckle and his Critics,* pp. 7–8.

There are two biographies of Buckle, Giles St. Aubyn's *A Victorian Eminence: The Life and Works of Henry Thomas Buckle* (London, 1958), and Alfred Henry Huth's *The Life and Writings of Henry Thomas Buckle* (2 vols., London, 1880; 1 vol. ed., New York, 1880). In addition, John Mackinnon Robertson published two important critical studies: *Buckle and his Critics: A Study in Sociology* (London, 1895) and *Introduction to the History of Civilization in England by Henry Thomas Buckle, New and Revised Edition, with Annotations and an Introduction* (London, 1904). These are the books to which the beginner must turn first in order to learn about Buckle's thought. The number of commentaries on Buckle's work is enormous. Among the most interesting is that of the great Czech scholar-statesman, Thomas G. Masaryk, whose *Theorie dějin dle zasad T. H. Bucklea* ("Theory of History according to the Principles of T. H. Buckle") of 1884 shows him to have been a keen student of Buckle.

It is perhaps worth adding that Buckle's contemporary, the American scientist and publicist John William Draper, published *A History of the Intellectual Development of Europe* in New York in 1863, in which he independently argued much the same case as Buckle had done, notably with regard to physical causation. Draper's book, like Buckle's, was at once translated into many languages, but it failed to create as much excitement in Europe as Buckle's book had done, perhaps because of a certain pedestrian quality in the presentation, perhaps because of a lack of scholarly apparatus. As a result, Draper came to be regarded in Europe as a sort of poor man's Buckle.

The present edition is based entirely on the editions of Buckle's *History* published during his lifetime. These consisted of two editions of volume one (the second differing from the first only by the addition of an analytical table of contents) and a single edition of volume two. All subsequent reprints have been more or less faithful copies of the second edition of volume one and the first edition of volume two. The text given here consists of the introductory matter contained in pages 224–31 of volume one of the first edition (London, 1857) and the Scottish sections of the first and only edition of volume two (London, 1861), viz. pages 157–601, plus Buckle's "Analytical Table of Contents." Chapters 1 and 2 of this edition (chapters 2 and 3 of the original) have been slightly shortened. Most passages relating to the Highlands of Scotland have been omitted because they were so manifestly based on prejudiced sources (Buckle was inclined to regard the Highlanders as ignorant barbarians). And there has been some pruning here and there. But no substantial changes have been made. All omissions are indicated by ellipses.

There is no modern book which covers quite the same ground as Buckle. T. C. Smout, *A History of the Scottish People, 1560–1830* (London, 1969), covers much the same period, but emphasises social history. Douglas Nobbs, *England and Scotland, 1560–1707* (London, 1952), discusses the differences in ideas and attitudes of the English and Scottish peoples after the Reformation, a topic of great interest to Buckle. On the Reformation itself the outstanding book is Gordon Donaldson, *The Scottish Reformation* (Cambridge, 1960). On the eighteenth-century enlightenment there is no single book which covers the whole ground, but Gladys Bryson, *Man and Society: the Scottish Inquiry of the Eighteenth Century* (Princeton, 1945, repr. New York, 1968), and Ernest C. Mossner, *The Life of David Hume* (Edinburgh and London, 1954), are good. There are a number of competent one-volume histories of Scotland, notably R. L. Mackie, *Short History of Scotland* (2d ed., London, 1962), J. D. Mackie, *History of Scotland* (London, 1966), and Janet R. Glover, *The Story of Scotland* (London, 1960), and there is a good *Church History of Scotland* by J. H. S. Burleigh (London, 1960); but the standard work on Scottish history is the *Edinburgh History of Scotland,* edited by Gordon Donaldson. Of this, two volumes have so far appeared: volume 3, *Scotland: James V–James VII,* by Gordon Donaldson (Edinburgh and London, 1965), and volume 4, *Scotland: 1689 to the Present,* by William Ferguson (Edinburgh and London, 1968).

H. J. HANHAM

ON SCOTLAND
AND THE
SCOTCH
INTELLECT

Analytical Table of Contents

3

CHAPTER II

CONDITION OF SCOTLAND IN THE
FIFTEENTH AND SIXTEENTH CENTURIES

From this moment, the nobles hated the Church more than ever. Their hatred brought about the Reformation

Active measures of the government against the nobles

The nobles revenged themselves by becoming Reformers

James V., on the other hand, threw himself entirely into the arms of the Church

As the nobles took the opposite side, and as the people had no influence, the success or failure of the Reformation in Scotland was simply a question of the success or failure of the aristocratic power

In 1542, the nobles openly refused obedience to James V.; and their treatment of him at this critical period of his life, broke his heart

Directly he died, they regained authority. The clergy were displaced, and measures favourable to Protestantism were adopted

In 1546, Cardinal Beaton was assassinated, and Knox began his career

Subsequent proceedings of Knox

While Knox was abroad, the nobles established the Reformation

He returned to Scotland in 1559, by which time the struggle was nearly over

In 1559, the queen regent was deposed; the nobles became supreme; and, in 1560, the Church was destroyed

Immediately this revolution was completed, the nobles and the preachers began to quarrel about the wealth of the Church

The nobles, thinking that they ought to have it, took it into their own hands

Thereupon, the Protestant preachers said that the nobles were instigated by the devil

Morton, who was at the head of the nobility, became enraged at the proceedings of the new clergy, and persecuted them

A complete rupture between the two classes

The clergy, finding themselves despised by the governing class, united themselves heartily with the people, and advocated democratic principles

In 1574, Melville became their leader. Under his auspices, that great struggle began, which never stopped until, sixty years later, it produced the rebellion against Charles I.

CHAPTER III

CONDITION OF SCOTLAND DURING THE
SEVENTEENTH AND EIGHTEENTH CENTURIES

7

CHAPTER V

AN EXAMINATION OF THE SCOTCH INTELLECT
DURING THE EIGHTEENTH CENTURY

Introduction

The greater the similarity between two nations, the more easily can we trace the consequences of any single divergence, and the more conspicuous do the laws of that divergence become. Such an opportunity occurs in the history of Scotland, as compared with that of England. Here we have two nations, bordering on each other, speaking the same language, reading the same literature, and knit together by the same interests. And yet it is a truth, which seems to have escaped attention, but the proof of which I shall fully detail, that until the last thirty or forty years, the Scotch intellect has been even more entirely deductive than the English intellect has been inductive. The inductive tendencies of the English mind, and the almost superstitious reverence with which we cling to them, have been noticed with regret by a few, and a very few, of our ablest men.[1] On the other hand, in Scotland, particularly during the eighteenth century, the great thinkers, with hardly an exception, adopted the deductive method. Now, the characteristic of deduction, when applied to branches of knowledge not yet ripe for it, is, that it increases the number of hypotheses from which we reason downwards, and brings into disrepute the slow and patient ascent peculiar to inductive inquiry. This desire to grasp at truth by speculative, and, as it were,

1. Particularly Coleridge and Mr. John Mill. But, with the greatest possible respect for Mr. Mill's profound work on Logic, I must venture to think that he has ascribed too much to the influence of Bacon in encouraging the inductive spirit, and too little to those other circumstances which gave rise to the Baconian philosophy, and to which that philosophy owes its success.

foregone conclusions, has often led the way to great discoveries; and no one, properly instructed, will deny its immense value. But when it is universally followed, there is imminent danger lest the observation of mere empirical uniformities should be neglected; and lest thinking men should grow impatient at those small and proximate generalizations, which, according to the inductive scheme, must invariably precede the larger and higher ones. Whenever this impatience actually occurs, there is produced serious mischief. For these lower generalizations form a neutral ground, which speculative minds and practical minds possess in common, and on which they meet. If this ground is cut away, the meeting is impossible. In such case, there arises among the scientific classes an undue contempt for inferences which the experience of the vulgar has drawn, but of which the laws seem inexplicable; while, among the practical classes, there arises a disregard of speculations so wide, so magnificent, and of which the intermediate and preliminary steps are hidden from their gaze. The results of this in Scotland are highly curious, and are, in several respects, similar to those which we find in Germany; since in both countries the intellectual classes have long been remarkable for their boldness of investigation and their freedom from prejudice, and the people at large equally remarkable for the number of their superstitions and the strength of their prejudices. In Scotland, this is even more striking than in Germany; because the Scotch, owing to causes which have been little studied, are, in practical matters, not only industrious and provident, but singularly shrewd. This, however, in the higher departments of life, has availed them nothing; and, while there is no country which possesses a more original, inquisitive, and innovating literature than Scotland does, so also is there no country, equally civilized, in which so much of the spirit of the Middle Ages still lingers, in which so many absurdities are still believed, and in which it would be so easy to rouse into activity the old feelings of religious intolerance.

The divergence, and indeed the hostility, thus established between the practical and speculative classes, is the most important fact in the history of Scotland, and is partly cause and partly effect of the predominance of the deductive method. For this descending scheme being opposed to the ascending or inductive scheme, neglects those lower generalizations which are the only ones that both classes understand, and, therefore, the only ones where they sympathize with each other. The inductive method, as popularized by Bacon, gave great prominence to these lower or proximate truths; and this, though it has often made the intellectual classes in England too utilitarian, has at all events saved them from that state of isolation in which they would otherwise have remained. But in Scotland the isolation has been almost complete, because the deductive method has been almost universal. Full evidence of this will be collected in [later chapters]; but, that I may not leave the subject entirely without illustration, I will notice very briefly the principal instances that occurred during those three generations in which Scotch literature reached its highest excellence.

During this period, which comprises nearly a century, the tendency was so unmistakeable, as to form a striking phenomenon in the annals of the human mind. The first great symptom was a movement begun by Simson, professor at the University of Glasgow, and continued by Stewart, professor at the University of Edinburgh. These able men made strenuous efforts to revive the pure Greek geometry, and depreciate the algebraic or symbolical analysis.[2] Hence there arose among them, and among their disciples, a love of the most refined methods of solution, and a contempt for those easier, but less elegant ones, which we owe to algebra.[3] Here we clearly see the isolating and esoteric character of a scheme which despises what ordinary understandings can

2. Simson was appointed in 1711; and even before he began to lecture, he drew up "a translation of the three first books of L'Hospital's Conic Sections, in which geometrical demonstrations are substituted for the algebraical of the original, according to Mr. Simson's early taste on this subject." *Trail's Life and Writings of Robert Simson*, 1812, 4to, p. 4. This was probably the rudiment of his work on Conic Sections, published in 1735. *Montucla, Histoire des Mathématiques*, vol. iii. p. 12. On the difference between the ancient and modern schemes, there are some ingenious, though perhaps scarcely tenable, remarks in Dugald Stewart's *Philosophy of the Mind*, vol. ii. p. 354 seq. and p. 380. See also *Comte, Philosophie Positive*, vol. i. pp. 383–395. Matthew Stewart, the mathematical professor at Edinburgh, was the father of Dugald. See, respecting him and his crusade against the modern analysis, *Bower's History of the University of Edinburgh*, vol. ii. pp. 357–360, vol. iii. p. 249; and a strange passage in *First Report of the British Association*, p. 59.

3. One of Simson's great reasons for recommending the old analysis, was that it was "more elegant" than the comparatively modern practice of introducing algebraic calculations into geometry. See *Trail's Simson*, 1812, 4to, pp. 27, 67; a valuable work, which Lord Brougham, in his hasty life of Simson, calls "a very

quickly master, and which had rather proceed from the ideal to the tangible, than mount from the tangible to the ideal. Just at the same time, the same spirit was displayed, in another branch of inquiry, by Hutcheson, who, though an Irishman by birth, was educated in the University of Glasgow, and was professor there. In his celebrated moral and æsthetic researches, he, in the place of inductive reasoning from palpable facts, substituted deductive reasoning from impalpable principles; ignoring the immediate and practical suggestions of the senses, and believing that by a hypothetical assumption of certain laws, he could descend upon the facts, instead of rising from the facts in order to learn the laws.[4] His philosophy exercised immense influence among metaphysicians;[5] and his method of working downwards, from the abstract to the concrete, was adopted by another and a still greater Scotchman, the illustrious Adam Smith. How Smith favoured the deductive form of investigation, is apparent in his *Theory of Moral Sentiments,* likewise in his *Essay on Language,*[6] and even

---

learned and exceedingly ill-written, indeed hardly readable" book. *Brougham's Men of Letters and Science,* vol. i. p. 482, 8vo, 1845. Dr. Trail's style is clearer, and his sentences are less involved, than Lord Brougham's; and he had moreover the great advantage of understanding the subject upon which he wrote.

4. Sir James Mackintosh (*Dissertation on Ethical Philosophy,* p. 208) says of Hutcheson, "To him may also be ascribed that proneness to multiply ultimate and original principles in human nature, which characterized the Scottish school till the second extinction of a passion for metaphysical speculation in Scotland." There is an able view of Hutcheson's philosophy in *Cousin, Histoire de la Philosophie,* I. série, vol. iv. pp. 31 seq.; written with clearness and eloquence, but perhaps overpraising Hutcheson.

5. On its influence, see a letter from Mackintosh to Parr, in *Memoirs of Mackintosh,* by his Son, vol. i. p. 334. Compare *Letters from Warburton to Hurd,* pp. 37, 82.

6. Which is added to his *Theory of Moral Sentiments,* edit. 1822, 2 volumes. Compare a letter which Smith wrote in 1763 on the origin of language (in *Nichol's Literary Illustrations of the Eighteenth Century,* vol. iii. pp. 515, 516), which exhibits, on a small scale, the same treatment, as distinguished from a generalization of the facts which are supplied by a comprehensive comparison of different languages. Dr. Arnold speaks slightingly of such investigations. He says, "Attempts to explain the phenomena of language *a priori* seem to me unwise." *Arnold's Miscellaneous Works,* p. 385. This would lead into a discussion too long for a note: but it appears to me that these *a priori* inferences are, to the philologist, what hypotheses are to the inductive natural philosopher; and if this be the case, they are extremely important, because no really fruitful experiment ever can be made unless it is preceded by a judicious hypothesis. In the absence of such an hypothesis, men may grope in the dark for centuries, accumulating facts without obtaining knowledge.

in his fragment on the *History of Astronomy,* in which he, from general considerations, undertook to prove what the march of astronomical discovery must have been, instead of first ascertaining what it had been.[7] The *Wealth of Nations,* again, is entirely deductive, since in it Smith generalizes the laws of wealth, not from the phenomena of wealth, nor from statistical statements, but from the phenomena of selfishness; thus making a deductive application of one set of mental principles to the whole set of economical facts.[8] The illustrations with which his great book abounds are no part of the real argument: they are subsequent to the conception; and if they were all omitted, the work, though less interesting, and perhaps less influential, would, in a scientific point of view, be equally valuable. To give another instance: the works of Hume, his metaphysical essays alone excepted, are all deductive; his profound economical inquiries are essentially *a priori,* and might have been written without any acquaintance

7. See, for instance, his attempt to prove, from general reasonings concerning the human mind, that there was a necessary relation in regard to the order in which men promulgated the system of concentric spheres and that of eccentric spheres and epicycles. *History of Astronomy,* in *Smith's Philosophical Essays,* 1795, 4to, pp. 31, 36, which it may be convenient to compare with *Whewell's Philosophy of the Inductive Sciences,* 1847, vol. ii. pp. 53, 60, 61. This striking fragment of Adam Smith's is probably little read now; but it is warmly praised by one of the greatest living philosophers, M. A. Comte, in his *Philosophie Positive,* vol. vi. p. 319.

8. The two writers who have inquired most carefully into the method which political economists ought to follow, are Mr. John Mill (*Essays on Unsettled Questions of Political Economy,* 1844, pp. 120–164) and Mr. Rae (*New Principles of Political Economy,* 1834, pp. 328–351). Mr. Rae, in his ingenious work, objects to Adam Smith that he transgressed the rules of the Baconian philosophy, and thus prevented his inferences from being as valuable as they would have been if he had treated his subject inductively. But Mr. Mill, with great force of reasoning, has proved that the deductive plan is the only one by which political economy can be raised to a science. He says, p. 143, political economy is "essentially an *abstract* science, and its method is the method *a priori*"; and at p. 146, that the *a posteriori* method is "altogether inefficacious." To this I may add, that the modern theory of rent, which is now the cornerstone of political economy, was got at, not by generalizing economical facts, but by reasoning downwards after the manner of geometricians. Indeed, those who oppose the theory of rent, always do so on the ground that it is contradicted by facts; and then, with complete ignorance of the philosophy of method, they infer that therefore the theory is wrong. See, for instance, *Jones on the Distribution of Wealth,* 8vo, 1831; a book containing some interesting facts, but vitiated by this capital defect of method. See also *Journal of Statistical Society,* vol. i. p. 317, vol. vi. p. 322; where it is said that economical theories should be generalized from statistical facts. Compare vol. xvii. p. 116, vol. xviii, p. 101.

with those details of trade and finance from which, according to the inductive scheme, they should have been generalized.[9] Thus, too, in his *Natural History of Religion,* he endeavoured simply by reflection, and independently of evidence, to institute a purely speculative investigation into the origin of religious opinions.[10] In the same way, in his *History of England,* instead of first collecting the evidence, and then drawing inferences from it, he began by assuming that the relations between the people and the government must have followed a certain order, and he either neglected or distorted the facts by which this supposition was contradicted.[11] These different writers, though varying in their principles, and in the subjects they studied, were all agreed as to their method; that is to say, they were all agreed to investigate

9. A striking instance has lately come to light of the sagacity with which Hume employed this method. See *Burton's Life and Correspondence of Hume,* vol. ii. p. 486; where we find, that immediately Hume had read the *Wealth of Nations,* he detected Smith's error concerning rent being an element of price: so that it now appears that Hume was the first to make this great discovery, as far as the idea is concerned; though Ricardo has the merit of proving it.

10. The historical facts he introduces are merely illustrations; as any one will see who will read *The Natural History of Religion,* in *Hume's Philos. Works,* Edinb. 1826, vol. iv. pp. 435–513. I may mention, that there is a considerable similarity between the views advocated in this remarkable essay and the religious stages of *Comte's Philosophie Positive;* for Hume's early form of polytheism is evidently the same as M. Comte's fetichism, from which both these writers believe that monotheism subsequently arose, as a later and more refined abstraction. That this was the course adopted by the human mind, is highly probable, and is confirmed by the learned researches of Mr. Grote. See his *History of Greece,* vol. i. pp. 462, 497, vol. v. p. 22. The opposite and more popular opinion, of monotheism preceding idolatry, was held by most of the great earlier writers, and is defended by many moderns, and among others by Dr. Whewell (*Bridgewater Treatise,* p. 256), who expresses himself with considerable confidence: see also *Letters from Warburton to Hurd,* p. 239. Compare *Thirlwall's History of Greece,* vol. i. p. 183, Lond. 1835, with the "einige Funken des Monotheismus" of Kant, *Kritik der reinen Vernunft,* in *Kant's Werke,* vol. ii. p. 455.

11. That is to say, he treated historical facts as merely illustrative of certain general principles, which he believed could be proved without the facts; so that, as M. Schlosser (*History of the Eighteenth Century,* vol. ii. p. 76) well says, "History with Hume was only a subordinate pursuit, only a means by which he might introduce his philosophy," &c. Considering how little is known of the principles which govern social and political changes, there can be no doubt that Hume was premature in the application of this method; but it is absurd to call the method dishonest, since the object of his History was, not to *prove* conclusions, but to *illustrate* them; and he therefore thought himself justified in selecting the illustrations. I am simply stating his views, without at all defending them; indeed, I believe that in this respect he was seriously in the wrong.

truth rather by descent than by ascent. The immense social importance of this peculiarity, I shall examine in [later chapters], where I shall endeavour to ascertain how it affected the national civilization, and caused some curious contrasts with the opposite, and more empirical, character of English literature. In the mean time, and merely to state what will be hereafter proved, I may add, that the deductive method was employed, not only by those eminent Scotchmen I have mentioned, but was carried into the speculative *History of Civil Society* by Ferguson; into the study of legislation by Mill; into the study of jurisprudence by Mackintosh; into geology by Hutton; into thermotics by Black and Leslie; into physiology by Hunter, by Alexander Walker, and by Charles Bell; into pathology by Cullen; into therapeutics by Brown and Currie.

I

Condition of Scotland to the End of the Fourteenth Century

In [giving] the . . . preceding view of the rise and decay of Spain, I have sought to exhibit the successive steps by which what was formerly one of the greatest nations of the earth, was broken, and cast down from its high estate. As we look back on that scene, the picture is, indeed, striking. A country rich in all natural productions, inhabited by a brave, a loyal, and a religious people, removed, too, by its geographical position from the hazards of European revolutions, did, by the operation of those general causes which I have indicated, suddenly rise to unparalleled grandeur; and then, without the occurrence of any new combination, but by a mere continuance of the same causes, fall with an equal velocity. Yet, these vicissitudes, strange and startling as they appear, were perfectly regular. They were the legitimate consequence of a state of society, in which the spirit of protection had reached its highest point, and in which, every thing being done for the people, nothing was done by the people. Whenever this happens, there may be great political progress, but there can be no really national progress. There may be accessions of territory, and vast increase of fame and of power. There may be improvements in the practice of administration, in the management of finances, in the organization of armies, in the art and theory of war, in the tricks of diplomacy, and in those various contrivances by which one nation is able to outwit and insult another. So far, however, from this benefiting the people, it will injure them in two different ways. In the first place, by increasing the reputation of the ruling classes, it encourages that blind and servile respect which men are too apt to feel for those who are above them, and which, wherever it has been generally practised, has been found fatal to the highest qualities of the citizen, and therefore to the permanent grandeur of the nation. And, in the second place, it multiplies the resources of the executive government, and thus renders the country unable, as well as unwilling, to correct the errors of those who are at the head of affairs. Hence, in Spain, as in all countries similarly circumstanced, it was at the very moment when things were most prosperous at the surface, that they were most rotten at the foundation. In presence of the most splendid political success, the nation hastened to its downfall, and the crisis was fast approaching, in which, the whole edifice being overturned, nothing would be left, except a memorable warning of the consequences which must ensue, when the people, giving themselves up to the passions of superstition and loyalty, abdicate their own proper functions, forego their own responsibility, renounce their highest duties, and degrade themselves into passive instruments to serve the will of the Church and the throne.

Such is the great lesson taught by the history of Spain. From the history of Scotland, we may gather another lesson, of a different, and yet of a similar, kind. In Scotland, the progress of the nation has been very slow, but, on the whole, very sure. The country is extremely barren; the executive government has, with rare exceptions, been always weak; and the people have never been burdened with those feelings of loyalty which circumstances had forced upon the Spaniards. Certainly, the last charge that will be brought against the Scotch, is that of superstitious attachment to their princes. . . .[1] There have been more rebellions

---

1. One of their own historians complacently says, "but the Scots were seldom distinguished for loyalty." *Laing's History of Scotland,* vol. iii. p. 199, edit. 1819. See also p. 366. To the same effect, Brodie (*History of the British Empire,* Edinburgh, 1822, vol. i. p. 383): "The little respect paid to royalty is conspicuous in every page of Scottish history." Or, as Wilkes expressed himself in the House of Commons, "Scotland seems, indeed, the natural *foyer* of rebellion, as Egypt is of the plague." *Parliamentary History,* vol. xix. p. 810, London, 1814; and Nimmo (*History of Stirlingshire,* Edinburgh, 1777, p. 219): "Never was any race of monarchs more unfortunate than the Scottish. Their reigns were generally turbulent and disastrous, and their own end often tragical."

in Scotland than in any other country; and the rebellions have been very sanguinary, as well as very numerous. The Scotch have made war upon most of their kings, and put to death many. To mention their treatment of a single dynasty, they murdered James I. and James III. They rebelled against James II. and James VII. They laid hold of James V., and placed him in confinement. Mary, they immured in a castle, and afterwards deposed. Her successor, James VI., they imprisoned; they led him captive about the country, and on one occasion attempted his life. Towards Charles I., they showed the greatest animosity, and they were the first to restrain his mad career. Three years before the English ventured to rise against that despotic prince, the Scotch boldly took up arms, and made war on him. . . .

While, however, in regard to loyalty, the opposition between Scotland and Spain is complete, there is, strange to say, the most striking similarity between those countries in regard to superstition. Both nations have allowed their clergy to exercise immense sway, and both have submitted their actions, as well as their consciences, to the authority of the Church. As a natural consequence, in both countries, intolerance has been, and still is, a crying evil; and in matters of religion, a bigotry is habitually displayed, discreditable indeed to Spain, but far more discreditable to Scotland, which has produced many philosophers of the highest eminence, who would willingly have taught the people better things, but who have vainly attempted to remove from the national mind that serious blemish which mars its beauty, and tends to neutralize its many other admirable qualities.

Herein lies the apparent paradox, and the real difficulty, of Scotch history. That knowledge should not have produced the effects which have elsewhere followed it; that a bold and inquisitive literature should be found in a grossly superstitious country, without diminishing its superstition; that the people should constantly withstand their kings, and as constantly succumb to their clergy; that while they are liberal in politics, they should be illiberal in religion; and that, as a natural consequence of all this, men who, in the visible and external department of facts and of practical life, display a shrewdness and a boldness rarely equalled, should nevertheless, in speculative life, and in matters of theory, tremble like sheep before their pastors, and yield assent to every absurdity they hear, provided their Church has sanctioned it; that these discrepancies should coëxist, seems at first sight a strange contradiction, and is surely a phenomenon worthy of our careful study. To indicate the causes of this anomaly, and to trace the results to which the anomaly has led, will be the business of the remaining part of this volume. . . .

In Scotland, as elsewhere, the course of events has been influenced by its physical geography; and by this I mean, not only its own immediate peculiarities, but also its relation to adjoining countries. It is close to Ireland; it touches England; and by the contiguity of the Orkney and Shetland Isles, it was eminently exposed to the attacks of that great nation of pirates, which for centuries inhabited the Scandinavian peninsula. Considered merely by itself, it is mountainous and sterile; nature has interposed such obstacles, that it was long impossible to open regular communications between its different parts, which, indeed, in regard to the Highlands, was not effected till after the middle of the eighteenth century.[2] Finally, and this, as we shall presently

2. In England, the travelling was bad enough; in Scotland, it was far worse. Morer, stating what he saw in 1689, says, "Stage-coaches they have none; yet there are a few Hackney's at Edinburgh, which they may hire into the country upon urgent occasions. The truth is, the roads will hardly allow 'em those conveniences, which is the reason that their gentry, men and women, chuse rather to use their horses." *Morer's Account of Scotland,* London, 1702, p. 24.

As to the northern parts, we have the following account, written in Inverness, between 1726 and 1730. "The Highlands are but little known even to the inhabitants of the low country of Scotland, for they have ever dreaded the difficulties and dangers of travelling among the mountains; and, when some extraordinary occasion has obliged any one of them to such a progress, he has, generally speaking, made his testament before he set out, as though he were entering upon a long and dangerous sea-voyage, wherein it was very doubtful if he should ever return." *Letters from a Gentleman in the North of Scotland,* edit. London, 1815, vol. i. p. 4. Between 1720 and 1730, military roads were cut through parts of the Highlands, but they were "laid down by a practical soldier, and destined for warlike purposes, with scarcely any view towards the ends for which free and peaceful citizens open up a system of internal transit." *Burton's History of Scotland,* vol. ii. p. 255. See also *Chalmers' Caledonia,* vol. ii. p. 36. This is confirmed by the fact, that, even between Inverness and Edinburgh, "until 1755, the mail was conveyed by men on foot." Account of Inverness-shire, in *M'Culloch's British Empire,* London, 1847, vol. i. p. 299; to which I may add, that in *Anderson's Essay on the Highlands,* Edinburgh, 1827, pp. 119, 120, it is stated, that "A postchaise was first seen in Inverness itself in 1760, and was for a considerable time, the only four-wheeled carriage in the district." As to the communications in the country about Perth, see *Penny's Traditions of Perth,* pp. 131, 132, Perth, 1836; and as to those from Aberdeen

see, was a matter of great importance, the most fertile land in Scotland is in the south, and was, therefore, constantly ravaged by the English borderers. Hence, the accumulation of wealth was hindered; the growth of towns was discouraged, by the serious hazards to which they were liable; and it was impossible to develop that municipal spirit, which might have existed, if the districts most favoured by nature had been situated in the north of Scotland, instead of in the south. If the actual state of things had been reversed, so that the Highlands were in the south,[3] and the Lowlands in the north, it can hardly be doubted, that, after the cessation in the thirteenth century of the great Scandinavian invasions, the most fertile parts of Scotland, being comparatively secure, would have been the seat of towns, which the active spirit of the people would have caused to prosper, and the prosperity of which would have introduced a new element into Scotch affairs, and changed the course of Scotch history. This, however, was not to be; and, as we have to deal with events as they actually are, I will now endeavour to trace the consequences of the physical peculiarities which have just been noticed; and, by coördinating their results, I will, so far as I am able, show their general meaning, and the way in which they have shaped the national character.

---

to Inverness, and from Aberdeen to Edinburgh, see *Kennedy's Annals of Aberdeen,* vol. ii. pp. 269, 270, London, 4to, 1818.

The history of the improvement of the roads during the latter half of the eighteenth century, has never been written; but it is of the greatest importance for its intellectual results, in causing national fusion, as well as for its economical results, in helping trade. Some idea may be formed of the extraordinary energy displayed by Scotland in this matter, by comparing the following passages: *Chalmers' Caledonia,* vol. ii. pp. 494, 865, 939, vol. iii. pp. 599, 799; *Crawfurd's History of the Shire of Renfrew,* part ii. pp. 128, 160; *Irving's History of Dumbartonshire,* pp. 245, 246; *Sinclair's Statistical Account of Scotland,* vol. i. pp. 109, 210, 367, 430, 496; vol. ii. p. 498; vol. iii. pp. 331, 352, 353; vol. iv. p. 313; vol. v. pp. 128, 234, 235, 315, 364, 365; vol. vi. pp. 107, 154, 180, 458; vol. vii. pp. 135, 251, 275, 299, 417; vol. viii. pp. 81, 243, 344, 345, 541; vol. ix. pp. 414, 530; vol. x. pp. 221, 237, 238, 466, 618; vol. xi. pp. 127, 380, 418, 432, 522, 541; vol. xii. p. 59; vol. xiii. pp. 42, 141, 488, 542, 663; vol. xiv. pp. 217, 227, 413, 443, 466, 506; vol. xv. pp. 54, 88, 276; vol. xvi. p. 120; vol. xvii. pp. 5, 267, 297, 377, 533; vol. xviii. p. 309; vol. xx. p. 156.

3. I use the word Highlands, in the common, though improper, sense of including all Scotland from the Pentland Firth to the beginning of the mountains, a few miles north of Glasgow, Stirling, Perth, and Dundee. All such distinctions are necessarily somewhat vague, because the boundaries of nature are never clearly marked. Compare *Macky's Scotland,* p. 124, London, 1732, with *Anderson's Guide to the Highlands,* Edinburgh, 1847, pp. 17, 18.

The earliest fact with which we are acquainted respecting the history of Scotland, is the Roman invasion under Agricola, late in the first century. But neither his conquests, nor those of his successors, made any permanent impression. The country was never really subjugated, and nothing was effected except a military occupation, which, in spite of the erection of numerous forts, walls, and ramparts, left the spirit of the inhabitants unbroken. . . .

The Romans, gradually losing ground, the proximity of Ireland caused repeated attacks from that fertile island, whose rich soil and great natural advantages gave rise to an exuberant, and therefore a restless, population. An overflow, which, in civilized times, is an emigration, is, in barbarous times, an invasion. Hence the Irish, or Scotti as they were termed, established themselves by force of arms in the west of Scotland, and came into collision with the Picts, who occupied the eastern part. A deadly struggle ensued, which lasted four centuries after the withdrawal of the Romans, and plunged the country into the greatest confusion. At length, in the middle of the ninth century, Kenneth M'Alpine, king of the Scotti, gained the upper hand, and reduced the Picts to complete submission.[4] The country was now united under one rule; and the conquerors, slowly absorbing the conquered, gave their name to the whole, which, in the tenth century, received the appellation of Scotland.[5]

4. The history of Scotland, in this period, is in great confusion, and perhaps will never be recovered. For the statements made in the text, I have chiefly used the following authorities: *Fordun's Scotichronicon,* vol. i.; *Buchanan's Rerum Scoticarum Historia,* lib. v. pp. 121–132, and the beginning of the sixth book. Also various parts of *Bede; Pinkerton's Enquiry into the Early History of Scotland; Chalmers' Caledonia;* the first volume of *Browne's History of the Highlands;* and, above all, Mr. Skene's acute and learned work on the Highlanders. In the last-named book, the western boundary of the Picts is traced with great ingenuity, though perhaps with some uncertainty. *Skene's Highlanders of Scotland,* vol. i. pp. 26–33, London, 1837.

5. Here, again, we are involved in doubt; it being uncertain when the name Scotia was first applied to Scotland. The date, therefore, which I have given, is only intended as an approximate truth. In arriving at it, I have compared the following different, and often conflicting, passages: *Chalmers' Caledonia,* vol. i. p. 339. *Browne's History of the Highlands,* vol. i. p. 34. *Pinkerton's Enquiry into the Early History of Scotland,* vol. i. pp. 253, 254, vol. ii. pp. 151, 228, 237, 240. *Spottiswoode's History of the Church of Scotland,* edit. Russell, 1851, vol. i. p. 16, note, where, however, Pinkerton's authority is appealed to for an assertion which he did not make. *Skene's Highlanders,* vol. i. pp. 45, 61, 244. *Anderson's Prize Essay on the Highlands,* p. 34.

But the kingdom was to have no rest. For, in the mean time, circumstances, which it would be tedious to relate, had raised the inhabitants of Norway to be the greatest maritime power in Europe. The use which that nation of pirates made of their strength, forms another and a very important link in the history of Scotland, and moreover illustrates the immense weight, which, in an early period of society, shoud be assigned to mere geographical considerations. The nearest land to the centre of the long coast of Norway is the Shetland Isles, whence it is an easy sail to the Orkneys. The northern pirates naturally seized these small, but, to them, most useful islands, and, as naturally, made them intermediate stations, from which they could conveniently pillage the coasts of Scotland. Being constantly reinforced from Norway, they, in the ninth and tenth centuries, advanced from the Orkneys, made permanent settlements in Scotland itself, and occupied not only Caithness, but also great part of Sutherland. Another body of them got possession of the Western Islands; and as Skye is only separated from the mainland by a very narrow channel, these pirates easily crossed over, and fixed themselves in Western Ross.[6] From their new abodes, they waged incessant and destructive war against every district within their reach; and, keeping a large part of Scotland in constant alarm, they, for about three centuries prevented the possibility of its social improvement. . . . Danger from that quarter being over, it might have been hoped, that Scotland would now enjoy peace, and would have leisure to develop the natural resources which she possessed, particularly those in the southern and more favoured districts.

This, however, was not to be. For, scarcely were the attacks from Norway at an end, when those from England began. Early in the thirteenth century, the lines of demarcation which separated Normans from Saxons, were [in England] becoming so obliterated, that in many cases it was impossible to distinguish them.[7] By the middle of the same century, the two races were fused into one powerful nation; and, as that nation had a comparatively

6. *Pinkerton's Enquiry into the Early History of Scotland*, vol. i. pp. 136, 317, vol. ii. pp. 179, 298. *Skene's Highlanders*, vol. i. pp. 90, 91, 94, 106, 114, 258, 259. *Chalmers' Caledonia*, vol. i. pp. 340–347.
7. *Buckle's History of Civilization*, vol. i. pp. 565, 566.

feeble neighbour, it was certain that the stronger people would try to oppress the weaker.[8] In an ignorant and barbarous age, military success is preferred to all other kinds of fame; and the English, greedy for conquest, set their eyes upon Scotland, which they were sure to invade at the first opportunity. That Scotland was near, made it tempting; that it was believed to be defenceless, made the temptation irresistible. In 1290, Edward I. determined to avail himself of the confusion into which Scotland was thrown by disputes respecting the succession to the crown. The intrigues which followed, need not be related; it is enough to say, that, in 1296, the sword was drawn, and Edward invaded a country which he had long desired to conquer. But he little recked of the millions of treasure, and the hundreds of thousands of lives, which were to be squandered, before that was was over.[9] The contest that ensued was of unexampled length and severity; and in its sad course, the Scotch, notwithstanding their heroic resistance, and the victories they occasionally gained, had to endure every evil which could be inflicted by their proud and insolent neighbour. The darling object of the English, was to subjugate the Scotch; and if anything could increase the disgrace of so base an enterprise, it would be that, having undertaken it, they ignominiously failed.[10] The suffering, however, was incalculable, and was aggravated by the important fact, that it was precisely the most fertile part of Scotland which was most exposed to the English ravages. . . .

By these disasters, the practice of agriculture was every where

8. In *Tytler's History of Scotland,* vol. i. p. 18, "the early part of the reign" of Alexander III. is indicated as the period in which "the first approaches were made towards the great plan for the reduction of Scotland" by the English. Alexander III. came to the throne in 1249. Earlier, the feeling was very different. Thus, late in the twelfth century, "the two nations, according to Fordun, seemed one people; Englishmen travelling at pleasure through all the corners of Scotland (?); and Scotchmen in like manner through England." *Ridpath's Border History,* p. 76. Compare *Dalrymple's Annals of Scotland,* vol. i. p. 158. At that time, England, being weak, was peaceably disposed.

9. An old Scotch writer says, with some exaggeration, "The year 1296, at which tyme, the bloodyest and longest warr that ever was betwixt two nationes fell out, and continued two hundreth and sextie years, to the undoeing and ruineing of many noble families, with the slaughter of a million of men." *Somerville's Memoire of the Somervilles,* vol. i. p. 61.

10. See some just and biting remarks in *Hume's History of the House of Douglas,* vol. i. p. 85.

interrupted, and in many places ceased for several generations.[11] The labourers either fled, or were murdered; and there being no one to till the ground, some of the fairest parts of Scotland were turned into a wilderness, overgrown with briers and thickets. Between the invasions, a few of the inhabitants, taking courage, issued from the mountains, and raised wretched huts in the place of their former abodes. But, even then, they were pursued to their very doors by wolves, searching for food, and maddened with hunger. If they escaped from these famished and ferocious animals, they and their families were exposed to a danger still more horrible. For, in those terrible days, when famine stalked abroad, despair perverted the souls of men, and drove them to new crime. There were cannibals in the land; and we have it on contemporary authority, that a man and his wife, who were at length brought to justice, subsisted during a considerable period on the bodies of children, whom they caught alive in traps, devouring their flesh, and drinking their blood.[12]

Thus the fourteenth century passed away. In the fifteenth century, the devastations of the English became comparatively rare; and, although the borders were the scene of constant hostilities,[13]

11. "Agriculture was ruined; and the very necessaries of life were lost, when the principal lords had scarcely a bed to lye on." *Chalmers' Caledonia*, vol. ii. p. 142. See also, in p. 867 of the same volume of this learned work, some curious extracts from Scotch charters and other sources, illustrating the horrible condition of the country. And on the difficulty of obtaining food, compare *Fordun's Scotichronicon*, vol. ii. pp. 242, 324; *Dalrymple's Annals*, vol. i. p. 307, vol. ii. pp. 238, 330; and *Tytler's History of Scotland*, vol. ii. p. 94.

12. Notices of Scotch cannibals will be found in *Lindsay of Pitscottie's Chronicles of Scotland*, edit. 1814, vol. i. p. 163; and in *Hollinshead's Scottish Chronicle*, 4to, 1805, vol. ii. pp. 16, 99. In *Fordun's Scotichronicon*, vol. ii. p. 331, the following horrible account is given; it refers to the neighbourhood of Perth in the year 1339: "Tota illa patria circumvicina eo tempore in tantum fuit vastata, quòd non remansit quasi domus inhabitata, sed feræ et cervi de montanis descendentes circa villam sæpiùs venabantur. Tanta tunc temporis facta est caristia, et victualium inopia, ut passim plebicula deficeret, et tanquam oves herbas depascentes, in foveis mortua reperirentur. Prope illinc in abditis latitabat quidam robustus rusticus, Crysticleik nomine, cum viragine sua, qui mulierculis et pueris ac juvenibus insidiabantur, et, tanquam lupi eos strangulantes, de ipsorum carnibus victitabant."

13. Even when the two nations were at peace, the borderers were at war. See *Ridpath's Border History*, pp. 240, 308, 394; and for other evidence of this chronic anarchy, compare *Hollinshead's Scottish Chronicle*, vol. ii. p. 30. *Lesley's History of Scotland*, pp. 40, 52, 67. *Sadler's State Papers*, vol. i. pp. 300, 301, 444, 449. *State Papers of the Reign of Henry VIII.*, 4to, 1836, vol. iv. pp. 366, 370, 569, 570, vol. v. pp. 17, 18, 161. *Historie of James the Sext*, pp. 21, 91, 146.

there is no instance, since the year 1400, of any of our kings invading Scotland.[14] An end being put to those murderous expeditions, which reduced the country to a desert, Scotland drew breath, and began to recover her strength.[15] But, though the material losses were gradually repaired; though the fields were again cultivated, and the towns rebuilt, there were other consequences, which were less easy to remedy, and from whose effects the people long smarted. These were, the inordinate power of the nobles, and the absence of the municipal spirit. The strength of the nobles, and the weakness of the citizens, are the most important peculiarities of Scotland during the fifteenth and sixteenth centuries; and they, as I am about to show, were directly encouraged by the ravages committed by the English troops. We shall, moreover, see that this combination of events increased the authority of the clergy, weakened the influence of the intellectual classes, and made superstition more prevalent than it would otherwise have been. It is in this way, that in Scotland, as in all other countries, every thing is linked together; nothing is casual or accidental; and the whole march of affairs is governed by general causes, which, owing to their largeness and remoteness, often escape attention, but which, when once recognized, are found to be marked by a simplicity and uniformity, which are the invariable characteristics of the highest truths that the mind of man has reached.

The first circumstance favourable to the authority of the nobles, was the structure of the country. Mountains, fens, lakes, and morasses, which even the resources of modern art have only recently made accessible, supplied the great Scottish chieftains with retreats in which they could with impunity defy the power

---

14. In 1400, Henry IV. made "the last invasion which an English monarch ever conducted into Scotland." *Tytler's History of Scotland,* vol. ii. p. 406. It is said, however, that it was not till the reign of Elizabeth, that an English sovereign "had the policy to disavow any claim of sovereignty over Scotland." *Chalmers' Caledonia,* vol. i. p. 650.

15. But very slowly. Pinkerton (*History of Scotland,* vol. i. pp. 166, 167) says: "The frequent wars between Scotland and England, since the death of Alexander III., had occasioned to the former country the loss of more than a century in the progress of civilization. While in England, only the northern provinces were exposed to the Scotish incursions, Scotland suffered in its most civilized departments. It is apparent that in the reign of Alexander III., the kingdom was more abundant in the useful arts and manufactures, than it was in the time of Robert III."

of the crown.[16] The poverty of the soil, also, made it difficult for armies to find means of subsistence; and from this cause alone, the royal troops were often unable to pursue the lawless and refractory barons.[17] During the fourteenth century, Scotland was constantly ravaged by the English; and in the intervals of their absence, it would have been a hopeless undertaking for any king to try to repress such powerful subjects, since he would have had to march through districts so devastated by the enemy, that they no longer yielded the common necessaries of life. Besides this, the war with the English lessened the authority of the crown, absolutely as well as relatively. Its patrimony, lying in the south, was incessantly wasted by the borderers, and before the middle of the fourteenth century greatly deteriorated in value.[18] In 1346, David II. fell into the hands of the English, and during his captivity of eleven years, the nobles carried all before them, and affected, says an historian, the style and title of princes.[19] The longer the war with England continued, the more these consequences were felt; so that before the close of the fourteenth century, a few of the leading Scotch families had raised themselves to such preeminence, that it was evident, either that a deadly struggle must

16. Owing to this, their castles were, by position, the strongest in Europe; Germany alone excepted. Respecting their sites, which were such as to make them in many instances almost unassailable, see *Chalmers' Caledonia,* vol. ii. pp. 122, 406, 407, 918, 919, vol. iii. pp. 268, 269, 356–359, 864; *Pennant's Scotland,* vol. i. pp. 175, 177; *Sinclair's Scotland,* vol. iii. p. 169, vol. vii. p. 510, vol. xi. pp. 102, 212, 407, 408, vol. xii. pp. 25, 58, vol. xiii. p. 598, vol. xv. p. 187, vol. xvi. p. 554, vol. xviii. p. 579, vol. xix, p. 474, vol. xx. pp. 56, 312; *Macky's Scotland,* pp. 183, 297; and some good remarks in *Nimmo's History of Stirlingshire,* p. 56. Neither England, nor France, nor Italy, nor Spain, afforded such immense natural advantages to their aristocracy.

17. "By retiring to his own castle, a mutinous baron could defy the power of his sovereign, it being almost impracticable to lead an army through a barren country, to places of difficult access to a single man." *History of Scotland,* book i. p. 59, in *Robertson's Works,* edit. London, 1831. Notwithstanding the immense materials which have been brought to light since the time of Robertson, his *History of Scotland* is still valuable; because he possessed a grasp of mind which enabled him to embrace general views, that escape ordinary compilers, however industrious they may be.

18. "The patrimony of the Crown had been seriously dilapidated during the period of confusion which succeeded the battle of Durham." *Tytler's History of Scotland,* vol. ii. p. 86.

19. "During the long captivity of David," the nobles had been completely insubordinate, and "affected the style and title of princes." *Tytler's History of Scotland,* vol. ii. p. 85. See also, on the state of the barons under David II., *Skene's Highlanders,* vol. ii. pp. 63–67.

ensue between them and the crown, or else that the executive government would have to abdicate its most essential functions, and leave the country a prey to these headstrong and ferocious chiefs.[20]

At this crisis, the natural allies of the throne would have been the citizens and free burgesses, who in most European countries were the eager and resolute opponents of the nobles, whose licentious habits interfered not only with their trade and manufactures, but also with their personal liberty. Here again, however, the long war with England was favourable to the aristocracy of Scotland. For, as the invaders ravaged the southern parts of Scotland, which were also the only tolerably fertile parts, it was impossible that towns should flourish in the places which nature had appointed for them. There being no large cities, there was no asylum for the citizens, and there could be no municipal spirit. There being no municipal spirit, the crown was deprived of that great resource, which enabled the English kings to curtail the power of the nobles, and to punish a lawlessness which long impeded the progress of society.

During the middle ages, the Scotch towns were so utterly insignificant, that but few notices have been preserved of them; contemporary writers concentrating their attention upon the proceedings of the nobles and clergy. Respecting the people, who found shelter in such miserable cities as then existed, our best accounts are very imperfect; it is, however, certain that, during the long English wars, the inhabitants usually fled at the approach of the invaders, and the wretched hovels in which they lived were burned to the ground.[21] Hence the population acquired a fluctuating and vagabond character, which prevented the formation of settled habits of industry, and thus took away one reason which men have for congregating together. This applied more especially

20. In 1299, "a superior baron was in every respect a king in miniature." *Tytler's History of Scotland,* vol. ii. p. 150. In 1377, "the power of the barons had been decidedly increasing since the days of Robert the First." p. 332. And, by 1398, it had risen still higher. p. 392.

21. On this burning of Scotch towns, which appears to have been the invariable practice of our humane forefathers, see *Chalmers' Caledonia,* vol. ii. pp. 592, 593; *Kennedy's Annals of Aberdeen,* vol. i. pp. 18, 27, 375, vol. ii. p. 304; *Mercer's History of Dunfermline,* pp. 55, 56; *Sinclair's Scotland,* vol. v. p. 485, vol. x. p. 584, vol. xix. p. 161; *Ridpath's Border History,* pp. 147, 221, 265.

to the southern Lowlands; for the north, there were other evils equally threatening. The ferocious Highlanders, who lived entirely by plunder, were constantly at hand; and to them were not unfrequently added the freebooters of the Western Isles. Any thing which bore even the semblance of wealth, was an irresistible excitement to their cupidity. They could not know that a man had property, without longing to steal it; and, next to stealing, their greatest pleasure was to destroy.[22] Aberdeen and Inverness were particularly exposed to their assaults; and twice during the fifteenth century, Inverness was totally consumed by fire, besides having to pay at other times a heavy ransom, to save itself from a similar fate.[23]

22. A curious description of them is given in a Scotch statute, of the year 1597. "They hawe lykwayis throche thair barbarus inhumanitie maid and presentlie makis the saidis hielandis and Iles qlk are maist comodious in thame selwes alsueill be the ferteillitie of the ground as be riche fischeingis altogidder vnproffitabill baithe to thame selffis and to all vthuris his hienes liegis within this realme; Thay nathair intertening onie ciuill or honest societie amangis thame selffis neyther zit admittit vtheris his hienesse lieges to trafficque within thair boundis vithe saiftie of thair liues and gudes; for remeid quhairof and that the saidis inhabitantis of the saidis hilandeis and Iles may the better be reduced to ane godlie, honest, and ciuill maner of living, it is statute and ordanit," &c. Acts of the Parliaments of Scotland, vol. iv. p. 138, edit, folio, 1816.

These little peculiarities of the Highlanders remained in full force until about the middle of the eighteenth century, as will appear in the course of this history. But, without anticipating what will be narrated in a subsequent chapter, I will merely refer the reader to two interesting passages in Pennant's Scotland, vol. i. p. 154, and in Heron's Scotland, vol. i. pp. 218, 219; both of which illustrate the state of things a little before 1745.

23. Inverness was burned in 1429. Gregory's History of the Western Highlands, p. 36; and again in 1455, Buchanan's Rerum Scoticarum Historia, lib. xi. p. 322. "The greatest part" of it was also burned in 1411. See Anderson on the Highlands, Edinb. 1827, p. 82.

Aberdeen, being richer, was more tempting, but was likewise more able to defend itself. Still, its burgh records supply curious evidence of the constant fear in which the citizens lived, and of the precautions which they took to ward off the attacks, sometimes of the English, and sometimes of the clans. See the Council Register of Aberdeen (published by the Spalding Club, Aberdeen, 1844–1848, 4to), vol. i. pp. 8, 19, 60, 83, 197, 219, 232, 268, vol. ii. p. 82. The last entry, which is dated July 31, 1593, mentions "the disordourit and lawles helandmen in Birss, Glentanner, and their about, nocht onlie in the onmerciful murthering of men and bairnis, bot in the maisterfull and violent robbing and spulzeing of all the bestiall, guidis, and geir of a gryt pairt of the inhabitantis of theas boundis, rasing of gryt, hairschip furth of the samen, being committit to ewous and nar this burgh, within xx mylis theirunto, deuysit and ordanit for preservatioun of this burgh and inhabitantis theireof, fra the tyran-

Such insecurity[24] both on the north and on the south, made peaceful industry impossible in any part of Scotland. No where could a town be built, without being in danger of immediate destruction. The consequence was, that, during many centuries, there were no manufactures; there was hardly any trade; and nearly all business was conducted by barter.[25] Some of the commonest arts were unknown. The Scotch were unable to make even the arms with which they fought. This, among such a warlike people, would have been a very profitable labour; but they were so ignorant of it, that, early in the fifteenth century, most of the armour which they wore was manufactured abroad, as also were their spears, and even their bows and arrows; and the heads of these weapons were entirely imported from Flanders.[26] Indeed, the Flemish artizans supplied the Scotch with ordinary farming implements, such as cart-wheels and wheel-barrows, which, about

---

nous invasion of the saidis hieland men, quha has no respect to God nor man; that the haill inhabitantis of this burgh, fensiball persones als weill onfrie as frie, salbe in reddiness weill armit for the defence of this burgh, thair awin lyvis, gudis, and geir, and resisting and repressing of the said heland men as occasioun salbe offered, at all tymes and houris as thay salbe requirt and chargit."

Even in 1668 we find complaints that Highlanders had forcibly carried off women from Aberdeen or from its neighbourhood. *Records of the Synod of Aberdeen,* p. 290. Other evidence of their attacks in the sixteenth and seventeenth centuries, may be seen in *Kennedy's Annals of Aberdeen,* vol. i. p. 133; *Spalding's History of the Troubles,* vol. i. pp. 25, 217; *Extracts from the Presbytery Book of Strathbogie,* pp. 62, 73.

24. Even Perth ceased to be the capital of Scotland, because "its vicinity to the Highlands" made it dangerous for the sovereign to reside there. *Lawson's Book of Perth,* p xxxi.

25. On the prevalence of barter, and lack of specie, in Scotland, see the *Spalding Club Miscellany,* vol. iv. pp. lvii.–lx., Aberdeen, 1849, 4to. In 1492, the treasury of Aberdeen was obliged to borrow 4*l.* 16*s.* Scots. *Kennedy's Annals of Aberdeen,* vol. i. p. 61. Compare *Sinclair's Statistical Account of Scotland,* vol. x. p. 542. Fynes Moryson, who was in Scotland late in the sixteenth century, says, "the gentlemen reckon their revenues not by rents of money, but by chauldrons of victuals." *Moryson's Itinerary,* part iii. p. 155. London, folio, 1617; a rare and extremely curious book, which ought to be reprinted. A hundred years after Moryson wrote, it was observed that, "in England, the rents are paid in money; in Scotland, they are, generally speaking, paid in kind, or victual, as they call it." *De Foe's History of the Union,* p. 130.

26. In the reign of James I. (1424–1436), "It appears that armour, nay spears, and bows and arrows, were chiefly imported." . . . "In particular, the heads of arrows and of spears seem to have been entirely imported from Flanders." *Pinkerton's History of Scotland,* vol. i. p. 163. We learn from Rymer's *Fœdera,* that, in 1368, two Scotchmen having occasion to fight a duel, got their armour from London. *Macpherson's Annals of Commerce,* vol. i. p. 575.

the year 1475, used to be regularly shipped from the Low Countries.[27] As to the arts which indicate a certain degree of refinement, they were then, and long afterwards, quite out of the
question.[28] Until the seventeenth century, no glass was manufactured in Scotland,[29] neither was any soap made there.[30] Even
the higher class of citizens would have deemed windows absurd
in their wretched abodes;[31] and as they were alike filthy in their
persons as in their houses, the demand for soap was too small to
induce any one to attempt its manufacture.[32] Other branches of

27. From the *Libel of English Policy,* supposed to have been written in the
reign of Edward IV., we learn that "the Scotish imports from Flanders were
mercery, but more haberdashery, cart-wheels, and wheel-barrows." *Pinkerton's
History of Scotland,* vol. i. p. 408. In *Mercer's History of Dunfermline,* p. 61,
we are told that, in the fifteenth century, "Even in the best parts of Scotland, the
inhabitants could not manufacture the most necessary articles. Flanders was the
great mart in those times, and from Bruges chiefly, the Scots imported even
horse-shoes, harness, saddles, bridles, cart-wheels, and wheel-barrows, besides
all their mercery and haberdashery."

28. Aberdeen was, for a long period, one of the most wealthy, and, in some
respects, the most advanced, of all the Scotch cities. But it appears, from
the council-registers of Aberdeen, that, "in the beginning of the sixteenth century, there was not a mechanic in the town capable to execute the ordinary re-
pairs of a clock." *Kennedy's Annals of Aberdeen,* vol. i. p. 99. On the Scotch
clocks in the middle of the sixteenth century, compare Mr. Morley's interesting
Life of Cardan, London, 1854, vol. ii. p. 128. Cardan was in Scotland in 1552.

29. About 1619, Sir George Hay "set up at the village of Wemyss, in Fife,
a small glass-work, being the first known to have existed amongst us." *Chambers' Annals,* vol. i. p. 506. See also p. 428.

30. "Before this time, soap was imported into Scotland from foreign countries, chiefly from Flanders." *Ibid.,* vol. i. p. 507, under the year 1619, where
mention is made of the manufactory set up at Leith. "The sope-workers of
Leith" are noticed in 1650, in *Balfour's Annales,* vol. iv. p. 68.

31. Ray, who visited Scotland in 1661, says, "In the best Scottish houses, even
the king's palaces, the windows are not glazed throughout, but the upper part
only; the lower have two wooden shuts or folds to open at pleasure and admit
the fresh air." . . . "The ordinary country-houses are pitiful cots, built of stone,
and covered with turves, having in them but one room, many of them no chim-
neys, the windows very small holes and not glazed." *Ray's Itineraries,* p. 153,
edited by Dr. Lankester, London, 1846. "About 1752, the glass window was
beginning to make its appearance in the small farm-houses." *Brown's History
of Glasgow,* vol. ii. p. 265, Edinburgh, 1797.

32. In 1650, it was stated of the Scotch, that "many of their women are so
sluttish, that they do not wash their linen above once a month, nor their hands
and faces above once a year." *Whitelock's Memorials,* p. 468, London, 1732,
folio. Six or seven years after this, a traveller in Scotland says, "the linen they
supplied us with, were it not to boast of, was little or nothing different from
those female complexions that never washed their faces to retain their christen-
dom." *Franck's Northern Memoirs,* edit. Edinburgh, 1821, p. 94. A celebrated
Scotchman notices, in 1698, the uncleanly habits of his countrymen, but gives a
comical reason for them; since, according to him, they were in a great measure

industry were equally backward. In 1620, the art of tan-
ning leather was for the first time introduced into Scotland;[33]
and it is stated, on apparently good authority, that no paper
was made there until about the middle of the eighteenth
century.[34]

In the midst of such general stagnation, the most flourishing
towns were, as may be easily supposed, very thinly peopled.
Indeed, men had so little to do, that if they had collected in
large numbers, they must have starved. Glasgow is one of the
oldest cities in Scotland, and is said to have been founded about
the sixth century.[35] At all events, in the twelfth century, it was,
according to the measure of that age, a rich and prosperous
place, enjoying the privilege of holding both a market and a

---

caused by the position of the capital. "As the happy situation of London has
been the principal cause of the glory and riches of England, so the bad situation
of Edinburgh has been one great occasion of the poverty and uncleanliness in
which the greater part of the people of Scotland live." *Second Discourse on the
Affairs of Scotland,* in *Fletcher of Saltoun's Political Works,* p. 119, Glasgow,
1749. Another Scotchman, among his reminiscences of the early part of the
eighteenth century, says, that "table and body linen [were] seldom shifted."
Memoires by Sir Archibald Grant of Monymusk, in *Spalding Club Miscellany,*
vol. ii. p. 100, Aberdeen, 1842, 4to. Finally, we have positive proof that in
some parts of Scotland, even at the end of the eighteenth century, the people
used, instead of soap, a substitute too disgusting to mention. See the account
communicated by the Rev. William Leslie to Sir John Sinclair, in *Sinclair's
Statistical Account of Scotland,* vol. ix. p. 177, Edinburgh, 1793.

33. *Chambers' Annals,* vol. i. p. 512.

34. A paper-mill was established near Edinburgh in 1675; but "there is reason to conclude this paper-mill was not continued, and that paper-making was
not successfully introduced into Scotland till the middle of the succeeding century." *Chambers' Annals,* vol. ii. p. 399. I have met with so many proofs of the
great accuracy of this valuable work, that I should be loath to question any
statement made by Mr. Chambers, when, as in this case, I have only my memory
to trust to. But I think that I have seen evidence of paper being successfully
manufactured in Scotland late in the seventeenth century, though I cannot recall
the passages. However, Arnot, in his *History of Edinburgh,* p. 599, edit. 4to,
says, "About forty years ago, printing or writing paper began to be manufactured in Scotland. Before that, papers were imported from Holland, or brought
from England." As Arnot's work was printed in 1788, this coincides with Mr.
Chambers' statement. I may add, that, at the end of the eighteenth century,
there were "two paper-mills near Perth." *Heron's Journey through Scotland,*
vol. i. p. 117, Perth, 1799; and that, in 1751 and 1763, the two first paper-mills
were erected north of the Forth. *Sinclair's Statistical Account of Scotland,* vol.
ix. p. 593, vol. xvi. p. 373. Compare *Lettice's Letters from Scotland in* 1792,
p. 420.

35. "This city was founded about the sixth century." *M'Ure's History of
Glasgow,* edit. 1830, p. 120. Compare *Denholm's History of Glasgow,* p. 2,
Glasgow, 1804.

fair.[36] It had also a municipal organization, and was governed by its own provosts and baillies.[37] Yet, even this famous town had no kind of trade before the fifteenth century, when the inhabitants began to cure salmon, and export it.[38] That was the only branch of industry with which Glasgow was acquainted. We need not, therefore, be surprised at hearing, that so late as the middle of the fifteenth century, the entire population did not exceed fifteen hundred persons, whose wealth consisted of some small cattle, and a few acres of ill-cultivated land.[39]

Other cities, though bearing a celebrated name, were equally backward at a still more recent period. Dunfermline is associated with many historic reminiscences; it was a favourite residence of Scotch kings, and many Scotch parliaments have been held there.[40] Such events are supposed to confer distinction; but the illusion vanishes, when we inquire more minutely into the condition of the place where they happened. In spite of the pomp of princes and legislators, Dunfermline, which at the end of the fourteenth century was still a poor village, composed of wooden huts,[41] had, by the beginning of the seventeenth century, ad-

36. In 1172, a market was granted to Glasgow; and in 1190, a fair. See the charters in the Appendix to *Gibson's History of Glasgow*, pp. 299, 302, Glasgow, 1777.

37. "By the sale of land made by Robert de Mythyngby to Mr. Reginald de Irewyne, A.D. 1268, it is evident that the town was then governed by provosts, aldermen, or wardens, and baillies, who seem to have been independent of the bishop, and were possessed of a common seal, distinct from the one made use of by the bishop and chapter." *Gibson's History of Glasgow*, p. 72.

38. "A Mr. William Elphinston is made mention of as the first promoter of trade in Glasgow, so early as the year 1420; the trade which he promoted was, in all probability, the curing and exporting of salmon." *Gibson's History of Glasgow*, p. 203. See also *M'Ure's History of Glasgow*, p. 93.

39. Gibson (*History of Glasgow*, p. 74), with every desire to take a sanguine view of the early state of his own city, says, that, in 1450, the inhabitants "might perhaps amount to fifteen hundred;" and that "their wealth consisted in a few burrow-roods very ill-cultivated, and in some small cattle, which fed on their commons."

40. "Dunfermline continued to be a favorite royal residence as long as the Scottish dynasty existed. Charles I. was born here; as also his sister Elizabeth, afterwards Queen of Bohemia, from whom her present Majesty is descended; and Charles II. paid a visit to this ancient seat of royalty in 1650. The Scottish parliament was often held in it." *M'Culloch's Geographical Dictionary*, London, 1849, vol. i. p. 723. Compare *Mercer's History of Dunfermline*, 1828, pp. 56, 58, and *Chalmers' History of Dunfermline*, 1844, p. 264.

41. In 1385, it was "only a sorry wooden village, belonging to the monastery." *Mercer's History of Dunfermline*, p. 62.

vanced so slowly that its whole population, including that of its wretched suburbs, did not exceed one thousand persons.[42] For a Scotch town, that was a considerable number. About the same time, Greenock, we are assured, was a village consisting of a single row of cottages, tenanted by poor fishermen.[43] Kilmarnock, which is now a great emporium of industry and of wealth, contained, in 1668, between five and six hundred inhabitants.[44] And, to come down still lower, even Paisley itself, in the year 1700, possessed a population which, according to the highest estimate, did not amount to three thousand.[45]

Aberdeen, the metropolis of the north, was looked up to as one of the most influential of the Scotch towns, and was not a little envied during the Middle Ages, for its power and importance. These, however, like all other words, are relative, and mean different things at different periods. Certainly, we shall not be much struck by the magnitude of that city, when we learn, from calculations made from its tables of mortality, that, so late as 1572, it could only boast of about two thousand nine hundred inhabitants.[46] Such a fact will dispel many a dream respecting the old Scotch towns, particularly if we call to mind, that it refers to a

---

42. See "Ms. Annals," in *Chalmers' History of Dunfermline*, p. 327. In 1624, we learn from *Balfour's Annales*, edit. 1825, vol. ii. p. 99, that "the quholl bodey of the towne, wich did consist of 120 tenements, and 287 families, was brunt and consumed."

43. "Greenock, which is now one of the largest shipping towns in Scotland, was, in the end of the sixteenth century, a mean fishing village, consisting of a single row of thatched cottages, which was inhabited by poor fishermen." *Chalmers' Caledonia*, vol. iii. p. 806, 4to, 1824.

44. In May 1668, Kilmarnock was burnt; and "the event is chiefly worthy of notice as marking the smallness of Kilmarnock in those days, when, as yet, there was no such thing as manufacturing industry in the country. A hundred and twenty families speaks to a population of between five and six hundred." *Chambers' Annals*, Edinburgh, 1858, vol. ii. p. 320. In 1658, their houses are described by an eye-witness as "little better than huts." *Franck's Northern Memoirs*, reprinted Edinburgh, 1821, p. 101.

45. "Betwixt two and three thousand souls." *Denholm's History of Glasgow*, p. 542, edit. Glasgow, 1804.

46. In 1572, the registers of Aberdeen show that seventy-two deaths occurred in the year. An annual mortality of 1 in 40 would be a very favourable estimate; indeed, rather too favourable, considering the habits of the people at that time. However, supposing it to be 1 in 40, the population would be 2880; and if, as I make no doubt, the mortality was more than 1 in 40, the population must of course have been less. Kennedy, in his valuable, but very uncritical, work, conjectures that "one fiftieth part of the inhabitants had died annually;" though it

date, when the anarchy of the Middle Ages was passing away, and Aberdeen had for some time been improving. That city—if so miserable a collection of persons deserves to be termed a city—was, nevertheless, one of the most densely peopled places in Scotland. From the thirteenth century to the close of the sixteenth, no where else were so many Scotchmen assembled together, except in Perth, Edinburgh, and possibly in Saint Andrews.[47] Respecting Saint Andrews, I have been unable to meet with any precise information;[48] but of Perth and Edinburgh, some particulars are preserved. Perth was long the capital of Scotland, and after losing that preëminence, it was still reputed to be the second city in the kingdom.[49] Its wealth was supposed to be astonishing; and every good Scotchman was proud of it, as one of the chief ornaments of his country.[50] But, according to an estimate recently

---

is certain that there was no town in Europe any thing like so healthy as that. On this hypothesis, which is contradicted by every sort of statistical evidence that has come down to us, the number would be 72 × 50 = 3600. See *Kennedy's Annals of Aberdeen*, vol. i. p. 103, London, 1818, 4to.

47. "St. Andrews, Perth, and Aberdeen, appear to have been the three most populous cities before the Reformation." *Lawson's Roman Catholic Church in Scotland*, 1836, p. 26. The same assertion is made in *Lyon's History of St. Andrews*, 1843, vol. i. p. 2. But neither of these writers appear to have made researches on the subject, or else they would not have supposed that Aberdeen was larger than Edinburgh.

48. I have carefully read the two histories of St. Andrews, by Dr. Grierson and by Mr. Lyon, but have found nothing in them of any value concerning the early history of that city. Mr. Lyon's work, which is in two thick volumes, is unusually superficial, even for a local history; and that is saying much.

49. "Of the thirteen parliaments held in the reign of King James I., eleven were held at Perth, one at Stirling, and one at Edinburgh. The National Councils of the Scottish clergy were held there uniformly till 1459. Though losing its pre-eminence by the selection of Edinburgh as a capital, Perth has uniformly and constantly maintained the second place in the order of burghs, and its right to do so has been repeatedly and solemnly acknowledged." *Penny's Traditions of Perth*, Perth, 1836, p. 231. See also p. 305. It appears, however, from Froissart, that Edinburgh was deemed the capital in the latter half of the fourteenth century.

50. I find one instance of its being praised by a man who was not a Scotchman. Alexander Necham "takes notice of Perth in the following distich, quoted in Camden's Britannia:

'Transis ample Tai, per rura, per oppida, per Perth:
Regnum sustentant illius urbis opes.'

Thus Englished in Bishop Gibson's Translation of Camden's Book:

'Great Tay, through Perth, through towns, through country flies:
Perth the whole kingdom with her wealth supplies.' "

Sinclair's Scotland, vol. xviii. p. 511.

made by a considerable authority in these matters, its entire population, in the year 1585, was under nine thousand.[51] This will surprise many readers; though, considering the state of society at that time, the real wonder is, not that there were so few, but that there were so many. For, Edinburgh itself, notwithstanding the officials and numerous hangers-on, which the presence of a court always brings, did not contain, late in the fourteenth century, more than sixteen thousand persons.[52] Of their general condition, a contemporary observer has left us some account. Froissart, who visited Scotland, and records what he saw, as well as what he heard, gives a lamentable picture of the state of affairs. The houses in Edinburgh were mere huts, thatched with boughs; and were so slightly put together, that when one of them was destroyed, it took only three days to rebuild it. As to the people who inhabited these wretched hovels, Froissart, who was by no means given to exaggeration, assures us, that the French, unless they had seen them, could not have believed that such destitution existed, and that now, for the first time, they understood what poverty really was.[53]

51. 1427 × 6 = 8562, the computed population in 1584 and 1585, exclusive of the extraordinary mortality caused by the plague. *Chambers' Annals of Scotland,* 1858, vol. i. p. 158.

52. "The inhabitants of the capital, in the reign of Robert II., hardly exceeded sixteen thousand." *Pinkerton's History of Scotland,* vol. i. p. 152.

53. When the French arrived in Edinburgh, the Scotch said, " 'Quel diable les a mandés? Ne savons-nous pas bien faire notre guerre sans eux aux Anglois? Nous ne ferons jà bonne besogne tant comme ils soient avec nous. On leur dise que ils s'en revoisent, et que nous sommes gens assez en Escosse pour parmaintenir notre guerre, et que point nous ne voulons leur compagnie. Ils ne nous entendent point, ni nous eux; nous ne savons parler ensemble; ils auront tantôt riflé et mangé tout ce qui est en ce pays: ils nous feront plus de contraires, de dépits, et de dommages, si nous les laissons convenir, que les Anglois ne feroient si ils s'étoient embattus entre nous sans ardoir. Et si les Anglois ardent nos maisons, que peut il chaloir? Nous les aurons tantôt refaites à bon marché, nous n'y mettons au refaire que trois jours, mais que nous ayons quatre ou six estaches et de la ramée pour lier par dessus.' "

"Ainsi disoient les Escots en Escosse à la venue des seigneurs de France." . . . .
"Et quand les Anglois y chevauchent ou que ils y vont, ainsi que ils y ont été plusieurs fois, il convient que leurs pourvéances, si ils veulent vivre, les suivent toujours au dos; car on ne trouve rien sur le pays: à grand 'peine y recuevre-l'en du fer pour serrer les chevaux, ni du cuir pour faire harnois, selles ni brides. Les choses toutes faites leur viennent par mer de Flandre, et quand cela leur défaut, ils n'ont nulle chose. Quand ces barons et ces chevaliers de France qui avoient appris ces beaux hôtels à trouver, ces salles parées, ces chasteaux et ces bons mols lits pour reposer, se virent et trouvèrent en celle povreté, si com-

After this period, there was, no doubt, considerable improvement; but it was very slow, and even late in the sixteenth century, skilled labour was hardly known, and honest industry was universally despised.[54] It is not, therefore, surprising, that the citizens, poor, miserable, and ignorant, should frequently purchase the protection of some powerful noble by yielding to him the little independence that they might have retained.[55] Few of the Scotch

---

mencèrent à rire et à dire: 'En quel pays nous a ci amenés l'amiral? Nous ne sçumes oncques que ce fût de povreté ni de dureté fors maintenant.' " *Les Chroniques de Froissart,* edit. Buchon, Paris, 1835, vol. ii. pp. 314, 315. "The hovels of the common people were slight erections of turf, or twigs, which, as they were often laid waste by war, were built merely for temporary accommodation. Their towns consisted chiefly of wooden cottages." .... "Even as late as 1600, the houses of Edinburgh were chiefly built of wood." *Chalmers' Caledonia,* vol. i. p. 802. Another account, written in 1670, says, "The houses of the commonalty are very mean, mud-wall and thatch, the best; but the poorer sort live in such miserable huts as never eye beheld." .... "In some parts, where turf is plentiful, they build up little cabbins thereof, with arched roofs of turf, without a stick of timber in it; when the house is dry enough to burn, it serves them for fuel, and they remove to another." *Harleian Miscellany,* vol. vi. p. 139, 4to, 1810.

54. "Our manufactures were carried on by the meanest of the people, who had small stocks, and were of no reputation. These were, for the most part, workmen for home-consumpt, such as masons, house-carpenters, armourers, blacksmiths, taylors, shoemakers, and the like. Our weavers were few in number, and in the greatest contempt, as their employments were more sedentary, and themselves reckoned less fit for war, in which all were obliged to serve, when the exigencies of the country demanded their attendance." *The Interest of Scotland Considered,* Edinburgh, 1733, p. 82. Pinkerton (*History of Scotland,* vol. ii. p. 392), referring to the Sloane manuscripts, says, "The author of an interesting memoir concerning the state of Scotland about 1590, observes, that the husbandmen were a kind of slaves, only holding their lands from year to year; that the nobility being too numerous for the extent of the country, there arose too great an inequality of rank and revenue; and there was no middle station between a proud landholder and those who, having no property to lose, were ready for any tumult. A rich yeomanry, numerous merchants and tradesmen of property, and all the denominations of the middle class, so important in a flourishing society, were long to be confined to England." Thirteen years later, we are told that the manufactures of Scotland "were confined to a few of the coarsest nature, without which the poorest nations are unable to subsist." *Laing's History of Scotland,* vol. iii. p. 7, under the year 1603.

55. Thus, for instance, "the town of Dunbar naturally grew up under the shelter of the castle of the same name." .... "Dunbar became the town, in demesn, of the successive Earls of Dunbar and March, partaking of their influences, whether unfortunate or happy." *Chalmers' Caledonia,* vol. ii. p. 416. "But when the regal government became at any time feeble, these towns, unequal to their own protection, placed themselves under the shelter of the most powerful lord in their neighbourhood. Thus, the town of Elgyn found it neces-

towns ventured to elect their chief magistrate from among their own people; but the usual course was, to choose a neighbouring peer as provost or baillie.[56] Indeed, it often happened that his office became hereditary, and was looked upon as the vested right of some aristocratic family.[57] To the head of that family, every thing gave way. His authority was so incontestable, that an injury done even to one of his retainers was resented, as if it had been done to himself.[58] The burgesses who were sent to parliament, were completely dependent on the noble who ruled the town. Down to quite modern times, there was in Scotland no real popular representation. The so-called representatives were obliged to vote as they were ordered; they were, in fact, delegates of the aristocracy; and as they possessed no chamber of their own, they sat and deliberated in the midst of their powerful masters, by whom they were openly intimidated.[59]

---

sary, at various periods between the years 1389 and 1452, to accept of many charters of protection, and discharges of taxes, from the Earls of Moray, who held it in some species of vassalage." *Sinclair's Scotland,* vol. v. p. 3. Compare *Pinkerton's History of Scotland,* vol. ii. p. 396; and two letters, written in 1543 and 1544, by the magistrates of Aberdeen, to the Earl of Huntly, and printed in the *Council Register of Aberdeen,* vol. i. pp. 190, 201, Aberdeen, 1844, 4to. They say to him, "Ye haf our band as protectour to wss."

56. *Tytler's History of Scotland,* vol. iv. p. 225. See also p. 131; and *Pinkerton's History of Scotland,* vol. ii. p. 179. Sometimes the nobles did not leave to the citizens even the appearance of a free election, but fought it out among themselves. An instance of this happened at Perth, in 1544, "where a claim for the office of provost was decided by arms, between Lord Ruthven on the one side, supported by a numerous train of his vassals, and Lord Gray, with Norman Lesley master of Rothes, and Charteris of Kinfauns, on the other." *Tytler,* vol. iv. p. 323.

57. For illustrations of this custom, see *Hollinshead's Scottish Chronicle,* vol. ii. p. 230. *Brown's History of Glasgow,* vol. ii. p. 154. *Denholm's History of Glasgow,* p. 249. *Mercer's History of Dunfermline,* p. 83.

58. "An injury inflicted on the 'man' of a nobleman was resented as much as if he himself had been the injured party." *Preface to the Council Register of Aberdeen,* vol. i. p. xii.

59. See, in *Macaulay's History of England,* vol. i. p. 93, 1st edit., a spirited description of Scotland in 1639. "The parliament of the northern kingdom was a very different body from that which bore the same name in England." . . . . "The three estates sat in one house. The commissioners of the burghs were considered merely as retainers of the great nobles," &c. To come down much later, Lord Cockburn gives a terrible account of the state of things in Scotland in 1794, the year in which Jeffrey was called to the bar. "There was then, in this country, no popular representation, no emancipated burghs, no effective rival of the established church, no independent press, no free public meetings, and no better trial by jury, even in political cases (except high treason), than what was

Under these circumstances, it would have been idle for the crown to have expected aid from a body of men who themselves had no influence, and whose scanty privileges existed only on suffrance. But there was another class, which was extremely powerful, and to which the Scotch kings naturally turned. That class was the clergy; and the interest which both parties had in weakening the nobles, caused a coalition between the church and the throne, against the aristocracy. During a long period, and indeed until the latter half of the sixteenth century, the kings almost invariably favoured the clergy, and increased their privileges in every way they could. The Reformation dissolved this alliance, and gave rise to new combinations, which I shall presently indicate. But while the alliance lasted, it was of great use to the clergy, by imparting to their claims a legitimate sanction, and making them appear the supporters of order and of regular government. The result, however, clearly proved that the nobles were more than equal to the confederacy which opposed them. Indeed, looking at their enormous power, the only wonder is, that

---

consistent with the circumstances, that the jurors were not sent into court under any impartial rule, and that, when in court, those who were to try the case were named by the presiding judge. The Scotch representatives were only forty-five, of whom thirty were elected for counties, and fifteen for towns. Both from its price and its nature (being enveloped in feudal and technical absurdities), the elective franchise in counties, where alone it existed, was far above the reach of the whole lower, and of a great majority of the middle, and of many even of the higher, ranks. There were probably not above 1500 or 2000 county electors in all Scotland; a body not too large to be held, hope included, in government's hand. The return, therefore, of a single opposition member was never to be expected." . . . . "Of the fifteen town members, Edinburgh returned one. The other fourteen were produced by clusters of four or five unconnected burghs electing each one delegate, and these four or five delegates electing the representative. Whatever this system may have been originally, it had grown, in reference to the people, into as complete a mockery as if it had been invented for their degradation. The people had nothing to do with it. It was all managed by town-councils, of never more than thirty-three members; and every town-council was self-elected, and consequently perpetuated its own interests. The election of either the town or the county member was a matter of such utter indifference to the people, that they often only knew of it by the ringing of a bell, or by seeing it mentioned next day in a newspaper; for the farce was generally performed in an apartment from which, if convenient, the public could be excluded, and never in the open air." *Cockburn's Life of Jeffrey,* Edinburgh, 1852, vol. i. pp. 74–76. On the state of Scotch representation between this and the Reform Bill, compare *Irving's History of Dumbartonshire,* 4to, 1860, pp. 275, 276, with *Moore's Memoirs,* edited by Lord John Russell, vol. iv. p. 268, vol. vi. p. 163, London, 1853–4.

the clergy could have prolonged the contest as they did; since they were not actually overthrown until the year 1560. That the struggle should have been so arduous, and should have extended over so considerable a period, is what, on a superficial view, no one could have expected. The reason of this, I shall now endeavour to explain; and I shall, I trust, succeed in proving, that in Scotland there was a long train of general causes, which secured to the spiritual classes immense influence, and which enabled them, not only to do battle with the most powerful aristocracy in Europe, but to rise up, after what seemed their final defeat, fresh and vigorous as ever, and eventually to exercise, as Protestant preachers, an authority nowise inferior to that which they had wielded as Catholic priests.

Of all Protestant countries, Scotland is certainly the one where the course of affairs has for the longest period been most favourable to the interests of superstition. How those interests were encouraged during the seventeenth and eighteenth centuries, I shall hereafter relate. At present, I purpose to examine the causes of their early growth, and to show the way in which they were not only connected with the Reformation, but gave to that great event some peculiarities which are extremely remarkable, and are diametrically opposed to what happened in England.

If the reader will bear in mind what I have elsewhere stated,[60] he will remember that the two principal sources of superstition are ignorance and danger; ignorance keeping men unacquainted with natural causes, and danger making them recur to supernatural ones. Or, to express the same proposition in other words, the feeling of veneration, which, under one of its aspects, takes the form of superstition, is a product of wonder and of fear;[61] and it is obvious that wonder is connected with ignorance, and that fear is connected with danger.[62] Hence it is, that whatever in

60. *History of Civilization,* vol. i. pp. 113–117, 342–347.
61. *Ibid.,* vol. i. p. 616.
62. We must discriminate between wonder and admiration. Wonder is the product of ignorance; admiration is the product of knowledge. Ignorance wonders at the supposed irregularities of nature; science admires its uniformities. The earlier writers rarely attended to this distinction, because they were misled by the etymology of the word "admiration." The Romans were very superficial thinkers upon all matters except jurisprudence; and their blundering use of "admirari" gave rise to the error, so common among our old writers, of "I admire," instead of "I wonder."

any country increases the total amount of amazement, or whatever in any country increases the total amount of peril, has a direct tendency to increase the total amount of superstition, and therefore to strengthen the hands of the priesthood.

By applying these principles to Scotland, we shall be able to explain several facts in the history of that country. In the first place, the features of its scenery offer a marked contrast to those of England, and are much more likely, among an ignorant people, to suggest effective and permanent superstitions. The storms and the mists, the darkened sky flashed by frequent lightning, the peals of thunder reverberating from mountain to mountain, and echoing on every side, the dangerous hurricanes, the gusts sweeping the innumerable lakes with which the country is studded, the rolling and impetuous torrent flooding the path of the traveller and stopping his progress, are strangely different to those safer and milder phenomena, among which the English people have developed their prosperity, and built up their mighty cities. Even the belief in witchcraft, one of the blackest superstitions which has ever defaced the human mind, has been affected by these peculiarities; and it has been well observed, that while, according to the old English creed, the witch was a miserable and decrepit hag, the slave rather than the mistress of the demons which haunted her, she, in Scotland, rose to the dignity of a potent sorcerer, who mastered the evil spirit, and, forcing it to do her will, spread among the people a far deeper and more lasting terror.[63]

63. "Our Scottish witch is a far more frightful being than her supernatural coadjutor on the south side of the Tweed. She sometimes seems to rise from the proper sphere of the witch, who is only the slave, into that of the sorcerer, who is master of the demon." . . . . "In a people, so far behind their neighbours in domestic organisation, poor and hardy, inhabiting a country of mountains, torrents, and rocks, where cultivation was scanty, accustomed to gloomy mists and wild storms, every impression must necessarily assume a corresponding character. Superstitions, like funguses and vermin, are existences peculiar to the spot where they appear, and are governed by its physical accidents." . . . . "And thus it is that the indications of witchcraft in Scotland are as different from those of the superstition which in England receives the same name, as the Grampian Mountains from Shooter's Hill or Kennington Common." *Burton's Criminal Trials in Scotland,* vol. i. pp. 240–243. This is admirably expressed, and exhausts the general view of the subject. The relation between the superstition of the Scotch and the physical aspects of their country is also touched upon, though with much inferior ability, in *Browne's History of the Highlands,* vol. i. p. 106, and in *Sinclair's Scotland,* vol. iv. p. 560. Hume, in his *Commentaries on the Law of Scotland,* vol. ii. p. 556, has an interesting passage

Similar results were produced by the incessant and sanguinary wars to which Scotland was exposed, and especially by the cruel ravages of the English in the fourteenth century. Whatever religion may be in the ascendant, the influence of its ministers is invariably strengthened by a long and dangerous war, the uncertainties of which perplex the minds of men, and induce them, when natural resources are failing, to call on the supernatural for help. On such occasions, the clergy rise in importance; the churches are more than usually filled; and the priest, putting himself forward as the exponent of the wishes of God, assumes the language of authority, and either comforts the people under their losses in a righteous cause, or else explains to them that those losses are sent as a visitation for their sins, and as a warning that they have not been sufficiently attentive to their religious duties; in other words, that they have neglected rites and ceremonies, in the performance of which the priest himself has a personal interest.

No wonder, therefore, that in the fourteenth century, when the sufferings of Scotland were at their height, the clergy flourished more than ever; so that as the country became poorer, the spiritual classes became richer in proportion to the rest of the nation. Even in the fifteenth, and first half of the sixteenth, century, when industry began somewhat to advance, we are assured that notwithstanding the improvement in the position of laymen, the whole of their wealth put together, and including the posses-

on the high pretensions of Scotch witchcraft, which never degenerated, as in other countries, into a mere attempt at deception, but always remained a sturdy and deep-rooted belief. He says, "For, among the many trials for witchcraft which fill the record, I have not observed that there is even one which proceeds upon the notion of a vain or cheating art, falsely used by an impostor to deceive the weak and credulous." Further information respecting Scotch witchcraft will be found in *Mackenzie's Criminal Laws of Scotland,* Edinburgh, folio, 1699, pp. 42–56; *Correspondence of Mrs. Grant of Laggan,* London, 1844, vol. iii. pp. 186, 187; *Southey's Life of Bell,* London, 1844, vol. i. p. 52; *Vernon Correspondence,* edited by James, London, 1841, vol. ii. p. 301; *Weld's History of the Royal Society,* London, 1848, vol. i. p. 89; *Letters from a Gentleman in the North of Scotland,* edit. 1815, vol. i. pp. 220, 221; *The Spottiswoode Miscellany,* vol. ii. p. 41, Edinburgh, 1845; *Lyon's History of St. Andrews,* Edinburgh, 1843, vol. ii. pp. 56, 57. The work of James I., and that of Sir Walter Scott, need hardly be referred to, as they are well known to every one who is interested in the history of witchcraft; but Pitcairn's *Criminal Trials,* though less read, are, in every respect, more valuable, on account of the materials they contain for a study of this department of Scotch superstition.

sions of all ranks, was barely equal to the wealth of the Church.[64] If the hierarchy were so rapacious and so successful during a period of comparative security, it would be difficult to overrate the enormous harvest they must have reaped in those earlier days, when danger being much more imminent, hardly any one died without leaving something to them; all being anxious to testify their respect towards those who knew more than their fellows, and whose prayers could either avert present evil, or secure future happiness.[65]

Another consequence of these protracted wars was, that a more than ordinary proportion of the population embraced the ecclesiastical profession, because in it alone there was some chance of safety; and the monasteries in particular were crowded with persons who hoped, though frequently in vain, to escape from the burnings and slaughterings to which Scotland was exposed. When the country, in the fifteenth century, began to recover from the effects of these ravages, the absence of manufactures and of

---

64. Pinkerton (*History of Scotland,* vol. i. p. 414) says, that, in the reigns of James II. and James III., "the wealth of the Church was at least equivalent to that of all the lay interest." See also *Life of Spottiswoode,* p. liii., in volume i. of his *History of the Church of Scotland.* "The numerous devices employed by ecclesiastics, both secular and regular, for enriching the several Foundations to which they were attached, had transferred into their hands more than half of the territorial property of Scotland, or of its annual produce."

In regard to the first half of the sixteenth century, it is stated by a high authority, that, just before the Reformation, "the full half of the wealth of the nation belonged to the clergy." *M'Crie's Life of Knox,* p. 10. And another writer says, "If we take into account the annual value of all these abbeys and monasteries, in conjunction with the bishoprics, it will appear at once that the Scottish Catholic hierarchy was more munificently endowed, considering the extent and resources of the kingdom, than it was in any other country in Europe." *Lawson's Roman Catholic Church in Scotland,* p. 22. See also, respecting the incomes of the Scotch bishops, which, considering the poverty of the country, were truly enormous, *Lyon's History of St. Andrews,* Edinburgh, 1843, vol. i. pp. 97, 125.

65. "They could employ all the motives of fear and of hope, of terror and of consolation, which operate most powerfully on the human mind. They haunted the weak and the credulous; they besieged the beds of the sick and of the dying; they suffered few to go out of the world without leaving marks of their liberality to the Church, and taught them to compound with the Almighty for their sins, by bestowing riches upon those who called themselves his servants." *History of Scotland,* book ii. p. 89, in *Robertson's Works,* London, 1831. It is interesting to observe the eagerness with which the clergy of one persuasion expose the artifices of those of another. By comparing their different statements, laymen gain an insight into the entire scheme.

commerce, made the Church the best avenue to wealth;[66] so that it was entered by peaceful men for the purpose of security, and by ambitious men as the surest means of achieving distinction.

Thus it was, that the want of great cities, and of that form of industry which belongs to them, made the spiritual classes more numerous than they would otherwise have been; and what is very observable is, that it not only increased their number, but also increased the disposition of the people to obey them. Agriculturists are naturally, and by the very circumstances of their daily life, more superstitious than manufacturers, because the events with which they deal are more mysterious, that is to say, more difficult to generalize and predict.[67] Hence it is, that, as a body, the inhabitants of agricultural districts pay greater respect to the teachings of their clergy than the inhabitants of manufacturing districts. The growth of cities has, therefore, been a main cause of the decline of ecclesiastical power; and the fact that, until the eighteenth century, Scotland had nothing worthy of being called a city, is one of many circumstances which explain the prevalence of Scotch superstition, and the inordinate influence of the Scotch clergy.

To this, we must add another consideration of great moment. Partly from the structure of the country, partly from the weakness of the crown, and partly from the necessity of being constantly in arms to repel foreign invaders, the predatory habits incidental to an early state of society were encouraged, and consequently the reign of ignorance was prolonged. Little was studied, and nothing was known. Until the fifteenth century, there was not even an university in Scotland, the first having been founded at St. Andrews in 1412.[68] The nobles, when they were not making war

66. Pinkerton observes, under the year 1514, that "ecclesiastical dignities presented almost the only path to opulence." *History of Scotland,* vol. ii. p. 123.

67. *Buckle's History of Civilization,* vol. i. pp. 344–348.

68. Arnot (*History of Edinburgh,* p. 386) says, that the University of St. Andrews was founded in 1412; and the same thing is stated in *Kennedy's Annals of Aberdeen,* vol. ii. p. 83. Grierson, in his *History of St. Andrews,* Cupar, 1838, p. 14, says, "In 1410, the city of St. Andrews first saw the establishment of its famous university, the most ancient institution of the kind that exists in Scotland;" but, at p. 144 of the same work, we are told, that the charter, "constituting and declaring it to be a university," is "dated at St. Andrews, the 27th of February 1411." See also *Lyon's History of St. Andrews,* vol. i. pp. 203–206, vol. ii. p. 223. At all events, "at the commencement of the fifteenth century, no

upon the enemy, occupied themselves in cutting each other's throats, and stealing each other's cattle.[69] Such was their ignorance, that, even late in the fourteenth century, there is said to be no instance of a Scotch baron being able to sign his own name.[70] And as nothing approaching to a middle class had been yet formed, we may from this gain some idea of the amount of knowledge possessed by the people at large.[71] Their minds must have been immersed in a darkness which we can now barely conceive. No trades, or arts, being practised which required skill, or dexterity, there was nothing to exercise their intellects. They consequently remained so stupid and brutal, that an intelligent observer, who visited Scotland in the year 1360, likens them to savages, so much was he struck by their barbarism and their unsocial manners.[72] Another writer, early in the fifteenth century,

---

university existed in Scotland; and the youth who were desirous of a liberal education were under the necessity of seeking it abroad." *M'Crie's Life of Melville,* vol. i. p. 211. The charter granted by the Pope, confirming the university, reached Scotland in 1413. *Lawson's Roman Catholic Church in Scotland,* Edinburgh, 1836, p. 12.

69. Those were times, when, as a Scotch lawyer delicately expresses himself, "thieving was not the peculiar habit of the low and indigent, but often common to them with persons of rank and landed estate." *Hume's Commentaries on the Law of Scotland,* 4to, 1797, vol. i. p. 126. The usual form of robbery being cattle-stealing, a particular name was invented for it; see p. 148, where we learn that it "was distinguished by the name of Hership or Herdship, being the driving away of numbers of cattle, or other bestial, by the masterful force of armed people."

70. Tytler, who was a great patriot, and disposed to exaggerate the merit of every thing which was Scotch, does nevertheless allow that, "from the accession of Alexander III. to the death of David II. (*i.e.,* in 1370), it would be impossible, I believe, to produce a single instance of a Scottish baron who could sign his own name." *Tytler's History of Scotland,* vol. ii. pp. 239, 240. Early in the sixteenth century, I find it casually mentioned, that "David Straiton, a cadet of the house of Laureston," .... "could not read." *Wodrow's Collections,* vol. i. pp. 5, 6. The famous chief, Walter Scott of Harden, was married in 1567; and "his marriage contract is signed by a notary, because none of the parties could write their names." *Chambers' Annals,* vol. i. p. 46. Crawfurd (*History of Renfrew,* part iii. p. 313) says: "the modern practice of subscribing names to writes of moment was not used in Scotland till about the year 1540;" but he forgets to tell us why it was not used. In 1564, Robert Scot of Thirlstane, "ancestor of Lord Napier," could not sign his name. See *Pitcairn's Criminal Trials in Scotland,* vol. iii. p. 394.

71. A Scotchman, of considerable learning, says: "Scotland was no less ignorant and superstitious at the beginning of the fifteenth century, than it was towards the close of the twelfth." *Dalrymple's Annals of Scotland,* vol. i. p. 428.

72. "Et sont ainsi comme gens sauvages qui ne se savent avoir ni de nulli

uses the same expression; and, classing them with the animals which they tended, he declares that Scotland is fuller of savages than of cattle.[73]

By this combination of events, and by this union of ignorance with danger, the clergy had, in the fifteenth century, obtained more influence in Scotland than in any other European country, Spain alone excepted. And as the power of the nobles had increased quite as rapidly, it was natural that the crown, completely overshadowed by the great barons, should turn for aid to the Church. During the fifteenth century, and part of the sixteenth, this alliance was strictly preserved;[74] and the political history of Scotland is the history of a struggle by the kings and the clergy against the enormous authority of the nobles. The contest, after lasting about a hundred and sixty years, was brought to a close in 1560, by the triumph of the aristocracy, and the overthrow of the Church. With such force, however, had the circumstance just narrated, engrained superstition into the Scotch character, that the spiritual classes quickly rallied, and, under their new name of Protestants, they became as formidable as under their old name of Catholics. Forty-three years after the establishment of the Reformation in Scotland, James VI. ascended the throne of England, and was able to array the force of the southern country against the refractory barons of the northern. From that moment the Scotch aristocracy began to decline; and, the equipoise to the clergy being removed, the Church became so powerful, that, during the seventeenth and eighteenth centuries, it was the most effectual obstacle to the progress of Scotland; and even now it exercises a sway which is incomprehensible to those who have not carefully studied the whole chain of its antecedents. To trace with minuteness the long course of affairs which has led to this unfortunate result, would be incompatible with the object of an Introduction, whose only aim is to establish broad and general principles. But, to bring the question clearly before the mind of

accointer." *Les Chroniques de Froissart,* edit. Buchon, Paris, 1835, vol. ii. p. 315.

73. "Plus pleine de sauvagine que de bestail." *Hist. de Charles VI, par Le Laboureur,* quoted in *Pinkerton's History of Scotland,* vol. i. p. 149.

74. Occasionally, we find evidence of it earlier, but it was hardly systematic. Compare *Tytler's History of Scotland,* vol. i. p. 66, with *Dalrymple's Annals,* vol. i. pp. 72, 110, 111, 194, vol. iii. p. 296; *Nimmo's History of Stirlingshire,* p. 88; *Chalmers' History of Dunfermline,* pp. 133, 134.

the reader, it will be necessary, that I should give a slight sketch of the relation which the nobles bore to the clergy in the fifteenth and sixteenth centuries, and of the way in which their relative position, and their implacable hatred of each other, brought about the Reformation. By this means, we shall perceive, that the great Protestant movement, which, in other countries, was democratic, was, in Scotland, aristocratic. We shall also see, that, in Scotland, the Reformation, not being the work of the people, has never produced the effects which might have been expected from it, and which it did produce in England. It is, indeed, but too evident, that, while in England, Protestantism has diminished superstition, has weakened the clergy, has increased toleration, and, in a word, has secured the triumph of secular interests over ecclesiastical ones, its result in Scotland has been entirely different; and that, in that country, the Church, changing its form, without altering its spirit, not only cherished its ancient pretensions, but unhappily retained its ancient power; and that, although that power is now dwindling away, the Scotch preachers still exhibit, whenever they dare, an insolent and domineering spirit, which shows how much real weakness there yet lurks in the nation, where such extravagant claims are not immediately silenced by the voice of loud and general ridicule.

II

Condition of Scotland in the Fifteenth and Sixteenth Centuries

Early in the fifteenth century, the alliance between the Crown and the Church, and the determination of that alliance to overthrow the nobles, became manifest. Indications of this may be traced in the policy of Albany, who was Regent from 1406 to 1419, and who made it his principal object to encourage and strengthen the clergy.[1] He also dealt the first great blow upon which any government had ventured against the aristocracy. Donald, who was one of the most powerful of the Scottish chieftains, and who, indeed, by the possession of the Western Isles, was almost an independent prince, had seized the earldom of Ross, which, if he could have retained, would have enabled him to set the Crown at defiance. Albany, backed by the Church, marched into his territories, in 1411, forced him to renounce the earldom, to make personal submission, and to give hostages for his future conduct.[2] So vigorous a proceeding on the part of the executive, was extremely unusual in Scotland;[3] and it was the first of a series of aggressions, which

1. "The Church was eminently favoured by Albany." *Pinkerton's History of Scotland,* vol. i. p. 86. But Pinkerton misunderstands his policy in regard to the nobles.

2. *Skene's Highlanders,* vol. ii. pp. 72–74; *Browne's History of the Highlands,* vol. i. p. 162, vol. iv. pp. 435, 436.

3. Chalmers (*Caledonia,* vol. i. pp. 826, 827), referring to the state of things before Albany, says, "There is not a trace of any attempt by Robert II. to limit the power of the nobles, whatever he may have added, by his improvident grants, to their independence. He appears not to have attempted to raise the royal prerogative from the debasement, in which the imprudence and misfortunes of David II. had left it." And, of his successor, Robert III., "So mild a prince, and so weak a man, was not very likely to make any attempt upon the power of others, when he could scarcely support his own."

ended in the Crown obtaining for itself, not only Ross, but also the Western Isles.[4] The policy inaugurated by Albany, was followed up with still greater energy by James I. In 1424, this bold and active prince procured an enactment, obliging many of the nobles to show their charters, in order that it might be ascertained what lands they held, which had formerly belonged to the Crown.[5] And, to conciliate the affections of the clergy, he, in 1425, issued a commission, authorizing the Bishop of Saint Andrews to restore to the Church whatever had been alienated from it; while he at the same time directed that the justiciaries should assist in enforcing execution of the decree.[6] This occurred in June; and what shows that it was part of a general scheme is, that in the preceding spring, the king suddenly arrested, in the parliament assembled at Perth, upwards of twenty of the principal nobles, put four of them to death, and confiscated several of their estates.[7] Two years afterwards, he, with equal perfidy, summoned the Highland chiefs to meet him at Inverness, laid hands on them also, executed three, and imprisoned more than forty, in different parts of the kingdom.[8]

4. In 1476, "the Earldom of Ross was inalienably annexed to the Crown; and a great blow was thus struck at the power and grandeur of a family which had so repeatedly disturbed the tranquillity of Scotland." *Gregory's History of the Western Highlands,* Edinburgh, 1836, p. 50. In 1493, "John, fourth and last Lord of the Isles, was forfeited, and deprived of his title estates." *Ibid.* p. 58.

5. As those who held crown lands were legally, though not in reality, the king's tenants, the act declared, that "gif it like the king, he may ger sumonde all and sindry his tenand at lauchfull day and place to schawe thar chartis." *The Acts of the Parliament of Scotland,* vol. ii. p. 4, § 9, edit. folio, 1814.

6. "On the 8th June 1425, James issued a commission to Henry, bishop of St. Andrews, authorising him to resume all alienations from the Church, with power of anathema, and orders to all justiciaries to assist. This curious paper is preserved in Harl. Ms. 4637, vol. iii. f. 189." *Pinkerton's History of Scotland,* vol. i. p. 116. Archbishop Spottiswoode, delighted with his policy, calls him a "good king," and says that he built for the Carthusians "a beautiful monastery at Perth, bestowing large revenues upon the same." *Spottiswoode's History of the Church of Scotland,* vol. i. p. 113. And Keith assures us that, on one occasion, James I. went so far as to give to one of the bishops "a silver cross, in which was contained a bit of the wooden cross, on which the apostle St. Andrew had been crucified." *Keith's Catalogue of Scotch Bishops,* Edinburgh, 1755, 4to, p. 67.

7. Compare *Balfour's Annales,* vol. i. pp. 153–156, with *Pinkerton's History,* vol. i. pp. 113–115. Between these two authorities there is a slight, but unimportant, discrepancy.

8. *Tytler's History of Scotland,* vol. iii. pp. 95–98; *Skene's Highlanders,* vol.

By these measures, and by supporting the Church with the same zeal that he attacked the nobles, the king thought to reverse the order of affairs hitherto established, and to secure the supremacy of the throne over the aristocracy.[9] But herein, he overrated his own power. Like nearly all politicians, he exaggerated the value of political remedies. The legislator and the magistrate may, for a moment, palliate an evil; they can never work a cure. General mischiefs depend upon general causes, and these are beyond their art. The symptoms of the disease they can touch, while the disease itself baffles their efforts, and is too often exasperated by their treatment. In Scotland, the power of the nobles was a cruel malady, which preyed on the vitals of the nation; but it had long been preparing; it was a chronic disorder; and, having worked into the general habit, it might be removed by time, it could never be diminished by violence. On the contrary, in this, as in all matters, whenever politicians attempt great good, they invariably inflict great harm. Overaction on one side produces reaction on the other, and the balance of the fabric is disturbed. By the shock of conflicting interests, the scheme of life is made insecure. New animosities are kindled, old ones are embittered, and the natural jar and discordance are aggravated, simply because the rulers of mankind cannot be brought to understand, that, in dealing with a great country, they had to do with an organization so subtle, so extremely complex, and withal so obscure, as to make it highly probable, that whatever they alter in it, they will alter wrongly, and that while their efforts to protect or to strengthen its particular parts are extremely hazardous, it does undoubtedly possess within itself a capacity of repairing its injuries, and that to bring such capacity into play, there is merely required that time

---

ii. p. 75; and an imperfect narrative in *Gregory's History of the Western Highlands,* p. 35.

9. Tytler (*History of Scotland,* vol. iii. p. 126), under the year 1433, says: "In the midst of his labours for the pacification of his northern dominions, and his anxiety for the suppression of heresy, the king never forgot his great plan for the diminution of the exorbitant power of the nobles." See also p. 84. "It was a principle of this enterprising monarch, in his schemes for the recovery and consolidation of his own power, to cultivate the friendship of the clergy, whom he regarded as a counterpoise to the nobles." Lord Somerville (*Memorie of the Somervilles,* vol. i. p. 173) says, that the superior nobility were "never or seldome called to counsell dureing this king's reign."

and freedom which the interference of powerful men too often prevents it from enjoying.

Thus it was in Scotland, in the fifteenth century. The attempts of James I. failed, because they were particular measures directed against general evils. Ideas and associations, generated by a long course of events, and deeply seated in the public mind, had given to the aristocracy immense power; and if every noble in Scotland had been put to death, if all their castles had been razed to the ground, and all their estates confiscated, the time would unquestionably have come, when their successors would have been more influential than ever, because the affection of their retainers and dependents would be increased by the injustice that had been perpetrated. For, every passion excites its opposite. Cruelty to-day, produces sympathy to-morrow. A hatred of injustice contributes more than any other principle to correct the inequalities of life, and to maintain the balance of affairs. It is this loathing at tyranny, which, by stirring to their inmost depth the warmest feelings of the heart, makes it impossible that tyranny should ever finally succeed. This, in sooth, is the noble side of our nature. This is that part of us, which, stamped with a godlike beauty, reveals its divine origin, and, providing for the most distant contingencies, is our surest guarantee that violence shall never ultimately triumph; that, sooner or later, despotism shall always be overthrown; and that the great and permanent interests of the human race shall never be injured by the wicked counsels of unjust men.

In the case of James I., the reaction came sooner than might have been expected; and, as it happened in his lifetime, it was a retribution, as well as a reaction. For some years, he continued to oppress the nobles with impunity;[10] but, in 1436, they turned upon him, and put him to death, in revenge for the treatment to which he had subjected many of them.[11] Their power now rose as suddenly as it had fallen. In the south of Scotland, the Douglases were supreme,[12] and the earl of that family possessed rev-

10. Compare *Chalmers' Caledonia,* vol. ii. p. 263, with *Buchanan's Rerum Scoticarum Historia,* lib. x. p. 286.

11. *Tytler's History of Scotland,* vol. iii. pp. 157, 158.

12. Lindsay of Pitscottie (*Chronicles,* vol. i. p. 2) says, that directly after the death of James I., "Alexander, Earle of Douglas, being uerie potent in kine

enues about equal to those of the Crown.[13] And, to show that his authority was equal to his wealth, he, on the marriage of James II., in 1449, appeared at the nuptials with a train composed of five thousand followers.[14] These were his own retainers, armed and resolute men, bound to obey any command he might issue to them. Not, indeed, that compulsion was needed on the part of a Scotch noble to secure the obedience of his own people. The servitude was a willing one, and was essential to the national manners. Then, and long afterwards, it was discreditable, as well as unsafe, not to belong to a great clan; and those who were so unfortunate as to be unconnected with any leading family, were accustomed to take the name of some chief, and to secure his protection by devoting themselves to his service.[15]

What the Earl of Douglas was in the south of Scotland, that were the Earls of Crawford and of Ross in the north.[16] Singly they were formidable; united they seemed irresistible. When, therefore, in the middle of the fifteenth century, they actually leagued

---

and friendis, contemned all the kingis officeris, in respect of his great puissance." The best account I have seen of the rise of the Douglases, is in Chalmers' learned, but ill-digested, work, *Caledonia,* vol. i. pp. 579–583.

13. In 1440, "the chief of that family had revenues, perhaps equivalent to those of the Scottish monarch." *Pinkerton's History of Scotland,* vol. i. p. 192.

14. "It may give us some idea of the immense power possessed at this period by the Earl of Douglas, when we mention, that on this chivalrous occasion, the military suite by which he was surrounded, and at the head of which he conducted the Scottish champions to the lists, consisted of a force amounting to five thousand men." *Tytler's History of Scotland,* vol. iii. p. 215. The old historian of his family says: "He is not easy to be dealt with; they must have mufles that would catch such a cat. Indeed, he behaved himself as one that thought he would not be in danger of them; he entertained a great family; he rode ever well accompanied when he came in publick; 1000 or 2000 horse were his ordinary train." *Hume's History of the House of Douglas,* vol. i. pp. 273, 264, reprinted Edinburgh, 1743.

15. In the seventeenth century, "To be without a chief, involved a kind of disrepute; and those who had no distinct personal position of their own, would find it necessary to become a Gordon or a Crichton, as prudence or inclination might point out." *Burton's Criminal Trials in Scotland,* vol. i. p. 207. Compare *Pitcairn's Criminal Trials in Scotland,* vol. iii. p. 250, on "the protective surname of Douglas;" and *Skene's Highlanders,* vol. ii. p. 252, on the extreme importance attached to the name of Macgregor.

16. "Men of the greatest puissance and force next the Douglasses, that were in Scotland in their times." *Hume's History of the House of Douglas,* vol. i. p. 344. The great power of the Earls of Ross in the north, dates from the thirteenth century. See *Skene's Highlanders,* vol. i. pp. 133, 134, vol. ii. p. 52.

together, and formed a strict compact against all their common enemies, it was hard to say what limit could be set to their power, or what resource remained to the government, except that of sowing disunion among them.[17]

But, in the mean time, the disposition of the nobles to use force against the Crown, had been increased by fresh violence. Government, instead of being warned by the fate of James I., imitated his unscrupulous acts, and pursued the very policy which had caused his destruction. Because the Douglases were the most powerful of all the great families, it was determined that their chiefs should be put to death; and because they could not be slain by force, they were to be murdered by treachery. In 1440, the Earl of Douglas, a boy of fifteen, and his brother, who was still younger than he, were invited to Edinburgh on a friendly visit to the king. Scarcely had they arrived, when they were seized by order of the chancellor, subjected to a mock trial, declared guilty, dragged to the castle-yard, and the heads of the poor children cut off.[18]

Considering the warm feelings of attachment which the Scotch entertained for their chiefs, it is difficult to overrate the consequences of this barbarous murder, in strengthening a class it was hoped to intimidate. But this horrible crime was committed by the government only, and it occured during the king's minority: the next assassination was the work of the king himself. In 1452, the

17. In 1445, the Earl of Douglas concluded "one offensiue and defensiue league and combinatione against all, none excepted, (not the king himselue), with the Earle of Crawfurd, and Donald, Lord of the Isles; wich was mutually sealled and subscriued by them three, the 7 day of Marche." *Balfour's Annales,* vol. i. p. 173. This comprised the alliance of other noble families. "He maid bandis with the Erle of Craufurd, and with Donald lorde of the Ylis, and Erle of Ross, to take part every ane with other, and with dyvers uther noble men also." *Lesley's History of Scotland,* from 1436 to 1561, p. 18.

18. An interesting account of this dastardly crime, is given in *Hume's History of the House of Douglas,* vol. i. pp. 274–288, where great, but natural, indignation is expressed. On the other hand, Lesley, bishop of Ross, narrates it with a cold-blooded indifference, characteristic of the ill-will which existed between the nobles and the clergy, and which prevented him from regarding the murder of two children as an offence. "And eftir he was set doun to the burd with the governour, chancellour, and otheris noble men present, the meit was sudantlie removed, and ane bullis heid presented, quhilk in thay daies was ane signe of executione; and incontinent the said erle, David his broder, and Malcolme Fleming of Cummernald, wer heidit before the castell yett of Edenburgh." *Lesley's History,* p. 16.

Earl of Douglas[19] was, with great show of civility, requested by James II. to repair to the court then assembled at Stirling. The earl hesitated, but James overcame his reluctance by sending to him a safe-conduct with the royal signature, and issued under the great seal.[20] The honour of the king being pledged, the fears of Douglas were removed. He hastened to Stirling, where he was received with every distinction. The evening of his arrival, the king, after supper was over, broke out into reproaches against him, and, suddenly drawing his dagger, stabbed him. Gray then struck him with a battle-ax, and he fell dead on the floor, in presence of his sovereign, who had lured him to court, that he might murder him with impunity.[21]

The ferocity of the Scotch character, which was the natural result of the ignorance and poverty of the nation, was, no doubt, one cause, and a very important one, of the commission of such crimes as these, not secretly, but in the open light of day, and by the highest men in the State. It cannot, however, be denied, that another cause was, the influence of the clergy, whose interest it was to humble the nobles, and who were by no means scrupulous as to the means that they employed.[22] As the crown became more alienated from the aristocracy, it united itself still closer with the Church. In 1443, a statute was enacted, the object of which was, to secure ecclesiastical property from the attacks made upon it by the nobles.[23] And although, in that state of society, it was easier

19. The cousin of the boys who were murdered in 1440. See *Hume's History of the House of Douglas*, vol. i. pp. 297, 316.

20. "With assurance under the broad seal." *Hume's House of Douglas*, vol. i. p. 351. See also *Nimmo's History of Stirlingshire*, Edinb. 1777, pp. 246, 322, 323.

21. *Hume's House of Douglas*, vol. i. pp. 351–353. The king "stabbed him in the breast with a dagger. At the same instant Patrick Gray struck him on the head with a pole-ax. The rest that were attending at the door, hearing the noise, entred, and fell also upon him; and, to show their affection to the king, gave him every man his blow after he was dead." Compare *Lindsay of Pitscottie's Chronicles of Scotland*, vol. i. p. 103. "He strak him throw the bodie thairwith; and thairefter the guard, hearing the tumult within the chamber, rushed in and slew the earle out of hand."

22. In *Nimmo's History of Stirlingshire*, pp. 99, 100, the alienation of the nobles from the Church is dated "from the middle of the fifteenth century;" and this is perhaps correct in regard to general dislike, though the movement may be clearly traced fifty years earlier.

23. See *Acts of the Parliaments of Scotland*, vol. ii. p. 33, edit. folio, 1814; respecting the "statute of haly kirk quhilk is oppressit and hurt."

to pass laws than to execute them, such a measure indicated the general policy of the government, and the union between it and the Church. Indeed, as to this, no one could be mistaken.[24] For nearly twenty years, the avowed and confidential adviser of the Crown was Kennedy, bishop of Saint Andrews, who retained power until his death, in 1466, during the minority of James III.[25] He was the bitter enemy of the nobles, against whom he displayed an unrelenting spirit, which was sharpened by personal injuries; for the Earl of Crawford had plundered his lands, and the Earl of Douglas had attempted to seize him, and had threatened to put him into irons.[26] The mildest spirit might well have been roused by this; and as James II., when he assassinated Douglas, was more influenced by Kennedy than by any one else, it is probable that the bishop was privy to that foul transaction. At all events, he expressed no disapprobation of it; and when, in consequence of the

24. In 1449, James II., "with that affectionate respect for the clergy, which could not fail to be experienced by a prince who had successfully employed their support and advice to escape from the tyranny of his nobles, granted to them some important privileges." *Tytler's History of Scotland,* vol. iii. p. 226. See also p. 309. Among many similar measures, he conceded to the monks of Paisley some important powers of jurisdiction that belonged to the Crown. Charter, 13th January 1451, 2, in *Chalmers' Caledonia,* vol. iii. p. 823.

25. *Pinkerton's History of Scotland,* vol. i. pp. 188, 209, 247, 254. *Keith's Catalogue of Scotch Bishops,* p. 19. *Ridpath's Border History,* p. 298. *Hollinshead's Scottish Chronicle,* vol. ii. p. 101. In *Somerville's Memorie of the Somervilles,* vol. i. p. 213, it is stated, under the year 1452, that fear of the great nobles "had once possest his majestie with some thoughts of going out of the countrey; but that he was perswaded to the contrary by Bishop Kennedie, then Arch-bishop of Saint Andrewes, whose counsell at that tyme and eftirward, in most things he followed, which at length proved to his majesties great advantage." See also *Lesley's History,* p. 23. "The king wes put to sic a sharp point, that he wes determinit to haif left the realme, and to haif passit in Fraunce by sey, were not that bischop James Kennedy of St. Androis causit him to tarrye."

26. "His lands were plundered by the Earl of Crawford and Alexander Ogilvie of Inveraritie, at the instigation of the Earl of Douglas, who had farther instructed them to seize, if possible, the person of the bishop, and to put him in irons." Memoir of Kennedy, in *Chambers' Lives of Scotchmen,* vol. iii. p. 307, Glasgow, 1834. "Sed Kennedus et ætate, et consilio, ac proinde auctoritate cæteros anteibat. In eum potissimum ira est versa. Crafordiæ comes et Alexander Ogilvius conflato satis magno exercitu, agros ejus in Fifa latè populati, dum prædam magis, quam causam sequuntur, omni genere cladis in vicina etiam prædia grassati, nemine congredi auso pleni prædarum in Angusiam revertuntur. Kennedus ad sua arma conversus comitem Crafordiæ disceptationem juris fugientem diris ecclesiasticis est prosecutus." *Buchanan, Rerum Scoticarum Historia,* lib. xi. p. 306.

murder, the Douglases and their friends rose in open rebellion, Kennedy gave to the king a crafty and insidious counsel, highly characteristic of the cunning of his profession. Taking up a bundle of arrows, he showed James, that when they were together, they were not to be broken; but that, if separated, they were easily destroyed. Hence he inferred, that the aristocracy should be overthrown by disuniting the nobles, and ruining them one by one.[27]

In this he was right, so far as the interests of his own order were concerned; but, looking at the interest of the nation, it is evident that the power of the nobles, notwithstanding their gross abuse of it, was, on the whole, beneficial, since it was the only barrier against despotism. The evil they actually engendered, was indeed immense. But they kept off other evils, which would have been worse. By causing present anarchy, they secured future liberty. For, as there was no middle class, there were only three orders in the commonwealth; namely, government, clergy, and nobles. The two first being united against the last, it is certain that if they had won the day, Scotland would have been oppressed by the worst of all yokes, to which a country can be subjected. It would have been ruled by an absolute king and an absolute Church, who, playing into each other's hands, would have tyrannized over a people, who, though coarse and ignorant, still loved a certain rude and barbarous liberty, which it was good for them to possess, but which, in the face of such a combination, they would most assuredly have forfeited.

Happily, however, the power of the nobles was too deeply

27. "This holie bischop schew ane similitud to the king, quhilk might bring him to experience how he might invaid againes the Douglass, and the rest of the conspiratouris. This bischop tuik furth ane great scheife of arrowes knitt togidder werrie fast, and desired him to put thame to his knie, and break thame. The king said it was not possible, becaus they war so many, and so weill fastened togidder. The bischop answeired, it was werrie true, bot yitt he wold latt the king sea how to break thame: and pulled out on be on, and tua be tua, quhill he had brokin thame all; then said to the king, 'Yea most doe with the conspiratouris in this manner, and thair complices that are risen againes yow, quho are so many in number, and so hard knit togidder in conspiracie againes yow, that yea cannot gett thame brokin togidder. Butt be sick pratick as I have schowin yow be the similitud of thir arrowes, that is to say, yea must conqueis and break lord by lord be thameselffis, for yea may not deall with thame all at once." *Lindsay of Pitscottie's Chronicles of Scotland,* vol. i. pp. 172, 173.

rooted in the popular mind to allow this catastrophe. In vain did James III. exert himself to discourage them,[28] and to elevate their rivals, the clergy.[29] Nothing could shake their authority; and, in 1482, they, seeing the determination of the king, assembled together, and such was their influence over their followers, that they had no difficulty in seizing his person, and imprisoning him in the Castle at Edinburgh.[30] After his liberation, fresh quarrels arose;[31] and in 1488, the principal nobles collected troops, met him in the field, defeated him, and put him to death.[32] He was succeeded by James IV., under whom the course of affairs was exactly the same; that is to say, on one side the nobles, and on the other side the Crown and the Church. Every thing that the king could do to uphold the clergy, he did cheerfully. In 1493, he obtained an act to secure the immunities of the sees of Saint Andrews and of Glasgow, the two most important in Scotland.[33] In 1503, he procured a general revocation of all grants and gifts prejudicial to the Church, whether they had been made by the Parliament or by the

28. "He wald nocht suffer the noblemen to come to his presence, and to governe the realme be thair counsell." *Lesley's History of Scotland*, p. 48. "Wald nocht use the counsall of his nobillis." p. 55. "Excluding the nobility." *Hume's History of the House of Douglas*, vol. ii. p. 33. "The nobility seeing his resolution to ruin them." p. 46. "Hes contening his nobility." *Balfour's Annales*, vol. i. p. 206.

29. Also to aggrandize them. See, for instance, what "has obtained the name of the golden charter, from the ample privileges it contains, confirmed to Archbishop Shevez by James III. on 9th July 1480." *Grierson's History of Saint Andrews*, p. 58, Cupar, 1838.

30. "Such was the influence of the aristocracy over their warlike followers, that the king was conveyed to the castle of Edinburgh, without commotion or murmur." *Pinkerton's History of Scotland*, vol. i. p. 308.

31. "The king and his ministers multiplied the insults which they offered to the nobility." . . . . "A proclamation was issued, forbidding any person to appear in arms within the precincts of the court; which, at a time when no man of rank left his own house without a numerous retinue of armed followers, was, in effect, debarring the nobles from all access to the king." . . . . "His neglect of the nobles irritated, but did not weaken them." *History of Scotland*, book i. p. 68, in *Robertson's Works*, edit. London, 1831.

32. *Balfour's Annales*, vol. i. pp. 213, 214; *Buchanan, Rerum Scoticarum Historia*, lib. xii. p. 358. Lindsay of Pitscottie (*Chronicles*, vol. i. p. 222) says: "This may be ane example to all kingis that cumes heirefter, not to fall from God." . . . . "For, if he had vsed the counsall of his wyse lordis and barrones, he had not cum to sick disparatioun."

33. *Acts of the Parliaments of Scotland*, folio, 1814, vol. ii. p. 232. "That the said abbaceis confirmit be thame sall neid na prouisioun of the court of Rome."

Council.[34] And, in 1508, he, by the advice of Elphinston, bishop of Aberdeen, ventured on a measure of still greater boldness. That able and ambitious prelate induced James to revive against the nobility several obsolete claims, by virtue of which the king could, under certain circumstances, take possession of their estates, and could, in every instance in which the owner held of the Crown, receive nearly the whole of the proceeds during the minority of the proprietor.[35]

To make such claims was easy; to enforce them was impossible. Indeed, the nobles were at this time rather gaining ground than losing it; and, after the death of James IV., in 1513, they, during the minority of James V., became so powerful, that the regent, Albany, twice threw up the government in despair, and at length abandoned it altogether.[36] He finally quitted Scotland in 1524, and with him the authority of the executive seemed to have vanished. The Douglases soon obtained possession of the person of the king, and compelled Beaton, archbishop of Saint Andrews, the most influential man in the Church, to resign the office of chancellor.[37] The whole command now fell into their hands; they

34. *Acts of the Parliaments of Scotland,* vol. ii. p. 240; and the summary of the statute (p. 21), "Revocation of donations, statutis, and all uthir thingis hurtand the croune or hali kirk." In the next year (1504), the king "greatly augmented" the revenues of the bishoprick of Galloway. *Chalmers' Caledonia,* vol. iii. p. 417.

35. *Pinkerton's History of Scotland,* vol. ii. p. 63; *Calderwood's History of the Kirk of Scotland,* vol. viii. p. 135, edit. Wodrow Society, Edinburgh, 1849. The latter authority states, that "The bishop devysed wayes to King James the Fourth, how he might attaine to great gaine and profit. He advised him to call his barons and all those that held any lands within the realme, to show their evidents by way of recognition; and, if they had not sufficient writings for their warrant, to dispone upon their lands at his pleasure; for the which advice he was greatlie hated. But the king, perceaving the countrie to grudge, agreed easilie with the possessors."

36. The Regency of Albany, little understood by the earlier historians, has been carefully examined by Mr. Tytler, in whose valuable, though too prolix, work, the best account of it will be found. *Tytler's History of Scotland,* vol. iv. pp. 98–160, Edinburgh, 1845. On the hostility between Albany and the nobles, see *Irving's History of Dumbartonshire,* p. 99; and, on the revival of their power in the north, after the death of James IV., see *Gregory's History of the Western Highlands,* pp. 114, 115.

37. *Tytler's History of Scotland,* vol. iv. pp. 180–182: "Within a few months, there was not an office of trust or emolument in the kingdom, which was not filled by a Douglas, or by a creature of that house." See also pp. 187,

or their adherents filled every office; secular interests predominated, and the clergy were thrown completely into the shade.[38] In 1528, however, an event occurred by which the spiritual classes not only recovered their former position, but gained a preëminence, which, as it turned out, was eventually fatal to themselves. Archbishop Beaton, impatient at proceedings so unfavourable to the Church, organized a conspiracy, by means of which James effected his escape from the Douglases, and took refuge in the castle of Stirling.[39] This sudden reaction was not the real and controlling cause, but it was undoubtedly the proximate cause, of the establishment of Protestantism in Scotland. For, the reins of government now passed into the hands of the Church; and the most influential of the nobles were consequently persecuted, and some of them driven from the country. But, though their political power was gone, their social power remained. They were stripped of their honours and their wealth. They became outcasts, traitors, and beggars. Still, the real foundation of their authority was unshaken, because that authority was the result of a long train of circumstances, and was based on the affections of the people.

194; and *Keith's Catalogue of Scotch Bishops*, pp. 22, 23. Beaton, who was so rudely dispossessed of the chancellorship, that, according to Keith, he was, in 1525, obliged "to lurk among his friends for fear of his life," is mentioned, in the preceding year, as having been the main supporter of Albany's government; "that most hath favoured the Duke of Albany." *State Papers of the Reign of Henry VIII.*, vol. iv. p. 97, 4to, 1836.

38. The complete power of the Douglases lasted from the cessation of Albany's regency to the escape of the king, in 1528. *Keith's History of the Affairs of Church and State in Scotland*, edit. Edinburgh, 1835, vol. i. pp. 33–35. Compare *Balfour's Annales*, vol. i. p. 257. "The Earle of Angus violentley takes one him the gouerniment, and retanes the king in effecte a prisoner with him; during wich tyme he, the Earle of Lennox, and George Douglas, his auen brother, frely disposses vpone all affaires both of churche and staite."

39. *Tytler's History of Scotland*, vol. iv. pp. 195, 196. The curious work, entitled *A Diurnal of Occurrents*, p. 10, says, "In the zeir of God 1500, tuantie aucht zeiris, the kingis grace by slicht wan away fra the Douglassis." From Stirling, he repaired to Edinburgh, on 6th July 1528, and went to "the busshop of Sainct Andros loegeing." See a letter written on the 18th of July 1528, by Lord Dacre to Wolsey, in *State Papers of Henry VIII.*, vol. iv. p. 501, 4to, 1836. Compare a proclamation on 10th September 1528, in *Pitcairn's Criminal Trials in Scotland*, vol. i. part i. pp. 138*, 139*, Edinburgh, 4to, 1833. I particularly indicate these documents, because Lindsay of Pitscottie (in his *Chronicles of Scotland*, vol. ii. p. 335) erroneously places the flight of James in 1527; and he is generally one of the most accurate of the old writers, if indeed he be the author of the work which bears his name.

Therefore it was, that the nobles, even those who were exiled and attainted, were able to conduct an arduous, but eventually successful, struggle against their enemies. The desire of revenge whetted their exertions, and gave rise to a deadly contest between the Scotch aristocracy and the Scotch Church. This most remarkable conflict was, in some degree, a continuation of that which began early in the fifteenth century. But it was far more bitter; it lasted, without interruption, for thirty-two years; and it was only concluded by the triumph of the nobles, who, in 1560, completely overthrew the Church, and destroyed, almost at a blow, the whole of the Scotch hierarchy.

The events of this struggle, and the vicissitudes to which, during its continuance, both parties were exposed, are related, though somewhat confusedly, in our common histories; it will be sufficient if I indicate the salient points, and, avoiding needless detail, endeavour to throw light on the general movement. The unity of the entire scheme will thus be brought before our minds, and we shall see, that the destruction of the Catholic Church was its natural consummation, and that the last act of that gorgeous drama, so far from being a strained and irregular sequence, was in fit keeping with the whole train of the preceding plot.

When James effected his escape, in 1528, he was a boy of sixteen, and his policy, so far as he can be said to have had any mind of his own, was of course determined by the clergy, to whom he owed his liberty, and who were his natural protectors. His principal adviser was the Archbishop of Saint Andrews; and the important post of chancellor, which, under the Douglases, had been held by a layman, was now conferred on the Archbishop of Glasgow.[40] These two prelates were supreme; while, at the same time, the Abbot of Holyrood was made treasurer, and the Bishop of Dunkeld was made privy seal.[41] All nobles, and even all followers, of the house of Douglas, were forbidden to approach within twelve miles of the court, under pain of treason.[42] An expedition

40. *State Papers of Henry VIII.*, vol. iv. p. 501.
41. "Archibald was depryvit of the thesaurarie, and placit thairin Robert Cairncorse, abbot of Halyrudhous. And als was tane fra the said Archibald the privie seill, and was givin to the bischope of Dunkell." *A Diurnal of Occurrents*, p. 11.
42. Tytler (*History of Scotland*, vol. iv. p. 196) says: "His first act was to summon a council, and issue a proclamation, that no lord or follower of the

was fitted out, and sent against the Earl of Caithness, who was defeated and slain.[43] Just before this occurred, the Earl of Angus was driven out of Scotland, and his estates confiscated.[44] An act of attainder was passed against the Douglases.[45] The government, moreover, seized, and threw into prison, the Earl of Bothwell, Home, Maxwell, the two Kerrs, and the barons of Buccleuch, Johnston, and Polwarth.[46]

All this was vigorous enough, and was the consequence of the Church recovering her power. Other measures, equally decisive, were preparing. In 1531, the king deprived the Earl of Crawford of most of his estates, and threw the Earl of Argyle into prison.[47] Even those nobles who had been inclined to follow him, he now discouraged. He took every opportunity of treating them with coldness, while he filled the highest offices with their rivals, the clergy.[48] Finally, he, in 1532, aimed a deadly blow at their order,

---

house of Douglas should dare to approach within *six* miles of the court, under pain of treason." For this, no authority is cited; and the historian of the Douglas family distintly states, "within *twelve* miles of the king, under pain of death." *Hume's House of Douglas,* vol. ii. p. 99. See also *Diurnal of Occurrents,* p. 10: "that nane of thame nor thair familiaris cum neir the king be tuelf myllis." The reason was, that "the said kingis grace haid greit suspicioun of the temporall lordis, becaus thaj favourit sum pairt the Douglassis." *Diurnal,* p. 12.

43. "The Erle of Caithnes and fyve hundreth of his men wes slayne an drownit in the see." *Lesley's History of Scotland,* p. 141.

44. *Tytler's History of Scotland,* vol. iv. pp. 203, 204.

45. *Acts of the Parliaments of Scotland,* vol. ii. p. 324, edit. folio, 1814.

46. *Tytler's History of Scotland,* vol. iv. p. 207.

47. *Tytler,* vol. iv. p. 212.

48. "His preference of the clergy to the temporal lords disgusted these proud chiefs." *Tytler's History of Scotland,* vol. iv. p. 230. See also p. 236. His reasons are stated by himself, in a curious letter, which he wrote so late as 1541, to Henry VIII. "We persaif," writes James, "be zoure saidis writingis yat Ze ar informyt yat yair suld be sum thingis laitlie attemptat be oure kirkmen to oure hurte and skaith, and contrar oure mynde and plesure. We can nocht understand, quhat suld move Zou to beleif the samyn, assuring Zou *We have nevir fund bot faithfull and trew obedience of yame at all tymes,* nor yai seik nor attemptis nouthir jurisdictioun nor previlegijs, forthir nor yai have usit sen the first institutioun of the Kirk of Scotland, quhilk We may nocht apoun oure conscience alter nor change in the respect We have to the honour and faith of God and Halikirk, and douttis na inconvenient be yame to come to Ws and oure realme yerthrou; for sen the Kirk wes first institute in our realme, the stait yairof hes nevir failzeit, bot *hes remanyt evir obedient to oure progenitouris, and in our tyme mair thankefull to Ws, nor evir yai wer of before."* This letter, which, in several points of view, is worth reading, will be found in *State Papers of Henry VIII.,* vol. v. pp. 188–190, 4to, 1836.

by depriving them of a large part of the jurisdiction which they were wont to exercise in their own country, and to the possession of which they owed much of their power. At the instigation of the Archbishop of Glasgow, he established what was called the College of Justice, in which suits were to be decided, instead of being tried, as heretofore, by the barons, at home, in their castles. It was ordered that this new tribunal should consist of fifteen judges, eight of whom must be ecclesiastics; and, to make the intention still more clear, it was provided that the president should invariably be a clergyman.[49]

This gave the finishing touch to the whole, and it, taken in connexion with previous measures, exasperated the nobles almost to madness. Their hatred of the clergy became uncontrollable; and, in their eagerness for revenge, they not only threw themselves into the arms of England, and maintained a secret understanding with Henry VIII., but many of them went even further, and showed a decided leaning towards the principles of the Reformation. As the enmity between the aristocracy and the Church grew more bitter, just in the same proportion did the desire to reform the Church become more marked. The love of innovation was encouraged by interested motives, until, in the course of a few years, an immense majority of the nobles adopted extreme Protestant opinions; hardly caring what heresy they embraced, so long as they were able, by its aid, to damage a Church from which they had recently received the greatest injuries, and with which they and their progenitors had been engaged in a contest of nearly a hundred and fifty years.[50]

In the mean time, James V. united himself closer than ever

49. *Tytler's History of Scotland,* vol. iv. pp. 212, 213, and *Arnot's History of Edinburgh,* 4to, 1788, p. 468: "fifteen ordinary judges, seven churchmen, seven laymen, and a president, whom it behoved to be a churchman." The statute, as printed in the folio edition of 1814 (*Acts of the Parliaments of Scotland,* vol. ii. p. 335), says, "xiiij psoufis half spuale half temporall wᵗ ane president." Mr. Lawson (*Roman Catholic Church in Scotland,* Edinburgh, 1836, p. 81) supposes that it was the Archbishop of St. Andrews who advised the erection of this tribunal.

50. Keith, who evidently does not admire this part of the history of his country, says, under the year 1546, "Several of our nobility found it their temporal interest, as much as their spiritual, to sway with the new opinions as to religious matters." *Keith's Affairs of Church and State,* vol. i. pp. 112, 113. Later, and with still more bluntness: "The noblemen wanted to finger the patrimony of the kirkmen." vol. iii. p. 11.

with the hierarchy. In 1534, he gratified the Church, by personally assisting at the trial of some heretics, who were brought before the bishops and burned.[51] The next year, he was offered, and
he willingly accepted, the title of Defender of the Faith, which
was transferred to him from Henry VIII.; that king being supposed to have forfeited it by his impiety.[52] At all events, James
well deserved it. He was a stanch supporter of the Church, and
his privy-council was chiefly composed of ecclesiastics, as he
deemed it dangerous to admit laymen to too large a share in the
government.[53] And, in 1538, he still further signalized his policy,
by taking for his second wife Mary of Guise; thus establishing an
intimate relation with the most powerful Catholic family in Europe, whose ambition, too, was equal to their power, and who
made it their avowed object to uphold the Catholic faith, and to
protect it from those rude and unmannerly invasions which were
now directed against it in most parts of Europe.[54]

    This was hailed by the Church as a guarantee for the intentions

51. "In the month of August (1534), the bishops having gotten fitt oppor-
tunitie, renewed their battell aganest Jesus Christ. David Stratilon, a gentel-
man of the House of Lawrestoune, and Mr. Norman Gowrlay, was brought to
judgement in the Abby of Halyrudhouse. The king himself, all cloathed with
reid, being present, grait pains war taken upon David Stratoun to move him
to recant and burn his bill; bot he, ever standing to his defence, was in end
adjudged to the fire. He asked grace at the king. The bishops answred proudlie,
that 'the king's hands war bound, and that he had no grace to give to such as
were by law condemned.' So was he, with Mr. Norman, after dinner, upon
the 27th day of Agust, led to a place beside the Rude of Greenside, between
Leth and Edinbrug, to the intent that the inhabitants of Fife, seeing the fire,
might be striken with terrour and feare." *Pitcairn's Criminal Trials in Scotland,*
vol. i. part i. p. 210*. Also *Calderwood's Historie of the Kirk of Scotland,* vol.
i. pp. 106, 107.

52. "It appears, by a letter in the State-paper Office, that Henry remonstrated
against this title being given to James." *Tytler's History of Scotland,* vol. iv. p.
223. See also p. 258.

53. In 1535, "his privy council were mostly ecclesiastics." *Ibid.* vol. iv.
p. 222. And Sir Ralph Sadler, during his embassy to Scotland in 1539–40,
writes: "So that the king, as far as I can perceive, is of force driven to use the
bishops and his clergy as his only ministers for the direction of his realm. They
be the men of wit and policy that I see here; they be never out of the king's
ear. And if they smell any thing that in the least point may touch them, or that
the king seem to be content with any such thing, straight they inculk to him,
how catholic a prince his father was, and feed him both with fair words and
many, in such wise as by those policies they lead him (having also the whole
governance of his affairs) as they will." *State Papers and Letters of Sir Ralph
Sadler,* Edinb., 1809, 4to, vol. i. p. 47.

54. *State Papers of Henry VIII.,* vol. v. p. 128. *A Diurnal of Occurrents,* p.
22. The Reverend Mr. Kirkton pronounces that the new queen was "ane egge

of the king. And so indeed it proved to be. David Beaton, who negotiated the marriage, became the chief adviser of James during the rest of his reign. He was made Archbishop of Saint Andrews in 1539,[55] and, by his influence, a persecution hotter than any yet known, was directed against the Protestants. Many of them escaped into England,[56] where they swelled the number of the exiles, who were waiting till the time was ripe to take a deadly revenge. They, and their adherents at home, coalesced with the disaffected nobles, particularly with the Douglases,[57] who were by far the most powerful of the Scotch aristocracy, and who were connected with most of the great families, either by old associations, or by the still closer bond of interest which they all had in reducing the power of the Church.[58]

At this juncture, the eyes of men were turned towards the Douglases, whom Henry VIII. harboured at his court, and who were now maturing their plans.[59] Though they did not yet dare

---

of the bloody nest of Guise." *Kirkton's History of the Church of Scotland,* edited by Sharpe, Edinburgh, 1817, 4to, p. 7.

55. "At his return home, he was made coadjutor, and declared future successor to his uncle in the primacy of St. Andrews, in which see he came to be fully invested upon the death of his uncle the next year, 1539." *Keith's Catalogue of Scotch Bishops,* pp. 23, 24.

56. *M'Crie's Life of Knox,* p. 20. *Spottiswoode's History of the Church of Scotland,* vol. i. p. 139. *Lawson's Roman Catholic Church in Scotland,* p. 178. *Wodrow's Collections upon the Lives of the Reformers,* vol. i. p. 100.

57. Tytler (*History of Scotland,* vol. iv. p. 241), says, that the cruelties of 1539 forced "many of the persecuted families to embrace the interests of the Douglases."

58. It is asserted of the Douglases, that, early in the sixteenth century, their "alliances and power were equal to one-half of the nobility of Scotland." *Brown's History of Glasgow,* vol. i. p. 8. See also, on their connexions, *Hume's House of Douglas,* vol. i. pp. xix. 252, 298, vol. ii. p. 293.

59. Henry VIII., "in the year 1532, sought it directly, among the conditions of peace, that the Douglas, according to his promise, should be restored. For King Henry's own part, he entertained them with all kind of beneficence and honour, and made both the Earl and Sir George of his Privy Council." *Hume's History of the House of Douglas,* vol. ii. pp. 105, 106. James was very jealous of any communication taking place between the Douglases and his other subjects; but it was impossible for him to prevent it. See a letter which he wrote to Sir Thomas Erskin (in *Miscellany of the Spalding Club,* vol. ii. p. 193, Aberdeen, 1842, 4to), beginning, "I commend me rycht hartly to you, and weit ye that it is murmuryt hyr that ye sould a spolkyn with Gorge and Archebald Dougles in Ingland, quhylk wase again my command and your promys quhan we departyt." See also the cases of Lady Trakware, John Mathesone, John Hume, and others, in *Pitcairn's Criminal Trials in Scotland,* vol. i. part i. pp. 161*, 177*, 202*, 243*, 247*.

to return to Scotland, their spies and agents reported to them all that was done, and preserved their connexions at home. Feudal covenants, bonds of manrent, and other arrangements, which, even if illegal, it would have been held disgraceful to renounce, were in full force; and enabled the Douglases to rely with confidence on many of the most powerful nobles, who were, moreover, disgusted at the predominance of the clergy, and who welcomed the prospect of any change which was likely to lessen the authority of the Church.[60]

60. "The Douglases were still maintained with high favour and generous allowances in England; their power, although nominally extinct, was still far from being destroyed; their spies penetrated into every quarter, followed the king to France, and gave information of his most private motions; their feudal covenants and bands of manrent still existed, and bound many of the most potent nobility to their interest; whilst the vigour of the king's government, and his preference of the clergy to the temporal lords, disgusted these proud chiefs, and disposed them to hope for a recovery of their influence from any change which might take place." *Tytler's History of Scotland,* vol. iv. pp. 229, 230. These bonds of manrent, noticed by Tytler, were among the most effective means by which the Scotch nobles secured their power. Without them, it would have been difficult for the aristocracy to have resisted the united force of the Crown and the Church. On this account, they deserve special attention. Chalmers (*Caledonia,* vol. i. p. 824) could find no bond of manrent earlier than 1354; but in Lord Somerville's *Memorie of the Somervilles,* edit. Edinburgh, 1815, vol. i. p. 74, one is mentioned in 1281. This is the earliest instance I have met with; and they did not become very common till the fifteenth and sixteenth centuries. Compare *Hume's History of the House of Douglas,* vol. ii. p. 19. *Somerville's Memorie of the Somervilles,* vol. i. p. 234. *Pitcairn's Criminal Trials of Scotland,* vol. iii. p. 83. *Irving's History of Dumbartonshire,* pp. 142, 143. *Skene's Highlanders,* vol. ii. p. 186. *Gregory's History of the Western Highlands,* p. 126. *Kennedy's Annals of Aberdeen,* vol. i. p. 55. *Miscellany of the Spalding Club,* vol. ii. pp. cvi. 93, 251, vol. iv. pp. xlviii. 179. As these covenants were extremely useful in maintaining the balance of power, and preventing the Scotch monarchy from becoming despotic, acts of parliament were of course passed against them. See one in 1457, and another in 1555, respecting "lige" and "bandis of manrent and mantenance," in *Acts of the Parliaments of Scotland,* folio 1814, vol. ii. pp. 50, 495. Such enactments being opposed to the spirit of the age, and adverse to the exigencies of society, produced no effect upon the general practice, though they caused the punishment of several individuals. Manrent was still frequent until about 1620 or 1630, when the great social revolution was completed, by which the power of the aristocracy was subordinated to that of the Church. Then, the change of affairs effected, without difficulty, and indeed spontaneously, what the legislature had vainly attempted to achieve. The nobles, gradually sinking into insignificance, lost their spirit, and ceased to resort to those contrivances by which they had long upheld their order. Bonds of manrent became every year less common, and it is doubtful if there is any instance of them after 1661. See *Chalmers' Caledonia,* vol. iii. pp. 32, 33. It is, however, so dangerous to assert a negative, that I do not wish to

With such a combination of parties, in a country where, there being no middle class, the people counted for nothing, but followed wherever they were led, it is evident that the success or failure of the Reformation in Scotland was simply a question of the success or failure of the nobles. They were bent on revenge. The only doubt was, as to their being strong enough to gratify it. Against them, they had the Crown and the Church. On their side, they had the feudal traditions, the spirit of clanship, the devoted obedience of their innumerable retainers, and, what was equally important, that love of names, and of family associations, for which Scotland is still remarkable, but which, in the sixteenth century, possessed an influence difficult to exaggerate.

The moment for action was now at hand. In 1540, the government, completely under the control of the clergy, caused fresh laws to be enacted against the Protestants, whose interests were by this time identical with those of the nobles. By these statutes, no one, even suspected of heresy, could for the future hold any office; and all Catholics were forbidden to harbour, or to show favour to, persons who professed the new opinions.[61] The clergy, now flushed with conquest, and greedy for the destruction of their ancient rivals, proceeded to still further extremities. So unrelenting was their malice, that, in that same year, they presented to James a list containing the names of upwards of three hundred members of the Scotch aristocracy, whom they formally accused as heretics, who ought to be put to death, and whose estates they recommended the king to confiscate.[62]

---

rely on this date, and some few cases may exist later; but if so, they are very few, and it is certain that, speaking generally, the middle of the seventeenth century is the epoch of their extinction.

61. *Acts of the Parliaments of Scotland,* vol. ii. pp. 370, 371. "That na mañ quhatsueuir stait or conditioũ he be luge ressauve cherish nor favor ony heretike." . . . . "And alswa that na persoũ that hes bene suspectit of heresie howbeit thai be ressauit to penance and grace sall in this realme exers haif nor brouk ony honest estait degre office nor judicato* spuall nor teporale in burgh nor w*out nor na salbe admittit to be of our counsale."

62. Lindsay of Pitscottie (*Chronicles,* vol. ii. p. 383) says, that they "devysed to put ane discord and variance betwixt the lordis and gentlmen with thair prince; for they delaited, and gave vp to the king in writt, to the number of thrittie scoir of earles, lordis, and barrones, gentlmen and craftismen, that is, as thei alledgit, wer all heretickis, and levied not after the Pope's lawis, and ordinance of the hollie kirk; quhilk his grace sould esteme as ane capitall cryme, to ony man that did the same" . . . . "all thair landis, rentes, guidis, and geir

These hot and vindictive men little knew of the storm which they were evoking, and which was about to burst on their heads, and cover them and their Church with confusion. Not that we have reason to believe that a wiser conduct would have ultimately saved the Scotch hierarchy. On the contrary, the probability is, that their fate was sealed; for the general causes which governed the entire movement, had been so long at work, that, at this period, it would have been hardly possible to have baffled them. But, even if we admit as certain, that the Scotch clergy were doomed, it is also certain that their violence made their fall more grievous, by exasperating the passions of their adversaries. The train, indeed, was laid; their enemies had supplied the materials, and all was ready to explode; but it was themselves who at last applied the match, and sprung the mine to their own destruction.

In 1542, the nobles, seeing that the Church and the Crown were bent on their ruin, took the most decisive step on which they had yet ventured, and peremptorily refused to obey James in making war upon the English. They knew that the war in which they were desired to participate, had been fomented by the clergy, with the twofold object of stopping all communication with the exiles, and of checking the introduction of heretical opinions.[63] Both

---

apperteanis propperlie to your grace, for thair contempt of our hollie father the Pope, and his lawis, and high contempt of your grace's authoritie." This document was found among the king's papers after his death, when it appeared that, of the six hundred names on the list, more than three hundred belonged to the principal nobility: "Eum timorem auxerunt codicilli post regis interitum reperti, e quibus supra trecentorum è prima nobilitate nomina continebantur." *Buchanan, Rerum Scoticarum Historia,* lib. xv. p. 424. Compare *Sadler's State Papers,* 1809, vol. i. p. 94; and *Watson's Historicall Collections of Ecclesiastick Affairs in Scotland,* 1657, p. 22. According to Watson, it "was called the bloudy scroll."

63. In the autumn of 1542, James "was encouraged by the clergy to engage in a war against King Henry, who both assured him of victory, since he fought against an heretical prince, and advanced an annuity of 50,000 crowns for prosecuting the war." *Crawfurd's History of the Shire of Renfrew,* 1782, 4to, part i. p. 48. Compare, in *State Papers of Henry VIII.,* vol. v. p. 154, a letter written, in 1539, by Norfolk to Cromwell: "By diverse other waies I am advertised that the clergie of Scotlande be in such feare that their king shold do theire, as the kinges highnes hath done in this realme, that they do their best to bring their master to the warr; and by many waies I am advertised that a great parte of the temporaltie there wold their king shold followe our insample, which I pray God yeve hym grace to come unto." Even after the battle of Solway, the policy of the clergy was notoriously the same. "And undoubtedlie, the kyrkemen labor, by all the means they can, to empeche the unitie and establishment of thiese two

these intentions they resolved to frustrate, and, being assembled on the field, they declared with one voice that they would not invade England. Threats and persuasions were equally useless. James, stung with vexation, returned home, and ordered the army to be disbanded. Scarcely had he retired, when the clergy attempted to rally the troops, and to induce them to act against the enemy. A few of the peers, ashamed at what seemed a cowardly desertion of the king, appeared willing to march. The rest, however, refused; and, while they were in this state of doubt and confusion, the English, taking them unawares, suddenly fell upon their disorderly ranks, utterly routed them, and made a large number prisoners. In this disgraceful action, ten thousand Scotch troops fled before three hundred English cavalry.[64] The news being brought to James, while he was still smarting from the disobedience of the nobles, was too much for his proud and sensitive mind. He reeled under the double shock; a slow fever wasted his strength; he sunk into a long stupor; and, refusing all comfort, he died in December 1542, leaving the Crown to his infant daughter, Mary, during whose reign the great contest between the aristocracy and the Church was to be finally decided.[65]

The influence of the nobles was increased by the death of James V., and yet more by the bad repute into which the clergy fell for having instigated a war, of which the result was so disgraceful.[66] Their party was still further strengthened by the exiles, who, as

---

realmes; uppon what groundes ye can easelie conjecture." Letter from Sadler to Parr, dated Edinburgh, 27th March 1543, in *State Papers of Henry VIII.*, vol. v. p. 271, 4to, 1836.

64. "Ten thousand Scottish troops fled at the sight of three hundred English cavalry, with scarce a momentary resistance." *Tytler's History of Scotland,* vol. iv. p. 264.

65. The best account of these events will be found in *Tytler's History of Scotland,* vol. iv. pp. 260–267. I have also consulted *Ridpath's Border History,* pp. 372, 373. *Hollinshead's Scottish Chronicle,* vol. ii. pp. 207–209. *Lesley's History,* pp. 163–166. *Lindsay of Pitscottie's Chronicles,* vol. ii. pp. 399–406. *Calderwood's History of the Kirk of Scotland,* vol. i. pp. 145–152. *Buchanan, Rerum Scoticarum Historia,* lib. xiv. pp. 420, 421.

66. "This defeat being so very dishonourable, especially to the clergy, who stirred up the king to that attempt, and promised him great success from it; and there being such a visible evidence of the anger of God, fighting by his providence against them, all men were struck with fear and astonishment; the bishops were ashamed to show their faces for a time." *Stevenson's History of the Church of Scotland,* reprinted, Edinburgh, 1840, p. 30.

soon as they heard the glad tidings, prepared to leave England.[67] Early in 1543, Angus and Douglas returned to Scotland,[68] and were soon followed by other nobles, most of whom professed to be Protestants, though, as the result clearly proved, their Protestantism was inspired by a love of plunder and of revenge. The late king had, in his will, appointed Cardinal Beaton to be guardian of the queen, and governor of the realm.[69] Beaton, though an unprincipled man, was very able, and was respected as the head of the national church; he being Archbishop of Saint Andrews, and primate of Scotland. The nobles, however, at once arrested him,[70] deprived him of his regency, and put in his place the Earl of Arran, who, at this time, affected to be a zealous Protestant, though, on a fitting occasion, he afterwards changed his opinions.[71] Among the supporters of the new creed, the most power-

67. We may readily believe the assertion of an old chronicler, that "the nobilitie did not greatlie take his death grievouslie, because he had fined manie, imprisoned more, and caused no small few (for avoiding his displeasure) to flie into England, and rather to commit themselves to the enemie than to his anger." *Hollinshead's Scottish Chronicle,* vol. ii. p. 210.

68. *Hume's History of the House of Douglas,* vol. ii. p. 111.

69. It has been often said, that this will was forged; but for such an assertion I cannot find the slightest evidence, except the declaration of Arran (*Sadler's State Papers,* Edinburgh, 1809, vol. i. p. 138), and the testimony, if testimony it can be called, of Scotch historians, who do not profess to have examined the handwriting, and who, being themselves Protestants, seem to suppose that the fact of a man being a cardinal, qualifies him for every crime. There is no doubt that Beaton was thoroughly unprincipled, and therefore was capable of the forgery. Still, we have no proof; and the will is such as we might have expected from the king. In regard to Arran, his affirmation is not worth the paper it is written on: for he hated Beaton; he was himself very unscrupulous; and he succeeded to the post which Beaton had to vacate on the ground that the will was forged. If such circumstances do not disqualify a witness, some of the best-established principles of evidence are false. The reader who cares to look further into this subject, may compare, in favour of the will being forged, *Buchanan, Rerum Scoticarum Historia,* lib. xv. p. 422, Abredoniæ, 1762; *Knox's History of the Reformation,* edit. Laing, Edinburgh, 1846, vol. i. pp. 91, 92; *Irving's History of Dumbartonshire,* second edition, 4to, 1860, p. 102; and, in favour of its being genuine, *Lyon's History of St. Andrews,* Edinburgh, 1843, vol. i. pp. 304, 305. Some other writers on the subject leave it doubtful: *Tytler's History of Scotland,* 1845, vol. iv. p. 274; *Lawson's Roman Church in Scotland,* 1836, p. 99; and a note in *Keith's Church and State in Scotland,* 1844, vol. i. p. 63.

70. On the 26th of January 1542-3, "the said cardinall was put in pressoune in Dalkeith." *A Diurnal of Occurrents,* p. 26. See also, respecting his imprisonment, a letter written, on the 16th of March, by Angus and Douglas, in *State Papers of Henry VIII.,* vol. v. p. 263. He was then in "firmance."

71. His appointment was confirmed by parliament on the 12th of March. *Acts of the Parliaments of Scotland,* vol. ii. p. 411: "tuto^r lau^{t}full to the quenis

ful were the Earl of Angus and the Douglases. They were now freed from a proscription of fifteen years; their attainder was reversed, and their estates and honours were restored to them.[72] It was evident that not only the executive authority, but also the legislative, had passed from the Church to the aristocracy. And they, who had the power, were not sparing in the use of it. Lord Maxwell, one of the most active of their party, had, like most of them, in their zeal against the hierarchy, embraced the principles of the Reformation.[73] In the spring of 1543, he obtained the sanction of the Earl of Arran, the governor of Scotland, for a proposal which he made to the Lords of the Articles, whose business it was to digest the measures to be brought before Parliament. The proposal was, that the people should be allowed to read the Bible in a Scotch or English translation. The clergy arrayed all their force against what they rightly deemed a step full of danger to themselves, as conceding a fundamental principle of Protestantism. But all was in vain. The tide had set in, and was not to be turned. The proposition was adopted by the Lords of the Articles. On their authority, it was introduced into Parliament. It was passed.

---

grace and gounour of this realme." He excluded the clergy from power. On 20th March, in the same year, Sir Ralph Sadler writes to Henry VIII., that Sir George Douglas "brought me into the council-chamber, where I found a great number of noblemen and others at a long board, and divers standing, but *not one bishop nor priest among them.* At the upper end of the board sat the governour." *Sadler's State Papers,* vol. i. p. 78.

72. *Acts of the Parliaments of Scotland,* vol. ii. pp. 415, 419, 424, 423*; and *Tytler's History of Scotland,* vol. iv. p. 285.

73. "Had become a convert to its doctrines." *Tytler's Hist. of Scotland,* vol. iv. p. 286. But he, as well as the other nobles, neither knew nor cared much about doctrines; and he was, moreover, very venal. In April 1543, Sir Ralph Sadler writes to Henry VIII.: "And the lord Maxwell told me apart, 'That, indeed, he lacked silver, and had no way of relief but to your majesty;' which he prayed me to signify unto the same. I asked him what would relieve him? and he said, 300*l.*; 'for the which,' he said, 'as your majesty seemed, when he was with your grace, to have him in more trust and credit than the rest of your majesty's prisoners, so he trusted to do you as good service as any of them; and amongst them they will do you such service, as, if the war succeed, ye shall make an easy conquest of this realm; as *for his part he shall deliver into your hands, at the entry of your army, the keys of the same on the west marches, being all the strongholds there in his custody.*' I offered him presently to write to my lord of Suffolk for 100*l.* for him, if he would; but he said, 'he would stay till he heard again from your majesty in that behalf.' " *Sadler's State Papers,* vol. i. p. 165.

It received the assent of the government; and, amid the lamentations of the Church, it was proclaimed, with every formality, at the market-cross of Edinburgh.[74]

Scarcely had the nobles thus attained the upper hand, when they began to quarrel among themselves. They were resolved to plunder the Church; but they could not agree as to how the spoil should be shared. Neither could they determine as to the best mode of proceeding; some being in favour of an open and immediate schism, while others wished to advance cautiously, and to temporize with their opponents, that they might weaken the hierarchy by degrees. The more active and zealous section of the nobles were known as the English party,[75] owing to their intimate connexion with Henry VIII., from whom many of them received supplies of money. But, in 1544, war broke out between the two countries, and the clergy, headed by Archbishop Beaton, roused, with such success, the old feelings of national hatred against the English, that the nobles were compelled for a moment to bend before the storm, and to advocate an alliance from France. Indeed, it seemed for a few months as if the Church and aristocracy had forgotten their old and inveterate hostility, and were about to unite their strength in one common cause.[76]

This, however, was but a passing delusion. The antagonism

74. *Acts of the Parliaments of Scotland,* vol. ii. pp. 415, 425. *Sadler's State Papers,* vol. i. p. 83. Knox, in his *History of the Reformation* (edit. Laing, vol. i. p. 100), archly says, "The cleargy hearto long repugned; butt in the end, convicted by reassonis, *and by multitud of votes in thare contrare,* thei also condiscended; and so, by Act of Parliament, it was maid free to all man and woman to reid the Scriptures in thair awin toung, or in the Engliss toung; and so war all Actes maid in the contrair abolished."

75. Or, as Keith calls them, "English lords." *History of the Affairs of Church and State in Scotland,* vol. i. p. 80.

76. In May 1544, the English attacked Scotland, *Tytler's History,* vol. iv. p. 316; and in the same month, the "Anglo-Scottish party" consisted only of the Earls of Lennox and of Glencairn, since even "Angus, George Douglas, and their numerous and powerful adherents, joined the cardinal." p. 319. As to the part taken by the Scotch clergy, see, in *Sadler's State Papers,* vol. i. p. 173, a letter to Henry VIII., written on the 1st of May 1543: "And as to the kirkmen, I assure your majesty they seek the war by all the means they can, and do daily entertain the noblemen with money and rewards to sustain the wars, rather than there should be any agreement with your majesty; thinking, verily, that if peace and unity succeed, that they shall be reformed, and lose their glory, which they had rather die, and put all this realm in hazard, than they would forego." See also p. 184, note.

between the two classes was irreconcilable.[77] In the spring of 1545, the leading Protestant nobles formed a conspiracy to assassinate Archbishop Beaton,[78] whom they hated more than any one else, partly because he was the head of the Church, and partly because he was the ablest and most unscrupulous of their opponents. A year, however, elapsed before their purpose could be effected; and it was not till May 1546, that Lesley, a young baron, accompanied by the Laird of Grange, and a few others, burst into Saint Andrews, and murdered the primate in his own castle.[79]

77. Buchanan records a very curious conversation between the Regent and Douglas, which, as I do not remember to have met with elsewhere, I shall transcribe. The exact date of it is not mentioned, but, from the context, it evidently took place in 1544 or 1545. "Ibi cum Prorex suam deploraret solitudinem, et se a nobilitate derelictum quereretur, Duglassius ostendit 'id ipsius culpa fieri, non nobilium, qui et fortunas omnes et vitam ad publicam salutem tuendam conferrent, quorum consilio contempto ad sacrificulorum nutum circumageretur, qui foris imbelles, domi seditiosi, omniumque periculorum expertes alieni laboris fructu ad suas voluptates abuterentur. Ex hoc fonte inter te et proceres facta est suspitio, quæ (quòd neutri alteris fidatis) rebus gerendis maxime est impedimento.'" *Rerum Scoticarum Historia,* lib. xv. p. 435. Buchanan was, at this time, about thirty-eight years old; and that some such conversation as that which he narrates actually took place, is, I think, highly probable, though the historian may have thrown in some touches of his own. At all events, he was too great a rhetorician to invent what his contemporaries would deem unlikely to happen; so that, from either point of view, the passage is valuable as an evidence of the deep-rooted hostility which the nobles bore towards the Church.

78. *Tytler's History of Scotland,* vol. iv. p. 337. "The plot is entirely unknown either to our Scottish or English historians; and now, after the lapse of nearly three centuries, has been discovered in the secret correspondence of the State-paper Office." The first suggestion of the murder was in April 1544. See *State Papers of Henry VIII.,* vol. v. p. 377, and the end of the Preface to vol. iv. But Mr. Tytler and the editor of the *State Papers* appear to have overlooked a still earlier indication of the coming crime, in *Sadler's Papers.* See, in that collection, vol. i. p. 77, a conversation, held in March 1543, between Sir Ralph Sadler and the Earl of Arran; Sadler being conducted by the Earl of Glencairn. On that occasion, the Earl of Arran used an expression concerning Beaton, the meaning of which Sir Ralph evidently understood. "'By God,' quoth he, 'he shall never come out of prison whilst I may have mine own will, *except it be to his farther mischief.'* I allowed the same well" (replied Sadler), "and said, 'It were pity, but he should receive such reward as his merits did require.'"

79. *State Papers of Henry VIII.,* vol. v. p. 560. *A Diurnal of Occurrents,* p. 42. *Calderwood's History of the Kirk of Scotland,* vol. i. pp. 221–223. Lindsay of Pitscottie (*Chronicles,* vol. ii. p. 484) relates a circumstance respecting the murder, which is too horrible to mention, and of which it is enough to say, that it consisted of an obscene outrage committed on the corpse of the victim. Though such facts cannot now be published, they are so characteristic of the age, that they ought not be passed over in complete silence.

The horror with which the Church heard of this foul and bar-barous deed,[80] may be easily imagined. But the conspirators, noth-ing daunted, and relying on the support of a powerful party, jus-tified their act, seized the castle of Saint Andrews, and prepared to defend it to the last. And in this resolution they were upheld by a most remarkable man, who now first appeared to public view, and who, being admirably suited to the age in which he lived, was destined to become the most conspicuous character of those troublous times.

That man was John Knox. To say that he was fearless and in-corruptible, that he advocated with unflinching zeal what he be-lieved to be the truth, and that he devoted himself with untiring energy to what he deemed the highest of all objects, is only to render common justice to the many noble attributes which he un-doubtedly possessed. But, on the other hand, he was stern, unre-lenting, and frequently brutal; he was not only callous to human suffering, but he could turn it into a jest, and employ on it the re-sources of his coarse, though exuberant, humour;[81] and he loved power so inordinately, that, unable to brook the slightest opposi-tion, he trampled on all who crossed his path, or stood even for a moment in the way of his ulterior designs.

The influence of Knox in promoting the Reformation, has in-deed been grossly exaggerated by historians, who are too apt to ascribe vast results to individual exertions; overlooking those large and general causes, in the absence of which the individual exertion would be fruitless. Still, he effected more than any single man;[82]

80. Respecting which, two Scotch Protestant historians have expressed them-selves in the following terms: "God admonished men, by this judgement, that he will in the end be avenged upon tyranns for their crueltie, howsoever they strenthen themselves." *Calderwood's History of the Kirk of Scotland,* vol. i. p. 224. And, whoever considers all the circumstances, "must acknowledge it was a stupendous act of the judgment of the Lord, and that the whole was overruled and guided by Divine Providence." *Stevenson's History of the Church and State of Scotland,* p. 38.

81. Even the editor of *M'Crie's Life of Knox,* Edinburgh, 1841, p. xxxv., notices "the ill-timed merriment he displays in relating the foul deed" of Beaton's murder.

82. Shortly before his death, he said, with honest and justifiable pride, "What I have bene to my countrie, albeit, this vnthankfull aige will not knowe, yet the aiges to come wilbe compelled to bear witnes to the treuth." *Bannatyne's Jour-nal,* Edinburgh, 1806, p. 119. Bannatyne was Knox's secretary. It is to be re-

although the really important period of his life, in regard to Scotland, was in and after 1559, when the triumph of Protestantism was already secure, and when he reaped the benefit of what had been effected during his long absence from his own country. His first effort was a complete failure, and, more than any one of his actions, has injured his reputation. This was the sanction which he gave to the cruel murder of Archbishop Beaton, in 1546. He repaired to the Castle of Saint Andrews; he shut himself up with the assassins; he prepared to share their fate; and, in a work which he afterwards wrote, openly justified what they had done.[83] For this, nothing can excuse him; and it is with a certain sense of satisfied justice that we learn, that, in 1547, the castle being taken by the French, Knox was treated with great severity, and was made to work at the galleys, from which he was not liberated till 1549.[84]

During the next five years, Knox remained in England, which he quitted in 1554, and arrived at Dieppe.[85] He then travelled abroad; and did not revisit Scotland till the autumn of 1555, when he was eagerly welcomed by the principal nobles and their adherents.[86] From some cause, however, which has not been sufficiently explained, but probably from an unwillingness to play a subordinate part among those proud chiefs, he, in July 1556,

---

gretted that no good life of Knox should have yet been published. That by M'Crie is an undistinguishing and injudicious panegyric, which, by provoking a reaction of opinion, has damaged the reputation of the great reformer. On the other hand, the sect of Episcopalians in Scotland are utterly blind to the real grandeur of the man, and unable to discern his intense love of truth, and the noble fearlessness of his nature.

83. *Tytler's History of Scotland,* vol. iv. pp. 374, 375. *M'Crie's Life of Knox,* pp. 27, 28. *Lawson's Roman Catholic Church in Scotland,* p. 154. *Presbytery Displayed,* 1663, 4to, p. 28. *Shields' Hind let loose,* 1687, pp. 14, 39, 638. In his *History of the Reformation,* edit. Laing, vol. i. pp. 177, 180, he calls it a "godly fact," and says, "These ar the workis of our God;" which, in plain language, is terming the Deity an assassin. But, bad as this is, I agree with M'Crie, that there is no trustworthy evidence for deeming him privy to the murder. Compare, however, *A Diurnal of Occurrents,* p. 42, with *Lyon's History of St. Andrews,* vol. ii. p. 364.

84. *M'Crie's Life of Knox,* pp. 38, 43, 350. *Argyll's Presbytery Examined,* 1848, p. 19.

85. *M'Crie's Life of Knox,* pp. 44, 71.

86. *Ibid.,* p. 99. As to the nobles, who received him, and heard him preach, see p. 102.

again left Scotland, and repaired to Geneva, where he had been invited to take charge of a congregation.[87] He stayed abroad till 1559, by which time the real struggle was almost over; so completely had the nobles succeeded in sapping the foundations of the Church.

For, the course of events having been long prepared, was now rapid indeed. In 1554, the queen dowager had succeeded Arran as regent.[88] She was that Mary of Guise whose marriage with James V. we have noticed as one of the indications of the policy then prevailing. If left alone, she would probably have done little harm;[89] but her powerful and intolerant family exhorted her to suppress the heretics, and, as a natural part of the same scheme, to put down the nobles. By the advice of her brothers, the Duke of Guise and the Cardinal of Lorraine, she, in 1555, proposed to establish a standing army, to supply the place of the troops, which consisted of the feudal barons and their retainers. Such a force, being paid by the Crown, would have been entirely under its control; but the nobles saw the ulterior design, and compelled Mary to abandon it, on the ground that they and their vassals were able to defend Scotland without further aid.[90] Her next attempt was to

87. "Influenced by motives which have never been fully comprehended, he departed to Geneva, where, for a time, he became pastor of a Protestant congregation." *Russell's History of the Church in Scotland,* 1834, vol. i. p. 193. M'Crie, who sees no difficulty, simply says, "In the month of July 1556, he left Scotland, and, having arrived at Dieppe, he proceeded with his family to Geneva." *Life of Knox,* p. 107.

88. Knox, in his savoury diction, likens her appointment to putting a saddle on the back of a cow. "She maid Regent in the year of God 1554; and a croune putt upone hir head, als semlye a sight (yf men had eis), as to putt a sadill upoun the back of ane unrewly kow." I copy this passage from Mr. Laing's excellent edition of *Knox's History of the Reformation,* vol. i. p. 242; but in *Watson's Historicall Collections of Ecclesiastick Affairs in Scotland,* 1657, p. 73, there is a slightly different version. " 'As seemly a sight,' saith John Knox, in the new gospel language, 'as to put the saddle upon the back of an unruly sow.' "

89. The Duke of Argyll, in his *Presbytery Examined,* p. 9, calls her "ambitious and intriguing." Not only, however, is she praised by Lesley (*History,* pp. 289, 290), which might have been expected, but even Buchanan does justice to her, in a passage unusually gracious for so Protestant and democratic a writer. "Mors ejus varie mentes hominum affecit. Nam et apud quosdam eorum, quibuscum armis contendit, non mediocre sui desiderium reliquit. Erat enim singulari ingenio prædita, et animo ad æquitatem admodum propenso." *Buchanan, Rerum Scoticarum Historia,* lib. xvi. p. 487.

90. *History of Scotland,* book ii. p. 91, in Robertson's Works, 1831. *Tytler's*

consolidate the interests of the Catholic party, which she effected, in 1558, by marrying her daughter to the dauphin. This increased the influence of the Guises,[91] whose niece, already queen of Scotland, would now, in the ordinary course of affairs, become queen of France. They urged their sister to extreme measures, and promised to assist her with French troops. On the other hand, the nobles remained firm, and prepared for the struggle. In December 1557, several of them had drawn up a covenant, agreeing to stand by each other, and to resist the tyranny with which they were threatened.[92] They now took the name of Lords of the Congregation, and sent forth their agents to secure the subscriptions of those who wished for a reformation of the Church.[93] They, moreover, wrote to Knox, whose style of preaching, being very popular, would, they thought, be useful in stirring up the people to rebellion.[94] He was then in Geneva, and did not arrive in Scotland till May 1559,[95] by which time the result of the impending contest was hardly doubtful, so successful had the nobles been in

---

History, vol. v. pp. 22, 23. It appears, from Lesley (History, pp. 254, 255), that some of the nobles were in favour of this scheme, hoping thereby to gain favour. "Albeit sum of the lordis of the nobilitie for pleasour of the quene seamed to aggre thairto for the tyme, yit the barronis and gentill men was nathing content thairwith" . . . . "affirming that thair foirfatheris and predicessouris had defendit the samyn" (i.e. the realm) "mony hundreth yeris, vailyeantlie with their awin handis."

91. "It completed the almost despotic power of the house of Guise." Tytler's History of Scotland, vol. v. p. 27.

92. This covenant, which marks an important epoch in the history of Scotland, is dated 3d of December 1557. It is printed in Stevenson's History of the Church of Scotland, p. 47; in Calderwood's History of the Kirk, vol. i. pp. 326, 327; and in Knox's History of the Reformation, vol. i. pp. 273, 274.

93. In 1558, "the lords of the congregation had sent agents through the kingdom to solicit the subscriptions of those who were friendly to a reformation." Stephen's History of the Church of Scotland, London, 1848, vol. i. p. 58.

94. Keith (Affairs of Church and State in Scotland, vol. iii. p. 82) calls him "a trumpeter of rebellion," which he undoubtedly was, and very much to his credit too, though the courtly bishop imputes it to him as a fault. The Scotch, if it had not been for their rebellious spirit, would long since have lost their liberties.

95. "He sailed from Dieppe on the 22nd of April 1559, and landed safely at Leith in the beginning of May." M'Crie's Life of Knox, p. 139. Knox himself says, "the secound of Maij." History of the Reformation, edit. Laing, vol. i. p. 318. "He was called home by the noblemen that enterprised the Reformation." Spottiswoode's History of the Church of Scotland, edit. Russell, vol. ii. p. 180.

strengthening their party, and so much reason had they to expect the support of Elizabeth.

Nine days after Knox entered Scotland, the first blow was struck. On the 11th of May 1559, he preached in Perth. After the sermon, a tumult arose, and the people plundered the churches, and pulled down the monasteries.[96] The queen-regent, hastily assembling troops, marched towards the town. But the nobles were on the alert. The Earl of Glencairn joined the Congregation with two thousand five hundred men; and a treaty was concluded, by which both sides agreed to disarm, on condition that no one should be punished for what had already happened.[97] Such, however, was the state of the public mind, that peace was impossible. In a few days, war again broke out; and this time the result was more decisive. The Lords of the Congregation mustered in great force. Perth, Stirling, and Linlithgow, fell into their hands. The queen-regent retreated before them. She evacuated Edinburgh; and, on the 29th of June, the Protestants entered the capital in triumph.[98]

All this was done in seven weeks from the breaking out of the first riot. Both parties were now willing to negotiate, with the view of gaining time; the queen-regent expecting aid from France, the Lords expecting it from England.[99] But the proceed-

96. *Penny's Traditions of Perth*, p. 310. *Knox's History of the Reformation,* vol. i. pp. 321–323. *Lyon's History of St. Andrews,* vol. i. p. 329; and a spirited narrative in *Buchanan's Rerum Scoticarum Historia,* lib. xvi. pp. 471, 472. Some interesting circumstances are also preserved in *Lesley's History,* pp. 271, 272; but, though Lesley was a contemporary, he erroneously places the riot in 1558. He, moreover, ascribes to Knox language more inflammatory than that which he really used.

97. *Tytler's History of Scotland,* vol. v. pp. 59, 62, 63. Of the Earl of Glencairn, Chalmers (*Caledonia,* vol. iii. p. 485) says, that he was a "religious ruffian, who enjoyed pensions, from Henry VIII, for injuring the country of his birth, and benefits." This, besides being ungrammatical, is foolish. Glencairn, like the other aristocratic leaders of the Reformation, was, no doubt, influenced by sordid motives; but, so far from injuring his country, he rendered it great service.

98. *Tytler's History of Scotland,* vol. v. pp. 64–73.

99. It is stated of the queen-regent, that, in July 1559, "shee had sent alreadie to France for more men of warr." See the curious pamphlet entitled "A Historie of the Estate of Scotland, from July 1558 to April 1560," in *Miscellany of the Wodrow Society,* p. 63, Edinburgh, 1844. All sorts of rumours were circulated; and a letter, dated 12th October 1559, says, "Summe thinke the regent will departe secretlie. Summe that she will to Ynchkeith, for that three shippes are a preparing. Summe say that she is verie sicke. Summe saye the devill cannot kill her." *Sadler's State Papers,* vol. i. p. 499.

ings of Elizabeth being tardy, the Protestants, after waiting for some months, determined to strike a decisive blow before the reinforcements arrived. In October, the principal peers, headed by the Duke of Chastelherault, the Earl of Arran, the Earl of Argyle, and the Earl of Glancairn, assembled at Edinburgh. A great meeting was held, of which Lord Ruthven was appointed president, and in which the queen-regent was solemnly suspended from the government, on the ground that she was opposed to "the glory of God, to the liberty of the realm, and to the welfare of the nobles."[100]

In the winter, an English fleet sailed into the Frith, and anchored near Edinburgh.[101] In January 1560, the Duke of Norfolk arrived at Berwick, and concluded, on the part of Elizabeth, a treaty with the Lords of the Congregation, by virtue of which, the English army entered Scotland on the 2d of April.[102] Against this

100. *Tytler's History of Scotland,* vol. v. p. 104. This was on the 22d of October 1559. Compare *Sadler's State Papers,* vol. i. p. 512. "This Mondaye, the 22 of October, was the douagier deprived from her authoritie by commen consent of all lords and barons here present." On this occasion, "Johne Willocke," the preacher, delivered himself of a discourse in favour of her deposition. Among other arguments, he said, "that in deposing of princes, and these that have beene in authoritie, God did not alwayes use his immediat power, but sometimes he used other meanes, which His wisdome thought good, and justice approved. As by Asa, He removed Maacha, his owne mother, from honour and authoritie, which before she had used; by Jehu He destroyed Joram, and the whole posteritie of Achab." *Therefore* "he" (the orator) "could see no reasoun why they, the borne counsellers, the nobilitie and barons of the realme might not justlie deprive her from all regiment." *Calderwood's History of the Kirk,* vol. i. pp. 540, 541; and *Knox's History of the Reformation,* vol. i. pp. 442, 443.

101. The *Diurnal of Occurrents,* pp. 55, 272, says, that the fleet arrived on 24th of January 1559–60; "aucht greit schippis of Ingland in the raid of Leith." And a letter (in *Sadler's State Papers,* vol. i. p. 697), dated the 23d of January, says, "the shippes arrived yesterdaye in the Frythe to the number of ix. or x., as yet, and the remanent followith." The date, therefore, of the 10th of January, given in a note to *Keith's Church and State in Scotland,* vol. i. p. 255, is evidently erroneous. Important as the event was, its exact date is not mentioned either by Tytler (*History of Scotland,* vol. v. pp. 114, 115), or by Chalmers (*Caledonia,* vol. ii. p. 631).

102. *Chalmers' Caledonia,* vol. ii. p. 632. *Knox's History of the Reformation,* vol. ii. p. 57. The Berwick treaty, in February, is printed in *Keith's Church and State in Scotland,* vol. i. pp. 258–262. So great was the influence of the nobles, that the English troops were well received by the people, in spite of the old and bitter animosity between the two nations. "Especially in Fyfe they were thankfully receaved, and well entreated, with such quietnes and gentle entertainement betwixt our nation and them, as no man would have thought that ever there had beine any variance." *A Historie of the Estate of Scotland,* from 1558 to 1560, in *Miscellany of the Wodrow Society,* p. 78.

combination, the government could effect nothing, and in July, was glad to sign a peace, by which the French troops were to evacuate Scotland, and the whole power of administration was virtually consigned to the Protestant Lords.[103]

The complete success of this great revolution, and the speed with which it was effected, are of themselves a decisive proof of the energy of those general causes by which the whole movement was controlled. For more than a hundred and fifty years, there had been a deadly struggle between the nobles and the Church; and the issue of that struggle was, the establishment of the Reformation, and the triumph of the aristocracy. They had, at last, carried their point. The hierarchy was overthrown, and re-placed by new and untried men. All the old notions of apostolic succession, of the imposition of hands, and of the divine right of ordination, were suddenly discarded. The offices of the Church were performed by heretics, the majority of whom had not even been ordained.[104] Finally, and to crown the whole, in the summer of that same year, 1560, the Scotch parliament passed two laws, which utterly subverted the ancient scheme. By one of these laws, every statute which had ever been enacted in favour of the Church, was at once repealed.[105] By the other law, it was declared that

---

103. "Vpoun the vi. day of Julij, it wes concludit and finallie endit betuix the saids ambassatouris, tuitching all debaittis, controversies and materis con-cernyng the asseiging of Leith, depairting of the Frenchemen thairfra, and randering of the same; and the said peax daitit this said day." *A Diurnal of Occurrents*, pp. 277, 278. See also p. 60; and *Keith's Affairs of Church and State in Scotland*, vol. i. p. 295.

104. "That Knox himself was in priest's orders, is a fact which his biog-rapher, the late Dr. M'Crie, has placed beyond dispute; and some of the other leaders were also priests; but the greater number of the preachers, and all those who subsequently became ministers, were totally without any orders whatever, not even such as the superintendents could have given them; for their own sup-posed call, the election of the people, and the *civil* ceremony of induction to the living, was all that was then 'judged necessary.'" *Stephen's History of the Church of Scotland*, 1848, vol. i. pp. 145, 146. "A new-fashioned sort of min-istry, unknown in the Christian Church for all preceding generations." *Keith's Church and State in Scotland*, vol. iii. p. 204. Compare *Argyll's Presbytery Examined*, pp. 34–36.

105. "The thre estaitis of parliament hes anullit and declarit all sik actes maid in tymes bipast not aggreing wᵗ goddis word and now contrair to the con-fessiouñ of oure fayᵗ according to the said word publist in this parliament. Tobe of nane avale force nor effect. And decernis the said actis and every ane of thame to haue na effect nor strenth in tyme to cum." *Acts of the Parliaments of Scotland*, 1814, folio, vol. ii. p. 535. This was on 24th August 1560.

whoever said mass, or was present while it was said, should, for the first offence, lose his goods; for the second offence be exiled; and, for the third offence, be put to death.[106]

Thus it was, that an institution, which had borne the brunt of more than a thousand years, was shivered, and fell to pieces. And, from its fall, great things were augured. It was believed, that the people would be enlightened, that their eyes were opening to their former follies, and that the reign of superstition was about to end. But what was forgotten then, and what is too often forgotten now, is, that in these affairs there is an order and a natural sequence, which can never be reversed. This is, that every institution, as it actually exists, no matter what its name or pretences may be, is the effect of public opinion far more than the cause; and that it will avail nothing to attack the institution, unless you can first change the opinion. In Scotland, the Church was grossly superstitious; but it did not, therefore, follow, that to overthrow the establishment, would lessen the evil. They who think that superstition can be weakened in this way, do not know the vitality of that dark and ill-omened principle. Against it, there is only one weapon, and that weapon is knowledge. When men are ignorant, they must be superstitious; and wherever superstition exists, it is sure to organize itself into some kind of system, which it makes its home. If you drive it from that home, it will find another. The spirit transmigrates; it assumes a new form; but still it lives. How idle, then, is that warfare which reformers are too apt to wage, in which they slay the carcass, and spare the life! The husk, forsooth, they seek out, and destroy; but within that husk is a seed of deadly poison, whose vitality they are unable to impair, and which, shifted from its place, bears fruit in another direction, and shoots up with a fresh, and often more fatal, exuberance.

The truth is, that every institution, whether political or religious, represents, in its actual working, the form and pressure of the age. It may be very old; it may bear a venerated name; it may

106. "That na maner of person nor personis say mess nor zit heir mess nor be pñt thairat vnder the pane of confiscatiouñ of all thair gud movable and vnmovable and pvneissing of thair bodeis at the discretioun of the magistrat within quhais jurisdictiouñ sik personis happynis to be apprehendit ffor the first falt: Banissing of the Realme for the secund falt, and justifying to the deid for the thrid falt." *Ibid.*, 24th August 1560, vol. ii. p. 535.

aim at the highest objects; but whoever carefully studies its history, will find that, in practice, it is successively modified by successive generations, and that, instead of controlling society, it is controlled by it. When the Protestant Reformation was effected, the Scotch were excessively ignorant, and, therefore, in spite of the Reformation, they remained excessively superstitious. How long that ignorance continued, and what its results were, we shall presently see; but before entering into that inquiry, it will be advisable to trace the immediate consequences of the Reformation itself, in connexion with the powerful class by whose authority it was established.

The nobles, having overthrown the Church, and stripped it of a large part of its wealth, thought that they were to reap the benefit of their own labour. They had slain the enemy, and they wished to divide the spoil.[107] But this did not suit the views of the Protestant preachers. In their opinion, it was impious to secularise ecclesiastical property, and turn it aside to profane purposes. They held, that it was right, indeed, for the lords to plunder the Church; but they took for granted that the proceeds of the robbery were to enrich themselves. They were the godly men; and it was the business of the ruling classes to endow them with benefices, from which the old and idolatrous clergy were to be expelled.[108]

In accordance with these opinions, Knox and his colleagues, in August 1560, presented a petition to Parliament, calling on the nobles to restore the Church property which they had seized, and

107. As Robertson says, in his measured, and somewhat feeble, style, "Among the Scottish nobility, some hated the persons, and others coveted the wealth, of the dignified clergy; and by abolishing that order of men, the former indulged their resentment, and the latter hoped to gratify their avarice." *History of Scotland,* book iii. p. 116, in *Robertson's Works,* edit. 1831. The contemporary narrative, in *A Diurnal of Occurrents,* p. 269, sounds much more vigorous to my ear. "In all this tyme" (1559), "all kirkmennis goodis and geir wer spoulzeit and reft fra thame, in euerie place quhair the samyne culd be apprehendit; for euerie man for the maist pairt that culd get any thing pertenyng to any kirkmen, thocht the same as wele won geir."

108. "Knox never dreamed that the revenues of the Church were to be secularized; but that he and his colleagues were simply to remove the old incumbents, and then take possession of their benefices." *Stephen's History of the Church of Scotland,* vol. i. p. 106. "The ecclesiastical revenues, which they never contemplated for a moment were to be seized by the Protestant nobility." *Lawson's Roman Catholic Church in Scotland,* p. 233.

to have it properly applied to the support of the new ministers.[109] To this request, those powerful chiefs did not even vouchsafe a reply.[110] They were content with matters as they actually stood, and were, therefore, unwilling to disturb the existing arrangement. They had fought the fight; they had gained the victory, and shared the spoil. It was not to be supposed that they would peaceably relinquish what they had won with infinite difficulty. Nor was it likely that, after being engaged in an arduous struggle with the Church for a hundred and fifty years, and having at length conquered their inveterate enemy, they should forego the fruits of their triumph for the sake of a few preachers, whom they had but recently called to their aid; low-born and obscure men, who should rather deem it an honour that they were permitted to associate with their superiors in a common enterprise, but were not to presume on that circumstance, nor to suppose that they, who only entered the field at the eleventh hour, were to share the booty on any thing approaching to terms of equality.[111]

But the aristocracy of Scotland little knew the men with whom they had to deal. Still less, did they understand the character of their own age. They did not see that, in the state of society in which they lived, superstition was inevitable, and that, therefore, the spiritual classes, though depressed for a moment, were sure speedily to rise again. The nobles had overturned the Church; but the principles on which Church authority is based, remained intact. All that was done, was to change the name and the form. A new hierarchy was quickly organized, which succeeded the old one in the affections of the people. Indeed, it did more. For, the

---

109. Compare *Knox's History of the Reformation,* vol. ii. pp. 89–92, with *M'Crie's Life of Knox,* p. 179. Of this document, M'Crie says, "There can be no doubt that it received the sanction, if it was not the composition, of the reformer." . . . . "It called upon them" (the nobles) "to restore the patrimony of the Church, of which they had unjustly possessed themselves."

110. "Making no answer to the last point." *Spottiswoode's History of the Church of Scotland,* vol. i. p. 327. "Without taking any notice." *Keith's Affairs of Church and State,* vol. i. p. 321.

111. "They viewed the Protestant preachers as low-born individuals, not far raised above the condition of mechanics or tradesmen, without influence, authority, or importance." *Lawson's Roman Catholic Church in Scotland,* p. 251. "None were more unmerciful to the poore ministers than they that had the greatest share of the kirk rents." *Calderwood's History of the Kirk of Scotland,* vol. ii. p. 42.

Protestant clergy, neglected by the nobles, and unendowed by the state, had only a miserable pittance whereupon to live, and they necessarily threw themselves into the arms of the people, where alone they could find support and sympathy.[112] Hence, a closer and more intimate union than would otherwise have been possible. Hence, too, as we shall presently see, the Presbyterian clergy, smarting under the injustice with which they were treated, displayed that hatred of the upper classes, and that peculiar detestation of monarchical government, which they showed whenever they dared. In their pulpits, in their presbyteries, and in their General Assemblies, they encouraged a democratic and insubordinate tone, which eventually produced the happiest results, by keeping alive, at a critical moment, the spirit of liberty; but which, for that very reason, made the higher ranks rue the day, when, by their ill-timed and selfish parsimony, they roused the wrath of so powerful and implacable a class.

The withdrawal of the French troops, in 1560, had left the nobles in possession of the government;[113] and it was for them to decide to what extent the Reformed clergy should be endowed. The first petition, presented by Knox and his brethren, was passed over in contemptuous silence. But the ministers were not so easily put aside. Their next step was, to present to the Privy Council what is known as the First Book of Discipline, in which they again urged their request.[114] To the tenets contained in this book, the council had no objection; but they refused to ratify it, because, by doing so, they would have sanctioned the principle

112. In 1561, "Nothwithstanding the full establishment of the Reformation, the Protestant ministers were in a state of extreme poverty, and dependent upon the precarious assistance of their flocks." *Tytler's History of Scotland,* vol. v. p. 207. Compare a letter, written by Knox, in 1566, on "the extreame povertie wherein our ministers are brought." *Knox's History of the Reformation,* vol. ii. p. 542.

113. "The limited authority which the Crown had hitherto possessed, was almost entirely annihilated, and the aristocratical power, which always predominated in the Scottish government(?), became supreme and incontrollable." *Russell's History of the Church in Scotland,* 1834, vol. i. p. 223.

114. See the *First Book of Discipline,* reprinted in *A Compendium of the Laws of the Church of Scotland,* part i., second edition, Edinburgh, 1837. They summed up their requests in one comprehensive passage (p. 119), that "the haill rentis of the Kirk abusit in Papistrie sal be referrit againe to the Kirk." In another part (p. 106), they frankly admit that, "we doubt not but some of our petitions shall appear strange unto you at the first sight."

that the new church had a right to the revenues of the old one.[115] A certain share, indeed, they were willing to concede. What the share should be, was a matter of serious dispute, and caused the greatest ill-will between the two parties. At length, the nobles broke silence, and, in December 1561, they declared that the Reformed clergy should only receive one-sixth of the property of the Church; the remaining five-sixths being divided between the government and the Catholic priesthood.[116] The meaning of this was easily understood, since the Catholics were now entirely dependent on the government, and the government was, in fact, the nobles themselves, who were, at that period, the monopolizers of political power.

Such being the case, it naturally happened, that, when the arrangement was made known, the preachers were greatly moved. They saw how unfavourable it was to their own interests, and, therefore, they held that it was unfavourable to the interests of religion. Hence, in their opinion, it was contrived by the devil, whose purposes it was calculated to serve.[117] For, now, they who travailed in the vineyard of the Lord, were to be discouraged, and were to suffer, in order that what rightly belonged to them might

115. "The form of polity recommended in the First Book of Discipline never obtained the proper sanction of the State, chiefly in consequence of the avarice of the nobility and gentry, who were desirous of securing to themselves the revenues of the Church." *Miscellany of the Wodrow Society,* p. 324. See also *Argyll's Presbytery Examined,* p. 26. Many of the nobles, however, did sign it (*Knox's History of the Reformation,* vol. ii. p. 129); but, says Spottiswoode (*History of the Church of Scotland,* vol. i. p. 373), "Most of those that subscribed, getting into their hands the possessions of the Church, could never be induced to part therewith, and turned greater enemies in that point of church patrimony than were the papists, or any other whatsoever."

116. *M'Crie's Life of Knox,* p. 204. *Knox's History of the Reformation,* vol. ii. pp. 298–301, 307–309. *Buchanan's Rerum Scoticarum Historia,* lib. xvii. p. 500. The nominal arrangement, which was contrived with considerable art, was, that one-third of the church revenues should be divided into two parts; one part for the government, and another part for the preachers. The remaining two-thirds were gravely assigned to the Catholic priesthood, who, at that very moment, were liable, by Act of Parliament, to the penalty of death, if they performed the rites of their religion. Men, whose lives were in the hands of the government, were not likely to quarrel with the government about money matters; and the result was, that nearly every thing fell into the possession of the nobles.

117. "The Ministeris, evin in the begynnyng, in publict Sermonis opponed thame selves to suche corruption, for thei foirsaw the purpose of the Devill." *Knox's History of the Reformation,* vol. ii. p. 310.

be devoured by idle bellies.[118] The nobles might benefit for a time, but the vengeance of God was swift, and would most assuredly overtake them.[119] From the beginning to the end, it was nothing but spoliation. In a really Christian land, the patrimony of the Church would be left untouched.[120] But, in Scotland, alas!

118. "For it seemeth altogether unreasonable that idle belleis sall devoure and consume the patrimonie of the Kirk, whill the faithfull travellers in the Lord's vineyarde suffer extreme povertie, and the needie members of Christ's bodie are altogether neglected." *Calderwood's History of the Kirk,* vol. ii. pp. 484, 485. This was in 1569; and, in 1571, the celebrated Ferguson, in one of his sermons, declared that the holders of church property, most of whom were the nobility, were "ruffians." See an extract from his sermon, in *Chalmers' History of Dunfermline,* p. 309, Edinburgh, 1844. "For this day Christ is spuilzeit amang us, quhil y^t quhilk aucht to mantene the Ministerie of the Kirk and the pure, is geuin to prophane men, flattereris in court, ruffianes, and hyrelingis."

119. In September 1571, John Row "preiched, wha in plane pulpet pronunced to the lordis, for thair covetusnes, and becaus they wold not grant the just petitiones of the Kirk, Godis heastie vengeance to fall upon them; and said, moreover, 'I cair not, my lordis, your displeasour; for I speik my conscience befoir God, wha will not suffer sic wickitnes and contempt vnpunished." *Bannatyne's Journal,* edit. Edinburgh, 1806, p. 257.

120. In 1576, the General Assembly declared, that their right to "the patrimonie of the Kirk" was "ex jure divino." *Acts of the General Assemblies of the Kirk of Scotland,* vol. i. p. 360, Edinburgh, 1839, 4to. More than a hundred years later, a Scotch divine evinces how deeply the members of his profession felt this spoliation of the Church, by going out of his way to mention it. See *Jacob's Vow,* by Dr. *John Cockburn,* Edinburgh, 1696, pp. 422, 423, 425. But this is nothing in comparison to a recent writer, the Reverend Mr. Lyon, who deliberately asserts that, because these and similar acts occurred in the reign of Mary, therefore the queen came to a violent end; such being the just punishment of sacrilege. "The practice" (of saying masses for the dead) "ceased, of course, at the Reformation; and the money was transferred by Queen Mary to the civil authorities of the town. This was, undoubtedly, an act of sacrilege; for, though sacrificial masses for the dead was an error, yet the guardians of the money so bequeathed, were under an obligation to apply it to a sacred purpose. This, and other sacrilegious acts on the part of Mary, of a still more decided and extensive character, have been justly considered as the cause of all the calamities which subsequently befell her." *History of St. Andrews, by the Rev. C. J. Lyon, M.A., Presbyter of the Episcopal Church, St. Andrews,* Edinburgh, 1843, vol. i. p. 54. Elsewhere (vol. ii. p. 400) the same divine mentions, that the usual punishment for sacrilege is a failure of male issue. "The following examples, selected from the diocese of St. Andrews, according to its boundaries before the Reformation, will corroborate the general doctrine contended for throughout this work, that sacrilege has ever been punished in the present life, and *chiefly* by the failure of male issue." The italics are in the text. See also vol. i. p. 118. For the sake of the future historian of public opinion, it may be well to observe, that the work containing these sentiments is not a reprint of an older book, but was published for the first time in 1843, having apparently been just written.

Satan had prevailed,[121] and Christian charity had waxen cold.[122] In Scotland, property, which should be regarded as sacred, had been broken up and divided; and the division was of the worst kind, since, by it, said Knox, two-thirds are given to the devil, and the other third is shared between God and the devil. It was as if Joseph, when governor of Egypt, had refused food to his brethren, and sent them back to their families with empty sacks.[123] Or, as another preacher suggested, the Church was now, like the Maccabees of old, being oppressed, sometimes by the Assyrians, and sometimes by the Egyptians.[124]

But neither persuasions nor threats[125] produced any effect on

121. "The General Assemblie of the Kirk of Scotland, convenit at Edinburgh the 25 of December 1566, to the Nobilitie of this Realme that professes the Lord Jesus with them, and hes renouncit that Roman Antichryst, desyre constancie in faith, and the spirit of righteous judgment. Seeing that Sathan, be all our negligence, Right Honourable, hes so farre prevailit within this Realme within these late dayes, that we doe stand in extream danger, not only *to lose our temporall possessiouns,* but also to be depryvit of the glorious Evangell," &c. *Keith's Church and State,* vol. iii. pp. 154, 155.

122. In 1566, in their piteous communication to the English bishops and clergy, they said, "The days are ill; iniquitie abounds; christian charity, alas, is waxen cold." *Acts and Proceedings of the General Assemblies of the Kirk of Scotland,* vol. i. p. 87, Edinburgh, 1839, 4to.

123. "I see twa partis freely gevin to the Devill, and the thrid maun be devided betwix God and the Devill: Weill, bear witnes to me, that this day I say it, or it be long the Devill shall have three partis of the thrid; and judge you then what Goddis portioun shalbe." . . . . "Who wold have thought, that when Joseph reulled Egypt, that his brethren should have travailled for vittallis, and have returned with empty seckis untol thair families? Men wold rather have thought that Pharao's pose, treasure, and garnallis should have bene diminished, or that the houshold of Jacob should stand in danger to sterve for hungar." *Knox's History of the Reformation,* vol. ii. pp. 310, 311.

124. In May 1571, "This Sonday, Mr.Craig teiched the 130 Psalme; and, in his sermond, he compared the steat of the Kirk of God in this tovne vnto the steat of the Maccabeis; wha were oppressed sumtymes by the Assyrianis, and sumtymes by the Egiptianis." *Bannatyne's Journal,* p. 150.

125. The first instance I have observed of any thing like menace, is in 1567, when "the Assembly of the Church being convened at Edinburgh," admonished all persons "as well nobleman as barons, and those of the other Estates, to meet and give their personal appearance at Edinburgh on the 20th of July, for giving their advice, counsel, and concurrence in matters then to be proponed; especially for purging the realm of popery, the establishing of the policy of the Church, and *restoring the patrimony thereof to the just possessors.* Assuring those that should happen to absent themselves at the time, due and lawful advertisement being made, that they should be reputed hinderers of the good work intended, and as *dissimulate professors be esteemed unworthy of the fellowship of Christ's flock.*" *Spottiswoode's History of the Church of Scotland,* vol. ii. p. 64. This

the obdurate minds of the Scotch nobles. Indeed, their hearts, instead of being softened, became harder. Even the small stipends, which were allotted to the Protestant clergy, were not regularly paid, but were mostly employed for other purposes.[126] When the ministers complained, they were laughed at, and insulted, by the nobles, who, having gained their own ends, thought that they could dispense with their former allies.[127] The Earl of Morton, whose ability, as well as connexions, made him the most powerful man in Scotland, was especially virulent against them; and two of the preachers, who offended him, he put to death, under circumstances of great cruelty.[128] The nobles, regarding him as their chief, elected him Regent in 1572;[129] and, being now pos-

---

evidently alludes to the possibility of excommunicating those who would not surrender to the Protestant preachers, the property stolen from the Catholic Church; and, in 1570, we find another step taken in the same direction. Under that year, the following passage occurs in *Acts and Proceedings of the General Assemblies of the Kirk of Scotland*, vol. i. p. 181. "Q. If those that withold the duty of the Kirk, *wherethrough Ministers want their stipends,* may be excommunicate? A. All things beand done that the civill ordour requyres of them that withaldis the duetie of the Kirk, quherby Ministers wants their stipends; *the Kirk may proceed to excommunication, for their contempt.*"

126. In 1562, "the poore ministers, exhorters, and readers, compleaned at church assembleis, that neither were they able to live upon the stipends allowed, nor gett payment of that small portioun which was allowed." *Calderwood's History of the Kirk*, vol. ii. p. 172. Compare *Acts of the General Assemblies*, 1839, 4to, vol. i. p. 53; "To requyre payment to ministers of there stipends for the tyme by past, according to the promise made." This was in December 1564. In December 1565, the General Assembly said (p. 71), "that wher oft and divers tymes promise hes bein made to us, that our saids brethren, travelers and preachers in the Kirk of God, sould not be defraudit of their appointit stipends, neither zet in any wayes sould be molestit in their functioun; zet nottheles universallie they want ther stipends appointit for diverse tymes by past." On the state of things in 1566, see "The Supplication of the Ministers to the Queen," in *Knox's History of the Reformation*, vol. ii. p. 529. See also, in the *Miscellany of the Spalding Club*, vol. iv. pp. 92–101, Aberdeen, 1849, 4to, a letter written by John Erskine in December 1571, especially p. 97; "the gretest of the nobilitie haifing gretest rentis in possessione, and plaicet of God in maist hie honouris, ceasis nocht, maist wiolentlie blindit with awarice, to spoilye and draw to thame selfis the possessiones of the Kirk."

127. "The ministers were called proud knaves, and receaved manie injurious words from the lords, speciallie from Morton, who ruled all. He said, he sould lay their pride, and putt order to them." *Calderwood's History of the Kirk*, vol. iii. pp. 137, 138. This was in 1571.

128. *Chambers' Annals of Scotland*, vol. i. pp. 79, 80.

129. "The nobilitie wnderwrittin convenit in Edinburgh, and chesit and electit James erle of Mortoun regent." *A Diurnal of Occurrents*, p. 320.

sessed of supreme power, he employed it against the Church. He seized upon all the benefices which became vacant, and retained their profits in his own hands.[130] His hatred of the preachers passed all bounds. He publicly declared, that there would be neither peace nor order in the country, until some of them were hung.[131] He refused to sanction the General Assemblies by his presence; he wished to do away with their privileges, and even with their name; and with such determination did he pursue his measures, that, in the opinion of the historian of the Scotch Kirk, nothing but the special interference of the Deity could have maintained its existing polity.[132]

The rupture between Church and State was now complete. It remained to be seen, which was the stronger side. Every year, the clergy became more democratic; and, after the death of Knox, in 1572, they ventured upon a course which even he would hardly have recommended, and which, during the earlier period of the Reformation, would have been impracticable.[133] But, by this time, they had secured the support of the people; and the treatment

130. In 1573, "when any benefeces of Kirk vaikit, he keapit the proffet of thair rents sa lang in his awin hand, till he was urgit be the Kirk to mak donatioun tharof, and that was not gevin but proffeit for all that." *The Historie and Life of King James the Sext,* edit. Edinburgh, 1825, 4to, p. 147. Even in 1570, when Lennox was regent, "the Earle of Mortoun was the chiefe manager of every thing under him;" and was "master of the church rents," and made "gifts of them to the nobility." *Wodrow's Collections upon the Lives of the Reformers of the Church of Scotland,* vol. i. part i. pp. 27, 126, Glasgow, 1834, 4to.

131. "During all these Assembleis and earnest endeavoures of the brethrein, the regent was often required to give his presence to the Assemblie, and further the caus of God. He not onlie refused, but threatned some of the most zealous with hanging, alledging, that otherwise there could be no peace nor order in the countrie." *Calderwood's History of the Kirk,* vol. iii. pp. 393, 394. "Uses grait thretning against the maist zelus breithring, schoring to hang of thame, utherwayes ther could be na peace nor ordour in the countrey." *The Autobiography and Diary of James Melvill,* edited by R. Pitcairn, Edinburgh, 1842, pp. 59, 60.

132. "He mislyked the Generall Assembleis, and would have had the name changed, that he might take away the force and priviledge thereof; and no question he had stayed the work of policie that was presentlie in hands, if God had not stirred up a factioun against him." *Calderwood's History of the Kirk of Scotland,* vol. iii. p. 396. See also *The Autobiography of James Melvill,* p. 61.

133. "During the two years following the death of Knox, each day was ripening the more determined opposition of the Church. The breach between the clergy with the great body of the people, and the government or higher nobility, was widening rapidly." *Argyll's Presbytery Examined,* p. 70.

they were receiving from the government, and from the nobles, embittered their minds, and drove them into desperate counsels. While their plans were yet immature, and while the future was looming darkly before them, a new man arose, who was well qualified to be their chief, and who at once stepped into the place which the death of Knox left vacant. This was Andrew Melville, who, by his great ability, his boldness of character, and his fertility of resource, was admirably suited to be the leader of the Scottish Church in that arduous struggle in which it was about to embark.[134]

In 1574, Melville, having completed his education abroad, arrived in Scotland.[135] He quickly rallied round him the choicest spirits in the Church; and, under his auspices, a struggle began with the civil power, which continued, with many fluctuations, until it culminated, sixty years later, in open rebellion against Charles I. To narrate all the details of the contest, would be inconsistent with the plan of this Introduction; and, notwithstanding the extreme interest of the events which now ensued, the greater part of them must be omitted; but I will endeavour to indicate the general march, and to put the reader in possession of such facts as are most characteristic of the age in which they occurred.

Melville had not been in Scotland many months, before he began his opposition, at first by secret intrigues, afterwards with open and avowed hostility.[136] In the time of Knox, episcopacy had been recognized as part of the Protestant Church, and had received the sanction of the leading Reformers.[137] But that institution did not harmonize with the democratic spirit which was

134. "Next to her Reformer, who, under God, emancipated her from the degrading shackles of papal superstition and tyranny, I know no individual from whom Scotland has received such important services, or to whom she continues to owe so deep a debt of national respect and gratitude, as Andrew Melville." *M'Crie's Life of Andrew Melville,* vol. ii. p. 473, Edinburgh, 1819. His nephew, himself a considerable person, says, "Scotland receavit never a graitter benefit at the hands of God nor this man." *The Autobiography of James Melvill,* p. 38.

135. He left Scotland in 1564, at the age of nineteen, and returned "in the beginning of July 1574, after an absence of ten years from his native country." *M'Crie's Life of Andrew Melville,* vol. i. pp. 17, 57. See also *Scot's Apologetical Narration of the State of the Kirk of Scotland,* edit. Wodrow Society, p. 34; and *Howie's Biographia Scoticana,* p. 111, Glasgow, 1781.

136. He appears to have first set to work in November 1574. See *Stephen's History of the Church of Scotland,* vol. i. p. 261, London, 1848.

137. "The compilers of the Book of Discipline" (*i.e.* the First Book, in

now growing up. The difference of ranks between the bishops and the inferior clergy was unpleasant, and the ministers determined to put an end to it.[138] In 1575, one of them, named John Dury, was instigated, by Melville, to bring the subject before the General Assembly at Edinburgh.[139] After he had spoken, Melville also expressed himself against episcopacy; but, not being yet sure of the temper of the audience, his first proceedings were somewhat cautious. Such hesitation was, however, hardly necessary; for, owing to the schism between the Church and the upper classes, the ministers were becoming the eager enemies of those maxims of obedience, and of subordination, which they would

---

1560) "were distinguished by prelatical principles to the end of their days." .... "That Knox himself was no enemy to prelacy, considered as an ancient and apostolical institution, is rendered clear by his 'Exhortation to England for the speedy embracing of Christ's Gospel.' " *Russell's History of the Church in Scotland,* 1834, vol. i. p. 240. "The associates of Knox, it is obvious, were not Presbyterians, and had no intention of setting up a system of parity among the ministers of their new establishment." p. 243. See also p. 332. Even in 1572, the year of Knox's death, I find it stated, that "the whole Diocie of Sanct Andrews is decerned be the Assembly to pertain to the Bishop of the same." *Acts and Proceedings of the General Assemblies of the Kirk of Scotland,* vol. i. p. 264, 4to, 1839. The Scotch Presbyterians have dealt very unfairly with this part of the history of their Church.

138. Some little time after this, David Ferguson, who died in 1598, and was minister at Dunfermline, and very frankly to James VI., "Yes, Sir, ye may have Bishops here, but *ye must remember to make us all equall:* make us all Bishops, els will ye never content us." *Row's History of the Kirk of Scotland from 1558 to 1637,* edit. Wodrow Society, p. 418. Compare *Calderwood's History of the Kirk,* vol. iv. p. 214: in 1584, "these monstruous titles of superioritie." In 1586, "that tyrannicall supremacie of bishops and archbishops over ministers," p. 604.

139. "He stirred up John Dury, one of the ministers of Edinburgh, in an Assembly which was then convened, to propound a question touching the lawfulness of the episcopal function, and the authority of chapters in their election. He himself, as though he had not been acquainted with the motion, after he had commended the speaker's zeal, and seconded the purpose with a long discourse of the flourishing estate of the church of Geneva, and the opinions of Calvin and Theodore Beza concerning church government, came to affirm, 'That none ought to be esteemed office-bearers in the Church whose titles were not found in the book of God. And, for the title of bishops, albeit the same was found in Scripture, yet was it not to be taken in the sense that the common sort did conceive, there being no superiority allowed by Christ amongst ministers,' " &c. *Spottiswoode's History of the Church of Scotland,* vol. ii. p. 200. See also *Acts of the General Assemblies,* vol. i. p. 331, where it appears that six bishops were present on this memorable occasion. The question raised was, "Whither if the Bischops, as they are now in the Kirk of Scotland, hes thair function of the word of God or not, or if the Chapiter appointit for creating of them aucht to be tollerated in this reformed Kirk." p. 340.

have upheld, had the higher ranks been on their side. As it was, the clergy were only favoured by the people; they, therefore, sought to organize a system of equality, and were ripe for the bold measures proposed by Melville and his followers. This was clearly shown, by the rapidity of the subsequent movement. In 1575, the first attack was made in the General Assembly at Edinburgh. In April 1578, another General Assembly resolved, that, for the future, bishops should be called by their own names, and not by their titles.[140] The same body also declared, that no see should be filled up, until the next Assembly.[141] Two months afterwards, it was announced that this arrangement was to be perpetual, and that no new bishop should ever be made.[142] And, in 1580, the Assembly of the Church at Dundee, pulling the whole fabric to the ground, unanimously resolved that the office of bishop was a mere human invention; that it was unlawful; that it must be immediately done away with; and that every bishop should at once resign his office, or be excommunicated if he refused to do so.[143]

The minister and the people had now done their work, and,

---

140. "It was ordained, That Bischops and all vthers bearand Ecclesiasticall functioun, be callit be thair awin names, or Brethren, in tyme comeing." *Acts of the General Assemblies of the Kirk of Scotland,* vol. ii. p. 404.

141. "Therfor the Kirk hes concludit, That no Bischops salbe electit or made heirafter, befor the nixt Generall Assemblie." *Ibid.,* vol. ii. p. 408.

142. "Anent the Act made in the last Assemblie, the 28 of Aprile 1578, concerning the electioun of Bischops, suspendit quhill this present Assemblie, and the farther ordour reservit thereto: The General Assemblie, all in ane voyce, hes concludit, That the said act salbe extendit for all tymes to come, ay and quhill the corruptioun of the Estate of Bischops be alluterlie tane away." *Ibid.,* vol. ii. p. 413.

143. "Forsameilke as the office of a Bischop, as it is now vsit, and commounly takin within this realme, hes no sure warrand, auctoritie, nor good ground out of the (Book and) Scriptures of God; but is brocht in by the folie and corruptions of (men's) invention, to the great overthrow of the Kirk of God: The haill Assemblie of the Kirk, in ane voyce, after libertie givin to all men to reason in the matter, *none opponing themselves in defending the said pretendit office,* Finds and declares the samein pretendit office, vseit and termeit, as is above said, vnlaufull in the selfe, as haveand neither fundament, ground nor warrant within the word of God: and ordaines, That all sick persons as bruiks, or sall bruik heirafter the said office, salbe chargeit simpliciter to demitt, quyt and leave of the samein, as ane office quhervnto they are not callit be God; and siclyke to desist and cease from all preaching, ministration of the sacraments, or vsing any way the office of pastors, quhill, they receive *de novo* admission from the Generall Assemblie, vnder the paine of excommunicatioun to be denuncit agains them; quherin if they be found dissobedient, or contraveine this act in any point, the sentence of excommunicatioun, after dew admonitions, to be execute agains them." *Acts of the General Assemblies,* vol. ii. p. 453.

so far as they were concerned, had done it well.[144] But the same circumstances which made them desire equality, made the upper classes desire inequality.[145] A collision, therefore, was inevitable, and was hastened by this bold proceeding of the Church. Indeed, the preachers, supported by the people, rather courted a contest, than avoided it. They used the most inflammatory language against episcopacy; and, shortly before abolishing it, they completed, and presented to Parliament, the Second Book of Discipline, in which they flatly contradicted what they had asserted in their First Book of Discipline.[146] For this, they are often taunted with inconsistency.[147] But the charge is unjust. They were perfectly consistent; and they merely changed their maxims, that they might preserve their principles. Like every corporation, which has ever existed, whether spiritual or temporal, their supreme and paramount principle was to maintain their own power. Whether or not this is a good principle, is another matter; but all history proves that it is an universal one. And when the leaders of the Scotch Church found that it was at stake, and that the question at issue was, who should possess authority, they, with

144. As Calderwood triumphantly says, "the office of bishops was damned." *History of the Kirk,* vol. iii. p. 469. "Their whole estat, both the spirituall and civill part, was damned." p. 526. James Melville (*Autobiography,* p. 52) says that, in consequence of this achievement, his uncle Andrew "gatt the nam of επισκοπομαστιξ, *Episcoporum exactor,* the flinger out of Bischopes."

145. Tytler (*History of Scotland,* vol. vi. p. 302) observes that, while "the great body of the burghers, and middle and lower classes of the people," were Presbyterians, "a large proportion of the nobility supported episcopacy." Instead of "a large proportion," he would not have been far wrong, if he had said "all." Indeed, "Melville himself says the whole peerage was against him." *Stephen's History of the Church of Scotland,* vol. i. p. 269. Forbes ascribes the aristocratic movement against presbytery to "godles atheists," who insisted "that there could be nothing so contrair to the nature of a monarchie," &c., "than that paritie of authoritie in pastours." *Forbes, Certaine Records touching the Estate of the Kirk,* p. 349, edit. Wodrow Society. See also p. 355. "That Democratie (as they called it) whilk allwayes behoved to be full of sedition and troublle to ane Aristocratie, and so in end to a Monarchie." The reader will observe this important change in the attitude of classes in Scotland. Formerly, the clergy had been the allies of the crown against the nobles. Now, the nobles allied themselves with the crown against the clergy. The clergy, in self-defence, had to ally themselves with the people.

146. On the difference between the two productions, there are some remarks worth looking at, in *Argyll's Presbytery Examined,* 1848, pp. 38–43. But this writer, though much freer from prejudice than most Presbyterian authors, is unwilling to admit how completely the Second Book of Discipline contradicts the First.

147. By the Scotch Episcopalians.

perfect consistency, abandoned opinions that they had formerly held, because they now perceived that those opinions were unfavourable to their existence as an independent body.

When the First Book of Discipline appeared, in 1560, the government was in the hands of the nobles, who had just fought on the side of the Protestant preachers, and were ready to fight again on their side. When the Second Book of Discipline appeared, in 1578, the government was still held by the nobles; but those ambitious men had now thrown off the mask, and, having effected their purpose in destroying the old hierarchy, had actually turned round, and attacked the new one. The circumstances having changed, the Church changed with them; but in the change there was nothing inconsistent. On the contrary, it would have been the height of inconsistency for the ministers to have retained their former notions of obedience and of subordination; and it was perfectly natural that, at this crisis, they should advocate the democratic idea of equality, just as before they had advocated the aristocratic idea of inequality.

Hence it was, that, in their First Book of Discipline, they established a regularly ascending hierarchy, according to which the general clergy owed obedience to their ecclesiastical superiors, to whom the name of superintendents was given.[148] But, in the Second Book of Discipline, every vestige of this was swept away; and it was laid down in the broadest terms, that all the preachers

---

148. See the *First Book of Discipline*, reprinted in the first volume of *A Compendium of the Laws of the Church of Scotland*, 2d edit., Edinburgh, 1837. The superintendents were "to set, order, and appoint ministers," p. 61; and it would seem (p. 88) that no minister could be deposed without the consent of his superintendent; but this could hardly be intended to interfere with the supreme authority of the General Assembly. See also the summary, p. 114, where it is said of the superintendents, that "in thair visitatioun thei sal not onlie preiche, but als examine the doctrine, life, diligence, and behavior of the ministeris, reideris, elderis, and deaconis." According to Spottiswoode (*History of the Church of Scotland*, vol. ii. p. 607), "the superintendents held their office during life, and their power was episcopal; for they did elect and ordain ministers, they presided in synods, and directed all church censures, neither was any excommunication pronounced without their warrant." See further, on their authority, *Knox's History of the Reformation*, vol. ii. p. 161. "That punyschment suld be appointed for suche as dissobeyid or contemned the superintendentes in thair functioun." This was in 1561; and, in 1562, "It was ordained, that if ministers be disobedient to superintendents in any thing belonging to edification, they must be subject to correction." *Acts of the General Assemblies of the Kirk*, vol. i. p. 14. Compare p. 131: "sick things as superintendents may and aught decyde in their synodall conventiouns."

being fellow-labourers, all were equal in power; that none had authority over others; and that, to claim such authority, or to assert preëminence, was a contrivance of man, not to be permitted in a divinely constituted Church.[149]

The government, as may be supposed, took a very different view. Such doctrines were deemed, by the upper classes, to be anti-social, and to be subversive of all order.[150] So far from sanctioning them, they resolved, if possible, to overthrow them; and, the year after the General Assembly had abolished episcopacy, it was determined that, upon that very point, a trial of strength should be made between the two parties.

In 1581, Robert Montgomery was appointed archbishop of Glasgow. The ministers who composed the chapter of Glasgow, refused to elect him; whereupon the Privy Council declared that the King, by virtue of his prerogative, had the right of nomination.[151] All was now confusion and uproar. The General Assem-

149. "For albeit the Kirk of God be rewlit and governit be Jesus Christ, who is the onlie King, hie Priest, and Heid thereof, yet he useis the ministry of men, as the most necessar middis for this purpose." . . . . "And to take away all occasion of tyrannie, he willis that they sould rewl with mutuall consent of brether and *equality of power,* every one according to thair functiones." *Second Book of Discipline,* in *A Compendium of the Laws of the Church of Scotland,* vol. i. pp. 126, 127. "As to Bischops, if the name επισκοπος be properly taken, *they ar all ane with the ministers,* as befoir was declairit. For it is *not a name of superioritie and lordschip,* bot of office and watching." p. 142. To understand the full meaning of this, it should be mentioned, that the superintendents, established by the Kirk in 1560, not unfrequently assumed the title of "Lordship," as an ornament to the extensive powers conferred upon them. See, for instance, the notes to *Wodrow's Collections upon the Lives of the Reformers of the Church of Scotland,* vol. i. part ii. p. 461. But, in the Second Book of Discipline, in 1578, the superintendents are, if I rightly remember, not even once named.

150. Just as in England, we find that the upper classes are mostly Episcopalians, their minds being influenced, often unconsciously, by the, to them, pleasing spectacle of an inequality of rank, which is conventional, and does not depend upon ability. On the other hand, the strength of the Dissenters lies among the middle and lower classes, where energy and intellect are held in higher respect, and where a contempt naturally arises for a system, which, at the mere will of the sovereign or minister of the day, concedes titles and wealth to persons whom nature did not intend for greatness, but who, to the surprise of their contemporaries, have greatness thrust upon them. On this difference of opinion in Scotland, corresponding to the difference of social position, see the remarks on the seventeenth century, in *Hume's Commentaries on the Law of Scotland,* vol. ii. p. 544, Edinburgh, 1797, 4to.

151. Record of Privy Council, in *M'Crie's Life of Melville,* vol. i. p. 267. "The brethrein of Glasgow were charged, under paine of horning, to admitt Mr. Robert Montgomrie." *Calderwood's History of the Kirk,* vol. iii. p. 596.

bly forbad the archbishop to enter Glasgow.[152] He refused to obey their order, and threw himself upon the support of the Duke of Lennox, who had obtained the appointment for him, and to whom he, in return, had surrendered nearly all the revenues of the see, reserving for himself only a small stipend.[153] This was a custom which had grown up within the last few years, and was one of many contrivances by which the nobles plundered the Church of her property.[154]

This, however, was not the question now at issue.[155] The point to be decided was one, not of revenue, but of power. For, the clergy knew full well, that if they established their power, the revenue would quickly follow. They, therefore, adopted the most energetic proceedings. In April 1582, the General Assembly met at St. Andrews, and appointed Melville as moderator.[156] The government, fearing the worst, ordered the members, on pain of rebellion, to take no steps respecting the archbishopric.[157] But the representatives of the Church were undaunted. They summoned Montgomery before them; they ratified the sentence by which he had been suspended from the ministry; and they declared that

---

152. "Charges the said Mr. Robert to continue in the ministrie of the Kirk of Striveling," &c. *Acts of the General Assemblies,* vol. ii. p. 547. This was in October 1581; the Record of the Privy Council was in April 1582. Moysie, who was a contemporary, says that, in March 1581, 2, not only the dean and chapter, but all the clergy (the "haill ministrie") declared from the pulpit that Montgomery's appointment "had the warrand of the deuill and not of the word of God, bot wes damnit thairby." *Moysie's Memoirs,* Edinburgh, 1830, 4to, p. 36.

153. "The title whereof the said duke had procured to him, that he, having the name of bishop, and eight hundreth merks money for his living and sustentatioun, the whole rents, and other duteis of the said benefice, might come to the duke's utilitie and behove." *Calderwood's History of the Kirk,* vol. iv. p. 111. See also p. 401.

154. *Scot's Apologetical Narration of the State of the Kirk,* pp. 24, 25. *Calderwood's History of the Kirk,* vol. iii. p. 302. *Wodrow's Collections upon the Lives of the Reformers,* vol. i. part i. p. 206. *Lyon's History of St. Andrews,* vol. i. p. 379. *Gibson's History of Glasgow,* p. 59. *Hume's History of the House of Douglas,* vol. ii. pp. 216, 217. *Chalmers' Caledonia,* vol. iii. p. 624.

155. "But the Church passing this point" (*i.e.* the simony) "made quarrel to him for accepting the bishopric." *Spottiswoode's History of the Church of Scotland,* vol. ii. p. 282.

156. *Acts of the General Assemblies of the Kirk,* vol. ii. p. 548.

157. "A messenger-at-arms entered the house, and charged the moderator and members of the assembly, on the pain of rebellion, to desist from the process." *M'Crie's Life of Melville,* vol. i. p. 268.

he had incurred the penalties of deposition and of excommunication.[158]

A sentence of excommunication was, in those days, so ruinous,
that Montgomery was struck with terror at the prospect before
him. To avoid the consequences, he appeared before the Assembly, and solemnly promised that he would make no further attempt to possess himself of the archbishopric.[159] By doing this, he
probably saved his life; for the people, siding with their clergy,
were ripe for mischief, and were determined, at all hazards, to
maintain what they considered to be the rights of the Church, in
opposition to the encroachments of the State.

The government, on the other hand, was equally resolute.[160]
The Privy Council called several of the ministers before them;
and Dury, one of the most active, they banished from Edinburgh.[161] Measures still more violent were about to be taken,
when they were interrupted by one of those singular events which
not unfrequently occurred in Scotland, and which strikingly
evince the inherent weakness of the Crown, notwithstanding the
inordinate pretensions it commonly assumed.

This was the Raid of Ruthven, which happened in 1582, and
in consequence of which the person of James VI. was held in
durance for ten months.[162] The clergy, true to the policy which

158. "The Assemblie and brether present, after voteing in the said matter,
depryvit the said Mr. Robert from all functioun of the Ministrie in the Kirk of
God, dureing the will of the Kirk of God; and farther, descernit the fearefull
sentence of excommunicatioun to be pronuncit against him in the face of the
haill Assemblie, be the voyce and mouth of the Moderatour present; to the
effect, that, *his proud flesh being cast into the hands of Satan,* he may be win
againe, if it be possible, to God; and the said sentence (to) be intimat be every
particular minister, at his awin particular kirk, solemnelie in the first sermoun
to be made be them, after thair returning." *Acts of the General Assemblies of
the Kirk,* vol. ii. p. 562.

159. *Ibid.,* vol. ii. p. 565. Calderwood (*History of the Kirk,* vol. iii. p. 604)
says, "After long reluctatioun, at lenth he condescended."

160. M'Crie (*Life of Melville,* vol. i. p. 274) says, "In all these contendings,
the ministers had no countenance or support from any of the nobility." It would
have been strange if they had, seeing that the whole movement was essentially
democratic.

161. *Melville's Autobiography,* p. 129. *Calderwood's History of the Kirk,*
vol. iii. p. 620. *M'Crie's Life of Melville,* vol. i. p. 270.

162. He was seized in August 1582, and was let loose again in June 1583.
Tytler's History of Scotland, vol. vi. pp. 321, 360. It is a pity that this valuable,
and really able, work should be so superficial in regard to the ecclesiastical affairs of Scotland. Mr. Tytler appears not to have studied at all the proceedings

now governed them, loudly approved of the captivity of the king, and pronounced it to be a godly act.[163] Dury, who had been driven from his pulpit, was brought back to the capital in triumph;[164] and the General Assembly, meeting at Edinburgh, ordered that the imprisonment of James should be justified by every minister to his own congregation.[165]

In 1583, the king recovered his liberty, and the struggle became more deadly than ever; the passions of both parties being exasperated by the injuries each had inflicted on the other. The Ruthven conspiracy, having been declared treason, as it undoubtedly was, Dury preached in its favour, and openly defended it; and although, under the influence of momentary fear, he afterwards withdrew what he had said,[166] it was evident, from other circumstances, that his feelings were shared by his brethren.[167] A number of them being summoned before the king for their seditious language, bad him take heed what he was about, and

of the presbyteries, or even of the General Assemblies; neither does he display any acquaintance with the theological literature of his country. And yet, from the year 1560 to about 1700, these sources disclose more of the genuine history of the Scotch people than all other sources put together.

163. "The pulpit resounded with applause of the godly deed." *Arnot's History of Edinburgh,* p. 37.

164. "As he is comming from Leith to Edinburgh, upon Tuisday the 4th of September, there mett him at the Gallow Greene two hundreth men of the inhabitants of Edinburgh. Their number still increassed, till he came within the Neather Bow. There they beganne to sing the 124 Psalme, 'Now may Israel say,' &c., and sang in foure parts, knowne to the most part of the people. They came up the street till they came to the Great Kirk, singing thus all the way, to the number of two thowsand. They were muche moved themselves, and so were all the beholders. The duke was astonished, and more affrayed at the sight than at anie thing that ever he had seene before in Scotland, and rave his beard for anger." *Calderwood's History of the Kirk,* vol. iii. pp. 646, 647.

165. *Acts of the General Assemblies,* vol. ii. pp. 595, 596. This was ordered by the General Assembly which met at Edinburgh on the 9th of October 1582, p. 585. See also *Watson's Historicall Collections of Ecclesiastick Affairs in Scotland,* p. 192, "requiring the ministers in all their churches to commend it unto the people."

166. *Spottiswoode's History of the Church of Scotland,* vol. ii. p. 308.

167. James, after his escape, "convocat all his peceabill Prelatis and Nobles, and thair he notefeit unto theyme the greif that he consavit of his unlaughfull detentioun the yeir bygayne, and therefore desyrit thame to acknawlege the same; and thay be thair generall voittis decernit the rayd of Ruthven to be manifest treasoun. The Ministers on the uther part, perswadit the people that it was a godly fact, and that whasoever wald not allow thareof in his hart, was not worthie to be estemit a Christien." *The Historie of King James the Sext,* p. 202, published by the Bannatyne Club, Edinburgh, 1825, 4to.

reminded him that no occupant of the throne had ever prospered after the ministers had begun to threaten him.[168] Melville, who exercised immense influence over both clergy and people, bearded the king to his face, refused to account for what he had delivered in the pulpit, and told James that he perverted the laws both of God and of man.[169] Simpson likened him to Cain, and warned him to beware of the wrath of God.[170] Indeed, the spirit now displayed by the Church was so implacable, that it seemed to delight in venting itself in the most repulsive manner. In 1585, a clergyman, named Gibson, in a sermon which he preached in Edinburgh, denounced against the king the curse of Jeroboam, that he should die childless, and that his race should end with him.[171] The year after this happened, James, finding that Elizabeth was evidently determined to take his mother's life, bethought him of

168. "Disregard not our threatening; for there was never one yet in this realm, in the place where your grace is, who prospered after the ministers began to threaten him." *Tytler's History of Scotland,* vol. vi. p. 364. See also, in *Calderwood's History of the Kirk,* vol. v. pp. 540, 541, a letter from one of the clergy in Fife, addressed to the king, in 1597. "And now, Sir, lett me be free with you in writting other men's reports, and that of the wisest politicians. They say, our bygane historeis report, and experience teacheth, that *raro et fere nunquam* has a king and a prince continued long together in this realme; for *Filius ante diem patrios inquirit in annos.* And they say, Sir, farther, that whatsoever they were of your Majestie's predecessors in governement that oppouned themselves directlie or indirectlie to God's ordinance in his Kirk, it has beene their wracke and subversioun in the end. I might herein be more particular; but I leave it to your Majestie's owne grave and modest consideratioun, for it concerneth you most neere."

169. "Saying, 'He perverted the laws both of God and man.'" *Spottiswoode's History of the Church of Scotland,* vol. ii. p. 309. Also *Tytler's History of Scotland,* vol. vi. p. 371.

170. "Mr. Patrick Simson, preaching before the king upon Gen. iv. 9, 'The Lord said to Cain, Where is Abel, thy brother?' said to the king, before the congregation, 'Sir, I assure you, in God's name, the Lord will ask at you where is the Earl of Moray your brother?' The king replyed, before all the congregation, 'Mr. Patrik, my chalmer doore wes never steeked upon you: ye might have told me anything ye thought in secret.' He replyed, 'Sir, the scandall is publict.'" *Row's History of the Kirk,* p. 144. "Having occasion, *anno* 1593, to preach before the king, he publicly exhorted him to beware that he drew not the wrath of God upon himself in patronizing a manifest breach of divine laws." *Howie's Biographia Scoticana,* p. 120.

171. "Saying, 'That Captain James, with his lady Jesabel, and William Stewart (meaning the colonel), were taken to be the persecutors of the Church; but that now it was seen to be the king himself, against whom he denounced the curse that fell on Jeroboam—that he would die childless, and be the last of his race.'" *Spottiswoode's History of the Church of Scotland,* vol. ii. p. 335.

what was valued in that age as an unfailing resource, and desired the clergy to offer up prayers on behalf of Mary. This, they almost unanimously refused.[172] And not only did they abstain from supplication themselves, but they resolved that no one else should do what they had declined. The archbishop of Saint Andrews being about to officiate before the king, they induced a certain John Cowper to station himself in the pulpit beforehand, so as to exclude the prelate. Nor was it until the captain of the guard threatened to pull Cowper from the place he had usurped, that the service could go on, and the king be allowed to hear his own mother prayed for, in this sad crisis of her fate, when it was still uncertain whether she would be publicly executed, or whether, as was more generally believed, she would be secretly poisoned.[173]

In 1594, John Ross stated in the pulpit, that the advisers of the

172. "The king, perceiving by all these letters, that the death of his mother was determined, called back his ambassadors, and at home gave order to the ministers to remember her in their public prayers, which they denied to do." . . . "Upon their denial, charges were directed to command all bishops, ministers, and other office-bearers in the Church to make mention of her distress in their public prayers, and commend her to God in the form appointed. But of all the number only Mr. David Lindsay at Leith and the king's own ministers gave obedience." *Spottiswoode's History of the Church,* vol. ii. pp. 355, 356. "They, with only one exception, refused to comply." *Russell's History of the Church in Scotland,* vol. ii. p. 23. Compare *Watson's Historicall Collections of Ecclesiastick Affairs in Scotland,* p. 208; and *Historie of James the Sext,* p. 225.

173. "They stirred up Mr. John Cowper, a young man not entered as yet in the function, to take the pulpit before the time, and exclude the bishop. The king coming at the hour appointed, and seeing him in the place, called to him from his seat, and said, 'Mr. John, that place is destined for another; yet since you are there, if you will obey the charge that is given, and remember my mother in your prayers, you shall go on.' He replying, 'that he would do as the Spirit of God should direct him,' was commanded to leave the place: and making as though he would stay, the captain of the guard went to pull him out; whereupon he burst forth in these speeches: 'This day shall be a witness against the king in the great day of the Lord:' and then denouncing a wo to the inhabitants of Edinburgh, he went down, and the bishop of St. Andrews entering the pulpit did perform the duty required." *Spottiswoode's History of the Church of Scotland,* vol. ii. p. 356. "The Kingis Majestie, to testefie his earnest and naturall affection to his mother, causit pray for hir oppinly efter him selff; quhairvpone arrose a great dissensioun betuix sum of the ministrie and his Majestie, namely the ministrie of Edinburgh. Quhairvpone the king appoynted Patrik, archbischop of St. Androis to teache, bot he wes preuented be Mr. John Covpar minister, quho come befoir and filled the pulpit. And as the said Mr. John wes beginnand the prayer, the Kingis Majestie commandit him to stay: so as Mr. John raschit michtely vpone the pulpit, saying, 'This day sall bear witnes agaiins yow in the day of the lord: woe be to ye Edinburgh, for the last of xi plaiges salbe the worst." *Moysie's Memoirs,* p. 59.

king were all traitors, and that the king himself was likewise a traitor. He was also a rebel and a reprobate. That such should be the case, was not surprising, considering the parentage of James. For, his mother was a Guise, and a persecutor of the saints. He avoided open persecution, and spoke them fair; but his deeds did not correspond to his words; and, so great was his dissimulation, that he was the most arrant hypocrite then living in Scotland.[174]

In 1596, David Black, one of the most influential of the Protestant ministers, delivered a sermon, which made much noise. He said, in his discourse, that all kings were children of the devil; but that in Scotland the head of the court was Satan himself. The members of the council, he added, were cormorants, and the lords of the session miscreants. The nobility had degenerated: they were godless; they were dissemblers; they were the enemies of the Church. As to the queen of England, she was nothing but an atheist. And as to the queen of Scotland, all he would say was, that they might pray for her if they list, and because it was the fashion to do so; but that there was no reason for it, inasmuch as no good would ever come from her to them.[175]

174. See *The Historie of King James the Sext,* pp. 316–318, from "a just copie of his sermon" supplied by Ross himself. "His text was upon the 6 chapter of the Prophet Jeremias, verse 28. 'Brethren, we have manie, and almaist innumerable enormiteis in this cuntrie to be lamentit, as the misgovernement of our king be sinistrous counsall of sum particular men. They ar all rebellious traitors, evin the king the maist singular person, and particularlie everie estait of the land.' . . . 'Our king in sindrie poyntis hes bene rebellious aganis the Majestie of God.' . . . 'To this howre, we gat never gude of the Guysien blude, for Queyne Marie his mother was an oppin persecutor of the sanctis of God, and althoght the king be not an oppin persecutor, we have had many of his fayre wordis, wherein he is myghtie aneugh, bot for his gude deiddis, I commend me to thayme.' . . . 'Admit, that our king be a Christien king, yit but amen dement, he is a reprobat king. Of all the men in this nation, the king himself is the maist fynest, and maist dissembling hypocreit.' " A very short notice of this sermon is given by Calderwood (*History of the Kirk,* vol. v. p. 299), who probably had not seen the original notes.

175. The accusation, which was fully proved, was, that "he had publictlie sayd in pulpit, that the papist erles wes come home be the kingis knavledge and consent, quahairin his Hienes treacherie wes detectit; that all kingis war deuilis and come of deuilis, that the deuill wes the head of the court and in the court; that he prayit for the Queine of Scotland for the faschione, because he saw na appearance of guid in hir tyme." *Moysie's Memoirs,* p. 128. "Having been heard to affirm, that the popish lords had returned into the country by the king's permission, and that thereby the king had discovered the "treacherous

For preaching this sermon, Black was summoned by the Privy Council. He refused to attend, because it was for a spiritual tribunal, and not for a temporal one, to take notice of what was uttered in the pulpit. The Church, to be sure, he would obey; but, having received his message from God, he was bound to deliver it, and it would be a dereliction of duty, if he were to allow the civil power to judge such matters.[176] The king, greatly enraged, ordered Black to be cast into prison; and it is difficult to see what other course was open to him; though it was certain that neither this, nor any measure he could adopt, would tame the indomitable spirit of the Scotch Church.[177]

In December the same year, the Church proclaimed a fast; and Welsh preached in Edinburgh a sermon, with the view of rousing the people against their rulers. The king, he told his audience, had formerly been possessed by a devil, and that devil being put out,

---

hypocrisy of his heart;' that 'all kings were the devil's bairns, and that the devil was in the court, and the guiders of it.' He was proved to have used in his prayer these indecent words, when speaking of the queen, 'We must pray for her for fashion's sake; but we might as well not, for she will never do us any good.' He called the Queen of England an atheist, and the Lords of Session *bribers;* and said that the nobility at large 'were degenerate, godless, dissemblers, and enemies of the church.' " *Grierson's History of Saint Andrews,* p. 30, Cupar, 1838. Among the charges against him were, "Fourthly, that he had called the queen of England an atheist. Fifthly, that he had discussed a suspension granted by the lords of session in pulpit, and called them miscreants and bribers. Sixthly, that, speaking of the nobility, he said they were "degenerated, godless, dissemblers, and enemies to the church.' Likewise, speaking of the council, that he had called them "holiglasses, cormorants, and men of no religion.' " *Spottiswoode's History of the Church,* vol. iii. p. 21.

176. See the original papers on "The Declinatour of the King and Counsel's Judicatour in Maters Spirituall, namelie in Preaching of the Word," in *Calderwood's History of the Kirk,* vol. v. pp. 457–459, 475–480. Tytler (*History of Scotland,* vol. vii. pp. 326–332) has given extracts from them, and made some remarks on their obvious tendency. See also, on the Declinature of Jurisdiction claimed by the Scotch Church, *Hallam's Constitutional History,* 4th edit. 1842, vol. ii. p. 461; and *Mackenzie's Laws and Customs of Scotland in Matters Criminal,* Edinburgh, 1699, folio, pp. 181, 182.

177. M'Crie, in his *Life of Melville,* vol. ii. pp. 70 seq., has given an account of the punishment of Black, but, as usual, conceals the provocation; or, at least, softens it down until it hardly becomes a provocation. According to him, "David Black had been served with a summons to answer before the privy council for certain expressions used by him in his sermons." Certain expressions, indeed! But why name the penalty, and suppress the offence? This learned writer knew perfectly well what Black had done, and yet all the information bestowed on the reader is a note at p. 72, containing a mutilated extract from Spottiswoode.

seven worse ones had come in its place. It was, therefore, evident that James was demented, and it became lawful to take the sword of justice from his hands; just as it would be lawful for servants or children to seize the head of their family, if it had pleased heaven to afflict him with madness. In such case, the preacher observed, it would be right to lay hold of the madman, and to tie him hand and foot, that he might do no further harm.[178]

The hatred felt by the clergy was at this period so bitter, and the democratic spirit in them so strong,[179] that they seemed unable to restrain themselves; and Andrew Melville, in an audience with the king, in 1596, proceeded to personal insults, and, seizing him by the sleeve, called him God's silly vassal.[180] The large amount of truth contained in this bitter taunt, increased its pungency. But the ministers did not always confine themselves to words.[181] Their participation in the Ruthven conspiracy is unquestionable; and it is probable that they were privy to the last great peril to

178. "Saying, 'He was possessed with a devil; that one devil being put out, seven worse were entered in place; and that the subjects might lawfully rise, and take the sword out of his hand:' which he confirmed by the example of a father that falling into a frenzy, might be taken by the children and servants of the family, and tied hand and foot from doing violence." *Spottiswoode's History of the Church of Scotland,* vol. iii. p. 34. See also *Arnot's History of Edinburgh,* pp. 46, 47.

179. This did not escape the attention of the English government; and Elizabeth, who was remarkably well informed respecting Scotch affairs, wrote to James, in 1590, a warning, which was hardly necessary, but which must have added to his fears. "And lest fayre semblance, that easely may begile, do not brede your ignorance of suche persons as ether pretend religion or dissemble deuotion, let me warne you that ther is risen, bothe in your realme and myne, a secte of perilous consequence, suche as wold have no kings but a presbitrye, and take our place while the inioy our privilege, with a shade of Godes word, wiche non is iuged to folow right without by ther censure the be so demed. Yea, looke we wel unto them." *Letters of Elizabeth and James VI.,* edited by John Bruce, Camden Society, 1849, 4to, p. 63.

180. The Reverend James Melville, who was present at the scene, describes it with exuberant delight. "To the quhilk, I beginning to reply, in my manner, Mr. Andro doucht nocht abyd it, bot brak af upon the king in sa zealus, powerfull, and unresistable a maner, that whowbeit the king used his authoritie in maist crabbit and colerik maner, yit Mr. Andro bure him down, and outtered the Commission as from the mightie God, calling the king bot 'God's sillie vassall;' and taking him be the sleive," &c. *Autobiography and Diary of James Melvill,* p. 370. See also *Shields' Hind let loose,* 1687, p. 52; and *M'Crie's Life of Melville,* vol. ii. p. 66.

181. In 1593, 4, some of them formed a plot to seize him. See the evidence from the State-paper Office, in *Tytler's History of Scotland,* vol. vii. p. 249, edit. Edinburgh, 1845.

which James was exposed, before he escaped from that turbulent land, which he was believed to govern. Certain it is, that the Earl of Gowrie, who, in 1600, entrapped the king into his castle in order to murder him, was the hope and the mainstay of the Presbyterian clergy, and was intimately associated with their ambitious schemes.[182] Such, indeed, was their infatuation on behalf of the assassin, that, when his conspiracy was defeated, and he himself slain, several of the ministers propagated a report that Gowrie had fallen a victim to the royal perfidy, and that, in point of fact, the only plot which ever existed was one concocted by the king, with fatal art, against his mild and innocent host.[183]

An absurdity of this sort[184] was easily believed in an ignorant, and, therefore, a credulous, age. That the clergy should have propagated it, and that in this, as in many other cases, they should have laboured with malignant industry to defame the character of their prince,[185] will astonish no one, who knows how quickly the wrath of the Church can be roused, and how ready the spiritual classes always are to cover, even with the foulest calumny, those who stand in their way. The evidence which has been collected, proves that the Presbyterian ministers carried their violence against the constituted authorities of the state, to an indecent, if not to a criminal, length; and we cannot absolve them from the charge of being a restless and unscrupulous body, greedy after power, and grossly intolerant of whatever opposed their own views. Still, the real cause of their conduct was, the spirit of their age, and the peculiarities of their position. None of us can be sure that, if we were placed exactly as they were placed, we should have acted differently. Now, indeed, we cannot read of

182. "He was the darling hope of the Presbyterian party." *Ibid.,* vol. vii. p. 410.

183. "Gowry's conspiracy was by them charged on the king, as a contrivance of his to get rid of that earl." *Burnet's History of his own Time,* edit. Oxford, 1823, vol. i. p. 31. See also *Tytler's History of Scotland,* vol. vii. pp. 439, 440; and on the diffusion of "this absurd hallucination," see *The Spottiswoode Miscellany,* vol. ii. p. 320, Edinburgh, 1845.

184. See a good note in *Pitcairn's Criminal Trials in Scotland,* vol. ii. p. 179. Edinburgh, 1833, 4to. Compare *Lawson's Book of Perth,* Edinburgh, 1847, p. xxxix.

185. Their language, and their general bearing, so enraged James, as to extort from him a passionate declaration, in 1592, that "it would not be weill till noblemen and gentlemen gott licence to breake ministers' heads." *Calderwood's History of the Kirk,* vol. v. p. 148.

their proceedings, as they are recorded in their own Assemblies, and by the historians of their own Church, without an uneasy feeling of dislike, I had almost said of disgust, at finding ourselves in presence of so much of superstition, of chicanery, of low, sordid arts, and yet, withal, of arrogant and unbridled insolence. The truth, however, is, that in Scotland, the age was evil, and the evil rose to the surface. The times were out of joint, and it was hard to set them right. The long prevalence of anarchy, of ignorance, of poverty, of force, of fraud, of domestic tumult, and of foreign invasion, had reduced Scotland to a state which it is scarcely possible for us to realize. Hereafter, I shall give some evidence of the effect which this produced on the national character, and of the serious mischief which it wrought. In the mean time, we should, in fairness to the Scotch clergy, admit that the condition of their country affords the best explanation of their conduct. Every thing around them was low and coarse; the habits of men, in their daily life, were violent, brutal, and utterly regardless of common decency; and, as a natural consequence, the standard of human actions was so depressed, that upright and well-meaning persons did not shrink from doing what to us, in our advanced state of society, seems incredible. Let us, then, not be too rash in this matter. Let us not be too forward in censuring the leading actors in that great crisis through which Scotland passed, during the latter half of the sixteenth century. Much they did, which excites our strongest aversion. But one thing they achieved, which should make us honour their memory, and repute them benefactors of their species. At a most hazardous moment, they kept alive the spirit of national liberty.[186] What the nobles and the crown had

186. "At the period of which we speak" (about the year 1584) "the pulpit was, in fact, the only organ by which public opinion was, or could be, expressed; and the ecclesiastical courts were the only assemblies in the nation which possessed any thing that was entitled to the name of liberty or independence. Parliament had its business prepared to its hand, and laid before it in the shape of acts which required only its assent. Discussion and freedom of speech were unknown in its meetings. The courts of justice were dependent on the will of the sovereign, and frequently had their proceedings regulated, and their decisions dictated, by letters or messages from the throne. It was the preachers who first taught the people to express an opinion on the conduct of their rulers; and the assemblies of the Church set the earliest example of a regular and firm opposition to the arbitrary and unconstitutional measures of the Court." *M'Crie's Life of Melville,* vol. i. p. 302.

put in peril, that did the clergy save. By their care, the dying spark was kindled into a blaze. When the light grew dim, and flickered on the altar, their hands trimmed the lamp, and fed the sacred flame. This is their real glory, and on this they may well repose. They were the guardians of Scotch freedom, and they stood to their post. Where danger was, they were foremost. By their sermons, by their conduct, both public and private, by the proceedings of their Assemblies, by their bold and frequent attacks upon persons, without regard to their rank, nay, even by the very insolence with which they treated their superiors, they stirred up the minds of men, woke them from their lethargy, formed them to habits of discussion, and excited that inquisitive and democratic spirit, which is the only effectual guarantee the people can ever possess against the tyranny of those who are set over them. This was the work of the Scotch clergy; and all hail to them who did it. It was they who taught their countrymen to scrutinize, with a fearless eye, the policy of their rulers. It was they who pointed the finger of scorn at kings and nobles, and laid bare the hollowness of their pretensions. They ridiculed their claims, and jeered at their mysteries. They tore the veil, and exposed the tricks of the scene which lay behind. The great ones of the earth, they covered with contempt; and those who were above them, they cast down. Herein, they did a deed which should compensate for all their offences, even were their offences ten times as great. By discountenancing that pernicious and degrading respect which men are too apt to pay to those whom accident, and not merit, has raised above them, they facilitated the growth of a proud and sturdy independence, which was sure to do good service at a time of need. And that time came quicker than any one had expected. Within a very few years, James became master of the resources of England, and attempted, by their aid, to subvert the liberties of Scotland. The shameful enterprise, which he began, was continued by his cruel and superstitious son. How their attempts failed; how Charles I., in the effort, shipwrecked his fortune, and provoked a rebellion, which brought to the scaffold that great criminal, who dared to conspire against the people, and who, as the common enemy and oppressor of all, was at length visited with the just punishment of his sins, is known to every reader of our history. It is also well known, that, in conducting the struggle, the English were greatly indebted to the Scotch, who had, more-over, the merit of being the first to lift their hand against the tyrant. What, however, is less known, but is undoubtedly true, is, that both nations owe a debt they can never repay to those bold men, who, during the latter part of the sixteenth century, disseminated, from their pulpits and Assemblies, sentiments which the people cherished in their hearts, and which, at a fitting moment, they reproduced, to the dismay, and eventually to the destruction, of those who threatened their liberties.

III

Condition of Scotland during the Seventeenth and Eighteenth Centuries

Scarcely had James mounted the throne of England, when he began seriously, and on a large scale, to attempt to subjugate the Scotch Church, which, as he clearly saw, was the principal obstacle that stood between him and despotic power. While he was merely King of Scotland, he made several efforts, which were constantly baffled; but now that he wielded the vast resources of England, the victory seemed easy.[1] As early as 1584, he had gained a temporary triumph, by forcing many of the clergy to recognize episcopacy.[2] But that institution was so repugnant to their levelling and democratic principles, that nothing could overcome their abhorrence of it;[3] and, completely overawing the king, they compelled him to give way, and to retrace his steps. The result was, that, in 1592, an Act of Parliament was passed, which subverted

1. Lord Dartmouth says (Note in *Burnet's History of his own Time,* vol. i. p. 15): "The Earl of Seafield told me that King James frequently declared that he never looked upon himself to be more than King of Scotland in name, till he came to be King of England; but now, he said, one kingdom would help him to govern the other, or he had studied kingcraft to very little purpose from his cradle to that time." Compare *Burnet's Memoirs of the Dukes of Hamilton,* Oxford, 1852, p: 36. "No sooner was he happily settled on the throne of England, but he went more roundly to work."

2. Compare *Tytler's History of Scotland,* vol. vi. p. 430, with *Acts of the Parliaments of Scotland,* vol. iii. p. 303, § 20; also the Act (p. 293, § 4), likewise in 1584, limiting the power of the General Assemblies. James, who flattered himself that he had now settled every thing, signalized his triumph by personally abusing the clergy; "calling them lownes, smaicks, seditious knaves, and so furth." See a letter, dated 2d of January 1585-6, in *Miscellany of the Wodrow Society,* p. 438, Edinburgh, 1844.

3. "Bishops were always looked at with a frown." *Kirkton's History of the Church of Scotland,* p. 129.

the authority of the bishops, and established Presbyterianism; a scheme based on the idea of equality, and, therefore, suited to the wants of the Scotch Church.[4]

To this statute, James had assented with the greatest reluctance.[5] Indeed, his feeling respecting it was so strong, that he determined, on the first opportunity, to procure its repeal, even if he used force to effect his purpose. The course he adopted, was characteristic both of the man and of the age. In December 1596, one of those popular tumults arose in Edinburgh, which are natural in barbarous times, and which, under ordinary circumstances, would have been quelled, and nothing more thought of it.[6] But James availed himself of this, to strike what he deemed a decisive

4. See this remarkable statute, in *Acts of the Parliaments of Scotland,* vol. iii. pp. 541, 2. As some of the historians of the Scotch Church have greatly misrepresented it, I will quote that part which expressly repeals the Act of 1584, in favour of the bishops. "Item oure said souerane lord and estaittis of Parliament foirsaid, abrogatis cass and anullis the xx act of the same pliamet haldin at Edinburgh the said zeir 1584 zeiris granting comissioun to bishoppis and vtheris iuges constitute in ecclesiastical causs To ressaue his hienes presentatioun to benefices, To gif collatioun thairvpoun and to put ordo^r in all causs ecclesiasticall qlk his Maiestie and estaittis foirsaid declairis to be expyrit in the self and to be null in tyme cuming and of nane availl force nor effect."

5. "The King repented after that he had agreed unto it." *Calderwood's History of the Kirk,* vol. v. p. 162. But this gives a faint idea of his real feelings. It is perhaps hardly necessary to adduce evidence of the opinions entertained on this point, by a prince, one of whose favourite sayings was, "No Bishop, no King." The reader will, however, find, in the *Clarendon State Papers* (vol. ii. p. 260, Oxford, 1773, folio), a letter from Charles I., which is worth looking at, because it frankly avows that James, in loving episcopacy and hating presbyterianism, was actuated rather by political motives, than by religious ones. Charles writes: "The prudentiall part of any consideration will never be found opposit to the conscientious, nay heere, they go hand in hand; for (according to lawyers lodgique) show me any president where ever Presbiteriall governement and Regall was together, without perpetuall rebellions. *Which was the cause that necessitated the King, my Father, to change that governement in Scotland.*" Compare what is said by a Scotch Presbyterian of the seventeenth century, in *Biographies, edited for the Wodrow Society* by the Rev. W. K. Tweedie, Edinburgh, 1845, vol. i. p. 13. "The reason why King James was so violent for Bishops was neither their divine institution (which he denied they had), nor yet the profit the Church should reap by them (for he knew well both the men and their communications), but merely because he believed they were useful instruments to turn a limited monarchy into absolute dominion, and subjects into slaves, the design in the world he minded most."

6. "Had it not been laid hold of by designing politicians as a handle for accomplishing their measures, it would not now have been known that such an event had ever occurred." *M'Crie's Life of Melville,* vol. ii. p. 85. "Harmless as this uproar was, it afforded the court a pretext for carrying into execution its designs against the liberties and government of the Church." p. 89.

blow. His plan was nothing less than to turn into the capital of his own monarchy, large bodies of armed and licensed banditti, who, by threatening to plunder the city, should oblige the clergy and their flocks to agree to whatever terms he chose to dictate. This magnanimous scheme was well worthy of the mind of James, and it was strictly executed. From the north, he summoned the Highland nobles, and from the south, the border barons, who were to be accompanied by their fierce retainers,—men who lived by pillage, and whose delight it was to imbrue their hands in blood. At the express command of James, these ferocious brigands, on the 1st of January 1597, appeared in the streets of Edinburgh, gloating over the prospect before them, and ready, when their sovereign gave the word, to sack the capital, and raze it to the ground.[7] Resistance was hopeless. Whatever the king demanded, was conceded; and James supposed that the time was now come, in which he could firmly establish the authority of the bishops, and, by their aid, control the clergy, and break their refractory spirit.[8]

In this undertaking, three years were consumed. To insure its success, the king, supported by the nobles, relied, not only on force, but also on an artifice, which now seems to have been employed for the first time. This was, to pack the General Assemblies, by inundating them with clergymen drawn from the north of Scotland, where, the old clannish and aristocratic spirit being supreme, the democratic spirit, found in the south, was unknown. Hitherto, these northern ministers had rarely attended at the great meetings of the Church; but James, in 1597, sent Sir Patrick Murray on a special mission to them, urging them to be present, in order that they might vote on his side.[9] They, being a very

7. *Tytler's History of Scotland*, vol. vii. pp. 342–345. *Calderwood's History of the Kirk*, vol. v. pp. 514, 515, 530, 531.

8. "Intimidated by these menaces, and distressed at the loss of the courts of justice, they came to the resolution of making surrender of their political and religious liberties to the King." *M'Crie's Life of Melville*, vol. ii. p. 92. This is said of the magistrates of Edinburgh. Among other threats, one was, the "razing and ploughing of Edinburgh, and sowing it with salt." *Wodrow's Life of Bruce*, p. 48, prefixed to *Bruce's Sermons*, edited by the Rev. William Cunningham, Edinburgh, 1843. On this occasion, Elizabeth wrote a letter to James, which is printed in *Letters of Queen Elizabeth and James VI.*, 1849, 4to, pp. 120, 121.

9. *M'Crie's Life of Melville*, vol. ii. p. 100. Scot (*Apologetical Narration*

ignorant body, knowing little or nothing of the questions really at issue, and being, moreover, accustomed to a state of society in which men, notwithstanding their lawlessness, paid the most servile obedience to their immediate superiors, were easily worked upon, and induced to do what they were bid. By their help, the crown and the nobles so strengthened their party in the General Assembly, as to obtain in many instances a majority; and innovations were gradually introduced, calculated to destroy the democratic character of the Scotch Church.[10]

In 1597, the movement began. From then, until 1600, successive Assemblies sanctioned different changes, all of which were marked by that aristocratic tendency which seemed about to carry every thing before it. In 1600, the General Assembly met at Montrose; and government determined on making a final effort to compel the Church to establish an episcopal polity. Andrew Melville, by far the most influential man in the Church, and the leader of the democratic party, had been elected, as usual, a member of the Assembly; but the king, arbitrarily interposing, refused to allow him to take his seat.[11] Still, neither by threats, nor by force, nor by promises, could the court carry their point. All that they obtained was, that certain ecclesiastics should be allowed to sit in parliament; but it was ordered that such persons should every year lay their commissions at the feet of the General Assembly, and render an account of their conduct. The Assembly was to have the power of deposing them; and, to keep them in

---

of the State of the Kirk, p. 88) says, "Sir Patrick Murray, the diligent apostle of the North, made their acquaintance with the King." Also, *The Autobiography and Diary of James Melville,* p. 403.

10. *Tytler's History of Scotland,* vol. vii. pp. 350, 359. But by far the best account of the influence of these northern clergy, will be found in *M'Crie's Life of Melville* (vol. ii. pp. 100–105, 109, 131, 152), drawn, in several instances, from manuscript authorities. Compare *Calderwood's History of the Kirk,* vol. v. p. 695.

11. This is related by his nephew, James Melville. "Mr. Andro Melvill come to the Assembly, by Commissioune of his Presbytrie, but wes commandit to keip his ludgeing; quho, being callit to the King in private, and demandit, Quhy he wes so trublesume as to come to the Assembly being dischairgit? He answerit, He had a calling in the Kirk of God, and of Jesus Chryst, the King of kings, quhilk he behovit to dischairge at all occasiounes, being orderlie callit thairto, as he wes at this tyme; and that for feir of a grytter punischment then could any earthly King inflict." *The Autobiography and Diary of James Melvill,* p. 542.

greater subjection, they were forbidden to call themselves bishops, but were to be content with the inferior title of Commissioners of the Church.[12]

After sustaining this repulse, James seems to have been disheartened; as he made no further effort, though he still laboured underhand at the restoration of episcopacy.[13] If he had persevered,

12. As, owing to the passions of the rival classes, every step of this part of Scotch history is the subject of angry controversy, and as even Mr. Tytler (*History of Scotland,* vol. vii. p. 360) asserts that "the final establishment of Episcopacy" took place at the Assembly of Montrose, in 1600, I subjoin a few extracts from the enactments of that Assembly, in order that the reader may judge for himself, and may test the accuracy of what I have stated in the text. "Concerning the maner of choosing of him that sall have vote in Parliament in name of the Kirk: It is condiscendit vpon, that *he sall first be recommendit be the Kirk to his Majestie;* and that the Kirk sall nominat sixe for every place that sall have neid to be filled, of quhom his Majestie sall choose ane, of quhom he best lykes; and his Majestie promises, obleises, and binds himselfe to choose no vther but ane of that number: And in cace his Majestie refuses the haill vpon ane just reason of ane insufficiency, and of greater sufficiencie of vthers that are not recommendit, the Kirk sall make ane new recommendatioun of men according to the first number, of the quhilk, ane salbe chosin be his Majestie without any farther refuisall or new nominatioun; and he that salbe chosin be his Majestie, salbe admittit be the Synods." *Acts of the General Assemblies of the Kirk of Scotland,* vol. iii. p. 954. "As to the cautions to keip him, that sall have vote in Parliament, from corruptiouns: They be these following: 1. *That he presume not, an any tyme, to propone at Parliament, Counsell or Conventioun, in name of the Kirk, any thing without expresse warrand and directioun from the Kirk,* and sick things as he sall answer (for) to be for the weill of the Kirk, vnder the paine of depositioun from his office." . . . 2. "He sall be bound at every Generall Assemblie, to give ane accompt anent the discharge of his commissioun sen the Assemblie gangand befor; and *sall submitt himselfe to thair censure, and stand at thair determinatioun quhatsumever, without appellatioun; and sall seik and obtain ratificatioun of his doings at the said Assemblie, vnder the paine of infamie and excommunicatioun.*" . . . 6. "In the administration of discipline, collatioun of benefices, visitatioun, and all vther points of ecclesiasticall government, he sall neither vsurpe nor acclaime to himselfe *any power or jurisdictioun farther than any vther of the rest of his breither,* unlesse he be imployit be his breither, vnder the paine of deprivatioun." p. 955. "Anent his name that for the Kirk sall (have) vote in Parliament: It is advyseit, be vniforme consent of the haill brether, that he salbe callit Commissioner of such a place." p. 956. "Therfor the Generall Assemblie having reasonit at length the said questioun, tuiching the continuance of him that sall have vote in Parliament, after votting of the same, finds and decernes, that *he sall annuatim give count of his commission obtainit from the Assemblie, and lay downe the samein at thair feitt,* to be continuit or alterit therfra be his Maiestie and the Assemblie, as the Assemblie, with consent of his Maiestie, sall think most expedient for the weill of the Kirk." p. 959.

13. "While James remained in Scotland, the scheme of introducing episcopacy, though never lost sight of, was cautiously prosecuted." *M'Crie's Life of Melville,* vol. ii. p. 178.

it might have cost him his crown. For, his resources were few; he was extremely poor;[14] and recent events had shown that the clergy were stronger than he had supposed. When he thought himself most sure of success, they had subjected him to a mortifying defeat; and this was the more remarkable, as it was entirely their own work; they being by this time so completely separated from the nobles, that they could not rely upon even a single member of that powerful body.

While affairs were in this state, and while the liberties of Scotland, of which the Church was the guardian, were trembling in the balance, Elizabeth died, and the King of Scotland became also King of England. James at once determined to employ the resources of his new kingdom to curb his old one. In 1604, that is, only the year after his accession to the English throne, he aimed a deadly blow at the Scotch Church, by attacking the independence of their Assemblies; and, by his own authority, he prorogued the General Assembly of Aberdeen.[15] In 1605, he again prorogued it; and, to make his intentions clear, he, this time, refused to fix a day for its future meeting.[16] Hereupon, some of the ministers,

---

14. James, during the whole of his reign, was chiefly dependent on the money which Elizabeth gave him, and which she dealt out rather niggardly. Such were his necessities, that he was forced to pawn his plate, and, even then, he was often unable to defray his ordinary household expenses. See *Tytler's History of Scotland*, vol. vi. pp. 265, 266, 272; vol. vii. pp. 158, 378–380. *Miscellany of the Spalding Club*, vol. ii. pp. xlv. 114. *Gregory's History of the Western Highlands*, pp. 241, 277. See also a clamorous begging-letter from James to Elizabeth, written in 1591, in *Letters of Queen Elizabeth and James VI.*, 1849, 4to, pp. 68, 69. In 1593, she apologizes for sending him only a small sum: "The small token you shall receave from me I desire yt may serve to make you remember the tyme and my many weighty affaires, wich makes it les than else I would, and I dowt nothing but when you heare all, yow will beare with this." p. 84. A letter from James Hudson, written about the year 1591, states that "both the king's table and queen's had like to have been unserved by want; and that the king had nothing he accounted certain to come into his purse, but what he had from the Queen of England." *Ridpath's Border History*, p. 465, Berwick, 1848, 4to.

15. *Laing's History of Scotland*, edit. 1819, vol. iii. p. 28. *Calderwood's History of the Kirk*, vol. vi. pp. 264, 323. *Bower's History of the University of Edinburgh*, vol. i. p. 175, Edinburgh, 1817. *Stevenson's History of the Church of Scotland*, p. 88.

16. "Adde thereunto, that the letter of the commissioner and last moderator, conteaned no certane tyme nor day whereto the said Assemblie sould be prorogued; so that it imported a casting loose and deserting, yea, and tyning of the possessioun of our Assemblie; than the which what could be more dangerous to the libertie and freedom of the Kirk of Jesus Christ, at suche a tyme, namelie

deputed by presbyteries, took upon themselves to convene it, which they had an undoubted right to do, as the act of the king was manifestly illegal. On the day appointed, they met in the session-house of Aberdeen. They were ordered to disperse. Having, as they conceived, by the mere fact of assembling, sufficiently asserted their privileges, they obeyed. But James, now backed by the power of England, resolved that they should feel the change of his position, and, therefore, of theirs. In consequence of orders which he sent from London, fourteen of the clergy were committed to prison.[17] Six of them, who denied the authority of the privy-council, were indicted for high treason. They were at once put upon their trial. They were convicted. And sentence of death was only deferred, that the pleasure of the king might first be taken, as to whether he would not be satisfied with some punishment that fell short of sacrificing the lives of these unhappy men.[18]

Their lives, indeed, were spared; but they were subjected to a close imprisonment, and then condemned to perpetual exile.[19] In

of the treatie of the Unioun, when all the estates of the realme, and everie particular are zealous and carefull of their rights and possessiouns?" *Calderwood's History of the Kirk,* vol. vi. pp. 309, 310.

17. See a list of them in *Calderwood's History of the Kirk,* vol. vi. p. 347, where the fourteen names are preserved with pious care.

18. *Pitcairn's Criminal Trials in Scotland,* vol. ii. pp. 494–502. *Forbes' Certaine Records touching the Estate of the Kirk,* edit. Wodrow Society, Edinburgh, 1846, pp. 463–496. "Delayed the giving forth of the sentence of condemnation till the King's mind were further knowne." See also *Calderwood's History of the Kirk,* vol. vi. pp. 434, 449. When they were found guilty, "the peiple said, 'Certainely this wes a worke of darknes, to mak Chrystis faithfull Ministeres tratouris to the King! God grant he be niver in greater dangeris nor off sic traitouris.'" *Melvill's Autobiography and Diary,* p. 626.

19. *M'Crie's Life of Melville,* vol. ii. pp. 207, 208. *Pitcairn's Criminal Trials,* vol. ii. p. 504. In connexion with these transactions, a letter is preserved in the Winwood Papers, which is much too curious to be passed over in silence. It is addressed by the Earl of Salisbury to Sir Charles Cornwallis, and is dated 12th September 1605. Salisbury, who was then at the head of affairs, writes, "True it is that his Majestie seeking to *adorne that kingdome of Scotland with Prelates as they are in England,* some of the Ministers have spurned against it; and althouge his Majestie had ever warranted their calling of General Assemblies upon no other condition, then that they should make him acquainted, receive his warrant, and a commissioner for his Majestie resident in their councells, yet have they (followed with some poor plebecall numbers) presumed to hold their General Assemblies in some parte of the Realme contrarie to his commandement. Whereupon his Majestie hath shewed himself displeased, and cyted divers of them before his councell," &c. *Memorials of Affairs of State, from the Papers of Sir Ralph Winwood,* London, 1725, folio, vol. ii.

other parts of the country, similar measures were adopted. Nearly all over Scotland, numbers of the clergy were either imprisoned or forced to fly.[20] Terror and proscription were universal. Such was the panic, that it was generally believed that nothing could prevent the permanent establishment of despotism, unless there were some immediate and providential interference on behalf of the Church and the people.[21]

Nor can it be denied that there were plausible grounds for these apprehensions. The people had no friends except among the clergy, and the ablest of the clergy were either in prison or in exile.[22] To deprive the Church entirely of her leaders, James, in 1606, summoned to London, Melville and seven of his colleagues, under pretence of needing their advice.[23] Having got possession of their persons, he detained them in England.[24] They were for-

---

p. 132. And yet the man who could write such nonsense as this, and who could only see, in the great democratic movement of the Scotch mind, a disinclination to the *adornment* of episcopacy, was deemed one of the most eminent statesmen of his time, and his reputation has survived him. If great statesmen discern so little of what is before them and around them, we are tempted to inquire, how much confidence ought to be placed in the opinions of those average statesmen by whom countries are ruled. For my own part, I can only say, that I have had occasion to read many thousand letters written by diplomatists and politicians, and I have hardly ever found an instance of one of them who understood the spirit and tendency of the age in which he lived.

20. "Ministers in all parts of the country were thrown into prison, or declared rebels, and forced to abscond." *M'Crie's Life of Melville*, vol. ii. p. 250. Liberty of speech was so completely suppressed, that, in 1605, when the most zealous and intelligent clergy were banished, "a strait command" (was) "gevin to magistrats, and uther officiers of burrowis, that in cace any preacher sould speik opinlie aganis that baneisment, or for defence or mentenence of that assemblie, or pray publiklie for ther saiftie, that they sould be noted and manifested to the secret counsell, and corrected for their fault." *The Historie of King James the Sext*, p. 380.

21. See an eloquent and touching passage, in *Calderwood's History of the Kirk*, vol. vi. pp. 696, 697.

22. "The godliest, wisest, learnedest, and most zealous men of the ministrie in Scotland, were either banished, warded, or detained in Ingland, of purpose that they might not be a lett to the grand designe in hand." *Row's History of the Kirk*, p. 238.

23. *Scot's Apologetical Narration of the State of the Kirk*, pp. 164, 165. Compare *The Autobiography and Diary of James Melvill*, pp. 642–645.

24. "Quhen we wer gone out of the Palice a lytle way towardis Kingstoune, Mr. Alexander Hay sendis back for us, and withall, in the Uttir Court, reidis to us a chairge from the King not to returne to Scotland, nor to com neire the King, Quein, nor Prince their Courtis, without a speciall calling for and licence." *Melvill's Autobiography*, p. 661.

bidden to return to Scotland; and Melville, who was most feared, was committed to custody. He was then imprisoned in the Tower, where he remained four years, and from which he was only liberated on condition of living abroad, and abandoning altogether his native country.[25] The seven ministers who had accompanied him to London, were also imprisoned; but, being considered less dangerous than their leader, they, after a time, were allowed to return home. The nephew of Melville was, however, ordered not to travel more than two miles from Newcastle; and his six companions were confined in different parts of Scotland.[26]

Every thing now seemed ripe for the destruction of those ideas of equality, of which, in Scotland, the Church was the sole representative. In 1610, a General Assembly was held at Glasgow; and, as the members of it were nominated by the crown,[27] whatever the government wished, was conceded. By their vote, episcopacy was established, and the authority of the bishops over the ministers was fully recognized.[28] A little earlier, but in the same year, two courts of High Commission were erected, one at Saint Andrews, and one at Glasgow. To them, all ecclesiastical courts were subordinate. They were armed with such immense power, that they could cite any one they pleased before them,

25. *M'Crie's Life of Melville,* vol. ii. pp. 246, 252, 260, 337–339, 403, 407–411, 414. This truly great and fearless man died in exile, in 1622. p. 458.

26. *Melvill's Autobiography and Diary,* p. 709. *Scot's Apologetical Narration,* p. 194. *M'Crie's Life of Melville,* vol. ii. pp. 252, 253, 267, 268.

27. "Royal missives were sent to the presbyteries, nominating the individuals whom they should chuse as their representatives to it." *M'Crie's Life of Melville,* vol. ii. pp. 387, 388. On the character of its members, compare *Wodrow's History of the Sufferings of the Church of Scotland,* edit. Glasgow, 1838, vol. i. p. 256. *Stevenson's History of the Church of Scotland,* pp. 320, 321. *Crookshank's Church of Scotland,* Edinburgh, 1812, vol. i. p. 28; and *Calderwood's History of the Kirk,* vol. vii. pp. 97, 98.

28. *Acts of the General Assemblies of the Kirk,* vol. iii. pp. 1096, 1097. The Assembly even forbad the democratic notion of equality to be advocated. See p. 1101. "Because it is vncivill that laws and constitutiouns, either Civill or Ecclesiasticall, being anes establischit and in force, by publick and opin consent, sould be controllit and callit in questioun by any person: therfor, it is statute by vniforme consent of this haill Assemblie, that none of the Ministrie either in pulpitt in his preaching, or in the publick exercise, speake and reason against the acts of this present Assemblie, nor dissobey the same, vnder the paine of deprivatioun, being tryit and convict thereof; and *speciallie, that the questioun of equalitie and inequalitie in the Kirk, be not treattit in pulpitt vnder the said paine."*

could examine him respecting his religious opinions, could have him excommunicated, and could fine or imprison him, just as they thought proper.[29] Finally, and to complete the humiliation of Scotland, the establishment of episcopacy was not considered complete, until an act was performed, which nothing but its being very ignominious, could have saved from being ridiculed as an idle and childish farce. The archbishop of Glasgow, the bishop of Brechin, and the bishop of Galloway, had to travel all the way to London, in order that they might be touched by some English bishops. Incredible as it may appear, it was actually supposed that there was no power in Scotland sufficiently spiritual to turn a Scotchman into a prelate. Therefore it was, that the arch-

29. Mr. Russell (*History of the Church in Scotland,* vol. ii. p. 88), misled, probably, by a passage in *Spottiswoode's History of the Church,* vol. iii. p. 210, says, "A Court of High Commission was instituted." But it is certain that there were two such courts; one for the diocese of Saint Andrews, and one for that of Glasgow. See the "commissioun givin under the great seale to the two archbishops," dated 15th of February 1610, in *Calderwood's History of the Kirk,* vol. vii. pp. 57–62. See also p. 210. They were not united till December 1615. See *Scot's Apologetical Narration of the State of the Kirk,* pp. 218, 239; and *Crookshank's History of the Sufferings of the Church of Scotland,* vol. i. p. 28. By the royal commission, these despotic tribunals were authorized (*Calderwood,* vol. vii. p. 59) "to call before them at suche tymes and places as they sall thinke meete, anie person or persons dwelling and remaining within their provinces respective above writtin of St. Andrews or Glasgow, or within anie dioceis of the same, being offenders ather in life or religioun, whom they hold anie way to be scandalous, and that they take tryell of the same; and if they find them guiltie and impenitent, refusing to acknowledge their offence, they sall give command to the preacher of that parish where they dwell, to proceed with sentence of excommunicatioun against them; which, if it be protracted, and their command by that minister be not presentlie obeyed, they sall conveene anie suche minister before them, and proceed in censuring of him for his disobedience, ather by suspensioun, deprivatioun, or wairding, according as in their discretioun they sall hold his obstinacie and refuse of their directioun to have deserved. And further, to fyne at their discretiouns, imprisoun, or warde anie suche persoun, who being convicted before them, they sall find upon tryell to have deserved anie suche punishment." Hereupon, Calderwood justly remarks, p. 62: "This commissioun and executioun thereof, as it exalted the aspyring bishops farre above any prelat that ever was in Scotland, so it putt the king in possessioun of that which he had long tyme hunted for; to witt, of the royall prerogative, and absolute power to use the bodeis and goods of the subjects at pleasure, without forme or processe of the commoun law, even then when the Lower Hous in England was compleaning in their parliament upon the injurie thereof. So our bishops were fitt instruments to overthrow the liberteis both of the Kirk and countrie."

bishop of Glasgow and his companions, performed what was then an arduous journey to a strange and distant capital, for the sake of receiving some hidden virtue, which, on their return home, they might communicate to their brethren. To the grief and astonishment of their country, these unworthy priests, abandoning the traditions of their native land, and forgetting the proud spirit which animated their fathers, consented to abjure their own independence, to humble themselves before the English Church, and to submit to mummeries, which, in their hearts, they must have despised, but which were now inflicted upon them by their ancient and inveterate foes.[30]

We may easily imagine what would be the future conduct of men, who, merely for their own aggrandizement, and to please their prince, could thus renounce the cherished independence of the Scotch Church. They who crouch to those who are above them, always trample on those who are below them. Directly they returned to Scotland, they communicated the consecration they had received in England to their fellow-bishops,[31] who were of the like mould to themselves, in so far as all of them aided James in his attempt to subjugate the liberties of their native country. Being now properly ordained, their spiritual life was complete; it remained for them to secure the happiness of their temporal life. This they did, by gradually monopolizing all authority, and treating with unsparing severity those who opposed them. The full triumph of the bishops was reserved for the reign of Charles I., when a number of them obtained seats in the privy-council, where they behaved with such overbearing insolence, that even Clarendon, notwithstanding his notorious partiality for their order, cen-

---

30. See *Stevenson's History of the Church of Scotland,* p. 93, and *Kirkton's History,* p. 15. Kirkton indignantly says, that James "perswaded a few unworthy men to perjure themselves, and after their episcopall consecration by the English bishops in England, to exercise that odious office in Scotland against their own oath and the consciences of their brethren." Compare the contemptuous notice, in *Row's History of the Kirk,* p. 283, on the "anoynting of oyle and other ceremonies," and on "the foolish guyses in it." Indeed, on this subject, every Scotch writer who cared for the liberty of his country, expressed himself either with contempt or indignation.

31. Calderwood, with ill-suppressed bitterness, says, "efter the same maner that they were consecrated themselfs, *als neere as they could imitate."* *History of the Kirk,* vol. vii. p. 152. Compare *Wodrow's Collections,* vol. i. part i. p. 293. "The Bishops ordeaned in England keeped as near the manner taken with themselves there as they could."

sures their conduct.[32] In the time, however, of James I., they carried nearly every thing before them.[33] They deprived the towns of their privileges, and forced them to receive magistrates of their own choosing.[34] They accumulated wealth, and made an ostentatious display of it; which was the more disgraceful, as the country was miserably poor and their fellow-subjects were starving around them.[35] The Lords of the Articles, without whose sanc-

32. "Some of them, by want of temper, or want of breeding, did not behave themselves with that decency in their debates, towards the greatest men of the kingdom, as in discretion they ought to have done, and as the others reasonably expected from them." *Clarendon's History of the Rebellion,* edit. Oxford, 1843, p. 35. In 1633, "nine of them were privy councillors;" and "their pride was cried out upon as unsupportable." *Burnet's Memoirs of the Dukes of Hamilton,* p. 38. Sir John Scot imputes to them "insolence, pride and avarice." *Scot's Staggering State of the Scots Statesmen,* Edinburgh, 1754, p. 41. See also *Spalding's History of the Troubles,* vol. i. pp. 46, 46, Edinburgh, 1828, 4to.

33. So early as 1613, a letter from James Inglish (preserved in *Wodrow's Collections,* vol. ii. part i. p. 110, Glasgow, 1845, 4to) complains that "the libertys of the Lord's Kirk are greatly abridged by the pride of Bishops, and their power daily increases over her." Civil rights were equally set at nought by the bishops; and, among other enactments which they obtained, one was, "that no man should be permitted to practise or profess any physic, unless he had first satisfied the bishop of the diocese touching his religion." *Spottiswoode's History of the Church of Scotland,* vol. iii. p. 236. This at once gave them the control of the whole medical profession.

34. "Not satisfied with ruling the church-courts, they claimed an extensive civil authority within their dioceses. The burghs were deprived of their privileges, and forced to receive such magistrates as their episcopal superiors, in concert with the court, were pleased to nominate." . . . "Archbishop Gladstanes, in a letter to the King, June the 9th, 1611, says: 'It was your pleasure and direction, that I sould be possessed with the like privileges in the electione of the magistrats there (in St. Andrews), as my lord of Glasgow is endued with in that his city. Sir, whereas they are troublesome, I will be answerable to your Majesty and Counsell for them, after that I be possessed of my right.' Ms. in Bibl. Jurid. Edin. M. 6, 9. n°. 72." *M'Crie's Life of Melville,* vol. ii. p. 422.

35. And their prodigality was equal to their rapacity. When Archbishop Gladstanes died, in 1615, it was ascertained that, "notwithstanding of the great rent of his bishoprick, he died in the debt of twentie thowsand pounds." *Calderwood's History of the Kirk,* vol. vii. p. 197. See also p. 303. Also the case of the Bishop of Galloway, who died in 1619, and of whom Calderwood says (*History of the Kirk,* vol. vii. p. 350), "It is thought, that if just calculation were made of the commoditie extorted by him through his diocie, by advice of his two covetous counsellours, Andro Couper, his brother, and Johne Gilmour, wrytter in Edinburgh, for his use and theirs, by racting of rents, getting of grassoumes, setting of tacks, of teithes, and other like meanes, wold surmount the soume of an hundreth thousand merks, or, in the opinion of others, almost the double; so that manie within that diocie, and the annexed prelacies, sall hardlie recover their estates in their time." Compare *Stevenson's History of the Church,* pp. 212, 392.

tion no measure could be presented to parliament, had been hitherto elected by laymen; but the bishops now effected a change, by virtue of which the right of nomination devolved on themselves.[36] Having thus gained possession of the legislature, they obtained the enactment of fresh penalties against their countrymen. Great numbers of the clergy they suspended; others they deprived of their benefices; others they imprisoned. The city of Edinburgh, being opposed to the rites and ceremonies lately introduced, and being, like the rest of the country, hostile to episcopacy, the bishops fell on it also, displaced several of its magistrates, seized some of the principal citizens, and threatened to deprive it of the courts of justice, and of the honour of being the seat of government.[37]

In the midst of all this, and while things seemed to be at their worst, a great reaction was preparing. And the explanation of the reaction is found in that vast and pregnant principle, on which I have often insisted, but which our common historians are unable to understand; namely, that a bad government, bad laws, or laws badly administered, are, indeed, extremely injurious at the time, but can produce no permanent mischief; in other words, they may harm a country, but can never ruin it. As long as the people are sound, there is life, and while there is life, there will be reaction. In such case, tyranny provokes rebellion, and despotism causes freedom. But if the people are unsound, all hope is gone, and the nation perishes. In both instances, government is, in the long-run, inoperative, and is nowise responsible for the ultimate result. The ruling classes have, for the moment, immense power, which they invariably abuse, except when they are restrained, either by fear, or by shame. The people may inspire them with fear; public opinion may inspire them with shame. But whether or not that shall happen, depends on the spirit of the

36. On this change, which was completed in 1621, see *Laing's History of Scotland,* vol. iii. p. 88; *Calderwood's History of the Kirk,* vol. vii. p. 490; and *Baillie's Letters and Journals,* vol. i. p. 486, edit. Laing, Edinburgh, 1841.

37. *Calderwood's History of the Kirk,* vol. vii. pp. 472–474, 507, 509, 511, 517–520, 530–543, 549–553, 566, 567, 614, 621. *Laing's History of Scotland,* vol. iii. pp. 90, 91. Laing, very unjustly, accuses the bishops of being so merciful as to disapprove of some of these transactions. But whoever has read much of the Scotch literature of the seventeenth century, will cheerfully exonerate the bishops from a charge, which they would themselves have repelled, and to which they are nowise amenable.

people, and on the state of opinion. These two circumstances are themselves governed by a long chain of antecedents, stretching back to a period, always very distant, and sometimes so remote as to baffle observation. When the evidence is sufficiently abundant, those antecedents may be generalized; and their generalization conducts us to certain large and powerful causes, on which the whole movement depends. In short periods, the operation of these causes is imperceptible, but in long periods, it is conspicuous and supreme; it colours the national character; it controls the great sweep and average of affairs. In Scotland, as I have already shown, general causes made the people love their clergy, and made the clergy love liberty. As long as these two facts coëxisted, the destiny of the nation was safe. It might be injured, insulted, and trampled upon. It might be harmed in various ways; but the greater the harm, the surer the remedy, because the higher the spirit of the country would be roused. All that was needed was, a little more time, and a little more provocation. We, who, standing at a distance, can contemplate these matters from an elevation, and see how events pressed on and thickened, cannot mistake the regularity of their sequence. Notwithstanding the apparent confusion, all was orderly and methodical. To us, the scheme is revealed. There is the fabric, and it is of one hue, and one make. The pattern is plainly marked, and fortunately it was worked into a texture, whose mighty web was not to be broken, either by the arts, or the violence, of designing men.

It was, therefore, of no avail that tyranny did her utmost. It was of no avail that the throne was occupied by a despotic and unscrupulous king, who was succeeded by another, more despotic and more unscrupulous than himself. It was of no avail that a handful of meddling and intrusive bishops, deriving their consecration from London, and supported by the authority of the English church, took counsel together, and conspired against the liberties of their native land. They played the part of spies and of traitors, but they played it in vain. Yet, every thing that government could give them, it gave. They had the law on their side, and they had the right of administering the law. They were legislators, councillors, and judges. They had wealth; they had high-sounding titles; they had all the pomp and attributes for which they bartered their independence, and with which they hoped to dazzle the eyes of the vulgar. Still, they could not turn back the stream; they could not even stop it; they could not prevent it from coming on, and swallowing them up in its course. Before that generation passed away, these little men, big though they were in their own conceit, succumbed, and fell. The hand of the age was upon them, and they were unable to resist. They were struck down, and humbled; they were stripped of their offices, their honours, and their splendour; they lost all which minds like theirs hold most dear. Their fate is an instructive lesson. It is a lesson, both to the rulers of nations, and to those who write the history of nations. To rulers, in so far as it is one of many proofs how little they can do, and how insignificant is the part which they play in the great drama of the world. To historians, the result should be especially instructive, as convincing them that the events on which they concentrate their attention, and which they believe to be of supreme importance, are in reality of trifling value, and, so far from holding the first rank, ought to be made subservient to those large and comprehensive studies, by whose aid alone, we can ascertain the conditions which determine the tread and destiny of nations.

The events that now happened in Scotland, may be quickly told. The patience of the country was well-nigh exhausted, and the day of reckoning was at hand.[38] In 1637, the people began to rise. In the summer of that year, the first great riot broke out in Edinburgh.[39] The flame quickly spread, and nothing could stop it. By October, the whole nation was up, and an accusation was preferred against the bishops, which was signed by nearly every corporation, and by men of all ranks.[40] In November, the Scotch,

38. In October 1637, Baillie, who was carefully watching the course of affairs, writes, "No man may speak any thing in publick for the king's part, except he would have himself marked for a sacrifice to be killed one day. I think our people possessed with a bloody devill, farr above any thing that ever I could have imagined, though the masse in Latine had been presented." And, in a postscript, dated 3d October, he adds: "My fears in my former went no farther then to ane ecclesiastik separation, but now I am more affravit for a bloudie civill warr." *Baillie's Letters and Journals*, edit. Laing, Edinburgh, 1841, vol. i. pp. 23, 25.

39. *Laing's History of Scotland*, vol. iii. p. 131. *Chambers' Annals*, vol. ii. pp. 101–104. *Spalding's History of the Troubles in Scotland*, vol. i. pp. 47, 48.

40. "The accusation, among themselves a bond of union, and to their enemies a signal of hostility, was subscribed by the nobility, the gentry, the clergy, and afterwards by all ranks, and almost by every corporation in the kingdom." *Laing's History of Scotland*, vol. iii. p. 137.

in defiance of the Crown organized a system of representation of their own, in which every class had a share.[41] Early in 1638, the National Covenant was framed; and the eagerness with which it was sworn to, showed that the people were determined, at all hazards, to vindicate their rights.[42] It was now evident that all was over. During the summer of 1638, preparations were made, and, in the autumn, the storm broke. In November, the first General Assembly seen in Scotland for twenty years, met at Glasgow.[43] The Marquis of Hamilton, the king's commissioner, ordered the members to separate.[44] They refused.[45] Nor would they disband, until they had done the work expected from them.[46] By their vote, the democratic institution of presbyteries was restored to its old power; the forms of consecration were done away with; the bishops were degraded from their functions, and episcopacy was abolished.[47]

Thus, the bishops fell, even more rapidly than they had risen.[48]

41. *Ibid.,* vol. iii. p. 138.

42. "It was signed by a large majority of the people, in a paroxysm of enthusiasm beyond all example in our history." *Chambers' Annals,* vol. ii. p. 105. Kirkton, who was a contemporary, says, "And though only eleven private men (and some of them very inconsiderable) had the boldness first to begin this work, without ever asking leave of king or council, yet was it very quickly taken by all the people of Scotland, with hands lifted up in most solemn manner." *Kirkton's History of the Church of Scotland,* p. 33. Lord Somerville, taking a somewhat different view of affairs, remarks, that "the generalitie of the natione entered into a hellish covenant, wherein they mutually obleidged themselves to extirpate episcopacy, and to defend each other against all persones whatsoever, noe not excepting the persone of his sacred majestie; but upon conditiones of ther oune frameing." *Somerville's Memorie of the Somervilles,* vol. ii. p. 187.

43. There had been no General Assembly since 1618. *Argyll's Presbytery Examined,* p. 102; and the *Spottiswoode Miscellany,* vol. i. p. 88. But "the provincial synods, presbyteries, and sessions still remained, and in these, good men mutually comforted one another." *Stevenson's History of the Church of Scotland,* p. 162.

44. "The assembly went on at such a rate, that the marquis judged it no longer fit to bear with their courses." *Burnet's Memoirs of the Dukes of Hamilton,* p. 128. "In end, seeing nothing said in reason did prevail, he, in his majesty's name, dissolved the assembly, and discharged their further proceeding under pain of treason." p. 135.

45. *Stevenson's History of the Church of Scotland,* p. 310.

46. "Notwithstanding the Proclamation, the Assembly presently thereafter met, and sat daily for divers weeks, until they had done their affairs, and were themselves pleas'd to dissolve." *Guthry's Memoirs,* p. 41, edit. London, 1702.

47. *Acts of the General Assembly of the Church of Scotland,* from 1638 to 1842, Edinburgh, 1843, pp. 9–18. *Stevenson's History of the Church of Scotland,* pp. 332, 338.

48. See, on their fall, some highly characteristic remarks in *Baillie's Letters*

As, however, their fall was merely a part of the democratic movement, matters could not stop there.[49] Scarcely had the Scotch expelled their bishops, when they made war upon their king. In 1639, they took up arms against Charles. In 1640, they invaded England. In 1641, the king, with the hope of appeasing them, visited Scotland, and agreed to most of their demands. It was too late. The people were hot, and a cry for blood had gone forth. War again broke out. The Scotch united with the English, and Charles was every where defeated. As a last chance, he threw himself upon the mercy of his northern subjects.[50] But his offences were of that rank and luxuriant growth, that it was impossible to forgive them. Indeed, the Scotch, instead of pardoning him, turned him to profit. He had not only trampled on their liberties, he had also put them to an enormous expense. For the injury, he could offer no adequate atonement; but the expense they had incurred, might be defrayed. And as it is an old and

---

and Journals, vol. i. p. 168. In 1639, Howell writes from Edinburgh, "The Bishops are all gone to wrack, and they have had but a sorry funeral; the very name is grown so contemptible, that a black dog, if he hath any white marks about him, is called *Bishop.* Our Lord of Canterbury is grown here so odious, that they call him commonly in the pulpit, the Priest of Baal, and the Son of Belial." *Howell's Letters,* edit. London, 1754, p. 276.

49. "That people, after they had once begun, pursued the business vigorously, and with all imaginable contempt of the government." *Clarendon's History of the Rebellion,* p. 45. Now, for the first time, the English government began to tremble. On 13th December 1639, Secretary Windebank writes, "His Majesty near these six weeks last past hath been in continual consultations with a select Committee of some of his Council (of which I have had the honour to be one), how to redress his affairs in Scotland, the fire continuing there, and growing to that danger, that *it threatens not only the Monarchical Government there, but even that of this kingdom.*" *Clarendon State Papers,* vol. ii. p. 81, Oxford, 1773, folio. This is the earliest intimation I have met with of Charles and his advisers being aware of their real peril. But though the king was capable of fear, he was incapable of compunction. There is no evidence on record, to show that he even felt remorse for having planned and executed those arbitrary and unprincipled measures, by which he inflicted immense misery upon Scotland and England, but more especially upon Scotland.

50. "The kinge was now so waik, haueing nether toune, fort, nor armie, and Oxford being a waik and onfortified toune, from whence he looked daylie to be taken perforce, he therefor resolues to cast himself into the arms of the Scots; who, being his natiue people, and of late so ongratfullie dealt with by the Inglish, he hoped their particular credit, and the credit of the wholl natione depending thereupon, they would not baslie rander him to the Inglish." *Gordon's Britane's Distemper,* p. 193, published by the Spalding Club, Aberdeen, 1844, 4to.

recognized maxim, that he who cannot pay with his purse, shall pay with his body, the Scotch saw no reason why they should not derive some advantage from the person of their sovereign, particularly as, hitherto, he had caused them nothing but loss and annoyance. They, therefore, gave him up to the English, and, in return, received a large sum of money, which they claimed as arrears due to them for the cost of making war on him.[51] By this arrangement, both of the contracting parties benefited. The Scotch, being very poor, obtained what they most lacked. The English, a wealthy people, had indeed to pay the money, but they were recompensed by getting hold of their oppressor, against whom they thirsted for revenge; and they took good care never to let him loose, until they had exacted the last penalty of his great and manifold crimes.[52]

51. That it may not be supposed, that, as an Englishman, I misrepresent this transaction by looking at it from an English point of view, I will merely quote what Scotch writers have said respecting it. "Giveing up the king to the will and pleasure of the English parliament, that soe they might come by ther money." *Somerville's Memorie of the Somervilles,* vol. ii. p. 366. "The Scots sold their unfortunate king, who had fled to them for protection, to the commissioners of the English Parliament, for 200,000*l.* sterling." *Lyon's History of St. Andrews,* vol. ii. 38. "The incident itself was evidence of a bargain with a *quid pro quo.*" *Burton's History of Scotland,* vol. i. p. 493. "The sale of the king to the parliament." *Napier's Life of Montrose,* Edinburgh, 1840, p. 448. "The king was delivered up, or rather sold, to the parliament's commissioners." *Brown's History of Glasgow,* vol. i. p. 91. "Their arrears were undoubtedly due; the amount was ascertained before the dispute concerning the disposal of his person, and the payment was undertaken by the English parliament, five months previous to the delivery, or surrender of the king. But the coincidence, however unavoidable, between that event and the actual discharge and departure of their army, still affords a presumptive proof of the disgraceful imputation of having sold their king; 'as the English, unless previously assured of receiving his person, would never have relinquished a sum so considerable as to weaken themselves, while it strengthened a people with whom a material question remained to be discussed.' " *Laing's History of Scotland,* vol. iii. pp. 369, 370.

52. A letter from Sir Edw. Hyde to Lord Hatton, dated April 12, 1649 (in the *Clarendon State Papers,* vol. ii. p. 479, Oxf. 1773, fol.), says of Charles II., that the Scotch "sold his father to those who murdered him." But this is not true. Charles I., though certainly bought by the English, was not murdered by them. He was tried in the face of day; he was found guilty; he was executed. And most assuredly never did a year pass, without men far less criminal than he, suffering the same fate. Possibly, they are right who deem all capital punishment needless. That, however, has never been proved; and if this last and most terrible penalty is ever to be exacted, I cannot tell where we should find a more fitting subject to undergo it, than a despot who seeks to subjugate the liberties of the people over whom he is called to rule, inflicts cruel and illegal punish-

After the execution of Charles I., the Scotch recognized his son as his successor. But before they would crown the new king, they subjected him to a treatment which hereditary sovereigns are not much accustomed to receive. They made him sign a public declaration, expressing his regret for what had happened, and acknowledging that his father, moved by evil counsels, had unjustly shed the blood of his subjects. He was also obliged to declare, that by these things he felt humbled in spirit. He had, moreover, to apologize for his own errors, which he ascribed partly to his inexperience, and partly to the badness of his education.[53] To evince the sincerity of this confession, and in order that the confession might be generally known, he was commanded to keep a day of fasting and humiliation, in which the whole nation would weep and pray for him, in the hope that he might escape the consequences of the sins committed by his family.[54]

---

ment on those who oppose him, and, sooner than renounce his designs, engages in a civil war, setting fathers against their children, disorganizing society, and causing the land to run with blood. Such men are outlaws; they are the enemies of the human race; who shall wonder if they fall, or, having fallen, who shall pity them?

53. The declaration was signed by Charles on the 16th August 1650. An abridgment of it is given in *Balfour's Annales of Scotland*, vol. iv. pp. 92–94; but the entire document is preserved by Sir Edward Walker. See *Journal of Affairs in Scotland,* in *Walker's Historical Discourses,* London, folio, 1705, pp. 170–176. In it, Charles is made to state that, "though his Majesty as a dutiful son be obliged to honour the memory of his Royal Father, and have in estimation the person of his Mother; yet doth he desire to be deeply humbled and afflicted in spirit before God, because of his Father's hearkening unto and following evil councils, and his opposition to the work of reformation, and to the solemn league and covenant by which so much of the blood of the Lord's people hath shed in these kingdoms." He went on to say, that though he might palliate his own misconduct by pleading "his education and age," he thinks it better to "ingeniously acknowledge all his own sins and the sins of his father's house." Burnet (*History of his own Time,* vol. i. p. 97) says of this declaration: "In it there were many hard things. The king owned the sin of his father in marrying into an idolatrous family: he acknowledged the bloodshed in the late wars lay at his father's door: he expressed a deep sense of his own ill education," &c.

54. In reference to this event, the following entry occurs in Lamont's Journal: "1650, Dec. 22.—The fast appointed by the commission of the kirke to be keiped througe the kingdome before the coronatione, was keiped att Largo the forsaide day by Mr. Ja. Magill; his lecture, Reu. 3. from v. 14 to the end of the chapt.; his text Reu. 2. 4, 5. Vpon the Thursday following, the 26 of this instant, the fast was keiped in likemaner; his lecture 2. Chro. 29 to v 12; his text 2. Chron. 12, 12. The causes of the first day (not read) was, the great contempt of the gospell, holden forth in its branches; of the second day (which

The spirit, of which acts like these are but symptoms, continued to animate the Scotch during the rest of the seventeenth century. And fortunately for them it did so. For, the reigns of Charles II. and James II. were but repetitions of the reigns of James I. and Charles I. From 1660 to 1688, Scotland was again subjected to a tyranny, so cruel and so exhausting, that it would have broken the energy of almost any other nation. . . .[55]

The people, deserted by every one except their clergy, were ruthlessly plundered, murdered, and hunted, like wild-beasts, from place to place. From the tyranny of the bishops, they had so recently smarted, that they abhorred episcopacy more than ever; and yet that institution was not only forced upon them, but government put at its head Sharp, a cruel and rapacious man, who, in 1661, was raised to the archbishopric of St. Andrews.[56]

---

were read), the sinns of the king, and of his father's house, where sundry offences of K. James the 6 were aknowledged, and of K. Charles the 1, and of K. Ch. the 2, nowe king." *The Dairy of Mr. John Lamont of Newton,* p. 25, Edinburgh, 1830, 4to. See also *Baillie's Letters and Journals,* vol. iii. p. 107; *Nicoll's Diary,* Edinburgh, 4to, 1836, p. 38; *Row's Continuation of Blair's Autobiography,* edit. Wodrow Society, p. 255; *Bower's History of the University of Edinburgh,* vol. i. p. 253; *Presbytery Book of Strathbogie,* edit. Spalding Club, p. 169; and, above all, the *Registers of the Presbytery of Lanark,* published by the Abbotsford Club, Edinburgh, 1839, 4to, pp. 88, 89.

55. Wodrow, who had before him the records of the Privy Council, besides other evidence now lost, says, that the period from 1660 to 1688 was "a very horrid scene of oppression, hardships, and cruelty, which, were it not incontestably true, and well vouched and supported, could not be credited in after ages." *Wodrow's History of the Church of Scotland from the Restoration to the Revolution,* vol. i. p. 57. And the Reverend Alexander Shields, quaintly, but truly, observes, "that the said Government was the most untender, unpeaceable, tyrannical, arbitrary and wicked, that ever was in Scotland in any age or period." *Shields' Scots Inquisition,* Edinburgh, 1745, p. 24.

56. He was made "primate" in 1661, but did not arrive in Scotland till April 1662. *Wodrow's History of the Church of Scotland,* vol. i. pp. 236, 247; and *Nicoll's Diary,* pp. 363, 364. "That he was decent, if not regular, in his deportment, endued with the most industrious diligence, and not illiterate, was never disputed; that he was vain, vindictive, perfidious, at once haughty and servile, rapacious and cruel, his friends have never attempted to disown." *Laing's History of Scotland,* vol. iv. pp. 98, 99. The formal establishment of episcopacy was in the autumn of 1661, as we learn from an entry in Lamont's Diary. "1661. Sept. 5 being Thursday, (the chancelour, Glencairne, and the E. of Rothes, haueing come downe from court some dayes before,) the cownsell of state satt att Edb., and the nixt day, being Fryday, they caused emitte and be proclaimed ouer the Crosse, a proclamation in his Maj. name, for establishing Episcopacie againe in the church of Scotlande; which was done with great solemnitie, and was afterwarde printed. *All persons, wither men or woemen,*

He set up a court of ecclesiastical commission, which filled the prisons to overflowing; and when they would hold no more, the victims were transported to Barbadoes, and other unhealthy settlements. The people, being determined not to submit to the dictation of government respecting their religious worship, met together in private houses; and, when that was declared illegal, they fled from their houses to the fields. But there, too, the bishops were upon them.[57] Lauderdale, who, for many years, was at the head of affairs, was greatly influenced by the new prelates and aided them with the authority of the executive.[58] Under their united auspices, a new contrivance was hit upon; and a body of soldiers, commanded by Turner, a drunken and ferocious soldier, was let loose upon the people.[59] The sufferers, galled to madness,

---

were discharged to speake against that office, under the paine of treason." The Diary of Mr. John Lamont, p. 140. This, as we learn from another contemporary, was on account of "the Kinges Majestie having stedfastlie resolvit to promove the estait, power, and dignitie of Bischops, and to *remove all impedimentes contrary thairto." Nicoll's Diary,* 4to, p. 353; on 21st November 1661. This curious diary, written by John Nicoll, and extending from 1650 to 1667, was printed at Edinburgh, in 1836, by the Bannatyne Club, and is now not often met with.

57. They were invested with such immense power, that "the old set of bishops made by the parliament, 1612, were but pigmies to the present high and mighty lords." *Wodrow's History of the Church of Scotland,* vol. i. p. 262. See also, at p. 286, the remarks of Douglas: "It is no wonder then the complaint against their bishops be, that their little finger is thicker than the loins of the former."

58. In 1663, Middleton was dismissed; and was succeeded by Lauderdale, who "was dependent upon the prelates, and was compelled to yield to their most furious demands." *Laing's History of Scotland,* vol. iv. p. 33. "The influence, or rather the tyranny, which was thus at the discretion of the prelates, was unlimited; and they exercised it with an unsparing hand." *Bower's History of the University of Edinburgh,* vol. i. p. 284.

59. "Sir James Turner, that commanded them, was naturally fierce, but was mad when he was drunk; and that was very often." *Burnet's History of his own Time,* vol. i. p. 364. Kirkton (*History of the Church,* p. 221) says: "Sir James Turner hade made ane expedition to the west countrey *to subdue it to the bishops,* in the year 1664; another in the year 1665; and a third in the year 1666; and this was the worst." Full particulars will be found in *Wodrow's History of the Church of Scotland,* vol. i. pp. 373–375, 411, vol. ii. pp. 8, 17, vol. iii. pp. 264, 265. "This method of dragooning people to the church, as it is contrary to the spirit of Christianity, so it was a stranger in Scotland, till Bishop Sharpe and the prelates brought it in." vol. i. p. 401.

Sir James Turner, whose Memoirs, written by himself, were not published till thirty years ago, relates an anecdote of his own drunkenness in a strain of maudlin piety well worthy of his career. *Turner's Memoirs of his own Life,*

rose in arms. This was made the pretence, in 1667, for fresh military executions, by which some of the fairest parts of western Scotland were devastated, houses burned, men tortured, women ravished.[60] In 1670, an act of parliament was passed, declaring that whoever preached in the fields without permission should be put to death.[61] Some lawyers were found bold enough to defend

---

Edinburgh, 1829, 4to, pp. 42, 43. At p. 206, this impudent man writes: "And yet I confesse, my humour never was, nor is not yet, one of the calmest; when it will be, God onlie knoues; yet by many sad passages of my life. I know that *it hath beene good for me to be afflicted*." Perhaps, however, he may take the benefit of his assertion (p. 144), "that I was so farre from exceeding or transgressing my commission and instructions, that I never came the full length of them." Considering the cruelties he committed, what sort of instructions could his superiors have given to him?

60. "Sir James Turner lately had forced Galloway to rise in arms, by his cruelty the last and former years; but he was an easy master, compared with General Dalziel, his ruffians, and Sir William Bannatyne, this year." *Wodrow's Church of Scotland,* vol. ii. p. 62. Dalziel "cruelly tortured whom he would." p. 63. One woman "is brought prisoner to Kilmarnock, where she was sentenced to be let down to a deep pit, under the house of the dean, full of toads and other vile creatures. Her shrieks thence were heard at a great distance." p. 64. Two countrymen were "bound together with cords, and hanged by their thumbs to a tree, there to hang all night." *Ibid.* Sir William Bannatyne's soldiers seized a woman, "and bound her, and put lighted matches betwixt her fingers for several hours; the torture and pain made her almost distracted; she lost one of her hands, and in a few days she died." *Ibid.* "Oppressions, murders, robberies, rapes." p. 65. "He made great fires, and laid down men to roast before them, when they would not, or could not, give him the money he required, or the informations he was seeking." p. 104. See also *Crookshank's History of the Church of Scotland,* vol. i. pp. 204–207. This History is based upon Wodrow's great work, but contains many facts with which Wodrow was unacquainted. See *Crookshank,* vol. i. p. 11. Respecting the outrages in 1667, there are some horrible details in a book published in that very year, under the title of *Naphtali, or the Wrestlings of the Church of Scotland.* See, especially, the summary at p. 174: "wounding, beating, stripping and imprisoning mens persons, violent breaking of their houses both by day and night, and beating and wounding of wives and children, ravishing and deflowring of women, forcing wives and other persons by fired matches and other tortures to discover their husbands and nearest relations, although it be not within the compass of their knowledge, and driving and spoiling all their goods that can be carried away, without respect to guilt or innocency."

61. "That whosoever without licence or authoritie forsaid shall preach, expound Scripture, or pray at any of these meetings in the ffield, or in any house wher ther be moe persons nor the house contains, so as some of them be without doors (which is heerby declared to be a feild conventicle), or who shall convocat any number of people to these meetings, shall be punished with death and confiscation of ther goods." *Acts of the Parliaments of Scotland,* vol. viii. p. 9, edit. 1820, folio. This was on the 13th August 1670.

innocent men, when they were tried for their lives; it was therefore determined to silence them also, and, in 1674, a great part of the Faculty of Advocates was expelled from Edinburgh.[62] In 1678, by the express command of government, the Highlanders were brought down from their mountains, and, during three months, were encouraged to slay, plunder, and burn at their pleasure, the inhabitants of the most populous and industrius parts of Scotland. . . .

It was in this way, that the English government sought to break the spirit, and to change the opinions, of the Scotch people. The nobles looked on in silence, and, so far from resisting, had not even the courage to remonstrate. The parliament was equally servile, and sanctioned whatever the government demanded. Still, the people were firm. Their clergy, drawn from the middle classes, clung to them; they clung to their clergy, and both were unchanged. The bishops were hated as allies of the government, and were with reason regarded as public enemies. They were known to have favoured, and often to have suggested, the atrocities which had been committed;[63] and they were so pleased with the punishment inflicted upon their opponents, that no one was surprised, when, a few years later, they, in an address to James II., the most cruel of all the Stuarts, declared that he was the darling of heaven, and hoped that God might give him the hearts of his subjects, and the necks of his enemies. . . .[64]

The short reign of James II. was ushered in by an act of singular barbarity. A few weeks after this bad man came to the throne,

62. The immediate pretence being, to do away with appeals. See *Laing's History of Scotland,* vol. iv. pp. 72–74.

63. "Indeed, the whole of the severity, hardships, and bloodshed from this year" (1661), "until the revolution, was either actually brought on by the bishops, procured by them, or done for their support." *Wodrow's History of the Church of Scotland,* vol. i. p. 223. "It was our prelates who pushed the council to most of their severities." p. 247. "The bishops, indeed, violently pushed prosecutions." *Crookshank's History of the Church,* vol. i. p. 298. In 1666, "As to the Prelates, they resolved to use all severities, and to take all imaginable cruel and rigorous ways and courses, first against the rest of the prisoners, and then against the whole west of Scotland." *Row's Continuation of Blair's Autobiography,* pp. 505, 506, edit. Edinburgh, 1848. This interesting work is edited by Dr. M'Crie, and published by the Wodrow Society.

64. In 1688, "the bishops concurred in a pious and convivial address to James, as the darling of heaven, that God might give him the hearts of his subjects and the necks of his enemies." *Laing's History of Scotland,* vol. iv. p. 193.

all the children of Annandale and Nithsdale, between the ages of six and ten, were seized by the soldiers, separated from their parents, and threatened with immediate death.[65] The next step was, to banish, by wholesale, large numbers of adults, who were shipped off to unhealthy settlements; many of the men first losing their ears, and the women being branded, some on the hand, some on the cheek.[66] Those, however, who remained behind, were equal to the emergency, and were ready to do what remained to be done. In 1688, as in 1642, the Scotch people and the English people united against their common oppressor, who saved himself by sudden and ignominious flight. He was a coward as well as a despot, and from him there was no further danger. The bishops, indeed, loved him; but they were an insignificant body, and had

65. "Upon the 10th of March, all freeholders, heritors, and gentlemen in Nithsdale and Annandale, and, I suppose, in most other shires of the kingdom, but I name those as being the scene of the severities now used, were summoned to attend the king's standard; and the militia in the several shires were raised. Wherever Claverhouse came, he resolved upon narrow and universal work. He used to set his horse upon the hills and eminences, and that in different parties, that none might escape; and there his foot went through the lower, marshy, and mossy places, where the horse could not do so well. The shire be parcelled out in so many divisions, and six or eight miles square would be taken in at once. In every division, the whole inhabitants, men and women, young and old, without distinction, were all driven into one convenient place." . . . "All the children in the division were gathered together by themselves, under ten years, and above six years of age, and a party of soldiers were drawn out before them. Then they were bid pray, for they were going to be shot. Some of them would answer, Sir, we cannot pray." . . . "At other times, they treated them inhumanly, threatening them with death, and at some little distance would fire pistols without ball in their face. Some of the poor children were frightened almost out of their wits, and others of them stood all out with a courage perfectly above their age. These accounts are so far out of the ordinary way of mankind, that I would not have insert them, had I not before me several informations agreeing in all these circumstances, written at this time by people who knew the truth of them." *Wodrow's History of the Church of Scotland,* vol. iv. pp. 255, 256.

66. "Numbers were transported to Jamaica, Barbadoes, and the North American settlements; but the women were not unfrequently burnt in the cheek, and the ears of the men were lopt off, to prevent, or to detect, their return." *Laing's History of Scotland,* vol. iv. p. 162. "Great multitudes banished." *Wodrow's History of the Church,* vol. iv. p. 211. In July 1685, "the men are ordered to have their ears cropt, and the women to be marked in their hand." p. 217. "To have the following stigma and mark, that they may be known as banished persons if they shall return to this kingdom, *viz.* that the men have one of their ears cut off by the hand of the hangman, and that the women be burnt by the same hand on the cheek with a burned iron." p. 218. These are extracts from the proceedings of the privy-council.

enough to do to look to themselves. His only powerful friends were the Highlanders. . . .

The decay of the Scotch nobility, in the eighteenth century, may be traced to two special causes, in addition to those general causes which were weakening the aristocracy nearly all over Europe. With the general causes, which were common to England and to most parts of the Continent, we are not now concerned. It is enough to say, that they were entirely dependent on that advance of knowledge, which, by increasing the authority of the intellectual class, undermines, and must eventually overthrow, mere hereditary and accidental distinctions. But those causes which were confined to Scotland, had a more political character, and though they were purely local, they harmonized with the whole train of events, and ought to be noticed, as links of a vast chain, which connects the present state of that singular country with its past history.

The first cause was the Union of Scotland with England, in 1707, which struck a heavy blow at the Scotch aristocracy. By it, the legislature of the smaller country was absorbed in that of the larger, and the hereditary legislators suddenly sunk into insignificance. In the Scotch parliament, there were a hundred and forty-five peers, all of whom, except sixteen, were, by the Act of Union, deprived of the power of making laws.[67] These sixteen were sent off to London, and took their seats in the House of Lords, of which they formed a small and miserable fraction. On every subject, however important to their own country, they were easily outvoted; their manners, their gesticulations, and particularly

67. Laing (*History of Scotland,* vol. iv. p. 345) says, that in 1706, "the commons in the Scottish parliament were 160; the peers 145." Of these peers, the Treaty of Union declared that "sixteen shall be the number to sit and vote in the House of Lords." *De Foe's History of the Union between England and Scotland,* London, 1786, 4to, pp. 205, 538. The English House of Lords consisted of 179 members. See *The Lockhart Papers,* London, 1817, 4to, vol. i. pp. 343, 547. It was impossible to mistake the result of this sweeping measure, by which, as was said at the time, "Scotland was to retrench her nobility." *De Foe's History of the Union,* p. 495. Compare p. 471: "The nobility being thereby, as it were, degraded of their characters." In 1710, a Scotchman writes in his journal: "It was one of the melancholyest sights to any that have any sense of our antient Nobility, to see them going throu for votes, and making partys, and giving their votes to others who once had their oun vote; and I suspect many of them reu the bargain they made, in giving their oun pouer away." *Wodrow's Analecta,* vol. i. p. 308.

their comical mode of pronouncing English, were openly ridiculed;[68] and the chiefs of this old and powerful aristocracy found
themselves, to their utter amazement, looked on as men of no account, and they were often obliged to fawn and cringe at the levee
of the minister, in order to procure a place for some needy dependent. Their friends and relations applied to them for offices,
and generally applied in vain. Indeed, the Scotch nobles, being
very poor, wanted for themselves more than the English government was inclined to give, and, in the eagerness of their
clamour, they lost both dignity and reputation.[69] They were ex-

68. The Scotch, consequently, became so eager to do away with this source
of mirth, that even as late as the year 1761, when the notorious lecturer, Sheri-
dan, visited Edinburgh, "such was the rage for speaking with an English accent,
that more than three hundred gentlemen, among whom were the most eminent
in the country for rank and learning, attended him." *Ritchie's Life of Hume,*
London, 1807, p. 94. It was, however, during about twenty years immediately
after thie Union, that the Scotch members of Parliament, both Lords and Commons, were most jeered at in London, and were treated with marked disrespect,
socially and politically. Not only were they mocked and lampooned, but they
were also made tools of. In September 1711, Wodrow writes (*Analecta,* vol. i.
p. 348, 4to, 1842): "In the beginning of this (month), I hear a generall dis-
satisfaction our Nobility, that wer at last Parliament, have at their treatment at
London. They complean they are only made use of as tools among the English,
and cast by when their party designes are over." The next year (1712), the
Scotch members of the House of Commons met together, and expressed their
"high resentment of the uncivil, haughty treatment they mett with from the
English." *The Lockhart Papers,* London, 1817, 4to, vol. i. p. 417. See, further,
Burton's History of Scotland, vol. ii. p. 27. "Without descending to rudeness,
the polished contemporaries of Wharton and St. John could madden the sensitive and haughty Scots by light shafts of raillery, about their pronunciation or
knowledge of parliamentary etiquette." Some curious observations upon the
way in which the Scotch pronounced English, late in the seventeenth century,
will be found in *Morer's Short Account of Scotland,* London, 1702, pp. 13, 14.
The author of this book was chaplain to a Scotch regiment.

69. Among many illustrations with which contemporary memoirs abound,
the following is by no means the worst. Burnet, as a Scotchman, thinks proper
to say that those of his countrymen who were sent to parliament, "were persons
of such distinction, that they very well deserved" the respect and esteem with
which they were treated. To which, Lord Dartmouth adds: "and were very im-
portunate to have their deserts rewarded. A Scotch earl pressed Lord Godolphin
extremely for a place. He said there was none vacant. The other said, his lordship could soon make one so, if he pleased. Lord Godolphin asked him, if he
expected to have any body killed to make room? He said, No; but Lord Dartmouth commonly voted against the court, and every body wondered that he had
not turned out before now. Lord Goldolphin told him, he hoped his lordship
did not expect that he should be the person to propose it; and advised him
never to mention it any more, for fear the queen should come to hear of it;
for if she did, his lordship would run great risk never to have a place as long

posed to mortifying rebuffs, and their true position being soon known, weakened their influence at home, among a people already prepared to throw off their authority. To this, however, they were comparatively indifferent, as they looked for future fortune, not to Scotland, but to England. London became the centre of their intrigues and their hopes.[70] Those who had no seat in the House of Lords, longed to have one, and it was notorious, that the

as she lived. But he could not forbear telling every where, how ill the lord treasurer had used him." *Burnet's History of his own Time*, vol. v. p. 349, Oxford, 1823. Compare the account, in 1710, in *Wodrow's Analecta*, vol. i. p. 293. "Argyle is both picked (*i.e.* piqued) at Marlburrou, and his brother Yla, for refuising him a regiment; and Godolphin should have said to the Queen that my Lord Yla was not to be trusted with a regiment! The Earl of Marr was one of the greatest cronnies Godolphine had, till the matter of his pension, after the Secretary office was taken from him, came about. Godolphine caused draw it during pleasure; Marr expected it during life, which the Treasurer would not yield to, and therefore they brake." The history of the time is full of these wretched squabbles, which show what the Scotch nobles were made of. Indeed, their rapacity was so shameless, that, in 1711, several of them refused to perform their legislative duties in London, unless they received some offices which they expected. "About the midle of this moneth, I hear ther was a meeting of severall of our Scots Peers, at the Viscount of Kilsyth's, where they concerted not to goe up to this parliament till peremptorly writ for; and (also) some assurance be given of the places they were made to hope for last session and missed." *Wodrow's Analecta*, vol. i. p. 365. In 1712, the same Scotchman writes (*Analecta*, vol. ii. p. 8): "Our Scots Peers' secession from the House of Peers makes much noise; but they doe not hold by it. They somtimes come and somtimes goe, and *they render themselves base in the eyes of the English*." See also a letter "concerning the Scots Peerage," in *Somers Tracts*, vol. xii. p. 607, edit. Scott, London, 1814, 4to.

70. A Scotch writer, twenty years after the Union, says: "Most of our gentlemen and people of quality, who have the best estates in our country, live for the most part at London." *Reasons for Improving the Fisheries and Linen Manufacture of Scotland*, London, 1727, p. 22. I do not know who wrote this curious little treatise; but the author was evidently a native of Scotland. See p. 25. I have, however, still earlier evidence to adduce. A letter from Wodrow, dated 9th of August 1725, complains of "the general sending our youth of quality to England;" and a letter to him, in 1716, describes the Anglicizing process going on among the Scotch aristocracy, only nine years after the Union. "Most of our Lords and others here do so much depend on the English for their posts, and *seeking somewhat or other,* that their mouths are almost quite stopped; and really *most of them go into the English way in all things*." *Wodrow's Correspondence*, vol. ii. p. 196, vol. iii. p. 224. The Earl of Mar lost popularity in Scotland, on account of the court he paid to Lord Godolphin; for, he "appears to have passed much more time in intrigues in London than among the gardens of Alloa." *Thomson's Memoirs of the Jacobites*, vol. i. p. 36. Even Earl Ilay, in his anxiety to advance himself at the English court, "used to regret his being a Scots peer, and to wish earnestly he was a commoner." *Letters of Lord Grange*, in *The Miscellany of the Spalding Club*, vol. iii. p. 39, Aberdeen, 4to, 1846.

darling object of nearly every Scotch noble was to be made an English peer.[71] The scene of their ambition being shifted, they were gradually weaned from their old associations. Directly this was apparent, the foundation of their power was gone. From that moment, their real nationality vanished. It became evident that their patriotism was but a selfish passion. They ceased to love a country which could give them nothing, and, as a natural consequence, their country ceased to love them.

Thus it was that this great tie was severed. In this, as in all similar movements, there were, of course, exceptions. Some of the nobles were disinterested, and some of the dependents were faithful. But, looking at the Lowlands as a whole, there can be no doubt that, before the middle of the eighteenth century, that bond of affection was gone, which, in former times, made tens of thousands of Scotchmen ready to follow their superiors in any cause, and to sacrifice their lives at a nod. That spirit, which was once deemed ardent and generous, but which a deeper analysis shows to be mean and servile, was now almost extinct, except among the barbarous Highlanders, whose ignorance of affairs long prevented them from being influenced by the stream of events. That the proximate cause of this change was the Union, will probably be denied by no one who has minutely studied the history of the period. And that the change was beneficial, can only be questioned by those sentimental dreamers, with whom life is a matter rather of feeling than of judgment, and who, despising real and tangible interests, reproach their own age with its material prosperity, and with its love of luxury, as if they were the result of low and sordid desires unknown to the loftier temper of bygone days. To visionaries of this sort, it may well appear that the barbarous and ignorant noble, surrounded by a host of devoted retainers, and living with rude simplicity in his own dull and wretched castle, forms a beautiful picture of those unmercenary and uncalculating times, when men, instead of seeking for knowledge, or

71. Indeed, their expectation ran so high, as to induce a hope, not only that those Commissioners of the Union who were Scotch peers should be made English ones, but that "the whole nobility of Scotland might in time be admitted." *Laing's History of Scotland,* vol. iv. p. 346. Compare *The Lockhart Papers,* vol. i. pp. 298, 343: "the Scots Peerage, many of whom had been bubled with the hopes of being themselves created British Peers." Also *The Gordon Letters,* in *The Miscellany of the Spalding Club,* vol. iii. pp. 227, 228.

for wealth, or for comfort, were content with the frugal innocence of their fathers, and when, protection being accorded by one class, and gratitude felt by the other, the subordination of society was maintained, and its different parts were knit together by sympathy, and by the force of common emotions, instead of, as now, by the coarse maxims of a vulgar and selfish utility.

Those, however, whose knowledge gives them some acquaintance with the real course of human affairs, will see that in Scotland, as in all civilized countries, the decline of aristocratic power forms an essential part of the general progress. It must, therefore, be esteemed a fortunate circumstance, that, among the Scotch, where that power had long been enormous, it was weakened in the eighteenth century, not only by general causes, which were operating elsewhere, but also by two smaller and more special causes. The first of these minor causes was, as we have just seen, the Union with England. The other cause was, comparatively speaking, insignificant, but still it produced decided effect, particularly in the northern districts. It consisted in the fact, that some of the oldest Highland nobles were concerned in the rebellion of 1745, and that, when that rebellion was put down, those who escaped from the sword were glad to save their lives by flying abroad, leaving their dependents to shift for themselves. . . .[72]

Owing to these circumstances, the course of affairs in Scotland, during the eighteenth century, and especially during the first half of it, was marked by a more rapid decline of the influence of the higher ranks than was seen in any other country. It was, therefore, an easy task for the English government to procure a law, which, by abolishing hereditary jurisdictions, deprived the Scotch aristocracy, in 1748, of the last great ensign of their power.[73] The law, being suited to the spirit of the times, worked well; and in the Highlands, in particular, it was one immediate cause of the estab-

72. The Chevalier de Johnstone, in his plaintive remarks on the battle of Culloden, says: "The ruin of many of the most illustrious families in Scotland immediately followed our defeat." *Johnstone's Memoirs of the Rebellion in 1745*, p. 211. He, of course, could not perceive that, sad as such ruin was to the individual sufferers, it was an immense benefit to the nation. Mr. Skene, referring to the year 1748, says of the Highlanders: "their long-cherished ideas of clanship gradually gave way under the absence and ruin of so many of their chiefs." *Skene's Highlanders*, vol. i. p. 147.

73. *Burton's History of Scotland*, vol. ii. pp. 535–537. *Struthers' History of Scotland*, Glasgow, 1828, vol. ii. pp. 519–525.

lishment of something like the order of a settled state.[74] But, in this instance, as in every other, the real and overruling cause is to be found in the condition of the surrounding soicety. A few generations earlier, hardly any one would have thought of abolishing these mischievous jurisdictions, which were then deemed beneficial, and were respected, as belonging to the great families by natural and inalienable right. Such an opinion was the inevitable result of the state of things then existing. This being the case, it is certain that, if the legislature had, at that time, been so rash as to lay its hand on what the nation respected, popular sympathy would have been aroused, and the nobles would have been strengthened by what was intended to weaken them.[75] In 1748, however, matters were very different. Public opinion had changed; and this change of opinion was not only the cause of the new law, but was the reason of the new law being effective. And so it always is. They, indeed, whose knowledge is almost confined to what they see passing around them, and who, on account of their ignorance, are termed practical men, may talk as they will about the reforms which government has introduced, and the improvement to be expected from legislation. But whoever will take a wider and more commanding view of affairs, will soon discover that such hopes are chimerical. They will learn that lawgivers are nearly always the obstructors of society, instead of its helpers; and that, in the extremely few cases in which their measures have turned out well, their success has been owing to the fact, that, contrary to their usual custom, they have implicitly obeyed the spirit of their time, and have been, as they always should be, the mere servants of the people, to whose wishes they are bound to give a public and legal sanction.

Another striking peculiarity of Scotland, during the remarkable period we are now considering, was the sudden rise of trad-

74. Macpherson (*Annals of Commerce,* vol. iii. p. 259) says, "This excellent statute may not unfitly be termed a new magna charta to the free people of Scotland."

75. I cannot, therefore, agree with Macpherson, who asserts, in his valuable work, that the abolition of these jurisdictions "should undoubtedly have been made an essential preliminary of the consolidating union of the two kingdoms of England and Scotland, concluded forty years before." *Macpherson's Annals of Commerce,* vol. iii. p. 257. Compare *De Foe's History of the Union between England and Scotland,* pp. 458, 459, London, 1786, 4to.

ing and manufacturing interests. This preceded, by a whole generation, the celebrated statute of 1748, and was one of the causes of it, in so far as it weakened the great families, against whom that statute was directed. The movement may be traced back, as I have already noticed, to the end of the seventeenth century, and it was in active operation before the first twenty years of the eighteenth century had passed away. A mercantile and money-making spirit was diffused to an extent formerly unknown, and men becoming valued for their wealth as well as for their birth, a new standard of excellence was introduced, and new actors appeared on the scene. Heretofore, persons were respected solely for their parentage; now they were also respected for their riches. The old aristocracy, made uneasy by the change, did every thing they could to thwart and discourage these young and dangerous rivals.[76] Nor can we wonder at their feeling somewhat sore. The tendency which was exhibited, was, indeed, fatal to their pretensions. Instead of asking who was a man's father, the question became, how much he had got. And certainly, if either question is to be put, the latter is the more rational. Wealth is a real and substantial thing, which ministers to our pleasures, increases our comfort, multiplies our resources, and not unfrequently alleviates our pains. But birth is a dream and a shadow, which, so far from benefiting either body or mind, only puffs up its possessor with an imaginary excellence, and teaches him to despise those whom nature has made his superiors, and who, whether engaged in adding to our knowledge or to our wealth, are, in either case, ameliorating the condition of society, and rendering to it true and valuable service.

This antagonism between the aristocratic and trading spirit, lies in the nature of things, and is essential, however it may be disguised at particular periods. Therefore, it is, that the history of trade has a philosophic importance in reference to the progress of society, quite independent of practical considerations. On this account I have called the attention of the reader to what otherwise would be foreign to the objects of the present Introduction; and I will now trace, as briefly as possible, the beginning of that great

76. In 1740, "the rising manufacturing and trading interests of the country" were "looked down upon and discouraged by the feudal aristocracy." *Burton's Lives of Lovat and Forbes*, p. 361.

industrial movement, to the extension of which the overthrow of the Scotch aristocracy is to be partly ascribed.

The Union with England, which was completed in 1707, produced immediate and striking effects on trade. Its first effect was, to throw open to the Scotch a new and extensive commerce with the English colonies in America. Before the Union, no goods of any kind could be landed in Scotland from the American plantations, unless they had first been landed in England, and paid duty there; nor even, in that case, might they be conveyed by any Scotch vessel.[77] This was one of many foolish regulations by which our legislators interfered with the natural course of affairs, and injured the interests of their own country, as well as those of their neighbours. Formerly, however, such laws were considered to be extremely sagacious, and politicians were constantly contriving protective schemes of this sort, which, with the best intentions, inflicted incalculable harm. But if, as seems probable, one of their objects, in this instance, was to retard the improvement of Scotland, they were more than usually successful in effecting the purpose at which they aimed. For, the whole of the western coast, being cut off from direct intercourse with the American colonies, was debarred from the only foreign trade it could advantageously follow; since the European ports lay to the east, and could not be reached by the inhabitants of Western Scotland wtihout a long circumnavigation, which prevented them from competing, on equal terms, with their countrymen, who, sailing from the other side, were already near the chief seats of commerce. The consequence was, that Glasgow and the other western ports remained almost stationary; having comparatively few means of gratifying

77. "Whereas Scotland had, before this, prohibited all the English woollen manufactures, under severe penalties, and England, on the other hand, had excluded the Scots from trading with Scots ships to their colonies in America, directly from Scotland, and had confiscated even their own English ships trading to the said Colonies from England, if navigated or manned with above one-third Scots seamen," &c. *De Foe's History of the Union,* p. 603. In 1696, the wise men in our English parliament passed a law, "that on no pretence whatever any kind of goods from the English American plantations should hereafter be put on shore, either in the kingdoms of Ireland or Scotland, without being first landed in England, and having also paid the duties there, under forfeiture of ship and cargo." *Macpherson's Annals of Commerce,* vol. ii. p. 684. Certainly, the more a man knows of the history of legislation, the more he will wonder that nations should have been able to advance in the face of the formidable impediments which legislators have thrown in their way.

that enterprising spirit, which rose among them late in the seventeenth century, and not daring to trade with those prosperous colonies which were just before them across the Atlantic, but from which they were entirely excluded by the jealous precautions of the English parliament.[78]

When, however, by the Act of Union, the two countries became one, these precautions were discontinued, and Scotland was allowed to hold direct intercourse with America and the West India Islands. The result which this produced on the national industry, was almost instantaneous, because it gave vent to a spirit which had begun to appear among the people late in the seventeenth century, and because it was aided by those still more general causes, which, in most parts of Europe, predisposed that age to increased industry. The west of Scotland, being nearest to America, was the first to feel the movement. In 1707, the inhabitants of Greenock, without the interference of government, imposed on themselves a voluntary assessment, with the object of constructing a harbour. In this undertaking, they displayed so much zeal, that, by the year 1710, the whole of the works were completed; a pier and capacious harbour were erected, and Greenock was suddenly raised from insignificance to take an important part in the trade of the Atlantic.[79] For a while, the merchants were content to

78. "A spirit for commerce appears to have been raised among the inhabitants of Glasgow between the periods of 1660 and 1707, when the Union with England took place." . . . . But, "whatever their trade was, at this time, it could not be considerable; the ports to which they were obliged to trade, lay all to the eastward; the circum-navigation of the island would, therefore, prove an almost insurmountable bar to the commerce of Glasgow; the people upon the east coast, from their situation, would be in possession of almost the whole commerce of Scotland." *Gibson's History of Glasgow,* p. 205, Glasgow, 1777.

79. "The importance of the measure induced the inhabitants of Greenock to make a contract with the superior, by which they agreed to an assessment of 1s. 4d. sterling on every sack of malt, brewed into ale, within the limits of the town; the money, so levied, to be applied in liquidating the expence of forming a proper harbour at Greenock. The work was begun, at the epoch of the Union, in 1707; and a capacious harbour, containing upwards of ten Scotish acres, was formed by building an extensive circular pier, with a straight pier, or tongue, in the middle, by which the harbour was divided into two parts. This formidable work, the greatest of the kind, at that time, in Scotland, incurred an expence of more than 100,000 marks Scots." *Chalmers' Caledonia,* vol. iii. p. 807, London, 1824, 4to. In *M'Culloch's Geographical and Statistical Dictionary,* London, 1849, vol. i. p. 930, it is stated, that "the inhabitants took the matter (1707)

carry on their traffic with ships hired from the English. Soon, however, they became bolder; they began to build on their own account; and, in 1719, the first vessel belonging to Greenock sailed for America.[80] From that moment, their commerce increased so rapidly, that, by the year 1740, the tax which the citizens had laid on themselves sufficed, not only to wipe off the debt which had been incurred, but also to leave a considerable surplus available for municipal purposes.[81] At the same time, and by the action of the same causes, Glasgow emerged from obscurity. In 1718, its enterprising inhabitants launched in the Clyde the first Scotch vessel which ever crossed the Atlantic; thus anticipating the people of Greenock by one year.[82] Glasgow and Greenock be-

---

into their own hands, and agreed with their superior to assess themselves at a certain rate, to build a proper pier and harbour. The work was finished in 1710, at an expense of 5,555l."

80. "The trade of Greenock has kept pace with the improvements made on its harbour. The union of the kingdoms (1707) opened the colonies to the enterprising inhabitants of this town, and generally of the west of Scotland; but it was not till 1719 that the first vessel belonging to Greenock crossed the Atlantic." *M'Culloch's Geographical and Statistical Dictionary,* vol. i. p. 930.

81. "Such was the effect of the new harbour in increasing the trade, and the population, of the town, that the assessment, and port-dues, cleared off the whole debt before 1740, and left, in that year, a clear surplus of 27,000 marks Scots, or 1500l. sterling." *Chalmers' Caledonia,* vol. iii. p. 807. "After the Union, however, the trade of the port increased so rapidly, that, in the year 1740, the whole debt was extinguished, and there remained a surplus, the foundation of the present town's funds, of 27,000 merks." *Sinclair's Statistical Account of Scotland,* vol. v. p. 576, Edinburgh, 1793.

82. "By the Union, however, new views were opened up to the merchants of the city; they thereby obtained the liberty of a free commerce to America and the West Indies, from which they had been before shut out; they chartered English vessels for these voyages, having none at first fit for the purpose; sent out cargoes of goods for the use of the colonies, and returned home laden with tobacco. The business doing well, vessels were built belonging to the city, and in the year 1718, the first ship, the property of Glasgow, crossed the Atlantic." *Denholm's History of Glasgow,* p. 405, 3d edit. Glasgow, 1804. Brown (*History of Glasgow,* vol. ii. p. 330, Edinburgh, 1797) says, that the Glasgow merchants "chartered Whitehaven ships for many years;" but that, "in 1716, a vessel of sixty tons burden was launched at Crawford's dike, being the first Clyde ship that went to the British settlements in America with goods and a supercargo." But this date is probably two years too early. Mr. M'Culloch, in his excellent *Geographical and Statistical Dictionary,* London, 1849, vol. ii. p. 659, says: "But for a while, the merchants of Glasgow, who first embarked in the trade to America, carried it on by means of vessels belonging to English ports; and it was not till 1718 that a ship built in Scotland (in the Clyde), the

came the two great commercial outlets of Scotland, and the chief centres of activity.[83] Comforts, and, indeed, luxuries, hitherto only attainable at enormous cost, began to be diffused through the country. The productions of the tropics could now be procured direct from the New World, which, in return, offered a rich and abundant market for manufactured goods. This was a further stimulus to Scotch industry, and its effects were immedaitely apparent. The inhabitants of Glasgow, finding a great demand among the Americans for linen, introduced its manufacture into their city in 1725, whence it extended to other places, and, in a short time, gave employment to thousands of workmen.[84] It is also from the year 1725, that Paisley dates its rise. So late as the beginning of the eighteenth century, this rich and prosperous city was still a straggling village, containing only a single street.[85] But, after the Union, its poor, and hitherto idle, inhabitants began to be moved by the activity which they saw on every side. Gradually, their views expanded; and the introduction among

property of Scotch owners, sailed for the American colonies." Gibson, also (*History of Glasgow,* 1777, p. 206), says: "In 1718, the first vessel of the property of Glasgow crossed the Atlantic." And, to the same effect, *Sinclair's Statistical Account of Scotland,* vol. v. p. 498, Edinburgh, 1793.

83. The progress was so rapid, that in a work printed in 1732, it is stated, that "this city of Glasgow is a place of the greatest trade in the kingdom, especially to the Plantations; from whence they have twenty or thirty sail of ships every year, laden with tobacco and sugar; an advantage this kingdom never enjoyed till the Union. They are purchasing a harbour on the Frith near Alloway, to which they have but twelve miles by land; and then they can re-ship their sugars and tobacco, for Holland, Germany, and the Baltick Sea, without being at the trouble of sailing round England or Scotland." *Macky's Journey through Scotland,* pp. 294, 295, 2d edit. London, 1732. The first edition of this book was also printed in 1732. See *Watt's Bibliotheca Britannica,* vol. i. p. 631 m., Edinburgh, 1824, 4to.

84. Gibson, who was a Glasgow merchant, says, in his *History of Glasgow,* p. 236, "that the commerce to America first suggested the idea of introducing manufactures into Glasgow, is to me very evident; and that they were only attempted to be introduced about the year 1725 is apparent." Denholm (*History of Glasgow,* p. 412) says: "The linen manufacture, which began here in the year 1725, was, for a long time, the staple, not only of this city, but of the west of Scotland." Compare *Heron's Journey through the Western Counties of Scotland,* Perth, 1799, vol. ii. p. 412.

85. "Consisting only of one principal street about half a mile in length." *Sinclair's Statistical Account of Scotland,* vol. vii. p. 62. But the local historian mentions, with evident pride, that this one street contained "handsome houses." *Crawfurd's History of the Shire of Renfrew,* part iii. p. 305, edit. Paisley, 1782, 4to.

them, in 1725, of the manufacture of thread, was the first step in that great career in which they never stopped, until they had raised Paisley to be a vast emporium of industry, and a successful promoter of every art by which industry is nurtured.[86]

Nor was it merely in the west, that this movement was displayed. In Scotland generally, the spirit of trade became so rife, that it began to encroach on the old theological spirit, which had long been supreme. Hitherto, the Scotch had cared for little except religious polemics. In every society, these had been the chief subject of conversation; and on them, men had wasted their energies, without the least benefit either to themselves or to others. But, about this time, it was observed, that the improvement of manufactures became a common topic of discourse.[87] Such a statement, made by a well-informed writer, who witnessed what he relates, is a curious proof of the change which was beginning, though very faintly, to steal over the Scotch mind. It shows that there was, at all events, a tendency to turn aside from subjects which are inaccessible to our understanding, and the discussion of which has no effect except to exasperate those who dispute, and to make them more intolerant than ever of theological opinions different from their own. Unhappily, there were, as I shall presently point out, other causes at work, which prevented this tendency from producing all the good that might have been expected. Still, so far as it went, it was a clear gain. It was a blow to superstition, inasmuch as it was an attempt to occupy the human mind with mere secular considerations. In a country like Scotland, this alone was extremely important. We must also add, that, though it was the effect of increased industry, it, as often happens, reacted upon, and strengthened, its cause. For, by diminishing, how-

---

86. *Denholm's History of Glasgow*, pp. 546, 547; and *Sinclair's Statistical Account of Scotland*, vol. vii. pp. 62–64. See also, on the rise of Paisley, *Heron's Journey through the Western Counties of Scotland*, vol. ii. pp. 399, 400; *Pennant's Tour in Scotland*, vol. ii. p. 144; and *Crawfurd's History of the Shire of Renfrew*, part iii. p. 321. At an earlier period, Paisley was famous in a different way. In the middle ages, it swarmed with monks. Keith (*Catalogue of Scotch Bishops*, p. 252, Edinburgh, 1755, 4to) tells us that, "it formerly was a Priory, and afterwards changed into an Abbey of Black Monks."

87. The author of *The Interest of Scotland Considered*, Edinburgh, 1733, says (p. xvi.) that since 1727, "we have happily turned our eyes upon the improvement of our manufactures, which is now a common subject in discourse, and this contributes not a little to its success."

ever little, the inordinate respect formerly paid to theological pursuits, it was, in the same proportion, an inducement to ambitious
and enterprising men to abstain from those pursuits, and to engage in temporal matters, where ability, being less fettered by
prejudice, has more scope, and enjoys more freedom of action. Of
those men, some rose to the first rank in literature; while others,
taking a different but equally useful turn, became as eminent in
trade. Hence, Scotland, during the eighteenth century, possessed,
for the first time, two powerful and active classes, whose aim was
essentially secular; the intellectual class, and the industrious class.
Before the eighteenth century, neither of these classes exercised
an independent sway, or could, indeed, be said to have a separate
existence. The intellect of the country was absorbed by the church;
the industry of the country was controlled by the nobles. The
effect which this change produced on the literature of Scotland,
will be traced in the last chapter of the present volume. Its effect
on industry was equally remarkable, and, for the well-being of
the nation, was equally valuable. But it does not possess that general scientific interest which belongs to the intellectual movement;
and I shall, therefore, in addition to the evidence already given,
confine myself to a few more facts illustrative of the history of
Scotch industry down to the middle of the eighteenth century, by
which time there was no longer any doubt that the flood of
material prosperity had fairly set in.

During the seventeenth century, the only Scotch manufacture
of any importance was that of linen, which, however, like every
other branch of industry, was very backward, and was exposed
to all sorts of discouragement.[88] But, after the Union, it received
a sudden impetus, from two causes. One of these causes, as I have
already noticed, was the demand from America, consequent upon
the trade of the Atlantic being thrown open. The other cause
was, the removal of the duty which England had imposed upon
the importation of Scotch linen. These two circumstances, occur-
ring nearly at the same time, produced such effect on the national

88. Morer, who was in Scotland in 1688 and 1689, says, "But that which
employs great part of their land is hemp, of which they have mighty burdens,
and on which they bestow much care and pains to dress and prepare it for making their linen, the most noted and beneficial manufacture of the kingdom."
Morer's Short Account of Scotland, London, 1702, pp. 3, 4.

industry, that De Foe, who had a wider knowledge of the details of trade than any man of that age, said that it seemed as if, for the future, the Scotch poor could never lack employment.[89] Unfortunately, this was not the case, and never will be, until society is radically changed. But the movement which provoked so bold a remark from so cautious an observer as De Foe, must have been very striking; and we know, from other sources, that, between 1728 and 1738, the manufacture of linen for exportation alone was more than doubled.[90] After that period, this and other departments of Scotch industry advanced with a constantly accelerating speed. It is mentioned, by a contemporary who was likely to be well informed, that, between 1715 and 1745, the trade and manufactures of Scotland increased more than they had done for ages before.[91] Such a statement, though valuable as corroborating other evidence, is too vague to be entirely relied on; and historians, who usually occupy themselves with insignificant details about courts and princes and statesmen, desert us in matters which are really important, so that it is now hardly possible to recon-

89. "The duties upon linen from Scotland being taken off in England, made so great a demand for Scots linen more than usual, that it seemed the poor could want no employment." *De Foe's History of the Union between England and Scotland,* p. 604. Compare *Macpherson's Annals of Commerce,* vol. ii. p. 736: "a prodigious vent, not only in England, but for the American plantations." This concerns a later period.

90. The surplus of linen made above the consumption, was, in 1728, 2,183,978 yards; in 1738, 4,666,011." *Chalmers' Caledonia,* vol. i. p. 873. On the increase between 1728 and 1732, see the Table in *The Interest of Scotland Considered,* Edinburgh, 1733, p. 97. In a work published in 1732, it is stated that "they make a great deal of linnen all over the kingdom, not only for their own use, but export it to England, and to the Plantations. In short, the women are all kept employ'd, from the highest to the lowest of them." *Macky's Journey through Scotland,* London, 1732, p. 271. This refers merely to the women of Scotland, whom Macky represents as much more industrious than the men.

91. In 1745, Craik writes to Lord Nithisdale, "The present family have now reigned over us these thirty years, and though during so long a time they may have fallen into errors, or may have committed faults, (as what Government is without?) yett I will defy the most sanguine zealot to find in history a period equal to this in which Scotland possessed so uninterrupted a felicity, in which liberty, civil and religious, was so universally enjoyed by all people of whatever denomination—nay, by the open and avowed ennemys of the family and constitution, or a period in which all ranks of men have been so effectually secured in their property. Have not trade, manufactures, agriculture, and the spirit of industry in our country extended themselves further during this period and under this family than for ages before?" *Thomson's Memoirs of the Jacobites,* London, 1845, vol. ii. pp. 60, 61.

struct the history of the Scotch people during this, the first epoch
of their material prosperity. I have, however, gathered a few
facts, which appear to rest on good authority, and which supply us
with something like precise information as to dates. In 1739,
the manufacture of linen was introduced into Kilbarchan,[92] and,
in 1740, into Arbroath.[93] From the year 1742, the manufactures
of Kilmarnock date their rise.[94] In 1748, the first linen was manufactured in Cullen;[95] and in the same year in Inverary.[96] In 1749,
this great branch of industry and source of wealth was established,
on a large scale, in Aberdeen;[97] while, about 1750, it began to
diffuse itself in Wemyss, in the county of Fife.[98] These things
happening, within eleven years, in parts of the country so distant
from each other, and so totally unconnected, indicate the existence
of general causes, which governed the whole movement; though
in this, as in all instances, every thing is popularly ascribed to the
influence of a few powerful individuals. We have, however, other
proofs that the progress was essentially national. Even in Edinburgh, where hitherto no claims had been respected except those
of the nobles or clergy, the voice of this new trading interest
began to be heard. In that poor and warlike capital, a society was
now first established for the encouragement of manufactures; and
we are assured that this was but a single manifestation of the
enthusiasm which was generally felt on the subject.[99] Coinciding
with this movement, and indeed forming part of it, we can discern the earnest symptoms of a monied class, properly so called.
In 1749, there was established, at Aberdeen, the first county bank
ever seen in Scotland; and, in the very same year, a similar estab-

92. *Crawfurd's History of the Shire of Renfrew,* part ii. p. 114.

93. *Sinclair's Statistical Account of Scotland,* vol. vii. p. 341, compared with
vol. xii. pp. 176, 177.

94. *Chalmers' Caledonia,* vol. iii. p. 483.

95. *Sinclair's Statistical Account of Scotland,* vol. xii. p. 145.

96. *Ibid.,* vol. v. p. 297.

97. *Kennedy's Annals of Aberdeen,* vol. ii. pp. 199, 200.

98. *Sinclair's Statistical Account of Scotland,* vol. xvi. p. 520: "About the
year 1750." I need hardly say, that some of these dates, depending upon tradition, are given by the authors approximatively.

99. "Betwixt the year 1750 and 1760, a great degree of patriotic enthusiasm
arose in Scotland to encourage arts and manufactures; and the *Edinburgh Society* was established in 1755 for the express purpose of improving these."
Bower's History of the University of Edinburgh, vol. iii. pp. 126, 7.

lishment was formed at Glasgow.[100] These represented the east and the west, and, by the advances which they were able to make, each assisted the trade of its own district. Between eastern and western Scotland, the intercourse, as yet, was difficult and costly. But this likewise was about to be remedied by an enterprise, the mere conception of which would formerly have excited ridicule. After the Union, the idea arose of uniting the east with the west by a canal, which should join the Forth to the Clyde. The plan was deemed chimerical, and was abandoned. As soon, however, as the manufacturing and commercial classes had gained sufficient influence they adopted it, with that energy which is characteristic of their order, and which is more common among them than among any other rank of society. The result was, that, in 1768, the great work was fairly begun;[101] and the first step was taken towards what, in a material point of view, was an enterprise of vast importance, but, in a social and intellectual point of view, was of still superior value, inasmuch as, by supplying a cheap and easy transit through the heart of the most populous part of Scotland, it had a direct tendency to make different districts and different places feel that each had need of others, and thus encouraging the notion that all belonged to one common scheme, it assisted in diminishing local prejudice and assuaging local jeal-

100. "The first country-bank that any where appeared, was the Aberdeen Bank, which was settled in 1749: it was immediately followed by a similar establishment in Glasgow during the same year." *Chalmers' Caledonia,* vol. iii. p. 9, 4to, 1824. Kennedy (*Annals of Aberdeen,* 4to, 1818, vol. ii. p. 195) says: "Banking was originally projected in Aberdeen about the year 1752, by a few of the principal citizens who were engaged in commerce and manufactures. They commenced business, upon a limited scale, in an office on the north side of the Castle Street, issued notes of hand, of five pounds and of twenty shillings sterling, and discounted bills and promissory notes, for the accommodation of the public." It is uncertain if Chalmers knew of this passage; but he was a more accurate writer than Kennedy, and I, therefore, prefer his authority. Besides, Kennedy vaguely says, "about the year 1752."

101. "After having been frequently proposed, since the Union, this canal was at length begun in 1768, and finished in 1790. The trade upon it is already great, and is rapidly increasing." *Sinclair's Statistical Account of Scotland,* vol. ii. pp. 279, 280, Edinburgh, 1792. See also vol. xii. p. 125; *Irving's History of Dumbartonshire,* 1860, 4to, p. 247; and an interesting contemporary notice in *Nimmo's History of Stirlingshire,* Edinburgh, 1777, pp. 468–481. In 1767, Watt was employed as a surveyor. See *Muirhead's Life of Watt,* 2nd edit. London, 1859, p. 167.

ousy; while, in the same proportion, by enticing men to move out of the narrow circle in which they had habitually lived, it prepared them for a certain enlargement of mind, which is the natural consequence of seeing affairs under various aspects, and which is never found in any country in which the means of travelling are either very hazardous or very expensive.

Such was the state of Scotland towards the middle of the eighteenth century; and surely a fairer prospect was never opened to any country. The land was at peace. It had nothing to fear, either from foreign invasion, or from domestic tyranny. The arts, which increase the comfort of man, and minister to his happiness, were sedulously cultivated; wealth was being created with unexampled speed, and the blessings which follow in the train of wealth were being widely diffused; while the insolence of the nobility was so effectually curbed, that industrious citizens could, for the first time, feel their own independence, could know that what they earned, that likewise they should enjoy, and could hold themselves erect, and with a manly brow, in the presence of a class before whom they had long crouched in abject submission.

Besides this, a great literature now arose, a literature of rare and surpassing beauty. To narrate the intellectual achievements of the Scotch during the eighteenth century, in a manner at all commensurate with their importance, would require a separate treatise, and I cannot now stop even to mention what all educated persons are at least partly acquainted with; each student recognizing the value of what was done in his own pursuit. In the last chapter of this volume, I shall, however, attempt to give some idea of the general results considered as a whole; at present, it is enough to say, that in every branch of knowledge this once poor and ignorant people produced original and successful thinkers. What makes this the more remarkable, is its complete contrast to their former state. Down even to the beginning of the eighteenth century, Scotland could only boast of two authors whose works have benefited mankind. They were Buchanan and Napier. Buchanan was the first political writer who held accurate views respecting government, and who clearly defined the true relation between the people and their rulers. He placed popular rights on a solid basis, and vindicated, by anticipation, all subsequent revolutions. Napier, equally bold in another department, succeeded, by a mighty effort of genius, in detecting, and pushing to its extreme consequence, a law of the progression of numbers, which is so simple and yet so potent, that it unravels the most tedious and intricate calculations, and, thus economizing the labours of the brain, has saved an enormous and incalculable waste. These two men were, indeed, great benefactors of their species; but they stand alone, and if all the other authors Scotland produced down to the close of the seventeenth century had never been born, or if, being born, they had never written, society would have lost nothing, but would be in exactly the same position as it now is.

Early, however, in the eighteenth century, a movement was felt all over Europe, and in that movement Scotland participated. A spirit of inquiry was abroad, so general and so searching, that no country could entirely escape from its action. Sanguine men were excited, and even grave men were stirred. It seemed as if a long night were about to close. Light broke forth where before there was nothing but darkness. Opinions which had stood the test of ages were suddenly questioned; and in every direction doubts sprung up, and proofs were demanded. The human mind, waxing bold, would not be satisfied with the old evidence. Things were examined at their foundation, and the basis of every belief was jealously scrutinized. For a time, this was confined to the higher intellects; but soon the movement spread, and, in the most advanced countries, worked upon nearly all classes. In England and in France, the result was extremely beneficial. It might have been hoped, that in Scotland likewise, the popular mind would gradually have become enlightened. But not so. Time rolled on; one generation succeeded another; the eighteenth century passed away; the nineteenth century came; and still the people made no sign. The gloom of the middle ages was yet upon them. While all around was light, the Scotch, enveloped in mist, crept on, groping their way, dismally, and with fear. While other nations were shaking off their old superstitions, this singular people clung to theirs with undiminished tenacity. Now, indeed, their grasp is gradually slackening, but with extreme slowness, and threatening reactions frequently appear. This, as it always has been, and still is, the curse of Scotland, so also is it the chief difficulty with which the historian of Scotland has to contend.

Every where else, when the rise of the intellectual classes, and that of the trading and manufacturing classes, have accompanied each other, the invariable result has been, a diminution of the power of the clergy, and, consequently, a diminution of the influence of superstition. The peculiarity of Scotland is, that, during the eighteenth century, and even down to the middle of the nineteenth century, the industrial and intellectual progress has continued without materially shaking the authority of the priesthood.[102] Strange and unequalled combination! The country of bold and enterprising merchants, of shrewd manufacturers, of far-seeing men of business, and of cunning artificers; the country, too, of such fearless thinkers as George Buchanan, David Hume, and Adam Smith, is awed by a few noisy and ignorant preachers, to whom it allows a license, and yields a submission, disgraceful to the age, and incompatible with the commonest notions of liberty. A people, in many respects very advanced, and holding upon political subjects enlightened views, do, upon all religious subjects, display a littleness of mind, an illiberality of sentiment, a heat of temper, and a love of persecuting others, which shows that the Protestantism of which they boast has done them no good; that, in the most important matters, it has left them as narrow as it found them; and that it has been unable to free them from prejudices which make them the laughing-stock of Europe, and which have turned the very name of the Scotch Kirk into a by-word and a reproach among educated men.

I shall now endeavour to explain how all this arose, and how such apparent inconsistencies are to be reconciled. That they may be reconciled, and that the inconsistencies are merely apparent and not real, will be at once admitted by whoever is capable of a scientific conception of history. For, in the moral world, as in the physical world, nothing is anomalous; nothing is unnatural; nothing is strange. All is order, symmetry, and law. There are opposites, but there are no contradictions. In the character of a nation, inconsistency is impossible. Such, however, is still the

102. I will quote, in a single passage, the opinions of an eminent German and of an eminent Scotchman. "Dr. Spurzheim, when he last visited Scotland, remarked that the Scotch appeared to him to be the most priest-ridden nation in Europe; Spain and Portugal not excepted. *After having seen other countries, I can understand the force of this observation.*" Notes on the United States of North America by George Combe, vol. iii. p. 32, Edinburgh, 1841.

backward condition of the human mind, and with so evil and jaundiced an eye do we approach the greatest problems, that not only common writers, but even men from whom better things might be hoped, are on this point involved in constant confusion, perplexing themselves and their readers by speaking of inconsistency, as if it were a quality belonging to the subject which they investigate, instead of being, as it really is, a measure of their own ignorance. It is the business of the historian to remove this ignorance, by showing that the movements of nations are perfectly regular, and that, like all other movements, they are solely determined by their antecedents. If he cannot do this, he is no historian. He may be an annalist, or a biographer, or a chronicler, but higher than that he cannot rise, unless he is imbued with that spirit of science which teaches, as an article of faith, the doctrine of uniform sequence; in other words, the doctrine that certain events having already happened, certain other events corresponding to them will also happen. To seize this idea with firmness, and to apply it on all occasions, without listening to any exceptions, is extremely difficult, but it must be done by whoever wishes to elevate the study of history from its present crude and informal state, and do what he may towards placing it in its proper rank, as the head and chief of all the sciences. Even then, he cannot perform his task unless his materials are ample, and derived from sources of unquestioned credibility. But if his facts are sufficiently numerous; if they are very diversified; if they have been collected from such various quarters that they can check and confront each other, so as to do away with all suspicion of their testimony being garbled; and if he who uses them possesses that faculty of generalization, without which nothing great can be achieved, he will hardly fail in bringing some part of his labours to a prosperous issue, provided he devotes all his strength to that one enterprise, postponing to it every other object of ambition, and sacrificing to it many interests which men hold dear. Some of the most pleasurable incentives to action, he must disregard. Not for him, are those rewards which, in other pursuits, the same energy would have earned; not for him, the sweets of popular applause; not for him, the luxury of power; not for him, a share in the councils of his country; not for him, a conspicuous and honoured place before the public eye. Albeit conscious of what he could do, he may not compete in the great contest; he cannot hope to win the prize; he cannot even enjoy the excitement of the struggle. To him, the arena is closed. His recompense lies within himself, and he must learn to care little for the sympathy of his fellow-creatures, or for such honours as they are able to bestow. So far from looking for these things, he should rather be prepared for that obloquy which always awaits those, who, by opening up new veins of thought, disturb the prejudices of their contemporaries. While ignorance, and worse than ignorance, is imputed to him, while his motives are misrepresented and his integrity impeached, while he is accused of denying the value of moral principles, and of attacking the foundation of all religion, as if he were some public enemy, who made it his business to corrupt society, and whose delight it was to see what evil he could do; while these charges are brought forward, and repeated from mouth to mouth, he must be capable of pursuing in silence the even tenor of his way, without swerving, without pausing, and without stepping from his path to notice the angry outcries which he cannot but hear, and which he is more than human if he does not long to rebuke. These are the qualities, and these the high resolves, indispensable to him, who, on the most important of all subjects, believing that the old road is worn out and useless, seeks to strike out a new one for himself, and, in the effort, not only perhaps exhausts his strength, but is sure to incur the enmity of those who are bent on maintaining the ancient scheme unimpaired. To solve the great problem of affairs; to detect those hidden circumstances which determine the march and destiny of nations; and to find, in the events of the past, a key to the proceedings of the future, is nothing less than to unite into a single science all the laws of the moral and physical world. Whoever does this, will build up afresh the fabric of our knowledge, re-arrange its various parts, and harmonize its apparent discrepancies. Perchance, the human mind is hardly ready for so vast an enterprise. At all events, he who undertakes it will meet with little sympathy, and will find few to help him. And let him toil as he may, the sun and noontide of his life shall pass by, the evening of his days shall overtake him, and he himself have to quit the scene, leaving that unfinished which he had vainly hoped to complete. He may lay the foundation; it will be for his successors to raise the edifice. Their hands will give the last touch; they will

reap the glory; their names will be remembered when he is forgotten. It is, indeed, too true, that such a work requires, not only
several minds, but also the successive experience of several generations. Once, I own, I thought otherwise. Once, when I first
caught sight of the whole field of knowledge, and seemed, however dimly, to discern its various parts and the relation they bore
to each other, I was so entranced with its surpassing beauty, that
the judgment was beguiled, and I deemed myself able, not only
to cover the surface, but also to master the details. Little did I
know how the horizon enlarges as well as recedes, and how vainly
we grasp at the fleeting forms, which melt away and elude us in
the distance. Of all that I had hoped to do, I now find but too
surely how small a part I shall accomplish. In those early aspira-
tions, there was much that was fanciful; perhaps there was much
that was foolish. Perhaps, too, they contained a moral defect, and
savoured of an arrogance which belongs to a strength that refuses
to recognize its own weakness. Still, even now that they are defeated and brought to nought, I cannot repent having indulged in
them, but, on the contrary, I would willingly recall them, if I
could. For, such hopes belong to that joyous and sanguine period
of life, when alone we are really happy; when the emotions are
more active than the judgment; when experience has not yet hardened our nature; when the affections are not yet blighted and
nipped to the core; and when the bitterness of disappointment
not having yet been felt, difficulties are unheeded, obstacles are
unseen, ambition is a pleasure instead of a pang, and the blood
coursing swiftly through the veins, the pulse beats high, while the
heart throbs at the prospect of the future. Those are glorious days;
but they go from us, and nothing can compensate their absence.
To me, they now seem more like the visions of a disordered fancy,
than the sober realities of things that were, and are not. It is painful to make this confession; but I owe it to the reader, because I
would not have him to suppose that either in this, or in the future
volumes of my History, I shall be able to redeem my pledge, and
to perform all that I promised. Something, I hope to achieve,
which will interest the thinkers of this age; and something, perhaps, on which posterity may build. It will, however, only be a
fragment of my original design. In the two last chapters I have attempted, and in the two next chapters I shall still further attempt,

to solve a curious problem in the history of Scotland, which is intimately connected with other problems of a yet graver import: but though the solution will, I believe, be complete, the evidence of the solution will, most assuredly, be imperfect. I regret to add, that such imperfection is henceforth an essential part of my plan. It is essential, because I despair of supplying those deficiencies in my knowledge, of which I grow more sensible in proportion as my views become more extensive. It is also essential, because, after a fair estimate of my own strength, of the probable duration of my life, and of the limits to which industry can safely be pushed, I have been driven to the conclusion, that this Introduction, which I had projected as a solid foundation on which the history of England might subsequently be raised, must either be greatly curtailed, and consequently shorn of its force, or that, if not curtailed, there will hardly be a chance of my being able to narrate, with the amplitude and fulness of detail which they richly deserve, the deeds of that great and splendid nation with which I am best acquainted, and of which it is my pride to count myself a member. It is with the free, the noble, and the high-minded English people, that my sympathies are most closely connected; on them my affections naturally centre; from their literature, and from their example, my best lessons have been learnt; and it is now the most cherished and the most sacred desire of my heart, that I may succeed in writing their history, and in unfolding the successive phases of their mighty career, while I am yet somewhat equal to the task, and before my faculties have begun to dwindle, or the power of continuous attention has begun to decay.

IV

An Examination of the Scotch Intellect
during the Seventeenth Century

The remaining part of this volume, I purpose to devote to an attempt to unravel still further the two-fold paradox, which forms the prominent peculiarity of the history of Scotland. The paradox consists, as we have seen, in the fact, first, that the same people have long been liberal in politics, and illiberal in religion; and, secondly, that the brilliant, inquisitive, and sceptical literature, which they produced in the eighteenth century, was unable to weaken their superstition, or to instil into them wiser and larger maxims on religious matters. From an early period, there were, as I have endeavoured to show, many circumstances which predisposed the Scotch to superstition, and, so far, had a general connexion with the subject before us. But the remarkable phenomenon with which we are immediately concerned, may, I think, be traced to two distinct causes. The first cause was, that, for a hundred and twenty years after the establishment of Protestantism, the rulers of Scotland either neglected the church or persecuted it, thereby driving the clergy into the arms of the people, from whom alone they could obtain sympathy and support. Hence an alliance between the two parties, more intimate than would otherwise have been possible; and hence, too, the rise of that democratic spirit which was the necessary consequence of such an union, and which the clergy encouraged, because they were opposed and thwarted by the upper classes. So far, the result was extremely beneficial, as it produced a love of independence and a hatred of tyranny, which, twice during the seventeenth century, saved the country from the yoke of a cruel despotism. But these very circumstances, which guarded the people against political despotism, exposed them all the more to ecclesiastical despotism. For, having no one to trust except their preachers, they trusted them entirely, and upon all subjects. The clergy gradually became supreme, not only in spiritual matters, but also in temporal ones. Late in the sixteenth century, they had been glad to take refuge among the people; before the middle of the seventeenth century, they ruled the people. How shamefully they abused their power, and how, by encouraging the worst kind of superstition, they prolonged the reign of ignorance, and stopped the march of society, will be related in the course of this chapter; but, in fairness to them, we ought to acknowledge, that the religious servitude into which the Scotch fell during the seventeenth century, was, on the whole, a willing one, and that, mischievous as it was, it had at least a noble origin, inasmuch as the influence of the Protestant clergy is mainly to be ascribed to the fearlessness with which they came forward as leaders of the people, at a period when that post was full of danger, and when the upper classes were ready to unite with the crown in destroying the last vestiges of national liberty.

To trace the operation of this cause of Scotch superstition, will be the business of the present chapter; while, in the next and concluding chapter, I shall examine the other cause, which I have as yet hardly mentioned. This latter inquiry will involve some considerations respecting the philosophy of method, still imperfectly appreciated among us, and on which the history of the Scotch mind will throw considerable light. For, it will appear, that, during the eighteenth century, the ablest Scotchmen, with hardly an exception, adopted a method of investigating truth, which cut them off from the sympathies of their countrymen, and prevented their works from producing the effect which they might otherwise have done. The result was, that though a very sceptical literature was produced, scepticism made no progress, and therefore superstition was undiminished. The highly-educated minds, indeed, were affected; but they formed a class apart, and there were no means of communication between them and the people. That this was owing to the method which literary men employed, I hope to prove in the next chapter; and if I succeed in doing so, it will be evident, that I have been guilty of no exaggeration in terming this the second great cause of the prolongation of Scotch superstition, since it was sufficiently powerful to prevent the intellectual classes from exercising their natural functions as the disturbers of old opinions.

We have already seen, that, almost immediately after the Reformation, ill-feeling arose between the upper classes and the spiritual leaders of the Protestant church, and that this ill-feeling increased until, in 1580, it vented itself by the abolition of episcopacy. This bold and decisive measure made the breach irreparable. The preachers had now committed themselves too far to recede, even if they had desired to do so; and from that moment, uniting themselves heartily with the people, they took up a position which they have never since abandoned. During the remaining twenty-three years that James was in Scotland, they were occupied in exciting the people against their rulers; and as they became more democratic, so did the crown and nobles grow more hostile, and display, for the first time, a disposition to combine together in defence of their common interests. In 1603, James ascended the throne of England, and the struggle began in earnest. It lasted, with few interruptions, eighty-five years, and during its continuance, the Presbyterian clergy never wavered; they were always steady to the good cause; always on the side of the people. This greatly increased their influence; and what favoured it still more was, that, besides being the champions of popular liberty, they were also the champions of national independence. When James I. and the two Charles's attempted to force episcopacy upon Scotland, the Scotch rejected it, not only because they hated the institution, but also because they looked on it as the mark of a foreign domination, which they were determined to resist. Their nearest and most dangerous enemy was England; and they spurned the idea of receiving bishops who must, in the first instance, be consecrated in London, and who, it was certain, would never have been admitted into Scotland unless England had been the stronger country. It was, therefore, on patriotic, as well as religious, grounds, that the Scotch clergy, during the seventeenth century, struggled against episcopacy;[1] and when they overthrew

1. In 1638, one of the most eminent of the Scotch clergy writes: "Our maine feare" is "to have our religion lost, our throats cutted, our poore countrey made ane English province, to be disposed upon for ever hereafter at the will of a

it, in 1638, their bold and determined conduct associated, in the popular mind, the love of country with the love of the church. Subsequent events strengthened this association.[2] In 1650, Cromwell invaded Scotland, overthrew the Scotch in the battle of Dunbar, and intrusted to Monk the task of curbing their spirit, by building fortresses, and establishing a long chain of military posts.[3] The nation, cowed and broken, gave way, and, for the first time for three centuries, felt the pressure of a foreign yoke. The clergy alone remained firm.[4] Cromwell, who knew that they were the chief obstacle to completing his conquest, hated them, and did everything he could to ruin them.[5] But their power was

Bishope of Canterburie." *Baillie's Letters and Journals,* vol. i. p. 66. Compare p. 450. "This kirk is a free and independant kirk, no less then the kingdom is a free and independant kingdom; and as our own Patriots can best judge what is for the good of the kingdom, so our own Pastors should be most able to judge what form of worship beseemeth our Reformation, and what serveth most for the good of the People." Two generations later, one of the most popular arguments against the Union was, that it might enable the English to force episcopacy upon Scotland. See *De Foe's History of the Union between England and Scotland,* pp. 222, 284, 359. "The danger of the Church of Scotland, from the suffrages of English bishops," &c.

2. The hatred which the Scotch naturally felt against the English for having inflicted so much suffering upon them, was intense about the middle of the seventeenth century, notwithstanding the temporary union of the two nations against Charles. In 1652, "the criminal record is full of cases of murder of English soldiers. They were cut off by the people whenever a fitting opportunity occurred, and were as much detested in Scotland as the French soldiers were in Spain during the Peninsular war." *The Spottiswoode Miscellany,* vol. ii. p. 98, Edinburgh, 1845. See also p. 167: "a nationall quarrell and not for the Stuarts."

3. *Browne's History of the Highlands,* vol. ii. pp. 75–77: "the English army was augmented to twenty thousand men, and citadels erected in several towns, and a long chain of military stations drawn across the country to curb the inhabitants."

4. Clarendon, under the year 1655, says, "Though Scotland was vanquished, and subdued, to that degree, that there was no place nor person who made the least show of opposing Cromwell; who, by the administration of Monk, made the yoke very grievous to the whole nation; yet the preachers kept their pulpit license; and, more for the affront that was offered to presbytery, than the conscience of what was due to majesty, many of them presumed to pray for the king; and generally, though secretly, exasperated the minds of the people against the present government." *Clarendon's History of the Rebellion,* p. 803.

5. And, what they must have felt very acutely, he would not go to hear them preach. A writer of that time informs us that, even in 1648, when Cromwell was in Edinburgh, "he went not to their churches; but it is constantle reported that ewerie day he had sermons in his oune ludginge, himself being the preacher, whensoewer the spirit came upon him; which took him lyk the fitts

too deeply seated to be shaken. From their pulpits, they continued to influence and animate the people. In face of the invaders, and in spite of them, the Scotch church continued to hold its General Assemblies, until the summer of 1653. Then, indeed, they had to yield to brute force; and the people, to their unutterable grief, beheld the venerated representatives of the Scotch kirk driven from their place of meetings by English soldiers, and led like criminals through the streets of Edinburgh.[6]

---

of an ague, somtyms twise, sometyms thryse in a day." *Gordon's Britane's Distemper,* p. 212. In 1650, according to another contemporary, "he made stables of all the churches for hes horsses quhersoeuer he came, and burned all the seatts and pewes in them; riffled the ministers housses, and distrayed ther cornes." *Balfour's Annales of Scotland,* vol. iv. p. 88. The clergy, on the other hand, employing a resource with which their profession has always been familiar, represented Cromwell as opposing Providence, because he was opposing them. Rutherford (*Religious Letters,* reprinted Glasgow, 1824, p. 346) says, that he fought "against the Lord's secret ones;" and Row (*Continuation of Blair's Autobiography,* p. 335), under the year 1658, triumphantly observes: "In the beginning of September this year, the Protector, that old fox, died. It was observed, as a remarkable cast of divine providence, that he died upon the 3d of September, which he, glorying of routing of our armies at Dunbar and Worcester on that day, used to call *his day.* On that very same day the Just Judge called him to an account," &c.

6. See contemporary notices of this, in *Nicoll's Diary,* p. 110; and in *The Diary of Mr. John Lamont of Newton,* pp. 56, 57. But the best account is that given by Baillie, in a letter to Calamy, dated Glasgow, 27th July 1653. He writes: "That on the 20th of July last, when our Generall Assemblie wes sett in the ordinarie tyme and place, Lieutenant-Colonell Cotterall besett the church with some rattes of musqueteirs and a troup of horse; himself (after our fast, wherein Mr. Dickson and Mr. Dowglas had two gracious sermons) entered the Assemblie-house, and, immediately after Mr. Dickson the Moderator his prayer, required audience; wherein he inquired, If we did sitt there by the authority of the Parliament of the Commonwealth of England? or of the Commanders-in-chiefe of the English forces? or of the English Judges in Scotland? The Moderator replyed, That we were ane Ecclesiasticall synod, ane Spirituall court of Jesus Christ, which medled not with any thing Civile; that our authoritie wes from God, and established by the lawes of the land yet standing unrepealed; that, by the Solemn League and Covenant, the most of the English army stood obliedged to defend our Generall Assemblie. When some speeches of this kind had passed, the Lieutenant-Colonell told us, his order was to dissolve us; whereupon he commanded all of us to follow him, else he would drag us out of the rowme. When we had entered a Protestation of this unheard-of and unexampled violence, we did ryse and follow him; he ledd us all through the whole streets a myle out of the towne, encompassing us with foot-companies of musqueteirs, and horsemen without; all the people gazing and mourning as at the saddest spectacle they had ever seen. When he had ledd us a myle without the towne, he then declared what further he had in commission, That we should not dare to meet any more above three in number;

Thus it was that in Scotland, after the latter part of the sixteenth century, every thing tended to increase the reputation of the clergy, by raising them to the foremost rank among the defenders of their country. And it was but natural that the spiritual classes, finding themselves in the ascendant, should conduct the contest according to views habitual to their profession, and should be anxious for religious advantages, rather than for temporal benefits. The war which the Scotch waged against Charles I. partook more of the character of a crusade than any war ever carried on by a Protestant nation.[7] The main object was, to raise up presbyters, and to destroy bishops. Prelacy was the accursed thing, and that must be rooted out at every hazard. To this, all other considerations were subordinate.[8] The Scotch loved liberty, and hated

and that against eight o'clock to-morrow, we should depart the towne, under paine of being guiltie of breaking the publick peace: And the day following, by sound of trumpet, we were commanded off towne under the paine of present imprisonment. Thus our Generall Assemblie, the glory and strength of our Church upon earth, is, by your souldiarie, crushed and trod under foot, without the least provocatione from us, at this time, either in word or deed." *Baillie's Letters and Journals,* vol. iii. pp. 225, 226.

7. In August 1640, the army marched into England; and "it was very refreshfull to remark, that after we came to ane quarter at night, there was nothing almost to be heard throughout the whole army but singing of psalms, prayer, and reading of Scripture by the souldiers in their severall hutts." *Select Biographies,* edited by Mr. Tweedie for the Wodrow Society, vol. i. p. 163. "The most zealous among them boasted, they should carry the triumphant banners of the covenant to Rome itself." *Arnot's History of Edinburgh,* p. 124. In 1644, the celebrated divine, Andrew Cant, was appointed by the Commissioners of the General Assembly "to preach at the opening of the Parliament, wherein he satisfied their expectation fully. For, the main point he drove at in his sermon, was to state an opposition betwixt King Charles and King Jesus (as he was pleased to speak), and upon that account to press resistance to King Charles for the interest of King Jesus. It may be wondered that such doctrine should have relish'd with men brought up in the knowledge of the Scriptures; and yet, such was the madness of the times, that none who preach'd in public since the beginning of the Troubles, had been so cried up as he was for that sermon." *Guthry's Memoirs,* pp. 136, 137.

8. "The rooting out of prelacy and the wicked hierarchy therein so obviously described, is the main duty." *Naphtali, or the Wrestlings of the Church of Scotland,* pp. 53, 54. This refers to the Covenant of 1643. So, too, the continuator of *Row's History of the Kirk,* p. 521, says, under the year 1639, that the object of the war was, "to withstand the prelaticall fatcion and malignant, countenanced by the kinge in his owne persone." Compare the outbreak of the Reverend Samuel Rutherford, against "the accursed and wretched prelates, the Antichrist's first-born, and the first fruit of his foul womb." *Rutherford's Religious Letters,* p. 179.

England. Yet, even these two passions, notwithstanding their strength, were as nothing in comparison with their intense desire to extend and to propagate, if need be at the point of the sword, their own Presbyterian polity. This was their first and paramount duty. They fought, indeed, for freedom, but, above all, they fought for religion. In their eyes, Charles was the idolatrous head of an idolatrous church, and that church they were resolved to destroy. They felt that their cause was holy, and they went forth full of confidence, convinced that the sword of Gideon was drawn on their side, and that their enemies would be delivered up to them.

The rebellion, therefore, against Charles, which, on the part of the English, was essentially secular,[9] was, on the part of the Scotch, essentially religious. This was because with us, the laymen were stronger than the clergy; while with them, the clergy were stronger than the laymen. In 1643, both nations having united against the king, it was thought advisable that an intimate alliance should be concluded; but, in the negotiations which followed, it is noticed, by a contemporary observer, that though the English merely wished for a civil league, the Scotch demanded a religious covenant.[10] And as they would only continue the war on condition that this was granted, the English were obliged to give way. The result was the Solemn League and Covenant, by which what seemed a cordial union was effected between the two countries.[11] Such a compact was, however, sure to be short-lived, as each party had different objects; the aim of the English being political, while that of the Scotch was religious. The consequences of this differ-

9. Our civil war was not religious; but was a struggle between the Crown and the Parliament. See a note in *Buckle's History of Civilization*, vol. i. pp. 329, 330.

10. In September 1643, Baillie, writing an account of the proceedings of the Westminster Assembly in the preceding month, says, "In our committees also we had hard enough debates. The English were for a civill League, we for a religious Covenant." Letter to Mr. William Spang, dated 22d September 1643, in *Baillie's Letters and Journals*, vol. ii. p. 90.

11. "The Solemn League and Covenant," which "is memorable as the first approach towards an intimate union between the kingdoms, but, according to the intolerant principles of the age, a federal alliance was constructed on the frail and narrow basis of religious communion." *Laing's History of Scotland*, vol. iii. pp. 258, 259. The passage, however, which I have quoted, in the last note, from Baillie, shows that England was not responsible for the intolerant principles, or, consequently, for the narrow basis.

ence were soon apparent. In January 1645, negotiations having been opened with the king, commissioners met at Uxbridge, with the view of concluding a peace. The attempt failed, as might have been expected, seeing that, not only were the pretensions of the king irreconcilable with those of his opponents, but that the pretensions of his opponents were irreconcilable with each other. At Uxbridge, during the conferences, the Scotch expressed their readiness to concede to him what he required, if he would gratify them in regard to the Church; while the English, occupying themselves with civil and political questions, cared less, says Clarendon, for what concerned the Church than for any thing else.[12] A better illustration could hardly be found of the secular character of the English rebellion, as compared with the spiritual character of the Scotch rebellion. Indeed, the Scotch, so far from concealing this, boasted of it, and evidently thought that it proved how superior they were to their worldly-minded neighbours. In February 1645, the General Assembly issued an address to the nation, including not only those who were at home, but also those who served in armies out of Scotland. In this document, which proceeding from such a quarter, necessarily exercised great influence, political considerations, as having to do merely with the temporal happiness of men, are treated as insignificant, and almost despicable. That Rupert was defeated, and that York and Newcastle were taken, were but trifling matters. They were only the means of accomplishing an end, and that end was the reformation of religion in England, and the establishment there of the pure Presbyterian polity.[13]

12. The Chancellor of Scotland "did as good as conclude 'that if the king would satisfy them in the business of the Church, they would not concern themselves in any of the other demands.' " . . . "And it was manifest enough, by the private conferences with other of the commissioners, that the parliament took none of the points in controversy less to heart, or were less united in, than in what concerned the Church." *Clarendon's History of the Rebellion*, edit. Oxford, 1843, p. 522. See also p. 527: "that the Scots would insist upon the whole government of the Church, and in all other matters would defer to the king."

13. See this extraordinary document in *Acts of the General Assembly of the Church of Scotland from 1638 to 1842*, pp. 122–128, Edinburgh, 1843. It is entitled "A solemne and seasonable warning to the noblemen, barons, gentlemen, burrows, ministers, and commons of Scotland; as also to armies without and within this kingdom." In it (p. 123) occurs the following passage: "And for our part, our forces sent into that kingdom, in pursuance of that Covenant,

A war, undertaken with such holy objects, and conceived in so elevated a spirit, was supposed to be placed under the immediate protection of the Deity, on whose behalf it was carried on. In the language of the time, it was a war for God, and for God's church. Every victory that was obtained, was the result, not of the skill of the general, nor of the valour of the troops, but was an answer to prayer.[14] When a battle was lost, it was either because God was vexed at the sins of the people,[15] or else to show them that they

---

have been so mercifully and manifestly assisted and blessed from heaven (though in the mids of many dangers and distresses, and much want and hardship), and have been so farre instrumentall to the foyling and scattering of two principall armies; first, the Marquesse of Newcastle his army; and afterward Prince Rupert's and his together; and to the reducing of two strong cities, York and Newcastle, that we have what to answer the enemy that reproacheth us concerning that businesse, and that which may make iniquitie it self to stop her mouth. But which *is more unto us than all victories or whatsomever temporall blessing,* the reformation of religion in England, and uniformity therein between both kingdoms (a principal end of that Covenant), is so far advanced, that the English Service-Book with the Holy-Dayes and many other ceremonies contained in it, together with the Prelacy, the fountain of all these, are abolished and taken away by ordinance of parliament, and a directory for the worship of God in all the three kingdoms agreed upon in the Assemblies, and in the Parliaments of both kingdoms, without a contrary voice in either; the government of the kirk by congregational elderships, classical presbyteries, provincial and national assemblies, is agreed upon by the Assembly of Divines at Westminster, which is also voted and concluded in both Houses of the Parliament of England."

14. In 1644, "God ansuered our Wednesday's prayers: Balfour and Waller had gotten a glorious victorie over Forth and Hopton, and routed them totallie, horse and foot." *Baillie's Letters and Journals,* vol. ii. p. 155. In the same year, thanksgivings being offered at Aberdeen for the victory of Leslie over Rupert, "oure minister Mr. William Strathauchin declairit out of pulpit that this victory wes miraculous, wrocht by the fynger of God." *Spalding's History of the Troubles,* vol. ii. p. 254. In 1648, the Commissioners of the General Assembly, in an address to the Prince of Wales, stated that the Deity had been "fighting for his people;" meaning by his people, the Scotch people. They added, that the fact of their enemies having been repulsed, was a proof of "how sore the Lord hath been displeased with their way." *Clarendon State Papers,* vol. ii. p. 424, Oxford, 1773, folio.

15. Two Scotch notices are now before me of the fatal battle of Dunbar. According to one, the defeat was intended to testify against "the great sin and wickedness" of the people. *Naphtali, or the Wrestlings of the Church of Scotland,* p. 75. According to the other, it was owing to the anger of the Deity at the Scotch showing any favour to the partizans of Charles. For, says the Reverend Alexander Shields, "both at that time, and since that time, the Lord never countenanced an expedition where that malignant interest was taken in unto the state of the quarrel. Upon this, our land was invaded by Oliver Cromwell, who defeat our army at Dunbar, where the anger of the Lord was

must not trust to the arms of the flesh.[16] Nothing was natural; all was supernatural. The entire course of affairs was governed, not by their own antecedents, but by a series of miracles. To assist the Scotch, winds were changed, and storms were lulled. Such intelligence as was important for them to receive, was often brought by sea; and, on those occasions, it was expected that, if the wind were unfavourable, Providence would interfere, would shift it from one quarter to another, and, when the news had safely arrived, would allow it to return to its former direction.[17]

It was in this way that, in Scotland, every thing conspired to strengthen that religious element which the force of circumstances had, at an early period, made prominent, and which now threatened to absorb all the other elements of the national character. The clergy were supreme; and habits of mind natural and becoming to themselves, were diffused among all classes. The theories of a single profession outweighed those of all other professions; and not only war, but also trade, literature, science, and

---

evidently seen to smoke against us, for espousing that interest." *Shields' Hind let loose*, p. 75. These opinions were formed after the battle. Before the battle, a different hypothesis was broached. Sir Edward Walker, who was in Scotland at the time, tells us, that the clergy assured the people that "they had an army of saints, and that they could not be beaten." *Journal of Affairs in Scotland in 1650*, in *Walker's Historical Discourses*, London, 1705, folio, p. 165.

16. "Each new victory of Montrose was expressly attributed to the admonitory 'indignation of the Lord' against his chosen people for their sin, in 'trusting too much to the arm of flesh.'" *Napier's Life of Montrose*, Edinburgh, 1840, p. 283. Compare *Guthrie's Considerations contributing unto the Discovery of the Dangers that threaten Religion*, pp. 274, 275, reprinted Edinburgh, 1846. Guthrie was at the height of his reputation in the middle of the seventeenth century. Lord Somerville says of the Scotch, when they were making war against Charles I., that it was "ordinary for them, dureing the wholl tyme of this warre, to attribute ther great successe to the goodnesse and justice of their cause, untill Divyne Justice trysted them with some crosse dispensatione, and then you might have heard this language from them, that it pleased the Lord to give his oune the heavyest end of the tree to bear, that the saints and people of God must still be sufferers while they are here away; that that malignant party was God's rod to punish them for their unthankfullnesse," &c. *Somerville's Memorie of the Somervilles*, vol. ii. pp. 351, 352.

17. Baillie mentions, in 1644, an instance of these expectations being fulfilled. He says (*Letters and Journals*, vol. ii. p. 138), "These things were brought in at a very important nick of time, by God's gracious providence: Never a more quick passage from Holy Island to Yarmouth in thirtie houres; they had not cast anchor halfe an houre till the wind turned contrare." Compare p. 142: "If this were past, we look for a new lyfe and vigoure in all affaires, especiallie if it please God to send a sweet northwind, carrying the certain news of the taking of Newcastle, which we dailie expect."

art, were held of no account unless they ministered to the general feeling. A state of society so narrow and so one-sided, has never been seen in any other country equally civilized. Nor did there appear much chance of abating this strange monopoly. As the seventeenth century advanced, the same train of events was continued; the clergy and the people always making common cause against the crown, and being, by the necessity of self-preservation, forced into the most intimate union with each other. Of this, the preachers availed themselves to strengthen their own influence; and for upwards of a century their exertions stopped all intellectual culture, discouraged all independent inquiry, made men in religious matters fearful and austere, and coloured the whole national character with that dark hue, which, though now gradually softening, it still retains.

The Scotch, during the seventeenth century, instead of cultivating the arts of life, improving their minds, or adding to their wealth, passed the greater part of their time in what were called religious exercises. The sermons were so long and so frequent, that they absorbed all leisure, and yet the people were never weary of hearing them. When a preacher was once in the pulpit, the only limit to his loquacity was his strength. Being sure of a patient and reverential audience, he went on as long as he could. If he discoursed for two hours without intermission, he was valued as a zealous pastor, who had the good of his flock at heart; and this was about as much as an ordinary clergyman could perform, because, in uttering his sentiments, he was expected to display great vehemence, and to evince his earnestness by toiling and sweating abundantly.[18] This boundary was, however, often passed by those who were equal to the labour; and Forbes, who was vigorous as

18. No one, perhaps, carried this further than John Menzies, the celebrated professor of divinity at Aberdeen. "Such was his uncommon fervour in the pulpit, that, we are informed, he 'used to change his shirt always after preaching, and to wet two or three napkins with tears every sermon.'" Note in *Wodrow's Correspondence*, vol. ii. p. 222. James Forbes, also, was "an able and zealous preacher, who after every sermon behooved to change his shirt, he spoke with such vehemency and sweating." *Select Biographies*, published by the Wodrow Society, vol. i. p. 333. Lord Somerville, who wrote in 1679, mentions "their thundering preachings." *Memorie of the Somervilles*, vol. ii. p. 388. A traditionary anecdote, related by the Dean of Edinburgh, refers to a later period, but is characteristic of the class. "Another description I have heard of an energetic preacher more forcible than delicate—'Eh, our minister had a great power o'watter, for he grat, and spat, and swat like mischeef.'" *Reminiscences of Scottish Life and Character*, by E. B. Ramsay, Dean of Edinburgh, p. 201.

well as voluble, thought nothing of preaching for five or six hours.[19] But, in the ordinary course of nature, such feats were rare; and, as the people were in these matters extremely eager, an ingenious contrivance was hit upon whereby their desires might be satisfied. On great occasions, several clergymen were present in the same church, in order that, when one was fatigued, he might leave the pulpit, and be succeeded by another, who, in his turn, was followed by a third; the patience of the hearers being apparently inexhaustible.[20] Indeed, the Scotch, by the middle of the seventeenth century, had grown accustomed to look up to their minister as if he were a god, and to dwell with rapture upon every word that dropt from his lips. To hear a favourite preacher, they would incur any fatigue, and would undertake long journeys without sleep or food.[21] Their power of attention was marvellous.

19. He "was a very learned and pious man; he had a strange faculty of preaching five or six hours at a time." *Burnet's History of his own Time*, vol. i. p. 38. Even early in the eighteenth century, when theological fervour was beginning to decline, and sermons were consequently shorter, Hugh Thomson came near to Forbes. "He was the longest preacher ever I heard, and would have preached four (or) five hours, and was not generally under two hours; that almost every body expected." . . . . "He was a piouse good man, and a fervent affectionat preacher, and, when I heard him, he had a vast deal of heads, and a great deal of matter, and generally very good and practicall, but very long." *Wodrow's Analecta*, vol. iv. p. 203.

20. In 1653, Lamont casually mentions, in his journal, that "the one came doune from the pulpit and the other went vp, in the tyme that the psalme after the first sermon was singing, so that ther was no intermission of the exercise, nether were the peopell dismissed till both sermons were ended." *The Diary of Mr. John Lamont of Newton*, p. 58. Burnet (*History of his own Time*, vol. i. p. 92) says, "I remember in one fast day there were six sermons preached without intermission. I was there myself, and not a little weary of so tedious a service."

21. When Guthrie preached at Fenwick, "his church, although a large country one, was overlaid and crowded every Sabbath-day, and very many, without doors, from distant parishes, such as Glasgow, Paisley, Hamilton, Lanerk, Kilbryde, Glasford, Strathaven, Newmills, Egelsham, and many other places, who hungered for the pure gospel preached, and got a meal by the word of his ministry. It was their usual practice to come to Fenwick on Saturday, and to spend the greatest part of the night in prayer to God, and conversation about the great concerns of their souls, to attend the public worship on the Sabbath, to dedicate the remainder of that holy day in religious exercises, and then to go home on Monday the length of ten, twelve or twenty miles without grudging in the least at the long way, want of sleep or other refreshments; neither did they find themselves the less prepared for any other business through the week." *Howie's Biographia Scoticana*, 2d edit., Glasgow, 1781, p. 311. One woman went forty miles to hear Livingstone preach. See her own statement, in *Wodrow's Analecta*, vol. ii. p. 249.

The same congregation would sometimes remain together for ten hours, listening to sermons and prayers, interspersed with singings and readings.[22] In an account of Scotland in 1670, it is stated that, in a single church in Edinburgh, thirty sermons were delivered every week.[23] Nor is this at all unlikely, considering the religious enthusiasm of the age. For, in those times, the people delighted in the most harassing and ascetic devotions. Thus, for instance, in 1653, when the sacrament was administered, they pursued the following course. On Wednesday, they fasted, and listened to prayers and sermons for more than eight hours. On Saturday, they heard two or three sermons; and on Sunday, the number of sermons was so great that they stayed in church more than twelve hours; while, to conclude the whole, three or four additional ones were preached on Monday by way of thanksgiving.[24]

Such eagerness, and yet such patience, indicate a state of society altogether peculiar, and for which we find no parallel in the history of any civilized country. This intense desire to hear whatever the preachers had to say, was, in itself, a homage of the most flattering kind, and was naturally accompanied by a belief that they were endowed with a light which was withheld from their less gifted countrymen. It is not surprising that the clergy, who, at no period, and in no nation, have been remarkable for their meekness, or for a want of confidence in themselves, should, under circumstances so eminently favourable to their pretensions, have been somewhat elated, and should have claimed an authority even greater than that which was conceded

22. Spalding gives the following account of what happened at Aberdeen in 1644. "So heir in Old Abirdene, upone the sevint of July, we had ane fast, entering the churche be nyne houris, and continewit praying and preiching whill tua houris. Efter sermon, the people sat still heiring reiding whill efternone's sermon began and endit, whiche continewit till half hour to sex. Then the prayer bell rang to the evening prayeris, and continewit whill seven." *Spalding's History of the Troubles,* vol. ii. p. 244, edit. Edinburgh, 1829, 4to. See also p. 42: "the people keipit churche all day." This was also at Aberdeen, in 1642.

23. "Out of one pulpit now they have thirty sermons per week, all under one roof." *A Modern Account of Scotland,* in *The Harleian Miscellany,* vol. vi. p. 138, edit. Park, London, 1810, 4to.

24. "But where the greatest part was more sound, they gave the sacrament with a new and unusual solemnity. On the Wednesday before, they held a fast day, with prayers and sermons for about eight or ten hours together: on the Saturday they had two or three preparation sermons: and on the Lord's day they had so very many, that the action continued above twelve hours in some places: and all ended with three or four sermons on Monday for thanksgiving." *Burnet's History of his own Time,* vol. i. p. 108.

to them. And as this is intimately connected with the subsequent history of Scotland, it will be necessary to collect some evidence respecting their conduct, which will have the further advantage of exhibiting the true character of spiritual domination, and of showing how it works, not only on the intellectual, but also on the practical, life of a people.

According to the Presbyterian polity, which reached its height in the seventeenth century, the clergyman of the parish selected a certain number of laymen on whom he could depend, and who, under the name of elders, were his councillors, or rather the ministers of his authority. They, when assembled together, formed what was called the Kirk-Session, and this little court, which enforced the decisions uttered in the pulpit, was so supported by the superstitious reverence of the people, that it was far more powerful than any civil tribunal. By its aid, the minister became supreme. For, whoever presumed to disobey him was excommunicated, was deprived of his property, and was believed to have incurred the penalty of eternal perdition.[25] Against such weapons,

25. "The power of those kirk-sessions, which are now private assemblages, in whose meetings and proceedings the public take no interest whatever, is defined to be the cognizance of parochial matters and cases of scandal; but in the sixteenth and seventeenth centuries, especially during the Covenanting reign of terror after the outbreak of the Civil War against Charles I., the kirk-sessions of Scotland were the sources of excessive tyranny and oppression—were arbitrary, inquisitorial, and revengeful, to an extent which exceeds all belief. It is truly stated by the author of the 'Memoirs of Locheill'—'Every parish had a tyrant, who made the greatest Lord in his district stoop to his authority. The kirk was the place where he kept his court; the pulpit his throne or tribunal from whence he issued out his terrible decrees; and twelve or fourteen sour ignorant enthusiasts, under the title of Elders, composed his council. If any, of what quality soever, had the assurance to disobey his orders, the dreadful sentence of excommunication was immediately thundered out against him, his goods and chattels confiscated and seized, and he himself being looked upon as actually in the possession of the devil, and irretrievably doomed to eternal perdition.' " Introduction to *The Kirk-Session Register of Perth*, in *The Spottiswoode Miscellany*, vol. ii. pp. 229, 230, Edinburgh, 1845. In regard to the perdition which the sentence of excommunication was supposed to involve, one of the most influential Scotch divines of that time merely expresses the prevailing notion, when he asserts, that whoever was excommunicated was thereby given up to Satan. "That he who is excommunicated may be truly said to be delivered to Sathan is undeniable." *Gillespie's Aaron's Rod Blossoming, or the Divine Ordinance of Church Government Vindicated*, 1646, 4to, p. 239. "Excommunication, which is a shutting out of a Church-member from the Church, whereby Sathan commeth to get dominion and power over him." *Ibid.*, p. 297. "Sure I am an excommunicate person may truly be said to be delivered to Sathan." p. 424.

in such a state of society, resistance was impossible. The clergy interfered with every man's private concerns, ordered how he should govern his family, and often took upon themselves the personal control of his household.[26] Their minions, the elders, were every where; for each parish was divided into several quarters, and to each quarter one of these officials was allotted, in order that he might take special notice of what was done in his own district.[27] Besides this, spies were appointed, so that nothing could escape their supervision.[28] Not only the streets, but even private houses, were searched, and ransacked, to see if any one was absent

26. Clarendon, under the year 1640, emphatically says (*History of the Rebellion*, p. 67), "The preacher reprehended the husband, governed the wife, chastised the children, and insulted over the servants, in the houses of the greatest men." The theory was, that "ministers and elders must be submitted unto as fathers." *Shield's Enquiry into Church Communion*, 2d edit., Edinburgh, 1747, p. 66. In the middle of the seventeenth century, one of the most famous of the Scotch preachers openly asserted the right of his profession to interfere in family matters, on the ground that such was the custom in the time of Joshua. "The Ministers of God's house have not only the ministry of holy things, as Word and Sacraments, committed to their charge, but also the power of ecclesiastical government to take order with scandalous offences within the familie; both these are here promised to Joshua and the Priests." *Hutcheson's Exposition of the Minor Prophets*, vol. iii. p. 72, London, 1654. In 1603, the Presbytery of Aberdeen took upon themselves to order that every master of a house should keep a rod, that his family, including his servants, might be beaten if they used improper language. "It is concludit that thair salbe in ewerie houss a palmar." *Selections from the Records of the Kirk Session, Presbytery, and Synod of Aberdeen*, printed for the Spalding Club, 4to, Aberdeen, 1846, p. 194. It also appears (p. 303) that, in 1674, the clergyman was expected to exercise supervision over all visitors to private houses; since he ought to be informed, "iff ther be anie persone receaved in the familie without testimoniall presented to the minister."

27. In 1650, it was ordered, "That everie paroche be divydit in severall quarteris, and each elder his owne quarter, over which he is to have speciall inspectioun, and that everie elder visit his quarter once everie month at least, according to the act of the Generall Assemblie, 1649, and in thair visitatioun tak notice of all disorderlie walkeris, especiallie neglectouris of God's worship in thair families, sueareris, haunteris of aill houses, especiallie at vnseasonable tymes, and long sitteris thair, and drinkeris of healthis; and that by dilate these to the Sessioun." *Selections from the Minutes of the Synod of Fife*, printed for the Abbotsford Club, Edinburgh, 1837, 4to, p. 168. "The elders each one in his own quarter, for trying the manners of the people." *The Government and Order of the Church of Scotland*, Edinburgh, 1690, p. 14. This scarce little volume is reprinted from the edition of 1641. See the advertisement at the beginning.

28. In 1652, the Kirk-Session of Glasgow "brot boyes and servants before them, for breaking the Sabbath, and other faults. They had clandestine censors, and gave money to some for this end." *Wodrow's Collections*, vol. ii. part ii. p. 74, Glasgow, 1848, 4to.

from church while the minister was preaching.[29] To him, all must listen, and him all must obey. Without the consent of his tribunal, no person might engage himself, either as a domestic servant, or as a field labourer.[30] If any one incurred the displeasure of the clergy, they did not scruple to summon his servants and force them to state whatever they knew respecting him, and whatever they had seen done in his house.[31] To speak disrespectfully of a preacher was a grievous offence;[32] to differ from him was a heresy;[33] even to pass him in the streets without saluting him,

---

29. "It is thocht expedient that ane baillie with tua of the sessioun pas throw the towne everie Sabboth day, and nott sic as thay find absent fra the sermones ather afoir or efter none; and for that effect that thay pas and *sersche sic houss as they think maist meit*, and pas athort the streittis." *Selections from the Records of the Kirk Session, Presbytery, and Synod of Aberdeen*, p. 26. "To pas throw the towne to caus the people resort to the hering of the sermones." p. 59. "Ganging throw the towne on the ordinar preiching dayes in the weik, als weill as on the Saboth day, to caus the people resort to the sermones." p. 77. See also p. 94; and *Wodrow's Collections*, vol. ii. part ii. p. 37: "the Session allous the searchers to go into houses and apprehend absents from the kirk."

30. "Another peculiarity was the supervision weilded over the movements of people to such a degree that they could neither *obtain lodging nor employment* except by a licence from the Kirk-Session, or, by defying this police court, expose themselves to fine and imprisonment." *Lawson's Book of Perth*, p. xxxvii., Edinburgh, 1847.

31. In 1652, Sir Alexander Irvine indignantly writes, that the presbytery of Aberdeen, "when they had tried many wayes, bot in vaine, to mak probable this their vaine imaginatione, they, at lenthe, when all other meanes failed thame, by ane unparalelled barbaritie, enforced my serwandis to reweall upon oathe what they sawe, herd, or knewe done within my house, beyond which no Turkische inquisitione could pase." *The Miscellany of the Spalding Club*, vol. iii. p. 206, Aberdeen, 1846, 4to.

32. In 1656, a servant was ordered to be brought before the Kirk-Session of Aberdeen "for her rayleing against Mr. Andrew Cant, minister, in saying that becaus the said Mr. Andrew spak against Yuill, he spak lyke ane old fool." *Selections from the Records of the Kirk Session, Presbytery, and Synod of Aberdeen*, p. 138. In 1642, the Presbytery of Lanark had up a certain James Baillie, because he stated the extremely probable circumstance, "that two fooles mett togither, when the Minister and his sone mett togither." *Selections from the Registers of the Presbytery of Lanark*, printed for the Abbotsford Club, Edinburgh, 1839, 4to, p. 30.

33. In 1644, "If you dissent from them in a theological tenet, it is heresy." *Presbytery Displayed*, 1644, p. 39, reprinted London, 1663, 4to. In 1637, "If ye depart from *what I taught you in a hair-breadth* for fear or favour of men, or desire of ease in this world, I take heaven and earth to witness, that ill shall come upon you in end." *Rutherford's Religious Letters*, p. 116. In 1607, "Mr. William Cowper, Minister, complained upon Robert Keir that he had disdainfully spoken of his doctrine. The (Kirk) Session ordained him to be warned to the morrow." *Lawson's Book of Perth*, p. 247.

was punished as a crime.[34] His very name was regarded as sacred, and not to be taken in vain. And that it might be properly protected, and held in due honour, an Assembly of the Church, in 1642, forbad it to be used in any public paper unless the consent of the holy man had been previously obtained.[35]

These and similar proceedings, being upheld by public opinion, were completely successful. Indeed, they could hardly have been otherwise, seeing that it was generally believed that whoever gainsaid the clergy, would be visited, not only with temporal penalties, but also with spiritual ones. For such a crime, there was punishment here, and there was punishment hereafter. The preachers willingly fostered a delusion by which they benefited. They told their hearers, that what was spoken in the pulpit was binding upon all believers, and was to be regarded as immediately proceeding from the Deity.[36] This proposition being established, other propositions naturally followed. The clergy believed that they alone were privy to the counsels of the Almighty, and that, by virtue of this knowledge, they could determine what any man's future state would be.[37] Going still further, they claimed the

34. In 1619, a man was summoned before the Kirk-Session of Perth, because, among other things, he would not perform "that civil duty of salutation, as becomes him to his pastor;" but "passed by him without using any kind of reverence." *The Chronicle of Perth,* Edinburgh, 1831, 4to, p. 80. The complaint was preferred by the minister himself. Indeed, the Scotch clergy took these things so much to heart, that they set up a theory to the effect that whoever showed them any disrespect, was prompted thereto by Satan. "It is Satan's great engine to draw men to contemne God and his word, under pretext of disrespect and prejudice against the Messengers only." . . . "It may let us see their guilt who despise most eminent ordinary Messengers." *Hutcheson's Exposition of the Minor Prophets,* vol. i. pp. 205, 233.

35. The General Assembly of Saint Andrews, in 1642, passed "an act against using ministers' names in any of the public papers, without their own consent." *Stevenson's History of the Church of Scotland,* p. 503.

36. "Directions for a believer's walk, given by Christ's ministers from his word, are his own, and are accounted by him as if he did immediately speak them himself." *Durham's Exposition of the Song of Solomon,* p. 102. I quote from the Glasgow reprint of 1788. That my references may be easily verified, and any error, if error there be, detected, I mention that the exact edition used will, in every case, be found specified in the List of Authors at the beginning of the [1st edition]. But, if it will give the reader any additional confidence, I will venture to observe, that I am always scrupulously careful in reference to quotations, having looked out each passage afresh, as the sheets came from the printer's hands. Some of the circumstances narrated in this chapter are so monstrous, that I hope to be excused in saying that I have taken all possible pains to secure their literal accuracy.

37. "Yea, such was their arrogance, that, as if they had been privy to

power, not only of foretelling his future state, but also of controlling it; and they did not scruple to affirm that, by their censures, they could open and shut the kingdom of heaven.[38] As if this were not enough, they also gave out that a word of theirs could hasten the moment of death, and by cutting off the sinner in his prime, could bring him at once before the judgment-seat of God.[39]

Utterly horrible as such a pretension now appears, it was made, not only with impunity, but with advantage; and numerous instances are recorded, in which the people believed that it was strictly enforced. The celebrated John Welsh, sitting one night at table, round which a party were assembled at supper, began to discourse to the company respecting the state of their souls. Those who were present listened with humility; but to this gen-

---

the councils of God, or the dispensers of his vengeance to the world, they presumed to pronounce upon their future state, and doomed them, both body and soul to eternal torments." *Wishart's Memoirs of the Marquis of Montrose,* p. 237. "Ye heard of me the whole counsel of God." *Rutherford's Religious Letters,* p. 16. "I am free from the blood of all men; for I have communicated to you the whole counsel of God." *Ibid.,* p. 191. "This is the great business of Gospel Ministers, to declare the whole counsel of God." *Halyburton's Great Concern of Salvation,* p. 4. "Asserting that he had declared the whole counsel of God, and had keeped nothing back." *Life of the Rev. Alexander Peden,* p. 41, in vol. i. of *Walker's Biographia Presbyteriana.*

38. "The power of the keys is given to the ministers of the church, wherewith not only by the preaching of the word, but also to church censures, (sic) they open and shut the kingdom of heaven." *Dickson's Truth's Victory over Error,* p. 282. "To preach the Word, impugne, rebuik, admonishe, exhort and correct, and that under no less paine then casting both bodie and soull into eternall hell's fire." *Forbes' Certaine Records touching the Estate of the Kirk,* p. 519. "The next words, 'Whatsoever ye shall bind on Earth shall be bound in Heaven,' being spoken to the Apostles, and in them to other Ministers of Jesus Christ." *Gillespie's Aaron's Rod Blossoming,* p. 366. "The keys of the kingdom of Heaven" . . . . "are committed and intrusted to the pastors and other ruling officers of the Church." *Ibid.,* p. 260.

39. "Gird up the loins of your mind, and make you ready for meeting the Lord; I have often summoned you, and now I summon you again, to compear before your Judge, to make a reckoning of your life." *Rutherford's Religious Letters,* p. 235. "Mr. Cameron, musing a little, said, 'You, and all who do not know my God in mercy, shall know him in his judgments, which shall be sudden and surprising in a few days upon you; and I, as a sent servant of Jesus Christ, whose commission I bear, and whose badge I wear upon my breast, give you warning, and leave you to the justice of God.' Accordingly, in a few days after, the said Andrew, being in perfect health, took his breakfast plentifully, and before he rose fell a-vomiting, and vomitted his heart's blood in the very vessel out of which he had taken his breakfast; and died in a most frightful manner." *Howie's Biographia Scoticana,* p. 406.

eral feeling there was one exception. For, it so happened that a Roman Catholic was in the room, and he, of course, disagreed with the opinions expressed by the Presbyterian divine. If he had been a cautious man, he would have kept his disagreement to himself; but being a hot-headed youth, and being impatient at seeing a single person engross the conversation, he lost his temper, and not only ridiculed Welsh, but actually made faces at him. Thereupon, Welsh charged the company to take heed, and see what the Lord was about to do to him who mocked. Scarcely had this threat been uttered, when it was carried into execution. He who had dared to jest at the minister, suddenly fell, sank under the table, and died there in presence of the whole party.[40]

This happened early in the seventeenth century, and being bruited abroad, it became a great terror to all evil-doers. But, after a time, its effect appears to have been weakened; since another man was equally rash some forty or fifty years afterwards. It seems that a Scotch clergyman, of considerable repute, Mr.

40. "Sitting at supper with the Lord Ochiltree (who was uncle to Mr. Welsh's wife), as his manner was, he entertained the company with godly and edifying discourse, which was well received by all the company save only one debauched Popish young gentleman, who sometimes laughed, and sometimes mocked and made faces; whereupon Mr. Welsh brake out into a sad abrupt charge upon all the company to be silent, and observe the work of the Lord upon that profane mocker, which they should presently behold: upon which immediately the profane wretch sunk down and died beneath the table, but never returned to life again, to the great astonishment of all the company." *History of Mr. John Welsh, Minister of the Gospel at Ayr,* in *Select Biographies,* vol. i. p. 29. "Mr. Welsh being by the Captaine, set at the upper end, intertained the company with grave and edifying discourse which all delighted to hear, save this young Papist who with laughter and derision laboured to silence him, which was little regarded by Mr. Welsh. But after supper while the guests sate a little, this youth stood up at the lower end of the table, and while Mr. Welsh proceeded from grave to gracious entertainment of his company, the youth came to that height of insolence as with the finger to point at him and with the face to make flouting grimaces, whereby he grieved the holy man, so as on a suddain he was forced to a silence. The whole company, who had heard him with delight, were silent with him. Within a little, Mr. Welsh, as moved by the spirit of God, broke forth into these words: 'Gentlemen, the spirit of God is provoked against us, and I shall intreat you not to be afraid to see what God shall do among you before you rise from the table, for he will smite some of you with death before you go hence.' All were silently astonished, waiting to see the issue with fear. And while every man feared himselfe, except the insolent youth, he fel down dead suddenly at the foot of the table to shew the power of God's jealousie against the mockers of his Spirit and the offers of his grace." *Fleming's Fulfilling the Scripture,* pp. 374, 375.

Thomas Hog, was, like Welsh, sitting at supper, when it so chanced that the servant forgot to lay the knives. Mr. Hog, thinking the opportunity a favourable one, observed that such forgetfulness was of little moment, and that, while we thought so much of our comforts here, it was far more necessary to consider our condition hereafter. A gentleman present, amused, either by the manner of Mr. Hog, or by the skill with which he introduced the topics of his own profession, was unable to restrain himself, and burst into a violent fit of laughter. The minister, however, was not to be checked, and he continued after such a fashion, that the laughter was repeated louder than ever. At length Mr. Hog turned round, and told his merry comrade that very shortly he should seek for mercy, but find it not. That same night, the scoffer was taken ill, and in great alarm sent for Mr. Hog. It was, however, useless. Before the clergyman could reach his room, the sinner was lying dead, a lost and ruined man.[41]

41. "When they sat doun to supper, it seems, knives were forgote; and when the servant was rebuked, Mr. Hogg said, there was noe matter, for he had one in his pocket, and it was a necessary companion for a travailer; and, as his use was upon evry thing, he took occasion to raise a spirituall discourse from it: 'If we wer soe carefull about accommodations in our way here, what care should we take in our spirituall journey!' and the like; at which the factour takes a kink of laughing. Mr. Hogg looked at him with a frown, and went on in his discourse. Within a litle, at somewhat or other, he laughed out yet louder, and Mr. Hogg stoped a litle, and looked him very stern in the face, and went on in his discourse, upon the free grace of God; and, at some expression or other, the man fell a laughing and flouting very loud: Upon which Mr. Hogg stoped, and directed his discourse to him, to this purpose: 'Alace!' sayes he, 'my soul is afflicted to say what I must say to you, sir, and I am constrained and pressed in spirit to say it, and cannot help it. Sir, you nou dispise the grace of God, and mock at it; but I tell you, in the name of the Lord, that the time is coming, and that very shortly, when you (will) seek ane offer of grace, but shall not find it!' Upon which the man arose, laughing and flouting, and went to his room. After he was away, the lady asked Mr. Hogg, What he thought would come upon him? He answered, he kneu noe more then he had said, and that he was constrained and oblidged to say it against his inclination; and he could not accompt for some of these impressions he sometimes felt, and after Providences would clear, and that shortly; but what it was, when, or where, he kneu not. The man told some of the servants that a phanatick Minister had been pronouncing a curse on him, but he did not value him nor it either. After Mr. Hogg had been somtime with the lady, he went to his room; and after he had, as he used to doe, spent some time in prayer, he putt off his cloaths, and just as he was stepping into his bedd, a servant comes and knocks at the dore and cryes, 'For the Lord's sake, Mr. Hogg, come doun staires, presently, to the factour's room!' He put on his cloaths, as quickly as possible, and came doun, but the wretch was dead before he reached him!" *Analecta, or Materials for a History of Remarkable*

Nor was it merely in private houses that such examples were made. Sometimes the clergyman denounced the offender from the pulpit, and the punishment was a public as the offence. It is said that Gabriel Semple, when preaching, had a strange habit of putting out his tongue, and that this excited the mirth of a drunken man, who went into the church, and, by way of derision, put out his tongue also. But, to his horror, he found that, though he could put it out, he could not draw it in again. The result was, that the tongue stiffened; it lost all sensibility; and, paralysis coming on, the man died a few days after his transgression.[42]

Occasionally, the penalty was less severe, though the miracle was equally conspicuous. In 1682, a certain woman took upon herself to scold the famous divine, Peden, who was justly regarded as one of the great lights of the Scotch Church. "I wonder," said that eminent man, "I wonder your tongue is not sore with so much idle clatter." She indignantly replied, that she had never suffered, either from a sore tongue, or from a sore mouth. He told her that she soon would. And the consequence of his saying so was, that her tongue and gums swelled to that degree, that for some days she was unable to take her usual food.[43]

She escaped with her life; others were more sharply handled. A clergyman was interrupted in the midst of his sermon by three gentlemen leaving the church. It is not stated that there was any

---

Providences, mostly relating to Scotch Ministers and Christians, by the Rev. Robert Wodrow, vol. i. pp. 265, 266. Compare *The Life of Mr. Thomas Hog,* in *Howie's Biographia,* p. 543, where a version is given, slightly different, but essentially the same.

42. "He tells me, that when in the South country, he heard this story, which was not doubted about Geddart" (i.e., Jedburgh): "Mr. Gabriel Semple had gote a habite, when speaking and preaching, of putting out his tongue, and licking his lipps very frequently. Ther was a fellou that used to ape him, in a way of mock; and one day, in a drunken caball, he was aping him and putting out his tongue; and it turned stiffe and sensless, and he could not drau it in again, but in a feu dayes dyed. This accompt is soe odd, that I wish I may have it confirmed from other hands." *Wodrow's Analecta,* vol. ii. p. 187.

43. "About the same time, wading Douglas-water very deep," (he) "came to a house there; the goodwife of the house insisted (as most part of women do not keep a bridle-hand) in chiding of him; which made him to fret, and said, I wonder that your tongue is not sore with so much idle clatter. She said, I never had a sore tongue nor mouth all my days. He said, It will not be long so. Accordingly, her tongue and gooms swelled so, that she could get no meat taken for some days." *Account of the Life and Death of Mr. Walter Smith,* p. 93, in vol. ii. of *Walker's Biographia Presbyteriana.*

thing offensive in their manner; but their object in going was to amuse themselves at some fair or race, and the minister, no doubt, thought that they should have been content with the gratification of hearing him. At all events, he was dissatisfied, and, after the sermon was over, he censured their conduct, and threatened them with the divine displeasure. His words were remembered, and, to the awe of his parishioners, every tittle was fulfilled. Of the three gentlemen, all died violent deaths; one of them broke his neck by falling from his horse, and another was found in his room with his throat cut.[44]

Cases of this sort were frequent during the seventeenth century; and as in that credulous age they were firmly believed and widely circulated, the power of the clergy was consolidated by them. The Laird of Hilton once ventured to pull a minister out of a pulpit which was not his own, and into which he had unlawfully intruded. "For the injury you have done to the servant of God," cried the enraged preacher, "you shall be brought into this church like a sticked sow." And so indeed he was. Yet a little while, and Hilton became entangled in a quarrel, was run through the body, and his corpse, still bleeding, was carried into the very church where the outrage had been committed.[45]

44. "I hear from Lady Henriett Campbell, who was present at a Communion at Jeddart (Jedburgh), some years before Mr. Gabriel Semple's death, that, either on the fast day, or Saturnday, ther wer three gentlmen either in the parish or noturely knouen thereabout, who rose in the time of the last sermon, and with their servants went out of (the church), either to some fair or some race, not farr off. After sermon, when Mr. Semple rose to give the ordinary advertisments, he began with taking nottice of this, and said, he had remarked three gentlmen rise in time of sermon, and contemptuously and boldly leave God's service to goe to a fair, or race, as he supposed; but sayes, 'It's born in upon me, and I am perswaded of it, the Lord will not suffer them to goe off time, without some remarkable judgment, and I am much mistaken if the most part that have seen them committ the sin, will not hear of the punishment of such open despite to the ordinances of Christ.' This peremptoryness did very much surprize Lady H(enriett), and coming home from sermon with my Lord Lothian and his Lady, in coach, she expressed her surprize at it. My Lord Lothian said, 'The Minister is a man of God, and I am perswaded not one word of his will fall to the ground!' Within some feu moneths, my Lord or my Lady, writing to Lady H(enriett), signifyed to her, that one of these gentlmen was found in his room, (if I forgett not), with his throat cutt; and a second, being drunk, fell off his horse, and broke his neck; and some while after, shee heard the third had dyed some violent death." *Wodrow's Analecta*, vol. i. pp. 344, 345.

45. "In the time of sermon, the Laird of Hiltoun comes in, and charges him in the midst of his work, to come out of (the) pulpite, in the king's name. Mr.

Even when a clergyman was in prison, he retained the same power. His authority was delegated to him from on high, and no temporal misfortune could curtail it. In 1673, the Reverend Alexander Peden, when in confinement, heard a young girl laughing at him outside the door of his room, while he was engaged in those vociferous devotions for which he was celebrated. The mirth of the poor child cost her dear. Peden denounced against her the judgment of God. In consequence of that denuciation, the wind blew her from a rock on which she was walking, and swept her into the sea, where she was quickly drowned.[46]

Sometimes the vengeance of the clergy extended to the innocent offspring of the man who had offended them. A certain minister, whose name has not been preserved, met with opposition in his parish, and fell into pecuniary and other difficulties. He applied for aid to a trader, who, being wealthy, ought, he thought, to afford him assistance. The trader, however, thought otherwise, and refused. Upon this, the clergyman declared that God would visit him. The result was, that his business not only declined, but his mind became impaired, and he died an idiot. He had two sons and two daughters. Both his sons went mad. One of his daughters, likewise, lost her reason. The other daughter being married, even her husband became destitute, and the children of that mar-

---

Douglasse refused; whereupon the Laird comes to the pulpit, and pulls him out by force! When he sau he behoved to yeild, he said, 'Hiltoun, for this injury you have done to the servant of God, knou what you are to meet with! In a litle time you shall be brought into this very church, like a sticked sou!' And in some litle time after, Hilton was run throu the body, and dyed by, if I mistake not, Annandale's brother, either in a douell or a drunken toilzie, and his corpes wer brought in, all bleeding, into that church. 'Touch not mine annoynted, and doe my prophets noe harm!'" *Wodrow's Analecta*, vol. ii. p. 154. In the same work (vol. iv. p. 268), the Reverend Mr. Wodrow writes, that he had been subsequently informed, "that the story is very true about the denuntiation upon the Laird of Hiltoun, as I have (I think) published it; and ther is a man yet alive who was witnes to it, and in the church at the time."

46. "While prisoner in the Bass, one Sabbath morning, being about the publick worship of God, a young lass, about the age of thirteen or fourteen years, came to the chamber-door, mocking with loud laughter: He said, Poor thing, thou mocks and laughs at the worship of God; but ere long, God shall write such a sudden, surprising judgment on thee, that shall stay thy laughing, and thou shalt not escape it. Very shortly thereafter, she was walking upon the rock, and there came a blast of wind, and sweeped her off the rock into the sea, where she was lost." *Life and Death of Mr. Alexander Peden*, p. 43, in vol. i. of *Walker's Biographia Presbyteriana*. See also *Howie's Biographia Presbyteriana*, p. 487.

riage became beggars, that the heinous crime might be visited to the third generation.[47]

To prosecute a minister, or even to assert one's rights against him before a civil tribunal, was not only a hazard, but a certain ruin. About the year 1665, James Fraser was sued in a court of law for a large sum of money, said to be due from his father's estate. As usually happens in these cases, the party sued, considered that he was unjustly treated, and that his opponent had no right to make the claim. So far, all was natural. But the peculiarity was, that Fraser, against whom the action was brought,

47. "He (Mr. Fordyce, in Aberdeen) tells me this following accompt, which he had from personall observation: When he lived near Frazerburge, in the North, there was a Minister setled there *jure devoluto,* the toun being biggotted against Presbytery to a pitch, and only two or three that had any seeming liking that way. After the Minister is setled, he expected much encouragment from one Ougstoun, I think his name was, who had professed much respect for him and that way. A while after, in some difficulty, the Minister came to him, and desired his countenance and assistance in the difficulty. He at first put the Minister off with delay; and within a litle plainly mocked him, and would doe nothing. The Minister came from him to my informer, who lived a litle from the place, and gave him ane account (of) what had befallen him, and said, 'I expected much from that man, and reaconed upon his help and assistance, in soe comfortless a setlement as I have ventured on; and he has not only disappointed me, but mocked me!' And the Minister was like to sink under the thoughts of this carriage; and after some silence, he said, very peremptorly, 'I am much mistaken, yea, I'le say it, God hath sent me, and spoken by me. God will visite that man, and something more than ordinary will befall him and his!' My informer was very much stunned and greived at such a peremptory declaration. However, it was accomplished, to my informer's personall knowledge. The man was a trader, who was very rich, worth near four or five thousand pounds sterling in stock. He had two sons and two daughters. Within some litle time, one of his sons turned distracted, and I think continoues soe still. The other son, in some distemper, turned silly, and litle better, and dyed. His daughters, one was maryed, and her husband lost all his stock at sea, twice or thrice; his good-father stocked him once or twice, and all was still lost, and they and their children are miserable. The other daughter fell into a distemper, wherein she lost her reason. The man himself, after that time, never throve; his means wasted away insensibly; and throu all things, he fell under melancholy, and turned silly, and dyed stupide. All this fell out in some feu years after what passed above; and my relator kneu all this particularly, and had occasion to be upon the man's bussiness and affairs." *Wodrow's Analecta,* vol. ii. pp. 175, 176. See also, in another work by this eminent Scotch divine, an account of what happened, when "a rash young man" having destroyed the property of a clergyman, named Boyd, "it was observed that that family did never thrive afterwards, but were in a decaying condition till they are reduced almost to nothing." *Wodrow's Collections upon the Lives and Ministers of the Church of Scotland,* vol. ii. part i. p. 215.

was a young man preparing for the ministry, and, therefore, under the immediate protection of Providence. Such an one was not to be vexed with impunity; and we are assured by Fraser himself, that God specially interposed to prevent his ruin; that one of his opponents was made unable to appear in court, and that the Lord, laying his hand upon the others, put them to death, in order that every obstacle might be at once removed.[48]

While stories of this sort were generally believed, it was but natural that an opinion should grow up that it was dangerous to meddle with a minister, or in any way to interfere with his conduct.[49] The clergy, intoxicated by the possession of power,

48. See Fraser's Life of Himself, in vol. ii. of *Select Biographies*, edited by the Rev. W. K. Tweedie. "Nothing now remained of all my father's great fortune but a small wadset of sixteen chalders, liferented likewise by my mother. And about the same time a new (though an unjust) adversary charges both her and me for 36,000 merks, and a reduction of our rights; so that our whole livelihood was either gone or at the stake. For four years did this adversary vex us, and was like to have undone us as to our temporal condition, had not the Lord prevented." p. 196. "I, ignorant what defences to make, had in my company a registrate horning, which I accidentally and without premeditation (God putting it in my mind at the same time) did cast in, by which he, being the king's rebel, was incapacitate from pursuing me. And the Lord so ordered it that he never after compeared to trouble me, by which means I was delivered from a loss and a fashery, and had but one court to wait upon." p: 202. "My condition during this time was a wrestling condition with the sons of Zeruiah that were too strong for me; little or no overcoming, yet violent wrestling." . . . . "For I humbled myself under the sense of the calamities of our family, and my own particular wants; I besought him to keep us from utter destruction. And the Lord was pleased to hear; *he destroyed by death my chief adversaries,* I found shifts to pay my many petty debts, gained our law-action, and was restored to some of my ancient possessions again." pp. 227, 228.

49. "So hazardous a thing it is to meddle with Christ's sent servants." *Life of Mr. William Guthrie, Minister at Fenwick,* by the Rev. William Dunlop, reprinted in *Select Biographies,* vol. ii. p. 62. To arrest a clergyman on a civil or criminal process, was an act full of danger, inasmuch as the Deity would hardly fail to avenge it. This applied even to the officers who executed the arrest, as well as to him by whom it was ordered. See, for instance, *Some Remarkable Passages of the Life and Death of Mr. John Semple, Minister of the Gospel,* p. 171 (in *Walker's Biographia Presbyteriana,* vol. i.). "Some time thereafter, he gat orders to apprehend Mr. Semple; he intreated to excuse him, for Mr. Semple was the minister and man he would not meddle with; for he was sure, if he did that, some terrible mischief would suddenly befal him. Mr. Arthur Coupar, who was Mr. Semple's precentor, told these passages to a Reverend Minister in the church, yet alive, worthy of all credit, who told me." Durham boasts that, "when Ministers have most to do, and *meet with most opposition,* God often furnisheth them accordingly with more boldness, gifts, and assistance than ordinary. Christ's witnesses are a terrible party; for as few

reached to such a pitch of arrogance, that they did not scruple to declare, that whoever respected Christ, was bound, on that very account, to respect them.[50] They denounced the judgments of God upon all who refused to hear the opinions they propounded in their pulpits.[51] Nor did this apply merely to persons who usually formed their audience. Such was their conceit, and so greedy were they after applause, that they would not allow even a stranger to remain in their parish, unless he, too, came to listen to what they chose to say.[52] Because they had adopted the Presby-

---

as these witnesses are, none of their opposits do gain at their hand; *whoever hurteth them shall in this manner be killed.* Though they be despicable in sackcloth, yet *better oppose a king in his strength, and giving orders from his throne covered in cloath of state, than them:* though they may burn some and imprison others, yet their opposers will pay sickerly for it. This is not because of any worth that is in them, or for their own sake; But 1. for His sake and for His authority that sendeth them. 2. for the event of their word, which will certainly come to passe, and that more terribly, and as certainly, as ever any temporall judgement was brought on by Moses or Elias." *Durham's Commentarie upon the Book of the Revelation,* p. 416.

50. "These who are trusted by Christ to be keepers of the vineyard, and his ministers, ought also to be respected by the people over whom they are set; and Christ allows this on them. Where Christ is respected and gets his due, there the keepers will be respected and get their due." *Durham's Exposition of the Song of Solomon,* pp. 450, 451. Fergusson complacently says, that to affront a clergyman by not believing his statement, or "message," as he terms it, is a "dishonour done to God." *Fergusson's Exposition of the Epistles of Paul,* p. 422.

51. "As it is true concerning vs, that necessitie lyeth vpon vs to preach, and woe will bee to vs if wee preach not; so it is true concerning you, that a necessitie lyeth vpon you to heare, and *woe will be to you if you heare not.*" *Cowper's Heaven Opened,* p. 156.

52. The following order was promulgated by the Kirk-Session of Aberdeen on the 12th July 1607. "The said day, inrespect it wes delatit to the sessioun that thair is sindrie landvart gentillmen and vtheris cum to this towne, quha mackis thair residence thairin, and resortis not to the preching nather on Saboth nor vlk dayes; thairfor, it is ordanit that thrie elderis of everie quarter convene with the ministrie in the sessioun hous, immediatlie efter the ending of the sermone on Tuysday nixt, and thair tak vp the names of the gentillmen and vtheris skipperis duelling in this burgh, quha kepis nocht the Kirk, nor resortis not to the hering of Godis word; and thair names being taken vp, ordains ane off the ministeris, with a baillie, to pas vnto thame and admoneis thame to cum to the preichingis, and keip the Kirk, vthervayes to remowe thame aff the towne." *Selections from the Records of the Kirk Session, Presbytery and Synod of Aberdeen,* p. 58. It was not enough to go occasionally to church; the attendance must be regular; otherwise the clergy were dissatisfied, and punished the delinquents. In the Presbytery Book of Strathbogie it is recorded that, on the 29th September 1649, "Mr. Johne Reidfurd being posed quhat diligence he had vsed to the Lady Frendraught, reported, shoe had hard three sermons, and so, as he thought, shoe intended to continow ane hearer. The bretheren, con-

terian polity, they asserted that the Almighty had never failed to punish every one who tried to supersede it;[53] and as this was the perfection of the church, those who were blind to its merits, were given over to wrath, and were, indeed, the slaves of Satan.[54] The clergy, who held this language respecting their opponents, exhausted the choicest epithets of praise on themselves, and on their own pursuits. When one of them got into the pulpit, or took a pen in his hand, he seemed as if he could not find words strong enough to express his sense of the surpassing importance of that class of

---

sidering her long continowed contumacie and delay of her process, by *heiring a sermon now and then,* thought not *that kind of heiring satisfactorie,* quherfor Mr. Robert Watson, and Mr. Robert Irving, ver ordained to goe with Mr. Johne Reidfurd, and requyre the said Lady to subscryv the Covenant, quherby shoe might testifie her conformitie vith the Kirk of Scotland, quhilk, if shoe refused, the said Mr. Johne vas ordained to pronunce the sentence of excommunicatioun against hir before the Provinciall Assemblie, as he vold be answerable therto." *Extracts from the Presbytery Book of Strathbogie,* p. 115. Neither distance, nor illness, might be pleaded as a valid excuse. Under no circumstances, would the preachers tolerate the affront of any one displaying an unwillingness to hear their sermons. In 1650, "compeired the Lord Oliphant, being summondit for not keeping his parish kirk of Abercherdour, vho declared his inabilitie of bodie many tymes, and the want of houses for accommodating him and his familie so farr distant from the same, vas the onlie caus, quhilk he promised to amend in tym comming. Mr. John Reidfurd ordained to report the same to the presbytrie, and vpon his continowed absence, to processe him." *Presbytery Book of Strathbogie,* p. 149. See more on this subject in *Registers of the Presbytery of Lanark,* pp. 5, 33, 67; *Minutes of the Presbyteries of St. Andrews and Cupar,* pp. 67, 68, 90, 153; *Minutes of the Synod of Fife,* pp. 18, 55, 132; and *Spalding's History of the Troubles,* vol. ii. p. 57. Spalding also mentions (p. 114) that at Aberdeen, in 1643, the clergy discoursed every Tuesday, Thursday, and Saturday, in the afternoon; on which occasions, "the people is compellit to attend their Lectureis, or then cryit out against."

53. "And it may be truly said, as the Church of Scotland hath had no detractors, but such as were ignorant of her, or mis-informed about her, or whom faction, partiality, prejudice, wickedness, or love of unlawful liberty did inspire; so no person or party hath endeavoured hithertil to root out Presbytery, but the Lord hath made it a burdensome stone unto them." *Naphtali,* sig. B 2 rev. "The Lord's wrath shall so meet his enemies in the teeth, wheresoever they turn, that they shall be forced to forsake their pursuing of the Church." *Dickson's Explication of the First Fifty Psalms,* p. 115.

54. "The true children of the Kirk are indeed the excellent ones of the earth, and princes indeed, wherever they live, in comparison of all other men who are but the beastly slaves of Satan." *Dickson's Explication of the First Fifty Psalms,* p. 312. Another high authority carefully identifies "the true religion" with "the true presbyterial profession." See *An Enquiry into Church Communion by Mr. Alexander Shields, Minister of the Gospel at Saint Andrews,* p. 126. His remark applies to the "Burgess-oaths."

which he was himself a member.[55] They alone knew the truth; they alone were able to inform and enlighten mankind. They had their instruction direct from heaven; they were, in fact, the ambassadors of Christ; from him they received their appointment; and since no one else could reward them, so no one else had a right to rule them.[56] As they were messengers sent by the Almighty, they were rightly termed angels, and it was the duty of the people to listen to their minister, as if he really were an angel who had descended upon earth.[57] His parishioners, therefore, were

55. Fergusson gives an ingenious turn to this, and says that it was their duty to praise their own profession, not for their own sake, but for the sake of others. "It is the duty of Christ's ministers to commend and magnify their office, not for gaining praise and esteem to themselves, 2 Cor. iii. 1, but that the malice of Satan and his instruments may be hereby frustrated, 2 Cor. xi. 12, who labours to bring that sacred calling into contempt; that so it may have the less of success upon people's hearts." *Fergusson's Exposition of the Epistles of Paul,* p. 180.

56. "Neither is there any mediate authoritie betweene the Lord and his ambassadours, in the affaires of their message; he only sendeth them; he alone gives them to be pastors and doctors, etc.; he alone shall judge them; he alone shall reward them; to him alone they must give an accompt of their dispensation; and he himselfe alone doth immediatlie rule them by his spirit and word." *Forbes' Certaine Records touching the Estate of the Kirk,* p. 435. In reference to these amazing pretensions, the Scotch clergy were constantly terming themselves the ambassadors of the Deity; thereby placing themselves infinitely above all other men. See, for instance, *Durham's Commentarie upon the Book of the Revelation,* pp. 86, 100, 160. *Durham's Law Unsealed,* pp. 85, 96. *Halyburton's Great Concern of Salvation,* p. 402. *Fergusson's Exposition of the Epistles of Paul,* pp. 77, 273. *Shields' Enquiry into Church Communion,* p. 72. *Binning's Sermons,* vol. ii. p. 118, vol. iii. p. 178. *Abernethy's Physicke for the Soule,* p. 122. *Monro's Sermons,* p. 207. *Gillespie's Aaron's Rod Blossoming,* pp. 240, 413. *Cowper's Heaven Opened,* p. 166. *Rutherford's Free Disputation against Pretended Liberty of Conscience,* p. 41. *Dickson's Truth's Victory over Error,* p. 274. *Gray's Great and Precious Promises,* pp. 50, 74. *Fleming's Fulfilling of the Scripture,* p. 429. *Cockburn's Jacob's Vow, or Man's Felicity and Duty,* p. 401. *Hutcheson's Exposition of the Book of Job,* pp. 461, 479.

57. "Ministers are called Angels, because they are God's Messengers, intrusted by Him with a high and heavenly imployment; and it is a title that should put Ministers in mind of their duty, to do God's will on earth as the Angels do it in heaven, in a spiritual and heavenly way, cheerfully, willingly and readily; and it *should put people in mind of their duty, to take this word off Ministers hands, as from Angels.*" *Durham's Commentarie upon the Book of the Revelation,* p. 496. "Therefore are Ministers called Angels, and Angels, Ministers." p. 596. Cockburn says that this is the reason why "we should behave ourselves decently and reverently" in church; "for if the presence of Kings overawe us, how much more should the presence of God and Angels." *Cockburn's Jacob's Vow, or Man's Felicity and Duty,* p. 356. Another Scotch divine asserts that he and his brethren are able to instruct the angels, and free them from their ignorance. See the audacious passage in *Fergusson's Exposition of*

bound, not only to acknowledge him and provide for him, but also to submit to him.[58] Indeed, no one could refuse obedience, who considered who the clergy were, and what functions they performed. Besides being ambassadors and angels, they were watchmen, who spied out every danger, and whose sleepless vigilance protected the faithful.[59] They were the joy and delight of the earth. They were musicians, singing the songs of sweetness; nay, they were sirens, who sought to allure men from the evil path, and save them from perishing.[60] They were chosen arrows,

---

the Epistles of Paul, p. 180: "*This may commend the ministers of the gospel not a little unto men,* and beget reverence in them towards the same, that even the blessed angels are in some sort bettered by it, and that it is therefore respected by them: for Paul commendeth his office from this, that by occasion thereof 'unto the principalities and powers, was made known the manifold wisdom of God.' Though angels be most knowing creatures, as enjoying the immediate sight and presence of God, Matt. xviii. 10, yet *they are ignorant of some things, which, by God's way of dispensing the Gospel to his church, they come to a more full knowledge off.*" After this, it is a slight matter to find Monro insisting that "the people should consider our character as the most difficult and most sacred." *Monro's Sermons,* p. 202.

58. "He is obliged to minister unto them in the gospel; and they are obliged to submit to him, strengthen him, acknowledge him, communicate to him in all good things, and to provide for him," &c. *Durham's Commentarie upon the Book of the Revelation,* p. 90. That the clergy are "rulers and governors," and that their business is "ruling and watching over the flock," is likewise affirmed in *Gillespie's Aaron's Rod Blossoming,* pp. 172, 313. Compare *The Correspondence of the Rev. Robert Wodrow,* vol. i. p. 181: "rule over the people and speak the word;" and *Rutherford's Free Disputation against Pretended Liberty of Conscience,* p. 41: "the commanding power in the Ambassadour of Christ." See also the "reverential estimation" inculcated in *Boston's Sermons,* p. 186.

59. "Called watchmen by a name borrowed from the practice of centinels in armies or cities." They are "Satan's greatest eye-sores." *Hutcheson's Exposition on the Minor Prophets,* vol. ii. p. 158, vol. iii. p. 208. "They being made watchmen, do thereby become the butt of Satan's malice." . . . . "The Enemy's principal design is sure to be against the watchman, because he prevents the surprising of his people by Satan, at least 'tis his business to do so." *Halyburton's Great Concern of Salvation,* p. 24. Compare *Guthrie's Considerations contributing unto the Discovery of the Dangers that threaten Religion,* p. 259; *Fergusson's Exposition of the Epistles of Paul,* pp. 97, 106; *Durham's Exposition of the Song of Solomon,* pp. 278, 443; and *Wodrow's Correspondence,* vol. i. pp. 84, 244.

60. One of the most popular of the Scotch preachers in the seventeenth century, actually ranks himself, in this respect, as doing the same work as the Son of God. "Christ and his ministers are the musicians that do apply their songs to catch men's ears and hearts, if so be they may stop their course and not perish. These are blessed syrens that do so." *Binning's Sermons,* vol. iii. p. 265.

stored up in the quiver of God.[61] They were burning lights and shining torches. Without them darkness would prevail; but their presence illumined the world, and made things clear.[62] Hence they were called stars, which title also expressed the eminence of their office, and its superiority over all others.[63] To make this still more apparent, prodigies were vouchsafed, and strange lights might occasionally be seen, which, hovering round the form of the minister, confirmed his supernatural mission.[64] The profane wished to jest at these things, but they were too notorious to be denied; and there was a well-known case, in which, at the death of a clergyman, a star was miraculously exhibited in the firmament, and was seen by many persons, although it was then mid day.[65]

Nor was this to be regarded as a solitary occurrence. On the

61. Rutherford terms himself, "a chosen arrow hid in his quiver." *Howie's Biographia Scoticana,* p. 230. To read the coarse materialism contained in this and other extracts, will, I know, shock, and so far offend, many pure and refined minds, whose feelings I would not needlessly wound. But no one can understand the history of the Scotch intellect, who refuses to enter into these matters; and it is for the reader to choose whether or not he will remain ignorant of what I, as an historian, am bound to disclose. His remedy is easy. He has only either to shut the book, or else to pass on at once to the next chapter.

62. "The Lord calleth men to be preachers, and hath them in his hand as starres, holding them out sometime to one part of the world, and sometime to another, that we may communicate light to them that are sitting in darkness." *Cowper's Heaven Opened,* p. 360.

63. "Ministers are called Stars, for these reasons: I. To signifie and point out the eminence and dignity of the office, that it is a glorious and shineing office. II. To point out what is the especiall end of this office; It is to give light: as the use of Stars is to give light to the world; so it's Ministers main imployment to shine and give light to others; to make the world, which is a dark night, to be lightsome." *Durham's Commentarie upon the Book of the Revelation,* p. 43. See also pp. 151, 368; and *Dickson's Truth's Victory over Error,* p. 176.

64. The Rev. James Kirkton says of the Rev. John Welsh, that some one who observed him walking, "saw clearly a strange light surround him, and heard him speak strange words about his spiritual joy." *Select Biographies,* edited by the Rev. W. K. Tweedie, vol. i. p. 12. But more than this remains to be told. The hearts of the Scotch clergy were so lifted up with pride, that they believed —horrible to relate—that they had audible and verbal communications from the Almighty God, which bystanders could hear. One of these stories, relating also to Welsh, will be found, as tradition handed it down, in *Howie's Biographia Scoticana,* p. 148. I cannot quote such blasphemy; and those who doubt my statement had better refer to the second edition of Howie's work, published at Glasgow in 1781. It may probably be met with in the British Museum.

65. "Mr. Johne M'Birnie at Aberdeen, (but first at the South Ferrie, over aganis the Castell of Broughtie,) a most zealous and painfull pastor, a great opposer of hierarchie. He was a shyning torch and a burning starre; wherefore the Lord miraculouslie made, at his death, a starre to appeare in heaven at the

contrary, it usually happened, that when a Scotch minister departed from this life, the event was accompanied by portents, in
order that the people might understand that something terrible
was going on, and that they were incurring a serious, perhaps an
irretrievable, loss. Sometimes the candles would be mysteriously
extinguished, without any wind, and without any one touching
them.[66] Sometimes, even when the clergyman was preaching, the
supernatural appearance of an animal would announce his approaching end in face of the congregation, who might vainly
mourn what they were unable to avert.[67] Sometimes the body of
the holy man would remain for years unchanged and undecayed;
death not having the power over it which it would have had over
the corpse of a common person.[68] On other occasions, notice was
given to him of his death, years before it occurred;[69] and, to strike
greater awe into the public mind, it was remarked, that when one

---

noone-tyde of the day; whilk many yet alive testifies that they did evidentlie see
it, (at Whitsunday 1609)." *Row's History of the Kirk of Scotland*, p. 421.

66. Mr. James Stirling, minister of Barony, Glasgow, writes respecting his
father, Mr. John Stirling, minister at Kilbarchan, that the "day he was burryed
ther wer two great candles burning in the chamber, and they did go out most
surprisingly without any wind causing them to go out." *Analecta, or Materials
for a History of Remarkable Providences,* by the Rev. Robert Wodrow, vol. iii.
p. 37.

67. "This night, Glanderston told me, that it was reported for a truth at
Burroustoness, that about six weeks since Mr. David Williamson was preaching
in his own church in Edinburgh, and in the middle of the sermon, a ratton came
and sat doun on his Bible. This made him stope; and after a little pause, he told
the congregation that this was a message of God to him, and broke off his
sermon, and took a formall fareweel of his people, and went home, and continoues sick." *Wodrow's Analecta,* vol. i. p. 12.

68. "The same person" (*i.e.* the Rev. Mr. White) "adds, that some years
ago, when Mr. Bruce's grave was opened, to lay in his grandchild, his body was
almost fresh and uncorrupted, to the great wonder of many; and if I right remember, the grave was again filled up, and another made. The fresh body had
no noisome smell. It was then nearly eighty years after he was buried. My informer was minister of Larbert when this happened." *Wodrow's Life of Bruce,*
p. 150, prefixed to *Bruce's Sermons.*

69. "He" (John Lockhart) "tells me Mr. Robert Paton, minister at Barn-
weel, his father-in-lau, had a particular for-notice, seven or eight years before,
of his death: That he signifyed so much to my informer." . . . "When my informer came, he did not apprehend any hazard, and signifyed so much to his
father-in-lau, Mr. Paton. He answered, 'John, John, I am to dye at this time;
and this is the time God warned me of, as I told you.' In eight or ten dayes he
dyed. Mr. Paton was a man very much (beloved) and mighty in prayer." *Wodrow's Analecta,* vol. iii. p. 451. Compare the case of Henderson (in *Wodrow's
Correspondence,* vol. iii. p. 33), where the notice was much shorter, but "all
fell out as he had foretold."

minister died, others were taken away at the same time, so that, the bereavement being more widely felt, men might, by the magnitude of the shock, be rendered sensible of the inestimable value of those preachers whose lives were happily spared.[70]

It was, moreover, generally understood, that a minister, during his abode in this world, was miraculously watched over and protected. He was peculiarly favoured by angels, who, though they did good offices to all members of the true church, were especially kind to the clergy;[71] and it was well known, that the celebrated Rutherford, when only four years old, having fallen into a well, was pulled out by an angel, who came there for the purpose of saving his life.[72] Another clergyman, who was in the habit of oversleeping himself, used to be roused to his duty in the morning, by three mysterious knocks at his door, which, if they did not produce a proper effect, were repeated close to his bed. These knocks never failed on Sunday, and on days when he had to administer the communion; and they lasted during the whole of his ministry; until he became old and infirm, when they entirely ceased.[73]

70. "Generally, I observe that Ministers' deaths are not single, but severall of them together." *Wodrow's Analecta,* vol. iii. p. 275.

71. The Rev. William Row (in his *Continuation of Blair's Autobiography,* p. 153) says, "Without all doubt, though it cannot be proven from Scripture, that every one has a tutelar angel, yet it is certain that the good angels do many good offices to the people of God, *especially to his ministers and ambassadors,* which we do not see, and do not remark or know."

72. "Mr. James Stirling, and Mr. Robert Muir, and severall others in the company, agreed on this account of Mr. Rutherford. When about four years old, he was playing about his father's house, and a sister of his, somewhat older than he, with him. Mr. Rutherford fell into a well severall fathoms deep, and not full, but faced about with heuen stone, soe that it was not possible for any body to get up almost, far less a child. When he fell in, his sister ran into the house near by, and told that Samuell was fallen into the well; upon which his father and mother ran out, and found him sitting on the grasse beside the well; and when they asked him, Hou he gote out? he said, after he was once at the bottome, he came up to the tope, and ther was a bonny young man pulled him out by the hand. Ther was noe body near by at the time; and soe they concluded it was noe doubt ane angell. The Lord had much to doe with him." *Wodrow's Analecta,* vol. i. p. 57. See also vol. iii. p. 88, 89, where this circumstance is again mentioned as "a tradition anent him" in the place of his birth.

73. "Mr. William Trail, minister at ****, tells me that his father, Mr. William Trail, minister at Borthwick, used every morning, when he had publick work on his hand, to hear three knocks at his chamber dore; and if, throu wearynes, or heaviness, he did sitt these, ther wer ordinarily three knocks at his bed-head, which he never durst sitt, butt gott up to his work. This was ordinarily about three in the morning. This, at first, in his youth, frighted him; but at

By the propagation of these and similar stories, in a country already prepared for their reception, the Scotch mind became imbued with a belief in miraculous interposition, to an extent which would be utterly incredible if it were not attested by a host of contemporary and unimpeachable witnesses. The clergy, partly because they shared in the general delusion, and partly because they derived benefit from it, did every thing they could to increase the superstition of their countrymen, and to familiarize them with notions of the supernatural world, such as can only be paralleled in the monastic legends of the middle ages.[74] How they laboured to corrupt the national intellect, and how successful they were in that base vocation, has been hitherto known to no modern reader; because no one has had the patience to peruse their interminable discourses, commentaries, and the other religious literature in which their sentiments are preserved. As, however, the preachers were, in Scotland, more influential than all other classes put together, it is only by comparing their statements with what is to be found in the general memoirs and correspondence of the time,

---

lenth it turned easy to him, and he believed these knocks and awaknings proceeded from a good art. That these never failed him on Sabbaths and at Communions, when he was oblidged to rise early: That when he turned old and infirm, toward the close of his dayes, they intirely ceased and left him." *Wodrow's Analecta,* vol. ii. p. 307. This work, in four quarto volumes, is invaluable for the history of the Scotch mind; being a vast repertory of the opinions and traditions of the clergy, during the seventeenth, and early part of the eighteenth, century. Wodrow was a man of ability, certainly above the average; his honesty is unimpeachable, as the jealous scrutiny which the episcopalians have made of his great work on the History of the Church of Scotland, decisively proves; and he was in the constant habit of personal and epistolary communication with the leading characters of his age. I have, therefore, freely used his *Analecta;* also his *Collections upon the Lives of Ministers,* which is likewise in four quarto volumes; and his *Correspondence,* in three thick octavo volumes. It would be difficult to find a more competent witness respecting the sentiments of his ecclesiastical brethren. It would be impossible to find a more candid one.

74. In illustration of this, a volume might be filled with extracts from the writings of the Scotch divines of the seventeenth century. The following passage is, perhaps, as good as any. "Yea, it can hardly be instanced any great change, or revolution in the earth, which hath not had some such extraordinary herald going before. Can the world deny how sometimes these prodigious signes have been shaped out to point at the very nature of the stroke then imminent, by a strange resemblance to the same, such as a flaming sword in the air, the appearance of armies fighting even sometimes upon the earth, to the view of many most sober and judicious onlookers, also showers of blood, the noise of drummes, and such like, which are known usually to go before warr and commotions." *Fleming's Fulfilling of the Scripture,* 1681, p. 216.

that we can at all succeed in re-constructing the history of a period, which, to the philosophic student of the human mind, is full of great, though melancholy, interest. I shall, therefore, make no apology for entering into still further details respecting these matters; and I hope to put the reader in possession of such facts as will connect the past history of Scotland with its present state, and will enable him to understand why it is, that so great a people are, in many respects, still struggling in darkness, simply because they still live under the shadow of that long and terrible night, which, for more than a century, covered the land. It will also appear, that their hardness and moroseness of character, their want of gaiety, and their indifference to many of the enjoyments of life, are traceable to the same cause, and are the natural product of the gloomy and ascetic opinions inculcated by their religious teachers. For, in that age, as in every other, the clergy, once possessed of power, showed themselves harsh and unfeeling masters. They kept the people in a worse than Egyptian bondage, inasmuch as they enslaved mind as well as body, and not only deprived men of innocent amusements, but taught them that those amusements were sinful. And so thoroughly did they do their work, that, though a hundred and fifty years have elapsed since their supremacy began to wane, the imprint of their hands is every where discernible. The people still bear the marks of the lash; the memory of their former servitude lives among them; and they crouch before their clergy, as they did of old, abandoning their rights, sacrificing their independence, and yielding up their consciences, to the dictates of an intolerant and ambitious priesthood.

Of all the means of intimidation employed by the Scotch clergy, none was more efficacious than the doctrines they propounded respecting evil spirits and future punishment. On these subjects, they constantly uttered the most appalling threats. The language, which they used, was calculated to madden men with fear, and to drive them to the depths of despair. That it often had this consequence, and produced most fatal results, we shall presently see. And, what made it more effectual was, that it completely harmonized with those other gloomy and ascetic notions which the clergy inculcated, and according to which, pleasures being regarded as sinful, sufferings were regarded as religious. Hence that love of inflicting pain, and that delight in horrible and revolting ideas, which characterized the Scotch mind during the seventeenth century. A few specimens of the prevailing opinions will enable the reader to understand the temper of the time, and to appreciate the resources which the Scotch clergy could wield, and the materials with which they built up the fabric of their power.

It was generally believed, that the world was overrun by evil spirits, who not only went up and down the earth, but also lived in the air, and whose business it was to tempt and hurt mankind.[75] Their number was infinite, and they were to be found at all places and in all seasons. At their head was Satan himself, whose delight it was to appear in person, ensnaring or terrifying every one he met.[76] With this object, he assumed various forms. One day, he would visit the earth as a black dog;[77] on another day, as a

75. Durham, after mentioning "old abbacies or monasteries, or castles when walls stand and none dwelleth in them," adds, "If it be asked, If there be such a thing, as the haunting of evill spirits in these desolate places? We answer 1. That there are evill spirits rangeing up and down through the earth is certain, even though hell be their prison properly, yet have they a sort of dominion and abode both in the earth and air; partly, as a piece of their curse, this is laid on them to wander; partly as their exercise to tempt men, or bring spirituall or temporall hurt to them," &c. *Durham's Commentarie upon the Book of the Revelation*, p. 582. So, too, Hutcheson (*Exposition of the Book of Job*, p. 9): "We should remember that we sojourn in a world where Devils are, and do haunt among us;" and Fleming (*Fulfilling of the Scripture*, p. 217): "But the truth itself is sure, that such a party is at this day, encompassing the earth, and trafficking up and down there, to prove which by arguments were to light a candle to let men see that it is day, while it is known what *ordinary familiar converse many have therewith*." One of their favourite abodes was the Shetland Islands, where, in the middle of the seventeenth century, "almost every family had a Brouny or evil spirit so called." See the account given by the Rev. John Brand, in his work entitled *A Brief Description of Orkney, Zetland, Pightland-Firth and Caithness*, pp. 111, 112, Edinburgh, 1701.

76. "There is not one whom he assaulteth not." *Abernethy's Physicke for the Soule*, p. 101. "On the right hand and on the left." *Cowper's Heaven Opened*, p. 273. Even early in the eighteenth century, the "most popular divines" in Scotland, affirmed that Satan "frequently appears clothed in a corporeal substance." *Memoirs of Charles Lee Lewes, written by Himself*, vol. iii. pp. 29, 30, London, 1805.

77. "This night James Lochheid told me, that last year, if I mistake not, at the Communion of Bafron, he was much helped all day. At night, when dark somewhat, he went out to the feilds to pray; and a terrible slavish fear came on him, that he almost lost his senses. Houever, he resolved to goe on to his duty. By (the time) he was at the place, his fear was off him; and lying on a knou-side, a black dogg came to his head and stood. He said he kneu it to be Satan, and shooke his hand, but found nothing, it evanishing." . . . . "Lord help

raven;[78] on another, he would be heard in the distance, roaring like a bull.[79] He appeared sometimes as a white man in black clothes;[80] and sometimes he came as a black man in black clothes, when it was remarked that his voice was ghastly, that he wore no shoes, and that one of his feet was cloven.[81] His stratagems were endless. For, in the opinion of divines, his cunning increased with his age; and having been studying for more than five thousand years, he had now attained to unexampled dexterity.[82] He

---

against his devices, and strenthen against them!" *Wodrow's Analecta*, vol. i. p. 24. The *Registers of the Presbytery of Lanark*, p. 77, contain a declaration, in 1650, that "the devill appeared like a little whelpe," and afterwards, "like a brown whelpe."

78. The celebrated Peden was present when "there came down the appearance of a raven, and sat upon one man's head." . . . . Thereupon, "going home, Mr. Peden said to his land-lord, I always thought there was Devilry among you, but I never thought that he did appear visibly among you, till now I have seen it. O, for the Lord's sake quit this way." *The Life and Death of Mr. Alexander Peden, late Minister of the Gospel at New Glenluce in Galloway*, pp. 111, 112, in vol. i. of *Walker's Biographia Presbyteriana*.

79. "I heard a voice just before me on the other side of the hedge, and it seemed to be like the groaning of an aged man. It continued so some time. I knew no man could be there; for, on the other side of the hedge, where I heard the groaning, there was a great stank or pool. I nothing doubted but it was Satan, and I guessed his design; but still I went on to beg the child's life. At length he roared and made a noise like a bull, and that very loud. From all this I concluded, that I had been provoking God some way or other in the duty, and that he was angry with me, and had let the enemy loose on me, and might give him leave to tear me in pieces. This made me intreat of God, to shew me wherefore he contended, and begged he would rebuke Satan. The enemy continued to make a noise like a bull, and seemed to be coming about the hedge towards the door of the summer-seat, bellowing as he came along." *Stevenson's Rare, Soul-Strengthening, and Comforting Cordial for Old and Young Christians*, p. 29. This book was published, and prepared for the press, by the Rev. William Cupples. See Mr. Cupples' letter at the beginning.

80. In 1684, with "black cloaths, and a blue band, and white handcuffs." *Sinclair's Satan's Invisible World Discovered*, p. 8.

81. "He observed one of the black man's feet to be cloven, and that the black man's apparel was black, and that he had a blue band about his neck, and white hand-cuffs, and that he had hoggers upon his legs without shoes; and that the black man's voice was hollow and ghastly." *Satan's Invisible World Discovered*, p. 9. "The devil appeared in the shape of a black man." p. 31. See also *Brand's Description of Orkney*, p. 126: "all in black."

82. "The acquired knowledge of the Devill is great, hee being an advancing student, and still learning now above five thousand yeares." *Rutherford's Christ Dying and Drawing Sinners to Himselfe*, p. 204. "He knowes very well, partly by the quicknesse of his nature, and partly by long experience, being now very neere six thousand yeeres old." *Cowper's Heaven Opened*, p. 219. "Hee, being compared with vs, hath many vantages; as that he is more subtill in nature, being of greater experience, and more ancient, being now almost six thousand

could, and he did, seize both men and women, and carry them away through the air.[83] Usually, he wore the garb of laymen, but it was said, that, on more than one occasion, he had impudently attired himself as a minister of the gospel.[84] At all events, in one dress or other, he frequently appeared to the clergy, and tried to coax them over to his side.[85] In that, of course, he failed; but,

---

yeeres old." *Ibid.*, p. 403. "The diuell here is both diligent and cunning, and (now almost of sixe thousand yeeres) of great experience." *Abernethy's Physicke for the Soule*, p. 142. "Satan, such an ingenious and experimented spirit." *Binning's Sermons*, vol. i. p. 67. "His great sleight and cunning." *Ibid.*, p. 110. Other eulogies of his skill may be seen in *Fergusson's Exposition of the Epistles of Paul*, p. 475; and in *Fleming's Fulfilling of the Scripture*, p. 45. A "minister," whose name is not mentioned, states that he is "of an excellent substance, of great natural parts, long experience, and deep understanding." *Sinclair's Satan's Invisible World Discovered*, p. 78.

83. In Professor Sinclair's work (*Satan's Invisible World Discovered*, p. 141), we find, in 1684, "an evident instance, that the devil can transport the bodies of men and women through the air. It is true, he did not carry her far off, but not for want of skill and power." Late in the seventeenth century, it was generally believed that one of Satan's accomplices was literally "strangled in his chair by the devil, least he should make a confession to the detriment of the service." *Crawfurd's History of the Shire of Renfrew,* part iii. p. 319.

84. See the account of a young preacher being deceived in this way, in *Wodrow's Analecta*, vol. i. pp. 103, 104. The Rev. Robert Blair detected the cheat, and "with ane awful seriousness appearing in his countenance, began to tell the youth his hazard, and that the man whom he took for a Minister was the Divel, who had trepanned him, and brought him into his net; advised him to be earnest with God in prayer, and likewise not to give way to dispair, for ther was yet hope." The preacher had, on this occasion, been so far duped as to give the devil "a written promise" to do whatever he was requested. As soon as the Rev. Mr. Blair ascertained this fact, he took the young man before the Presbytery, and narrated the circumstance to the members. "They were all strangely affected with it, and resolved unanimously to dispatch the Presbitry business presently, and to stay all night in town, and on the morrow to meet for prayer in one of the most retired churches of the Presbitry, acquainting none with their business, (but) taking the youth alongst with them, whom they keeped alwise close by them. Which was done, and after the Ministers had prayed all of them round, except Mr. Blair, who prayed last, in time of his prayer there came a violent rushing of wind upon the church, so great that they thought the church should have fallen down about their ears, and with that the youth's paper and covenant" (*i.e.* the covenant which he had signed at the request of Satan) "droops down from the roof of the church among the Ministers."

85. "The devil strikes at them, that in them he may strike at the whole congregation." *Boston's Sermons*, p. 186. Fleming (*Fulfilling of the Scripture,* p. 379) gives an account of his appearing to one of the Scotch clergy. Compare *Wodrow's Analecta*, vol. iv. p. 110. In 1624, Bruce writes, "I heard his voice as vively as ever I heard any thing, not being sleeping, but waking." *Life of Bruce*, p. 8, prefixed to *Bruce's Sermons*. The only remedy was immediate resistance. "It is the duty of called ministers to go on with courage in the work of

out of the ministry, few, indeed, could withstand him. He could raise storms and tempests; he could work, not only on the mind, but also on the organs of the body, making men hear and see whatever he chose.[86] Of his victims, some he prompted to commit suicide,[87] others to commit murder.[88] Still, formidable as he was, no Christian was considered to have attained to a full religious experience, unless had literally seen him, talked to him, and fought with him.[89] The clergy were constantly preaching about

the Lord, notwithstanding of any discouragement of that kind, receiving manfully the first onset chiefly of Satan's fury, as knowing their ceding to him will make him more cruel." *Fergusson's Exposition of the Epistles of Paul,* p. 74. In the seventeenth century, the Scotch clergy often complimented each other on having baffled him, and thereby put him in a passion. Thus, in 1626, Dickson writes to Boyd: "The devil is mad against you, he fears his kingdom." *Life of Robert Boyd,* in *Wodrow's Collections upon the Lives of Ministers,* vol. ii. part i. p. 238. See also pp. 165, 236.

86. "He can delude ears, eyes, &c., either by misrepresenting external objects, or by inward disturbing of the faculties and organes, whereby men and women may, and do often, apprehend that they hear, see, &c. such and such things, which, indeed, they do not." *Durham's Commentarie upon the Book of the Revelation,* p. 128. "Raise tempests." *Binning's Sermons,* vol. i. p. 122. "His power and might, whereby through God's permission, he doth raise up storms, commove the elements, destroy cattle," &c. *Fergusson's Exposition of the Epistles of Paul,* p. 264. "Hee can work curiously and strongly on the walls of bodily organs, on the shop that the understanding soule lodgeth in, and on the necessary tooles, organs, and powers of fancie, imagination, memory, humours, senses, spirits, bloud," &c. *Rutherford's Christ Dying,* p. 212. Semple, giving notice of his intention to administer the sacrament, told the congregation "that the Devil would be so envious about the good work they were to go about, that he was afraid he would be permitted to raise a storm in the air with a speat of rain, to raise the waters, designing to drown some of them; but it will not be within the compass of his power to drown any of you, no not so much as a dog." *Remarkable Passages of the Life and Death of Mr. John Semple, Minister of the Gospel,* pp. 168, 169, in vol. i. of *Walker's Biographia Presbyteriana.*

87. *Sinclair's Satan's Invisible World Discovered,* p. 137. *Memoirs of the Life and Experiences of Marion Laird of Greenock, with a Preface by the Rev. Mr. Cock,* pp. 43, 44, 45, 84, 172, 222, 223.

88. "I shall next show how the murderer Satan visibly appeared to a wicked man, stirred him up to stab me, and how mercifully I was delivered therefrom." *The Autobiography of Mr. Robert Blair, Minister of St. Andrews,* p. 65. See also *Fleming's Fulfilling of the Scripture,* pp. 379, 380.

89. "One Mr. Thomas Hogg, a very popular presbyterian preacher in the North, asked a person of great learning, in a religious conference, whether or not he had seen the Devil? It was answered him, 'That he had never seen him in any visible appearance.' 'Then, I assure you,' saith Mr. Hogg, 'that you can never be happy till you see him in that manner; that is, untill you have both a personal converse and combat with him.' " *Scotch Presbyterian Eloquence,* pp. 28, 29.

him, and preparing their audience for an interview with their great enemy. The consequence was, that the people became almost crazed with fear. Whenever the preacher mentioned Satan, the consternation was so great, that the church resounded with sighs and groans.[90] The aspect of a Scotch congregation in those days, is, indeed, hard for us to conceive. Not unfrequently the people, benumbed and stupefied with awe, were rooted to their seats by the horrible fascination exercised over them, which compelled them to listen, though they are described as gasping for breath, and with their hair standing on end.[91] Such impressions were not easily effaced. Images of terror were left on the mind, and followed the people to their homes, and in their daily pursuits. They believed that the devil was always, and literally, at hand; that he was haunting them, speaking to them, and tempting them. There was no escape. Go where they would, he was there. A sudden noise, nay, even the sight of an inanimate object, such as a stone, was capable of reviving the association of ideas, and of bringing back to the memory the language uttered from the pulpit.[92]

Nor is it strange that this should be the case. All over Scotland, the sermons were, with hardly an exception, formed after the same plan, and directed to the same end. To excite fear, was the

90. "Ye go to the kirk, and when ye hear the devil or hell named in the preaching, ye sigh and make a noise." *The Last and Heavenly Speeches of John, Viscount Kenmure,* in *Select Biographies,* vol. i. p. 405.

91. Andrew Gray, who died in 1656, used such language, "that his contemporary, the foresaid Mr. Durham, observed, That many times he caused the very hairs of their head to stand up." *Howie's Biographia Scoticana,* p. 217. James Hutcheson boasted of this sort of success. "As he expressed it, 'I was not a quarter of ane hour in upon it, till I sau a dozen of them all gasping before me.' He preached with great freedome *all day,* and fourteen or twenty dated their conversion from that sermon." *Wodrow's Analecta,* vol. i. p. 131. When Dickson preached, "many were so choaked and taken by the heart, that through terrour, the spirit in such a measure convincing them of sin, in hearing of the word they have been made to fall over, and thus carried out of the church." *Fleming's Fulfilling of the Scripture,* p. 347. There was hardly any kind of resource which these men disdained. Alexander Dunlop "entered into the ministry at Paislay, about the year 1643 or 1644." . . . . "He used in the pulpit, to have a kind of a groan at the end of some sentences. Mr. Peebles called it a holy groan." *Wodrow's Analecta,* vol. iii. pp. 16, 21.

92. A schoolmaster, recording his religious experiences (*Wodrow's Analecta,* vol. i. p. 246), says: "If any thing had given a knock, I would start and shiver, the seeing of a dogg made me affrayed, the seeing of a stone in the feild made me affrayed, and as I thought a voice in my head saying, 'It's Satan.'"

paramount object.[93] The clergy boasted, that it was their special mission to thunder out the wrath and curses of the Lord.[94] In their eyes, the Deity was not a beneficent being, but a cruel and remorseless tyrant. They declared that all mankind, a very small portion only excepted, were doomed to eternal misery. And when they came to describe what that misery was, their dark imaginations revelled and gloated at the prospect. In the pictures which they drew, they reproduced and heightened the barbarous imagery of a barbarous age. They delighted in telling their hearers, that they would be roasted in great fires, and hung up by their tongues.[95] They were to be lashed with scorpions, and see their

93. Only those who are extensively read in the theological literature of that time, can form an idea of this, its almost universal tendency. During about a hundred and twenty years, the Scotch pulpits resounded with the most frightful denunciations. The sins of the people, the vengeance of God, the activity of Satan, and the pains of hell, were the leading topics. In this world, calamities of every kind were announced as inevitable; they were immediately at hand; that generation, perhaps that year, should not pass away without the worst evils which could be conceived, falling on the whole country. I will merely quote the opening of a sermon which is now lying before me, and which was preached, in 1682, by no less a man than Alexander Peden. "There is three or four things that I have to tell you this day; and the first is this, A bloody sword, a bloody sword, a bloody sword, for thee, O Scotland, that shall reach the most part of you to the very heart. And the second is this, Many a mile shall ye travel in thee, O Scotland! and shall see nothing but waste places. The third is this, The most fertile places in thee, O Scotland! shall be waste as the mountain tops. And fourthly, The women with child in thee, O Scotland shall be dashed in pieces. And fifthly, There hath been many conventicles in thee, O Scotland! but ere it be long, God shall have a conventicle in thee, that shall make thee Scotland tremble. Many a preaching hath God wared on thee, O Scotland! but ere it be long God's judgments shall be as frequent in Scotland as these precious meetings, wherein he sent forth his faithful servants to give faithful warning in his name of their hazard in apostatizing from God, and in breaking all his noble vows. God sent out a Welsh, a Cameron, a Cargill, and a Semple to preach to thee; but ere long God shall preach to thee by a bloody sword." *Sermons by Eminent Divines,* pp. 47, 48.

94. To "thunder out the Lord's wrath and curse." *Durham's Commentarie upon the Book of the Revelation,* p. 191. "It is the duty of Ministers to preach judgments." *Hutcheson's Exposition on the Minor Prophets,* vol. i. p. 93. "If ministers when they threaten be not the more serious and fervent, the most terrible threatening will but little affect the most part of hearers." *Fergusson's Exposition of the Epistles of Paul,* p. 421.

95. The clergy were not ashamed to propagate a story of a boy who, in a trance, had been mysteriously conveyed to hell, and thence permitted to revisit the earth. His account, which is carefully preserved by the Rev. Robert Wodrow (*Analecta,* vol. i. p. 51) was, that "ther wer great fires and men roasted in them, and then cast into rivers of cold water, and then into boyling water; others hung up by the tongue."

companions writhing and howling around them.[96] They were to be thrown into boiling oil and scalding lead.[97] A river of fire and brimstone, broader than the earth, was prepared for them;[98] in that, they were to be immersed; their bones, their lungs, and their liver, were to boil, but never be consumed.[99] At the same time, worms were to prey upon them; and while these were gnawing at their bodies, they were to be surrounded by devils, mocking and making pastime of their pains.[100] Such were the first stages of suffering, and they were only the first. For the torture, besides being unceasing, was to become gradually worse. So refined was the cruelty, that one hell was succeeded by another; and, lest the sufferer should grow callous, he was, after a time, moved on, that he might undergo fresh agonies in fresh places, provision being made that the torment should not pall on the sense, but should be varied in its character, as well as eternal in its duration.[101]

All this was the work of the God of the Scotch clergy.[102] It

96. "Scortched in hell-fire and hear the howling of their fellow-prisoners, and see the ugly devils, the bloody scorpions with which Satan lasheth miserable soules." *Rutherford's Christ Dying*, pp. 491, 492.

97. "Boiling oil, burning brimstone, scalding lead." *Sermons by Eminent Divines*, p. 362.

98. "A river of fire and brimstone broader than the earth." *Rutherford's Religious Letters*, p. 35. "See the poor wretches lying in bundles, boiling eternally in that stream of brimstone." *Halyburton's Great Concern of Salvation*, p. 53.

99. "Tongue, lungs, and liver, bones and all, shall boil and fry in a torturing fire." *Rutherford's Religious Letters*, p. 17. "They will be universal torments, every part of the creature being tormented in that flame. When one is cast into a fiery furnace, the fire makes its way into the very bowels, and leaves no member untouched: what part then can have ease, when the damned swim in a lake of fire burning with brimstone?" *Boston's Human Nature in its Fourfold State*, p. 458.

100. "While wormes are sporting with thy bones, the devils shall make pastime of thy paines." *Abernethy's Physicke for the Soule*, p. 97. "They will have the society of devils in their torments, being shut up with them in hell." *Boston's Human Nature in its Four-fold State*, p. 442. "Their ears filled with frightful yellings of the infernal crew." *Ibid.*, p. 460.

101. This fundamental doctrine of the Scotch divines is tersely summed up in *Binning's Sermons*, vol. iii. p. 130: "You shall go out of one hell into a worse; eternity is the measure of its continuance, and the degrees of itself are answerable to its duration." The author of these sermons died in 1653.

102. And, according to them, the barbarous cruelty was the natural result of His Omniscience. It is with pain, that I transcribe the following impious passage. "Consider, Who is the contriver of these torments. There have been some very exquisite torments contrived by the wit of men, the naming of which, if ye understood their nature, were enough to fill your hearts with horror; but *all these fall as far short of the torments ye are to endure, as the wisdom of man*

was not only his work, it was his joy and his pride. For, according to them, hell was created before man came into the world; the Almighty, they did not scruple to say, having spent his previous leisure in preparing and completing this place of torture, so that, when the human race appeared, it might be ready for their reception.[103] Ample, however, as the arrangements were, they were insufficient; and hell, not being big enough to contain the countless victims incessantly poured into it, had, in these latter days, been enlarged.[104] There was now sufficient room. But in that vast expanse there was no void, for the whole of it reverberated with the shrieks and yells of undying agony.[105] They rent the air with horrid sound, and, amid their pauses, other scenes occurred, if possible, still more excruciating. Loud reproaches filled the ear: children reproaching their parents, and servants reproaching their masters. Then, indeed, terror was rife, and abounded on every side. For, while the child cursed his father, the father, consumed by remorse, felt his own guilt; and both children and fathers made hell echo with their piercing screams, writhing in convulsive agony at the torments which they suffered, and knowing that other torments more grievous still were reserved for them.[106]

---

falls short of that of God." . . . *"Infinite wisdom has contrived that evil." The Great Concern of Salvation, by the late Reverend Mr. Thomas Halyburton,* edit. Edinburgh, 1722, p. 154.

103. "Men wonder what he could be doing all that time, if we may call it time which hath no beginning, and how he was employed." . . . "Remember that which a godly man answered some wanton curious wit, who, in scorn, demanded the same of him—'He was preparing hell for curious and proud fools,' said he." *Binning's Sermons,* vol. i. p. 194.

104. "Hell hath inlarged itselfe." *Abernethy's Physicke for the Soule,* p. 146.

105. "Eternal shriekings." *Sermons by Eminent Divines,* p. 394. "Screakings and howlings." *Gray's Great and Precious Promises,* p. 20. "O! the screeches and yels that will be in hell." *Durham's Commentarie upon the Book of the Revelation,* p. 654. "The horrible scrieches of them who are burnt in it." *Cowper's Heaven Opened,* p. 175.

106. "When children and servants shall go, as it were, in sholes to the Pit, cursing their parents and their masters who brought them there. And parents and masters of families shall be in multitudes plunged headlong in endless destruction, because they have not only murdered their own souls, but also imbrued their hands in the blood of their children and servants. O how doleful will the reckoning be amongst them at that day! When the children and servants shall upbraid their parents and masters. 'Now, now, we must to the Pit, and we have you to blame for it; your cursed example, and lamentable negligence has brought us to the Pit.'" . . . "And on the other hand, how will the shrieks of

Even now such language freezes the blood, when we consider what must have passed through the minds of those who could bring themselves to utter it. The enunciation of such ideas unfolds the character of the men, and lays bare their inmost spirit. We shudder, when we think of the dark and corrupted fancy, the vindictive musings, the wild, lawless, and uncertain thoughts which must have been harboured by those who could combine and arrange the different parts of this hideous scheme. No hesitation, no compunction, no feelings of mercy, ever seem to have entered their breasts. It is evident, that their notions were well matured; it is equally evident, that they delighted in them. They were marked by a unity of conception, and were enforced with a freshness and vigour of language, which shows that their heart was in their work. But before this could have happened, they must have been dead to every emotion of pity and of tenderness. Yet, they were the teachers of a great nation, and were, in every respect, the most influential persons in that nation. The people, credulous and grossly ignorant, listened and believed. We, at this distance of time, and living in another realm of thought, can form but a faint conception of the effect which these horrible conceits produced upon them. They were convinced that, in this world, they were incessantly pursued by the devil, and that he, and other evil spirits, were constantly hovering around them, in bodily and visible shape, tempting them, and luring them on to destruction. In the next world, the most frightful and unheard-of punishments awaited them; while both this world and the next were governed by an avenging Deity, whose wrath it was impossible to propitiate. No wonder that, with these ideas before them, their reason should often give way, and that a religious mania should set in, under whose influence they, in black despair, put an end to their lives.[107]

---

parents fill every ear? 'I have damn'd myself, I have damn'd my children, I have damn'd my servants. While I fed their bodies, and clothed their backs, I have ruined their souls, and brought double damnation on myself.' " *Halyburton's Great Concern of Salvation,* pp. 527, 528. See this further worked out in *Boston's Human Nature in its Four-fold State,* pp. 378, 379: "curses instead of salutations, and tearing of themselves, and raging against one another, instead of the wonted embraces."

107. William Vetch, "preaching in the town of Jedburg to a great congregation, said, 'There are two thousand of you here today, but I am sure fourscore

Little comfort, indeed, could men then gain from their religion. Not only the devil, as the author of all evil, but even He whom we recognise as the author of all good, was, in the eyes of the Scotch clergy, a cruel and vindictive being, moved with anger like themselves. They looked into their own hearts, and there they found the picture of their God. According to them,

---

of you will not be saved;' upon which, three of his ignorant hearers being in despair, despatch'd themselves soon after." *Scotch Presbyterian Eloquence*, p. 23. See also the life, or rather panegyric, of Vetch in *Howie's Biographia Scoticana*, where this circumstance is not denied, but, on the contrary, is stated to be no "disparagement to him," p. 606. The frame of mind which the teachings of the clergy encouraged, and which provoked self-murder, is vividly depicted by Samuel Rutherford, the most popular of all the Scotch divines of the seventeenth century. "Oh! hee lieth down, and hell beddeth with him; hee sleepeth, and hell and hee dreame together; he riseth, and hell goeth to the fields with him; hee goes to his garden, there is hell." . . . "The man goes to his table, O! hee dare not eat, hee hath no right to the creature; to eat is sin and hell; so hell is in every dish. To live is sinne, *hee would faine chuse strangling;* every act of breathing is sin and hell. Hee goes to church, there is a dog as great as a mountaine before his eye: Here be terrors." *Rutherford's Christ Dying,* 1647, 4to, pp. 41, 42. Now, listen to the confessions of two of the tortured victims of the doctrines enunciated by the clergy; victims who, after undergoing ineffable agony, were more than once, according to their own account, tempted to put an end to their lives. "The cloud lasted for two years and some months." . . . "The arrows of the Almighty did drink up my spirits; night and day his hand lay heavy upon me, so that even my bodily moisture was turned into the drought of summer. When I said sometimes that my couch would ease my complaint, I was filled with tossings to the dawning of the day." . . . "Amidst all my downcastings, I had the roaring lion to grapple with, who likes well to fish in muddy waters. He strongly suggested to me that I should not eat, because I had no right to food; or if I ventured to do it, the enemy assured me, that the wrath of God would go down with my morsel; and that I had forfeited a right to the divine favour, and, therefore, had nothing to do with any of God's creatures." . . . "However, so violent were the temptations of the strong enemy, that I frequently forgot to eat my bread, and durst not attempt it; and when, through the persuasion of my wife, I at any time did it, the enemy through the day did buffet me in a violent way, assuring me that the wrath of God had gone over me with what I had taken." . . . "The enemy after all did so pursue me, that he violently suggested to my soul, that, some time or other, God would suddenly destroy me as with a thunder-clap: which so filled my soul with fear and pain, that, every now and then, I looked about me, to receive the divine blow, still expecting it was a coming; yea, many a night I durst not sleep, lest I had awakened in everlasting flames." *Stevenson's Rare Cordial,* pp. 11–13. Another poor creature, after hearing one of Smiton's sermons, in 1740, says, "Now, I saw myself to be a condemned criminal; but I knew not the day of my execution. I thought that there was nothing between me and hell, but the brittle thread of natural life." . . . "And in this dreadful confusion, I durst not sleep, least I had awakened in everlasting flames." . . . "And Satan violently assaulted me to take away my own life, seeing there was no mercy for me." . . . "Soon after this, I was again vio-

He was a God of terror, instead of a God of love.[108] To Him, they imputed the worst passions of their own peevish and irritable nature. They ascribed to Him, revenge, cunning, and a constant disposition to inflict pain. While they declared that nearly all mankind were sinners beyond the chance of redemption, and were, indeed, predestined to eternal ruin, they did not scruple to accuse the Deity of resorting to artifice against these unhappy victims; lying in wait for them, that He might catch them unawares.[109] The Scotch clergy taught their hearers, that the Almighty was so sanguinary, and so prone to anger, that He raged even against walls and houses and senseless creatures, wreaking His fury more than ever, and scattering desolation on every side.[110] Sooner than miss His fell and malignant purposes, He would, they said, let loose avenging angels, to fall upon men and upon their families.[111] Independently of this resource, He had various ways whereby He could at once content Himself and plague His creatures, as was particularly shown in the devices which He employed to bring famine on a people.[112] When a

---

lently assaulted by the tempter to take away my own life; he presented to me a knife therewith to do it; no person being in the house but myself. The enemy pursued me so close, that I could not endure so much as to see the knife in my sight, but laid it away." . . . "One evening, as I was upon the street, Satan violently assaulted me to go into the sea and drown myself; it would be the easiest death. Such a fear of Satan then fell upon me, as made my joints to shake, so that it was much for me to walk home; and when I came to the door, I found nobody within; I was afraid to go into the house, lest Satan should get power over me." *Memoirs of the Life and Experiences of Marion, Laird of Greenock,* pp. 13, 14, 19, 45, 223, 224.

108. Binning says, that "since the first rebellion" (that is, the fall of Adam), "there is nothing to be seen but the terrible countenance of an angry God." *Binning's Sermons,* vol. iii. p. 254.

109. "He will, as it were, lie in wait to take all advantages of sinners to undo them." *Hutcheson's Exposition on the Minor Prophets,* vol. i. p. 247.

110. "His wrath rages against walls, and houses, and senselesse creatures more now then at that time" (*i.e.* at the time when the Old Testament was written). "See what desolation he hath wrought in Ireland, what eating of horses, of infants, and of killed souldiers, hath beene in that land, and in Germany." *Rutherford's Free Disputation against Pretended Liberty of Conscience,* pp. 244, 245.

111. "Albeit there were no earthly man to pursue Christ's enemies; yet avenging angels, or evil spirits shall be let forth upon them and their families to trouble them." *Dickson's Explication of the First Fifty Pslams,* p. 229.

112. "God hath many wayes and meanes whereby to plague man, and *reach his contentments.*" *Hutcheson's Exposition on the Minor Prophets,* vol. i. p. 286. "God hath variety of means whereby to plague men, and to bring upon

country was starving, it was because God, in His anger, had smitten the soil, had stopped the clouds from yielding their moisture, and thus made the fruits of the earth to wither.[113] All the intolerable sufferings caused by a want of food, the slow deaths, the agony, the general misery, the crimes which that misery produced, the anguish of the mother as she saw her children wasting away and could give them no bread, all this was His act, and the work of His hands.[114] In His anger, He would sometimes injure the crops by making the spring so backward, and the weather so cold and rainy, as to insure a deficiency in the coming harvest.[115] Or else, He would deceive men, by sending them a

---

them any affliction he intendeth against them; and particularly he hath several wayes whereby to bring on famine. He can arme all his creatures to cut off men's provision, one of them after another; he can make the change of aire, and small insects do that worke when he pleaseth." *Ibid.*, vol. i. p. 422. The same divine, in another elaborate treatise, distinctly imputes to the Deity a sensation of pleasure in injuring even the innocent. "When God sends out a scourge, of sword, famine, or pestilence, suddenly to overthrow and cut people off, not only are the wicked reached thereby (which is here supposed), but even the innocent, that is such as are righteous and free of gross provocations; for, in any other sense, none are innocent, or free of sin, in this life. Yea, further, in trying of the innocent by these scourges, *the Lord seems to act as one delighted with it,* and little resenting the great extremities wherewith they are pressed." *Hutcheson's Exposition of the Book of Job,* 1669, folio, p. 123. Compare p. 359. "It pleaseth the Lord to exercise great variety in afflicting the children of men," &c. But, after all, mere extracts can give but a faint idea of the dark and malignant spirit which pervades these writings.

113. "The present death and famine quhilk seases vpon many, quhairby God his heavie wrath is evidentlie perceaved to be kindlit against vs." *Selections from the Minutes of the Synod of Fife,* p. 98. "Smiting the fruits of the ground." *Hutcheson's Exposition on the Minor Prophets,* vol. i. p. 277. "Makes fruits to wither." *Ibid.,* vol. ii. p. 183. "Hee restraines the clouds, and bindeth up the wombe of heaven, in extreme drought." *Rutherford's Christ Dying,* p. 52. "Sometime hee maketh the heauen aboue as brasse, and the earth beneath as iron; so that albeit men labour and sow, yet they receiue no encrease: sometime againe he giues in due season the first and latter raine, so that the earth renders abundance, but the Lord by blasting windes, or by the caterpiller, canker-worme and grasse-hopper doth consume them, who come out as exacters and officers sent from God to poind men in their goods." *Cowper's Heaven Opened,* p. 433.

114. "Under the late dearth this people suffered greatly, the poor were numerous, and many, especially about the town of Kilsyth, were at the point of starving; yet, as I frequently observed to them, I could not see any one turning to *the Lord who smote them,* or crying to him because of their sins, while *they howled upon their beds for bread." Robe's Narratives of the Extraordinary Work of the Spirit of God,* p. 68.

115. *Nicoll's Diary,* pp. 152, 153. Much rain in the autumn, was "the Lord's displeasure upon the land." *Minutes of the Presbyteries of Saint Andrews and Cupar,* p. 179.

favourable season, and, after letting them toil and sweat in the hope of an abundant supply, He would, at the last moment, suddenly step in, and destroy the corn just as it was fit to be reaped.[116] For, the God of the Scotch Kirk was a God who tantalized His creatures as well as punished them; and when He was provoked, He would first allure men by encouraging their expectations, in order that their subsequent misery might be more poignant.[117]

Under the influence of this horrible creed, and from the unbounded sway exercised by the clergy who advocated it, the Scotch mind was thrown into such a state, that, during the seventeenth, and part of the eighteenth, century, some of the noblest feelings of which our nature is capable, the feelings of hope, of love, and of gratitude, were set aside, and were replaced by the dictates of a servile and ignominious fear. The physical sufferings to which the human frame is liable, nay, even the very accidents to which we are casually exposed, were believed to proceed, not from our ignorance, nor from our carelessness, but from the rage of the Deity. If a fire chanced to break out in Edinburgh, the greatest alarm was excited, because it was the voice of God crying out against a luxurious and dissolute city.[118] If a boil or a sore appeared on your body, that, too, was a divine punishment, and it was more than doubtful whether it might lawfully be cured.[119]

116. "Men sweat, till, sow much, and the sun and summer, and clouds, warme dewes and raines smile upon cornes and meddowes, yet God steppeth in betweene the mouth of the husbandman and the sickle, and blasteth all." *Rutherford's Christ Dying,* p. 87. Compare *Bailie's Letters,* vol. iii. p. 52, on the "continuance of very intemperate rain upon the corns," as one of the "great signs of the wrath of God."

117. "When the Lord is provoked, he can not only send an affliction, but so order it, by faire appearances of a better lot, and heightening of the sinners expectation and desire, as may make it most sad." *Hutcheson's Exposition on the Minor Prophets,* vol. iii. pp. 9, 10.

118. In 1696, there was a fire in Edinburgh; whereupon Moncrief, in his sermon next day, "told us, 'That God's voice was crying to this city, and that he was come to the very ports, and was crying over the walls to us; that we should amend our ways, lest he should come to our city, and consume us in a terrible manner.' I cannot tell what this Dispensation of Providence wrought on me," &c. *Memoirs or Spiritual Exercises of Elizabeth Wast, written by her own Hand,* pp. 41, 42. See also, at pp. 122, 123, the account of another conflagration, where it is said, "there was much of God to be seen in this fire." Compare a curious passage in *Calderwood's History of the Kirk of Scotland,* vol. vii. pp. 455, 456.

119. The Rev. James Fraser had a boil, and afterwards a fever. "During this sickness he miraculously allayed the pain of my boil, and speedily, and that without means, cured it; for however I bought some things to prevent it, yet

The small-pox, being one of the most fatal as well as one of the most loathsome of all diseases, was especially sent by God; and, on that account, the remedy of inoculation was scouted as a profane attempt to frustrate His intentions.[120] Other disorders, which, though less terrible, were very painful, proceeded from the same source, and all owed their origin to the anger of the Almighty.[121] In every thing, His power was displayed, not by

looking on it as a punishment from God, I knew not if I could be free to take the rod out of his hand, and to counterwork him." *Memoirs of the Rev. James Fraser of Brea, Minister of the Gospel at Culross, written by Himself,* in *Select Biographies,* vol. ii. p. 223. Durham declaims against "Sinful shunning and shifting off suffering;" and Rutherford says, "No man should rejoice at weakness and diseases; but I think we may have a sort of gladness at boils and sores, because, without them, Christ's fingers, as a slain Lord, should never have touched our skin." *Durham's Law Unsealed,* p. 160; *Rutherford's Religious Letters,* p. 265. I do not know what effect these passages may produce upon the reader; but it makes my flesh creep to quote them. Compare *Stevenson's Rare, Soul-strengthening, and Comforting Cordial,* p. 35.

120. It was not until late in the eighteenth century, that the Scotch clergy gave up this notion. At last, even they became influenced by the ridicule to which their superstition exposed them, and which produced more effect than any argument could have done. The doctrines, however, which they and their predecessors had long inculcated, had so corrupted the popular mind, that instances will, I believe, be found even in the nineteenth century, of the Scotch deeming precautions against small-pox to be criminal, or, as they called it, flying in the face of Providence. The latest evidence I can at this moment put my hand on, is in a volume published in 1797. It is stated by the Rev. John Paterson, that, in the parish of Auldearn, in the county of Nairn, "Very few have fallen a sacrifice to the small-pox, though the people are in general averse to inoculation, from the general gloominess of their faith, which teaches them, that all diseases which afflict the human frame are instances of the Divine interposition, for the punishment of sin; any interference, therefore, on their part, they deem an usurpation of the prerogative of the Almighty." *Sinclair's Statistical Account of Scotland,* vol. xix, p. 618, Edinburgh, 1797. See also vol. xiv, p. 52, Edinburgh, 1795. This is well said. No doubt, so abject, and so pernicious, a superstition among the people, was the result of "the general gloominess of their faith." But the Rev. John Paterson has forgotten to add, that the gloominess of which he complains, was in strict conformity with the teachings of the most able, the most energetic, and the most venerated of the Scotch clergy. Mr. Paterson renders scant justice to his countrymen, and should rather have praised the tenacity with which they adhered to the instructions they had long been accustomed to receive.

121. The Rev. John Welsh, when suffering from a painful disorder, and also from other troubles, writes: "My douleurs ar impossible to expresse." . . . . "It is the Lord's indignation." See his letter, in *Miscellany of the Wodrow Society,* vol. i. p. 558. See also *Cowper's Heaven Opened,* p. 128. A pain in one's side was the work of "the Lord" (*Memoirs of Marion Laird,* p. 95); so was a sore throat (*Wast's Memoirs,* p. 203); and so was the fever in pleurisy, *Robe's Narratives of the Extraordinary Work of the Spirit of God,* p. 66.

increasing the happiness of men, nor by adding to their comforts, but by hurting and vexing them in all possible ways. His hand, always raised against the people, would sometimes deprive them of wine by causing the vintage to fail;[122] sometimes, would destroy their cattle in a storm;[123] and sometimes, would even make dogs bite their legs when they least expected it.[124] Sometimes, He would display His wrath by making the weather excessively dry;[125] sometimes, by making it equally wet.[126] He was always punishing; always busy in increasing the general suffering, or, to use the language of the time, making the creature smart under the rod.[127] Every fresh war was the result of His special interference; it was not caused by the meddling folly or insensate ambition of statesmen, but it was the immediate work of the Deity, who was thus made responsible for all the devastations, the murders, and other crimes more horrible still, which war produces.[128] In the intervals of peace, which, at that period, were

122. In January 1653, "This tyme, and mony monethis befoir, thair wes great skairshtie of wynes. In this also appered Godis justice toward this natioun for abusing of that blissing many yearis befoir." *Nicoll's Diary,* p. 105.

123. This idea was so deeply rooted, that we actually find a public fast and humiliation ordered, on account of "this present uncouth storme of frost and snaw, quhilk hes continewit sa lang that the bestiall ar dieing thik fauld." *Records of the Kirk Session, Presbytery, and Synod of Aberdeen,* p. 82.

124. "There was a dog bit my leg most desperately. I no sooner received this, but I saw the hand of God in it." *Wast's Memoirs,* p. 114.

125. "The evident documents of Goddis wrath aganes the land, be the extraordinarie drouth." *Records of the Kirk Session, Presbytery, and Synod of Aberdeen,* p. 78.

126. "The hynous synnes of the land produced much takines of Godis wraith; namelie, in this spring tyme, for all Februar and a great pairt of Marche wer full of havie weittis." *Nicoll's Diary,* p. 152.

127. *Halyburton's Great Concern of Salvation,* p. 85. *Fleming's Fulfilling of Scripture,* pp. 101, 149, 176. *Balfour's Annales,* vol. i. p. 169. *Boston's Sermons,* p. 52. *Boston's Human Nature in its Four-fold State,* pp. 67, 136. *Memoirs of Marion Laird,* pp. 63, 90, 113, 163. *Hutcheson's Exposition of the Book of Job,* pp. 62, 91, 140, 187, 242, 310, 449, 471, 476, 527, 528.

128. "War is one of the sharp scourges whereby God punisheth wicked nations; and it cometh upon a people, not accidentally, but *by the especial providence of God,* who hath peace and war in his own hand." *Hutcheson's Exposition on the Minor Prophets,* vol. ii. p. 3. In 1644, "Civill war wracks Spaine, and lately wracked Italie: it is coming by appearance shortlie upon France. The just Lord, who beholds with patience the wickednesse of nations, at last *arises in furie.*" . . . . "The Swedish and Danish fleets, after a hott fight, are making for a new onsett: great blood is feared shall be shortly shed there, both by sea and land. The *anger of the Lord* against all christendome is great." *Baillie's Letters and Journals,* vol. ii. pp. 190, 223.

very rare, He had other means of vexing mankind. The shock of an earthquake was a mark of His displeasure;[129] a comet was a sign of coming tribulation;[130] and when an eclipse appeared, the panic was so universal, that persons of all ranks hastened to church to deprecate His wrath.[131] What they heard there, would increase their fear, instead of allaying it. For the clergy taught their hearers, that even so ordinary an event as thunder, was meant to excite awe, and was sent for the purpose of showing to men with how terrible a master they had to deal.[132] Not to tremble at thunder, was, therefore, a mark of impiety; and, in this respect, man was unfavourably contrasted with the lower animals, since they were invariably moved by this symptom of divine power.[133]

These visitations, eclipses, comets, earthquakes, thunder, famine, pestilence, war, disease, blights in the air, failures in the crops, cold winters, dry summers, these, and the like, were, in the opinion of the Scotch divines, outbreaks of the anger of the

129. "Earthquakes, whereby God, when he is angry, overthrows and over-turns very mountains." *Hutcheson's Exposition of the Book of Job,* p. 114. "The ministris and sessioun convening in the sessioun hous, considering the fearfull erthquak that wes yisternicht, the aucht of this instant, throughout this haill citie about nine houris as evin, to be a document that God is angrie aganes the land and aganes this citie in particular, for the manifauld sinnis of the people," &c. *Records of the Kirk Session, Presbytery, and Synod of Aberdeen,* p. 64.

130. "Whatever natural causes may be adduced for those alarming appearances, the system of comets is yet so uncertain, and they have so frequently preceded desolating strokes and turns in public affairs, that they seem designed in providence to stir up sinners to seriousness. Those preachers from heaven, when God's messengers were silenced, neither prince nor prelate could stop." *Wodrow's History of the Church of Scotland,* vol. i. p. 421.

131. "People of all sortes rane to the churches to deprecat God's wrath." *Balfour's Annales,* vol. i. p. 403. This was in 1598.

132. "By it, he manifests his power and shows himself terrible." *Durham's Commentarie upon the Book of the Revelation,* p. 33. Compare *Row's History of the Kirk,* p. 333; and a passage in *Laird's Memoirs,* p. 69, which shows how greedily their credulous hearers imbibed such notions: "There were several signal evidences that the Lord's righteous judgments were abroad in the earth; great claps of thunder," &c.

133. "The stupidity and senselessnesse of man is greater than that of the brute creatures, which are all more moved with the thunder, then the hearts of men for the most part." *Dickson's Explication of the First Fifty Psalms,* p. 193. Hutcheson makes a similar remark concerning earthquakes. "The shaking and trembling of insensible creatures, when God is angry, serves to condemn men, who are not sensible of it, nor will stoop under his hand." *Hutcheson's Exposition of the Book of Job,* p. 115.

Almighty against the sins of men; and that such outbreaks were incessant is not surprising, when we consider that, in the same age, and according to the same creed, the most innocent, and even praiseworthy, actions were deemed sinful, and worthy of chastisement. The opinions held on this subject are not only curious, but extremely instructive. Besides forming an important part of the history of the human mind, they supply decisive proof of the danger of allowing a single profession to exalt itself above all other professions. For, in Scotland, as elsewhere, directly the clergy succeeded in occupying a more than ordinary amount of public attention, they availed themselves of that circumstance to propagate those ascetic doctrines, which, while they strike at the root of human happiness, benefit no one except the class which advocates them. That class, indeed, can hardly fail to reap advantage from a policy, which, by increasing the apprehensions to which the ignorance and timidity of men make them too liable, does also increase their eagerness to fly for support to their spiritual advisers. And the greater the apprehension, the greater the eagerness. Of this, the Scotch clergy, who were perfect masters of their own art, were well aware. Under their influence, a system of morals was established, which, representing nearly every act as sinful, kept the people in perpetual dread, lest unwittingly they were committing some enormous offence, which would bring upon their heads a signal and overwhelming punishment.

According to this code, all the natural affections, all social pleasures, all amusements, and all the joyous instincts of the human heart were sinful, and were to be rooted out. It was sinful for a mother to wish to have sons;[134] and, if she had any, it was sinful to be anxious about their welfare.[135] It was a sin to please

134. Lady Colsfeild "had born two or three daughters, and was sinfully anxious after a son, to heir the estate of Colsfeild." *Wodrow's Analecta,* vol. iii. p. 293.

135. Under the influence of this terrible creed, the amiable mother of Duncan Forbes, writing to him respecting his own health and that of his brother, speaks of "my sinful God-provoking anxiety, both for your souls and bodies." *Burton's Lives of Lovat and Forbes,* p. 274. The theological theory, underlying and suggesting this, was, that "grace bridles these affections." *Boston's Human Nature in its Four-fold State,* p. 184. Hence its rigid application on days set apart for religious purposes. The Rev. Mr. Lyon (*History of Saint Andrews,* vol. i. p. 458) mentions that some of the Scotch clergy, in drawing up regulations for the government of a colony, inserted the following clause: "No husband shall kiss his wife, and no mother shall kiss her child on the Sabbath day."

yourself, or to please others; for, by adopting either course, you were sure to displease God.[136] All pleasures, therefore, however slight in themselves, or however lawful they might appear, must be carefully avoided.[137] When mixing in society, we should edify the company, if the gift of edification had been bestowed upon us; but we should by no means attempt to amuse them.[138] Cheerfulness, especially when it rose to laughter, was to be guarded against; and we should choose for our associates grave and sorrowful men, who were not likely to indulge in so foolish a practice.[139] Smiling, provided it stopped short of laughter, might

136. "The more you please yourselves and the world, the further you are from pleasing God." *Binning's Sermons,* vol. ii. p. 55. Elsewhere (vol. ii. p. 45): "Amity to ourselves is enmity to God."

137. "Pleasures are most carefully to be auoided: because they both harme and deceiue." *Abernethy's Physicke for the Soule,* p. 251. At p. 268, the same authority says, "Beate downe thy body, and bring it to subiection by abstaining, not only from vnlawfull pleasures, but also from lawful and indifferent delights."

138. According to *Hutcheson's Exposition of Job,* p. 6, "there is no time wherein men are more ready to miscarry, and discover any bitter root in them, then when they are about the liberal use of the creatures, and amidst occasions of mirth and cheerfulness." How this doctrine ripened, cannot be better illustrated than from the sentiments entertained, so late as the early part of the eighteenth century, by Colonel Blackader, a Scotch officer, who was also an educated man, who had seen much of the world, and might, to some degree, be called a man of the world. In December 1714, he went to a wedding, and, on his return home, he writes: "I was cheerful, and perhaps gave too great a swing to raillery, but I hope not light or vain in conversation. I desire always to have my speech seasoned with salt, and ministering profit to the hearers. Sitting up late, and merry enough, though I hope innocent; but I will not justify myself." *The Life and Diary of Lieut.-Col. J. Blackader, by Andrew Crichton,* p. 453. On another occasion (p. 511), in 1720, he was at an evening party. "The young people were merry. I laid a restraint upon myself for fear of going too far, and joined but little, only so as not to show moroseness or ill-breeding. We sat late, but the conversation was innocent, and no drinking but as we pleased. However, much time is spent; which I dare not justify. *In all things we offend.*" At p. 159, he writes, "I should always be mixing something that may edify in my discourse;" and, says his biographer (p. 437), "Conversation, when it ceased to accomplish this object, be regarded as *degenerating into idle entertainment,* which ought to be checked rather than encouraged."

139. "Frequent the gravest company, and the fellowship of those that are sorrowfull." *Abernethy's Physicke for the Soule,* p. 416. Compare the attacks on "too much carnal mirth and laughter," in *Durham's Law Unsealed,* p. 323; in *Fleming's Fulfilling of the Scripture,* p. 226; and in *Fergusson's Exposition of the Epistles of Paul,* p. 227. See also *Gray's Spiritual Warfare,* p. 42. Cowper says, "Woe be unto them that now laugh, for assuredly they shall weepe, the end of their joy shall be endlesse mourning and gnashing of teeth, they shall shed tears abundantly with Esau, but shall find no place for mercy." *Cowper's*

occasionally be allowed; still, being a carnal pastime, it was a sin to smile on Sunday.[140] Even on week-days, those who were most imbued with religious principles hardly ever smiled, but sighed, groaned, and wept.[141] A true Christian would be careful, in his movements, to preserve invariable gravity, never running, but walking soberly, and not treading out in a brisk and lively manner, as unbelievers are wont to do.[142] So, too, if he wrote to a friend, he

---

Heaven Opened, p. 271. Hutcheson, in a strain of unusual liberality, permits occasional laughter. He says, "There is a faculty of laughing given to men, which certainly is given for use, at least at sometimes; and diversions are sometime needfull for men who are serious and employed in weighty affairs." . . . . "And particularly, laughter is sometime lawful for magistrates and others in publick charge, not only that they may recreate themselves, but that, thereby, and by the like insinuating carriage, they may gain the affection of the people." *Hutcheson's Exposition of the Book of Job,* edit. folio, 1669, pp. 389, 390.

140. In 1650, when Charles II. was in Scotland, "the clergy reprehended him very sharply, if he smiled on those days" (Sundays). *Clarendon's History of the Rebellion,* book xiii. p. 747, edit. Oxford, 1843.

141. It is said of Donald Cargill, that "his very countenance was edifying to beholders; often sighing with deep groans." *A Cloud of Witnesses for the Royal Prerogatives of Jesus Christ,* p. 423. The celebrated James Durham was "a person of the utmost gravity, and scarce smiled at anything." *Howie's Biographia Scoticana,* p. 226. Of Livingston, we are told "that he was a very affectionate person, and weeped much; that it was his ordinary way, and might be observed almost every Sabbath, that when he came into the pulpite he sate doun a litle, and looked first to the one end of the kirk, and then to the other; and then, ordinarly, the tear shott in his eye, and he weeped, and oftimes he began his preface and his work weeping." *Wodrow's Analecta,* vol. ii. p. 249. James Alexander "used to weep much in prayer and preaching; he was every way most savoury." *Ibid.,* vol. iii. p. 39. As to the Rev. John Carstairs, "his band in the Sabbath would have been all wett, as if it had been douked, with tears, before he was done with his first prayer." p. 48. Aird, minister of Dalserf, "weeping much" (*Ibid.,* vol. iii. p. 56), "Mr. James Stirling tells me was a most fervent, affectionat, weeping preacher." p. 172; and the Rev. Alexander Dunlop was noted for what was termed "a holy groan." vol. iii. p. 21. See also, on weeping as a mark of religion, *Wast's Memoirs,* pp. 83, 84; and *Robe's Narratives of the Extraordinary Work of the Spirit of God,* pp. 21, 31, 75, 150. One passage from the most popular of the Scotch preachers, I hesitate as to the propriety of quoting; but it is essential that their ideas should be known, if the history of Scotland is to be understood. Rutherford, after stating whom it is that we should seek to imitate, adds: "Christ did never laugh on earth that we read of, but he wept." *Rutherford's Christ Dying,* 1647, 4to, p. 525. I publish this with no irreverent spirit; God forbid that I should. But I will not be deterred from letting this age see the real character of a system which aimed at destroying all human happiness, exciting slavish and abject fear, and turning this glorious world into one vast theatre of woe.

142. "Walk with a sober pace, not 'tinkling with your feet.'" *Memoirs of the Rev. James Fraser, written by Himself,* in *Select Biographies,* vol. ii. p. 280. "It is somewhat like this, or less than this, which the Lord condemneth, *Isa.*

must beware lest his letter should contain any thing like jocose-ness; since jesting is incompatible with a holy and serious life.[143]

It was, moreover, wrong to take pleasure in beautiful scenery; for a pious man had no concern with such matters, which were beneath him, and the admiration of which should be left to the unconverted.[144] The unregenerate might delight in these vanities, but they who were properly instructed, saw Nature as she really was, and knew that as she, for about five thousand years, had been constantly on the move, her vigour was well-nigh spent, and her pristine energy had departed.[145] To the eye of ignorance, she still

---

iii. 16, 'Walking and mincing, or tripping and making a tinkling with their feet.' What is that but disdaining the grave way of walking, to affect an art in it? as many do now in our days; and shall this be displeasing to the Lord, and not the other? seeing he loveth, and is best pleased with, the native way of carry-ing the body." *Durham's Law Unsealed*, p. 324. "The believer hath, or at least ought to have, and, if he be like himself, will have, a well ordered walk, and will be in his carriage stately and princely." *Durham's Exposition of the Song of Solomon*, p. 365.

143. "At home, writing letters to a friend. My vein is inclined to jest and humour. The letter was too comical and jocose; and after I had sent it away, I had a check that it was too light, and jesting foolishly. I sent and got it back, and destroyed it. My temper goes too far that way, and I ought to check it, and be more on my guard, and study edification in every thing." *Crichton's Life and Diary of Blackader*, pp. 536, 537. Even amongst young children, from eight years old and upwards, toys and games were bad; and it was a good sign when they were discarded. "Some very young, of eight and nine years of age, some twelve and thirteen. They still inclined more and more to their duty, so that they meet three times a day, in the morning, at night, and at noon. Also they have forsaken all their childish fancies and plays; so these that have been awakened are known by their countenance and conversation, their walk and behaviour." *Robe's Narratives of the Extraordinary Work of the Spirit of God*, pp. 79, 80.

144. "To the unmortified man, the world smelleth like the garden of God" . . . "the world is not to him an ill-smelled stinking corps." *Rutherford's Christ Dying*, p. 498. But those who were properly mortified, knew that "the earth is but a potter's house" (*Ibid.*, p. 286); "an old thred-bare-worn case" (*Ibid.*, p. 530); a "smoky house" (*Rutherford's Religious Letters*, p. 100); a "plaistered, rotten world" (*Ibid.*, p. 132); and "an ashy and dirty earth" (*Ibid.*, p. 169). "The earth also is spotted (like the face of a woman once beautiful, but now deformed with scabs of leprosie) with thistles, thornes, and much barren wilder-nesse." *Cowper's Heaven Opened*, p. 255.

145. "Wearinesse and motion is laid on Moon and Sunne, and all creatures on this side of the Moon. Seas ebbe and flow, and that's trouble; winds blow, rivers move, heavens and stars these five thousand yeares, except one time, have not had six minutes rest." . . . . "The Sunne that never rests, but moves as swiftly in the night as in the day." *Rutherford's Christ Dying*, pp. 12, 157. "This is the world's old age; it is declining; albeit it seem a fair and beautiful

seemed fair and fresh; the fact, however, was, that she was worn out and decrepit; she was suffering from extreme old age; her frame, no longer elastic, was leaning on one side, and she soon would perish.[146] Owing to the sin of man, all things were getting worse, and nature was degenerating so fast, that already the lilies were losing their whiteness, and the roses their smell.[147] The heavens were waxing old;[148] the very sun, which lighted the earth, was becoming feeble.[149] This universal degeneracy was sad to think of; but the profane knew it not. Their ungodly eyes were still pleased by what they saw. Such was the result of their obstinate determination to indulge the senses, all of which were evil; the eye being, beyond comparison, the most wicked. Hence, it was especially marked out for divine punishment; and, being constantly sinning, it was afflicted with fifty-two different diseases, that is, one disease for each week in the year.[150]

On this account, it was improper to care for beauty of any kind; or, to speak more accurately, there was no real beauty. The world afforded nothing worth looking at, save and except the Scotch Kirk, which was incomparably the most beautiful thing under

thing in the eyes of them who know no better, and unto them who are of yesterday and know nothing, it looks as if it had been created yesterday; yet the truth is, and a believer knows, it is near the grave." *Binning's Sermons,* vol. iii. p. 372.

146. "This, then, I say, is the state all things ye see, are in,—it is their old age. The creation now is an old rotten house that is all dropping through and leaning to the one side." *Binning's Sermons,* vol. iii. p. 398.

147. "The lilies and roses, which, no doubt, had more sweetnesse of beauty and smell, before the sin of man made them vanity-sick." *Rutherford's Christ Dying,* p. 185.

148. "The heavens that are supposed to be incorruptible, yet they wax old as doth a garment." *Binning's Sermons,* vol. i. p. 95.

149. "The neerer the sun drawes to the end of his daily course, the lesse is his strength, for we see the Sunne in the evening decayes in heat; so it is, the longer by reuolution he turnes about in his sphere, he waxes alway the weaker; and, to vse the similitude of the holy spirit, as a garment the older it groweth the lesse beautifull." *Cowper's Heaven Opened,* p. 255.

150. "It is so delicate by nature, that since it was the first sense that offended, it is, aboue all the rest, made subject (as a condigne punishment) to as many maladies, as there are weekes in a yeere." *Abernethy's Physicke for the Soule,* p. 501. The Scotch divines were extremely displeased with our eyes. Rutherford contemptuously calls them "two clay windows." *Rutherford's Christ Dying,* p. 570. Gray, going still further, says, "these cursed eyes of ours." *Gray's Great and Precious Promises,* p. 53.

heaven.[151] To look at that was a lawful enjoyment, but every other pleasure was sinful. To write poetry, for instance, was a grievous offence, and worthy of especial condemnation.[152] To listen to music was equally wrong; for men had no right to disport themselves in such idle recreation. Hence the clergy forbad music to be introduced even during the festivities of a marriage;[153] neither would they permit, on any occasion, the national entertainment of pipers.[154] Indeed, it was sinful to look at any exhibition in the streets, even though you only looked at it from your own window.[155] Dancing was so extremely sinful, that an edict, expressly prohibiting it, was enacted by the General Assembly, and read in every church in Edinburgh.[156] New Year's Eve had

151. "The true visible Kirk where God's ordinances are set up, as he hath appointed, where his word is purely preached, is the most beautifull thing under heaven." *Dickson's Explication of the First Fifty Psalms,* p. 341.

152. I have one very late, and, on that account, very curious, instance of the diffusion of this feeling in Scotland. In 1767, a vacancy occurred in the mastership of the grammar-school of Greenock. It was offered to John Wilson, the author of "Clyde." But, says his biographer, "the magistrates and minister of Greenock thought fit, before they would admit Mr. Wilson to the superintendance of the grammar school, to stipulate that he should abandon 'the profane and unprofitable art of poem-making.'" *Lives of Eminent Scotsmen by the Society of Ancient Scots,* 1821, vol. v. p. 169.

153. "Sept. 22, 1649.—The quhilk day the Sessioune caused mak this act, that ther sould be no pypers at brydels, and who ever sould have a pyper playing at their brydell on their mariage day, sall loose their consigned money, and be farder punisched as the Sessioune thinks fitt." *Extracts from the Registers of the Presbytery of Glasgow, and of the Kirk Sessions of the Parishes of Cambusnethan Humbie and Stirling,* p. 34. This curious volume is a quarto, and without date; unless, indeed, one of the title-pages is wanting in my copy.

154. See the Minutes of the Kirk Session of Glasgow, in *Wodrow's Collections upon the Lives of Ministers,* vol. ii. part ii. p. 76; also the case of "Mure, pyper," in *Selections from the Minutes of the Presbyteries of Saint Andrews and Cupar,* p. 72.

155. This notion lingered on, probably to the beginning of this century; certainly to late in the last. In a work published in Scotland in 1836, it is stated, that a clergyman was still alive, who was "severely censured," merely because, when Punch was performing, "the servant was sent out to the showman to request him to come below the windows of her master's house, that the clergyman and his wife might enjoy the sight." *Traditions of Perth by George Penny,* Perth, 1836, p. 124.

156. "17 Feb. 1650. Ane act of the commissioun of the Generall Assemblie was red in all the churches of Edinburgh dischargeing promiscuous dansing." *Nicoll's Diary,* p. 3. See also *Acts of the General Assembly of the Church of Scotland,* 1638–1842, p. 201; *Register of the Kirk Session of Cambusnethan,* p. 35; *Minutes of the Presbyteries of St. Andrews and Cupar,* pp. 55, 181; *Minutes of the Synod of Fife,* pp. 150, 169, 175; and a choice passage in *A Collection of Sermons by Eminent Divines,* p. 51.

long been a period of rejoicing in Scotland, as in other parts of Europe. The Church laid her hands on this also, and ordered that no one should sing the songs usual on that day, or should admit such singers into his own private house.[157]

At the christening of a child, the Scotch were accustomed to assemble their relations, including their distant cousins, in whom, then as now, they much abounded. But this caused pleasure, and pleasure was sinful. It was, therefore, forbidden; the number of guests was limited; and the strictest supervision was exercised by the clergy, to prevent the possibility of any one being improperly happy on such occasions.[158]

Not only at baptisms, but also at marriages, the same spirit was displayed. In every country, it has been usual to make merry at marriages; partly from a natural feeling, and partly, perhaps, from a notion that a contract, so often productive of misery, might, at all events, begin with mirth. The Scotch clergy, however, thought otherwise. At the weddings of the poor, they would allow no rejoicing;[159] and at the weddings of the rich, it was the

157. See *Selections from the Records of the Kirk Session, Presbytery, and Synod of Aberdeen*, pp. 77, 78, forbidding any one to "giwe ony meatt or drink to these sangsteris or lat thame within thair houss." The singers were to be "put in prisoun."

158. In 1643 the Presbytery of St. Andrews ordered that "because of the great abuse that is likewayes among them by conveening multitudes at baptismes and contracts, the ministers and sessions are appointed to take strict order for restraineing these abuses, that in number they exceid not sixe or seven. As also ordaines that the hostlers quho mak such feists salbe censured by the sessions." *Minutes of the Presbyteries of St. Andrews and Cupar*, p. 11. See also *Records of the Kirk Session, Presbytery, and Synod of Aberdeen*, pp. 109, 110, complaining of the custom "that everie base servile man in the towne, when he hes a barne to be baptesed, invitis tuelff or sextene persones to be his gossopes and godfatheris to his barne," &c.; and enacting "that it shall not be lesume to any inhabitant within this burt quhasoever, to invite any ma persones to be godfatheris to thair barne in ony tyme cumming bot tua or four at the most, lyk as the Kirk officier is expresslie commandit and prohibitt that from hence furth he tak vp no ma names to be godfatheris, nor giwe any ma vp to the redar bot four at the most, vnder all hiest censure he may incur be the contrarie, and this ordinance to be intimat out of pulpitt, that the people pretend no ignorance thairof."

159. They forbad music and dancing; and they ordered that not more than twenty-four persons should be present. See the enactment, in 1647, respecting "Pennie bryddells," in *Minutes of the Presbyteries of St. Andrews and Cupar*, p. 117. In 1650, "The Presbyterie being sadly weghted with the report of the continwance, and exhorbitant and unnecessary numerous confluences of people at pennie brydles, and of inexpedient and wnlawfull pypeing and dancing at the same, so scandalous and sinfull in this tyme of our Churches lamentable conditioun; and being apprehensive that ministers and Kirk Sessiouns have

custom for one of them to go for the express purpose of preventing an excess of gaiety. A better precaution could hardly be devised; but they did not trust exclusively to it. To check the lusts of the flesh, they, furthermore, took into account the cookery, the choice of the meats, and the number of the dishes. They were, in fact, so solicitous on these points, and so anxious that the nuptial feast should not be too attractive, that they fixed its cost, and would not allow any person to exceed the sum which they thought proper to name.[160]

Nothing escaped their vigilance. For, in their opinion, even the best man was, at his best time, so full of turpitude, that his actions could not fail to be wicked.[161] He never passed a day without sinning, and the smallest sin deserved eternal wrath.[162] Indeed, every thing he did was sinful, no matter how pure his motives.[163] Man had been gradually falling lower and lower, and had now sunk to a point of debasement, which made him inferior to the beasts that perish.[164] Even before he was born, and while

---

not bein so vigilant and active (as neid werre), for repressing of these disorders, doe therfor most seriously recommend to ministers and Kirk Sessiouns to represse the same." *Ibid.*, pp. 169, 170. See, further, *Registers of the Presbytery of Lanark*, p. 29; and *Extracts from the Presbytery Book of Strathbogie*, pp. 4, 144.

160. See two curious instances of limitation of price, in *Irving's History of Dumbartonshire*, p. 567; and in *Wodrow's Collections upon the Lives of Ministers*, vol. ii. part ii. p. 34.

161. "What a vile, haughty, and base creature he is—how defiled and desperately wicked his nature—how abominable his actions; in a word, what a compound of darkness and wickedness he is—a heap of defiled dust, and a mass of confusion—a sink of impiety and iniquity, *even the best of mankind,* those of the rarest and most refined extraction, *take them at their best estate."* *Binning's Sermons*, vol. ii. p. 302. Compare *Boston's Human Nature in its Four-fold State*, pp. 26, 27.

162. "The least sin cannot but deserve God's wrath and curse eternally." *Dickson's Truth's Victory over Error*, p. 71. "All men, even the regenerate, sin daily." *Ibid.*, p. 153.

163. "Our best works have such a mixture of corruption and sin in them, that they deserve his curse and wrath." *Ibid.*, p. 130.

164. "But now, falling away from God, hee hath also so farre degenerated from his owne kind, that he is become inferiour to the beasts." *Cowper's Heaven Opened*, p. 251. "O! is not man become so brutish and ignorant, that he may be sent unto the beasts of the field to be instructed of that which is his duty?" *Gray's Spiritual Warfare*, p. 28. "Men are naturally more brutish than beasts themselves." *Boston's Human Nature in its Four-fold State*, p. 58. "Worse than the beast of the field." *Halyburton's Great Concern of Salvation*, p. 71.

he was yet in his mother's womb, his guilt began.[165] And when he grew up, his crimes multiplied thick and fast; one of the most heinous of them being the practice of teaching children new words,—a horrible custom, justly visited by divine wrath.[166] This, however, was but one of a series of innumerable and incessant offences; so that the only wonder was, that the earth could restrain herself at the hideous spectacle which man presented, and that she did not open her mouth, as of old, and swallow him even in the midst of his wickedness.[167] For it was certain, that in the whole creation, there was nothing so deformed and monstrous as he.[168]

Such being the case, it behoved the clergy to come forward, and to guard men against their own vices, by controlling their daily actions, and forcing them to a right conduct. This they did vigorously. Aided by the elders, who were their tools and the creatures of their power, they, all over Scotland, organized themselves into legislative bodies, and, in the midst of their little senate, they enacted laws which the people were bound to obey. If they refused, woe be to them. They became unruly sons of the Church, and were liable to be imprisoned, to be fined, or to be whipped,[169] or to be branded with a hot iron,[170] or to do penance

165. "Infants, even in their mother's belly, have in themselves sufficient guilt to deserve such judgments;" *i.e.,* when women with child are "ript up." *Hutcheson's Exposition on the Minor Prophets,* vol. i. p. 255.

166. "And in our speech, our Scripture and old Scots names are gone out of request; instead of *Father* and *Mother, Mamma* and *Papa,* training children to speak nonsense, and what they do not understand. These few instances, amongst many that might be given, are additional causes of God's wrath." *The Life and Death of Mr. Alexander Peden, late Minister of the Gospel at New Glenluce, in Galloway,* in *Walker's Biographia Presbyteriana,* vol. i. p. 140.

167. "Yea, if the Lord did not restraine her, shee would open her mouth and swallow the wicked, as she did Corah, Dathan, and Abiram." *Cowper's Heaven Opened,* p. 257. Compare *Hutcheson's Exposition on the Minor Prophets,* vol. i. p. 507.

168. "There is nothing so monstrous, so deformed in the world, as man." *Binning's Sermons,* vol. i. p. 234. "There is not in all the creation such a miserable creature as man." *Ibid.,* vol. iii. p. 321. "Nothing so miserable." *Abernethy's Physicke for the Soule,* p. 37.

169. "December 17th, 1635. Mention made of a correction house, which the Session ordeans persons to be taken to, both men and women, and appoints them to be whipt every day during the Session's will." *Wodrow's Collections upon the Lives of Ministers,* vol. ii. part ii. p. 67.

170. On the 22d October 1648, the Kirk Session of Dunfermline ordered that a certain Janet Robertson "shall be cartit and scourged through the town, and markit with an hot iron." *Chalmers' History of Dunfermline,* p. 437.

before the whole congregation, humbling themselves, bare-footed, and with their hair cut on one side,[171] while the minister, under pretence of rebuking them, enjoyed his triumph.[172] All this was natural enough. For the clergy were the delegates of heaven, and the interpreters of its will. They, therefore, were the best judges of what men ought to do; and any one whom they censured was bound to submit with humility and repentance.[173]

The arbitrary and irresponsible tribunals, which now sprung up all over Scotland, united the executive authority with the legislative, and exercised both functions at the same time. Declaring that certain acts ought not to be committed, they took the law into their own hands, and punished those who had committed them. According to the principles of this new jurisprudence, of which the clergy were the authors, it became a sin for any Scotchman to travel in a Catholic country.[174] It was a sin for any Scotch inn-

171. "As they punish by pecuniary fines, so corporally too, by imprisoning the persons of the delinquents, using them disgracefully, carting them through cities, making them stand in Iogges, as they call them, pillaries (which in the country churches are fixed to the two sides of the main door of the Parish Church), cutting the halfe of their hair, shaving their beards, &c., and it is more than ordinary, by their 'original' and 'proper power,' to banish them out of the bounds and limits of the parish, or presbytery, as they list to order it." *Presbytery Displayed*, p. 4.

172. The Scotch clergy of the seventeenth century were not much given to joking; but on one of these occasions a preacher is said to have hazarded a pun. A woman, named Ann Cantly, being made to do penance, "Here" (said the minister), "Here is one upon the stool of repentance, they call her *Cantly; she saith herself, she is an honest woman, but I trow *scantly.*" *Scotch Presbyterian Eloquence*, p. 125. From what I have read of Scotch theology, I can bear testimony to the accuracy of this book, so far as its general character is concerned. Indeed, the author, through fear of being entirely discredited, has often rather understated his case.

173. As Durham says, in his *Exposition of the Song of Solomon*, p. 451, "It is no burden to an honest believer to acknowledge Christ's ministers, to obey their doctrine, and submit to their censures."

174. A man, named Alexander Laurie, was brought before the Kirk Session of Perth, "and being inquired by the minister if, in his last being out of this country, he had been in Spain, answered that he was in Portugal, but was never present at mass, neither gave reverence to any procession, and that he was never demanded by any concerning his religion. The said Alexander being removed and censured, it was thought good by the (Kirk) Session that he should be admonished not to travel in these parts again, except that they were otherwise reformed in religion." *Extracts from the Kirk-Session Register of Perth,* in *The Spottiswoode Miscellany,* vol. ii. p. 274. Still earlier, that is, in 1592, the clergy attempted to interfere even with commerce, "allegeing that the marchands could not mak vayage in Spayne without danger of thair sawlis, and therefore

keeper to admit a Catholic into his inn.[175] It was a sin for any Scotch town to hold a market either on Saturday or on Monday, because both days were near Sunday.[176] It was a sin for a Scotch woman to wait at a tavern;[177] it was a sin for her to live alone;[178] it was also a sin for her to live with unmarried sisters.[179] It was a sin to go from one town to another on Sunday, however pressing the business might be.[180] It was a sin to visit your friend on Sunday;[181] it was likewise sinful either to have your garden wa-

---

willit thayme in the nayme of God to absteyne." *The Historie of King James the Sext*, p. 254.

175. See the case of Patrick Stewart, and Mr. Lawson's note upon it, in *Lawson's Book of Perth*, p. 238. In this instance, the "Roman Catholic gentleman" had been excommunicated, which made matters still worse.

176. The Presbytery of Edinburgh, "by their transcendent sole authority, discharged any market to be kept on Monday; the reason was, because it occasioned the travelling of men and horse the Lord's-day before, which prophaned the Sabbath." *Presbytery Displayed*, p. 10. In 1650, Saturday was also taken in by another ecclesiastical senate. "The Presbyterie doe appoint the severall brethren in burghes, to deale with such as have not changed ther Mondayes and Satterdayes mercats to other dayes of the weeke, that they may be doe the same *primo quoque tempore*." *Minutes of the Presbyteries of St. Andrews and Cupar*, p. 53.

177. In 1650, "For 'the down-bearing of sin,'" women were not allowed to act as waiters in taverns, but "allenarly men-servands and boys.'" *Chambers' Annals*, vol. ii. p. 196. This order "wes red and publictlie intimat in all the kirkis of Edinburgh." *Nicoll's Diary*, p. 5.

178. "Forsameikle as dilatation being made, that Janet Watson holds an house by herself where *she may give occasion of slander,* therfore Patrick Pitcairn, elder, is ordained to admonish her in the session's name, either to marry, or then pass to service, otherwise that she will not be suffered to dwell by herself." *Kirk-Session Records of Perth*, in *The Chronicle of Perth*, p. 86.

179. "Ordains the two sisters, Elspith and Janet Stewart, that they be not found in the house again with their sister, but every one of them shall go to service, or where they may be best entertained without slander, under the penalty of warding their persons and banishment of the town." *Kirk-Session Register*, in *Lawson's Book of Perth*, p. 169.

180. "Compeirit William Kinneir, and confest his travelling on the Sabbath day, which he declairit was out of meer necessitie, haveing two watters to croce, and ane tempestuos day, quhilk moowit him to fear that he wold not get the watters crost, and so his credit might faill. He was sharpelie admonished; and promist newer to doe the lyke again." *Selections from the Records of the Kirk-Session of Aberdeen*, p. 136.

181. "Compearit Thomas Gray, and confest that one Sunday in the morning, he went to Culter to visit a friend, and stayed thair all night. The sessioune warnit him, *apud acta,* to the next day, and appointed Patrick Gray, his master, to be cited to the next day, to give furder informatioune in the matter. (Sharply rebuked before the pulpit.)" *Selections from the Records of the Kirk-Session of Aberdeen*, p. 146.

tered,[182] or your beard shaved.[183] Such things were not to be tolerated in a Christian land. No one, on Sunday, should pay attention to his health, or think of his body at all. On that day, horse-exercise was sinful;[184] so was walking in the fields, or in the meadows, or in the streets, or enjoying the fine weather by sitting at the door of your own house.[185] To go to sleep on Sunday, before the duties of the day were over, was also sinful, and deserved church censure.[186] Bathing, being pleasant as well as wholesome, was a particularly grievous offence; and no man could be allowed to swim on Sunday.[187] It was, in fact, doubtful

182. "It was reported that Margaret Brotherstone did water her kaill wpon the Sabbath day, and thairwpon was ordained to be cited." .... "Compeired Margaret Brotherstone, and confessed her breach of Sabbath in watering of her kaill, and thairwpon ordained to give evidence in publick of her repentance the next Lord's day." *Extracts from the Register of the Kirk-Session of Humbie,* p. 42.

183. Even so late as the middle of the eighteenth century, "clergymen were sometimes libelled" .... "for shaving" on Sunday. *Sinclair's Statistical Account of Scotland,* vol. xvi. p. 34, Edinburgh, 1795. At an earlier period, no one might be shaved on that day. See *The Spottiswoode Miscellany,* vol. ii. p. 276; and *Lawson's Book of Perth,* pp. 224, 225.

184. "Compeired John Gordon of Avachie, and confessed that he had transgressed in travailing on the Sabbath day with horse, going for a milston. Referred to the session of Kinor for censure." *Extracts from the Presbytery Book of Strathbogie,* p. 236. See also the case mentioned in *Letters from a Gentleman in the North of Scotland,* vol. i. p. 172; "This riding on horseback of a Sunday was deemed a great scandal."

185. In 1647, the punishment was ordered of whoever was guilty of "sitting or walking idle upon the streetes and feildes" on Sunday. *Selections from the Minutes of the Synod of Fife,* p. 152. In 1742, "sitting idle at their doors" and "sitting about doors" was profane. *Robe's Narratives of the Extraordinary Work of the Spirit of God,* pp. 109, 110. In 1756, at Perth, "to stroll about the fields, or even to walk upon the inches, was looked upon as extremely sinful, and an intolerable violation of the fourth commandment." *Penny's Traditions of Perth,* p. 36.

186. In 1656, "Cite Issobell Balfort, servand to William Gordone, tailyeor, beeing found sleeping at the Loche side on the Lord's day in tyme of sermon." *Selections from the Records of the Kirk-Session of Aberdeen,* p. 137. It was a sin even for children to feel tired of the interminable sermons which they were forced to hear. Halyburton, addressing the young people of his congregation, says, "Have not you been glad when the Lord's day was over; or, at least, *when the preaching was done,* that ye might get your liberty? Has it not been a burden to you, to sit so long in the church? Well, *this is a great sin."* See this noticeable passage, in *Halyburton's Great Concern of Salvation,* p. 100.

187. In 1719, the Presbytery of Edinburgh indignantly declares, "Yea, some have arrived at that height of impiety, as not to be ashamed of washing in waters, and swimming in rivers upon the holy Sabbath." *Register of Presbytery of Edinburgh,* 29th April 1719, in *Arnot's History of Edinburgh,* p. 204.

whether swimming was lawful for a Christian at any time, even on week-days, and it was certain that God had, on one occasion, shown His disapproval, by taking away the life of a boy while he was indulging in that carnal practice.[188]

That it was a sin to cleanse one's body, might, indeed, have been taken for granted; seeing that the Scotch clergy looked on all comforts as sinful in themselves, merely because they were comforts.[189] The great object of life was, to be in a state of constant affliction.[190] Whatever pleased the senses, was to be suspected.[191] A Christian must beware of enjoying his dinner; for none but the ungodly relished their food.[192] By a parity of reasoning, it was wrong for a man to wish to advance himself in life, or in any way to better his condition.[193] Either to make

188. So late as 1691, the Kirk-Session of Glasgow attempted to prevent all boys from swimming, whatever the day might be. But as the Church was then on the decline, it was necessary to appeal to the civil authority for help. What the result was, I have not been able to ascertain. There is, however, a curious notice, in *Wodrow's Collections upon the Lives of Ministers,* vol. ii. part ii. p. 77, stating that, on "August 6th, 1691, the Session recommends it to the magistrates to think on some overtures for discharging boyes from swimming, in regard one was lately lost." I have met with other evidence respecting this; but I cannot remember the passages.

189. The Rev. James Fraser says, "The world is a dangerous thing and a great evil, and the comforts of it a hell." *Select Biographies,* vol. ii. p. 220. Compare *Gray's Spiritual Warfare,* p. 22.

190. "It is good to be continually afflicted here." *Select Biographies,* vol. ii. p. 220. Gray, advocating the same doctrine, sums up his remarks by a suggestion, that, "I think David had never so sweet a time as then, when he was pursued as a partridge by his son Absalom." *Gray's Great and Precious Promises,* p. 14.

191. "Suspect that which pleaseth the senses." *Abernethy's Physicke for the Soule,* p. 63.

192. Durham, in his long catalogue of sins, mentions as one, "the preparing of meat studiously, that is, when it is too riotously dressed, for pleasing men's carnal appetite and taste, or palate, by the fineness of it, and other curiosities of that kind." *Durham's Law Unsealed,* p. 333. See also p. 48, on "palate-pleasers;" and Dickson's opinion of the "rarest dishes and best meats." *Dickson's Explication of the Psalms,* p. 84. According to another of the Scotch divines, whoever makes one good meal and has enough left for a second, is in imminent peril. "He that is full, and hath enough to make him fuller, will easily deny God, and be exalted against him: his table shall be a snare to his body, and a snare to his soule." *Abernethy's Physicke for the Soule,* p. 421.

193. For, says Abernethy (*Physicke for the Soule,* p. 488), "men are loth to lend their eare to the Word, when they abound in prosperity." So, too, Hutcheson, in his *Exposition of the Book of Job,* p. 387: "Such is the weakness even of godly men, that they can hardly live in a prosperous condition, and not be overtaken with some security, carnal confidence, or other miscarriage."

money, or to save it, was unsuited to Christians; and even to possess much of it was objectionable, because it not only ministered to human pleasures, but encouraged those habits of foresight and of provision for the future, which are incompatible with complete resignation to the Divine will. To wish for more than was necessary to keep oneself alive, was a sin as well as a folly, and was a violation of the subjection we owe to God.[194] That it was contrary to His desire, was, moreover, evident, from the fact that He bestowed wealth liberally upon misers and covetous men; a remarkable circumstance, which, in the opinion of Scotch divines, proved that He was no lover of riches, otherwise He would not give them to such base and sordid persons.[195]

To be poor, dirty, and hungry, to pass through life in misery, and to leave it with fear, to be plagued with boils, and sores, and diseases of every kind, to be always sighing and groaning, to have the face streaming with tears and the chest heaving with

194. See this theory worked out in *Cockburn's Jacob's Vow, or Man's Felicity and Duty*, pp. 71–75. He says, "And certainly to crave and be desirous of more than what is competent for the maintenance and support of our lives, is both inconsistent with that dependence and subjection we owe to God, and doth also bespeak a great deal of vanity, folly, and inconsiderateness." Boston, striking at the very foundation of that practice of providing for the future, which is the first and most important maxim in all civil wisdom, and which peculiarly distinguishes civilized nations from barbarians, asks his hearers, "Why should men rack their heads with cares how to provide for to-morrow, while they know not if they shall then need anything?" *Boston's Human Nature in its Four-fold State*, p. 300. Hutcheson thinks that those who are guilty of such impious prudence, deserve to be starved. "When men are not content with food and rayment, but would still heap up more, it is just with God to leave them not so much as bread; and to suffer men to have an evil eye upon them, and to pluck at them, even so long as they have meat." *Hutcheson's Exposition of the Book of Job*, p. 296. Binning, going still further, threatens eternal ruin. "Ye may have things necessary here,—food and raiment; and if ye seek more, if ye will be rich, and will have superfluities, then ye shall fall into many temptations, snares, and hurtful lusts which shall drown you in perdition." *Binning's Sermons*, vol. iii. p. 355.

195. "If God loved riches well, do ye think he would give them so liberally, and heap them upon some base covetous wretches? Surely no." *Binning's Sermons*, vol. iii. p. 366. Gray, in his zeal against wealth, propounds another doctrine, which I do not remember to have seen elsewhere. He says, "All that the owner of riches hath, is, the seeing of them; which a man, who is a passer by, may likeways have, though he be not possessor of them." *Gray's Spiritual Warfare*, p. 128. I hope that the reader will not suspect me of having maliciously invented any of these passages. The books from which they are quoted, are, with only two or three exceptions, all in my library, and may be examined by persons who are curious in such matters.

sobs, in a word, to suffer constant affliction, and to be tormented in all possible ways; to undergo these things was deemed a proof of goodness, just as the contrary was a proof of evil. It mattered not what a man liked; the mere fact of his liking it, made it sinful. Whatever was natural, was wrong. The clergy deprived the people of their holidays, their amusements, their shows, their games, and their sports; they repressed every appearance of joy, they forbad all merriment, they stopped all festivities, they choked up every avenue by which pleasure could enter, and they spread over the country an universal gloom.[196] Then, truly, did darkness sit on the land. Men, in their daily actions and in their very looks, became troubled, melancholy, and ascetic. Their countenance soured, and was downcast. Not only their opinions, but their gait, their demeanour, their voice, their general aspect, were influenced by that deadly blight which nipped all that was genial and warm. The way of life fell into the sear and yellow leaf; its tints gradually deepened; its bloom faded, and passed off; its spring, its freshness, and its beauty, were gone; joy and love either disappeared or were forced to hide themselves in obscure corners, until at length the fairest and most endearing parts of our nature, being constantly repressed, ceased to bear fruit, and seemed to be withered into perpetual sterility.

Thus it was, that the national character of the Scotch was, in the seventeenth century, dwarfed and mutilated. With nations, as with individuals, the harmony and free development of life can only be attained by exercising its principal functions boldly and without fear. Those functions are of two kinds; one set of them increasing the happiness of the mind, another set increasing the happiness of the body. If we could suppose a man completely perfect, we should take for granted that he would unite these two forms of pleasure in the highest degree, and would extract, both from body and mind, every enjoyment consistent

196. "The absence of external appearances of joy in Scotland, in contrast with the frequent holidayings and merry-makings of the continent, has been much remarked upon. We find in the records of ecclesiastical discipline clear traces of the process by which this distinction was brought about. To the puritan kirk of the sixteenth and seventeenth centuries, every outward demonstration of natural good spirits was a sort of sin, to be as far as possible repressed." . . . . "The whole sunshine of life was, as it were, squeezed out of the community." *Chambers' Annals of Scotland*, vol. i. p. 336, vol. iii. p. 156.

with his own happiness, and with the happiness of others. But, as no such character is to be found, it invariably occurs, that even the wisest of us are unable to hold the balance; we, therefore, err, some in over-indulging the body, some in over-indulging the mind. Comparing one set of indulgences with the other, there can be no doubt that the intellectual pleasures are, in many respects, superior to the physical; they are more numerous, more varied, more permanent, and more ennobling; they are less liable to cause satiety in the individual, and they produce more good to the species. But for one person who can enjoy intellectual pleasures, there are at least a hundred who can enjoy physical pleasures. The happiness derived from gratifying the senses, being thus diffused over a wider area, and satisfying, at any given moment, a greater number of persons than the other form of happiness is capable of, does, on that account, possess an importance which many who call themselves philosophers are unwilling to recognize. Too often have philosophic and speculative thinkers, by a foolish denunciation of such pleasures, done all in their power to curtail the quantity of happiness of which humanity is susceptible. Forgetting that we have bodies as well as minds, and forgetting, too, that in an immense majority of instances the body is more active than the mind, that it is more powerful, that it plays a more conspicuous part, and is fitted for greater achievements, such writers commit the enormous error of despising that class of actions to which ninety-nine men out of every hundred are most prone, and for which they are best fitted. And for committing this error they pay the penalty of finding their books unread, their systems disregarded, and their scheme of life adopted, perhaps, by a small class of solitary students, but shut out from that great world of reality for which it is unsuited, and in which it would produce the most serious mischief.

If, then, we review the history of opinion in connexion with the history of action, we may probably say, that the ascetic notions of philosophers, such, for instance, as the doctrines of the Stoics, and similar theories of mortification, have not worked the harm which might have been expected, and have not succeeded in abridging, to any perceptible extent, the substantial happiness of mankind. There are, I apprehend, two reasons why they have failed. In the first place, these philosophers have, with hardly an exception, had little real acquaintance with human nature, and have, therefore, been unable to touch those chords, and appeal to those hidden motives, by influencing which one man gains over another to his side. And, in the second place, they, fortunately for us, have never possessed authority, and have, therefore, been unable either to enforce their doctrine by penalties, or to recommend it by rewards.

But, though philosophers have failed in their effort to lessen the pleasures of mankind, there is another body of men, who, in making the same attempt, have met with far greater success. I mean, of course, the theologians, who, considered as a class, have, in every country and in every age, deliberately opposed themselves to gratifications which are essential to the happiness of an overwhelming majority of the human race. Raising up a God of their own creation, whom they hold out as lover of penance, of sacrifice, and of mortification, they, under this pretence, forbid enjoyments which are not only innocent, but praiseworthy. For, every enjoyment by which no one is injured, is innocent; and every innocent enjoyment is praiseworthy, because it assists in diffusing that spirit of content and of satisfaction which is favourable to the practice of benevolence towards others. The theologians, however, for reasons which I have already stated, cultivate an opposite spirit, and, whenever they have possessed power, they have always prohibited a large number of pleasurable actions, on the ground that such actions are offensive to the Deity. That they have no warrant for this, and that they are simply indulging in preemptory assertions on subjects respecting which we have no trustworthy information, is well known to those who, impartially, and without preconceived bias, have studied their arguments, and the evidence which they adduce. On this, however, I need not dilate; for, inasmuch as men are, almost every year, and certainly every generation, becoming more accustomed to close and accurate reasoning, just in the same proportion is the conviction spreading, that theologians proceed from arbitrary assumptions, for which they have no proof, except by appealing to other assumptions, equally arbitrary and equally unproven. Their whole system reposes upon fear, and upon fear of the worst kind; since, according to them, the Great Author of our being has used His omnipotence in so cruel a manner as to endow

His creatures with tastes, instincts, and desires, which He not only forbids them to gratify, but which, if they do gratify, shall bring on themselves eternal punishment.

What the theologians are to the closet, that are the priests to the pulpit. The theologians work upon the studious, who read; the clergy act upon the idle, who listen. Seeing, however, that the same man often performs both offices, and seeing, too, that the spirit and tendency of each office are the same, we may, for practical purposes, consider the two classes as identical; and, putting them together, and treating them as a whole, it must be admitted by whoever will take a comprehensive view of what they have actually done, that they have been, not only the most bitter foes of human happiness, but also the most successful ones. In their high and palmy days, when they reigned supreme, when credulity was universal and doubt unknown, they afflicted mankind in every possible way; enjoining fasts, and penances, and pilgrimages, teaching their simple and ignorant victims every kind of austerity, teaching them to flog their own bodies, to tear their own flesh, and to mortify the most natural of their appetites. This was the state of Europe in the middle ages. It is still the state of every part of the world where the priesthood are uncontrolled. Such ascetic and self-tormenting observances are the inevitable issue of the theological spirit, if that spirit is unchecked. Now, and owing to the rapid march of our knowledge, it is constantly losing ground, because the scientific and secular spirit is encroaching on its domain. Therefore, in our time, and especially in our country, its most repulsive features are disguised, and it is forced to mask its native ugliness. Among our clergy, a habit of grave and decent compromise has taken the place of that bold and fiery war which their predecessors waged against a sensual and benighted world. Their threats have perceptibly diminished. They now allow us a little pleasure, a little luxury, a little happiness. They no longer tell us to mortify every appetite, and to forego every comfort. The language of power has departed from them. Here and there, we find vestiges of the ancient spirit; but this is only among uneducated men, addressing an ignorant audience. The superior clergy, who have a character to lose, are grown cautious; and, whatever their private opinion may be, they rarely venture on those terrific denunciations with which their pulpits once resounded, and which, in times of yore, made the people shrink with fear, and humbled every one except him by whom the denunciation was uttered.

Still, though much of this has vanished, enough remains to show what the theological spirit is, and to justify a belief, that nothing but the pressure of public opinion prevents it from breaking out into its former extravagance. Many of the clergy persist in attacking the pleasures of the world, forgetting that, not only the world, but all which the world contains, is the work of the Almighty, and that the instincts and desires, which they stigmatize as unholy, are part of His gifts to man. They have yet to learn, that our appetites, being as much a portion of ourselves as any other quality we possess, ought to be indulged, otherwise the whole individual is not developed. If a man suppresses part of himself, he becomes maimed and shorn. The proper limit to self-indulgence is, that he shall neither hurt himself nor hurt others. Short of this, every thing is lawful. It is more than lawful; it is necessary. He who abstains from safe and moderate gratification of the senses, lets some of his essential faculties fall into abeyance, and must, on that account, be deemed imperfect and unfinished. Such an one is incomplete; he is crippled; he has never reached his full stature. He may be a monk; he may be a saint; but a man he is not. And now, more than ever, do we want true and genuine men. No previous age has had so much work to do, and, to accomplish that work, we need robust and vigorous natures, whose every function has been freely exercised without let or hindrance. Never before, was the practice of life so arduous; never were the problems presented to the human mind so numerous, or so complicated. Every addition to our knowledge, every fresh idea, opens up new difficulties, and gives birth to new combinations. Under this accumulated pressure, we shall assuredly sink, if we imitate the credulity of our forefathers, who allowed their energies to be cramped and weakened by those pernicious notions, which the clergy, partly from ignorance, and partly from interest, have, in every age, palmed on the people, and have, thereby, diminished the national happiness, and retarded the march of national prosperity.

In the same way, we constantly hear of the evils of wealth, and of the sinfulness of loving money; although it is certain that, after the love of knowledge, there is no one passion which has done so much good to mankind as the love of money. It is to the love of money that we owe all trade and commerce; in other words, the possession of every comfort and luxury which our own country is unable to supply. Trade and commerce have made us familiar with the productions of many lands, have awakened curiosity, have widened our ideas by bringing us in contact with nations of various manners, speech, and thought, have supplied an outlet for energies which would otherwise have been pent up and wasted, have accustomed men to habits of enterprise, forethought and calculation, have, moreover, communicated to us many arts of great utility, and have put us in possession of some of the most valuable remedies with which we are acquainted, either to save life or to lessen pain. These things we owe to the love of money. If theologians could succeed in their desire to destroy that love, all these things would cease, and we should relapse into comparative barbarism. The love of money, like all our appetites, is liable to abuse; but to declaim against it as evil in itself, and, above all, to represent it as a feeling, the indulgence of which provokes the wrath of God, is to betray an ignorance, natural, perhaps, in former ages, but shameful in our time, particularly when it proceeds from men who give themselves out as public teachers, and profess that it is their mission to enlighten the world.

Injurious, however, as all this is to the best interests of society, it is nothing in comparison with the doctrines formerly advocated by the Scotch divines. What their ideas were, I have shown from their own sermons, the reading of which has been the most painful literary task I ever undertook, since, in addition to the narrowness and the dogmatism which even the best of such compositions contain, there is, in these productions, a hardness of heart, as austerity of temper, a want of sympathy with human happiness, and a hatred of human nature, such as have rarely been exhibited in any age, and, I rejoice to think, have never been exhibited in any Protestant country. These things, I have resuscitated from the oblivion in which they had long been buried, partly because it was necessary to do so in order to understand the history of the Scotch mind, and partly because I desired to show what the tendency of theologians is, when that tendency is uncontrolled. Protestants, generally, are too apt to suppose that there is something in their creed which protects them against those hurtful extravagancies which have been, and, to a certain extent, still are, practised in the Catholic Church. Never was a greater mistake. There is but one protection against the tyranny of any class; and that is, to give that class very little power. Whatever the pretensions of any body of men may be, however smooth their language, and however plausible their claims, they are sure to abuse power, if much of it is conferred on them. The entire history of the world affords no instance to the contrary. In Catholic countries, France alone excepted, the clergy have more authority than in Protestant countries. Therefore, in Catholic countries, they do more harm than in Protestant countries, and their peculiar views are developed with greater freedom. The difference depends, not on the nature of the creed, but on the power of the class. This is very apparent in Scotland, where the clergy, being supreme, did, Protestants though they were, imitate the ascetic, the unsocial, and the cruel doctrines, which, in the Catholic Church, gave rise to convents, fastings, scourgings, and all the other appliances of an uncouth and ungenial superstition.

Indeed, the Scotch divines, in some of their theories, went beyond any section of the Catholic Church, except the Spanish. They sought to destroy, not only human pleasures, but also human affections. They held that our affections are necessarily connected with our lusts, and that we must, therefore, wean ourselves from them as earthly vanities.[197] A Christian had no business with love or sympathy. He had his own soul to attend to, and that was enough for him. Let him look to himself. On Sunday, in particular, he must never think of benefiting others; and the Scotch clergy did not hesitate to teach the people, that on that day it was sinful to save a vessel in distress, and that it was a proof of religion to leave ship and crew to perish.[198] They might go; none but their wives and children would suffer, and that was nothing

197. "A Christian should mortifie his affections, which are his predominant lusts, to which our affections are so much joined, and our soul doth so much go out after." *Gray's Spiritual Warfare,* p. 29. "That blessed work of weaning of affections from all things that are here." *Grant's Great and Precious Promises,* p. 86.

198. "One of our more northern ministers, whose parish lies along the coast between Spey and Findorn, made some fishermen do penance for sabbath-breaking, in going out to sea, though purely with endeavour to save a vessel in distress by a storm." *Letters from a Gentleman in the North of Scotland,* vol. i. p. 173.

in comparison with breaking the Sabbath. So, too, did the clergy teach, that on no occasion must food or shelter be given to a starving man, unless his opinions were orthodox.[199] What need for him to live? Indeed, they taught that it was a sin to tolerate his notions at all, and that the proper course, was, to visit him with sharp and immediate punishment.[200] Going yet further, they broke the domestic ties, and set parents against their offspring. They taught the father to smite the unbelieving child, and to slay his own boy sooner than allow him to propagate error.[201] As if

199. "The master of a family may, and ought to, deny an act of humanity or hospitality to strangers that are false teachers." *Rutherford's Free Disputation against Pretended Liberty of Conscience,* p. 176. "The Holy Ghost forbiddeth the master of every Christian family to owne a hereticke as a guest." *Ibid.,* p. 219. See also p. 235.

200. "We hold that tolleration of all religions is not farre from blasphemy." *Rutherford's Free Disputation against Pretended Liberty of Conscience,* p. 20. "If wolves be permitted to teach what is right in their own erroneous conscience, and there be no 'Magistrate to put them to shame,' *Judg.* xviii. 7, and no King to punish them, then godlinesse and all that concernes the first Table of the Law must be marred." *Ibid.,* p. 230. "Wilde and atheisticall liberty of conscience." p. 337. "Cursed tolleration." p. 400. See also, in the same work (pp. 110, 244), Rutherford's remarks on the murder of Servetus. In 1645, Baillie, who was then in London, writes, "The Independents here plead for a tolleration both for themselfes and other sects. My Dissuasive is come in time to doe service here. We hope God will assist us to remonstrate the wickedness of such an tolleration." And on account of the Independents wishing to show common charity towards persons who differed in opinions from themselves, Baillie writes next year (1646), "The Independents has the least zeale to the truth of God of any men we know." *Baillie's Letters and Journals,* vol. ii. pp. 328, 361. Blair, who was in London in 1649, was sorely vexed with "the most illegal, irreligious, and wicked proceedings and actings of the sectarian army;" one of their crimes being the attempt "to ruin religion by their toleration." *Continuation of the Autobiography of Mr. Robert Blair, Minister of St. Andrews* p. 213. For other evidence of this persecuting spirit, see *Dickson's Truth's Victory over Error,* pp. 159, 163, 199–202; *Abernethy's Physicke for the Soule,* p. 215; *Durham's Exposition of the Song of Solomon,* p. 147; *Durham's Commentarie upon the Book of the Revelation,* pp. 141, 143, 330; and *Shields' Hind let loose,* p. 168.

201. "A third benefit (which is a branch of the former), is zeal in the godly against false teachers, who shall be so tender of the truth and glory of God, and the safety of the Church (all which are endangered by error), that it shall overcome natural affection in them; so that parents shall not *spare their own children,* being seducers, but shall either by an heroick act (such as was in Phinehas, *Numb.* xxv. 8), *themselves judge him worthy to die, and give sentence and execute it,* or cause him to be punished, by bringing him to the Magistrate," &c. . . . . . "The toleration of a false religion in doctrine or worship, and the exemption of the erroneous from civil punishment, is no more lawful under the New Testament than it was under the Old." *An Exposition of the Prophecie of Zechariah,* in *Hutcheson's Exposition on the Minor Prophets,* vol. iii. p. 203, 8vo, 1654.

this were not enough, they tried to extirpate another affection, even more sacred and more devoted still. They laid their rude and merciless hands on the holiest passion of which our nature is capable, the love of a mother for her son. Into that sanctuary, they dared to intrude; into that, they thrust their gaunt and ungentle forms. If a mother held opinions of which they disapproved, they did not scruple to invade her household, take away her children, and forbid her to hold communication with them.[202] Or if, perchance, her son had incurred their displeasure, they were not satisfied with forcible separation, but they laboured to corrupt her heart, and harden it against her child, so that she might be privy to the act. In one of these cases, mentioned in the records of the church of Glasgow, the Kirk-Session of that town summoned before them a woman, merely because she had received into her house her own son, after the clergy had excommunicated him. So effectually did they work upon her mind, that they induced her to promise, not only that she would shut her door against her child, but that she would aid in bringing him to punishment. She had sinned in loving him; she had sinned, even, in giving him shelter; but, says the record, "she promised not to do it again, and to tell the magistrates when he comes next to her."[203]

She promised not to do it again. She promised to forget him, whom she had borne of her womb and suckled at her breast. She promised to forget her boy, who had ofttimes crept to her knees, who had slept in her bosom, and whose tender frame she had watched over and nursed. All the dearest associations of the past, all that the most exquisite form of human affections can give or receive, all that delights the memory, all that brightens the prospect of life, all vanished, all passed away from the mind of this poor woman, at the bidding of her spiritual masters. At one fell swoop, all were gone. So potent were the arts of these men, that they persuaded the mother to conspire against her son, that she might deliver him up to them. They defiled her nature, by purging it of its love. From that day, her soul was polluted. She was lost to herself, as well as lost to her son. To hear of such things, is

202. *Selections from the Registers of the Presbytery of Lanark,* pp. x. 33, 56, 63, 65, 73.

203. I copy the exact words from *Wodrow's Collections upon the Lives of Ministers of the Church of Scotland,* vol. ii. part ii. p. 71. An order had been previously obtained from the government, "requiring the magistrates to expell furth of the Toun all excommunicated persons."

enough to make one's blood surge again, and raise a tempest in our inmost nature. But to have seen them, to have lived in the midst of them, and yet not to have rebelled against them, is to us utterly inconceivable, and proves in how complete a thraldom the Scotch were held, and how thoroughly their minds, as well as their bodies, were enslaved.

What more need I say? What further evidence need I bring to elucidate the real character of one of the most detestable tyrannies even seen on the earth? When the Scotch Kirk was at the height of its power, we may search history in vain for any institution which can compete with it, except the Spanish Inquisition. Be tween these two, there is a close and intimate analogy. Both were intolerant, both were cruel, both made war upon the finest parts of human nature, and both destroyed every vestige of religious freedom. One difference, however, there was, of vast importance. In political matters, the Church, which was servile in Spain, was rebellious in Scotland. Hence, the Scotch always had one direction in which they could speak and act with unrestrained liberty. In politics, they found their salvation. This saved them from the fate of Spain, by securing to them the exercise of those faculties which otherwise would have lain dormant, if, indeed, they had not been entirely destroyed by that long and enfeebling servitude in which their clergy retained them, and from which, but for this favourable circumstance, no escape would have been open.

V

An Examination of the Scotch Intellect during the Eighteenth Century

To complete the history and analysis of the Scotch mind, I have now to examine the peculiar intellectual movement which appeared in the eighteenth century, and which, for several reasons, deserves careful attention. It was essentially a reaction against the theological spirit which predominated during the seventeenth century. Such a reaction would hardly have been possible, except for the fact which I have already noticed, namely, that the political activity which produced the rebellion against the Stuarts, saved the Scotch mind from stagnating, and prevented that deep slumber into which the progress of superstition would naturally have thrown it. The long and stubborn conflict with a despotic government, kept alive a certain alertness and vigour of understanding, which survived the struggle that gave it birth. When the contest was ended, and peace was restored, the faculties which, for three generations, had been exercised in resisting the executive authority, sought other employment, and found another field in which they could disport themselves. Hence it was, that the boldness which, in the seventeenth century, was practical, became, in the eighteenth century, speculative, and produced a literature, which attempted to unsettle former opinions, and to disturb the ancient landmarks of the human mind. The movement was revolutionary, and bore the same relation to ecclesiastical tyranny, which the previous movement had borne to political tyranny. But this new rebellion had one striking characteristic. In nearly every other country, when the intellect has fairly arrayed itself against the exclusive pretensions of the Church, it has happened that the secular philosophy, which has been engendered, has been an inductive philosophy, taking for its basis individual and specific experience, and seeking, by that means, to overthrow the general and traditional notions, on which all church power is founded. The plan has been, to refuse to accept principles which could not be substantiated by facts; while the opposite and theological plan is, to force the facts to yield to the principles. In the former case, experience precedes theory; in the latter case, theory precedes experience, and controls it. In theology, certain principles are taken for granted; and, it being deemed impious to question them, all that remains for us is to reason from them downwards. This is the deductive method. On the other hand, the inductive method will concede nothing, but insists upon reasoning upwards, and demands that we shall have the liberty of ascertaining the principles for ourselves. In a complete scheme of our knowledge, and when all our resources are fully developed and marshalled into order, as they must eventually be, the two methods will be, not hostile, but supplementary, and will be combined into a single system. At present, however, we are very far from such a result; and not only is every mind more prone to one method than to another, but we find, historically, that different ages and different countries have been characterized by the extent to which one of these two schemes has predominated; and we also find, that a study of this antagonism is the surest way of understanding the intellectual condition of any period.

That the inductive philosophy is even more marked by its secular tendencies than by its scientific ones, will be evident to whoever observes the epochs in which it has been most active, and has possessed most adherents. Of this, the history of the French mind, in the eighteenth century, affords a good instance, where, after the death of Louis XIV., we may clearly trace the connexion between the growth of the inductive method, and the subsequent overthrow of the Gallican church. In England, too, the rise of the Baconian philosophy, with its determination to subordinate ancient principles to modern experience, was the heaviest blow which has ever been inflicted on the theologians, whose method is to begin, not with experience, but with principles, which are said to be inscrutable, and which we are bound to believe without further difficulty. And I need hardly remind the reader, that scarcely was that philosophy established among us, when it produced those bold inquiries which quickly ended in the downfall of the English Church under Charles I. From that terrible defeat, our clergy did, for a time, partly rally; but as their apparent success, in the reign of Charles II., was owing to political changes, and not to social ones, they were unable to recover their hold over society, and, unless the nation should retrograde, there is no possibility that they ever should recover it. Over the inferior order of minds, they still wield great influence; but the Baconian philosophy, by bringing their favourite method into disrepute, has sapped the very base of their system. From the moment that their mode of investigation was discredited, the secret of their power was gone. From the moment that men began to insist on inquiring into the validity of first principles, instead of accepting them without inquiry, and humbly submitting to them as matters of faith and of necessary belief; from that moment, the theologians, driven from one post to another, and constantly receding before the pressure of advancing knowledge, have been forced to abandon entrenchment after entrenchment, until what they have retained of their former territory is hardly worth the struggle. As a last resource, they, at the close of the eighteenth century, determined to use the weapons of their opponents; and Paley and his successors, enlarging the scheme which Ray and Derham had feebly sketched, endeavoured, by a skilful employment of the inductive method, to compensate their party for the failure of the deductive one. But their project, though ably conceived, has come to naught. It is now generally admitted, that nothing can be made of it, and that it is impossible to establish the old theological premises by a chain of inductive reasoning. Respecting this, the most eminent philosophers agree with the most eminent theologians; and, since the time of Kant in Germany, and of Coleridge in England, none of our ablest men, even among divines themselves, have recurred to a plan which Paley, indeed, pursued with vigour, but of which our Bridgewater Treatises, our Prize-Essays, and such schoolboy productions, are poor and barren imitations.[1]

1. Of course, I say this merely in reference to their theological bearings. Some of the Bridgewater Treaties, such as Bell's, Buckland's, and Prout's, had great scientific merit at the time of their appearance, and may even now be

No great thinkers now follow this course in matters of religion. On the contrary, they prefer the safer, as well as the more philosophic, method, of dealing with these subjects on transcendental grounds, frankly confessing that they elude the grasp of that inductive philosophy which, in the department of science, has achieved such signal triumphs.

The opposition of these two methods, and the inapplicability of the inductive method to theological pursuits being thus apparent, it is not strange that the Scotch should have adopted one of the methods with great zeal, and to the almost complete exclusion of the other. Scotland, being essentially theological, followed the theological plan. The intellectual history of that country, in the seventeenth century, is almost entirely the history of theology. With the single exception of Napier, who was born in the middle of the sixteenth century, all the most vigorous thinkers were divines. In physical science, scarcely any thing was done.[2] There was

---

studied with advantage; but the religious portion of them is pitiable, and shows either that their heart was not in their work, or else that the subject was too wide for them. At all events, it is to be hoped that we shall never again see men of equal eminence hiring themselves out as paid advocates, and receiving fees to support particular opinions. It is truly disgraceful that such great speculative questions, instead of being subjected to fair and disinterested argument, with a view of eliciting the truth, should be turned into a pecuniary transaction, in which any one of much money and little wit, can bribe as many persons as he likes, to prejudice the public ear in favour of his own theories.

2. "It is humiliating to have to remark, that the notices of comets which we derive from Scotch writers down to this time (1682) contain nothing but accounts of the popular fancies regarding them. Practical astronomy seems to have then been unknown in our country; and hence, while in other lands, men were carefully observing, computing, and approaching to just conclusions regarding these illustrious strangers of the sky, our diarists could only tell us how many *yards* long they seemed to be, what *effects* were apprehended from them in the way of war and pestilence, and how certain pious divines 'improved' them for spiritual edification. Early in this century Scotland had produced one great philosopher, who had supplied his craft with the mathematical instrument by which complex problems, such as the movement of comets, were alone to be solved. It might have been expected that the country of Napier, seventy years after his time, would have had many sons capable of applying his key to such mysteries of nature. But no one had arisen—nor did any rise for fifty years onward, when at length Colin Maclaurin unfolded in the Edinburgh University the sublime philosophy of Newton. There could not be a more expressive signification of the character of the seventeenth century in Scotland. Our unhappy contentions about external religious matters had absorbed the whole genius of the people, rendering to us the age of Cowley, of Waller, and of Milton, as barren of elegant literature, as that of Horrocks, of Halley, and

no poetry, no drama, no original philosophy, no fine compositions, no secular literature, now worth reading.[3] The only men
of real influence, were the clergy. They governed the nation, and
the pulpit was the chief engine of their power. From the pulpit,
they moved all classes and all sorts of intellects; the highest, as
well as the lowest. There, they instructed them, and threatened
them; saying whatever they liked, and knowing that what they
said would be believed.[4] But all their sermons, and all their con-
troversial writings, are eminently deductive; not one of them attempts an inductive argument. The bare idea of such a thing never
entered their heads. They assumed the truth of their own religious
and moral notions, most of which they had borrowed from antiquity; they made those notions the major premises of their syllogisms, and from them they reasoned downwards, till they obtained their conclusions. They never suspected that premises,
taken from ancient times, might be the result of the inductions of
those times, and that, as knowledge advanced, the inductions
might need revising. They assumed, that God has given to us first

---

of Newton, was of science." *Chambers' Domestic Annals of Scotland,* vol. ii.
pp. 444, 445.

3. "Thus, during the whole seventeenth century, the English were gradually
refining their language and their taste; in Scotland, the former was much de-
based, and the latter almost entirely lost." *History of Scotland,* book viii., in
Robertson's Works, p. 260.

"But the taste and science, the genius and the learning of the age, were
absorbed in the gulph of religious controversy. At a time when the learning
of Selden, and the genius of Milton, conspired to adorn England, the Scots
were reduced to such writers as Baillie, Rutherford, Guthrie, and the two
Gillespies." *Laing's History of Scotland,* vol. iii. p. 510. "From the Restoration
down to the Union, the only author of eminence whom Scotland produced was
Burnet." *Ibid.,* vol. iv. p. 406.

"The seventeenth century, fatal to the good taste of Italy, threw a total night
over Scotland." . . . . "Not one writer who does the least credit to the nation
flourished during the century from 1615 to 1715, excepting Burnet, whose name
would, indeed, honour the brightest period. In particular, no poet whose works
merit preservation arose. By a singular fatality, the century which stands highest
in English history and genius, is one of the darkest in those of Scotland."
Ancient Scotish Poems, edited by John Pinkerton, vol. i. pp. iii. iv., London,
1786.

4. Ray, who visited Scotland in 1661, could not suppress a little professional
envy, when he saw how much higher ecclesiastics were rated there than in
England. He says, "the people here frequent their churches much better than
in England, and have their ministers in more esteem and veneration." *Ray's
Memorials, edited by Dr. Lankester for the Ray Society,* p. 161.

principles, and that He, having revealed them, it would ill become to us to scrutinize them. That He had revealed them, they took for granted, and deemed it unnecessary to prove.[5] Their method being thus entirely deductive, all they were concerned with was, to beware that no error crept in between the premises and the conclusions. And this part of their task they accomplished with great ability. They were acute dialecticians, and rarely blundered in what is termed the formal part of logic. In dealing with their premises after they obtained them, they were extremely skilful; how they obtained them, they were very heedless. That was a point they never examined with any thing approaching to impartiality. According to their method, all that was requisite was, to draw inferences from what had been supernaturally communicated. On the other hand, the inductive method would have taught them that the first question was, whether or not they had been supernaturally communicated? They, as deductive reasoners, assumed the very preliminaries which inductive reasoners would have disputed. They proceeded from generals to particulars, instead of from particulars to generals. And they would not allow either themselves or others to sift the general propositions, which were to cover and control the particular facts. It was enough for them that the wider propositions were already established, and were to be treated according to the rules of the old and syllogistic logic. Indeed, they were so convinved of the impropriety of the inductive method, that they did not hesitate to assert, that it was by means of the syllogism that the Deity communicated His wishes to man.[6]

It was naturally to be expected, that the clergy, holding these views respecting the best means of arriving at truth, should do all in their power to bring over the nation to their side, and should

5. "Believing ignorance is much better than rash and presumptuous knowledge. Ask not a reason of these things, but rather adore and tremble at the mystery and majesty of them." *Binning's Sermons,* vol. i. p. 143. Even Biblical criticism was prohibited; and Dickson says of the different books of the Bible, "We are not to trouble ourselves about the name of the writer, or time of writing of any part thereof, especially because God of set purpose concealeth the name sundry times of the writer, and the time when it was written." *Dickson's Explication of the Psalms,* p. 291.

6. "Christ from heaven proposeth a syllogism to Saul's fury." *Rutherford's Christ Dying,* p. 180. "The conclusion of a practical syllogism, whereby the believer concludeth from the gospel that he shall be saved." *Durham's Law Unsealed,* p. 97. "All assurance is by practical syllogism, the first whereof must needs be a Scripture truth." *Gray's Precious Promises,* p. 139.

labour to make their own method of investigation entirely supersede the opposite method. Nor was this a very difficult task. The
prevailing credulity was one great point in their favour, inasmuch
as it made men more willing to accept propositions that to scrutinize them. When the propositions were accepted, nothing was
left but to reason from them; and the most active intellects in
Scotland, being constantly engaged in this process, acquired complete mastery over it, and the dexterity they displayed increased
its repute. Besides this, the clergy, who were its zealous champions, had monopolized all the sources of education, both public
and private. In no other Protestant country, have they exercised
such control over the universities; not only the doctrines taught,
but also the mode of teaching them, being, in Scotland, placed
under the supervision of the Church.[7] This power they, of course,
used to propagate their own plan of obtaining truth; and, as long
as their power remained undiminished, it was hardly possible that
the opposite, or inductive, plan should gain a hearing. Over
grammar-schools, the clergy possessed an authority fully equal to
that which they had in the universities.[8] They also appointed and
removed, at their own pleasure, teachers of every grade, from
village schoolmasters to tutors in private families.[9] In this way,

7. Bower (*History of the University of Edinburgh*, vol. i. p. 217) says,
"The history of the universities and of the church is, in modern Europe, and
perhaps in every other civilized portion of the globe, very nearly connected.
They are more nearly connected in Scotland than in any other civilized country
called Protestant; because the General Assembly have the legal power of
inquiring into the economy of the institutions, both as it respects the mode of
teaching, and the doctrines, whether religious, moral, or physical, which are
taught." Spalding, under the year 1639, gives an instance of the power of the
General Assembly in "the College of Old Aberdeen." *Spalding's History of the
Troubles,* vol. i. p. 178. See also, on the authority exercised by the General
Assembly over the universities, a curious little book, called *The Government
and Order of the Church of Scotland,* Edinburgh, 1690, p. 25.

8. In 1632, the "ministers" of Perth were greatly displeased because John
Row was made master of the grammar-school without their consent. *The
Chronicle of Perth,* p. 33, where it is stated that, consequently, "thair wes
much outcrying in the pulpett."

9. See, for instance, *Minutes of the Presbyteries of St. Andrews and Cupar,*
pp. 66, 83, 84, 118. One of the entries is, that in January 1648, "The Presbyterie ordained that all young students, who waittes on noblemen or gentlemen
within thir bounds, aither to teach ther children, or catechise and pray in ther
families, to frequent the Presbyterie, that the brether may cognosce what they ar
reading, and what proficiencie they make in ther studies, and to know also ther
behaviour in the said families, and of their affection to the Covenant and
present religione." p. 118. Compare *Selections from the Registers of the Presbytery of Lanark,* pp. 56, 65.

each generation, as it arose, was brought under their influence, and made subject to their notions. Taking the mind of Scotland while it was young and flexible, they bent it to their own method. Hence, that method became supreme; it reigned every where; not a voice was lifted up against it; and no one had an idea that there was more than one path by which truth could be reached, or that the human understanding was of any use, except to deal deductively with premises, which were not to be inductively examined.

The inductive or analytic spirit being thus unknown, and the deductive or synthetic spirit being alone favoured, it happened that, when, early in the eighteenth century, the circumstances already mentioned gave rise to a great intellectual movement, that movement, though new in its results, was not new in the method by which the results were obtained. A secular philosophy was, indeed, established, and the ablest men, instead of being theological, became scientific. But so completely had the theological plan occupied Scotland, that even philosophers were unable to escape from its method, and, as I am about to show, the inductive method exercised no influence over them. This most curious fact is the key to the history of Scotland in the eighteenth century, and explains many events which would otherwise appear incompatible with each other. It also suggests an analogy with Germany, where the deductive method has, for a long period, been equally prevalent, owing to precisely the same causes. In both countries, the secular movement of the eighteenth century was unable to become inductive; and this intellectual affinity between two such otherwise different nations, is, I have no doubt, the principal reason why the Scotch and German philosophies have so remarkably acted and reacted upon each other; Kant and Hamilton being the most finished specimens of their intercourse. To this, England forms a complete contrast. For more than a hundred and fifty years after the death of Bacon, the greatest English thinkers, Newton and Harvey excepted, were eminently inductive; nor was it until the nineteenth century that signs were clearly exhibited of a countermovement, and an attempt was made to return in some degree to the deductive method.[10] This, we are, in many respects, justified in doing, because, in the progress of our knowledge, we have, by

10. This I have already touched upon in the first volume, pp. 808, 809. Hereafter, and in my special history of the English mind, I shall examine it carefully and in detail. The revival of the old logic is a great symptom of it. Works

a long course of induction, arrived at several conclusions which we may safely treat deductively; that is to say, we may make them the major premises of new arguments. The same process has been seen in France, where the exclusively inductive philosophy of the eighteenth century preceded a partial resuscitation of deductive philosophy in the nineteenth century. In Scotland, however, there have been so such vicissitudes. In that country, men have always been deductive; even the most original thinkers being unable to liberate themselves from the universal tendency, and being forced to accept a method which time had consecrated, and which was interwoven with all the associations of the national mind.

To understand the investigation into which we are about to enter, the reader must firmly seize, and keep before his eyes, the essential difference between deduction, which reasons from principles, and induction, which reasons to principles. He must remember, that induction proceeds from the smaller to the greater; deduction, from the greater to the smaller. Induction is from particulars to generals, and from the senses to the ideas; deduction is from generals to particulars, and from the ideas to the senses. By induction, we rise from the concrete to the abstract; by deduction, we descend from the abstract to the concrete. Accompanying this distinction, there are certain qualities of mind, which, with extremely few exceptions, characterize the age, nation, or individual, in which one of these methods is predominant. The inductive philosopher is naturally cautious, patient, and somewhat creeping; while the deductive philosopher is more remarkable for boldness, dexterity, and often rashness. The deductive thinker invariably assumes certain premises, which are quite different from the hypotheses essential to the best induction. These premises are sometimes borrowed from antiquity; sometimes they are taken

---

like those of Whately, De Morgan, and Mansel, could not have been produced in the eighteenth century, or, at all events, if by some extraordinary combination of events they had been produced, they would have found no readers. As it is, they have exercised a very extensive and very salutary influence; and, although Archbishop Whately was not well acquainted with the history of formal logic, his exposition of its ordinary processes is so admirably clear, that he has probably contributed more than any other man towards impressing his contemporaries with a sense of the value of deductive reasoning. He has, however, not done sufficient justice to the opposite school, and has, indeed, fallen into the old academical error of supposing that all reasoning is by syllogism. We might just as well say that all movement is by descent.

from the notions which happen to prevail in the surrounding society; sometimes they are the result of a man's own peculiar organization; and sometimes, as we shall presently see, they are deliberately invented, with the object of arriving, not at truth, but at an approximation to truth. Finally, and to sum up the whole, we may say that a deductive habit, being essentially synthetic, always tends to multiply original principles or laws; while the tendency of an inductive habit is to diminish those laws by gradual and successive analysis.

These being the two fundamental divisions of human inquiry, it is surely a most remarkable fact in the history of Scotland, that, during the eighteenth century, all the great thinkers belonged to the former division, and that, in the very few instances of induction which their works contain, it is evident, from the steps they subsequently took, that they regarded such inductions as unimportant in themselves, and as only valuable in so far as they supplied the premises for another and deductive investigation. As the various departments of our knowledge have never yet been co-ordinated and treated as a whole, probably no one is aware of the universality of this movement in Scotland, and of the extent to which it pervaded every science, and governed every phase of thought. To prove, therefore, the force with which it acted, I now purpose to examine its working in all the principal forms of speculation, whether physical or moral, and to show that in each the same method was adopted. In doing this, I must, for the sake of clearness, proceed according to a natural arrangement of the different topics; but I will, whenever it is possible, also follow the chronological order in which the Scotch mind unfolded itself; so that we may understand, not only the character of that remarkable literature, but likewise the steps of its growth, and the astonishing vigour with which it emancipated itself from the shackles which superstition had imposed.

The beginning of the great secular philosophy of Scotland is undoubtedly due to Francis Hutcheson.[11] This eminent man,

11. See a letter from Sir James Mackintosh to Parr, in *Mackintosh's Memoirs*, London, 1835, vol. i. p. 344. "To Hutcheson the taste for speculation in Scotland, and all the philosophical opinions (except the Berkleian Humism) may be traced." M. Cousin (*Histoire de la Philosophie*, première série, vol. iv. p. 35, Paris, 1846) observes, that before Hutcheson "il n'avait paru en Ecosse ni un écrivain ni un professeur de philosophie un peu remarquable."

though born in Ireland, was of Scotch family, and was educated in the University of Glasgow, where he received the appointment of Professor of Philosophy in the year 1729.[12] By his lectures, and by his works, he diffused a taste for bold inquiries into subjects of the deepest importance, but concerning which it had previously been supposed nothing fresh was to be learned; the Scotch having hitherto been taught, that all truths respecting our own nature, which were essential to be known, had been already revealed. Hutcheson, however, did not fear to construct a system of morals according to a plan entirely secular, and no example of which had been exhibited in Scotland before his time. The principles from which he started, were not theological, but metaphysical. They were collected from what he deemed the natural constitution of the mind, instead of being collected, as heretofore, from what had been supernaturally communicated. He, therefore, shifted the field of study. Though he was a firm believer in revelation, he held that the best rules of conduct could be ascertained without its assistance, and could be arrived at by the unaided wit of man; and that, when arrived at, they were, in their aggregate, to be respected as the Law of Nature.[13] This confidence in the power of the human understanding was altogether new in Scotland, and its appearance forms an epoch in the national literature. Previously, men had been taught that the understanding was a rash and foolish thing, which ought to be repressed, and which was unfit to cope with the problems presented to it.[14] Hutcheson, however, held that it was quite able to deal with them, but that, to do so, it

12. *Tytler's Memoirs of Kames,* Edinburgh, 1814, vol. i. p. 223. *Hutcheson's Moral Philosophy,* vol. i. p. iii. London, 1755, 4to.

13. "The intention of Moral Philosophy is to direct men to that course of action which tends most effectually to promote their greatest happiness and perfection; as far as it can be done by observations and conclusions discoverable from the constitution of nature, without any aids of supernatural revelation: these maxims or rules of conduct are therefore reputed as laws of nature, and the system or collection of them is called the LAW OF NATURE." *Hutcheson's Moral Philosophy,* vol. i. p. 1.

14. "The natural understanding is the most whorish thing in the world." . . . "The understanding, even in the search of truth amongst the creatures, is a rash, precipitate, and unquiet thing." *Rutherford's Christ Dying,* p. 181. "Innocent Adam," indeed, says Boston, "Innocent Adam had a stock of gracious abilities, whereby he might have, by the force of moral considerations, brought himself to perform duty aright. But where is that with us?" *Boston's Sermons,* p. 65.

must be free and unfettered. Hence, he strenuously advocated that right of private judgment which the Scotch Kirk had not only assailed, but had almost destroyed. He insisted that each person had a right to form his opinion according to the evidence he possessed, and that, this right being inalienable, none but weak minds would abstain from exercising it.[15] Every one was to judge according to his own light, and nothing could be gained by inducing men to profess sentiments contrary to their convictions.[16] So far, however, was this from being understood, that we found all the little sects quarrelling among themselves, and abusing each other, merely because their views were different. In was strange to hear how the professors of one creed would stigmatize the professors of other creeds as idolatrous, and would demand that penalties shold be inflicted on them. In point of fact, all had much that was good; and their only real evil was, this love of persecution.[17]

15. "A like natural right every intelligent being has about his own opinions, speculative or practical, to judge according to the evidence that appears to him. This right appears from the very constitution of the rational mind, which can assent or dissent solely according to the evidence presented, and naturally desires knowledge. The same considerations show this right to be unalienable: it cannot be subjected to the will of another: though where there is a previous judgment formed concerning the superior wisdom of another, or his infallibility, the opinion of this other, to a weak mind, may become sufficient evidence. As to opinions about the Deity, religion, and virtue, this right is further confirmed by all the noblest desires of the soul; as there can be no virtue, but rather impiety in not adhering to the opinions we think just, and in professing the contrary." *Hutcheson's Moral Philosophy,* vol. i. pp. 295, 296. See also vol. ii. p. 311. "Every rational creature has a right to judge for itself in these matters: and as men must assent according to the evidence that appears to them, and cannot command their own assent in opposition to it, this right is plainly unalienable."

16. "Thus no man can really change his sentiments, judgments, and inward affections, at the pleasure of another, nor can it tend to any good to make him profess what is contrary to his heart." *Hutcheson's Moral Philosophy,* vol. i. pp. 261, 262.

17. "Arians and Socinians are idolaters and denyers of God, say the orthodox. They retort upon the orthodox, that they are Tritheists; and so do other sects; and thus they spirit up magistrates to persecute. While yet it is plain that in all these sects there are all the same motives to all social virtues from a belief of a moral providence, the same acknowledgments that the goodness of God is the source of all the good we enjoy or hope for, and the same gratitude and resignation to him recommended. Nor do any of their schemes excite men to vices, except that horrid tenet, too common to most of them, the right of persecuting." *Hutcheson's Moral Philosophy,* vol. ii. p. 316. See also vol. i. p. 160; and *Hutcheson's Inquiry into our Ideas of Beauty and Virtue,* London, 1738, p. 283.

But the vulgar deemed every one a heretic who did not believe what they believed; and this way of thinking had been too much countenanced by the clergy, many of whom felt their vanity offended at the idea of laymen pretending to be wiser than their spiritual teachers, and venturing to disagree with what they said.[18]

Such large views of liberty were far in advance of the country in which they were propounded, and could exercise no influence, except over a few thinking men. These, and similar doctrines, were, however, repeated by Hutcheson, in his lectures, every year.[19] And strange, indeed, they must have seemed. To those who received them, they were utterly subversive of the prevailing theological spirit, which regarded toleration as impious, and which, seeking to confine the human mind within the limits of foregone conclusions, deemed it a duty to chastize those who overstepped them. In opposition to this, Hutcheson let in the elements of inquiry, of discussion, and of doubt. There is also another point in which his philosophy is memorable, as the beginning of the great rebellion of the Scotch intellect. We saw, in the last chapter, how successfully the teachers of the people had inculcated doctrines of the darkest asceticism, and how naturally those doctrines had arisen out of the enormous authority possessed by the Church. Against such notions, Hutcheson set his face strenuously. He rightly supposed, that an admiration of every kind of beauty, so far from being sinful, is essential to a complete and well-balanced mind; and the most original part of his philosophy consists of the inquiries which he made into the working and origin of our ideas on that subject. Hitherto, the Scotch had been taught that the emotions which beauty excites, were owing to the corruption of our nature, and ought to be repressed. Hutcheson, on the other hand, insisted that they were good in themselves; that they were part of the general scheme of human affairs, and

18. "We all know the notions entertained by the vulgar concerning all hereticks; we know the pride of schoolmen and many ecclesiasticks; how it galls their insolent vanity that any man should assume to himself to be wiser than they in tenets of religion by differing from them." *Hutcheson's Moral Philosophy*, vol. i. p. 167.

19. "As he had occasion every year in the course of his lectures to explain the origin of government, and compare the different forms of it, he took peculiar care, while on that subject, to inculcate the importance of civil and religious liberty to the happiness of mankind." *Leechman's Life of Hutcheson*, p. xxxv., prefixed to Hutcheson's Moral Philosophy.

that they deserved a special and scientific study.[20] And with such skill did he investigate them, that, in the opinion of one of the highest living authorities, he is the originator of all subsequent inquiries into these matters; his being the first attempt to deal with the subject of beauty in a broad and comprehensive spirit.[21]

Not only in speculative views, but also in practical recommendations, Hutcheson displayed the same tendency; every where endeavouring to break down that gloomy fabric which superstition had built up.[22] His predecessors, and, indeed, nearly all his contemporaries who exercised much influence, represented pleasure as immoral, and opposed themselves to the fine arts, which they considered dangerous, as ministering to our pleasures, and thereby distracting our minds from serious concerns. Hutcheson, however, declared that the fine arts were to be cherished; for, he said, they are not only agreeable, but also reputable, and to employ our time with them is honourable.[23] That such is the case is obvious

20. "The ideas of beauty and harmony, like other sensible ideas, are necessarily pleasant to us, as well as immediately so." *Hutcheson's Inquiry into our Ideas of Beauty and Virtue,* p. 11. "Our sense of beauty seems designed to give us positive pleasure." p. 71. "Beauty gives a favourable presumption of good moral dispositions." p. 257. "But it is plain we have not in our power the modelling of our senses or desires, to form them for a private interest; they are fixed for us by the Author of our nature, subservient to the interest of the system; so that each individual is made, previously to his own choice, a member of a great body, and affected with the fortunes of the whole; or at least of many parts of it; nor can he break himself off at pleasure." *Hutcheson's Essay on the Passions,* pp. 105, 106.

21. "Fille de la scholastique, la philosophie moderne est demeurée longtemps étrangère aux grâces, et les *Recherches* d'Hutcheson présentent, je crois, le premier traité spécial sur le beau, écrit par un moderne. Elles ont paru en 1725. Cette date est presque celle de l'avènement de l'esthétique dans la philosophie européenne. L'ouvrage de père André, en France, est de 1741, celui de Baumgarten, en Allemagne, est de 1750. Ce n'est pas un petit honneur à Hutcheson d'avoir le premier soumis l'idée du beau à une analyse méthodique et régulière." *Cousin, Histoire de la Philosophie,* première série, vol. iv. p. 84.

22. In his *Inquiry into Beauty and Virtue,* p. 107, he so completely opposed the prevailing notions, as to assert that "our perception of pleasure is necessary, and nothing is advantageous or naturally good to us, but what is apt to raise pleasure mediately, or immediately." Compare what he says at p. 91 respecting "superstitious prejudices against actions apprehended as offensive to the Deity."

23. "Hence a taste for the ingenious arts of musick, sculpture, painting, and even for the manly diversions, is reputable." *Hutcheson's Moral Philosophy,* vol. i. p. 83. At p. 129 he says, that in them "our time is agreeably and honourably employed." See also vol. ii. p. 115.

enough to us, but it was long, indeed, since similar language had been heard in Scotland from a great public teacher, and it was completely opposed to the prevailing notions. But Hutcheson went even further. Not content with raising his voice in favour of wealth,[24] which the Scotch clergy stigmatized as one of the most pernicious and carnal of all things, he fearlessly asserted that all our natural appetites are lawful, and that the gratification of them is consistent with the highest virtue.[25] In his eyes, they were lawful, because they were natural; while, according to the theological theory, their being natural made them unlawful. And here lies the fundamental difference between the practical views of Hutcheson and those previously received. He, like every great thinker since the seventeenth century, loved human nature, and respected it; but he neither loved nor respected those who unduly trammelled it, and thereby weakened its vigour, as well as impaired its beauty. He placed more confidence in mankind, than in the rulers of mankind. The Scotch divines, who preceded him, were the libellers of their species; they calumniated the whole human race. According to them, there was nothing in us but sin and corruption; and, therefore, all our desires were to be checked. It is the peculiar glory of Hutcheson, that he was the first man in Scotland who publicly combated these degrading notions. With a noble and lofty aim did he undertake his task. Venerating the human mind, he was bent on vindicating its dignity against those who

24. "Wealth and power are truly useful, not only for the natural conveniences or pleasures of life, but as a fund for good offices." *Hutcheson's Moral Philosophy,* vol. i. p. 104. Compare *Hutcheson on Beauty and Virtue,* pp. 93–95; and his *Essay on the Passions and Affections,* pp. 8, 9, 99. "How weak also are the reasonings of some recluse moralists, who condemn in general all pursuits of wealth or power, as below a perfectly virtuous character; since wealth and power are the most effectual means, and the most powerful instruments, even of the greatest virtues, and most generous actions."

25. "The chief happiness of any being must consist in the full enjoyment of all the gratifications its nature desires and is capable of." *Hutcheson's Moral Philosophy,* vol. i. p. 100. "The highest sensual enjoyments may be experienced by those who employ both mind and body vigorously in social virtuous offices, and allow all the natural appetites to recur in their due seasons." p. 121. "Nay, as in fact it is for the good of the system that every desire and sense natural to us, even those of the lowest kinds, should be gratified as far as their gratification is consistent with the nobler enjoyments, and in a just subordination to them; there seems a natural notion of *right* to attend them all." pp. 254, 255.

disputed its titles. Unhappily, he could not succeed; the prejudices of his time were too strong. Still, he did all that was in his power. He opposed the tide which he was unable to stem; he attacked what it was impossible to destroy; and he cast from his philosophy, with vehement scorn, those base prejudices, which, by aspersing all that is great and magnanimous, had long blinded the eyes of their contemporaries, and, by bringing into fresh prominence the old and mischievous dogma of moral degeneracy, had represented our nature as a compound of vices, and had been unable to see how many virtues we really possess, how much of the spirit of self-sacrifice, and of free disinterested benevolence has always existed; how much of good even the worst of us retain; and how, among the ordinary and average characters of whom the world is composed, the desire of benefiting others is more frequent than the desire of hurting them, kindness is more common than cruelty, and the number of good deeds does, on the whole, far outweigh the number of bad ones.[26]

26. " 'Tis pleasant to observe how those authors who paint out our nature as a compound of sensuality, selfishness, and cunning, forget themselves on this subject in their descriptions of youth, when the natural temper is less disguised than in the subsequent parts of life. 'Tis made up of many keen, inconstant passions, many of them generous; 'tis fond of present pleasure, but 'tis also profusely kind and liberal to favourites; careless about distant interests of its own; full of confidence in others; studious of praise for kindness and generosity; prone to friendships, and void of suspicion." *Hutcheson's Moral Philosophy,* vol. ii. p. 11. "Men are often subject to anger, and upon sudden provocations do injuries to each other, and that only from self love without malice; but the greatest part of their lives is employed in offices of natural affection, friendship, innocent self love, or love of a country." *Hutcheson's Essay on the Passions,* pp. 97, 98. And at p. 165: "There are no doubt many furious starts of passion, in which malice may seem to have place in our constitution; but how seldom and how short, in comparison of years spent in fixed kind pursuits of the good of a family, a party, a country?" . . . . "Here men are apt to let their imaginations run out upon all the robberies, piracies, murders, perjuries, frauds, massacres, assassinations, they have ever either heard of, or read in history; thence concluding all mankind to be very wicked; as if a court of justice were the proper place for making an estimate of the morals of mankind, or an hospital of the healthfulness of a climate. Ought they not to consider that the number of honest citizens and farmers far surpasses that of all sorts of criminals in any state; and that the innocent or kind actions of even criminals themselves, surpass their crimes in numbers? That it is the rarity of crimes, in comparison of innocent or good actions, which engages our attention to them, and makes them be recorded in history; while incomparably more honest, generous, domestic actions are overlooked, only because they are so common; as one great danger, or one month's sickness, shall become a frequently repeated story, during a long life of health and safety."

Thus much as to the tendency of Hutcheson's philosophy.[27] We have now to ascertain his method, that is to say, the plan which he adopted in order to obtain his results. This is a very important part of our present inquiry; and we shall find that, in the study of moral philosophy, as in the study of all subjects not yet raised to sciences, there are not only two methods, but that each method leads to different consequences. If we proceed by induction, we arrive at one conclusion; if we proceed by deduction, we arrive at another. This difference in the results, is always a proof that the subject, in which the difference exists, is not yet capable of scientific treatment, and that some preliminary difficulties have to be removed, before it can pass from the empirical stage into the scientific one. As soon as those difficulties are got rid of, the results obtained by induction, will correspond with those obtained by deduction; supposing, of course, that both lines of argument are fairly managed. In such case, it will be of no importance whether we reason from particulars to generals, or from generals to particulars. Either plan will yield the same consequences, and this agreement between the consequences, proves that our investigation is, properly speaking, scientific. Thus, for instance, in chemistry, if, by reasoning deductively from general principles, we could always predict what would happen when we united two or more elements, even supposing those elements were new to us; and if, by reasoning inductively from each element, we could arrive at the same conclusion, one process would corroborate the other, and, by their mutual verification, the science would be complete. In chemistry, we cannot do this; therefore, chemistry is not yet a science, although, since the introduction into it, by Dalton, of the ideas of weight and number, there is every prospect of its becoming one. On the other hand, astronomy is a science, because, by employing the deductive weapon of mathematics, we can

27. In 1731, Wodrow, who was the last really great specimen of the old Presbyterian divines, and who was not a little shocked at the changes he saw going on around him, writes: "When Dr. Calamy heard of Mr. Hutcheson's being called to Glasgow, he smiled, and said, I think to Thomas Randy, that he was not for Scotland, as he thought from his book; and that he would be reckoned there as unorthodox as Mr. Simson. The Doctor has a strange way of fishing out privat storyes and things that pass in Scotland." *Wodrow's Analecta,* vol. iv. p. 227. It is interesting to compare with this, the remarks which that worldly-minded clergyman, the Rev. Alexander Carlyle, has made upon Hutcheson. See *Carlyle's Autobiography,* Edinburgh, 1860, 2d edit. pp. 82–85.

compute the motions and perturbations of bodies; and, by employing the inductive weapon of observation, the telescope reveals to us the accuracy of our previous, and, as it were, foregone, inferences. The fact agrees with the idea; the particular event confirms the general principle; the principle explains the event; and their unanimity authorizes us to believe that we must be right, since, proceed as we may, the conclusion is the same; and the inductive plan, of striking averages, harmonizes with the deductive plan, of reasoning from ideas.

But, in the study of morals there is no such harmony. Partly from the force of prejudice, and partly from the complexity of the subject, all attempts at a scientific investigation of morals have failed. It is not, therefore, surprising that, in this field, the inductive inquirer arrives at one conclusion, and the deductive inquirer at another. The inductive inquirer endeavours to attain his object by observing the actions of men, and subjecting them to analysis, in order to learn the principles which regulate them. The deductive inquirer, beginning at the other end, assumes certain principles as original, and reasons from them to the facts which actually appear in the world. The former proceeds from the concrete to the abstract; the latter, from the abstract to the concrete. The inductive moralist looks at the history of past society, or at the condition of the present, and takes for granted that the first step is, to assemble the facts, and then to generalize them. The deductive inquirer, using the facts rather to illustrate his principles, than to suggest them, appeals, in the first place, not to external facts, but to internal ideas, and he makes those ideas the major premiss of a syllogistic argument. Both parties agree, that we have the power of judging some actions to be right, and others to be wrong. But as to how we get that power, and as to what that power is, they are at utter variance. The inductive philosopher says, that its object is happiness, that we get it by association, and that it is due to action and reaction of social causes, which are susceptible of analysis. The deductive philosopher says, that this power of distinguishing between right and wrong, aims, not at happiness, but at truth; that it is inherent, that it cannot be analyzed, that it is a primary conviction, and that we may assume it and reason from it, but can never hope to explain it by reasoning to it.

It requires but a slight acquaintance with the works of Hutcheson to see that he belongs to the latter of these two schools. He assumes, that all men have what he terms a moral faculty, which, being an original principle, does not admit of analysis.[28] He further assumes, that the business of this faculty is to regulate all our powers.[29] From these two assumptions, he reasons downwards to the visible facts of our conduct, and deductively constructs the general scheme of life. His plan being entirely synthetic, he depreciates the analytic method, and complains of it as an artful attempt to diminish the number of our perceptive powers.[30] The truth is, that every such diminution would have taken away some of his original principles, and would thereby have prevented him from using them as the major premisses of separate arguments. And if you deprive a deductive reasoner of his major premisses, you leave him nothing on which to stand. Hutcheson, therefore, like all the philosophers of his school, was extremely jealous of the invasions of the inductive spirit, with its constant tendency to attack convictions supposed to be primary, and seek to resolve them into their elements. He repulsed such encroachments upon his major premisses, because the power and beauty of his method were displayed in reasoning from the premisses, and not in reasoning to them. According to him, the moral faculty, and the authority which it exercised, were impervious to analysis; it was impossible to track them higher, or to resolve them into simpler constituents; and it was in vain that many attempted to refer them to circumstances external to themselves, such as education, custom, or the association of ideas.[31]

Hence, the judgments which men pass upon the conduct of others, or of themselves, are, in their origin, altogether inexplic-

28. In his *Moral Philosophy,* vol. i. p. 52, he calls it "an original determination or sense in our nature, not capable of being referred to other powers of perception."

29. "This moral sense from its very nature appears to be designed for regulating and controlling all our powers." *Hutcheson's Moral Philosophy,* vol. i. p. 61.

30. See, in his *Moral Philosophy,* vol. i. p. 79, his complaint against those who "would reduce all our perceptive powers to a very small number, by one artful reference or another."

31. " 'Tis is vain here to alledge instruction, education, custom, or association of ideas, as the original of moral approbation." *Hutcheson's Moral Philosophy,* vol. i. p. 57. Compare his work on *Beauty and Virtue,* p. 84.

able; each judgment being merely a different form of one great moral faculty. Inasmuch, however, as that faculty escapes observation, and is only known by its results, it is evident that, for all purposes of reasoning, the judgments must be deemed primary, and arguments are to be constructed from them, as if they were the ultimate and highest conditions of our nature. In this way, Hutcheson was led to that love of multiplying original principles, which Sir James Mackintosh has justly noticed as a characteristic of his philosophy, and, after him, of the Scotch philosophy in general;[32] though the distinguished author of this remark has failed to perceive that such characteristic was but a single part of a far larger scheme, and was intimately connected with those habits of deductive thought which a long train of preceding circumstances had indelibly imprinted on the Scotch mind.

In Hutcheson, the tendency was so strong, as to make him believe, that, by arguing from a certain number of original principles, he could construct the theory and explain the march of human affairs, with little or no aid from the experience of the past, or, indeed, of the present. His views, for instance, respecting the nature and objects of legislation, criminal, as well as civil, might have been written by a recluse who had never quitted his hermitage, and whose purity was still unsoiled by the realities of the world. Starting from the so-called nature of things, his first steps were ideal, and from them he sought to advance to the actual. In his account of the duties of life, as they existed before the power of government was consolidated, he quotes no evidence to show what really happened among barbarous tribes who were in that state; but he contents himself with deductive inferences from the principles he had previously laid down.[33] Difficult questions relating to the laws of property, are treated in the same manner; that is to say, the conclusions respecting them are arrived at on speculative grounds, and not by comparing how the different

32. "To him may also be ascribed that proneness to multiply ultimate and original principles in human nature, which characterized the Scottish School till the second extinction of a passion for metaphysical speculation in Scotland." *Mackintosh's Dissertation on Ethical Philosophy,* edit. Whewell, Edinburgh, 1837, p. 208.

33. See his ingenious chapter, entitled "A deduction of the more special laws of nature and duties of life, previous to civil government, and other adventitious states." *Moral Philosophy,* vol. i. p. 227; and compare vol. ii. pp. 294–309, "How civil power is acquired."

enactments have worked in different countries.[34] Experience is either shut out, or made subordinate to theory; and facts are adduced to illustrate the inference, but not to suggest it. So, too, the proper relation between the people and their rulers, and the amount of liberty which the people should possess, instead of being inductively generalized from an historical inquiry into the circumstances which had produced most happiness, might, in the opinion of Hutcheson, be ascertained by reasoning from the nature of government, and from the ends for which it was instituted.[35]

The next great attempt to study the actions of men scientifically, and to generalize the principles of their conduct without the intervention of supernatural ideas, was made by Adam Smith, who, in 1759, published his *Theory of Moral Sentiments,* and, in 1776, his *Wealth of Nations.* To understand the philosophy of this, by far the greatest of all the Scotch thinkers, both works must be taken together, and considered as one; since they are, in reality, the two divisions of a single subject. In the *Moral Sentiments,* he investigates the sympathetic part of human nature; in the *Wealth of Nations,* he investigates its selfish part. And as all of us are sympathetic as well as selfish; in other words, as all of us look without as well as within, and as this classification is a primary and exhaustive division of our motives to action, it is evident, that if Adam Smith had completely accomplished his vast design, he would at once have raised the study of human nature to a science, leaving nothing for subsequent inquirers except to ascertain the minor springs of affairs, all of which would find their place in this general scheme, and be deemed subordinate to it. In his attempt to perform this prodigious task, and to traverse the enormous field which he saw lying before him, he soon perceived that an inductive investigation was impossible, because it would require the labour of many lives even to assemble the materials from which the generalization was to be made. Moved by this

34. See, for example, his remarks on "the right of possession." *Moral Philosophy,* vol. i. p. 344; on "rights by mortgage," p. 350; and on inheritance, p. 356.
35. In his *Moral Philosophy,* vol. ii. pp. 346, 347, he sums up a long argument on "the nature of civil laws," by saying: "Thus the general duties of magistrates and subjects are discoverable from the nature of the trust committed to them, and the end of all civil power."

reflection, and, probably, moved still more by the intellectual habits which prevailed around him, he resolved on adopting the deductive method instead of the inductive; but, in seeking for the premises from which he was to reason, and on which his structure was to be built, he resorted to a peculiar artifice, which is perfectly valid, and which he had an undoubted right to employ, though, to make it available, requires such delicate tact, and involves so many refinements, that extremely few writers have used it with effect on social questions, either before or since.

The plan to which I allude is, that when any subject becomes unmanageable by the inductive method, whether from the impossibility of experimenting upon it, or from its extreme natural complexity, or from the presence of immense and bewildering details collected around it, we may, in all such cases, make an imaginary separation of inseparable facts; and reason upon trains of events which have no real and independent existence, and which are nowhere to be found except in the mind of the inquirer. A result obtained in this way, cannot be strictly true; but, if we have reasoned accurately, it will be as near truth as were the premises from which we started. To make it perfectly true, we must confront it with other results, which we have arrived at in a similar way, and from the same subject. These separate inferences may eventually be coördinated into a single system; so that, while each inference contains only an imperfect truth, the whole of the inferences, when put together, will contain perfect truth.

Such hypothetical arguments are evidently based upon an intentional suppression of facts; and the artifice is necessary, because, without the suppression, the facts would be unmanageable. Each argument leads to a conclusion which approximates to truth; hence, whenever the premises are so comprehensive as almost to exhaust the facts to which they refer, the conclusion will be so near to complete truth as to be of the greatest value, even before it is coördinated with other conclusions drawn from the same department of inquiry.

Geometry exhibits the most perfect example of this logical stratagem. The object of the geometrician is, to generalize the laws of space; in other words, to ascertain the necessary and universal relations of its various parts. Inasmuch, however, as space would have no parts unless it were divided, the geometrician is

forced to assume such a division; and he takes the simplest possible form of it, a division by lines. Now, a line considered as a
fact, that is, as it is found in the actual world, must always have
two qualities, length and breadth. However slight these qualities
may be, every line has them both. But if the geometrician took
both into consideration, he would find himself in the presence
of a problem too complicated for the resources of the human
understanding to deal with; or, at all events, too complicated for
the present resources of our knowledge. He, therefore, by a scientific artifice, deliberately strikes off one of these qualities, and
asserts that a line is length without breadth. He knows that the
assertion is false but he also knows that it is necessary. For, if you
deny it, he can prove nothing. If you insist upon his letting into
his premises the idea of breadth, he is unable to proceed, and the
whole fabric of geometry falls to the ground. Since, however, the
breadth of the faintest line is so slight as to be incapable of mea-
surement, except by an instrument used under the microscope, it
follows that the assumption, that there can be lines without
breadth, is so nearly true, that our senses, when unassisted by art,
cannot detect the error. Formerly, and until the invention of the
micrometer, in the seventeenth century, it was impossible to detect
it at all. Hence, the conclusions of the geometrician approximate
so closely to truth, that we are justified in accepting them as true.
The flaw is too minute to be perceived. But that there is a flaw,
appears to me certain. It appears certain, that whenever something is kept back in the premises, something must be wanting
in the conclusion. In all such cases, the field of inquiry has not
been entirely covered; and part of the preliminary facts being suppressed, it must, I think, be admitted, that complete truth is un-
attainable, and that no problem in geometry has yet been exhaus-
tively solved.[36]

Still, the amazing triumphs effected in this branch of mathe-

36. That is, so far as the facts are concerned. Geometry, considered in the
most elevated manner, rests on ideas, and from that point of view is impreg-
nable, unless the axioms can be overthrown. But if geometricians will insist on
having definitions as well as axioms, they gain, no doubt, increased clearness,
but they lose something in accuracy. I apprehend that, without definitions,
geometry could not be a science of space, but would be a science of magnitudes,
ideally conceived, and consequently as pure as ratiocination could make it. This
does not touch the question as to the empirical origin of the axioms.

matics, show how powerful a weapon that form of deduction is, which proceeds by an artificial separation of facts, in themselves inseparable. So little, however, is the philosophy of the method understood, that when, late in the eighteenth century, political economy assumed a scientific form, many persons, who were otherwise well instructed, reproached its cultivators with their hard-heartedness; such objectors being unable to see, that the science could not be constructed if it were necessary to take in the whole range of generous and benevolent affections. The political economist aims at discovering the laws of wealth, which are far too complicated to be studied under every aspect. He, therefore, selects one of those aspects, and generalizes the laws as they are exhibited in the selfish parts of human nature. And he is right in doing so, simply because men, in the pursuit of wealth, consider their own gratification oftener than the gratification of others. Hence, he, like the geometrician, blots out one part of his premises, in order that he may manipulate the remaining part with greater ease. But we must always remember, that political economy, though a profound and beautiful science, is only a science of one department of life, and is founded upon a suppression of some of the facts in which all large societies abound. It suppresses, or, what comes to the same thing, it ignores, many high and magnanimous feelings which we could ill afford to lose. We are not, therefore, to allow its conclusions to override all other conclusions. We may accept them in science, and yet reject them in practice. Thus, the political economist, when confining himself to his own department, says, with good reason, that it is both absurd and mischievous for government to undertake to supply the working-classes with employment. This assertion, he, as a political economist, can prove; and yet, notwithstanding its scientific truth, it may be practically right for a government to do the exact opposite. It may be right for a government to supply the employment, when the people are so ignorant as to demand it, and when, at the same time, they are so powerful as to plunge the country into anarchy if the demand is refused. Here, the view of the politician takes in all the premises of which the political economist had only taken in a portion. In the same way, as a matter of economic science, it is wrong for any one to relieve the poor; since nothing is better established, than that to relieve poverty increases it, by encouraging improvidence. But, in spite of this, the antagonistic principle of sympathy will come into play, and will, in some minds, operate with such force, as to make it advisable, that he who feels it should give alms, because, if he abstains from giving them, the violence which he does to his own nature may inflict more mischief on himself, than his bestowal of charity would inflict on the general interests of society.

It will not, I hope, be considered that, in these remarks, I have digressed from the main argument of the present chapter, since, although, in making them, I have aimed at clearing up a general question respecting the nature of scientific proof, I have only done so with the more particular object of illustrating the philosophy of Adam Smith, and of explaining the method which that most profound and original thinker pursued. We shall now be able to see how entirely his plan was deductive, and what a peculiar form of deduction it was. In his two great works, he first lays down certain ideas, and from them he marches on to the facts of the external world. And, in each work, he reasons from only part of his premisses; supplying the other part in the other work. None of us are exclusively selfish, and none of us are exclusively sympathetic. But Adam Smith separates in speculation qualities which are inseparable in reality. In his *Moral Sentiments,* he ascribes our actions to sympathy; in his *Wealth of Nations,* he ascribes them to selfishness. A short view of these two works will prove the existence of this fundamental difference, and will enable us to perceive that each is supplementary to the other; so that, in order to understand either, it is necessary to study both.

In the *Theory of Moral Sentiments,* Adam Smith lays down one great principle from which he reasons, and to which all the others are subordinate. This principle is, that the rules which we prescribe to ourselves, and which govern our conduct, are solely arrived at by observing the conduct of others.[37] We judge our-

37. "Our continual observations upon the conduct of others, insensibly lead us to form to ourselves certain general rules concerning what is fit and proper either to be done or to be avoided." . . . . "It is thus that the general rules of morality are formed. They are ultimately founded upon experience of what, in particular instances, our moral faculties, our natural sense of merit and propriety, approve or disapprove of. We do not originally approve or condemn particular actions; because, upon examination, they appear to be agreeable or

selves, because we had previously judged them. Our notions are obtained from without, and not from within. If, therefore, we lived entirely alone, we could have no idea of merit or demerit, and it would be impossible for us to form an opinion as to whether our sentiments were right or wrong.[38] To acquire this knowledge, we must look abroad. Inasmuch, however, as we have no direct experience of what other persons actually feel, we can only gain the information by conceiving what we should feel if we were in their place.[39] Hence, all men are, in imagination, constantly changing situations with others; and though the change is ideal, and lasts but for a moment, it is the foundation of that great and universal impulse which is called Sympathy.[40]

By proceeding from these premises, a vast number of social phenomena may be explained. We naturally sympathize with joy more than with sorrow.[41] Hence, that admiration for prosperous and successful persons, which is quite independent of any benefit we expect from them; and hence, too, the existence of different

---

inconsistent with a certain general rule. The general rule, on the contrary, is formed by finding from experience that all actions of a certain kind, or circumstanced in a certain manner, are approved of or disapproved of." *Smith's Theory of Moral Sentiments,* vol. i. pp. 219, 220. At p. 153: "We either approve or disapprove of our own conduct, according as we feel that, when we place ourselves in the situation of another man, and view it, as it were, with his eyes and from his station, we either can or cannot entirely enter into and sympathize with the sentiments and motives which influenced it."

38. "Were it possible that a human creature could grow up to manhood in some solitary place, without any communication with his own species, he could no more think of his own character, of the propriety or demerit of his own sentiments and conduct, of the beauty or deformity of his own mind, than of the beauty and deformity of his own face." *Smith's Theory of Moral Sentiments,* vol. i. p. 154. "Our first moral criticisms are exercised upon the characters and conduct of other people." p. 156.

39. "As we have no immediate experience of what other men feel, we can form no idea of the manner in which they are affected, but by conceiving what we ourselves should feel in the like situation." *Smith's Theory of Moral Sentiments,* vol. i. p. 2.

40. "That imaginary change of situation, upon which their sympathy is founded, is but momentary." *Smith's Theory of Moral Sentiments,* vol. i. p. 21. Compare vol. ii. p. 206.

41. "I will venture to affirm that, when there is no envy in the case, our propensity to sympathize with joy is much stronger than our propensity to sympathize with sorrow." *Smith's Theory of Moral Sentiments,* vol. i. p. 58. "It is because mankind are disposed to sympathize more entirely with our joy than with our sorrow, that we make parade of our riches, and conceal our poverty." p. 65.

ranks and of social distinctions, all of which emanate from the same source.[42] Hence, also, the feeling of loyalty, which is a product, not of reason, nor of fear, nor of a sense of public convenience, but rather of sympathy with those above us, begetting an extraordinary compassion for even their ordinary sufferings.[43] Custom and fashion play a great part in the world, but they owe their origin entirely to sympathy;[44] and so do the various systems of philosophy which have flourished at different times, the disagreement between which depends on the fact, that each philosopher has sympathized with different ideas, some sympathizing with the notion of fitness or congruity, some with that of prudence, some with that of benevolence, and every one developing the conception paramount in his own mind.[45] To sympathy, again, we must ascribe the establishment of rewards and punishments, and the whole of our criminal laws, none of which would have existed but for our disposition to sympathize with those who either do good or suffer harm; for the circumstance of society being protected by penal laws, is a subsequent and subordinate discovery, which confirms our sense of their propriety, but did not suggest it.[46] The same principle causes the difference of character exhibited by different classes, such as the irritability of poets, compared with the coolness of mathematicians;[47] it likewise causes that social difference between the sexes, which makes men more remarkable for generosity, and women for humanity.[48] All

42. "Upon this disposition of mankind to go along with all the passions of the rich and the powerful, is founded the distinction of ranks, and the order of society. Our obsequiousness to our superiors more frequently arises from our admiration for the advantages of their situation, than from any private expectations of benefit from their good will." *Smith's Theory of Moral Sentiments,* vol. i. p. 69. See also vol. ii. p. 72.

43. See the striking remarks in *Theory of Moral Sentiments,* vol. i. p. 70–72.

44. *Theory of Moral Sentiments,* vol. ii. p. 23, seqq.

45. *Theory of Moral Sentiments,* vol. ii. pp. 131–244. This sketch of the different systems of philosophy is perhaps the ablest part of the book, notwithstanding two or three errors which it contains.

46. *Smith's Theory of Moral Sentiments,* vol. i. pp. 89, 92, 115, 116. The utmost which he will concede to the notion of social convenience, is that "we frequently have occasion to confirm our natural sense of the propriety and fitness of punishment, by reflecting how necessary it is for preserving the order of society." p. 122.

47. *Theory of Moral Sentiments,* vol. i. pp. 172–174.

48. "Humanity is the virtue of a woman, generosity of a man. The fair sex, who have commonly much more tenderness than ours, have seldom so much

these results illustrate the workings of sympathy, and are the remote, but still the direct, operations of that principle. Indeed, we can trace to it some of the minutest divisions of character; pride and vanity, for instance, being dependent on it, although those two passions are often confused together, and are sometimes strangely blended in the same mind.[49]

Sympathy, then, is the main-spring of human conduct. It arises, not so much from witnessing the passions of other persons, as from witnessing the situation which excites those passions.[50] To this single process we are indebted, not only for the highest principles, but also for the deepest emotions. For, the greatest affection of which we are capable, is merely sympathy fixed into habit; and the love which exists between the nearest relations, is not inherent, but is derived from this mighty and controlling principle, which governs the whole course of affairs.[51]

By this bold hypothesis, Adam Smith, at one stroke, so narrowed the field of inquiry, as to exclude from it all considerations of selfishness as a primary principle, and only to admit its great antagonist, sympathy. The existence of the antagonism, he distinctly recognizes. For, he will not allow that sympathy is in any way to be deemed a selfish principle.[52] Although he knew

---

generosity." *Smith's Theory of Moral Sentiments,* vol. ii. p. 19. Sufficient facts have not yet been collected to enable us to test the truth of this remark, and the loose experience of individual observers is worth very little on so wide a subject. Still, I venture to doubt the truth of Adam Smith's distinction. I suspect that women are, on the whole, more generous than men, as well as more tender. But to establish a proposition of this sort, would require the most extensive research, made by a careful and analytic mind; and, at present, there is not even any tolerably good work on the mental characteristics which distinguish the sexes, and there never will be one until physiology is united with biography.

49. *Theory of Moral Sentiments,* vol. ii. pp. 115–122.

50. "Sympathy, therefore, does not arise so much from the view of the passion, as from that of the situation which excites it." *Smith's Theory of Moral Sentiments,* vol. i. p. 6.

51. "What is called affection, is, in reality, nothing but habitual sympathy." *Smith's Theory of Moral Sentiments,* vol. ii. p. 63. "In some tragedies and romances, we meet with many beautiful and interesting scenes, founded upon what is called the force of blood, or upon the wonderful affection which near relations are supposed to conceive for one another, even before they know that they have any such connection. This force of blood, however, I am afraid, exists nowhere but in tragedies and romances." p. 66.

52. "Sympathy, however, cannot, in any sense, be regarded as a selfish principle." *Theory of Moral Sentiments,* vol. ii. p. 206. In vol. i. p. 9, he complains of "those who are fond of deducing all our sentiments from certain refinements of self-love."

that it is pleasurable, and that all pleasure contains an element of selfishness, it did not suit the method of his philosophy to subject the principle of sympathy to such an inductive analysis as would reveal its elements. His business was, to reason from it, and not to it. Concentrating his energy upon the deductive process, and displaying that dialectic skill which is natural to his countrymen, and of which he himself was one of the most consummate masters the world has ever seen, he constructed a system of philosophy, imperfect indeed, because the premises were imperfect, but approaching truth as closely as it was possible for any one to do who abstained from giving due consideration to the selfish part of human nature. Into the workings of its sympathetic part, he looked with a minuteness, and he reasoned from it with a subtlety, which make his work the most important that has ever been written on this interesting subject. But, inasmuch as his plan involved a deliberate suppression of preliminary and essential facts, the results which he obtained do not strictly correspond to those which are actually observed in the world.[53] This, however, as I have shown, is not a valid objection; since such discrepancy between the ideal and the actual, or between the abstract and the concrete, is the necessary consequence of that still early condition of our knowledge, which forces us to study complicated questions piecemeal, and to raise them to sciences by separate and fragmentary investigations.

That Adam Smith saw this necessity, and that his seeing it was the cause of the method he pursued, is evident from the fact, that in his next great work he followed the same plan, and, though he argued from new premises, he carefully avoided arguing from any of the old ones. Convinced that, in his theory of morals, he had reasoned as accurately as possible from the principles supplied by sympathy, his capacious and insatiable mind, deeming that nothing had been done while aught remained to do, urged him to pass on to the opposite passion of selfishness, and treat it in the same manner, so that the whole domain of thought might be covered. This he did in his *Wealth of Nations*, which, though

53. This is noticed by Sir James Mackintosh, whose sketch of Adam Smith is hasty, and somewhat superficial, but who, nevertheless, truly observes, that Smith "has exposed himself to objections founded on experience, to which it is impossible to attempt any answer." *Mackintosh's Dissertation on Ethical Philosophy,* pp. 239, 240. See also a letter from Hume to Adam Smith, in *Burton's Life and Correspondence of Hume,* vol. ii. p. 60.

even a greater work than his *Moral Sentiments,* is equally one-sided, in reference to the principles which it assumes. It assumes that selfishness is the main regulator of human affairs, just as his previous work had assumed sympathy to be so. Between the two works there elapsed an interval of seventeen years; the *Wealth of Nations* not being published till 1776. But what shows that to their author both were part of a single scheme, is the notable circumstance, that, so early as 1753, he had laid down the principles which his later work contains.[54] This was while his former work was still in meditation, and before it had seen the light. It is, therefore, clear, that the study which he made, first of one passion, and then of its opposite, was not a capricious or accidental arrangement, but was the consequence of that vast idea which presided over all his labours, and which, when they are rightly understood, gives to them a magnificent unity. And a glorious object of ambition it was. His aspiring and comprehensive genius, sweeping the distant horizon, and taking in the intermediate space at a glance, sought to traverse the whole ground in two separate and independent directions, indulging the hope, that, by supplying in one line of argument the premises which were wanting in the other, their opposite conclusions would serve as a broad and permanent basis on which one great science of human nature might be safely built.

The *Wealth of Nations* is, as I have elsewhere observed,[55] probably the most important book which has ever been written, whether we consider the amount of original thought which it contains, or its practical influence. Its practical recommendations were extremely favourable to those doctrines of freedom which the eighteenth century ushered in; and this secured to them an attention which otherwise they would not have received. While, therefore, the *Wealth of Nations* was the proximate cause of a great change in legislation,[56] a deeper analysis will show, that

54. "Mr. Smith's political lectures, comprehending the fundamental principles of his 'Inquiry,' were delivered at Glasgow as early as the year 1752 or 1753." *Dugald Stewart's Life of Adam Smith,* p. lxxviii., prefixed to *Smith's Posthumous Essays,* London, 4to, 1795.

55. *History of Civilization,* vol. i. p. 194.

56. "Perhaps the only book which produced an immediate, general, and irrevocable change in some of the most important parts of the legislation of all civilized states." *Mackintosh's Ethical Philosophy,* p. 232. But this is too strongly expressed, as the economical history of France and Germany decisively proves.

the success of the book, and, consequently, the alteration of the laws, depended upon the operation of more remote and general causes. It must also be confessed, that those same causes predisposed the mind of Adam Smith to the doctrines of liberty, and gave him a sort of prejudice in favour of conclusions which limited the interference of the legislator. Thus much he borrowed from his age; but one thing he did not borrow. His wide and organizing mind was all his own. This would have made him great under any circumstances; to make him powerful, required a peculiar conjunction of events. That conjunction he enjoyed, and he turned it to good account. The influence of his contemporaries was enough to make him liberal; his own capacity was enough to make him comprehensive. He had, in a most remarkable degree, that exuberance of thought, which is one of the highest forms of genius, but which leads those who possess it into distant excursions, which, though they have one common aim, are often stigmatized as digressions, simply because they who criticize are unable to discern the great principle which pervades the whole, and unites the various parts into a single scheme. This has been especially the case with Adam Smith, whose immortal work has often been exposed to such shallow objections. And certainly, the *Wealth of Nations* displays a breadth of treatment which those who cannot sympathize with, are very likely to ridicule. The phenomena, not only of wealth, but also of society in general, classified and arranged under their various forms; the origin of the division of labour, and the consequences which that division has produced; the circumstances which gave rise to the invention of money, and to the subsequent changes in its value; the history of those changes traced in different ages, and the history of the relations which the precious metals bear to each other; an examination of the connexion between wages and profits, and of the laws which govern the rise and fall of both; another examination of the way in which these are concerned, on the one hand, with the rent of land, and, on the other hand, with the price of commodities; an inquiry into the reason why profits vary in different trades, and at different times; a succinct, but comprehensive, view of the progress of towns in Europe since the fall of the Roman Empire; the fluctuations, during several centuries, in the prices of the food of the people, and a statement of how it is, that, in different stages of society, the relative cost of land and of meat

varies; the history of corporation laws and of municipal enactments, and their bearing on the four great classes of apprentices,
manufacturers, merchants, and landlords; an account of the immense power and riches formerly enjoyed by the clergy, and of
the manner in which, as society advances, they gradually lose
their exclusive privileges; the nature of religious dissent, and the
reason why the clergy of the established Church can never contend with it on terms of equality, and, therefore, call on the State
to help them, and wish to persecute when they cannot persuade;
why some sects profess more ascetic principles, and others more
luxurious ones; how it was, that, during the feudal times, the
nobles acquired their power, and how that power has, ever since,
been gradually diminishing; how the rights of territorial jurisdiction originated, and how they died away; how the sovereigns
of Europe obtained their revenue, what the sources of it are,
and what classes are most heavily taxed in order to supply it; the
cause of certain virtues, such as hospitality, flourishing in barbarous ages, and decaying in civilized ones; the influence of inventions and discoveries in altering the distribution of power
among the various classes of society; a bold and masterly sketch
of the peculiar sort of advantages which Europe derived from
the discovery of America and of the passage round the Cape; the
origin of universities, their degeneracy from their original plan,
the corruption which has gradually crept over them, and the
reason why they are so unwilling to adopt improvements, and to
keep pace with the wants of the age; a comparison between public
and private education, and an estimate of their relative advantages;—these, and a vast number of other subjects, respecting the
structure and development of society, such as the feudal system,
slavery, emancipation of serfs, origin of standing armies, and of
mercenary troops, effects produced by tithes, laws of primogeni-
ture, sumptuary laws, international treaties concerning trade, rise
of European banks, national debts, influence of dramatic repre-
sentations over opinions, influence of foreign travels over opinions, colonies, poor-laws,—all topics of a miscellaneous character,
and many of them diverging from each other,—all are fused into
one great system, and irradiated by the splendour of one great
genius. Into that dense and disorderly mass, did Adam Smith
introduce symmetry, method, and law. At his touch, anarchy dis-

appeared, and darkness was succeeded by light. Much, of course, he took from his predecessors, though nothing like so much as is commonly supposed. On this sort of borrowing, the best and strongest of us are dependent. But, after making every possible allowance for what he gathered from others, we must honestly say, that no single man ever took so great a step upon so important a subject, and that no single work which is now preserved, contains so many views, which were novel at the time, but which subsequent experience has ratified. What, however, for our present purpose, is most important to observe, is, that he obtained these results by arguing from principles which the selfish part of human nature exclusively supplied, and that he omitted those sympathetic feelings of which every human being possesses at least some share, but which he could not take into consideration, without producing a problem, the number of whose complications it would have been hopeless to unravel.

To avoid, therefore, being baffled, he simplified the problem, by erasing from his view of human nature those premises which he had already handled in his *Theory of Moral Sentiments*. At the beginning of the *Wealth of Nations,* he lays down two propositions: 1st, that all wealth is derived, not from land, but from labour; and 2d, that the amount of the wealth depends, partly on the skill with which the labour is conducted, and partly on the proportion between the number of those who labour and the number of those who do not labour. The rest of the work, is an application of these principles, to explain the growth and mechanism of society. In applying them, he every where assumes, that the great moving power of all men, all interests, and all classes, in all ages, and in all countries, is selfishness. The opposite power of sympathy he entirely shuts out; and I hardly remember an instance in which even the word occurs in the whole course of his work. Its fundamental assumption is, that each man exclusively follows his own interest, or what he deems to be his own interest. And one of the peculiar features of his book is, to show that, considering society as a whole, it nearly always happens that men, in promoting their own interest, will unintentionally promote the interest of others. Hence, the great practical lesson is, not to restrain selfishness, but to enlighten it; because there is a provision in the nature of things, by which the selfishness of

the individual accelerates the progress of the community. According to this view, the prosperity of a country depends on the
amount of its capital; the amount of its capital depends on the
habit of saving, that is, on parsimony, as opposed to generosity;
while the habit of saving is, in its turn, governed by the desire
we all feel of bettering our condition,—a desire so inherent in
our nature, that it comes with us from the womb, and only leaves
us in the grave.[57]

This constant effort of every man, to better his own condition,
is so salutary, as well as so powerful, that it is often capable of
securing the progress of society, in spite of the folly and extravagance of the rulers of mankind.[58] If it were not for this propensity,
improvement would be impossible. For human institutions are
constantly stopping our advance, by thwarting our natural inclinations.[59] And no wonder that this should be the case, seeing
that the men who are at the head of affairs, and by whom the
institutions are contrived, have, perhaps, a certain rough and
practical sagacity; but being, from the narrowness of their understandings, incapable of large views, their councils are determined
by those mere casual fluctuations which alone they are able to

57. "Parsimony, and not industry, is the immediate cause of the increase of
capital. Industry, indeed, provides the subject which parsimony accumulates;
but whatever industry might acquire, if parsimony did not save and store up,
the capital would never be the greater." . . . . "But the principle which prompts
to save, is the desire of bettering our condition; a desire which, though generally
calm and dispassionate, comes with us from the womb, and never leaves us till
we go into the grave." *Smith's Wealth of Nations,* book ii. chap. iii. pp. 138,
140, edit. Edinb. 1839.

58. "The uniform, constant, and uninterrupted effort of every man to better
his condition, the principle from which public and national, as well as private,
opulence is originally derived, is frequently powerful enough to maintain the
natural progress of things towards improvement, in spite both of the extravagance of government and of the greatest errors of administration. Like the unknown principle of animal life, it frequently restores health and vigour to the
constitution, in spite not only of the disease, but of the absurd prescriptions of
the doctor." *Wealth of Nations,* book ii. chap. iii. p. 141. "The natural effort of
every individual to better his own condition, when suffered to exert itself with
freedom and security, is so powerful a principle, that it is alone, and without
any assistance, not only capable of carrying on the society to wealth and prosperity, but of surmounting a hundred impertinent obstructions with which the
folly of human laws too often encumbers its operations." Book iv. chap. v.
p. 221.

59. See an admirable passage, p. 156, too long to quote, beginning, "If
human institutions had never thwarted those natural inclinations," &c.

perceive.[60] They do not see that we have prospered, not on account of their enactments, but in the teeth of them; and that the real cause of our prosperity is the fact that we enjoy undisturbed the fruit of our own labour.[61] Whenever this right is tolerably secure, every man will be bent on procuring for himself either present enjoyment or future profit; and if he does not aim at one of these objects, he is void of common understanding.[62] If he possess capital, he will probably aim at both, but, in doing so, he will never consider the interest of others; his sole motive will be his own private profit.[63] And it is well that such should be the case. For, by thus pursuing his personal interest, he aids society more than if his views were generous and exalted. Some people affect to carry on trade for the good of others; but this is mere affectation, though, to say the truth, it is an affectation not very common among merchants, and many words are not needed to dissuade them from so foolish a practice.[64]

In this way, Adam Smith completely changes the premisses which he had assumed in his earlier work. Here, he makes men naturally selfish; formerly, he had made them naturally sympathetic.[65] Here, he represents them as pursuing wealth for sordid objects, and for the narrowest personal pleasures; formerly, he

60. "That insidious and crafty animal, vulgarly called a statesman or politician, whose councils are directed by the momentary fluctuations of affairs." *Wealth of Nations,* book iv. chap. ii. p. 190.

61. "That security which the laws in Great Britain give to every man, that he shall enjoy the fruits of his own labour, is alone sufficient to make any country flourish, notwithstanding these and twenty other absurd regulations of commerce." *Wealth of Nations,* book iv. chap. v. p. 221.

62. "In all countries where there is a tolerable security, every man of common understanding will endeavour to employ whatever stock he can command, in procuring either present enjoyment or future profit." *Wealth of Nations,* book ii. chap. i. p. 115.

63. "The consideration of his own private profit is the sole motive which determines the owner of any capital to employ it either in agriculture, in manufactures, or in some particular branch of the wholesale or retail trade." *Wealth of Nations,* book ii. chap. v. p. 154.

64. "By pursuing his own interest, he frequently promotes that of the society more effectually than when he really intends to promote it. I have never known much good done by those who affected to trade for the public good. It is an affectation, indeed, not very common among merchants, and very few words need be employed in dissuading them from it." *Wealth of Nations,* book iv. chap. ii. p. 184.

65. In his *Theory of Moral Sentiments,* vol. i. p. 21, he says that mankind are "naturally sympathetic."

represented them as pursuing it out of regard to the sentiments of others, and for the sake of obtaining their sympathy.[66] In the *Wealth of Nations,* we hear no more of this conciliatory and sympathetic spirit; such amiable maxims are altogether forgotten, and the affairs of the world are regulated by different principles. It now appears, that benevolence and affection have no influence over our actions. Indeed, Adam Smith will hardly admit common humanity into his theory of motives. If a people emancipate their slaves, it is a proof, not that the people are acted on by high moral considerations, nor that their sympathy is excited by the cruelty inflicted on these unhappy creatures. Nothing of the sort. Such inducements to conduct are imaginary, and exercise no real sway. All that the emancipation proves, is, that the slaves were few in number, and, therefore, small in value. Otherwise, they would not have been emancipated.[67]

So, too, while, in his former work, he had ascribed the different systems of morals to the power of sympathy, he, in this work, ascribes them entirely to the power of selfishness. He observes, that, among the lower ranks of society, dissipation is more fatal to individuals, than it is among the higher ranks. The extravagance which dissipation produces, may injure the fortune of a wealthy man, but the injury is usually capable of being repaired, or, at all events, he can indulge his vices for years without completely destroying his fortune, and without bringing himself to utter ruin. To the labourer, a similar indulgence would be fatal in a single week; it would not merely reduce him to beggary, and perhaps send him to jail, but it would destroy his future prospects, by taking away that character for sobriety and regularity on which his employment depends. Hence, the better class of common people, guided by their interest, look with aversion on excesses which they know to be fatal; while the upper ranks, finding that a moderate amount of vice hurts neither their purse

66. "Nay, it is chiefly for this regard to the sentiments of mankind, that we pursue riches and avoid poverty." *Theory of Moral Sentiments,* vol. i. p. 66. "To become the natural object of the joyous congratulations and sympathetic attentions of mankind, is, in this manner, the circumstance which gives to prosperity all its dazzling splendour." p. 78.

67. "The late resolution of the Quakers in Pennsylvania, to set at liberty all their negro slaves, may satisfy us that their number cannot be very great. Had they made any considerable part of their property, such a resolution could never have been agreed to." *Wealth of Nations,* book iii. chap. ii. p. 159.

nor their reputation, consider such license to be one of the advantages which their fortune confers, and they value, as one of the privileges belonging to their station, the liberty of indulging themselves without being censured. Therefore it is, that they who dissent from the established Church have a purer system of morals, or, at all events, an austerer one, than they who agree with it. For, new religious sects usually begin among the common people, the thinking part of whom are, by their interest, driven to strict views of the duties of life. Consequently, the advocates of the new opinion profess a similar strictness, seeing that it is the surest means of increasing their proselytes. Thus it is that sectaries and heretics, governed by interest rather than by principle, adopt a code of morals which is suited to their own purpose, and the rigidity of which is strongly contrasted with the laxer code of more orthodox believers.[68] Owing to the operation of the same

68. "In every civilized society, in every society where the distinction of ranks has once been completely established, there have been always two different schemes or systems of morality current at the same time; of which the one may be called the strict or austere; the other the liberal, or, if you will, the loose system. The former is generally revered and admired by the common people; the latter is commonly more esteemed and adopted by what are called the people of fashion. The degree of disapprobation with which we ought to mark the vices of levity, the vices which are apt to arise from great prosperity, and from the excess of gaiety and good humour, seems to constitute the principal distinction between those two opposite schemes or systems. In the liberal, or loose system, luxury, wanton, and even disorderly mirth, the pursuit of pleasure to some degree of intemperance, the breach of chastity, at least in one of the two sexes, provided they are not accompanied with gross indecency, and do not lead to falsehood and injustice, are generally treated with a good deal of indulgence, and are easily either excused or pardoned altogether. In the austere system, on the contrary, these excesses are regarded with the utmost abhorrence and detestation. The vices of levity are always ruinous to the common people, and a single week's thoughtlessness and dissipation is often sufficient to undo a poor workman for ever, and to drive him, through despair, upon committing the most enormous crimes. The wiser and better sort of the common people, therefore, have always the utmost abhorrence and detestation of such excesses, which their experience tells them are so immediately fatal to people of their condition. The disorder and extravagance of several years, on the contrary, will not always ruin a man of fashion; and people of that rank are very apt to consider the power of indulging in some degree of excess, as one of the advantages of their fortune; and the liberty of doing so without censure or reproach, as one of the privileges which belong to their station. In people of their own station, therefore, they regard such excesses with but a small degree of disapprobation, and censure them either very slightly or not at all.

"Almost all religious sects have begun among the common people, from whom they have generally drawn their earliest, as well as their most numerous

principle, we also find, that among the orthodox themselves, the clergy embrace a stricter system of morals in countries where church benefices are nearly equal, than they do in countries where the benefices are very unequal. This is because, when all the benefices are nearly equal, none can be very rich, and, consequently, even the most conspicuous among the clergy will have but small incomes. But a man who has little to spend can have no influence, unless his morals are exemplary. Having no wealth to give him weight, the vices of levity would make him ridiculous. To avoid contempt, and also to avoid the expense which a looseness of conduct occasions, and which his narrow circumstances cannot afford, he has but one remedy, and that remedy he adopts. He retains his influence, and saves his pocket, by protesting against pleasures which he cannot conveniently enjoy; in this, as in all other cases, pursuing that plan of life which his own interest urges him to follow.[69]

In these striking generalizations, which, though they contain a large amount of truth, are far from containing the whole truth, no room is left for the magnanimous parts of our nature to act; but the system of morals, prevailing at any one time or in any one class, is solely scribed to the dictates of unalloyed selfishness.

---

proselytes. The austere system of morality has, accordingly, been adopted by those sects almost constantly, or with very few exceptions; for there have been some. It was the system by which they could best recommend themselves to that order of people, to whom they first proposed their plan of reformation upon what had been before established. Many of them, perhaps the greater part of them, have even endeavoured to gain credit by refining upon this austere system, and by carrying it to some degree of folly and extravagance; and this excessive rigour has frequently recommended them, more than any thing else, to the respect and veneration of the common people." . . . . "In little religious sects, accordingly, the morals of the common people have been almost always remarkably regular and orderly; generally much more so than in the established church. The morals of those little sects, indeed, have freqeuntly been rather disagreeably rigorous and unsocial." *Wealth of Nations*, book v. chap. i. pp. 332, 333.

69. "Where the church benefices are all nearly equal, none of them can be very great; and this mediocrity of benefice, though it may, no doubt, be carried too far, has, however, some very agreeable effects. Nothing but exemplary morals can give dignity to a man of small fortune. The vices of levity and vanity necessarily render him ridiculous, and are, besides, almost as ruinous to him as they are to the common people. In his own conduct, therefore, he is obliged to follow that system of morals which the common people respect the most. He gains their esteem and affection, by that plan of life which his own interest and situation would lead him to follow." *Wealth of Nations*, book v. chap. i. p. 340.

Adam Smith, by reasoning from this principle, with that exquisite subtlety which characterized his mind, explains many other circumstances which society presents, and which at first sight appear incongruous. According to the old notions, which, indeed, are not yet quite extinct, those who received wages were under a personal obligation to those who paid them; that is to say, they were under a moral obligation, over and above the obligation of performing certain services. It was believed, that a master could not only select what servants he chose, but could pay them what he chose; or, at all events, that it was the will of the masters, considered as a body, which fixed the usual and average rate of wages.[70] The lower classes were, therefore, much indebted to the higher ones for giving them so much as they did; and it was incumbent upon all persons, who received wages, to take them with humble thankfulness, and with a feeling of gratitude, on account of the favour bestowed upon them by the generosity of their superiors.

This doctrine, so convenient to the upper classes of society, and so natural to the universal ignorance which formerly prevailed on these matters, began to be shaken by the speculative thinkers of the seventeenth century; but it was reserved for the eighteenth century to overthrow it, by letting in the great idea of necessity, and proving, that the rate of wages established in a country, was the inevitable consequence of the circumstances in which that country was placed, and had no connexion with the wishes of any individual, or, indeed, with the wishes of any class. To all instructed persons, this is now a familiar truth. Its discovery has excluded the notion of gratitude from the pecuniary relation between employers and employed, and has made known that servants or workmen who receive wages, have no more reason to be grateful than those who pay them. For, no choice having been exercised in fixing the wages, no favour can be conferred in their payment. The whole process is compulsory, and is the result of what had previously happened. Scarcely had the eighteenth century passed away, when this most important discovery was completed. It was decisively proved, that the reward of

70. Besides the evidence supplied by economical treatises, the laws in our statute-book respecting wages, show the general conviction, that their rate could be fixed by the upper classes.

labour depends solely on two things; namely, the magnitude of that national fund out of which all labour is paid, and the number of the labourers among whom the fund is to be divided.

This vast step in our knowledge is due, mainly, though not entirely, to Malthus, whose work on Population, besides marking an epoch in the history of speculative thought, has already produced considerable practical results, and will probably give rise to others more considerable still. It was published in 1798; so that Adam Smith, who died in 1790, missed what to him would have been the intense pleasure of seeing how, in it, his own views were expanded rather than corrected. Indeed, it is certain, that without Smith there would have been no Malthus; that is, unless Smith had laid the foundation, Malthus could not have raised the superstructure. It was Adam Smith, who, far more than any other man, introduced the conception of uniform and necessary sequence into the apparently capricious phenomena of wealth, and who studied those phenomena by the aid of principles, of which selfishness alone supplied the data. According to his view, the employers of labour have, as employers, no benevolence, no sympathy, no virtue of any kind. Their sole aim is, their own selfish interest. They are constantly engaged in a tacit, if not in an open, combination, to prevent the lower ranks from being benefited by a rise of wages; and they sometimes combine for the purpose even of depressing those wages below their actual rate.[71] Having no bowels, they think only of themselves. The idea of their wishing to mitigate the inequalities of fortune, is to be exploded as one of the chimeras of that protective spirit, which imagined that society could not go on, unless the richer classes relieved the poorer ones, and sympathized with their troubles. This antiquated notion is further rebutted by the fact, that wages

71. "We rarely hear, it has been said, of the combinations of masters, though frequently of those of workmen. But whoever imagines, upon this account, that masters rarely combine, is as ignorant of the world as of the subject. Masters are always and every where in a sort of tacit, but constant and uniform, combination, not to raise the wages of labour above their actual rate. To violate this combination is every where a most unpopular action, and a sort of reproach to a master among his neighbours and equals. We seldom, indeed, hear of this combination, because it is the usual, and, one may say, the natural state of things which nobody ever hears of. Masters, too, sometimes enter into particular combinations to sink the wages of labour even below this rate." *Wealth of Nations,* book i. chap. viii. p. 28.

are always higher in summer than in winter, although the expenses which a labourer incurs in winter, being heavier than in summer, he ought, on principles of common humanity, to receive more money during the more expensive season.[72] In the same way, in years of scarcity, the dearness of food causes many persons to go to service, in order to support their families. The masters, instead of charitably paying such servants more on account of the unfortunate position in which they are placed, avail themselves of that position to pay them less. They make better terms for themselves; they lower wages just at the moment when sympathy for misfortune would have raised them; and, as they find that their servants, besides being worse remunerated, are, by poverty, made more submissive, they consider that scarcity is a blessing, and that dear years are to be commended as more favourable to industry than cheap ones.[73]

Adam Smith, therefore, though he failed in grasping the remote cause of the rate of wages, clearly saw that the proximate cause was, not the generosity of human nature, but its selfishness, and that the question was one of supply and demand; each side striving to extract as much as possible from the other.[74] By the aid of the same principle, he explained another curious fact, namely, the extravagant rewards bestowed on some of the most despicable classes of society, such, for instance, as opera-dancers, who always receive enormous pay for insignificant services. He observes, that one of the reasons why we pay them so highly, is, because we

72. "First, in almost every part of Great Britain, there is a distinction, even in the lowest species of labour, between summer and winter wages. Summer wages are always highest. But, on account of the extraordinary expense of fuel, the maintenance of a family is most expensive in winter. Wages, therefore, being highest when this expense is lowest, it seems evident that they are not regulated by what is necessary for this expense, but by the quantity and supposed value of the work." *Wealth of Nations,* book i. chap. viii. p. 31.

73. "In years of scarcity, the difficulty and uncertainty of subsistence make all such people eager to return to service. But the high price of provisions, by diminishing the funds destined for the maintenance of servants, disposes masters rather to diminish than to increase the number of those they have." . . . "Masters of all sorts, therefore, frequently make better bargains with their servants in dear than in cheap years, and find them more humble and dependent in the former than in the latter. They naturally, therefore, commend the former as more favourable to industry." *Wealth of Nations,* book i. chap. viii. p. 35.

74. "The workmen desire to get as much, the masters to give as little, as possible. The former are disposed to combine in order to raise, the latter in order to lower, the wages of labour." *Wealth of Nations,* b. i. c. viii. p. 27.

despise them. If to be a public dancer were a creditable occupation, more persons would be brought up to it, and the supply of public dancers becoming greater, competition would lower their wages. As it is, we look on them disdainfully. By way of compensating the disdain, we have to bribe them largely to induce them to follow their pursuit.[75] Here we see, that the reward which one class bestows on another, instead of being increased by sympathy, is increased by scorn; so that the more we contemn the tastes and the way of life of our fellow-creatures, the more liberal we are in recompensing them.

Passing to another, and somewhat different, class, Adam Smith threw new light on the cause of that hospitality for which the clergy were famous during the Middle Ages, and for the magnificence of which they have received great praise. He shows that, although they undoubtedly relieved a large amount of distress, this is not to be ascribed to them as a merit, since it resulted from the peculiarity of their position, and since, moreover, they did it for their own advantage. In the Middle Ages, the clergy possessed enormous wealth, and their revenues were mostly paid, not in money, but in kind, such as corn, wine, and cattle. Trade and manufactures being hardly known, the clergy could find no use for these commodities except to feed other people. By employing them in that way, they benefited themselves in the most effectual manner. They gained a reputation for extensive charity; they increased their influence; they multiplied the number of their adherents; and they not only advanced themselves to temporal power, but they secured to their spiritual threats a respect, which, without this contrivance, it would have been impossible for them to obtain.[76]

75. "It seems absurd at first sight, that we should despise their persons, and yet reward their talents with the most profuse liberality. While we do the one, however, we must of necessity do the other. Should the public opinion, or prejudice, ever alter with regard to such occupations, their pecuniary recompense would quickly diminish. More people would apply to them, and the competition would quickly reduce the price of their labour. Such talents, though far from being common, are by no means so rare as imagined. Many people possess them in great perfection, who disdain to make this use of them; and many more are capable of acquiring them, if any thing could be made honourably by them." *Wealth of Nations,* book i. chap. x. p. 44.

76. "Over and above the rents of those estates, the clergy possessed in the tithes a very large portion of the rents of all the other estates in every kingdom of Europe. The revenues arising from both those species of rents were, the

The reader will now be able to understand the nature of that method of investigation which is adopted in the *Wealth of Nations,* and of which I have gained more instances than I should otherwise have done, partly because the question of philosophic method lies at the very root of our knowledge, and partly because no attempt has hitherto been made to analyze the intellect of Adam Smith, by considering his two great works at the opposite, but yet the compensatory, parts of a single scheme. And, as he is by far the greatest thinker Scotland has produced, I need hardly apologize, in a history of the Scotch mind, for devoting so much attention to his system, and endeavouring to examine it at its base. But, having done so, it would be a needless prolixity to treat with equal fulness the productions of those other eminent Scotchmen who lived at the same time, and nearly all of whom pursued a method essentially, though not entirely, the same; that is to say, they preferred the deductive process of reasoning from principles, to the inductive process of reasoning to them. In that peculiar form of deduction which consists in a deliberate suppression of part of the principles, Adam Smith stands alone. For, though others attempted to follow that plan, they did so irregularly, and at intervals, and did not, like him, see the importance of keeping close to their method, and of invariably abstaining from letting into the premisses of their arguments, considerations which would complicate the problem that they wished to solve.

Among the contemporaries of Adam Smith, one of the first, in eminence as well as in reputation, is David Hume. His views respecting political economy were published in 1752,[77] that is,

---

greater part of them, paid in kind, in corn, wine, cattle, poultry, &c. The quantity exceeded greatly what the clergy could themselves consume; and there were neither arts nor manufactures, for the produce of which they could exchange the surplus. The clergy could derive advantage from this immense surplus in no other way than by employing it, as the great barons employed the like surplus of their revenues, in the most profuse hospitality, and in the most extensive charity. Both the hospitality and the charity of the ancient clergy, accordingly, are said to have been very great." . . . . "The hospitality and charity of the clergy, too, not only gave them the command of a great temporal force, but increased very much the weight of their spiritual weapons. Those virtues procured them the highest respect and veneration among all the inferior ranks of people, of whom many were constantly, and almost all occasionally, fed by them." *Wealth of Nations,* book v. chap. i. p. 336.

77. *Burton's Life of Hume,* vol. i. p. 354.

the very year in which Adam Smith taught the principles subsequently unfolded in the *Wealth of Nations*. But Hume, though a most accomplished reasoner, as well as a profound and fearless thinker, had not the comprehensiveness of Adam Smith, nor had he that invaluable quality of imagination without which no one can so transport himself into past ages as to realize the long and progressive movements of society, always fluctuating, yet, on the whole, steadily advancing. How unimaginative he was, appears, not only from the sentiments he expressed, but likewise from many traits in his private life.[78] It appears, also, in the very colour and mechanism of his language; that beautiful and chiselled style in which he habitually wrote, polished as marble, but cold as marble too, and wanting that fiery enthusiasm and those bursts of tempestuous eloquence, which, ever and anon, great objects naturally inspire, and which rouse men to their inmost depths. This it was, which, in his *History of England,*—that exquisite production of art, which, in spite of its errors, will be admired as long as taste remains among us,—prevented him from sympathizing with those bold and generous natures, who, in the seventeenth century, risked their all to preserve the liberty of their country. His imagination was not strong enough to picture the whole of that great century, with its vast discoveries, its longings after the unknown, its splendid literature, and, what was better than all these, its stern determination to vindicate freedom, and to put down tyranny. His clear and powerful understanding saw these things separately, and in their various parts, but could not fuse them into a single form, because he lacked that peculiar faculty which assimilates the past to the present, and enables the mind to discern both with almost equal ease. That Great Rebellion, which he ascribed to the spirit of faction, and the leaders of which he turned into ridicule, was but the continuation of a movement which can be clearly traced to the twelfth century, and of which such events as the invention of printing, and the establishment of the Reformation, were merely successive symptoms. For all this, Hume cared nothing. In regard to philosophy, and in regard to the purely speculative parts of religious doctrines, his penetrating genius enabled him to perceive that nothing could be done, except by a spirit of fearless and unrestrained liberty. But this was the liberty

78. See Mr. Burton's valuable *Life of Hume,* Edinburgh, 1846, vol. i. pp. 58, 267, vol. ii. pp. 14, 134.

of his own class; the liberty of thinkers, and not of actors. His absence of imagination prevented him from extending the range of his sympathy beyond the intellectual classes, that is, beyond the classes of whose feelings he was directly cognizant. It would, therefore, appear, that his political errors were due, not, as is commonly said, to his want of research, but rather to the coldness of his temperament.[79] It was this which made him stop where he did, and which gave to his works the singular appearance of a profound and original thinker, in the middle of the eighteenth century, advocating practical doctrines, so illiberal, that, if enforced, they would lead to despotism, and yet, at the same time, advocating speculative doctrines, so fearless and enlightened, that they were not only far in advance of his own age, but have, in some degree, outstripped even the age in which we live.

Among his speculative views, the most important are, his theory of causation as discarding the idea of power, and his theory of the laws of association. Neither of these theories are, in their primary conception, quite original, but his treatment made them as valuable as if they had been entirely his own. His theory of miracles, in connexion, on the one hand, with the principles of evidence, and, on the other hand, with the laws of causation, is worked out with consummate skill, and, after having received the modifications subsequently imposed by Brown, has now become the foundation on which the best inquirers into these matters take their stand.[80] His work on the principles of morals, by generaliz-

---

79. What confirms me in this view, is the fact, that the older Hume grew, and the more he read on history, the more he became imbued with these errors; which would not have been the case if the errors had, as many of his critics say, been the result of an insufficient acquaintance with the evidence. Mr. Burton, by comparing the different editions of his *History of England,* has shown that he gradually became less favourable to popular liberty; softening, or erasing, in later editions, those expressions which seemed favourable to freedom. *Burton's Life of Hume,* vol. ii. pp. 74–77. See also pp. 144, 434. In his *Own Life,* p. xi. (in vol. i. of *Hume's Works,* Edinb. 1826), he says: "In above a hundred alterations, which farther study, reading, or reflection, engaged me to make in the reigns of the two first Stuarts, I have made all of them invariably to the Tory side." In one of his essays, he observes (*Philosophical Works,* vol. iv. p. 172), that "there is no enthusiasm among philosophers;" a remark perfectly true, so far as he was concerned, but very unjust towards the class of men to whom it refers.

80. Brown, in his great work,—one of the greatest which this century has produced,—candidly confesses that his own book is "chiefly reflective of the lights, which he" (Hume) "has given." *Brown's Inquiry into the Relation of Cause and Effect,* London, 1835, p. 253. See also p. vii.

ing the laws of expediency, prepared the way for Bentham, who afterwards incorporated with them an estimate of the more remote consequences of human actions; Hume having chiefly confined himself to their more immediate consequences. The doctrine of utility was common to each; but while Hume applied it mainly to the individual, Bentham applied it to the surrounding society. Though Bentham was more comprehensive, yet Hume, having come first, was more original. The praise of originality must also be accorded to his economical theories, in which he advocated those principles of free trade, which politicians began to adopt many years after his death.[81] In opposition to the notions then prevailing, he distinctly asserted, that all commodities, though

81. While the politicians of his own time despised his views, the politicians of our time seem inclined to overrate them. Lord Brougham, for instance, in his Life of Hume, says, of his political economy, "Mr. Hume is, beyond all doubt, the author of the modern doctrines which now rule the world of science." *Brougham's Works,* Glasgow, 1856, vol. ii. p. 176. But so far from this being the case, the science of political economy has, since the time of Hume, received such additions, that if that illustrious philosopher were to rise from the dead, he would hardly be able to recognize it. To him, many of its largest and most fundamental principles were entirely unknown. Hume knew nothing of the causes which govern the accumulation of wealth, and compel that accumulation to proceed with different speed in different states of society; a fruitful and important study almost entirely neglected until entered upon by Rae. Neither did Hume know any thing of the law of the ratio between population and wages; nor of the ratio between wages and profits. He even supposes (*Philosophical Works,* vol. iii. p. 299, Edinburgh, 1826) that it is possible for the labouring classes by combination "to heighten their wages;" and again (p. 319) that the richer a nation is, and the more trade it has, the easier it will be for a poor country to undersell its manufactures, because the poor nation enjoys the advantage of a "low price of labour." Elsewhere, he asserts that coin can be depreciated without raising prices, and that a country, by taxing a foreign commodity, could increase its own population. "Were all our money, for instance, re-coined, and a penny's worth of silver taken from every shilling, the new shilling would probably purchase every thing that could have been bought by the old; the prices of every thing would thereby be insensibly diminished; foreign trade enlivened; and domestic industry, by the circulation of a great number of pounds and shillings, would receive some increase and encouragement." *Philosophical Works,* vol. iii. p. 324. "A tax on German linen encourages home manufactures, and thereby multiplies our people and industry." p. 365. These are cardinal errors, which go to the very root of political economy; and when we fairly estimate what has been done by Malthus and Ricardo, it will be evident that Hume's doctrines do not "rule the world of science." This is no disparagement of Hume, who, on the contrary, effected wonderful things, considering the then state of knowledge. The mistake is, in imagining that such a rapidly advancing science as political economy can be governed by doctrines propounded more than a century ago.

apparently bought by money, are in reality bought by labour.[82] Money, therefore, is not the subject of commerce, and is of no use except to facilitate it.[83] Hence, it is absurd for a nation to trouble itself about the balance of trade, or to make regulations to discourage the exportation of the precious metals.[84] Neither does the average rate of interest depend on their scarcity or abundance, but upon the operation of more general causes.[85] As a necessary consequence of these positions, Hume inferred that the established policy was wrong, which made trading states look upon each other as rivals, while, in point of fact, the question, if considered from a certain height, was one, not of rivalry, but of coöperation; every country being benefited by the increasing wealth of its neighbours.[86] Those who know the character of commercial legislation, and the opinions of even the most en-

82. "Every thing in the world is purchased by labour, and our passions are the only causes of labour." *Essay I. on Commerce,* in *Hume's Philosophical Works,* vol. iii. p. 294. Hence, he saw the fallacy of the assertion of the French economists, "that all taxes fall ultimately upon land." p. 388.

83. "Money is not, properly speaking, one of the subjects of commerce, but only the instrument which men have agreed upon to facilitate the exchange of one commodity for another." *Essay on Money,* in *Philosophical Works,* vol. iii. p. 317. "It is, indeed, evident that money is nothing but the representation of labour and commodities, and serves only as a method of rating or estimating them." p. 321.

84. See *Essay V. on the Balance of Trade,* in *Hume's Philosophical Works,* vol. iii. pp. 348–367.

85. *Hume's Philosophical Works,* vol. iii. pp. 333–335. Even now, a knowledge of this truth is so little diffused, that, lately, when Australia and California began to yield immense quantities of gold, a notion was widely circulated that the interest of money would consequently fall; although nothing can be more certain than that if gold were to become as plentiful as iron, the interest of money would be unaffected. The whole effect would fall upon price. The remarks on this subject in *Ritchie's Life of Hume,* London, 1807, pp. 332, 333, are interesting, as illustrating the slow progress of opinion, and the difficulty which minds, not specially trained, experience when they attempt to investigate these subjects.

86. "Nothing is more usual, among states which have made some advance in commerce, than to look on the progress of their neighbours with a suspicious eye, to consider all trading states as their rivals, and to suppose that it is impossible for any of them to flourish, but at their expense. In opposition to this narrow and malignant opinion, I will venture to assert, that the increase of riches and commerce in any one nation, instead of hurting, commonly promotes the riches and commerce of all its neighbours." . . . . "I go farther, and observe, that where an open communication is preserved among nations, it is impossible but the domestic industry of every one must receive an increase from the improvements of the others." *Essay on the Jealousy of Trade,* in *Hume's Philosophical Works,* vol. iii. pp. 368, 369.

lightened statesmen a century ago, will consider these views as extremely remarkable to have been propounded in the year 1752. But what is more remarkable still, is, that their author subsequently detected the fundamental error which Adam Smith committed, and which vitiates many of his conclusions. The error consists in his having resolved price into three components, namely, wages, profit, and rent; whereas it is now known that price is a compound of wages and profit, and that rent is not an element of it, but a result of it. This discovery is the cornerstone of political economy; but it is established by an argument so long and so refined, that most minds are unable to pursue it without stumbling, and the majority of those who acquiesce in it are influenced by the great writers to whom they pay deference, and whose judgment they follow. It is, therefore, a striking proof of the sagacity of Hume, that in an age when the science was but dawning, and when he could receive little help from his predecessors, he should have discovered a mistake of this sort, which lies so far beneath the surface. Directly the *Wealth of Nations* appeared, he wrote to Adam Smith, disputing his position that rent is a part of price;[87] and this letter, written in the year 1776, is the first indication of that celebrated theory of rent, which, a little later, Anderson, Malthus, and West, saw and imperfectly developed, but which it was reserved for the genius of Ricardo to build up on a broad and solid foundation.

It is very observable, that Hume and Adam Smith, who made such immense additions to our knowledge of the principles of trade, had no practical acquaintance with it.[88] Hume had, at an

87. This letter, which I have referred to in my first volume, p. 229, was published, for, I believe, the first time, in 1846, in *Burton's Life and Correspondence of Hume,* vol. ii. p. 486. It is, however, very difficult to determine what Adam Smith's opinion really was upon this subject, and how far he was aware that rent did not enter into price. In one passage in the *Wealth of Nations* (book i. chap. vi. p. 21) he says of wages, profit, and rent, "In every society, the price of every commodity finally resolves itself into some one or other, or all of those three parts; and *in every improved society, all the three enter, more or less, as component parts, into the price of the far greater part of commodities.*" But in book i. chap. xi. p. 61, he says, "High or low wages and profit are the causes of high or low price; high or low rent is the effect of it." This latter opinion we now know to be the true one; it is, however, incompatible with that expressed in the first passage. For, if rent is the effect of price, it cannot be a component of it.

88. Hence, when the *Wealth of Nations* appeared, one of our wise men

early period of his life, been in a mercantile house; but he threw up that employment in disgust, and buried himself in a provincial town, to think, rather than to observe.[89] Indeed, one of the capital defects of his mind, was a disregard of facts. This did not proceed, as is too often the case, from that worst form of moral obliquity, an indifference to truth; since he, on the contrary, was an ardent lover of it, and was, moreover, a man of the purest and most exemplary character, utterly incapable of falsehood, or of prevarication of any kind.[90] In him, a contempt for facts was

---

gravely said that "Dr. Smith, who had never been in trade, could not be expected to write well on that subject, any more than a lawyer upon physic." See *Boswell's Life of Johnson,* edit. Croker, 1848, p. 478, where this remark is ascribed to Sir John Pringle.

89. "He was sent to a mercantile house at Bristol in 1734; but he found the drudgery of this employment intolerable, and he retired to Rheims." *Brougham's Life of Hume,* Glasgow, 1856, p. 169. See also *Ritchie's Life of Hume,* p. 6. In *Roberts' Memoirs of Hannah More,* 2d ed. 1834, vol. i. p. 16, it is said that "two years of his life were spent in a merchant's counting-house in Bristol, whence he was dismissed on account of the promptitude of his pen in the correction of the letters intrusted to him to copy." The latter part of this story is improbable; the former part is certainly incorrect; since Hume himself says, "In 1734, I went to Bristol, with some recommendations to eminent merchants, but *in a few months* found that scene totally unsuitable to me. I went over to France, with a view of prosecuting my studies in a country retreat." *Own Life,* p. v.

90. What Sir James Mackintosh says of him is only a faint echo of the general voice of his contemporaries. "His temper was calm, not to say cold; but though none of his feelings were ardent, all were engaged on the side of virtue. He was free from the slightest tincture of malignity or meanness; his conduct was uniformly excellent." *Mackintosh's Memoirs,* vol. ii. p. 162. A greater than Mackintosh, and a man who knew Hume intimately, expresses himself in much warmer terms. "Upon the whole," writes Adam Smith, "Upon the whole, I have always considered him both in his lifetime and since his death, as approaching as nearly to the idea of a perfectly wise and virtuous man as perhaps the nature of human frailty will permit." *Hume's Philosophical Works,* vol. i. p. xxv. Some notices of Hume will be found in an interesting work just published, *Autobiography of Alexander Carlyle,* Edinburgh, 1860, pp. 272–278. But Carlyle, though a man of considerable practical skill, was incapable of large views, and was, therefore, unable, I will not say to measure, but even to conceive, the size of such an understanding as that possessed by David Hume. Of his want of speculative power, a decisive instance appears in his remarks on Adam Smith. He gravely says (*Autobiography,* p. 281), "Smith's fine writing is chiefly displayed in his book on *Moral Sentiment,* which is the pleasantest and most eloquent book on the subject. His *Wealth of Nations,* from which he was judged to be an inventive genius of the first order, is tedious and full of repetition. His separate essays in the second volume have the air of being occasional pamphlets, without much force or determination. On political subjects, his opinions were not very sound." It is rather too much when a village-preacher writes in this strain of the greatest man his country has ever produced.

merely the exaggerated result of a devotion to ideas. He not only believed, with perfect justice, that ideas are more important than facts, but he supposed that they should hold the first place in the order of study, and that they should be developed before the facts are investigated. The Baconian philosophy, which, though it allows a preliminary and tentative hypothesis, strongly insists upon the necessity of first collecting the facts, and then proceeding to the ideas, excited his aversion; and this, I have no doubt, is the reason why he, who was usually so lenient in his judgments, and who was so keen an admirer of intellectual greatness, is, nevertheless, grossly unfair towards Bacon, with whose method it was impossible for him to sympathize, though he could not deny its utility in physical science.[91] If Hume had followed the Baconian scheme, of always rising from particulars to generals, and from each generalization to that immediately above it, he would hardly have written one of his works. Certainly, his economical views would never have appeared, since political economy is as essentially a deductive science as geometry itself.[92] Reversing the inductive process, he was in favour of beginning with what he termed general arguments, by which he hoped to demonstrate the inaccuracy of opinions which facts were supposed to have proved.[93] He did not stop to investigate the facts from which the inference had been drawn, but he inverted the order by which the inference was to be obtained. The same dislike to make the facts of trade the basis of the science of trade, was displayed by Adam Smith, who expresses his want of confidence in statistics, or, as it

91. He speaks of him in the following extraordinary terms. "If we consider the variety of talents displayed by this man; as a public speaker, a man of business, a wit, a courtier, a companion, an author, a philosopher; he is justly the object of great admiration. If we consider him merely as an author and philosopher, the light in which we view him at present, though very estimable, *he was yet inferior to his contemporary Galileo, perhaps even to Kepler.*" . . . . "The national spirit which prevails among the English, and which forms their great happiness, is the cause why they bestow on all their eminent writers, and on Bacon among the rest, such praises and acclamations as may often appear partial and excessive." *Hume's History of England,* vol. vi. pp. 194, 195, London, 1789.

92. See the note in vol. i. pp. 228, 229 of *Buckle's History of Civilization.*

93. Thus, for instance, in his remarkable *Essay on the Balance of Trade,* he says (*Philosophical Works,* vol. iii. p. 349), "Every man who has ever reasoned on this subject, has always *proved his theory, whatever it was, by facts and calculations,* and by an enumeration of all the commodities sent to all foreign kingdoms;" therefore (p. 350), "It may here be proper to form a general argument to prove the impossibility of this event, so long as we preserve our people and our industry."

was then termed, political arithmetic.[94] It is, however, evident, that statistical facts are as good as any other facts, and, owing to their mathematical form, are very precise.[95] But when they concern human actions, they are the result of all the motives which govern those actions; in other words, they are the result, not merely of selfishness, but also of sympathy. And as Adam Smith, in the *Wealth of Nations,* dealt with only one of these passions, namely selfishness, he would have found it impossible to conduct his generalization from statistics, which are necessarily collected from the products of both passions. Such statistical facts were, in their origin, too complex to be generalized; especially as they could not be experimented upon, but could only be observed and arranged. Adam Smith, perceiving them to be unmanageable, very properly rejected them as the basis of his science, and merely used them by way of illustration, when he could select what he liked. The same remark applies to other facts which he drew from the history of trade, and, indeed, from the general history of society. All of these are essentially subsequent to the argument. They make the argument more clear, but not more certain. For, it is no exaggeration to say, that, if all the commercial and historical facts in the *Wealth of Nations* were false, the book would still remain, and its conclusions would hold equally good, though they would be less attractive. In it, every thing depends upon general principles, and they, as we have seen, were arrived at in 1752, that is, twenty-four years before the work was published, in which those principles were applied. They must, therefore, have been acquired independently of the facts which Adam Smith subsequently incorporated with them, and which he learnt during that long period of twenty-four years. And the ten years which he employed in composing his great work, were not spent in one of those busy haunts of men, where he might have observed all the

94. "I have no great faith in political arithmetic." *Wealth of Nations,* book iv. chap. v. p. 218.

95. Indeed, the only possible objection to them is that the language of their collectors is sometimes ambiguous; so that, by the same return, one statistician may mean one thing, and another statistician may mean something quite different. This is well exemplified in medical statistics; whence several writers, unacquainted with the philosophy of scientific proof, have supposed that medicine is incapable of mathematical treatment. In point of fact, however, the only real impediment is the shameful state of clinical and pathological terminology, which is in such confusion as to throw doubt upon all extensive numerical statements respecting disease.

phenomena of industry, and studied the way in which the operations of trade affect human character, and are affected by it. He did not resort to one of those vast marts and emporiums of commerce, where the events were happening which he was seeking to explain. That was not his method. On the contrary, the ten years, during which he was occupied in raising to a science the most active department of life, were passed in complete seclusion in Kirkaldy, his quiet little birth-place.[96] He had always been remarkable for absence of mind, and was so little given to observation, as to be frequently oblivious of what was passing around him.[97] In that obliviousness, he, amid the tranquil scenes of his childhood, could now indulge without danger. There, cheered, indeed, by the society of his mother, but with no opportunity of observing human nature upon a large scale, and far removed from the hum of great cities, did this mighty thinker, by the force of his own mind, unravel the numerous and complicated phenomena of wealth, detect the motives which regulate the conduct of the most energetic and industrious portion of mankind, and lay bare the schemes and the secrets of that active life from which he was shut out, while he, immured in comparative solitude, was unable to witness the very facts which he succeeded in explaining.

The same determination to make the study of principles precede that of facts, is exhibited by Hume in one of his most orig-

96. "Upon his return to England in the autumn of 1766, he went to reside with his mother at his native town of Kirkaldy, and remained there for ten years. All the attempts of his friends in Edinburgh to draw him thither were vain; and from a kind and lively letter of Mr. Hume upon the subject, complaining that, though within sight of him on the opposite side of the Frith of Forth, he could not have speech of him, it appears that no one was aware of the occupations in which those years were passed." *Brougham's Life of Adam Smith,* p. 189. Occasionally, however, he saw his literary friends. See *Dugald Stewart's Biographical Memoirs,* p. 73, Edinb. 1811, 4to.

97. "He was certainly not fitted for the general commerce of the world, or for the business of active life. The comprehensive speculations with which he had been occupied from his youth, and the variety of materials which his own invention constantly supplied to his thoughts, rendered him habitually inattentive to familiar objects and to common occurrences; and he frequently exhibited instances of absence, which have scarcely been surpassed by the fancy of La Bruyère." *Stewart's Biographical Memoirs,* p. 113. See also *Ramsay's Reminiscences,* 5th edit., Edinb. 1859, p. 236. Carlyle, who knew him well, says, "he was the most absent man in company that I ever saw, moving his lips, and talking to himself, and smiling, in the midst of large companies." *Autobiography of the Rev. Alexander Carlyle,* 2d edition, Edinburgh, 1860, p. 279.

inal works, the *Natural History of Religion*. In reference to the title of this treatise, we must observe, that, according to the Scotch philosophers, the natural course of any movement is by no means the same as its actual course. This discrepancy between the ideal and the real, was the unavoidable result of their method.[98] For, as they argued deductively from fixed premises, they could not take into account the perturbations to which their conclusions were liable, from the play and friction of the surrounding society. To do that, required a separate inquiry. It would have been needful to investigate the circumstances which caused the friction, and thus prevented the conclusions from being, in the world of fact, the same as they were in the world of speculation. What we call accidents, are constantly happening, and they prevent the real march of affairs from being identical with the natural march. And, as long as we are unable to predict those accidents, there will always be a want of complete harmony between the inferences of a deductive science and the realities of life; in other words, our inferences will tend towards truth, but never completely attain it.[99]

98. A Scotch philosopher of great repute, but, as it appears to me, of ability not quite equal to his repute, has stated very clearly and accurately this favourite method of his countrymen. "In examining the history of mankind, as well as in examining the phenomena of the material world, when we cannot trace the process by which an event *has been* produced, it is often of importance to be able to show how it *may have been* produced by natural causes." . . . . "To this species of philosophical investigation, which has no appropriated name in our language, I shall take the liberty of giving the title of *Theoretical or Conjectured History;* an expression which coincides pretty nearly in its meaning with that of *Natural History* as employed by Mr. Hume, and with what some French writers have called Histoire Raisonnée." *Dugald Stewart's Biographical Memoirs,* pp. 48, 49. Hence (p. 53), "in most cases, it is of more importance to ascertain the progress that is most simple, than the progress that is most agreeable to fact; for, paradoxical as the proposition may appear, it is certainly true, that *the real progress is not always the most natural.* It may have been determined by particular accidents, which are not likely again to occur, and which cannot be considered as forming any part of that general provision which nature has made for the improvement of the race."

99. Part of this view is well expressed in *Hume's Treatise of Human Nature,* book iii. part ii. "This, however, hinders not but that philosophers may, if they please, extend their reasoning to the supposed *state of nature;* provided they allow it to be a mere philosophical fiction, which never had, and never could have any reality." . . . . "The same liberty may be permitted to moral, which is allowed to natural philosophers; and 'tis very usual with the latter to consider any motion as compounded and consisting of two parts separate from each other, though, at the same time, they acknowledge it to be in itself uncompounded and inseparable." *Philosophical Works,* vol. ii. p. 263.

With peculiar propriety, therefore, did Hume term his work a *Natural History of Religion.* It is an admirable specimen of the deductive method. Its only fault is, that he speaks too confidently of the accuracy of the results to which, on such a subject, that method could attain. He believed, that, by observing the principles of human nature, as he found them in his own mind, it was possible to explain the whole course of affairs, both moral and physical.[100] These principles were to be arrived at by experiments made on himself; and having thus arrived at them, he was to reason from them deductively, and so construct the entire scheme. This, he contrasts with the inductive plan, which he calls a tedious and lingering process; and while others might follow that slow and patient method of gradually working their way towards first principles, his project was, to seize them at once, or, as he expresses himself, not to stop at the frontier, but to march directly on the capital, being possessed of which, he could gain an easy victory over other difficulties, and could extend his conquests over the sciences.[101] According to Hume, we are to reason, not in order to obtain ideas, but we are to have clear ideas before we reason.[102]

100. And, conversely, that whatever was demonstratively false," could "never be distinctly conceived by the mind." *Philosophical Works,* vol. iv. p. 33. Here, and sometimes in other passages, Hume, though by no means a Cartesian, reminds us of Descartes.

101. "Here, then, is the only expedient, from which we can hope for success in our philosophical researches, *to leave the tedious, lingering method,* which we have hitherto followed, and instead of taking now and then a castle or village on the frontier, to march up directly to the capital, or centre of these sciences, to human nature itself; which, being once masters of, we may every where else hope for an easy victory. From this station we may extend our conquests over all those sciences which more immediately concern human life, and may afterwards proceed, at leisure, to discover more fully those which are the objects of pure curiosity." *Hume's Philosophical Works,* vol. i. p. 8. See also, in vol. ii. pp. 73, 74, his remarks on the way "to consider the matter *a priori.*"

102. "No kind of reasoning can give rise to a new idea, such as this of power is; but wherever we reason, we must antecedently be possessed of clear ideas, which may be the objects of our reasoning." *Hume's Philosophical Works,* vol. i. p. 217. Compare vol. ii. p. 276, on our arriving at a knowledge of causes "by a kind of taste or fancy." Hence, the larger view preceding the smaller, and being essentially independent of it, will constantly contradict it; and he complains, for instance, that "difficulties, which seem unsurmountable in theory, are easily got over in practice." vol. ii. p. 357; and again, in vol. iii. p. 326, on the effort needed to "reconcile reason to experience." But, after all, it is rather by a careful study of his works, than by quoting particular passages, that his method can be understood. In the two sentences, however, just cited, the

By this means, we arrive at philosophy; and her conclusions are not to be impugned, even if they do happen to clash with science. On the contrary, her authority is supreme, and her decisions, being essentially true, must always be preferred to any generalization of the facts which the external world presents.[103]

Hume, therefore, believed, that all the secrets of the external world are wrapped up in the human mind. The mind was not only the key by which the treasure could be unlocked; it was also the treasure itself. Learning and science might illustrate and beautify our mental acquisitions, but they could not communicate real knowledge; they could neither give the prime original materials, nor could they teach the design according to which those materials must be worked.

In conformity with these views, the *Natural History of Religion* was composed. The object of Hume, in writing it, was to ascertain the origin and progress of religious ideas; and he arrives at the conclusion, that the worship of many Gods must, every where, have preceded the worship of one God. This, he regards as a law of the human mind, a thing not only that always has happened, but that always must happen. His proof is entirely speculative. He argues, that the earliest state of man is necessarily a savage state; that savages can feel no interest in the ordinary operations of nature, and no desire to study the principles which govern those operations; that such men must be devoid of curiosity on all subjects which do not personally trouble them; and that, therefore, while they neglect the usual events of nature, they will turn their minds to the unusual ones.[104] A violent tempest, a monstrous birth, excessive cold, excessive rain, sudden and fatal dis-

---

reader will see that theory and reason represent the larger view; while practice and experience represent the smaller.

103. " 'Tis certainly a kind of indignity to philosophy, whose sovereign authority ought every where to be acknowledged, to oblige her on every occasion to make apologies for her conclusions, and justify herself to every particular art and science, which may be offended at her. This puts one in mind of a king arraigned for high treason against his subjects." *Hume's Philosophical Works*, vol. i. pp. 318, 319.

104. "A barbarous, necessitous animal (such as a man is on the first origin of society), pressed by such numerous wants and passions, has no leisure to admire the regular face of nature, or make inquiries concerning the cause of those objects to which, from his infancy, he has been gradually accustomed. On the contrary, the more regular and uniform, that is the more perfect, nature appears, the more is he familiarized to it, and the less inclined to scrutinize

eases, are the sort of things to which the attention of the savage is confined, and of which alone he desires to know the causes. Directly he finds that such causes are beyond his control, he reckons them superior to himself, and, being incapable of abstracting them, he personifies them; he turns them into deities; polytheism is established; and the earliest creed of mankind assumes a form which can never be altered, as long as men remain in this condition of pristine ignorance.[105]

These propositions, which are not only plausible, but which are probably true, ought, according to the inductive philosophy, to have been generalized from a survey of facts; that is, from a collection of evidence respecting the state of religion, and of the speculative faculties among savage tribes. But this, Hume abstains from doing. He refers to none of the numerous travellers who have visited such people; he does not, in the whole course of his work, mention even a single book where facts respecting savage life are preserved. It was enough for him, that the progress from a belief in many Gods to a belief in one God, was the natural progress; which is saying, in other words, that it appeared to his mind to be the natural progress.[106] With that, he was satisfied.

---

and examine it. A monstrous birth excites his curiosity, and is deemed a prodigy. It alarms him from its novelty, and immediately sets him a trembling, and sacrificing, and praying. But an animal complete in all its limbs and organs, is to him an ordinary spectacle, and produces no religious opinion or affection. Ask him whence that animal arose? he will tell you, from the copulation of its parents. And these, whence? From the copulation of theirs. A few removes satisfy his curiosity, and set the objects at such a distance that he entirely loses sight of them. Imagine not that he will so much as start the question, whence the first animal, much less whence the whole system, or united fabric of the universe arose. Or, if you start such a question to him, expect not that he will employ his mind with any anxiety about a subject so remote, so uninteresting, and which so much exceeds the bounds of his capacity." *Natural History of Religion*, in *Hume's Philosophical Works*, vol. iv. p. 439. See also pp. 463–465.

105. "By degrees, the active imagination of men, uneasy in this abstract conception of objects, about which it is incessantly employed, begins to render them more particular, and to clothe them in shapes more suitable to its natural comprehension. It represents them to be sensible, intelligent beings like mankind; actuated by love and hatred, and flexible by gifts and entreaties, by prayers and sacrifices. Hence the origin of religion. And hence the origin of idolatry, or polytheism." *Hume's Philosophical Works*, vol. iv. p. 472. "The primary religion of mankind arises chiefly from an anxious fear of future events." p. 498.

106. "*It seems certain, that, according to the natural progress of human thought,* the ignorant multitude must first entertain some grovelling and fa-

In other parts of his essay, where he treats of the religious opinions of the ancient Greeks and Romans, he displays a tolerable, though by no means remarkable, learning; but the passages which he cites, do not refer to that entirely barbarous society in which, as he supposes, polytheism first arose. The premisses, therefore, of the argument are evolved out of his own mind. He reasons deductively from the ideas which his powerful intellect supplied, instead of reasoning inductively from the facts which were peculiar to the subject he was investigating.

Even in the rest of his work, which is full of refined and curious speculation, he uses facts, not to demonstrate his conclusions, but to illustrate them. He, therefore, selected those facts which suited his purpose, leaving the others untouched. And this, which many critics would call unfair, was not unfair of him; because he believed, that he had already established his principles without the aid of those facts. The facts might benefit the reader, by making the argument clearer, but they could not strengthen the argument. They were more intended to persuade than to prove; they were rather rhetorical than logical. Hence, a critic would waste his time if he were to sift them with a minuteness which would be necessary, supposing that Hume had built an inductive argument upon them. Otherwise, without going far, it might be curious to contrast them with the entirely different facts which Cudworth, eighty years before, had collected from the same source, and on the same subject. Cudworth, who was much superior to Hume

miliar notion of superior powers, before they stretch their conception to that perfect Being who bestowed order on the whole frame of nature. *We may as reasonably imagine, that men inhabited palaces before huts and cottages,* or studied geometry before agriculture, as assert that the Deity appeared to them a pure spirit, omniscient, omnipotent, and omnipresent, before he was apprehended to be a powerful though limited being, with human passions and appetites, limbs and organs. The mind rises gradually from inferior to superior. By abstracting from what is imperfect, it forms an idea of perfection; and slowly distinguishing the nobler parts of its own frame from the grosser, it learns to transform only the former, much elevated and refined, to its divinity. Nothing could disturb this *natural progress of thought,* but some obvious and invincible argument, which might immediately lead the mind into the pure principles of theism, and make it overleap, at one bound, the vast interval which is interposed between the human and the Divine nature. But though I allow, that the order and frame of the universe, when accurately examined, affords such an argument, yet *I can never think* that this consideration could have an influence on mankind, when they formed their first rude notions of religion." *Natural History of Religion,* in *Philosophical Works,* vol. iv. p. 438.

in learning, and much inferior to him in genius,[107] displayed, in his great work on the *Intellectual System of the Universe,* a prodigious erudition, to prove that, in the ancient world, the belief in one God was a prevailing doctrine. Hume, who never refers to Cudworth, arrives at a precisely opposite conclusion. Both quoted ancient writers; but while Cudworth drew his inferences from what he found in those writers, Hume drew his from what he found in his own mind. Cudworth, being more learned, relied on his reading; Hume, having more genius, relied on his intellect. Cudworth, trained in the school of Bacon, first collected the evidence, and then passed the judgment. Hume, formed in a school entirely different, believed that the acuteness of the judge was more important than the quantity of the evidence; that witnesses were likely to prevaricate; and that he possessed, in his own mind, the surest materials for arriving at an accurate conclusion. It is not, therefore, strange, that Cudworth and Hume, pursuing opposite methods, should have obtained opposite results, since such a discrepancy is, as I have already pointed out, unavoidable, when men investigate, according to different plans, a subject which, in the existing state of knowledge, is not amenable to scientific treatment.

The length to which this chapter has already extended, and the number of topics which I have still to handle, will prevent me from examining, in detail, the philosophy of Reid, who was the most eminent among the purely speculative thinkers of Scotland, after Hume and Adam Smith, though, in point of merit, he must be placed far below them. For, he had neither the comprehensiveness of Smith, nor the fearlessness of Hume. The range of his knowledge was not wide enough to allow him to be comprehensive; while a timidity, almost amounting to moral cowardice, made him recoil from the views advocated by Hume, not so much on account of their being false, as on account of their being dangerous. It is, however, certain, that no man can take high rank as a philosopher, who allows himself to be trammelled by con-

107. Not that he was by any means devoid of genius, though he holds a rank far below so great and original a thinker as Hume. He had, however, collected more materials than he was able to wield; and his work on the *Intellectual System of the Universe,* which is a treasure of ancient philosophy, is badly arranged, and, in many parts, feebly argued. There is more real power in his posthumous treatise on *Eternal and Immutable Morality.*

siderations of that kind. A philosopher should aim solely at truth, and should refuse to estimate the practical tendency of his speculations. If they are true, let them stand; if they are false, let them fall. But, whether they are agreeable or disagreeable, whether they are consolatory or disheartening, whether they are safe or mischievous, is a question, not for philosophers, but for practical men. Every new truth, which has ever been propounded, has, for a time, caused michief; it has produced discomfort, and often unhappiness, sometimes by disturbing social or religious arrangements, and sometimes merely by the disruption of old and cherished association of thought. It is only after a certain interval, and when the framework of affairs has adjusted itself to the new truth, that its good effects preponderate; and the preponderance continues to increase, until, at length, the truth causes nothing but good. But, at the outset, there is always harm. And, if the truth is very great, as well as very new, the harm is serious. Men are made uneasy; they flinch; they cannot bear the sudden light; a general restlessness supervenes; the face of society is disturbed, or perhaps convulsed; old interests, and old beliefs, are destroyed, before new ones have been created. These symptoms are the precursors of revolution; they have preceded all the great changes through which the world has passed; and while, if they are not excessive, they forebode progress, so, if they are excessive, they threaten anarchy. It is the business of practical men to moderate such symptoms, and to take care that the truths which philosophers discover, are not applied so rashly as to dislocate the fabric, instead of strengthening it. But the philosopher has only to discover the truth, and promulgate it; and that is hard work enough for any man, let his ability be as great as it may. This division of labour, between thinkers and actors, secures an economy of force, and prevents either class from wasting its power. It establishes a difference between science, which ascertains principles, and art, which applies them. It also recognizes, that the philosopher and the practical man, having each a separate part to play, each is, in his own field, supreme. But it is a sad confusion for either to interfere with the other. In their different sphere, both are independent, and both are worthy of admiration. Inasmuch, however, as practical men should never allow the speculative conclusions of philosophers, whatever be their truth, to be put in actual operation, unless society is, in some degree, ripe for their reception; so, on the other hand, philosophers are not to hesitate, and tremble, and stop short in their career, because their intellect is leading them to conclusions subversive of existing interests. The duty of a philosopher is clear. His path lies straight before him. He must take every pains to ascertain the truth; and, having arrived at a conclusion, he, instead of shrinking from it because it is unpalatable, or because it seems dangerous, should, on that very account, cling the closer to it, should uphold it in bad repute, more zealously than he would have done in good repute; should noise it abroad far and wide, utterly regardless what opinions he shocks, or what interests he imperils; should, on its behalf, court hostility and despise contempt, being well assured, that, if it is not true, it will die, but that, if it is true, it must produce ultimate benefit, albeit unsuited for practical adoption by the age or country in which it is first propounded.

But Reid, nothwithstanding the clearness of his mind and his great powers of argument, had so little of the real philosophic spirit, that he loved truth, not for its own sake, but for the sake of its immediate and practical results. He himself tells us, that he began to study philosophy, merely because he was shocked at the consequences at which philosophers had arrived. As long as the speculations of Locke and of Berkeley were not pushed to their logical conclusions, Reid acquiesced in them, and they were good in his eyes.[108] While they were safe and tolerably orthodox, he was not over-nice in inquiring into their validity. In the hands of Hume, however, philosophy became bolder and more inquisitive;

108. "I once believed this doctrine of ideas so firmly, as to embrace the whole of Berkeley's system in consequence of it; till, finding other consequences to follow from it, which gave me more uneasiness than the want of a material world, it came into my mind more than forty years ago, to put the question, What evidence have I for this doctrine that all the objects of my knowledge are ideas in my own mind? From that time to the present, I have been candidly and impartially, as I think, seeking for the evidence of this principle, but can find none, excepting the authority of philosophers." *Reid's Essays on the Powers of the Human Mind,* edit. Edinburgh, 1808, vol. i. p. 172. And, in a letter which he wrote to Hume in 1763, he, with a simple candour which must have highly amused that eminent philosopher, confesses that "your system appears to me not only coherent in all its parts, but likewise justly deduced from principles commonly received among philosophers; principles which I never thought of calling in question, until the conclusions you draw from them in the 'Treatise of Human Nature' made me suspect them." *Burton's Life and Correspondence of Hume,* vol. ii. p. 155.

she disturbed opinions which were ancient, and which it was pleasant to hold; she searched into the foundation of things, and by forcing men to doubt and to inquire, she rendered inestimable service to the cause of truth. But this was precisely the tendency at which Reid was displeased. He saw that such disturbance was uncomfortable; he saw that it was hazardous; therefore, he endeavoured to prove that it was groundless. Confusing the question of practical consequences with the totally different question of scientific truth, he took for granted that, because to his age the adoption of those consequences would be mischievous, they must be false. To the profound views of Hume respecting causation, he gravely objects, that if they were carried into effect, the operation of criminal law would be imperilled.[109] To the speculations of the same philosopher concerning the metaphysical basis of the theory of contracts, he replies, that such speculations perplex men, and weaken their sense of duty; they are, therefore, to be disapproved of, on account of their tendency.[110] With Reid, the main question always is, not whether an inference is true, but what will happen if it is true. He says, that a doctrine is to be judged by its fruits;[111]

109. "Suppose a man to be found dead on the high-way, his skull fractured, his body pierced with deadly wounds, his watch and money carried off. The coroner's jury sits upon the body, and the question is put, 'What was the cause of this man's death, was it accident, or *felo de se,* or murder by persons unknown?' Let us suppose an adept in Mr. Hume's philosophy to make one of the jury, and that he insists upon the previous question, whether there was any cause of the event, or whether it happened without a cause." *Reid's Essays on the Powers of the Mind,* vol. ii. p. 286. Compare vol. iii. p. 33: "This would put an end to all speculation, as well as to all the business of life."

110. "The obligation of contracts and promises is a matter so sacred, and of such consequence to human society, that speculations which have a *tendency to weaken that obligation,* and to perplex men's notions on a subject so plain and so important, ought to *meet with the disapprobation of all honest men.* Some such speculations, I think, we have in the third volume of Mr. Hume's 'Treatise of Human Nature,' and in his 'Enquiry into the Principles of Morals;' and my design in this chapter is, to offer some observations on the nature of a contract or promise, and on two passages of that author on this subject. I am far from saying or thinking, that Mr. Hume meant to weaken men's obligations to honesty and fair dealing, or that he had not a sense of these obligations himself. It is not the man I impeach, but his writings. Let us think of the first as charitably as we can, while we freely examine the import and *tendency* of the last." *Reid's Essays on the Powers of the Mind,* vol. iii. p. 444. In this, as in most passages, the italics are my own.

111. "Without repeating what I have before said of causes in the first of these Essays, and in the second and third chapters of this, I shall here mention some of the consequences that may be justly deduced from this definition of a cause, that we may judge of it by its fruits." *Reid's Essays,* vol. iii. p. 339.

forgetting that the same doctrine will bear fruits in different ages, and that the consequences which a theory produces in one state of society, are often diametrically opposed to those which it produces in another. He thus made his own age the standard of all future ones. He also trammelled philosophy with practical considerations; diverting thinkers from the pursuit of truth, which is their proper department, into the pursuit of expediency, which is not their department at all. Reid was constantly stopping to inquire, not whether theories were accurate, but whether it was advisable to adopt them; whether they were favourable to patriotism, or to generosity, or to friendship;[112] in a word, whether they were comfortable, and such as we should at present like to believe.[113] Or else, he would take other ground, still lower, and still more unworthy of a philosopher. In opposing, for instance, the doctrine, that our faculties sometimes deceive us,—a doctrine which, as he well knew, had been held by men whose honesty was equal to his own, and whose ability was superior to his own,—he does not scruple to enlist on his side the prejudices of a vulgar superstition; seeking to blacken the tenet which he was unable to refute. He actually asserts, that they who advocate it, insult the Deity, by imputing to the Almighty that He has lied. Such being the consequence of the opinion, it of course follows, that the opinion must be rejected without further scrutiny, since, to accept it, would produce fatal results on our conduct, and would, indeed, be subversive of all religion, of all morals, and of all knowledge.[114]

In 1764, Reid published his *Inquiry into the Human Mind;*

112. "Bishop Berkeley surely did not duly consider that it is by means of the material world that we have any correspondence with thinking beings, or any knowledge of their existence, and that by depriving us of the material world, he deprived us at the same time of family, friends, country, and every human creature; of every object of affection, esteem or concern, except ourselves. The good Bishop surely never intended this. He was too warm a friend, too zealous a patriot, and too good a Christian, to be capable of such a thought. *He was not aware of the consequences of his system*" (poor, ignorant Berkeley), "and therefore they ought not to be imputed to him; but we must impute them to the system itself. It stifles every generous and social principle." *Reid's Essays,* vol. ii. pp. 251, 252.

113. In his *Essays,* vol. i. p. 179, he says of Berkeley, one of the deepest and most unanswerable of all speculators, "But there is one *uncomfortable consequence* of his system which he seems not to have attended to, and from which it will be found difficult, if at all possible, to guard it."

114. "This doctrine is dishonourable to our Maker, and lays a foundation for universal scepticism. It supposes the Author of our being to have given us one faculty on purpose to deceive us, and another by which we may detect the

and in that, and in his subsequent work, entitled *Essays on the Powers of the Mind,* he sought to destroy the philosophy of Locke, Berkeley, and Hume. And as Hume was the boldest of the three, it was chiefly his philosophy which Reid attacked. Of the character of this attack, some specimens have just been given; but they rather concern his object and motives, while what we have now to ascertain is, his method, that is, the tactics of his warfare. He clearly saw, that Hume had assumed certain principles, and had reasoned deductively from them to the facts, instead of reasoning inductively from the facts to them. To this method, he strongly, and perhaps fairly, objects. He admits, that Hume had reasoned so accurately, that if his principles were conceded, his conclusions must likewise be conceded.[115] But, he says, Hume had no right to proceed in such a manner. He had no right to assume principles, and then to argue from them. The laws of nature were to be arrived at, not by conjecturing in this way, but by a patient induction of facts.[116] Discoveries depended solely on observation and experiment; and any other plan could only produce theories, ingenious, perhaps, and plausible, but quite worthless.[117] For, theory should yield to fact, and not fact to theory.[118] Speculators,

---

fallacy, and find that he imposed upon us." . . . "The genuine dictate of our natural faculties is the voice of God, no less than what he reveals from heaven; and to say that it is fallacious, is to impute a lie to the God of truth." . . . "Shall we impute to the Almighty what we cannot impute to a man without a heinous affront? Passing this opinion, therefore, as shocking to an ingenuous mind, and, in its consequences, subversive of all religion, all morals, and all knowledge," &c. *Reid's Essays,* vol. iii. p. 310. See also vol. i. p. 313.

115. "His reasoning appeared to me to be just; there was, therefore, a necessity to call in question the principles upon which it was founded, or to admit the conclusion." *Reid's Inquiry into the Human Mind,* p. v. "The received doctrine of ideas is the principle from which it is deduced, and of which, indeed, it seems to be a just and natural consequence." p. 53. See also *Reid's Essays,* vol. i. pp. 199, 200, vol. ii. p. 211.

116. "The laws of nature are the most general facts we can discover in the operations of nature. Like other facts, they are not to be hit upon by a happy conjecture, but justly deduced from observation. Like other general facts, they are not to be drawn from a few particulars, but from a copious, patient, and cautious induction." *Reid's Inquiry into the Human Mind,* pp. 262, 263.

117. "Such discoveries have always been made by patient observation, by accurate experiments, or by conclusions drawn by strict reasoning from observations and experiments; and such discoveries have always tended to refute, but not to confirm, the theories and hypotheses which ingenious men had invented." *Reid's Essays,* vol. i. p. 46.

118. "This is Mr. Hume's notion of a cause." . . . . "But theory ought to stoop to fact, and not fact to theory." *Reid's Essays,* vol. iii. p. 276.

indeed, might talk about first principles, and raise a system by reasoning from them. But the fact was, that there was no agreement as to how a first principle was to be recognized; since a principle which one man would deem self-evident, another would think it necessary to prove, and a third would altogether deny.[119]

The difficulties of deductive reasoning are here admirably portrayed. It might have been expected, that Reid would have built up his own philosophy according to the inductive plan, and would have despised that assumption of first principles, with which he taunts his opponents. But it is one of the most curious things in the history of metaphysics, that Reid, after impeaching the method of Hume, follows the very same method himself. When he is attacking the philosophy of Hume, he holds deduction to be wrong. When he is raising his own philosophy, he holds it to be right. He deemed certain conclusions dangerous, and he objects to their advocates, that they argued from principles, instead of from facts; and that they assumed themselves to be in possession of the first principles of truth, although people were not agreed as to what constituted a first principle. This is well put, and hard to answer. Strange, however, to say, Reid arrives at his own conclusions, by assuming first principles to an extent far greater than had been done by any writer on the opposite side. From them, he argues; his whole scheme is deductive; and his works scarcely contain a single instance of that inductive logic, which, when attacking his opponents, he found it convenient to recommend. It is difficult to conceive a better illustration of the peculiar character of the Scotch intellect in the eighteenth century, and of the firm hold, which, what may be called, the anti-Baconian method, had upon that intellect. Reid was a man of considerable ability, of immaculate honesty, and was deeply convinced that it was for the good of society that the prevailing philosophy should be overthrown. To the performance of that task, he dedicated his long and laborious life; he saw that the vulnerable point of the adverse system was its method; he indicated the deficiencies of that method, and declared, perhaps wrongly, but

119. "But yet there seems to be great difference of opinions among philosophers about first principles. What one takes to be self-evident, another labours to prove by arguments, and a third denies altogether." *Reid's Essays,* vol. ii. p. 218. "Mr. Locke seems to think first principles of very small use." p. 219.

at all events sincerely, that it could never lead to truth. Yet, and notwithstanding all this, such was the pressure of the age in which he lived, and so completely did the force of circumstances shape his understanding, that, in his own works, he was unable to avoid that very method of investigation which he rebuked in others. Indeed, so far from avoiding it, he was a slave to it. The evidence of this I will now give, because, besides its importance for the history of the Scotch mind, it is valuable as one of many lessons, which teach us how we are moulded by the society which surrounds us; how even our most vigorous actions are influenced by general causes of which we are often ignorant, and which few of us care to study; and, finally, how lame and impotent we are, when, as individuals, we try to stem the onward current, resisting the great progress instead of aiding it, and vainly opposing our little wishes to that majestic course of events, which admits of no interruption, but sweeps on, grand and terrible, while generation after generation passes away, successively absorbed in one mighty vortex.

Directly Reid, ceasing to refute the philosophy of Hume, began to construct his own philosophy, he succumbed to the prevailing method. He now assures us, that all reasoning must be from first principles, and that, so far from reasoning to those principles, we must at once admit them, and make them the basis of all subsequent arguments.[120] Having admitted them, they become a thread to guide the inquirer through the labyrinth of thought.[121] His opponents had no right to assume them, but he might do so, because to him they were intuitive.[122] Whoever denied them, was

120. "All reasoning must be from first principles; and for first principles no other reason can be given but this, that, by the constitution of our nature, we are under a necessity of assenting to them." *Reid's Inquiry*, p. 140. "All reasoning is from principles." . . . "Most justly, therefore, do such principles disdain to be tried by reason, and laugh at all the artillery of the logician when it is directed against them." p. 372. "All knowledge got by reasoning must be built upon first principles." *Reid's Essays*, vol. ii. p. 220. "In every branch of real knowledge there must be first principles, whose truth is known intuitively, without reasoning, either probable or demonstrative. They are not grounded on reasoning, but all reasoning is grounded on them." p. 360.

121. "For, when any system is grounded upon first principles, and deduced regularly from them, we have a thread to lead us through the labyrinth." *Reid's Essays*, vol. ii. p. 225.

122. "I call these 'first principles,' because they *appear to me* to have in themselves an intuitive evidence which *I cannot resist*." *Reid's Essays*, vol. iii. p. 375.

not fit to be reasoned with.[123] Indeed, to investigate them, or to seek to analyze them, was wrong as well as foolish, because they were part of the constitution of things; and of the constitution of things no account could be given, except that such was the will of God.[124]

As Reid obtained his first principles with such ease, and as he carefully protected them by forbidding any attempt to resolve them into simpler elements, he was under a strong temptation to multiply them almost indefinitely, in order that, by reasoning from them, he might raise a complete and harmonious system of the human mind. To that temptation he yielded with a readiness, which is truly surprising, when we remember how he reproached his opponents with doing the same thing. Among the numerous first principles which he assumes, not only as unexplained, but as inexplicable, are the belief in Personal Identity;[125] the belief in the External World;[126] the belief in the Uniformity of Nature;[127] the belief in the Existence of Life in Others;[128] the belief in Testimony,[129] also in the power of distinguishing truth from error,[130] and even in the correspondence of the face and voice to the thoughts.[131] Of belief generally, he asserts that there are many principles,[132] and he regrets that any one should have rashly at-

123. "If any man should think fit to deny that these things are qualities, or that they require any subject, *I leave him to enjoy his opinion, as a man who denies first principles, and is not fit to be reasoned with.*" *Reid's Essays,* vol. i. p. 38.

124. "No other account can be given of the constitution of things, but the will of Him that made them." *Reid's Essays,* vol. i. p. 115.

125. *Reid's Essays,* vol. i. pp. 36, 37, 340, 343; vol. ii. p. 245.

126. *Reid's Essays,* vol. i. pp. 115, 116, 288–299; vol. ii. p. 251.

127. Or, as he expresses it, "our belief of the continuance of the laws of nature." *Reid's Inquiry,* pp. 426–435; also his *Essays,* vol. i. p. 305; vol. ii. p. 268.

128. *Reid's Essays,* vol. ii. p. 259.

129. *Reid's Inquiry,* p. 422; and his *Essays,* vol. ii. p. 266.

130. "Another first principle is, 'That the natural faculties by which we distinguish truth from error are not fallacious.' " *Reid's Essays,* vol. ii. p. 256.

131. "Another first principle I take to be, 'That certain features of the countenance, sounds of the voice, and gestures of the body, indicate certain thoughts and dispositions of mind." *Reid's Essays,* vol. ii. p. 261. Compare his *Inquiry,* p. 416.

132. "We have taken notice of several original principles of belief in the course of this inquiry; and when other faculties of the mind are examined, we shall find more, which have not occurred in the examination of the five senses." *Reid's Inquiry,* p. 471.

tempted to explain them.[133] Such things are mysterious, and not to be pried into. We have also other faculties, which, being original and indecomposable, resist all inductive treatment, and can neither be resolved into simpler elements, nor referred to more general laws. To this class, Reid assigns Memory,[134] Perception,[135] Desire of Self-Approbation,[136] and not only Instinct, but even Habit.[137] Many of our ideas, such as those concerning Space and Time, are equally original;[138] and other first principles there are, which have not been enunciated, but from which we may reason.[139] They, therefore, are the major premisses of the argument; no reason having yet been given for them, they must be simple; and not having yet been explained, they are, of course, inexplicable.[140]

All this is arbitrary enough. Still, in justice to Reid, it must be said, that, having made these assumptions, he displayed remarkable ability in arguing from them, and that, in attacking the philosophy of his time, he subjected it to a criticism, which has been extremely serviceable. His lucidity, his dialectic skill, and the racy and masculine style in which he wrote, made him a formidable opponent, and secured to his objections a respectful hearing. To

133. "And if no philosopher had attempted to define and explain belief, some paradoxes in philosophy, more incredible than ever were brought forth by the most abject superstition, or the most frantic enthusiasm, had never seen the light." *Reid's Inquiry*, p. 45.

134. *Reid's Essays*, vol. i. pp. 329, 334; vol. ii. p. 247.

135. *Reid's Essays*, vol. i. pp. 9, 71, 303, 304.

136. *Reid's Essays*, vol. ii. p. 60.

137. "I see no reason to think, that we shall ever be able to assign the physical cause, either of instinct, or of the power of habit. Both seem to be parts of our original constitution. Their end and use is evident; but we can assign no cause of them, but the will of Him who made us." *Reid's Essays*, vol. iii. p. 119.

138. "I know of no ideas or notions that have a better claim to be accounted simple and original, than those of space and time." *Reid's Essays*, vol. i. p. 354.

139. "I do not at all affirm that those I have mentioned are all the first principles from which we may reason concerning contingent truths. Such enumerations, even when made after much reflection, are seldom perfect." *Reid's Essays*, vol. ii. p. 270.

140. "Why sensation should compel our belief of the present existence of the thing, memory a belief of its past existence, and imagination no belief at all, *I believe no philosopher can give a shadow of reason,* but that such is the nature of these operations. They are all simple and original, and *therefore inexplicable* acts of the mind." *Reid's Inquiry*, p. 40. "We can *give no reason* why the retina is, of all parts of the body, the only one on which pictures made by the rays of light cause vision; and *therefore we must resolve this solely into a law of our constitution.*" p. 258.

me, however, it appears, that notwithstanding the attempts, first of M. Cousin, and afterwards of Sir William Hamilton, to prop up his declining reputation, his philosophy, as an independent system, is untenable, and will not live. In this I may be mistaken; but what is quite certain is, that nothing can be more absurd than to suppose, as some have done, that he adopted the inductive, or, as it is popularly called, Baconian method. Bacon, indeed, would have smiled at such a disciple, assuming all sorts of major premisses, taking general principles for granted with the greatest recklessness, and reserving his skill for the task of reasoning from propositions for which he had no evidence, except that on a cursory, or, as he termed it, a common-sense, inspection, they appeared to be true.[141] This refusal to analyze preconceived notions, comes under the head of what Bacon stigmatized as the *anticipatio naturæ,* and which he deemed the great enemy of knowledge, on account of the dangerous confidence it places in the spontaneous and uncorrected conclusions of the human mind. When, therefore, we find Reid holding up the Baconian philosophy, as a pattern which it behoved all inquirers to follow;[142] and when we, moreover, find Dugald Stewart, who, though a somewhat superficial thinker, was, at all events, a careful writer, supposing that

141. In a recent work of distinguished merit, an instance is given of the loose manner in which he took for granted that certain phenomena were ultimate, in order that, instead of analyzing them, he might reason from them. "Dr. Reid has no hesitation in classing the voluntary command of our organs, that is, the sequence of feeling and action implied in all acts of will, among instincts. The power of lifting a morsel of food to the mouth, is, according to him, an instinctive or pre-established conjunction of the wish and the deed; that is to say, the emotional state of hunger, coupled with the sight of a piece of bread, is associated, through a primitive link of the mental constitution, with the several movements of the hand, arm, and mouth, concerned in the act of eating. *This assertion of Dr. Reid's may be simply met by appealing to the facts.* It is not true that human beings possess, at birth, any voluntary command of their limbs whatsoever. A babe of two months old cannot use its hands in obedience to its desires. The infant can grasp nothing, hold nothing, can scarcely fix its eyes on any thing." .... "If the more perfect command of our voluntary movements implied in every art be an acquisition, so is the less perfect command of these movements that grows upon a child during the first year of life." *Bain on the Senses and the Intellect,* London, 1855, pp. 292, 293.

142. See *Reid's Inquiry,* pp. 436, 446, as well as other parts of his works: see also an extract from one of his letters to Dr. Gregory, in *Stewart's Biographical Memoirs,* p. 432.

Reid had followed it,[143] we meet with fresh proof of how difficult it was for Scotchmen of the last age to imbibe the true spirit of inductive logic, since they believed, that a system which flagrantly violated its rules, had been framed in strict accordance with them.

Leaving mental philosophy, I now come to physical science, in which, if any where, we might expect that the inductive plan would predominate, and would triumph over the opposite, or deductive, one. How far this was the case, I will endeavour to ascertain, by an examination of the most important discoveries which have been made by Scotchmen concerning the organic and inorganic world. And, as my object is merely to indicate the turn and character of the Scotch mind, I shall avoid all details respecting the practical effects of those discoveries, and shall confine myself to such a narration as will exhibit their purely scientific aspect, so as to enable the reader to understand what additions were made to our knowledge of the laws of nature, and in what way the additions were made. The character of each discovery, and its process, will be stated, but nothing more. Neither here, nor in any part of this Introduction, do I pretend to investigate questions of practical utility, or to trace the connexion between the discoveries of science and the arts of life. That I shall do in the body of the work itself, where I hope to explain a number of minute social events, many of which are regarded as isolated, if not incongruous. For the present, I solely aim at those broad principles, which, by marking out the epochs of thought, underlie the whole fabric of society, and which must be clearly apprehended before history

143. "The idea of prosecuting the study of the human mind on a plan analogous to that which had been so successfully adopted in physics by the followers of Lord Bacon, if not first conceived by Dr. Reid, was, at least, first carried successfully into execution in his writings." *Stewart's Biographical Memoirs,* p. 419. "The influence of the general views opened in the *Novum Organon,* may be traced in almost every page of his writings; and, indeed, the circumstance by which they are so strongly and characteristically distinguished, is that they exhibit the first systematical attempt to exemplify, in the study of human nature, the same plan of investigation which conducted Newton to the properties of light, and to the law of gravitation." p. 421. From this passage one might hazard a supposition that Dugald Stewart did not understand Bacon much better than he did Aristotle or Kant. Of the two last most profound thinkers, he certainly knew little or nothing, except what he gathered secondhand. Consequently, he underrates them.

can cease to be a mere empirical assemblage of facts, of which the scientific basis being unsettled, the true order and coherence must be unknown.

Among the sciences which concern the inorganic world, the laws of heat occupy a conspicuous place. On the one hand, they are connected with geology, being intimately allied, and, indeed, necessarily bound up, with every speculation respecting the changes and present condition of the crust of the earth. On the other hand, they touch the great questions of life, both animal and vegetable; they have to do with the theory of species, and of race; they modify soil, food, and organization; and to them we must look for valuable help towards solving those great problems in biology, which, of late years, have occupied the attention of the boldest and most advanced philosophers.

Our present knowledge of the laws of heat, may be briefly stated as branching into five fundamental divisions. These are: latent heat; specific heat; the conduction of heat; the radiation of heat; and, finally, the undulatory theory of heat; by which last, we are gradually discarding our old material views, and are accustoming ourselves to look upon heat as simply one of the forms of force, all of which, such as light, electricity, magnetism, motion, gravitation, and chemical affinity, are constantly assuming each other's shape, but, in their total amount, are incapable either of increase or of diminution.[144] This grand conception, which is now placing the indestructibility of force on the same ground as the indestructibility of matter, has an importance far above its scientific value, considerable as that undoubtedly is. For, by teaching us, that nothing perishes, but that, on the contrary, the slightest

144. The theory of the indestructibility of force has been applied to the law of gravitation by Professor Faraday, in his *Discourse on the Conservation of Force,* 1857; an essay full of thought and power, and which should be carefully studied by every one who wishes to understand the direction which the highest speculations of physical science are now taking. I will quote only one passage from the opening, to give the reader an idea of its general scope, irrespective of the more special question of gravitation. "The progress of the strict science of modern times has tended more and more to produce the conviction that force can neither be created nor destroyed; and to render daily more manifest the value of the knowledge of that truth in experimental research." . . . . "Agreeing with those who admit the conservation of force to be a principle in physics, as large and sure as that of the indestructibility of matter, or the invariability of gravity, I think that no particular idea of force has a right to unlimited or unqualified acceptance, that does not include assent to it."

movement of the smallest body, in the remotest region, produces results which are perpetual, which diffuse themselves through all space, and which, though they may be metamorphosed, cannot be destroyed, it impresses us with such an exalted idea of the regular and compulsory march of physical affairs, as must eventually influence other and higher departments of inquiry. Our habits of thought are so connected and interwoven, that notions of law and of the necessary concatenation of things, can never be introduced into one field of speculation, without affecting other fields which lie contiguous to it. When, therefore, the modern doctrine of conservation of force,[145] becomes firmly coupled with the older doctrine of conservation of matter, we may rest assured, that the human mind will not stop there, but will extend to the study of Man, inferences analogous to those already admitted in the study of Nature. Having once recognized that the condition of the material universe, at any one moment, is simply the result of every

145. As an illustration of this doctrine, I cannot do better than quote the following passage from one of the most suggestive and clearly reasoned books which has been written in this century by an English physicist: "Wave your hand; the motion which has apparently ceased, is taken up by the air, from the air by the walls of the room, &c., and so by direct and reacting waves, continually comminuted, but never destroyed. It is true that, at a certain point, we lose all means of detecting the motion, from its minute subdivision, which defies our most delicate means of appreciation, but we can indefinitely extend our power of detecting it accordingly as we confine its direction, or increase the delicacy of our examination. Thus, if the hand be moved in unconfined air, the motion of the air would not be sensible to a person at a few feet distance; but if a piston of the same extent of surface as the hand be moved with the same rapidity in a tube, the blast of air may be distinctly felt at several yards distance. There is no greater absolute amount of motion in the air in the second than in the first case, but its direction is restrained, so as to make its means of detection more facile. By carrying on this restraint, as in the air-gun, we get a power of detecting the motion, and of moving other bodies at far greater distances. The puff of air which would in the air-gun project a bullet a quarter of a mile, if allowed to escape without its direction being restrained, as by the bursting of a bladder, would not be perceptible at a yard distance, though the same absolute amount of motion be impressed on the surrounding air." *Grove's Correlation of Physical Forces*, London, 1855, pp. 24, 25. In a work now issuing from the press, and still unfinished, it is suggested, with considerable plausibility, that Persistence of Force would be a more accurate expression than Conservation of Force. See Mr. Herbert Spencer's *First Principles*, London, 1861, p. 251. The title of this book gives an inadequate notion of the importance of the subjects with which it deals, and of the reach and subtlety of thought which characterize it. Though some of the generalizations appear to me rather premature, no well-instructed and disciplined intellect can consider them without admiration of the remarkable powers displayed by their author.

thing which has happened at all preceding moments, and that the most trivial disturbance would so violate the general scheme, as to render anarchy inevitable, and that, to sever from the total mass even the minutest fragment, would, by dislocating the structure, bury the whole in one common ruin, we, thus admitting the exquisite adjustment of the different parts, and discerning, too, in the very beauty and completeness of the design, the best proof that it has never been tampered with by the Divine Architect, who called it into being, in whose Omniscience both the plan, and the issue of the plan, resided with such clearness and unerring certainty, that not a stone in that superb and symmetrical edifice has been touched since the foundation of the edifice was laid, are, by ascending to this pitch and elevation of thought, most assuredly advancing towards that far higher step, which it will remain for our posterity to take, and which will raise their view to so commanding a height, as to insure the utter rejection of those old and eminently irreligious dogmas of supernatural interference with the affairs of life, which superstition has invented, and ignorance has bequeathed, and the present acceptance of which betokens the yet early condition of our knowledge, the penury of our intellectual resources, and the inveteracy of the prejudices in which we are still immersed.

It is, therefore, natural, that the physical doctrine of indestructibility applied to force as well as to matter, should be essentially a creation of the present century, notwithstanding a few allusions made to it by some earlier thinkers, all of whom, however, groped vaguely, and without general purpose. No preceding age was bold enough to embrace so magnificent a view as a whole, nor had any preceding philosophers sufficient acquaintance with nature to enable them to defend such a conception, even had they desired to entertain it. Thus, in the case now before us, it is evident, that while heat was believed to be material, it could not be conceived as a force, and, therefore, no one could grasp the theory of its metamorphosis into other forces; though there are passages in Bacon which prove that he wished to identify it with motion. It was first necessary to abstract heat into a mere property or affection of matter, and there was no chance of doing this until heat was better understood in its immediate antecedents, that is, until, by the aid of mathematics, its proximate laws had been generalized. But, with the single exception of Newton, whose efforts, notwithstanding his gigantic powers, were, on this subject, very unsatisfactory, and who, moreover, had a decided leaning towards the material theory, no one attempted to unravel the mathematical laws of heat till the latter half of the eighteenth century, when Lambert and Black began the career which Prevost and Fourier followed up. The mind, having been so slow in mastering the preliminaries and outworks of the inquiry, was not ripe for the far more difficult enterprise of idealizing heat itself, and so abstracting it, as to strip it of its material attributes, and leave to it nothing but the speculative notion of an immaterial force.

From these considerations, which were necessary to enable the reader to appreciate the value of what was done in Scotland, it will be seen how essential it was that the laws of the movement of heat should be studied before its nature was investigated, and before the emission theory could be so seriously attacked as to allow of the possibility of that great doctrine of the indestructibility of force, which, I make no doubt, is destined to revolutionize our habits of thought, and to give to future speculations a basis infinitely wider than any previously known. In regard to the movements of heat, we owe the laws of conduction and of radiation chiefly to France and Geneva, while the laws of specific heat, and those of latent heat, were discovered in Scotland. The doctrine of specific heat, though interesting, has not the scientific importance which belongs to the other departments of this great subject; but the doctrine of latent heat is extremely curious, not only in itself, but also on account of the analogies it suggests with various branches of physical inquiry.

What is termed latent heat, is exhibited in the following manner. If, in consequence of the application of heat, a solid passes into a liquid, as ice, for instance, into water, the conversion occupies a longer time than could be explained by any theory which had been propounded down to the middle of the eighteenth century. Neither was it possible to explain how it is, that ice never rises above the temperature of 32° until it is actually melted, no matter what the heat of the adjacent bodies may be. There were no means of accounting for these circumstances. And though practical men, being familiar with them, did not wonder at them, they caused great astonishment among thinkers, who were accustomed to analyze events, and to seek a reason for common and every-day occurrences.

Soon after the middle of the eighteenth century, Black, who was then one of the professors in the University of Glasgow, turned his attention to this subject.[146] He struck out a theory which, being eminently original, was violently attacked, but is now generally admitted. With a boldness and reach of thought not often equalled, he arrived at the conclusion, that whenever a body loses some of its consistence, as in the case of ice becoming water, or water becoming steam, such body receives an amount of heat which our senses, though aided by the most delicate thermometer, can never detect. For, this heat is absorbed; we lose all sight of it, and it produces no palpable effect on the material world, but becomes, as it were, a hidden property. Black, therefore, called it latent heat, because, though we conceive it as an idea, we cannot trace it as a fact. The body is, properly speaking, hotter; and yet its temperature does not rise. Directly, however, the foregoing process is inverted, that is to say, directly the steam is condensed into water, or the water hardened into ice, the heat returns into the world of sense; it ceases to be latent, and communicates itself to the surrounding objects. No new heat has been created; it has, indeed, appeared and disappeared, so far as our senses were deceived, since there has, in truth, been neither addition nor diminution.[147] That this remarkable theory paved the

146. He was appointed professor in 1756; and "it was during his residence in Glasgow, between the years 1759 and 1763, that he brought to maturity those speculations concerning the combination of heat with matter, which had frequently occupied a portion of his thoughts." *Thomson's History of Chemistry,* vol. i. pp. 319, 320.

147. *Black's Lectures on Chemistry,* vol. i. pp. 116, 117; and in various places. Dr. Robison, the editor of these Lectures, says, p. 513, "Nothing could be more simple than his doctrines of latent heat. The experience of more than a century had made us consider the thermometer as a sure and an accurate indicator of heat, and of all its variations. We had learned to distrust all others. Yet, in the liquefaction and vaporization of bodies, we had proofs uncontrovertible of the entrance of heat into the bodies. And we could, by suitable processes, get it out of them again. Dr. Black said that it was concealed in them,—*latet,*—it was as much concealed as carbonic acid is in marble, or water in zeolite,—it was concealed till Dr. Black detected it. He called it Latent Heat. He did not mean by this term that it was a different kind of heat from the heat which expanded bodies, but merely that it was concealed from our sense of heat, and from the thermometer." See also p. xxxvii.: "Philosophers had long been accustomed to consider the thermometer as the surest means for detecting the presence of heat or fire in bodies, and they distrusted all others."

way for the doctrine of the indestructibility of force, will be obvious to whoever has examined the manner in which, in the history of the human mind, scientific conceptions are generated. The process is always so slow, that no single discovery has ever been made, except by the united labours of several successive generations. In estimating, therefore, what each man has done, we must judge him, not by the errors he commits, but by the truths he propounds. Most of his errors are not really his own. He inherits them from his predecessors; and if he throws some of them off, we should be grateful, instead of being dissatisfied that he has not rejected all. Black, no doubt, fell into the error of regarding heat as a material substance, which obeys the laws of chemical composition.[148] But this was merely an hypothesis, which was bequeathed to him, and with which the existing state of thought forced him to encumber his theory. He inherited the hypothesis, and could not get rid of his troublesome possession. The real service which he rendered is, that, in spite of that hypothesis, which clung to him to the last, he, far more than any of his contemporaries, contributed towards the great conception of idealizing heat, and thus enabled his successors to admit it into the class of immaterial and supersensual forces. Once admitted into that class, the list of forces became complete; and it was comparatively easy to apply to the whole body of force, the same notion of indestructibility, which had previously been applied to the whole body of matter. But it was hardly possible to effect this object, while heat stood, as it were, midway between force and matter, yielding opposite results to different senses; amenable to the touch, but invisible to the eye. What was wanting, was to remove it altogether out of the jurisdiction of the senses, and to admit that, though we experience its effects, we can only conceive its existence. Towards accomplishing this, Black took a prodigious stride. Unconscious, perhaps, of the remote tendency of his own labours, he undermined that doctrine of material heat, which he seemed to support. For, by his advocacy of latent heat, he taught that its movements constantly baffle, not only some of our senses,

148. "Fluidity is the consequence of a certain combination of calorific matter with the substance of solid bodies," &c. *Black's Lectures,* vol. i. p. 133. Compare p. 192, and the remarks in *Turner's Chemistry,* 1847, vol. i. p. 31, on Black's views of the "chemical combination" of heat. Among the backward chemists, we still find traces of the idea of heat obeying chemical laws.

but all of them; and that, while our feelings make us believe that heat is lost, our intellect makes us believe that it is not lost. Here, we have apparent destructibility, and real indestructibility. To assert that a body received heat without its temperature rising, was to make the understanding correct the touch, and defy its dictates. It was a bold and beautiful paradox, which required courage as well as insight to broach, and the reception of which marks an epoch in the human mind, because it was an immense step towards idealizing matter into force. Some, indeed, have spoken of invisible matter; but that is a contradiction in terms, which will never be admitted, as long as the forms of speech remain unchanged. Nothing can be invisible, except force, mind, and the Supreme Cause of all. We must, therefore, ascribe to Black the signal merit that he first, in the study of heat, impeached the authority of the senses, and thereby laid the foundation of every thing which was afterwards done. Besides the relation which his discovery bears to the indestructibility of force, it is also connected with one of the most splendid achievements effected by this generation in inorganic physics; namely, the establishment of the identity of light and heat. To the senses, light and heat, though in some respects similar, are in most respects dissimilar. Light, for instance, affects the eye, and not the touch. Heat affects the touch, but, under ordinary circumstances, does not affect the eye. The capital difference, however, between them is, that heat, unlike light, possesses the property of temperature; and this property is so characteristic, that, until our understandings are invigorated by science, we cannot conceive heat separated from temperature, but are compelled to confuse one with the other. Directly, however, men began to adopt the method followed by Black, and were resolved to consider heat as supersensual, they entered the road which led to the discovery of light and heat being merely different developments of the same force. Ignoring the effects of heat on themselves, or on any part of the creation, which was capable of feeling its temperature, and would therefore be deceived by it, nothing was left for them to do, but to study its effects on the inanimate world. Then, all was revealed. The career of discovery was fairly opened; and analogies between light and heat, which even the boldest imagination had hardly suspected, were placed beyond a doubt. To the reflection of heat, which had been formerly known, were now added, the refraction of heat, its double refraction, its polarization, its depolarization, its circular polarization, the interference of its rays, and their retardation; while, what is more remarkable than all, the march of our knowledge on these points was so swift, that before the year 1836 had come to a close, the chain of evidence was completed by the empirical investigations of Forbes and Melloni, they themselves little witting that every thing which they accomplished was prepared before they were born, that they were but the servants and followers of him who indicated the path in which they trod, and that their experiments, ingenious as they were, and full of resource, were simply the direct practical consequence of one of those magnificent ideas which Scotland has thrown upon the world, and the memory of which is almost enough so to bribe the judgment, as to tempt us to forget, that, while the leading intellects of the nation were engaged in such lofty pursuits, the nation itself, untouched by them, passed them over with cold and contemptuous indifference, being steeped in that deadening superstition, which turns a deaf ear to every sort of reason, and will not hearken to the voice of the charmer, charm he never so wisely.

By thus considering the descent and relationship of scientific conceptions, we can alone understand what we really owe to Black's discovery of latent heat. In regard to the method of the discovery, little need be said, since every student of the Baconian philosophy must see, that the discovery was of a kind for which none of the maxims of that system had provided. As latent heat escapes the senses, it could not obey the rules of a philosophy, which grounds all truth on observation and experiment. The subject of the inquiry being supersensual, there was no scope for what Bacon called crucial experiments and separations of nature. The truth was in the idea; experiments, therefore, might illustrate it, might bring it up to the surface, and so enable men to grasp it, but could not prove it. And this, which appears on the very face of the discovery, is confirmed by the express testimony of Dr. Thomson, who knew Black, and was, indeed, one of the most eminent of his pupils. We are assured by this unimpeachable witness, that Black, about the year 1759, began to speculate concerning heat; that the result of those speculations was the theory of latent heat; that he publicly taught that theory in the year 1761; but that the experiments which were necessary to convince the world of it were not made till 1764,[149] though, as I need hardly add, according to the inductive method, it was a breach of all the rules of philosophy to be satisfied with the theory three years before the experiments were made, and it was a still greater breach, not only to be satisfied with it, but to have openly promulgated it as an original and unquestionable truth, which explained, in a new manner, the economy of the material world.

The intellect of Black belonged to a class, which, in the eighteenth century, was almost universal in Scotland, but was hardly to be found in England, and which, for want of a better word, we are compelled to call deductive, though fully admitting that even the most deductive minds have in them a large amount of induction, since, indeed, without induction, the common business of life could not be carried on. But for the purposes of scientific classification, we may say, that a man or an age is deductive, when the favourite process is reasoning from principles instead of reasoning to them, and when there is a tendency to underrate the value of specific experience. That this was the case with the illustrious discoverer of latent heat, we have seen, both from the nature of the discovery, and from the decisive testimony of his friend and pupil. And a further confirmation may be found in the circumstance, that, having once propounded his great idea, he,

---

149. "So much was he convinced of this, that he taught the doctrine in his lectures in 1761, before he had made a single experiment on the subject." . . . . "The requisite experiments were first attempted by Dr. Black in 1764." *Thomson's History of Chemistry,* vol. i. p. 324. See also pp. 319, 320; and on the history of the idea in Black's mind as early as the year 1754, see the interesting extracts from his note-books in Robison's appendix to *Black's Lectures,* vol. i. pp. 525, 526.

The statement by Dr. Thomson refers to the completion, or last stage, of the discovery, namely the vaporific combination of heat. But from a letter which Black wrote to Watt in 1780 (*Muirhead's Life of Watt,* London, 1859, p. 303), it appears that Thomson has even understated the question, and that Black, instead of first teaching his theory in 1761, taught it three years earlier, that is, *six* years before the decisive experiments were made. "I began," writes Black, "to give the doctrine of latent heat in my lectures at Glasgow in the winter 1757–58, which, I believe, was the first winter of my lecturing there; or if I did not give it that winter, I certainly gave it in the 1758–59; and I have delivered it every year since that time in my winter lectures, which I continued to give at Glasgow until winter 1766–67, when I began to lecture in Edinburgh."

instead of instituting a long series of laborious experiments by which it might be verified in its different branches, preferred reasoning from it according to the general maxims of dialectic; pushing it to its logical consequences, rather than tracking it into regions where the senses might either confirm or refute it.[150] By following this process of thought, he was led to some beautiful speculations, which are so remote from experience, that even now, with all the additional resources of our knowledge, we cannot tell whether they are true or false. Of this kind were his views respecting the causes of the preservation of man, whose existence would, he thought, be endangered, except for the power which heat possesses of lying latent and unobserved. Thus, for example, when a long and severe winter was followed by sudden warmth, it appeared natural that the ice and snow should melt with corresponding suddenness; and if this were to happen, the result would be such terrible inundations, that it would be hardly possible for man to escape from their ravages. Even if he escaped, his works, that is, the material products of his civilization, would perish. From this catastrophe, nothing saves him but the latent power of heat. Owing to this power, directly the ice and snow begin to melt at their surface, the heat enters their structure, where a large part of it remains in abeyance, and thus losing much of its power, the process of liquefaction is arrested. This dreadful agent is lulled, and becomes dormant. It is weakened at the outset of its career, and is laid up, as in a storehouse, from which it can afterwards emerge, gradually, and with safety to the human species.[151]

In this way, as summer advances, a vast magazine of heat is accumulated, and is preserved in the midst of water, where it can

150. And he distinctly states that, even in other matters, when he did make experiments, their object was to confirm theory, and not to suggest it. Thus, to give one of many instances, in his *Lectures,* vol. i. p. 354, he says, respecting salts, "When we examine the solidity of this reasoning by an experiment, *we have the pleasure to find facts agree exactly with the theory.*"

151. See a good summary of this idea in *Black's Lectures on Chemistry,* vol. i. p. 118. Contrasting his theory of heat with that previously received, he says, "But, were the ice and snow to melt as suddenly as they must necessarily do, were the former opinion of the action of heat in melting them well founded, the torrents and inundations would be incomparably more irresistible and dreadful. They would tear up and sweep away every thing, and that so suddenly, that mankind should have great difficulty to escape from their ravages."

do man no injury, since, indeed, his senses are unable to feel it. There the heat remains buried, until, in the rotation of the seasons, winter returns, and the waters are congealed into ice. In the process of congelation, that treasury of heat, which had been hidden all the summer, reappears; it ceases to be latent; and now, for the first time, striking the senses of man, it tempers, on his behalf, the severity of winter. The faster the water freezes, the faster the heat is disengaged; so that, by virtue of this great law of nature, cold actually generates warmth, and the inclemency of every season, though it cannot be hindered, is softened in proportion as the inclemency is more threatening.[152]

Thus, again, inasmuch as heat becomes latent, and flies from the senses, not only when ice is passing into water, but also when water is passing into steam, we find in this latter circumstance, one of the reasons why man and other animals can live in the tropics, which, but for this, would be deserted. They are constantly suffering from the heat which is collected in their bodies, and which, considered by itself, is enough to destroy them. But this heat causes thirst, and they consequently swallow great quantities of fluid, much of which exudes through the pores of the skin in the form of vapour. And as, according to the theory of latent heat, vapour cannot be produced without a vast amount of heat being buried within it, such vapour absorbs and carries off from the body, that which, if left in the system, would prove fatal. To this we must add, that, in the tropics, the evaporation of water is necessarily rapid, and the vapour which is thus produced, becomes another storehouse of heat, and a vehicle by which it is removed from the earth, and prevented from unduly interfering with the economy of life.[153]

152. "Dr. Black quickly perceived the vast importance of this discovery; and took a pleasure in laying before his students a view of the extensive and beneficial effects of this habitude of heat in the economy of nature. He made them remark how, by this means, there was accumulated, during the summer season, a vast magazine of heat, which, by gradually emerging, during congelation, from the water which covers the face of the earth, serves to temper the deadly cold of winter. Were it not for this quantity of heat, amounting to 145 degrees, which emerges from every particle of water as it freezes, and which diffuses itself through the atmosphere, the sun would no sooner go a few degrees to the south of the equator, than we should feel all the horrors of winter." *Robison's Preface to Black's Lectures,* vol. i. p. xxxviii.

153. As I am writing an account of Black's views, and not a criticism of them, I shall give them, without comment, in his own words, and in the words

From these and many other arguments, all of which were so essentially speculative, and dealt with such hidden processes of nature, that even now we are not justified either in confidently admitting them or in positively denying them, Black was led to that great doctrine of the indestructibility of heat,[154] which, as I have pointed out, has, in its connexion with the indestructibility of force, a moral and social importance even superior to its scientific value. Though the evidence of which he was possessed was far more scanty than what we now have, he, by the reach of his commanding intellect, rather than by the number and accuracy of his facts, became so penetrated with a conviction of the stability of physical affairs, that he not only applied that idea to the subtle phenomena of heat, but, what was much harder to do, he applied it to cases in which heat so entirely escapes the senses, that man has no cognizance of it, except through the medium of the imagi-

---

of one of his pupils. "Here we can also trace another magnificent train of changes, which are nicely accommodated to the wants of the inhabitants of this globe. In the equatorial regions, the oppressive heat of the sun is prevented from a destructive accumulation by copious evaporation. The waters, stored with their vaporific heat, are thus carried aloft into the atmosphere, till the rarest of the vapour reaches the very cold regions of the air, which immediately forms a small portion of it into a fleecy cloud. This also further tempers the scorching heat by its opacity, performing the acceptable office of a screen. From thence, the clouds are carried to the inland countries, to form the sources in the mountains, which are to supply the numberless streams that water the fields. And, by the steady operation of causes, which are tolerably uniform, the greater part of the vapours pass on to the circumpolar regions, there to descend in rains and dews; and in this beneficent conversion into rain, by the cold of those regions, each particle of steam gives up the 700 or 800 degrees of heat which were latent in it. These are immediately diffused, and soften the rigour of those less comfortable climates." . . . "I am persuaded that the heat absorbed in spontaneous evaporation greatly contributes to enable animals to bear the heat of the tropical climates, where the thermometer frequently continues to show the temperature of the human body. Such heats, indeed, are barely supportable, and enervate the animal, making it lazy and indolent, indulging in the most relaxed postures, and avoiding every exertion of body or mind. The inhabitants are induced to drink large draughts of diluting liquors, which transude through their pores most copiously, carrying off with them a vast deal of this troublesome and exhausting heat. There is in the body itself a continual laboratory, or manufacture of heat, and, were the surrounding air of such a temperature as not to carry it off, it would soon accumulate so as to destroy life. The excessive perspiration, supplied by diluting draughts, performs the same offiice as the cold air without the tropics, in guarding us from this fatal accumulation." *Black's Lectures,* vol. i. pp. xlvi, 214.

154. See his strong protest against the notion that heat is ever destroyed, in his *Lectures,* vol. i. pp. 125, 126, 164, 165.

nation. According to his view, heat passes through an immense variety of changes, during which it appears to be lost; changes which no eye can ever see, which no touch can ever experience, and which no instrument can ever measure. Still, and in the midst of all these changes, it remains intact. From it nothing can be taken, and to it nothing can be added. In one of those fine passages of his Lectures, which, badly reported as they are,[155] bear the impress of his elevated genius, Black, after stating what would probably happen, if the total amount of heat existing in the world were to be diminished, proceeds to speculate on the consequences of its being increased. Were it possible for any power to add to it ever so little, it would at once overstep its bounds; the equilibrium would be disturbed; the framework of affairs would be disjointed. The evil rapidly increasing, and acting with accumulated force, nothing would be able to stop its ravages. It must continue to gain ground, till all other principles are absorbed and conquered. Sweeping on, unhindered, and irresistible, before it, every animal must perish, the whole vegetable world must disappear, the waters must pass into vapour, and the solid parts of the globe be merged and melted, until, at length, the glorious fabric, loosened and dissolved, would fall away, and return to that original chaos out of which it had been evolved.[156]

These, like many other of the speculations of this great thinker, will find small favour with those purely inductive philosophers, who not only suppose, perhaps rightly, that all our knowledge is in its beginning built upon facts, but who countenance, what

155. They were published after his death from such scanty materials, that their editor, Dr. Robison, says (*Preface to Black's Lectures,* vol. i. p. x.): "When I then entered seriously on the task, I found that the notes were (with the exception of perhaps a score of lectures) in the same imperfect condition that they had been in from the beginning, consisting entirely of single leaves of paper, in octavo, full of erasions, interlinings, and alterations of every kind; so that, in many places, it was not very certain which of several notes was to be chosen."

156. "On the other hand, were the heat which at present cherishes and enlivens this globe, allowed to increase beyond the bounds at present prescribed to it; beside the destruction of all animal and vegetable life, which would be the immediate and inevitable consequence, the water would lose its present form, and assume that of an elastic vapour like air; the solid parts of the globe would be melted and confounded together, or mixed with the air and water in smoke and vapour; and nature would return to the original chaos." *Black's Lectures,* vol. i. pp. 246, 247.

seems to me, the very dangerous opinion, that every increase of knowledge must be preceded by an increase of facts. To such men it will appear, that Black had far better have occupied himself in making new observations, or devising new experiments, than in thus indulging his imagination in wild and unprofitable dreams. They will think, that these flights of fancy are suitable, indeed, to the poet, but unworthy of that severe accuracy, and of that close attention to facts, which ought to characterize a philosopher. In England, especially, there is, among physical inquirers, an avowed determination to separate philosophy from poetry, and to look upon them, not only as different, but as hostile. Among that class of thinkers, whose zeal and ability are beyond all praise, and to whom we owe almost unbounded obligations, there does undoubtedly exist a very strong opinion, that, in their own pursuit, the imagination is extremely dangerous, as leading to speculations, of which the basis is not yet assured, and generating a desire to catch too eagerly at distant glimpses before the intermediate ground has been traversed. That the imagination has this tendency is undeniable. But they who object to it on this account, and who would, therefore, divorce poetry from philosophy, have, I apprehend, taken a too limited view of the functions of the human mind, and of the manner in which truth is obtained. There is, in poetry, a divine and prophetic power, and an insight into the turn and aspect of things, which, if properly used, would make it the ally of science instead of the enemy. By the poet, nature is contemplated on the side of the emotions; by the man of science, on the side of the understanding. But the emotions are as much a part of us as the understanding; they are as truthful; they are as likely to be right. Though their view is different, it is not capricious. They obey fixed laws; they follow an orderly and uniform course; they run in sequences; they have their logic and method of inference. Poetry, therefore, is part of philosophy, simply because the emotions are a part of the mind. If the man of science despises their teaching, so much the worse for him. He has only half his weapons; his arsenal is unfilled. Conquests, indeed, he may make, because his native strength may compensate the defects of his equipment. But his success would be more complete and more rapid, if he were properly furnished and made ready for the battle. And I cannot but regard as the worst intellectual symptom of this great country, what I must venture to call the imperfect education of physical philosophers, as exhibited both in their writings and in their trains of thought. This is the more serious, because they, as a body, form the most important class in England, whether we look at their ability, or at the benefits we have received from them, or at the influence they are exercising, and are likely to exercise, over the progress of society. It cannot, however, be concealed, that they display an inordinate respect for experiments, an undue love of minute detail, and a disposition to overrate the inventors of new instruments, and the discoverers of new, but often insignificant, facts. Their predecessors of the seventeenth century, by using hypotheses more boldly, and by indulging their imagination more frequently, did certainly effect greater things, in comparison with the then state of knowledge, than our contemporaries, with much superior resources, have been able to achieve. The magnificent generalizations of Newton and Harvey could never have been completed in an age absorbed in one unvarying round of experiments and observations. We are in that predicament, that our facts have outstripped our knowledge, and are now encumbering its march. The publications of our scientific institutions, and of our scientific authors, overflow with minute and countless details, which perplex the judgment, and which no memory can retain. In vain do we demand that they should be generalized, and reduced into order. Instead of that, the heap continues to swell. We want ideas, and we get more facts. We hear constantly of what nature is doing, but we rarely hear of what man is thinking. Owing to the indefatigable industry of this and the preceding century, we are in possession of a huge and incoherent mass of observations, which have been stored up with great care, but which, until they are connected by some presiding idea, will be utterly useless. The most effective way of turning them to account, would be to give more scope to the imagination, and incorporate the spirit of poetry with the spirit of science. By this means, our philosophers would double their resources, instead of working, as now, maimed, and with only half their nature. They fear the imagination, on account of its tendency to form hasty theories. But, surely, all our faculties are needed in the pursuit of truth, and we cannot be justified in discrediting any part of the human mind. And I can hardly doubt, that one of the reasons why we, in England, made such wonderful discoveries during the seventeenth century, was because that century was also the great age of English poetry. The two mightiest intellects our country has produced are Shakspeare and Newton; and that Shakspeare should have preceded Newton was, I believe, no casual or unmeaning event. Shakspeare and the poets sowed the seed, which Newton and the philosophers reaped. Discarding the old scholastic and theological pursuits, they drew attention to nature, and thus became the real founders of all natural science. They did even more than this. They first impregnated the mind of England with bold and lofty conceptions. They taught the men of their generation to crave after the unseen. They taught them to pine for the ideal, and to rise above the visible world of sense. In this way, by cultivating the emotions, they opened one of the paths which lead to truth. The impetus which they communicated, survived their own day, and, like all great movements, was felt in every department of thought. But now it is gone; and, unless I am greatly mistaken, physical science is at present suffering from its absence. Since the seventeenth century, we have had no poet of the highest order, though Shelley, had he lived, would perhaps have become one. He had something of that burning passion, that sacred fire, which kindles the soul, as though it came fresh from the altar of the gods. But he was cut off in his early prime, when his splendid genius was still in its dawn. If we except his immature, though marvellous, efforts, we may assuredly say, that, for nearly two hundred years, England has produced no poetry which bears those unmistakable marks of inspiration which we find in Spenser, in Shakspeare, and in Milton. The result is, that we, separated by so long an interval from those great feeders of the imagination, who nurtured our ancestors, and being unable to enter fully into the feelings of poets, who wrote when nearly all opinions, and, therefore, nearly all forms of emotion, were very different to what they now are, cannot possibly sympathize with those immortal productions so closely as their contemporaries did. The noble English poetry of the sixteenth and seventeenth centuries is read more than ever, but it does not colour our thoughts; it does not shape our understandings, as it shaped the understandings of our forefathers. Between us and them is a chasm, which we cannot entirely bridge. We are so far removed from the associations amid which those poems were composed, that they do not flash upon us with that reality and distinctness of aim, which they would have done, had we lived when they were written. Their garb is strange, and belongs to another time. Not merely their dialect and their dress, but their very complexion and their inmost sentiments, tell of bygone days, of which we have no firm hold. There is, no doubt, a certain ornamental culture, which the most highly educated persons receive from the literature of the past, and by which they sometimes refine their taste, and sometimes enlarge their ideas. But the real culture of a great people, that which supplies each generation with its principal strength, consists of what it learnt from the generation immediately preceding. Though we are often unconscious of the process, we build nearly all our conceptions on the basis recognized by those who went just before us. Our closest contact is, not with our forefathers, but with our fathers. To them we are linked by a genuine affinity, which, being spontaneous, costs us no effort, and from which, indeed, we cannot escape. We inherit their notions, and modify them, just as they modified the notions of their predecessors. At each successive modification, something is lost and something is gained, until, at length, the original type almost disappears. Therefore it is, that ideas entertained several generations ago, bear about the same relation to us, as ideas preserved in a foreign literature. In both cases, the ideas may adorn our knowledge, but they are never so thoroughly incorporated with our minds, as to be the knowledge itself. The assimilation is incomplete, because the sympathy is incomplete. We have now no great poets; and our poverty in this respect is not compensated by the fact, that we once had them, and that we may, and do, read their works. The movement has gone by; the charm is broken; the bond of union, though not cancelled, is seriously weakened. Hence, our age, great as it is, and, in nearly all respects, greater than any the world has yet seen, has, notwithstanding its large and generous sentiments, its unexampled toleration, its love of liberty, and its profuse, and almost reckless, charity, a certain material, unimaginative, and unheroic character, which has made several observers tremble for the future. So far as I can understand our present condition, I do not participate in these fears, because I believe that the good we have already gained, is beyond all comparison greater than what we have lost. But that something has been lost, is unquestionable. We have lost much of that imagination, which, though, in practical life, it often misleads, is, in speculative life, one of the highest of all qualities, being suggestive as well as creative. Even practically, we should cherish it, because the commerce of the affections mainly depends on it. It is, however, declining; while, at the same time, the increasing refinement of society accustoms us more and more to suppress our emotions, lest they should be disagreeable to others. And as the play of the emotions is the chief study of the poet, we see, in this circumstance, another reason which makes it difficult to rival that great body of poetry which our ancestors possessed. Therefore, it is doubly incumbent on physical philosophers to cultivate the imagination. It is a duty they owe to their own pursuits, which would be enriched and invigorated by such an enlargement of their resources. It is also a duty which they owe to society in general; since they, whose intellectual influence is already greater than that of any other class, and whose authority is perceptibly on the increase, might have power enough to correct the most serious deficiency of the present age, and to make us some amends for our inability to produce such a splendid imaginative literature as that which our forefathers created, and in which the choicest spirits of the seventeenth century did, if I may so say, dwell and have their being.

If, therefore, Black had done nothing more than set the example of a great physical philosopher giving free scope to the imagination, he would have conferred upon us a boon, the magnitude of which it is not easy to overrate. And it is very remarkable, that, before he died, that department of inorganic physics, which he cultivated with such success, was taken up by another eminent Scotchman, who pursued exactly the same plan, though with somewhat inferior genius. I allude, of course, to Leslie, whose researches on heat are well known to those who are occupied with this subject; while, for our present purpose, they are chiefly interesting, as illustrating that peculiar method which, in the eighteenth century, seemed essential to the Scotch mind.

About thirty years after Black propounded his famous theory of heat, Leslie began to investigate the same topic, and, in 1804, published a special dissertation upon it.[157] In that work, and in some papers in his *Treatises on Philosophy,* are contained in his views, several of which are now known to be inaccurate.[158] though some are of sufficient value to mark an epoch in the history of science. Such was his generalization respecting the connexion between the radiation of heat and its reflection; bodies which reflect it most, radiating it least, and those which radiate it most, reflecting it least. Such, too, was another wide conclusion, which the best inquirers have since confirmed, namely, that, while heat is radiating from a body, the intensity of each ray is as the sine of the angle which it makes with the surface of that body.

These were important steps, and they were the result of experiments, preceded by large and judicious hypotheses. In relation, however, to the economy of nature, considered as a whole, they are of small account, in comparison with what Leslie effected towards consolidating the great idea of light and heat being identical, and thus preparing his contemporaries for that theory of the interchange of forces, which is the capital intellectual achievement of the nineteenth century. But it is interesting to observe, that, with all his ardour, he could not go beyond a certain length. He was so hampered by the material tendencies of his time, that he could not bring himself to conceive heat as a purely supersensual force, of which temperature was the external manifestation.[159] For this, the age was barely ripe. We, accordingly, find him asserting, that heat is an elastic fluid, extremely subtle, but still a fluid.[160] His real merit was, that, notwithstanding the diffi-

---

157. Mr. Napier, in his *Memoirs of Leslie*, pp. 16, 17 (prefixed to *Leslie's Treatises on Philosophy,* Edinb. 1838), says, that he "composed the bulk of his celebrated work on Heat in the years 1801 and 1802;" but that, in 1793, he propounded "some of its theoretical opinions, as well as the germs of its discoveries." It appears, however, from his own statement, that he was making experiments on heat, at all events, as early as 1791. See *Leslie's Experimental Inquiry into the Nature and Propagation of Heat,* London, 1804, p. 409.

158. For specimens of some of his most indefensible speculations, see *Leslie's Treatises on Philosophy,* pp. 38, 43.

159. Though he clearly distinguishes between the two. "It is almost superfluous to remark, that the term heat is of ambiguous import, denoting either a certain sensation, or the external cause which excites it." *Leslie on Heat,* p. 137.

160. "Heat is an elastic fluid extremely subtle and active." *Leslie on Heat,*

culties which beset his path, he firmly seized the great truth, that there is no fundamental difference between light and heat. As he puts it, each is merely a metamorphosis of the other. Heat is light in complete repose. Light is heat in rapid motion. Directly light is combined with a body, it becomes heat; but when it is thrown off from that body, it again becomes light.[161]

Whether this is true or false, we cannot tell; and many years, perhaps many generations, will have to elapse, before we shall be able to tell. But the service rendered by Leslie is quite independent of the accuracy of his opinion, as to the manner in which light and heat are interchanged. That they are interchanged, is the essential and paramount idea. And we must remember, that he made this idea the basis of his researches, at a period when some very important facts, or, I should rather say, some very conspicuous facts, were opposed to it; while the main facts which favoured it were still unknown. When he composed his work, the analogies between light and heat, with which we are now acquainted, had not been discovered; no one being aware, that double refraction, polarization, and other curious properties, are common to both. To grasp so wide a truth in the face of such obstacles, was a rare stroke of sagacity. But, on account of the obstacles, the inductive mind of England refused to receive the truth, as it was not generalized from a survey of all the facts. And Leslie, unfortunately for himself, died too soon to enjoy the exquisite pleasure of witnessing the empirical corroboration of his doctrine by direct experiment, although he clearly perceived, that the march of discovery, in reference to polarization, was leading the scientific world to a point, of which his keen eye had discerned the nature, when, to others, it was an almost invisible speck, dim in the distant offing.[162]

---

p. 150. At p. 31, "calorific and frigorific fluid." See also pp. 143, 144; and the attempt to measure its elasticity, in pp. 177, 178.

161. "Heat is only light in the state of combination." *Leslie on Heat*, p. 162. "Heat in the state of emission constitutes light." p. 174. "It is, therefore, the same subtle matter, that, according to its different modes of existence, constitutes either heat or light. Projected with rapid celerity, it forms light; in the state of combination with bodies it acts as heat." p. 188. See also p. 403, "different states of the same identical substance."

162. In 1814, that is ten years after his great work was published, and about twenty years after it was begun, he writes from Paris: "My book on heat is better known" here "than in England. I was even reminded of some passages

In regard to the method adopted by Leslie, he assures us, that, in assuming the principles from which he reasoned, he derived great aid from poetry; for he knew that the poets are, after their own manner, consummate observers, and that their united observations form a treasury of truths, which are nowise inferior to the truths of science, and of which science must either avail herself, or else suffer from neglecting them.[163] To apply these truths rightly, and to fit them to the exigencies of physical inquiry, is, no doubt, a most difficult task, since it involves nothing less than holding the balance between the conflicting claims of the emotions and the understanding. Like all great enterprises, it is full of danger, and, if undertaken by an ordinary mind, would certainly fail. But there are two circumstances which make it less dangerous in our time, than in any earlier period. The first circumstance is, that the supremacy of the human understanding, and its right to judge all theories for itself, is now more generally admitted than ever; so that there can be little fear of our leaning to the opposite side, and allowing poetry to encroach on science. The other circumstance is, that our knowledge of the laws of nature is much greater than that possessed by any previous age; and there is, consequently, less risk of the imagination leading us into error, inasmuch as we have a large number of well-ascertained truths, which we can confront with every speculation, no matter how plausible or ingenious it may appear.

---

in it which in England were considered as fanciful, but which the recent discoveries on the polarity of light have confirmed." *Napier's Memoirs of Leslie,* p. 28, prefixed to *Leslie's Philosophical Treatises,* edit. Edinb. 1838. Leslie died in 1832 (p. 40); and the decisive experiments of Forbes and Melloni were made between 1834 and 1836.

163. "The easiest mode of conceiving the subject, is to consider the heat that permeates all bodies, and unites with them in various proportions, as merely the subtle fluid of light in a state of combination. When forcibly discharged, or suddenly elicited from any substance, it again resumes its radiant splendour." . . . . "The same notion was embraced by the poets, and gives sublimity to their finest odes." . . . . "Those poetical images which have descended to our own times, were hence founded on a close observation of nature. Modern philosophy need not disdain to adopt them, and has only to expand and reduce to precision the original conceptions." *Leslie's Treatises on Philosophy,* pp. 308, 309. Again, at p. 416; "This is not the first occasion in which we have to admire, through the veil of poetical imagery, the sagacity and penetration of those early sages. It would be a weakness to expect nice conclusions in the infancy of science; but it is arrogant presumption to regard all the efforts of unaided genius with disdain."

On both these grounds, Leslie was, I apprehend, justified in taking the course which he did. At all events, it is certain, that, by following it, he came nearer than would otherwise have been possible, to the conceptions of the most advanced scientific thinkers of our day. He distinctly recognized that, in the material world, there is neither break nor pause; so that what we call the divisions of nature have no existence, except in our minds.[164] He was even almost prepared to do away with that imaginary difference between the organic and inorganic world, which still troubles many of our physicists, and prevents them from comprehending the unity and uninterrupted march of affairs. They, with their old notions of inanimate matter, are unable to see that all matter is living, and that what we term death is a mere expression by which we signify a fresh form of life. Towards this conclusion, all our knowledge is now converging; and it is certainly no small merit in Leslie, that he, sixty years ago, when really comprehensive views, embracing the whole creation, were scarcely known among scientific men, should have strongly insisted that all forces are of the same kind, and that we have no right to distinguish between them, as if some were living, and others were dead.[165]

We owe much to him, by whom such views were advocated. But they were then, and, in a certain, though far smaller, degree, they are now, so out of the domain of physical experience, that Leslie never could have obtained them by generalizing in the way which the inductive philosophy enjoins. His great work on heat was executed, as well as conceived, on the opposite plan;[166] and his prejudices on this point were so strong, that we are assured by his biographer, that he would allow no merit to Bacon, who organized the inductive method into a system, and to whose au-

164. "We should recollect that, in all her productions, Nature exhibits a chain of perpetual gradation, and that the systematic divisions and limitations are entirely artificial, and designed merely to assist the memory and facilitate our conceptions." *Leslie on Heat,* p. 506.

165. "All forces are radically of the same kind, and the distinction of them into *living* and *dead* is not grounded on just principles." *Leslie on Heat,* p. 133. Compare p. 299: "We shall perhaps find, that this prejudice, like many others, has some semblance of truth; and that even dead or inorganic substances must, in their recondite arrangements, exert such varying energies, and *so like sensation itself,* as if fully unveiled to our eyes, could not fail to strike us with wonder and surprise."

166. Mr. Napier, in his *Life of Leslie,* p. 17, says of it, very gravely, "It's hypotheses are not warranted by the sober maxims of inductive logic."

thority we in England pay a willing, and I had almost said a servile, homage.[167]

Another curious illustration of the skill with which the Scotch mind, when once possessed of a principle, worked from it deductively, appears in the geological speculations of Hutton, late in the eighteenth century. It is well known, that the two great powers which have altered the condition of our planet, and made it what it is, are fire and water. Each has played so considerable a part, that we can hardly measure their relative importance. Judging, however, from the present appearance of the crust of the earth, there is reason to believe, that the older rocks are chiefly the result of fusion, and that the younger are aqueous deposits. It is, therefore, not unlikely, that, in the order in which the energies of nature have unfolded themselves, fire preceded water, and was its necessary precursor.[168] But, all that we are as yet justified

167. "Notwithstanding the contrary testimony, explicitly recorded by the founders of the English experimental school, he denied all merit and influence to the immortal delineator of the inductive logic." *Napier's Life of Leslie,* p. 42.

168. The supposition, that volcanic agencies were formerly more potent than they are now, is by no means inconsistent with the scientific doctrine of uniformity, though it is generally considered to be so. It is one thing to assert the uniformity of natural laws; it is quite another thing to assert the uniformity of natural causes. Heat may once have produced far greater effects than it can do at present, and yet the laws of nature be unchanged, and the order and sequence of events unbroken. What I would venture to suggest to geologists is, that they have not taken sufficiently into account the theory of the interchange of forces, which seems to offer a solution of at least part of the problem. For, by that theory, a large portion of the heat which formerly existed may have been metamorphosed into other forces, such as light, chemical affinity, and gravitation. The increase of these forces consequent on the diminution of heat, would have facilitated the consolidation of matter; and until such forces possessed a certain energy, water, which afterwards became so prominent, could not have been formed. If the power of chemical affinity, for instance, were much weaker than it is, water would assuredly resolve itself into its component gases. Without wishing to lay too much stress on this speculation, I submit it to the consideration of competent judges, because I am convinced that any hypothesis, not absolutely inconsistent with the known laws of nature, is preferable to that dogma of interference, which what may be called the miraculous school of geologists wish to foist upon us, in utter ignorance of its incompatibility with the conclusions of the most advanced minds in other departments of thought. The remarks in Sir Roderick Murchison's great work (*Siluria,* London, 1854, pp. 475, 476) on the "grander intensity of former causation," and on the difficulty this opposes to the "uniformitarians," apply merely to those who take for granted that *each* force has always been equally powerful: they do not affect those who suppose that it is only the *aggregate* of force which remains unimpaired. Though the distribution of forces may be altered, their gross amount is

in asserting is, that these two causes, the igneous and the aqueous, were in full operation long before man existed, and are still busily working. Perhaps they are preparing another change in our habitation, suitable to new forms of life, as superior to man, as man is superior to the beings who occupied the earth before his time. Be this as it may, fire and water are the two most important and most general principles with which geologists are concerned; and though, on a superficial view, each is extremely destructive, it is certain that they can really destroy nothing, but can only decompose and recompose; shifting the arrangements of nature, but leaving nature herself intact. Whether one of these elements will ever again get the upper hand of its opponent, is a speculation of extreme interest. For, there is reason to suspect, that, at one period, fire was more active than water, and that, at another period, water was more active than fire. That they are engaged in incessant warfare, is a fact with which geologists are perfectly familiar, though, in this, as in many other cases, the poets were the first to discern the truth. To the eye of the geologist, water is constantly labouring to reduce all the inequalities of the earth to a single level; while fire, with its volcanic action, is equally busy in restoring those inequalities, by throwing up matter to the surface, and in various ways disturbing the crust of the globe.[169] And as the beauty of the material world mainly depends on that irregularity of aspect, without which scenery would have presented no variety of form, and but little variety of colour, we shall, I think, not be guilty of too refined a subtlety, if we say that fire, by saving us from the monotony to which water would have condemned us, has been the remote cause of that development of the imagina-

not susceptible of change, so far as the highest conceptions of our actual science extend. Consequently, there is no need for us to believe that, in different periods, the intensity of causation varies; though we may believe that some one agent, such as heat, had at one time more energy than it has ever had since.

169. "The great agents of change in the inorganic world may be divided into two principal classes, the aqueous and the igneous. To the aqueous belong rain, rivers, torrents, springs, currents, and tides; to the igneous, volcanos and earthquakes. Both these classes are instruments of decay as well as of reproduction; but they may also be regarded as antagonist forces. For the aqueous agents are incessantly labouring to reduce the inequalities of the earth's surface to a level; while the igneous are equally active in restoring the unevenness of the external crust, partly by heaping up new matter in certain localities, and partly by depressing one portion, and forcing out another, of the earth's envelope." *Lyell's Principles of Geology,* 9th edit., London, 1853, p. 198.

tion which has given us our poetry, our painting, and our sculpture, and has thereby not only wonderfully increased the pleasures of life, but has imparted to the human mind a completeness of function, to which, in the absence of such a stimulus, it could not have attained.

When geologists began to study the laws according to which fire and water had altered the structure of the earth, two different courses were open to them, namely, the inductive and the deductive. The deductive plan was to compute the probable consequences of fire and water, by reasoning from the sciences of thermotics and hydrodynamics; tracking each element by an independent line of argument, and afterwards coördinating into a single scheme the results which had been separately obtained. It would then only remain to inquire, how far this imaginary scheme harmonized with the actual state of things; and if the discrepancy between the ideal and the actual were not greater than might fairly be expected from the perturbations produced by other causes, the rationcination would be complete, and geology would, in its inorganic department, become a deductive science. That our knowledge is ripe for such a process, I am far, indeed, from supposing; but this is the path which a deductive mind would take, so far as it was able. On the other hand, an inductive mind, instead of beginning with fire and water, would begin with the effects which fire and water had produced, and would first study these two agents, not in their own separate sciences, but in their united action as exhibited on the crust of the earth. An inquirer of this sort would assume, that the best way of arriving at truth would be to proceed from effects to causes, observing what had actually happened, and rising from the complex results up to a knowledge of the simple agents, by whose power the results had been brought about.

If the reader has followed the train of thought which I have endeavoured to establish in this chapter, and in part of the preceding volume, he will be prepared to expect that when, in the latter half of the eighteenth century, geology was first seriously studied, the inductive plan of proceeding from effects to causes, became the favourite one in England; while the deductive plan of proceeding from causes to effects, was adopted in Scotland and in Germany. And such was really the case. It is generally admitted, that, in England, scientific geology owes its origin to William Smith, whose mind was singularly averse to system, and who, believing that the best way of understanding former causes was to study present effects, occupied himself, between the years of 1790 and 1815, in a laborious examination of different strata.[170] In 1815, he, after traversing the whole of England on foot, published the first complete geological map which ever appeared, and thus took the first great step towards accumulating the materials for an inductive generalization.[171] In 1807, and, therefore, before he had brought his arduous task to an end, there was formed in London the Geological Society, the express object of which, we are assured, was, to observe the condition of the earth, but by no means to generalize the causes which had produced that condition.[172] The resolution was, perhaps, a wise one. At all events, it was highly characteristic of the sober and patient spirit of the English intellect. With what energy and unsparing toil it has been executed, and how the most eminent members of the Geological

170. Dr. Whewell, comparing him with his great German contemporary, Werner, says, "In the German, considering him as a geologist, the ideal element predominated." . . . "Of a very different temper and character was William Smith. No literary cultivation of his youth awoke in him the *speculative love of symmetry and system;* but a singular clearness and precision of the classifying power, which he possessed as a native talent, was exercised and developed by exactly those geological facts among which his philosophical task lay." . . . "We see great vividness of thought and activity of mind, *unfolding itself exactly in proportion to the facts with which it had to deal.*" . . . "He dates his attempts to discriminate and connect strata from the year 1790." *Whewell's History of the Inductive Sciences,* London, 1847, vol. iii. pp. 562–564.

171. "The execution of his map was completed in 1815, and remains a lasting monument of original talent and extraordinary perseverance; for he had explored the whole country on foot without the guidance of previous observers, or the aid of fellow-labourers, and had succeeded in throwing into natural divisions the whole complicated series of British rocks." *Lyell's Principles of Geology,* p. 58. Geological maps of parts of England had, however, been published before 1815. See *Conybeare on Geology,* in *Second Report of the British Association,* p. 373.

172. "A great body of new data were required; and the Geological Society of London, founded in 1807, conduced greatly to the attainment of this desirable end. To multiply and record observations, and patiently to await the result at some future period, was the object proposed by them; and it was their favourite maxim, that the time was not yet come for a general system of geology, but that all must be content for many years to be exclusively engaged in furnishing materials for future generalizations." *Lyell's Principles of Geology,* p. 59. Compare *Richardson's Geology,* 1851, p. 40.

Society have, in the pursuit of truth, not only explored every part of Europe, but examined the shell of the earth in America and in Northern Asia, is well known to all who are interested in these matters; nor can it be denied, that the great works of Lyell and Murchison prove that the men who are capable of such laborious enterprises, are also capable of the still more difficult achievement of generalizing their facts and refining them into ideas. They did not go as mere observers, but they went with the noble object of making their observations subservient to a discovery of the laws of nature. That was their aim; and all honour be to them for it. Still, it is evident, that their process is essentially inductive; it is a procedure from the observation of complex phenomena, up to the elements to which those phenomena are owing; it is, in other words, a study of natural effects, in order to learn the operation of natural causes.

Very different was the process in Germany and Scotland. In 1787, that is, only three years before William Smith began his labours, Werner, by his work on the classification of mountains, laid the foundation of the German school of geology.[173] His influence was immense; and among his pupils we find the names of Mohs, Raumer, and Von Buch, and even that of Alexander Humboldt.[174] But the geological theory which he propounded, depended entirely on a chain of argument from cause to effect. He assumed, that all the great changes through which the earth had passed, were due to the action of water. Taking this for granted, he reasoned deductively from premisses with which his knowledge of water supplied him. Without entering into details respecting his system, it is enough to say, that, according to it, there was originally one vast and primeval sea, which, in the course of time, deposited the primitive rocks. The base of all was granite; then gneiss; and others followed in their order. In the bosom of the water, which at first was tranquil, agitations gradually arose, which, destroying part of the earliest deposits, gave birth to new

173. Cuvier, in his Life of Werner, says (*Biographie Universelle,* vol. L. pp. 376, 377), "La connaissance des positions respectives des minéraux dans la croûte du globe, et ce que l'on peut en conclure relativement aux époques de leur origine, forment une autre branche de la science qu'il appelle Géognosie. Il en présenta les premières bases en 1787, dans un petit écrit intitulé 'Classification et description des montagnes.'"

174. *Whewell's History of the Inductive Sciences,* vol. iii. p. 567.

rocks, formed out of their ruins. The stratified thus succeeded to the unstratified, and something like variety was established. Then came another period, in which the face of the waters, instead of being merely agitated, was convulsed by tempests, and, amid their play and collision, life was generated, and plants and animals sprung into existence. The vast solitude was slowly peopled, the sea gradually retired; and a foundation was laid for that epoch, during which man entered the scene, bringing with him the rudiments of order and of social improvement.[175]

These were the leading views of a system which, we must remember, exercised great sway in the scientific world, and won over to its side minds of considerable power. Erroneous and far-fetched though it was, it had the merit of calling attention to one of the two chief principles which have determined the present condition of our planet. It had the further merit of provoking a controversy, which was eminently serviceable to the interests of truth. For, the great enemy of knowledge is not error, but inertness. All that we want is discussion, and then we are sure to do well, no matter what our blunders may be. One error conflicts with another; each destroys its opponent, and truth is evolved. This is the course of the human mind, and it is from this point of view that the authors of new ideas, the proposers of new contrivances, and the originators of new heresies, are benefactors of their species. Whether they are right or wrong, is the least part of the question. They tend to excite the mind; they open up the faculties; they stimulate us to fresh inquiry; they place old subjects under new aspects; they disturb the public sloth; and they interrupt, rudely, but with most salutary effect, that love of routine, which, by inducing men to go grovelling on in the ways of their ances-

175. "Une mer universelle et tranquille dépose en grandes masses les roches primitives, roches nettement cristallisées, où domine d'abord la silice. Le granit fait la base de tout; au granit succède le gneiss, qui n'est qu'un granit commençant à se feuilleter." . . . "Des agitations intestines du liquide détruisent une partie de ces premiers dépôts; de nouvelles roches se forment de leurs débris réunis par des cimens. C'est parmi ces tempêtes que naît la vie." . . . "Les eaux, de nouveau tranquillisées, mais dont le contenu a changé, déposent des couches moins épaisses et plus variées, où les débris des corps vivans s'accumulent successivement dans un ordre non moins fixe que celui des roches qui les contiennent. Enfin, la dernière retraite des eaux répand sur le continent d'immenses alluvions de matières meubles, premiers sièges de la végétation, de la culture et de la sociabilité." *Eloge de Werner,* in *Cuvier, Recueil des Eloges Historiques,* vol. ii. pp. 321–323.

tors, stands in the path of every improvement, as a constant, an outlying, and, too often, a fatal obstacle.

The method adopted by Werner was evidently deductive, since he argued from a supposed cause, and reasoned from it to the effects. In that cause, he found his major premiss, and thence he worked downwards to his conclusion, until he reached the world of sense and of reality. He trusted in his one great idea, and he handled that idea with consummate skill. On that very account, did he pay less attention to existing facts. Had he chosen, he, like other men, could have collected them, and subjected them to an inductive generalization. But he preferred the opposite path. To reproach him with this, is irrational; for, in his journey after truth, he chose one of the only two roads which are open to the human mind. In England, indeed, we are apt to take for granted that one road is infinitely preferable to the other. It may be so; but on this, as on many other subjects, assertions are current which have never been proved. At all events, Werner was so satisfied with his method, that he would not be at the pains of examining the position of rocks and their strata, as they are variously exhibited in different countries; he did not even explore his own country, but, confining himself to a corner of Germany, he began and completed his celebrated system, without investigating the facts on which, according to the inductive method, that system should have been built.[176]

Exactly the same process, on the same subject, and at the same time, was going on in Scotland. Hutton, who was the founder of Scotch geology, and who, in 1788, published his *Theory of the Earth,* conducted the inquiry just as Werner did; though, when he began his speculations, he had no knowledge of what Werner was

176. "If it be true that delivery be the first, second, and third requisite in a popular orator, it is no less certain that to travel is of first, second, and third importance to those who desire to originate just and comprehensive views concerning the structure of our globe. Now, Werner had not travelled to distant countries: he had merely explored a small portion of Germany, and conceived, and persuaded others to believe, that the whole surface of our planet, and all the mountain chains in the world, were made after the model of his own province." . . . "It now appears that he had misinterpreted many of the most important appearances even in the immediate neighbourhood of Freyberg. Thus, for example, within a day's journey of his school, the porphyry, called by him primitive, has been found not only to send forth veins, or dykes, through strata of the coal formation, but to overlie them in mass." *Lyell's Principles of Geology,* p. 47.

doing.[177] The only difference between them was, that while Werner reasoned from the agency of water, Hutton reasoned from the agency of fire. The cause of this may, I think, be explained. Hutton lived in a country where some of the most important laws of heat had, for the first time, been generalized, and where, consequently, that department of inorganic physics had acquired great reputation. It was natural for a Scotchman to take more than ordinary interest in a subject in which Scotland had been so successful, and had obtained so much fame. We need not, therefore, wonder that Hutton, who, like all men, felt the intellectual bent of the time in which he lived, should have yielded to an influence of which he was, perhaps, unconscious. In obedience to the general mental habits of his country, he adopted the deductive method. In further obedience to the more special circumstances connected with his own immediate pursuits, he gathered the principles from which he reasoned from a study of fire, instead of gathering them, as Werner did, from a study of water.

Hence it is, that, in the history of geology, the followers of Werner are known as Neptunists, and those of Hutton as Plutonists.[178] And these terms represent the only difference between the two great masters. In the most important points, namely their method, they were entirely agreed. Both were essentially one-sided; both paid a too exclusive attention to one of the two principal agents which have altered, and are still altering, the crust of the earth; both reasoned from those agents, instead of reasoning to them; and both constructed their system without sufficiently studying the actual and existing facts; committing, in this respect, an error which the English geologists were the first to rectify.

As I am writing a history, not of science, but of scientific method, I can only briefly glance at the nature of those services which Hutton rendered to geology, and which are so considerable,

177. Though Hutton's *Theory of the Earth* was first published in 1788, the edition of 1795, which is the one I have used, contains a great number of additional illustrations of his views, and was evidently re-written. But the main features are the same; and we learn from his friend, Playfair, that "the great outline of his system" was completed "several years" before 1788. *Life of Hutton*, in *Plaifair's Works*, vol. iv. p. 50, Edinburgh, 1822.

178. Kirwan appears to have been the first who called Hutton's theory "the Plutonic System." See *Illustrations of the Huttonian Theory* in *Playfair's Works*, vol. i. p. 145. On the distinction between Neptunists and Plutonists, see the same work, pp. 504, 505.

that his system has been called its present basis.[179] This, however, is too strongly expressed; for, though Hutton was far from denying the influence of water,[180] he did not concede enough to it, and there is a tendency among several geologists to admit that the system of Werner, considered as an aqueous theory, contains a larger amount of truth than the advocates of the igneous theory are willing to allow. Still, what Hutton did was most remarkable, especially in reference to what are now termed metamorphic rocks, the theory of whose formation he was the first to conceive.[181] Into this, and into their connexion, on the one hand, with the sedimentary rocks, and, on the other hand, with those rocks whose origin is perhaps purely igneous, I could not enter without treading on debatable ground. But, putting aside what is yet uncertain, I will mention two circumstances respecting Hutton which are undisputed, and which will give some idea of his method, and of the turn of his mind. The first circumstance is, that, although he ascribed to subterranean heat, as exhibited in volcanic action, a greater and more constant energy than any previous inquirers had ventured to do,[182] he preferred speculating on the probable consequences of that action, rather than drawing inferences from the facts which the action presented; he being on this point so indifferent, that he arrived at his conclusions without inspecting even a single region of active volcanos, where he might have watched the workings of nature, and seen what she was really about.[183] The other circum-

179. "Has not only supplanted that of Werner, but has formed the foundation of the researches and writings of our most enlightened observers, and is justly regarded as the basis of all sound geology at the present day." *Richardson's Geology*, London, 1851, p. 38.

180. *Hutton's Theory of the Earth*, Edinb. 1795, vol. i. pp. 34, 41, 192, 290, 291, 593, vol. ii. pp. 236, 369, 378, 555.

181. "In his writings, and in those of his illustrator, Playfair, we find the germ of the metamorphic theory." *Lyell's Manual of Geology*, London, 1851, p. 92.

182. The shortest summary of this view is in his *Theory of the Earth*, Edin. 1795, vol. ii. p. 556. "The doctrine, therefore, of our Theory is briefly this; That whatever may have been the operation of dissolving water, and the chemical action of it upon the materials accumulated at the bottom of the sea, the general solidity of that mass of earth, and the placing of it in the atmosphere above the surface of the sea, has been the immediate operation of fire or heat melting and expanding bodies."

183. Although Hutton had never explored any region of active volcanos, he had convinced himself that basalt and many other trap rocks were of igneous origin." *Lyell's Principles of Geology*, London, 1853, p. 51. To this I may add, that he wrote his work without having examined granite. He says (*Theory of*

stance is equally characteristic. Hutton, in his speculations concerning the geological effects of heat, naturally availed himself of the laws which Black had unfolded. One of those laws was, that certain earths owe their fusibility to the presence of fixed air in them before heat has expelled it; so that, if it were possible to force them to retain their fixed air, or carbonic acid gas, as we now call it, no amount of heat could deprive them of the capability of being fused. The fertile mind of Hutton saw, in this discovery, a principle from which he could construct a geological argument. It occurred to him, that great pressure would prevent the escape of fixed air from heated rocks, and would thus enable them to be fused, nothwithstanding their elevated temperature. He then supposed that, at a period anterior to the existence of man, such a process had taken place under the surface of the sea, and that the weight of so great a column of water had prevented the rocks from being decomposed while they were subjected to the action of fire. In this way, their volatile parts were held together, and they themselves might be melted, which could not have happened except for this enormous pressure. By following this line of argument, he accounted for the consolidation of strata by heat; since, according to the premisses from which he started, the oily, or bituminous parts, would remain, in spite of the efforts of heat to disperse them.[184] This striking speculation led to the inference, that the volatile components of a substance, and its fixed components, may be made to cohere, in the very teeth of that apparently irresistible agent whose business it is to effect their separation. Such an inference was contrary to all experience; or, to say the least, no man had ever seen an instance of it.[185] Indeed, the event was only supposed to happen in consequence of circumstances

the Earth, vol. i. p. 214), "It is true, I met with it on my return by the east coast, when I just saw it, and no more, at Peterhead and Aberdeen; but that was all the granite I had ever seen when I wrote my _Theory of the Earth._ I have, since that time, seen it in different places; because I went on purpose to examine it, as I shall have occasion to describe in the course of this work." Hutton's theory of granite is noticed in _Bakewell's Geology,_ Lond. 1838, p. 101; but Mr. Bakewell does not seem to be aware that the theory was formed before the observations were made.

184. _Huttonian Theory,_ in _Playfair,_ vol. i. pp. 38–40, 509, 510. Compare _Playfair's Life of Hutton,_ p. 61.

185. Hence, the objections of Kirwan were invalid; because his argument against Hutton was "grounded on experiments, where that very separation of the volatile and fixed parts takes place, which it excluded in that hypothesis of subterraneous heat." _Huttonian Theory,_ in _Playfair,_ vol. i. p. 193, Edinb. 1822.

which were never met with on the surface of the globe, and which, therefore, were out of the range of all human observation.[186] The utmost that could be expected was, that, by means of our instruments, we might, perhaps, on a small scale, imitate the process which Hutton had imagined. It was possible, that a direct experiment might artificially combine great pressure with great heat, and that the result might be, that the senses would realize what the intellect had conceived.[187] But the experiment had never been tried, and Hutton, who delighted in reasoning from ideas rather than from facts, was not likely to undertake it.[188] He cast his speculation on the world, and left it to its fate.[189] Fortunately, however, for the reception of his system, a very ingenious and skilful experimenter of that day, Sir James Hall, determined to test the speculation by an appeal to facts; and as nature did not supply the

186. Hutton says (*Theory of the Earth*, Edinb. 1795, vol. i. p. 94), "The place of mineral operations is not on the surface of the earth; and we are not to limit nature with our imbecility, or estimate the powers of nature by the measure of our own." See also p. 159, "mineral operations proper to the lower regions of the earth." And p. 527, "The mineral operations of nature lie in a part of the globe which is necessarily inaccessible to man, and where the powers of nature act under very different conditions from those which we find take place in the only situation where we can live." Again, in vol. ii. p. 97, "The present Theory of the Earth holds for principle that the strata are consolidated in the mineral regions far beyond the reach of human observation." Similarly, vol. ii. p. 484, "we judge not of the progress of things from the actual operations of the surface."

187. Hutton, however, did not believe that this could be done. "In the Theory of the Earth which was published, I was anxious to warn the reader against the notion that subterraneous heat and fusion could be compared with that which we induce by our chemical operations on mineral substances here upon the surface of the earth." *Hutton's Theory of the Earth*, vol. i. p. 251.

188. See, in the *Life of Hutton*, in *Playfair's Works*, vol. iv. p. 62 note, a curious remark on his indifference to experimental verification. Innumerable passages in his work indicate this tendency, and show his desire to reason immediately from general principles. Thus, in vol. i. p. 17, "Let us strictly examine our principles in order to avoid fallacy in our reasoning." . . . . "We are now, in reasoning from principles, come to a point decisive of the question." vol. i. p. 177. "Let us now reason from our principles." vol. ii. p. 308. Hence, his constantly expressed contempt for experience; as in vol. ii. p. 367, where he says that we must "overcome those prejudices which contracted views of nature and *magnified opinions of the experience of man* may have begotten."

189. Playfair (*Life of Hutton*, p. 64) says that it drew "their attention" (*i.e.* the attention of "men of science"), "very slowly, so that several years elapsed before any one showed himself publicly concerned about it, either as an enemy or a friend." He adds, as one of the reasons of this, that it contained "too little detail of facts for a system which involved so much that was new, and opposite to the opinions generally received."

facts which he wanted, he created them for himself. He applied heat to powdered chalk, while, at the same time, with great delicacy of manipulation, he subjected the chalk to a pressure about equal to the weight of a column of water half a mile high. The result was, that, under that pressure, the volatile parts of the chalk were held together; the carbonic acid gas was unable to escape; the generation of quicklime was stopped; the ordinary operations of nature were baffled, and the whole composition, being preserved in its integrity, was fused, and, on subsequently cooling, actually crystallized into solid marble.[190] Never was triumph more complete. Never did a fact more fully confirm an idea.[191] But, in the mind of Hutton, the idea preceded the fact by a long interval; since, before the fact was known, the theory had been raised, and the system which was built upon it had, indeed, been published several years. It, therefore, appears that one of the chief parts of the Huttonian Theory, and certainly its most successful part, was conceived in opposition to all preceding experience; that it presupposed a combination of events which no one had ever observed, and the mere possibility of which nothing but artificial experiment could prove; and, finally, that Hutton was so confident of the validity of his own method of inquiry, that he disdained to make the experiment himself, but left to another mind that empirical branch of the investigation which he deemed of little moment, but which we, in England, are taught to believe is the only safe foundation of physical research.[192]

190. The account of these experiments was read before the Royal Society of Edinburgh in 1805, and is printed in their *Transactions,* vol. vi. pp. 71–185, Edinb. 1812, 4to. The general result was (pp. 148, 149), "That a pressure of 52 atmospheres, or 1700 feet of sea, is capable of forming a limestone in a proper heat; That under 86 atmospheres, answering nearly to 3000 feet, or about half a mile, a complete marble may be formed; and lastly, That, with a pressure of 173 atmospheres, or 5700 feet, that is little more than one mile of sea, the carbonate of lime is made to undergo complete fusion, and to act powerfully on other earths." See also p. 160: "The carbonic acid of limestone cannot be constrained in heat by a pressure less than that of 1708 feet of sea." There is a short, and not very accurate, notice of these instructive experiments in *Bakewell's Geology,* London, 1838, pp. 249, 250.

191. As Sir James Hall says, "The truth of the most doubtful principle which Dr. Hutton has assumed, has thus been established by direct experiment." *Transactions of the Royal Society of Edinburgh,* vol. vi. p. 175.

192. See the remarks of Sir James Hall, in *Transactions,* vol. vi. pp. 74, 75. He observes that Hutton's "system, however, involves so many suppositions, apparently in contradiction to common experience, which meet us on the very

I have now given an account of all the most important discoveries made by Scotland, in the eighteenth century, respecting the laws of the inorganic world. I have said nothing of Watt, because, although the steam-engine, which we owe to him, is of incalculable importance, it is not a discovery, but an invention. An invention it may justly be termed, rather than an improvement.[193] Notwithstanding what had been effected in the seventeenth century, by De Caus, Worcester, Papin, and Savery, and notwithstanding the later additions of Newcomen and others, the real originality of Watt is unimpeachable. His engine was, essentially, a new invention; but, under its scientific aspect, it was merely a skilful adaptation of laws previously known; and one of its most important points, namely, the economy of heat, was a practical application of ideas promulgated by Black.[194] The only discovery made by Watt, was that of the composition of water. Though his

threshold, that most men have hitherto been deterred from an investigation of its principles, and only a few individuals have justly appreciated its merits." . . . . "I conceived that the chemical effects ascribed by him to compression, ought, in the first place, to be investigated." . . . . "It occurred to me that this principle was susceptible of being established in a direct manner by experiment, and *I urged him to make the attempt; but he always rejected this proposal,* on account of the immensity of the natural agents, whose operation he supposed to lie far beyond the reach of our imitation; and he seemed to imagine that any such attempt must undoubtedly fail, and thus *throw discredit on opinions, already sufficiently established, as he conceived, on other principles."*

193. It may be traced back, certainly to the beginning of the seventeenth century, and probably still higher. Yet the popular opinion seems to be correct, that Watt was its real inventor; though, of course, he could not have done what he did, without his predecessors. This, however, may be said of all the most eminent and successful men, as well as of the most ordinary men.

194. On the obligations of Watt to Black, compare *Brougham's Life of Watt* (*Brougham's Works,* vol. i. pp. 25, 36–38, edit. Glasgow, 1855), with *Muirhead's Life of Watt,* second edit. London, 1859, pp. 66, 83. At p. 301, Mr. Muirhead says of Watt, that "his principal inventions connected with the steam-engine, with all their prodigious results, were founded, as we have seen, on the attentive observation of great philosophical truths; and the economy of fuel, increase of productive power, and saving of animal labour, which gradually ensued, all originated in the sagacious and careful thought with which he investigated the nature and properties of heat." But whatever investigations Watt made into heat, he discovered no new law respecting it, or, at all events, no new law which is large enough to be noted in the history of thermotics, considered purely as a science, and apart from practical application. Mr. Muirhead, in his interesting work which I have just quoted, has published (pp. 484–486) some remarks made on the subject by Watt, several years after the death of Black, which, though perfectly fair and candid, show that Watt had a rather confused notion of the real difference between an invention and a discovery.

claims are disputed by the friends of Cavendish, it would appear that he was the first who ascertained that water, instead of being an element, is a compound of two gases.[195] This discovery was a considerable step in the history of chemical analysis, but it neither involved nor suggested any new law of nature, and has, therefore, no claim to mark an epoch in the history of the human mind.[196] There is, however, one circumstance connected with it which is too characteristic to be passed over in silence. The discovery was made in 1783, by Watt, the Scotchman, and by Cavendish, the Englishman, neither of whom seems to have been aware of what the other was doing.[197] But between the two there was this difference. Watt, for several years previously, had been speculating on the subject of water in connexion with air, and having, by Black's law of latent heat, associated them together, he was prepared to believe that one is convertible into the other.[198] The idea of an

195. Mr. Muirhead, in his *Life of Watt*, pp. 301–370, seems to have put the priority of Watt beyond further doubt; though he is somewhat hard upon Cavendish, who, there can be little question, made the discovery for himself.

196. I would not wish to diminish one jot of the veneration in which the great name of Watt is justly held. But when I find the opinion of Dr. Withering, the botanist, quoted, to the effect that his "abilities and acquirements placed him next, if not superior, to Newton" (*Muirhead's Life of Watt*, p. 302), I cannot but protest against such indiscriminate eulogy, which would rank Watt in the same class as one of those godlike intellects of which the whole world has not produced a score, and which are entitled to be termed inspired, if ever human being was so. Another instance of this injudicious panegyric, will be found in the same otherwise excellent work (*Muirhead*, pp. 324, 325), where we read that Watt's discovery that water consists of oxygen and hydrogen, was "the commencement of a new era, the dawn of a new day in physical inquiry, the real foundation of the new system of chemistry; nay, even a discovery 'perhaps of greater importance than any single fact which human ingenuity has ascertained either before or since.'"

197. That there was no plagiarism on the part of Watt, we know from positive evidence; that there was none on the part of Cavendish, may be fairly presumed, both from the character of the man, and also from the fact that in the then state of chemical knowledge the discovery was imminent, and could not have been long delayed. It was antecedently probable that the composition of water would be ascertained by different persons at the same time, as we have seen in many other discoveries which have been simultaneously made, when the human mind, in that particular department of inquiry, had reached a certain point. We are too apt to suspect philosophers of stealing from each other, what their own abilities are sufficient to work out for themselves. It is, however, certain that Watt thought himself ill-treated by Cavendish. See *Watt's Correspondence on the Composition of Water,* London, 1846, pp. 48, 61.

198. On 26th November 1783, he writes: "For many years I have entertained an opinion that air was a modification of water; which was originally

intimate analogy between the two bodies having once entered his mind, gradually ripened; and when he, at last, completed the discovery, it was merely by reasoning from data which others possessed besides himself. Instead of bringing to light new facts, he drew new conclusions from former ideas.[199] Cavendish, on the other hand, obtained his result by the method natural to an Englishman. He did not venture to draw a fresh inference, until he had first ascertained some fresh facts. Indeed, his discovery was so completely an induction from his own experiments, that he omitted to take into consideration the theory of latent heat, from which Watt had reasoned, and where that eminent Scotchman had found the premises of his argument.[200] Both of these great

---

founded on the facts, that in most cases where air was actually made, which should be distinguished from those wherein it is only extricated from substances containing it in their pores, or otherwise united to them in the state of air, the substances were such as were known to contain water as one of their constituent parts, yet no water was obtained in the processes, except what was known to be only loosely connected with them, such as the water of the crystallization of salts. *This opinion arose from a discovery that the latent heat contained in steam diminished, in proportion as the sensible heat of the water from which it was produced, increased;* or, in other words, that the latent heat of steam was less when it was produced under a greater pressure, or in a more dense state, and greater when it was produced under a less pressure, or in a less dense state; which led me to conclude, that when a very great degree of heat was necessary for the production of the steam, the latent heat would be wholly changed into sensible heat; and that, in such cases, the steam itself might suffer some remarkable change. I now abandon this opinion, in so far as relates to the change of water into air, as I think that may be accounted for on better principles." See this remarkable passage, which is quite decisive as to the real history of Watt's discovery, in *Correspondence of James Watt on the Composition of Water,* London, 1846, pp. 84, 85. Compare p. cxxiv. and p. 248 note.

199. In the paper which he communicated to the Royal Soicety, announcing his discovery, he, well knowing the empirical character of the English mind, apologizes for this; and says, "I feel much reluctance to lay my thoughts on these subjects before the public in their present indigested state, and *without having been able to bring them to the test of such experiments as would confirm or refute them." Watt's Correspondence on the Discovery of the Composition of Water,* pp. 77, 78. Eleven months earlier, that is in December 1782, he writes (*Ibid.* p. 4): "Dr. Priestley has made a most surprising discovery, which *seems to confirm my theory* of water's undergoing some very remarkable change at the point where all its latent heat would be changed into sensible heat."

200. "He" (*i.e.* Cavendish) "here omits entirely the consideration of latent heat; an omission which he even attempts to justify, in one of the passages interpolated by Blagden. But it is well known to every one acquainted with the first principles of chemical science, even as it was taught in the days of Black, and it was indisputably familiar to Mr. Watt, that no aëriform fluid can be converted into a liquid, nor any liquid into a solid, without the evolution of

inquirers arrived at truth, but each accomplished his journey by a different path. And this antithesis is accurately expressed by one of the most celebrated of living chemists, who, in his remarks on the composition of water, truly says, that while Cavendish established the facts, Watt established the idea.[201]

Thus much, as to what was effected by the Scotch in the department of inorganic science. If we now turn to organic science, we shall find that, there also, their labours were very remarkable. To those who are capable of a certain elevation and compass of thought, it will appear, in the highest degree, probable, that, between the organic and inorganic world, there is no real difference. That they are separated, as is commonly asserted, by a sharp line of demarcation, which indicates where one abruptly ends, and the other abruptly begins, seems to be a supposition altogether untenable. Nature does not pause, and break off in this fitful and irregular manner. In her works, there is neither gap nor chasm. To a really scientific mind, the material world presents one vast and uninterrupted series, gradually rising from the lowest to the highest forms, but never stopping. In one part of that series, we find a particular structure, which, so far as our observations have yet extended, we, in another part, cannot find. We also observe particular functions, which correspond to the structure, and, as we believe, result from it. This is all we know. Yet, from these scanty facts, we, who, at present, are still in the infancy of knowledge, and have but skimmed the surface of things, are expected to infer, that there must be a point, in the chain of existence, where both structure and function suddenly cease, and, after which, we may vainly search for signs of life. It would be difficult to conceive a conclusion more repugnant to the whole march and analogy of modern thought. In every department, the speculations of the

---

heat, previously latent. This essential part of the process, Mr. Cavendish's theory does not embrace; but without it, no theory on the subject can be complete; and it will presently be seen, that Mr. Watt took it fully into account." *Muirhead's Life of Watt*, p. 315.

201. "Cavendish and Watt both discovered the composition of water. Cavendish established the facts; Watt the idea." .... "*The attaching too high a value to the mere facts, is often a sign of a want of ideas.*" *Liebig's Letters on Chemistry,* London, 1851, p. 48. The last sentence of this illustrious philosopher, which I have put in italics, should be well pondered in England. If I had my way, it should be engraved in letters of gold over the portals of the Royal Society and of the Royal Institution.

greatest thinkers are constantly tending to coördinate all phenomena, and to regard them as different, indeed, in degree, but by no means as different in kind. Formerly, men were content to ground their conviction of this difference in kind, on the evidence of the eye, which, on a cursory inspection, saw an organization in some bodies, and not in others. From the organization, they inferred the life, and supposed that plants, for instance, had life, but that minerals had none. This sort of argument was long deemed satisfactory; but, in the course of time, it broke down; more evidence was required, and, since the middle of the seventeenth century, it has been universally admitted, that the eye, by itself, is an untrustworthy witness, and that we must employ the microscope, instead of relying on the unaided testimony of our own puny and precarious senses. But the microscope is steadily improving, and we cannot tell what limits there are to its capacity for improvement. Consequently, we cannot tell what fresh secrets it may disclose. Neither can we say, that it may not be altogether superseded by some new artificial resource, which shall furnish us with evidence, as superior to any yet supplied, as our present evidence is superior to that of the naked eye. Even already, and notwithstanding the shortness of time during which the microscope has been a really effective instrument, it has revealed to us organizations, the existence of which no one had previously suspected. It has proved, that what, for thousands of years, had been deemed mere specks of inert matter, are, in truth, animals possessing most of the functions which we possess, reproducing their species in regular and orderly succession, and endowed with a nervous system, which shows that they must be susceptible of pain and enjoyment. It has detected life hidden in the glaciers of Switzerland; it has found it embedded in the polar ice, and, if it can flourish there, it is hard to say from what quarter it can be shut out. So unwilling, however, are most men to relinquish old notions, that the resources of chemistry have been called in, to ascertain the supposed difference between organic and inorganic matter; it being asserted, that, in the organic world, there is a greater complexity of molecular combination, than in the inorganic.[202] Chemists further assert,

202. "Organic substances, whether directly derived from the vegetable or animal kingdom, or produced by the subsequent modification of bodies which

that, in organic nature, there is a predominance of carbon, and, in inorganic, a predominance of silicon.[203] But chemical analysis, like microscopic observation, is making such rapid strides, that each generation, I had almost said each year, is unsettling some of the conclusions previously established; so that, now, and for a long time hence, we must regard those conclusions as empirical, and, indeed, as merely tentative. Surely a permanent and universal inference cannot be drawn from shifting and precarious facts, which are admitted to-day, and may be overthrown to-morrow. It would, therefore, appear that, in favour of the opinion, that some bodies are living, and that others are dead, we have nothing, except the circumstance, that our researches, so far as they have yet gone, have shown that cellular structure, growth, and reproduction, are not the invariable properties of matter, but are excluded from a large part of the visible world, which, on that account, we call inanimate. This is the whole of the argument on that side of the question. On the other side, we have the fact, that our sight, and the artificial instruments, by whose aid we have arrived at this conclusion, are confessedly imperfect; and we have the further fact, that, imperfect as they are, they have proved, that the organic kingdom is infinitely more extensive than the boldest dreamer had ever imagined, while they have not been able to enlarge the boundaries of the inorganic kingdom to any thing like the same amount. This shows, that, so far as our opinions are concerned, the balance is steadily inclining in one given direction; in other words, as our knowledge advances, a belief in the organic is enchoaching upon a belief in the inorganic.[204] When we, moreover, add, that all science is mani-

---

thus originate, are remarkable as a class for a degree of complexity of constitution far exceeding that observed in any of the compounds yet described." *Fownes' Chemistry*, 3d edit., London, 1850, p. 353. I quote this, as the first authority at hand, for a doctrine which is universally admitted by chemists, and which is indubitably true, *so far as our experiments have at present extended*.

203. "As the organic world is characterized by the predominance, in quantity, of carbon, so the mineral or inorganic world is marked by a similar predominance of silicon." *Turner's Chemistry*, edited by Lieberg and Gregory, vol. ii. p. 678, London, 1847.

204. I mean, of course, to apply this remark only to the globe we inhabit, and not to extra-terrestrial phenomena. Respecting the organization or non-organization of what exists out of this earth, we have no evidence, and can

festly converging towards one simple and general theory, which shall cover the whole range of material phenomena, and that, at each successive step, some irregularities are explained away, and some inequalities are reduced, it can hardly be doubted, that such a movement tends to weaken those old distinctions, the reality of which has been too hastily assumed; and that, in their place, we must, sooner or later, substitute the more comprehensive view, that life is a property of all matter, and that the classification of bodies into animate and inanimate, or into organic and inorganic, is merely a provisional arrangement, convenient, perhaps, for our present purposes, but which, like all similar divisions, will eventually be merged in a higher and wider scheme.

Until, however, that step is taken, we must be content to reason according to the evidence supplied by our imperfect instruments, or by our still more imperfect senses. We, therefore, recognize the difference between organic and inorganic nature, not as a scientific truth, but as a scientific artifice, by which we separate in idea, what is inseparable in fact; hoping, in this way, to pursue our course with the greater ease, and ultimately to obtain results, which will make the artifice needless. Assuming, then, this division, we may refer all investigations of organic bodies to one of two objects. The first object is, to ascertain the law of those bodies, in their usual, healthy, or, as we somewhat erroneously phrase it, normal course. The other object is, to ascertain their law, in their unusual, unhealthy, or abnormal course. When we attempt to do the first of these things, we are physiologists. When we attempt to do the second, we are pathologists.[205]

Physiology and pathology are thus the two fundamental divi-

---

hardly expect to have any for centuries. Inferences have, indeed, been drawn from telescopic observations; and attempts are now being made, abroad, to determine, by a still more refined process, the physical composition of some of the heavenly bodies. But without venturing, in this note, to enter into such discussions, or even to state their purport, I may say, that the difficulty of *verification* will long prove an insuperable barrier to our knowledge of the truth or falsehood of any results which may be obtained.

205. Mr. Simon, in his thoughtful and suggestive Lectures, says, "we may describe Pathology to consist in the Science of Life under other conditions than those of ideal perfection." *Simon's Lectures on Pathology*, London, 1850, p. 14. This is by far the best description I have met with; though, as it involves a negative, it cannot be accepted as a definition. Indeed, the context shows that Mr. Simon does not suppose it to be one.

sions of all organic science.[206] Each is intimately connected with the other; and eventually, no doubt, both will be fused into a single study, by discovering laws which will prove that here, as elsewhere, nothing is really abnormal, or irregular. Hitherto, however, the physiologists have immeasurably outstripped the pathologists in the comprehensiveness of their views, and, therefore, in the value of their results. For, the best physiologists distinctly recognize that the basis of their science must include, not only the animals below man, but also the entire vegetable kingdom, and that, without this commanding survey of the whole realm of organic nature, we cannot possibly understand even human physiology, still less general physiology. The pathologists, on the other hand, are so much in arrear, that the diseases of the lower animals rarely form part of their plan; while the diseases of plants are almost entirely neglected, although it is certain that, until all these have been studied, and some steps taken to generalize them, every pathological conclusion will be eminently empirical,

206. In my former volume, I adopted the commonly received division of organic statics and organic dynamics; the statics being anatomy, and the dynamics being physiology. But, I now think that our knowledge is not sufficiently advanced to make this so convenient as the division into physiological and pathological, or, into normal and abnormal, provided we remember that in reality nothing is abnormal. The practically useful, but eminently unscientific, doctrine, that there can be alteration of function without alteration of structure, has effaced some of the most essential distinctions between anatomy and physiology, and especially between morbid anatomy and morbid physiology. Until those distinctions are recognized, the scientific conceptions of professional writers must be confused, however valuable their practical suggestions may be. While men are capable of believing that it is *possible* for variations of function to proceed from any cause except variations of structure, the philosophic importance of anatomy will be imperfectly appreciated, and its true relation to physiology will remain undefined. Inasmuch, however, as, with our actual resources, the most careful dissection is often unable to detect (in insanity, for instance) those changes of structure which produce changes of function, superficial thinkers are placed under a strong temptation to deny their invariable connexion; and while the microscope is so imperfect, and chemistry so backward, it is impossible that experiments should always convince them of their mistake. Hence, I believe that until our means of empirical research are greatly improved, all such investigations, nothwithstanding their immense value in other respects, will tend to lead mere inductive minds into error, by making them rely too much on what they call the facts of the case, to the prejudice of the reason. This is what I mean by saying, that our knowledge is not sufficiently advanced to make it advisable to divide the sciences of organic bodies into physiological and anatomical. At present, and probably for some time yet, the humbler division into physiological and pathological, may be deemed safer, and more likely to produce solid results.

on account of the narrowness of the field from which it is collected.

The science of pathology being still so backward in the conception as well as in the execution, that even men of real ability believe that it can be raised from a mere study of the human frame, it will hardly be expected that the Scotch, notwithstanding the marvellous boldness of their speculations, should have been able, in the eighteenth century, to anticipate a method which the nineteenth century has yet to employ. But they produced two pathologists of great ability, and to whom we owe considerable obligations. These were, Cullen and John Hunter.[207] Cullen was eminent only as a pathologist; but Hunter, whose fine and discursive genius took a much wider range, was great both in physiology and in pathology. A short account of their generalizations respecting organic science, will be a fitting sequel to the notices I have already given of what was done by their countrymen for inorganic science, during the same period. It will complete our survey of the Scotch intellect, and will enable the reader to form some idea of the brilliant achievements of that most remarkable people, who, contrary to the course of affairs in all other modern nations, have shown that scientific discoveries do not necessarily weaken superstition, and that it is possible for two hostile principles to flourish side by side, without ever coming into actual collision, or without sensibly impairing each other's vigour.

In 1751, Cullen was appointed professor of medicine in the University of Glasgow;[208] from which, however, in 1756, he was removed to the University of Edinburgh,[209] where he delivered those celebrated lectures, on which his fame now depends. During the early part of his career, he paid great attention to inorganic physics, and propounded some remarkable speculations, which are supposed to have suggested the theory of latent heat to Black, who was his pupil.[210] But, to follow out those views, would have

207. Hunter, as we shall presently see, did take an extraordinarily comprehensive view of pathology, including the whole of the organic world, and even the aberrations of form in the inorganic.

208. *Thomson's Life of Cullen,* vol. i. p. 70, Edinburgh, 1832.

209. *Thomson's Life of Cullen,* vol. i. p. 96. Bower states that Cullen "was appointed to the chair in 1755." *Bower's History of the University of Edinburgh,* vol. ii. p. 216, Edinburgh, 1817.

210. "It seems impossible to peruse the passages I have quoted from Dr. Cullen's manuscript lectures and papers, and from his Essay on Evaporation,

required a number of minute experiments, which it did not suit the habit of his mind to make. Having, therefore, put forth his ideas, he left them to germinate, and passed on to his arduous attempt to generalize the laws of disease as they are exhibited in the human frame. In the study of disease, the phenomena being more obscure and less amenable to experiment, there was greater latitude for speculation; hence, he could more easily indulge in that love of theory, which was his ruling passion, and with an extreme devotion to which he has been reproached.[211] That the reproach is not altogether unjust, must, I think, be admitted, since we find him laying down the doctrine, that, inasmuch as, in the treatment of disease, theory could not be separated from practice, it was unimportant which came first.[212] This was tantamount to saying, that a medical practitioner might allow his theories to control his observations; for it is certain that, in an immense majority of cases, men are so tenacious of the opinions they imbibe, that whatever, in any pursuit, first occupies their understanding, is likely to mould all that comes afterwards. In ordinary minds, associations of ideas, if firmly established, become indissoluble; and the power of separating them, and of arranging them in new combinations, is one of the rarest of our endowments. An average intellect, when once possessed by a theory, can hardly ever escape from it. Hence, in practical matters, theory should be feared, just as, in scientific matters, it should be cherished; because practical pursuits are chiefly engrossed by the lower class of minds, where associations and the force of prejudice are extremely strong, while

---

without perceiving that his investigations with regard to the heat and cold occasioned by the combination, liquefaction, and evaporation of bodies, must not only have assisted to direct the attention of his pupil Dr. Black to similar inquiries, but must also have furnished him with several of the data from which his simple and comprehensive theory of Latent Heat was afterwards so philosophically deduced." *Thomson's Life of Cullen*, vol. i. p. 56.

211. "It is allowed by the admirers of this great man, that he was perhaps too fond of theory." *Bower's History of the University of Edinburgh*, vol. iii. p. 278.

212. In 1759, he wrote to Dr. Balfour Russell, one of his favourite pupils: "You will not find it possible to separate practice from theory altogether; and therefore, if you have a mind to begin with the theory, I have no objection." *Thomson's Life of Cullen*, vol. i. p. 130. Compare his *Introductory Lectures to the Practice of Physic*, where, asserting truly, "that reasoning in physic is unavoidable" (*Cullen's Works*, vol. i. p. 417), he boldly infers "that to render it safe, it is *necessary to cultivate theory in its full extent.*"

scientific pursuits concern the higher class, where such prepossessions are comparatively weak, and where close associations are more easily severed. The most powerful intellects are most accustomed to new arrangements of thought, and are, therefore, most able to break up old ones. On them, belief sits lightly, because they well know how little evidence we have for many of even our oldest beliefs. But the average, or, as we must say, without meaning offence, the inferior, minds, are not disturbed by these refinements. Theories, which they have once heartily embraced, they can hardly ever get rid of, and they often dignify them with the name of essential truths, and resent every attack upon them as a personal injury. Having inherited such theories from their fathers, they regard them with a sort of filial piety, and cling to them as if they were some rich acquisition, which no one has a right to touch.

To this latter class, nearly all men belong, who are more engaged in practical pursuits than in speculative ones. Among them, are the ordinary practitioners, whether in medicine or in any other department, extremely few of whom are willing to break up trains of thought to which they are inured.[213] Though they profess to despise theory, they are, in reality, enslaved by it. All that they can do, is to conceal their subjection, by terming their theory a necessary belief. It must, therefore, be deemed a remarkable proof of Cullen's love of deductive reasoning, that he, sagacious and clear-sighted as he was, should have supposed that, in so practical an art as medicine, theory could, with impunity, precede practice. For, it is most assuredly true, that, taking men in the average, their minds are so constructed, that it cannot precede it without controlling it. It is equally true, that such control must be hurtful. Even now, and notwithstanding the great steps which have been taken in morbid anatomy, in animal chemistry, and in

213. Even Cullen himself says, rather roughly, "The great horde of physicians are always servile imitators, who can neither perceive nor correct the faults of their system, and are always ready to growl at, and even to worry, the ingenious person that could attempt it. Thus was the system of Galen secured in the possession of the schools of physic, till soon after the irruption of the Goths and Vandals destroyed every vestige of literature in the western parts of Europe, and drove all that remained of it to seek a feeble protection at Constantinople." *Lectures introductory to the Practice of Physic,* in *Cullen's Works,* vol. i. p. 386, Edinburgh, 1827.

the microscopic investigation both of the fluids and solids of the human frame, the treatment of disease is a question of art, far more than a question of science. What chiefly characterizes the most eminent physicians, and gives them their real superiority, is not so much the extent of their theoretical knowledge,—though that, too, is often considerable,—but it is that fine and delicate perception which they owe, partly to experience, and partly to a natural quickness in detecting analogies and differences which escape ordinary observers. The process which they follow, is one of rapid, and, in some degree, unconscious, induction. And this is the reason why the greatest physiologists and chemists, which the medical profession possesses, are not, as a matter of course, the best curers of disease. If medicine were a science, they would always be the best. But medicine, being still essentially an art, depends mainly upon qualities which each practitioner has to acquire for himself, and which no scientific theory can teach. The time for a general theory has not yet come, and probably many generations will have to elapse before it does come. To suppose, therefore, that a theory of disease should, as a matter of education, precede the treatment of disease, is not only practically dangerous, but logically false. With its practical danger, I am not now concerned; but its logical aspect is a curious illustration of that passion for systematic and dialectic reasoning which characterized Scotland. It shows that Cullen, in his eagerness to argue from principles to facts, instead of from facts to principles, could, in the most important of all arts, recommend a method of procedure, for which even our knowledge is not ripe, but which, in his time, was so singularly rash and immature, that nothing can explain its adoption by a man of such vigorous understanding, except the circumstance of his living in a country in which that peculiar method reigned supreme.

It must, however, be admitted, that Cullen wielded the method with great ability, especially in his application of it to the science of pathology, to which it was far better suited than to the art of therapeutics. For, we must always remember, that the science which investigates the laws of disease, is quite a different thing from the art which cures it. The science has a speculative interest, which is irrespective of all practical considerations, and which depends simply on the fact, that, when it is completed, it will explain the aberrations of the whole organic world. Pathology aims at ascertaining the causes which determine every departure from the natural type, whether of form or of function. Hence it is, that no one can take a comprehensive view of the actual state of knowledge, without studying the theoretic relations between pathology and other departments of inquiry. To do this, is the business, not of practical men, but of philosophers, properly so-called. The philosophic pathologist is as different from the physician, as a jurist is different from an advocate, or as an agricultural chemist is different from a farmer, or as a political economist is different from a statesman, or as an astronomer, who generalizes the laws of the heavenly bodies, is different from a captain, who navigates his ship by a practical application of those laws. The two sets of functions may be united, and occasionally, though very rarely, they are, but there is no necessity for their being so. While, therefore, it would be absurdly presumptuous for an unprofessional person to pass judgment on the therapeutical system of Cullen, it is perfectly legitimate for any one, who has studied the theory of these matters, to examine his pathological system; because that, like all scientific systems, must be amenable to general considerations, which are to be taken, partly from the adjoining sciences, and partly from the universal logic of philosophic method.

It is from this latter, or logical, point of view, that Cullen's pathology is interesting for the purposes of the present chapter. The character of his investigations may be illustrated by saying, that his method in pathology is analogous to that which Adam Smith adopted at the same time, though in a very different field. Both were deductive; and both, before arguing deductively, suppressed some of the premises from which they reasoned. That this suppression is the key to Adam Smith's method, and was an intentional part of his plan, I have already shown; as also that, in each of his two works, he supplied the premises in which the other work was deficient. In this respect, he was far superior to Cullen. For, though Cullen, like Smith, began by mutilating his problem in order to solve it more readily, he, unlike Smith, did not see the necessity of instituting another and parallel inquiry, which should complete the scheme, by starting from the premises that had been previously omitted.

What I have termed the mutilation of the problem, was effected by Cullen in the following manner. His object was, to generalize the phenomena of disease, as they are exhibited in the human frame; and it was obvious to him, as to every one else, that the human frame consists partly of solids and partly of fluids. The peculiarity of his pathology is, that he reasons almost entirely from the laws of the solids, and makes so little account of the fluids, that he will only allow them to be the indirect causes of disease, which, in a scientific view, are to be deemed strictly subordinate to the direct causes, as represented by the solid constituents of our body.[214] This assumption, though false, was perfectly justifiable, since, by curtailing the problem, he simplified its study; just as Adam Smith, in his *Wealth of Nations,* simplified the study of human nature, by curtailing it of all its sympathy. But this most comprehensive thinker was careful, in his *Theory of Moral Sentiments,* to restore to human nature the quality of which the *Wealth of Nations* had deprived it; and, by thus establishing two different lines of argument, he embraced the whole subject. In the same way, it was incumbent on Cullen, after having constructed a theory of disease by reasoning from the solids, to have constructed another theory of reasoning from the fluids; so that a coördination of the two theories might have raised a science of pathology, as complete as the then state of knowledge allowed.[215] But to this, his mind was unequal. Able though he was, he lacked the grasp of intellect which characterized Adam Smith, and which

214. This idea runs through the whole of his writings. In the following passage, it is more succinctly stated than in any other: "In pathology, and in the prognosis of particular diseases, it is absolutely necessary to enter into the distinction of these causes. I call the one *direct* causes, those which act upon the nervous system directly; and the other *indirect* causes, those which produce the same effect, but by destroying those organs which are necessary to the support of the excitement, viz. the whole system of circulation." *Cullen's Works,* vol. i. p. 135. Even this passage, clear as it seems, can only be rightly interpreted by taking the context into consideration.

215. For, as is truly observed by probably the greatest pathologist of our time, "Humoral pathology is simply a requirement of common practical sense; and it has always held a place in medical science, although the limits of its domain have, no doubt, been variously circumscribed or interpreted at different times. Of late years, it has met with a new basis and support in morbid anatomy, which, in the inadequacy of its discoveries in the solids to account for disease and death, has been compelled to seek for an extension of its boundary through a direct examination of the blood itself." *Rokitansky's Pathological Anatomy,* vol. i. p. 362, London, 1854.

made that great man perceive, that every deductive argument, which is founded on a suppression of premises, must be compensated by a parallel argument, which takes those premises into account.[216] So little was Cullen aware of this, that, having built up that system of pathology which is known to medical writers as Solidism, he never took the pains to accompany it by another system, which gave the first rank to the fluids. On the contrary, he believed that his plan was complete and exhaustive, and that what is termed Humoral Pathology was a fiction, which had too long usurped the place of truth.[217]

Several of the views advocated by Cullen were taken from Hoffmann, and several of the facts from Gaubius; but that his pathology, considered as a whole, is essentially original, is evident from a certain unity of design which is inconsistent with extensive plagiarism, and which proves that he had thoroughly thought out his subject for himself. Without, however, stopping to inquire how much he borrowed from others, I will briefly indicate a few of the salient points of his system, in order to enable the reader to understand its general character.

According to Cullen, all the solids in the human body are either simple or vital. The simple solids retain, after death, the properties which they possessed during life. But the vital solids, which form the fundamental part of the nervous system, are marked by properties, which disappear directly death occurs.[218] Hence, the

216. Unless, as is the case in geometry, the premises, which are suppressed, are so slight as to be scarcely perceptible.

217. He was so indignant at the bare idea of a humoral pathology, that even Hoffmann, who before himself was the most eminent advocate of solidism, fell under his displeasure for allowing some little weight to the humoral doctrines. He says that Hoffmann "has not applied his fundamental doctrine so extensively as he might have done; and he has everywhere intermixed an humoral pathology, as incorrect and hypothetical as any other." *Cullen's Works,* vol. i. p. 410. At p. 470, "I have, therefore, assumed the general principles of Hoffmann. And, if I have rendered them more correct, and more extensive in their application, and, *more particularly, if I have avoided introducing the many hypothetical doctrines of the Humoral Pathology which disfigured both his and all the other systems that have hitherto prevailed,* I hope I shall be excused for attempting a system, which, upon the whole, may appear new."

218. "The solid parts of the body seem to be of two kinds: one whose properties are the same in the dead as in the living, and the same in the animate as in many inanimate bodies; the other, whose properties appear only in living bodies. In the last, a peculiar organization, or addition, is supposed to take place; in opposition to which the first are called the simple solids. Of these only, we shall treat here; and of the others, which may be called vital solids,

simple solids, having fewer functions than the vital, have also fewer diseases; and the maladies to which they are liable admit of easy classification.[219] The real difficulty lies in the vital solids, because on their peculiarities the whole nervous system depends, and nearly all disorders are immediately due to changes in them. Cullen, therefore, made the nervous system the basis of his pathology; and, in speculating on its functions, he assigned the chief place to an occult principle, which he termed the Animal Power, or Energy, of the brain.[220] This principle acted on the vital solids. When the principle worked well, the body was healthy; when it worked ill, the body was unhealthy. Since, then, the state of the vital solids was the main cause of disorder, and since the Energy of the brain was the main cause of the state of the vital solids, it became important to know what the influences were which acted on the Energy, because in them we should find the beginning of the series. Those influences were divided by Cullen into physical and mental. The physical were, heat, cold, and effluvia, the three most potent of the material disturbers of the human frame.[221] The mental influences, which excited the brain to act on the solids, were comprised under six different heads, namely, the will, the emotions, the appetites, the propensities, and, finally, the two great principles of habit and of imitation, on which he, with good reason, laid considerable stress.[222] In arguing from these mental causes, and in generalizing the relations between them and the

being the fundamental part of the nervous system, we shall treat under that title in the following section." *Cullen's Works,* vol. i. p. 10.

219. These diseases are laxity, flaccidity, &c. See the enumeration of "the diseases of the simple solids," in *Cullen's Works,* vol. i. p. 14.

220. *Cullen's Works,* vol. i. pp. 65, 600, vol. ii. p. 364. Dr. Thomson, who had access to papers and lectures of Cullen's, which have never been published, says (*Life of Cullen,* vol. i. p. 265), "His speculations with regard to the different functions of the nervous system, but more particularly with regard to that of the Animal Power or Energy of the brain, were incorporated with every opinion which he taught concerning the phenomena of the animal economy, the causes of diseases, and the operation of medicines; and they may be said to constitute a most important part, if not the sole basis, of that system of the Practice of Physic, which he made the subject of prelection, as well as of study, for a period of nearly forty years, before he ventured to give it to the public." I should mention, that Cullen, under the term 'brain,' included the contents of the vertebral column as well as of the cranium.

221. *Cullen's Works,* vol. i. pp. 40, 546, 558, 648, vol. ii. p. 321.

222. *Cullen's Works,* vol. i. pp. 86, 91, 100, 101, 108, 115, 116, 553, 592, vol. ii. pp. 35, 366. Compare the summary of causes in *Thomson's Life of Cullen,* vol. i. p. 289.

sensations of the body, he, faithful to his favourite method, proceeded deductively from the metaphysical principles then in vogue, without inquiring inductively into their validity, such an induction being, he thought, no part of his duty.[223] He was too anxious to get on with his dialectic, to be interrupted by so trifling a matter as the truth or falsehood of the premisses on which the reasoning rested. What he did in the metaphysical part of his pathology, he also did in its physical part. Although the blood and the nerves are the two leading features of the human economy, he did not search into them by a separate induction; he subjected them neither to chemical experiments in order to learn their composition, nor to microscopic observations in order to learn their structure.[224] This is the more observable, because though we must admit that animal chemistry was then generally neglected, and that its real meaning was scarcely understood until the wonderful labors of Berzelius revealed its importance, still the microscope was ready to Cullen's hands; it having been invented a

223. He says (*Works*, vol. i. pp. 31, 32), "Whoever has the smallest tincture of metaphysics will know the distinction pointed at here between the qualities of bodies as primary and secondary." . . . "*Whether these distinctions be well or ill founded, it is not my business to inquire.*" But though he did not deem it his business to inquire into the accuracy of these and similar distinctions, he thought himself justified in assuming them, and reasoning from them as if they could explain the working of those sensations, whose perversion formed the point of contact between metaphysics and pathology. See, for instance, in his *Works*, vol. i. p. 46, the long series of unproved and unprovable assertions respecting the combination and comparison of sensations giving rise to memory, imagination, and the like.

224. Cullen, with that admirable candour which was one of the most attractive peculiarities of his fine intellect, confesses his want of acquaintance with the microscope: "It leaves me, who am not conversant in such observations, altogether uncertain with respect to the precise nature of this part of the blood." *Cullen's Works*, vol. i. p. 195. A pathologist without a microscope is an unarmed man, indeed. In regard to his animal chemistry, one passage may be quoted as a specimen of the manner in which he arrived at conclusions speculatively, instead of subjecting the phenomena to experimental investigation. "We may remark it to be highly probable, that all animal matter is originally formed of vegetable; because all animals either feed directly and entirely on vegetables, or upon other animals that do so. From hence it is probable, that all animal substances may be traced to a vegetable origin; and *therefore,* if we would inquire into the production of animal matter, we *must first inquire* in what manner vegetable matter may be converted into animal?" *Cullen's Works*, vol. i. pp. 177, 178. The *therefore* and the *must,* resulting merely from an antecedent probability, are characteristic of that over-boldness, into which deduction is apt to degenerate, and which is strongly contrasted with the opposite vice of overtimidity, by which inductive reasoners are tainted.

hundred and fifty years before he completed his pathology, and having been in common scientific use for about a hundred years. But his love of synthesis overcame him. His system is constructed by reasoning from general principles; and of that process, he certainly was a consummate master. Between the premises and the conclusion, he hardly ever lets error creep in. And, in reference to the results of his speculations, he had one immense merit, which will always secure to him a conspicuous place in the history of pathology. By insisting on the importance of the solids, he, one-sided though he was, corrected the equal one-sidedness of his predecessors; for, with extremely few exceptions, all the best pathologists, from Galen downwards, had erred in ascribing too much to the fluids, and had upheld a purely humoral pathology. Cullen turned the minds of men in the other direction; and though, in teaching them that the nervous system is the sole primary seat of disease, he committed a great mistake, it was a mistake of the most salutary kind. By leaning on that side, he restored the balance. Hence, I have no doubt, he indirectly encouraged those minute researches into the nerves, which he would not himself stop to make, but which, in the next generation, gave rise to the capital discoveries of Bell, Shaw, Mayo, and Marshall Hall. At the same time, the old humoral pathology, which had prevailed for many centuries, was practically pernicious, because, assuming that all diseases are in the blood, it produced that constant and indiscriminate venesection, which destroyed innumerable lives, besides the irreparable injury it often inflicted both on body and mind; weakening those whom it was unable to slay. Against this merciless onslaught, which made medicine the curse of mankind, the Solid Pathology was the first effective barrier.[225]

225. Dr. Watson (*Principles and Practice of Physic*, 4th edit. London, 1857, vol. i. p. 41) says of the humoral pathology, that "the absurdity of the hypotheses, and *still more the dangerous practice which this doctrine generated,* began to be manifest, and led to its total abandonment." But, with every respect for this eminent authority, I venture to observe, that this supposition of Dr. Watson's is contradicted by the whole history of the human mind. There is no well-attested case on record of any theory having been abandoned, because it produced dangerous results. As long as a theory is believed, men will ascribe its evil consequences to any cause except the right one. And a theory which is once established, will always be believed, until there is some change in knowledge which shakes its foundation. Every practical change may, by careful analysis, be shown to depend, in the first instance, on some change of specula-

Practically, therefore, as well as speculatively, we must hail Cullen as a great benefactor of his species; and we must regard his appearance as an epoch in the history of human comfort, as well as in the history of human thought.

It may, perhaps, facilitate the conceptions of unprofessional readers, if I give, in as few words as possible, a specimen of the way in which Cullen employed his method, in investigating the theory of some one class of diseases. For this purpose, I will select his doctrine of fever, which, though now generally abandoned, once exercised more influence than any other part of his pathology. Here, as elsewhere, he reasons from the solids.[226] Disregarding the state of the blood, he says, that the cause of all fever is a diminished energy of the brain.[227] Such diminution may be produced by various sedatives, the most common of which are effluvia, whether marsh or human, intemperance, fear, and cold.[228]

tive opinions. Even at the present day, many doctrines are generally held in the most civilized countries, which are producing dangerous practical consequences, and have produced those consequences for centuries. But the mischief which the doctrine engenders does not weaken the doctrine itself. Nothing can do that, but the general progress of knowledge, which, by altering former opinions, modifies future conduct.

226. Some writers, who have taken notice of Cullen, have been deceived in this respect by his occasional use of the expression "nervous fluid," as if he were willing to let in the idea of humorism. But, in one place, he distinctly guards himself against such misconstruction. "Now, to avoid determining any thing with regard to these opinions, I have used the term of *nervous power;* but as this is a little ambiguous, I choose to express it by *nervous fluid;* not that I suppose, with Dr. Boerhaave, that the brain is an excretory, and that a fluid is secreted from it: *I mean nothing more than that there is a condition of the nerves which fits them for the communication of motion.* But I defer the consideration of these opinions for the present, and perhaps *ad Græcas calendas;* but nothing shall be rested upon the nervous fluid, it shall be considered merely as *a power* fitted for communicating motions." *Cullen's Works,* vol. i. p. 17. Without this passage, his remarks, on "the nervous fluid in the brain" (*Works,* vol. i. p. 129), might easily be misunderstood.

227. "Together with this, the languor, inactivity, and debility of the animal motions, the imperfect sensations, the feeling of cold, while the body is truly warm, and some other symptoms, all show that the energy of the brain is, on this occasion, greatly weakened; and I presume that, as the weakness of the action of the heart can hardly be imputed to any other cause, this weakness also is a proof of the diminished energy of the brain. So I conclude, that a debility of the nervous power forms the beginning of the cold fit, and lays the foundation of all the other phenomena." *Practice of Physic,* in *Cullen's Works,* vol. i. p. 492.

228. "To render our doctrine of fever consistent and complete, it is necessary to add here, that those remote causes of fever, human and marsh effluvia,

Directly the energy of the brain is impaired, the disease begins. Rapidly passing through the nervous system, its first palpable effect is a chill, or cold fit, which is accompanied by a spasm on the extremities of the arteries, particularly where they touch the surface of the body.[229] This spasm on the extreme vessels, irritates the heart and arteries, and the irritation continues till the spasm is relaxed.[230] At the same time, the increased action of the heart restores the energy of the brain; the system rallies; the extreme vessels are relieved; while, as a consequence of the whole movement, sweat is excreted, and the fever abates.[231] Shutting out,

---

seem to be of a debilitating or sedative quality." . . . . "Though we have endeavoured to show that fevers generally arise from marsh or human effluvia, we cannot, with any certainty, exclude some other remote causes, which are commonly supposed to have at least a share in producing those diseases. And I proceed, therefore, to inquire concerning these causes; the first of which that merits attention, is the power of cold applied to the human body." . . . "Besides cold, there are other powers that seem to be remote causes of fever; such as fear, intemperance in drinking, excess in venery, and other circumstances, which evidently weaken the system. But whether any of these sedative powers be alone the remote cause of fever, or if they only operate either as concurring with the operation of marsh or human effluvia, or as giving an opportunity to the operation of cold, are questions not to be positively answered." *Practice of Physic,* in *Cullen's Works,* vol. i. pp. 546, 552. One part of this view has been corroborated, since the time of Cullen. "The experiments of Chossat and others clearly prove cold to be a direct sedative." *Williams' Principles of Medicine,* second edit. London, 1848, p. 11. Compare *Watson's Principles and Practice of Physic,* 4th edit. London, 1857, vol. i. pp. 87–92, 249. Hence, perhaps, the "irresistible tendency to sleep caused by exposure to severe or long-continued cold." *Erichsen's Surgery,* second edit. London, 1857, p. 336; but as to this, Dr. Watson (*Principles of Physic,* vol. i. p. 89) is sceptical, and thinks that, in those cases which are recorded, the drowsiness ascribed to cold, is, in a great measure, the result of fatigue.

229. *Cullen's Works,* vol. i. p. 493. Compare, respecting his general theory of spasm, p. 84, and vol. ii. p. 400.

230. "The idea of fever, then, may be, that a spasm of the extreme vessels, however induced, proves an irritation to the heart and arteries; and that this continues till the spasm is relaxed or overcome." *Cullen's Works,* vol. i. p. 494.

231. "Such, however, is, at the same time, the nature of the animal economy, that this debility proves an indirect stimulus to the sanguiferous system; whence, by the intervention of the cold stage and spasm connected with it, the action of the heart and larger arteries is increased, and continues so till it has had the effect of restoring the energy of the brain, of extending this energy to the extreme vessels, of restoring, therefore, their action, and thereby especially overcoming the spasm affecting them; upon the removing of which, the excretion of sweat, and other marks of the relaxation of excretories take place." *Practice of Physic,* in *Cullen's Works,* vol. i. pp. 501, 502. See also p. 636, § cciii. Or, as he elsewhere expresses himself (vol. i. p. 561): "With regard

therefore, all consideration of the fluids of the body, the successive stages of languor, cold fit, and hot fit, might, in Cullen's opinion, be generalized by reasoning merely from the solids, which, furthermore, produced his well-known distinction between fevers, the continuance of which is owing to an excess of spasm, and those, the continuance of which is owing to an excess of debility.[232]

A similar process of thought gave birth to his *Nosology,* or general classification of diseases, which some have regarded as the most valuable part of his labours;[233] though, for reasons already mentioned, we must, I think, reject all such attempts as premature, and as likely to work more harm than good, unless they are simply used as a contrivance to aid the memory. At all events, the *Nosology* of Cullen, though it exhibits clear traces of his powerful and organizing mind, is fast falling into disrepute, and we may be sure, that, for a long time yet, a similar fate will await its successors. Our pathological knowledge is still too young for so great an enterprise.[234] We have every reason to expect, that, with the aid of chemistry, and of the microscope, it will continue

---

to the event of fevers, this is the fundamental principle: *in fevers, nature cures the disease;* that is, certain motions tending to death continue the disease, but, in consequence of the laws of the animal economy, other motions are excited by these which have a tendency to remove it."

232. "If we may trust to our conclusions with respect to the proximate cause, it follows, most naturally, from the view there given, that the continued fever is always owing to an excess of spasm, or to an excess of debility: as the one or other of these prevails, it will give one or other of the two forms, either the Synocha or inflammatory fever, or the Typhus or nervous fever." *Cullen's Works,* vol. i. p. 518.

233. "Cullen's most esteemed work is his *Nosology*." *Hamilton's History of Medicine,* London, 1831, vol. ii. p. 279. "His *Nosology* will probably survive all his other works; it is indisputably the best system which has yet appeared." *Lives of British Physicians,* London, 1830, p. 213. "Celle de Cullen, qui parut en 1772, et qui constitue un véritable progrès." *Renouard, Histoire de la Médecine,* Paris, 1846, vol. ii. p. 231. See also *Hooper's Medical Dictionary,* edited by Dr. Grant, London, 1848, p. 937. But, in the most celebrated medical works which have appeared in England during the last twelve or fifteen years, I doubt if there is any instance of the adoption of Cullen's nosological arrangement. Abroad, and particularly in Italy, it is more valued.

234. "I had rather not be cramped and hampered by attempting what abler heads than mine have failed to achieve, and what, in truth, I believe, in the present state of our science, to be impossible, a complete methodical system of nosology." *Watson's Principles and Practice of Physic,* London, 1857, vol. i. p. 9. This is the wisdom of a powerful understanding.

to grow more rapidly than it has hitherto done. Without venturing to predict the rate of its increase, we may form some idea of it, by considering what has been effected with resources very inferior to those we now possess. In a work of great authority, published in the year 1848, it is stated, that since the appearance of Cullen's *Nosology,* our mere enumeration of diseases has almost doubled, while our knowledge of the facts relating to disease has more than doubled.[235]

I have now only one more name to add to this splendid catalogue of the great Scotchmen of the eighteenth century.[236] But it is the name of a man, who, for comprehensive and original genius, comes immediately after Adam Smith, and must be placed far above any other philosopher whom Scotland has produced. I mean, of course, John Hunter, whose only fault was, an occasional obscurity, not merely of language, but also of thought. In this respect, and, perhaps, in this alone, Adam Smith had the advantage; for his mind was so flexible, and moved so freely, that even the vastest designs were unable to oppress it. With Hunter, on the contrary, it sometimes seemed as if the understanding was troubled by the grandeur of its own conceptions, and doubted what path it ought to take. He hesitated; the utterance of his intellect was indistinct.[237] Still, his powers were so extraordinary, that,

235. "Now, when the diseases of Cullen's nosology have been almost doubled, and the facts relating to them have been more than doubled." *Williams' Principles of Medicine,* London, 1848, p. 522.

236. I had intended giving some account of the once celebrated Brunonian system, which was founded by Dr. John Brown, who was first the pupil of Cullen, and afterwards his rival. But a careful perusal of his works has convinced me that the real basis of his doctrine, or the point from which he started, was not pathology, but therapeutics. His hasty division of all diseases into sthenic and asthenic, has no claim to be deemed a scientific generalization, but was a mere artificial arrangement, resulting from a desire to substitute a stimulating treatment in the place of the old lowering one. He, no doubt, went to the opposite extreme; but that being a purely practical subject, this Introduction has no concern with it. For the same reason, I omit all mention of Currie, who, though an eminent therapeutician, was a commonplace pathologist. That so poor and thinly-peopled a country as Scotland, should, in so short a period, have produced so many remarkable men, is extremely curious.

237. Mr. Ottley (*Life of Hunter,* p. 186) says, "In his writings we occasionally find an obscurity in the expression of his thoughts, a want of logical accuracy in his reasonings, and an incorrectness in his language, resulting from a deficient education." But, a deficient education will never make a man obscure. Neither will a good education make him lucid. The only cause of clearness of expression is clearness of thought; and clearness of thought is a natural gift,

among the great masters of organic science, he belongs, I apprehend, to the same rank as Aristotle, Harvey, and Bichat, and is somewhat superior either to Haller or Cuvier. As to this classification, men will differ, according to their different ideas of the nature of science, and, above all, according to the extent to which they appreciate the importance of philosophic method. It is from this latter point of view that I have, at present, to consider the character of John Hunter; and, in tracing the movements of his most remarkable mind, we shall find, that, in it, deduction and induction were more intimately united than in any other Scotch intellect, either of the seventeenth or eighteenth century. The causes of this unusual combination, I will now endeavour to ascertain. When they are understood, they will not only explain many peculiarities in his works, but will afford materials for speculation, to those who love to examine the development of ideas, and who are able to discern the way in which different schemes of national thought have given different shapes to national character, and have thereby modified the whole course of human affairs, to an extent of which the ordinary compilers of history have not the slightest suspicion.

Hunter remained in Scotland till the age of twenty, when he settled in London; and, though he was abroad for about three years, he abandoned his own country, and became, socially and intellectually, a native of England.[238] Hence, the early associations of his mind were formed in the midst of a deductive nation; the

which the most finished and systematic culture can but slightly improve. Uneducated men, without a thousandth part of John Hunter's intellect, are often clear enough. On the other hand, it as frequently happens that men, who have received an excellent education, cannot speak or write ten consecutive sentences which do not contain some troublesome ambiguity. In Hunter's works such ambiguities are abundant; and this is probably one of the reasons why no one has yet given a connected view of his philosophy. On his obscurity, compare *Cooper's Life of Sir Astley Cooper,* London, 1843, vol. i. pp. 151, 152; *Paget's Lectures on Surgical Pathology,* London, 1853, vol. i. p. 419; and the remarks of his enemy, Foot, in *Foot's Life of Hunter,* London, 1794, p. 59.

238. He was born in 1728, and came to London in 1748. *Adams' Life of John Hunter,* second edit. London, 1818, pp. 20, 203. According to Adams (pp. 30–35), he was abroad as surgeon in the English army from 1761 to 1763; though, in *Foot's Life of Hunter,* London, 1794, p. 78, he is said to have returned to England in 1762. Mr. Ottley says that he returned in 1763. *Ottley's Life of Hunter,* p. 22, in vol. i. of *Hunter's Works,* edited by Palmer, London, 1835.

later associations, in the midst of an inductive one. For twenty years he lived among a people, who are, perhaps, the acutest reasoners in Europe, if you concede to them the principles from which they reason; but who, on the other hand, owing to their proneness to this method, are so greedy after general principles, that they will accept them on almost any evidence, and are, therefore, at once very credulous and very logical. In that school, and surrounded by those habits, the intellect of John Hunter was nurtured during the most impressible period of his life. Then the scene suddenly shifted. Coming to England, he passed forty years in the heart of the most empirical nation in Europe; a nation utterly abhorring all general principles, priding itself on its common sense, boasting, and with good reason too, of its practical sagacity, proclaiming aloud the superiority of facts over ideas, and despising every theory, unless some direct and immediate benefit could be expected to accrue from it. The young and ardent Scotchman found himself transplanted into a country totally different from that which he had just quitted; and such a difference could not fail to influence his mind. He saw, on every side, marks of prosperity, and of long and uninterrupted success, not only in practical, but also in speculative, life; and he was told that these things were effected by a system which made facts the first consideration. He was ambitious of fame, but he perceived that the road to fame was not the same in England as in Scotland. In Scotland, a great logician would be deemed a great man; in England, little account would be made of the beauty of his logic, unless he was careful that the premises from which he argued, were trustworthy, and verified by experience. A new machine, a new experiment, the discovery of a salt, or of a bone, would, in England, receive a wider homage, than the most profound speculation from which no obvious results were apprehended. That this way of contemplating affairs has produced great good, is certain. But it is also certain, that it is a one-sided way, and satisfies only part of the human mind. Many of the noblest intellects crave for something which it cannot supply. In England, however, during the greater part of the eighteenth century, it was even more supreme than it is now, and was, indeed, so universal, that, from the year 1727 until nearly the close of the century, our country did not possess, in any branch of science, a speculator who had sufficient force to raise himself above those narrow views which were then deemed the perfection of wisdom.[239] Much was added to our knowledge, but its distant boundaries were not enlarged. Though there was an increase of curious and valuable details, and though several of the small and proximate laws of nature were generalized, it must be admitted, that those lofty generalizations, which we owe to the seventeenth century, remained stationary, and that no attempt was made to push beyond them. When John Hunter arrived in London, in 1748, Newton had been dead more than twenty years, and the English people, absorbed in practical pursuits, and now beginning, for the first time, to enter into political life, had become more averse than ever to inquiries which aimed at truth without regard to utility, and had accustomed themselves to value science chiefly for the sake of the direct and tangible benefit which they might hope to derive from it.

That Hunter must have been influenced by these circumstances, will be obvious to whoever considers how impossible it is for any single mind to escape from the pressure of contemporary opinion. But, inasmuch as all his early associations had inclined him in another direction, we perceive that, during his long residence in England, he was acted on by two conflicting forces. The country of his birth made him deductive; the country of his adoption made him inductive. As a Scotchman, he preferred reasoning from general principles to particular facts; as an inhabitant of England, he became inured to the opposite plan of reasoning from particular facts to general principles. In every country, men naturally give the first place to what is most valued. The English respect facts more than principles, and therefore begin with the facts. The Scotch consider principles as most important, and therefore begin with the principles. And, I make no doubt that one of the reasons why Hunter, in investigating a subject, is often obscure, is that, on such occasions, his mind was divided between these two hostile methods, and that, leaning sometimes to one and sometimes to the other, he was unable to determine which he should choose. The conflict darkened his understanding. Adam Smith, on the other hand, in common with all the great Scotchmen who remained in Scotland, was remarkably clear. He, like Hume, Black, and Cullen, never wavered in his method. These eminent men were not acted on by English influence. Of all the

239. See *Buckle's History of Civilization*, vol. i. pp. 808, 809.

most illustrious Scotchmen of the eighteenth century, Hunter alone underwent that influence, and he alone displayed a certain hesitation and perplexity of thought, which seems unnatural to so great a mind, and which, as it appears to me, is best explained by the peculiar circumstances in which he was placed.

One of the ablest of his commentators has justly observed, that his natural inclination was, to conjecture what the laws of nature were, and then reason from them, instead of reasoning to them by slow and gradual induction.[240] This process of deduction was, as I have shown, the favourite method of all Scotchmen, and, therefore, was precisely the course which we should have expected him to adopt. But, inasmuch as he was surrounded by the followers of Bacon,[241] this natural bias was warped, and a large part of his marvellous activity was employed in observations and experiments, such as no Scotch thinker, living in Scotland, would ever have engaged in. He himself declared, that thinking was his delight;[242] and there can be no doubt that, had he been differently situated, thinking would have been his principal pursuit. As it was, the industry with which he collected facts, is one of the most conspicuous features in his career. His researches covered the whole range of the animal kingdom, and were conducted with

240. "He followed his natural inclination. He preferred the more delusive, apparently the more direct, road, which has seduced so many philosophers. He sought to arrive at the general laws of nature at once by conjecture; rather than, by a close and detailed study of her inferior operations, to ascend, step by step, through a slow and gradual induction to those laws which govern her general procedure." Babington's Preface to Hunter's *Treatise on the Venereal Disease,* in *Hunter's Works,* vol. ii. p. 129. Compare the narrow and carping criticism in *Foot's Life of Hunter,* p. 163.

241. That I may not be suspected of exaggeration, I will quote what by far the greatest of all the historians of medicine has said upon this subject. ' La majorité des médecins qui prétendaient s'être formés d'après Bàcon, n'avaient hérité de lui qu'une répugnance invincible pour les hypothèses et les systèmes, une grande vénération pour l'expérience, et un désir extrême de multiplier le nombre des observations. Ce fut chez les Anglais que la méthode empirique en médecine trouva le plus de partisans, et c'est principalement aussi chez eux qu'elle s'est répandue jusqu'aux temps les plus rapprochés de nous. Sa propagation y fut favorisée, non-seulement par le profond respect que les Anglais continuent toujours de porter à l'immortel chancelier, mais encore par la haute importance que la nation entière attache au sens commun, *common sense,* et elle y demeura l'ennemie irréconciliable de tous systèmes qui ne reposent pas sur l'observation." *Sprengel, Historie de la Médecine,* vol. v. p. 411, Paris, 1815.

242. Clive says, "Much as Mr. Hunter did, he thought still more. He has often told me, his delight was, to think." *Abernethy's Hunterian Oration,* London, 1819, p. 26.

such untiring zeal, that he dissected upwards of five hundred different species, exclusive of dissections of different individuals, and exclusive, too, of dissections of a large number of plants.[243] The results were carefully arranged and stored up in that noble collection which he formed, and of the magnitude of which we may gain some idea from the statement, that, at his death, it contained upwards of ten thousand preparations illustrative of the phenomena of nature.[244] By this means, he became so intimately acquainted with the animal kingdom, that he made a vast number of discoveries, which, considered singly, are curious, but which, when put together, constitute an invaluable body of new truths. Of these, the most important are, the true nature of the circulation in crustacea and insects;[245] the organ of hearing in cephalopods;[246] the power possessed by mollusks of absorbing their

243. Mr. Owen, in his interesting Preface to the fourth volume of *Hunter's Works,* says (p. vii), "There is proof that Hunter anatomized at least five hundred different species of animals, exclusive of repeated dissections of different individuals of the same species, besides the dissections of plants to a considerable amount."

244. "Some idea may be formed of Hunter's extraordinary diligence, by the fact, that his museum contained at the time of his death, upwards of 10,000 preparations, illustrative of human and comparative anatomy, physiology, and pathology, and natural history." *Weld's History of the Royal Society,* London, 1848, vol. ii. p. 92.

245. 'I have tested the conflicting evidence of these observers by dissection of the heart in the lobster; and you will perceive by this preparation that it is more complicated than even the Danish naturalist supposed, and fully bears out the opinion of Hunter in regard to the mixed nature of the circulation in the crustacea." *Owen's Lectures on the Comparative Anatomy and Physiology of the Invertebrate Animals,* 2d edit. London, 1855, p. 318. "Cuvier, misled by the anomalous diffused condition of the venous system, supposed that there was no circulation of the blood in insects; yet the dorsal vessel was too conspicuous a structure to be overlooked. Such, however, was the authority of the great anatomist, that the nature of the heart began to be doubted, and the strangest functions to be attributed to it. Hunter, however, who was prepared to appreciate the true state of the circulating system in insects, by his discovery of the approximately diffused and irregular structure of the veins in the crustacea, has described, in his work on the blood, all the leading characters of the circulation in insects as it is recognized by comparative physiologists of the present day." *Ibid.,* p. 383. Compare *Hunter's Essays and Observations on Natural History,* London, 1861, vol. i. p. 108.

246. "The class called Sepia has the organ of hearing, though somewhat differently constructed from what it is in fishes." *An Account of the Organ of Hearing in Fishes,* in *Hunter's Works,* vol. iv. p. 294. At the bottom of the page Mr. Owen observes, in a note, "This is the first announcement of the existence of an organ of hearing in the Cephalopoda."

shells;[247] the fact that bees do not collect wax, but secrete it;[248] the semicircular canals of the cetacea;[249] the lymphatics of birds;[250] and the air-cells in the bones of birds.[251] We are also assured, that he anticipated the recent discoveries respecting the embryo of the kangaroo;[252] and his published works prove, that, in the human subject, he discovered the muscularity of the arteries,[253] the mus-

---

247. "Hunter discovered that the molluscous inhabitant of a shell had the power of absorbing part of its dwelling." *Owen's Lectures on the Comparative Anatomy and Physiology of the Invertebrate Animals*, London, 1855, p. 544. "Every shell-fish has the power of removing a part of its shell, so as to adapt the new and the old together, which is not done by any mechanical power, but by absorption." *Anatomical Remarks on a New Marine Animal*, in *Hunter's Works*, vol. iv. p. 469, edit. Palmer. In a note to this passage, it is said, that "the doctrine of the absorption of shell has been lately" (i.e. in 1833) "adduced as a new discovery."

248. "His keen observation did not fail to detect several errors which preceding naturalists had fallen into, especially with regard to the formation of the wax, which he proved to be secreted, not collected, by the animal." *Ottley's Life of Hunter*, p. 122. "The wax is formed by the bees themselves; it may be called an external secretion of oil, and I have found that it is formed between each scale of the under side of the belly." *Observations on Bees*, in *Hunter's Works*, vol. iv. p. 433.

249. "In the terminating part there are a number of perforations into the cochlea, and one into the semicircular canals, which afford a passage to the different divisions of the auditory nerve." *Observations on the Structure and Œconomy of Whales*, in *Hunter's Works*, vol. iv. pp. 383, 384. "The semicircular canals of the cetacea, described by Hunter in the paper on Whales, a structure which Cuvier rightly states that Camper overlooked, but incorrectly claims the discovery as his own." Preface to vol. iv. of *Hunter's Works*, p. xxi.

250. Dr. Adams, in his somewhat hastly *Life of Hunter*, says (pp. 27, 28), "Mr. Hewson always claimed the discovery of lymphatics in birds," But the truth is, that Hewson never claimed it. He says, "It may be necessary to mention here, that the dispute between Dr. Monro and me is, who first discovered the lacteals of birds? for as to the lymphatics in their necks (mentioned in this gentleman's note), these we both allow were discovered by Mr. John Hunter, about ten years ago." And, again, "These lymphatics in the necks of fowls were first discovered by Mr. John Hunter." *Hewson's Works*, edit. Gulliver (Sydenham Soc.), pp. 102, 145.

251. *Hunter's Works*, vol. iv. pp. xxi. 176.

252. "See Nos. 3731, 3734, 3735, in the Physiological series of the Hunterian Museum, in which there are evidences that Mr. Hunter had anticipated most of the anatomical discoveries which have subsequently been made upon the embryo of the Kangaroo." *Rymer Jones' Organization of the Animal Kingdom*, London, 1855, pp. 829, 830.

253. "The muscularity of arteries, of which John Hunter made physiological proof, is not a matter of eyesight." *Simon's Pathology*, London, 1850, p. 69. "To prove the muscularity of an artery, it is only necessary to compare its action with that of elastic substances." . . . "When the various uses of arteries are considered, such as their forming different parts of the body out of the blood,

cularity of the iris,[254] and the digestion of the stomach after death by its own juice.[255] Although, in his time, animal chemistry was not yet raised to a system, and was consequently little heeded by physiologists, Hunter endeavoured, by its aid, to search out the qualities of the blood, so as to ascertain the properties of its constituents.[256] He also examined it in different stages of embryonic life, and by minutely tracking it through its periods of development, he made the capital discovery, that the red globules of the blood are formed later than its other components. His contemporaries, however, were so little alive to the importance of this great physiological truth, that it fell dead upon them, and, being forgotten, it was, about fifty years afterwards, rediscovered, and was announced, in 1832, as a law of nature which had just been brought to light.[257] This is one of many instances in the history

---

their performing the different secretions, their allowing at one time the blood to pass readily into the smaller branches, as in blushing, and at another preventing it altogether, as in paleness from fear: and if to these we add the power of producing a diseased increase of any or every part of the body, we cannot but conclude that they are possessed of muscular powers." *Hunter's Works,* vol. iii. p. 157. See also vol. iv. p. 254. Mr. Gulliver, in his edition of *Hewson's Works,* London, 1846, says (p. 125), that Hunter's "experiments on the functions of the arteries are supported by the latest and best observations on their structure."

254. "The fact of the muscularity of the iris, which is here presumed from analogy by Mr. Hunter, has been since directly proved by the observations of Bauer and Jacob (*Phil. Trans.* 1822), and indirectly by Berzelius, who found that the iris possesses all the chemical properties of muscle." Palmer's note in *Hunter's Works,* vol. iii. p. 146, London, 1837.

255. *Adams' Life of Hunter,* pp. 59, 60, 245. *Hunter's Works,* vol. i. p. 43; vol. iv. pp. 116–121. *Watson's Principles of Physic,* vol. ii. p. 440.

256. "Hunter subjects the blood to both mechanical and chemical analysis, and endeavours to determine the characteristic properties of its different constituents." Owen's Preface to vol. iv. of *Hunter's Works,* p. xii. But this gives, perhaps, rather too high an idea of his animal chemistry; for such was then the miserable state of this extremely important branch of knowledge, that he arrived at the conclusion that "blood gives no analysis excepting that of common animal matter." *Principles of Surgery,* chap. iii. in *Hunter's Works,* vol. i. p. 229.

257. "In seeking to determine the respective importance of the different constituents of the blood, by the philosophical and most difficult inquiry into their respective periods of formation in the development of the embryo, Hunter made the interesting discovery that the vessels of the embryo of a red-blooded animal circulated in the first instance colourless blood, as in the invertebrate animals. 'The red globules,' he observes, 'seemed to be formed later in life than the other two constituents, for we see while the chick is in the egg the heart beating, and it then contains a transparent fluid before any red globules are formed, which fluid we may suppose to be the serum and the lymph.' I well

of our knowledge, which proves how useless it is for man to advance too far beyond the age in which he lives.[258] But Hunter, besides making the discovery, also saw its meaning. From it, he inferred, that the function of the red globules is to minister to the strength of the system, rather than to its repair.[259] This is now universally admitted; but it was not admitted till long after his death. Its recognition is chiefly owing to the rapid advance of animal chemistry, and to improvements in the microscope. For, by the employment of these resources, it has become manifest, that the red globules, the respiratory process, the production of animal heat, and the energy of the locomotive organs, are but different parts of a single scheme.[260] Their connexion with each other is established, not only by a comparison of different species, but also by a comparison of different members of the same species. In human beings, for example, the locomotive and other animal functions are more active in persons of a sanguine temperament,

---

remember the feelings of surprise with which I listened, while at Paris in 1832, to a memoir read before the Academy of Science, by M. M. Delpech and Coste, the object of which was the announcement of the same fact as a novel and important discovery. The statement of the French observers was received with all the consideration which its importance justly merited, without its being suspected that our great physiologist had, half a century before, embraced it, with all its legitimate deductions, in the extended circle of his investigations." Owen's Preface to vol. iv. of *Hunter's Works*, p. xiii.

258. Indeed, if we may rely on the references recently given by Mr. Gulliver, which, from his great general accuracy, there seems no reason to question, the fact that the pale blood precedes the red, was known even in the time of Glisson. See Gulliver's learned edition of *Hewson's Works*, London, 1846, p. 222. But, to the contemporaries of Glisson, such a fact was isolated, and consequently useless. Nothing is valuable while it appears to stand alone.

259. "From the above account it appears that whatever may be their utility in the machine, the red globules certainly are not of such universal use as the coagulating lymph, since they are not to be found in all animals, *nor so early in those that have them;* nor are they pushed into the extreme arteries, where we must suppose the coagulating lymph reaches; neither do they appear to be so readily formed. This being the case, *we must conclude them not to be the important part of the blood in contributing to growth, repair,* &c. *Their use would seem to be connected with strength."* A Treatise on the Blood, Inflammation, and Gun-shot Wounds, in *Hunter's Works*, vol. iii. p. 68. In another remarkable passage, he touches on the possibility of an increase in the amount of heat. "I will not pretend to determine how far this may assist in keeping up the animal heat." *Observations on the Structure and Œconomy of Whales*, in *Hunter's Works*, vol. iv. p. 364.

260. The evidence of this is collected in the notes to *Buckle's History of Civilization*, vol. i. pp. 53–55.

than in those of a lymphatic temperament; while, in sanguine temperaments, the globules are more numerous than in lymphatic ones. The knowledge of this fact we owe to Lecanu;[261] and to him we are also indebted for an analogous fact, corroborating the same view. He has shown, that the blood of women contains more water and fewer red globules than the blood of men;[262] so that here again we discern the relation between these globules and the energy of animal life. Inasmuch, however, as these researches were not made until many years after the death of Hunter, the coincidence between them and his speculative conclusions is a striking instance of his power of generalization, and of that un-rivalled knowledge of comparative anatomy, which supplied him with materials from which, in spite of the backwardness of animal chemistry, he was able to draw an inference, which later and minuter researches have decisively verified.[263]

261. "According to Lecanu, temperament has an influence upon the com-position of the blood. He infers from his analyses that the blood of lymphatic persons is poorer in solid constitutents, and especially in blood corpuscules, than that of persons of sanguineous temperament, while the quantity of albumen is much the same in both." *Simon's Animal Chemistry with reference to the Physiology and Pathology of Man*, London, 1845, vol. i. p. 236. Compare *Thomson's Chemistry of Animal Bodies*, Edinburgh, 1843, p. 370.

262. *Simon's Animal Chemistry*, vol. i. pp. 234, 235. Subsequent experiments have confirmed this. "The proportion of red globules *dried* to 1000 parts of blood, is in healthy males estimated at 127 parts by Andral and Gavarret; lower and higher figures have been given by other analysts, but this probably is the result of somewhat different modes of proceeding. *In females the proportion of globules is lower.* Becquerel and Rodier make the difference to be about 15 parts per 1000." *Jones and Sieveking's Pathological Anatomy*, London, 1854, p. 23. Hence, the greater specific gravity of male blood. See the interesting results of Dr. Davy's experiments in *Davy's Physiological and Anatomical Researches*, London, 1839, vol. ii. p. 32.

263. Hunter died in 1793. The researches of Lecanu were published in 1831 Another, and still more remarkable proof of the extent to which Hunter out-stripped his own age, appears in the following passage, which has just been published in his posthumous works, and in which he anticipates the grandest and most suggestive of all the ideas belonging to the physiology of the nine-teenth century. "If we were capable of following the progress of increase of the number of the parts of the most perfect animal, as they first formed in suc-cession, from the very first to its state of full perfection, we should probably be able to compare it with some one of the incomplete animals themselves, of every order of animals in the Creation, being at no stage different from some of the inferior orders. Or, in other words, if we were to take a series of animals, from the more imperfect to the perfect, we should probably find an imperfect animal, corresponding with some stage of the most perfect." *Essays and Observations by John Hunter, being his Posthumous Papers*, London, 1861, vol. i. p. 203.

Having thus, by a comprehensive survey of the animal world, associated its remarkable faculty of movement with the state of its blood, Hunter turned his attention to another aspect of the question, and took into consideration the movements of the vegetable world, in the hope that, by comparing these two divisions of nature, he might detect some law, which, being common to both, should unite into one study all the principles of organic motion. Though he failed in this great undertaking, some of his generalizations are very suggestive, and well illustrate the power and grasp of his mind. Looking at the organic kingdom as a whole, he supposed that its capacity of action, both in animals and in vegetables, was of three kinds. The first kind, was the action of the individual upon the materials it already possessed; and this gave rise to growth, secretion, and other functions, in which the juice of the plant was equivalent to the blood of the animal.[264] The second kind of action had for its object to increase these materials; it was always excited by want, and its result was, to nourish and preserve the individual.[265] The third kind was entirely due to external causes, including the whole material world, all the phenomena of which were a stimulus to some kind of action.[266] By

264. "The natural salutary actions, arising from stimuli, take place both in animals and vegetables, and may be divided into three kinds. The first kind of action, or self-motion, is employed simply in the œconomical operations, by which means the immediate functions are carried on, and the necessary operations performed, with the materials the animal or vegetable is in possession of, such as growth, support, secretion, &c. The blood is disposed of by the actions of the vessels, according to their specific stimulus, producing all the above effects. The juices of a plant are disposed of according to the different actions of the sap-vessels, arising also from their specific stimulus, which is different from that of blood vessels, but equally produces growth; but a vine will grow twenty feet in one summer, while a whale, probably, does not grow so much in as many years." *Croonian Lectures on Muscular Motion,* in *Hunter's Works,* vol. iv. p. 199.

265. "The second kind of action is in pursuit of external influence, and arises from a compound of internal and external stimulus; it is excited by the state of the animal or vegetable, which gives the stimulus of want, and being completed by external stimulus, produces the proper supplies of nourishment. It produces motions of whole parts: thus we see the *Hedysarum gyrans* moving its lesser foliola. This is an action apparently similar to breathing in animals, though, perhaps, it does not answer the same purpose; yet there is an alternate motion in both." *Croonian Lectures,* in *Hunter's Works,* vol. iv. p. 200.

266. "The third kind of motion is from external stimulus, and consists principally of the motion of whole parts, which is not inconsiderable in vegetables, as in the *Dionœa muscipula* and *Mimosa pudica* is very evident." . . . . "These actions are similar to what arise in many animals from external stimulus." *Ibid.,* vol. iv. p. 201.

combining, in different ways, these different sources of motion, and by studying every incitement to action, first, in reference to one of the three great divisions just indicated, and, secondly, in reference to the *power* of action, as distinguished from the *quantity* of action,[267] Hunter believed that some fundamental truths might be obtained, if not by himself, at all events by his successors. For, he thought that, though animals can do many things which plants cannot, still, the immediate cause of action is in both cases the same.[268] In animals, there is more variety of motion, but in plants there is more real power. A horse is certainly far stronger than a man. Yet a small vine can not only support, but can raise, a column of fluid five times higher than a horse can. Indeed, the power which a plant exercises of holding a leaf erect during an entire day, without a pause and without fatigue, is an effort of astonishing vigour, and is one of many proofs, that a principle of compensation is at work, so that the same energy which, in the animal world, is weakened by being directed to many objects, is, in the vegetable world, strengthened by being concentrated on a few.[269]

267. "I make a material difference between the power and the quantity of action. Some motions may be very small, yet act with great force; while others are of considerable extent, although very weak." *Ibid.,* vol. iv. p. 204.

268. "The immediate cause of motion in all vegetables is most probably the same, and it is probably the same in all animals; but how far they are the same in both classes, has not yet been determined. But I think it will appear, in the investigation of this subject, that vegetables and animals have actions evidently common to both, and that the causes of these actions are apparently the same in both; and most probably there is not an action in the vegetable, which does not correspond or belong to the animal, although the mode of action in the parts may not be the same, or muscular, in both." *Croonian Lectures,* in *Hunter's Works,* vol. iv. p. 196. Compare the section "Of Motion in Vegetables," in *Hunter's Essays,* London, 1861, vol. i. p. 24.

269. "The variety of motions is greater in animals, and more purposes are answered by them." . . . . "The first kind of action appears to be stronger in its power, although less in quantity, in vegetables than in animals; for a small vine was capable of sustaining, and even of raising, a column of sap 43 feet high, while a horse's heart was only capable of supporting a column of blood 8 feet 9 inches high; both of which columns must have been supported by the action of the internal parts, for we must suppose the heart equal, or nearly so, to the strength or action of the other parts of the vascular system; and when we consider that the sap of the tallest tree must be supported, and even raised from the root to the most distant branches, it must appear that the power of such vegetables far exceeds the power of any animal, and, indeed, it is such as the texture of a vegetable only can support. The power of supporting a leaf erect for a whole day, is as great an effort of action as that of the elevator palpebrarum

In pursuing these speculations, which, amid much that is uncertain, contain, I firmly believe, a large amount of important, though neglected, truth, Hunter was led to consider how motion is produced by various forces, such as magnetism, electricity, gravitation, and chemical attraction.[270] This carried him into inorganic science, where, as he clearly saw, the foundation of all organic science must be laid. Just as, on the one hand, the human frame could never be successfully studied, except by the aid of principles which had been collected from an investigation of animals below man,[271] so, on the other hand, the laws of those very animals must, he said, be approached through the laws of common or inorganic matter.[272] He, therefore, aimed at nothing less than to unite all the branches of physical science, taking them in the order of their relative complexity, and proceeding from the simplest to the most intricate. With this view, he examined the

---

muscle of the eye of an animal." *Hunter's Works,* vol. iv. pp. 203, 204. See also *Hunter's Essays,* vol. i. p. 342: "It is probable that the vegetable which can the least bear a suspension of its actions, can do so more than the animal which can bear it longest."

270. *Hunter's Works,* vol. iv. p. 255.

271. In his *Principles of Surgery,* he says (*Hunter's Works,* vol. i. p. 220), "The human body is what I mean chiefly to treat of; but I shall often find it necessary to illustrate some of the propositions which I shall lay down from animals of an inferior order, in whom the principles may be more distinct and less blended with others, or where the parts are differently constructed, in order to show, from many varieties of structure, and from many different considerations, what are the uses of the same parts in man; or, at least, to show that they are not for the uses which have been commonly assigned to them; and, as man is the most complicated part of the whole animal creation, it will be proper, in the first place, to point out general principles, common to all this species of matter, that I may be better understood, when I come to the more complicated machine, namely, the human."

272. "Before we endeavour to give an idea of an animal, it is necessary to understand the properties of that matter of which an animal is composed; but the better to understand animal matter, it is necessary to understand the properties of common matter; else we shall be often applying our ideas of common matter, which are familiar to us, to animal matter, an error hitherto too common, but which we should carefully avoid." *Principles of Surgery,* in *Hunter's Works,* vol. i. p. 211. "In the natural history of vegetables and animals, therefore, it will be necessary to go back to the first or common matter of this globe, and give its general properties; then see how far these properties are introduced into the vegetable and animal operations; or rather, perhaps, how far they are of use or subservient to their actions." *Hunter's Essays,* vol. i. p. 4. "Every property in man is similar to some property, either in another animal, or probably in a vegetable, or even in inanimate matter. Thereby (man) becomes classible with those in some of his parts." *Ibid.,* p. 10.

structure of the mineral kingdom, and, by an extensive comparison of crystals, he sought to generalize the principles of form, in the same way as, by a comparison of animals, he sought to generalize the principles of function. And, in doing this, he took into account, not only regular crystals, but also irregular ones.[273] For, he knew that, in nature, nothing is really irregular or disorderly; though our imperfect apprehension, or rather the backwardness of our knowledge, prevents us from discerning the symmetry of the universal scheme. The beauty of the plan, and the necessity of the sequence, are not always perceptible. Hence, we are too apt to fancy that the chain is broken, because we cannot see every link in it. From this serious error, Hunter was saved by his genius, even more than by his knowledge. Being satisfied that every thing which happens in the material world, is so connected and bound up with its antecedents, as to be the inevitable result of what had previously occurred, he looked with a true philosophic eye at the strangest and most capricious shapes, because to him they had a meaning and a necessary purpose. To him, they were neither strange nor capricious. They were deviations from the natural course; but it was a fundamental tenet of his philosophy, that nature, even in the midst of her deviations, still retains her regularity.[274] Or, as he elsewhere expresses it, deviation is, under certain circumstances, part of the law of nature.[275]

To generalize such irregularities, or, in other words, to show that they are not irregularities at all, was the main object of Hunter's life, and was the noblest part of his mission. Hence, notwithstanding his vast achievements in physiology, his favourite pursuit was pathology,[276] where, the phenomena being more complex, the intellect has more play. In this great field, he studied the aberrations of structure and of function, in the vegetable, as well

273. He made "a valuable collection of crystallizations, both of regular and irregular forms, which he was accustomed to use in his lectures to exemplify the difference between the laws which regulate the growth of organic and the increase of inorganic bodies." *Ottley's Life of Hunter*, p. 138.

274. "Nature is always uniform in her operations, and when she deviates is still regular in her deviations." *Principles of Surgery*, in *Hunter's Works*, vol. i. p. 485; see also vol. iv. pp. 44, 45.

275. "It certainly may be laid down, as one of the principles or laws of nature, to deviate under certain circumstances." *Hunter's Works*, vol. iv. p. 278.

276. Dr. Adams, who knew him personally, says that he studied "physiology, more particularly as connected with pathology." *Adams' Life of Hunter*, p. 77.

as in the animal, world;[277] while, for the abberations of form, which are the external manifestations of disturbed structure, he took into consideration the appearances presented by the mineral kingdom. There, the power of crystallization is the leading feature, and there, violations of symmetry constitute the essential disorder, whether the deformity of the crystal is subsequent to its production, or whether, being the result of what happened before its production, it is an original, and, if we may so say, congenital, defect. In either case, it is a deviation from the normal type, and, as such, is analogous to the monstrosities, both of animals and of vegetables.[278] The mind of Hunter, by sweeping

277. His *Principles of Surgery* contain some curious evidence of his desire to establish a connexion between animal and vegetable pathology. See, for instance, his remarks on "local diseases" (*Words,* vol. i. p. 341); on the influence of the seasons in producing diseases (vol. i. pp. 345, 346); and on the theory of inflammation exhibited in an oak-leaf (vol. ii. p. 391). But even now, too little is known of the diseases of the vegetable world to enable their study to be incorporated with the science of the diseases of the animal world; and, in the time of Hunter, the attempt was still less promising. Still, the effort shows the grandeur and range of the man's mind; and though little was effected, the method was right. So, too, in one of his essays on the *Power of Producing Heat,* he says, "In the course of a variety of experiments on animals and vegetables, I have frequently observed that the result of experiments in the one has explained the œconomy of the other, and pointed out some principle common to both." *Hunter's Works,* vol. iv. p. 136.

278. "Nature being pretty constant in the kind and number of the different parts peculiar to each species of animal, as also in the situation, formation, and construction of such parts, we call every thing that deviates from that uniformity a 'monster,' whether (it occur in) crystallization, vegetation, or animalization. There must be some principle for those deviations from the regular course of nature, in the economy of such species as they occur in. In the present inquiry it is the animal creation I mean to consider. Yet, as there may be in some degree an analogy between all the three (kingdoms of nature), I shall consider the other two, so far as this analogy seems to take place." . . . . "Monsters are not peculiar to animals: they are less so in them, perhaps, than in any species of matter. The vegetable (kingdom) abounds with monsters; and perhaps the uncommon formation of many crystals may be brought within the same species of production, and accounted for upon the same principle, viz. some influence interfering with the established law of regular formation. Monsters in crystals may arise from the same cause, as mentioned in the 'Introduction;' viz. either a wrong arrangement of the parts of which the crystal is to be composed, or a defect in the formation, from the first setting out being wrong, and (the formation) going on in the same (wrong) line. The principle of crystallization is in the solution; yet it requires more to set it a going, or into action, such, *e.g.,* as a solid surface. The deficiency in the production of a true crystal may be in the solution itself; or, I can conceive, that a very slight circumstance might alter the form of a crystal, and even give the disposition for one (crystal) to form

through this immense range of thought, attained to such commanding views of the philosophy of disease, that, in that department, he is certainly without a rival. As a physiologist, he was equalled, or perhaps excelled, by Aristotle; but as a pathologist, he stands alone, if we consider what pathology was when he found it, and what it was when he left it.[279] Since his death, the rapid advance of morbid anatomy and of chemistry has caused some of his doctrines to be modified, and some of them to be overturned. This has been the work of inferior men, wielding superior chemical and microscopical resources. To say that the successors of John Hunter are inferior to him, is no disparagement to their abilities, since he was one of those extremely rare characters who only appear at very long intervals, and who, when they do appear, remodel the fabric of knowledge. They revolutionize our modes of thought; they stir up the intellect to insurrection; they are the rebels and demagogues of science. And though the pathologists of the nineteenth century have chosen a humbler path, this must not blind us to their merits, or prevent us from being grateful for what they have done. We cannot, however, be too often reminded, that the really great men, and those who are the sole permanent benefactors of their species, are not the great experimenters, nor the great observers, nor the great readers, nor the great scholars, but the great thinkers. Thought is the creator and vivifier of all human affairs. Actions, facts, and external manifestations of every kind, often triumph for a while; but it is the progress of ideas which ultimately determines the progress of the world. Unless these are changed, every other change is superficial,

---

upon another. Quickness in the progress of crystallization produces irregularity and diminution in size." *Hunter's Essays,* London, 1861, vol. i. pp. 239–241. The reader must remember, that, when these remarks were written, the phenomena of crystallization had not been subjected to that exact mathematical treatment which subsequently revealed so many of their laws. Indeed, the goniometer was then so coarse an instrument, that it was impossible to measure the angles of crystals with accuracy.

279. Abernethy says, "He appears to me as a new character in our profession; and, briefly to express his peculiar merit, I may call him the first and great physionosologist, or expositor of the nature of disease." *Abernethy's Hunterian Oration,* p. 29, London, 1819. "He may be regarded as the first who applied the great truths of anatomical and physiological science to these most important subjects, by tracing the processes which nature employs in the construction of organic changes, in building up new formations, and in repairing the effects of injury or disease." *Hodgson's Hunterian Oration,* 1855, p. 32.

and every improvement is precarious. It is, however, evident that, in the present state of our knowledge, all ideas respecting nature must refer to the normal or to the abnormal; that is to say, they must be concerned either with what is regular, uniform, and obedient to recognized principles, or else with what is irregular, perturbed, and disobedient. Of these two divisions, the first belongs to science; the second, to superstition. John Hunter formed the superb conception of merging both classes of ideas into one, by showing that nothing is irregular, that nothing is perturbed, that nothing is disobedient. Centuries, perhaps, may elapse before that conception will be consummated. But what Hunter effected towards it, places him at the head of all pathologists, ancient or modern. For, with him, the science of pathology did not mean the laws of disease in man alone, or even in all animals, or even in the whole organic kingdom; but it meant the laws of disease and of malformation in the entire material world, organic and inorganic. His great object was, to raise a science of the abnormal. He determined to contemplate nature as a vast and united whole, exhibiting, indeed, at different times different appearances, but preserving, amidst every change, a principle of uniform and uninterrupted order, admitting of no deviation, undergoing no disturbance, and presenting no real irregularity, albeit to the common eye, irregularities abound on every side.

As pathology was the science to which Hunter was most devoted, so also was it that in which his natural love of deduction was most apparent. Here, far more than in his physiological inquiries, do we find a desire to multiply original principles from which he could reason; in opposition to the inductive method, which always aims at diminishing these principles by gradual and successive analysis. Thus, for instance, in his animal pathology, he attempted to introduce, as an ultimate principle from which he could argue, the idea that all diseases move more rapidly towards the skin than towards internal parts, by virtue of some hidden force, which also obliges vegetables to approach the surface of the earth.[280] Another favourite proposition, which he often used as

---

280. "The specific qualities in diseases also tend more rapidly to the skin than to the deeper-seated parts, except the cancer; although, even in this disease, the progress towards the superficies is more quick than its progress towards the centre." .... "In short, this is a law of nature, and it probably is upon the

a major premiss, and by its aid constructed deductively a pathological argument, was, that in no substance, be it what it may, can two processes go on in the same part at the same time.[281] By applying this universal proposition to the more limited phenomena of life, he inferred that two general diseases cannot co-exist in the same individual; and he relied so much on this ratiocination, that he refused to credit any testimony by which it was impugned.[282] There is reason to believe that his conclusion is erroneous, and that different diseases can so accompany each other, as to be united in the same individual, at the same time, and in the same part.[283]

---

same principle by which vegetables always approach the surface of the earth." *A Treatise on the Blood, Inflammation, and Gunshot Wounds*, in *Hunter's Works*, vol. iii. p. 285. "Granulations always tend to the skin, which is exactly similar to vegetation, for plants always grow from the centre of the earth towards the surface; and this principle was taken notice of when we were treating of abscesses coming towards the skin." *Ibid.*, pp. 489, 490.

281. "It may be admitted as an axiom, that two processes cannot go on at the same time in the same part of any substance." *Hunter's Works*, vol. iv. p. 96. Compare *Hunter's Essays*, vol. ii. p. 333: "As it appears, in general, that Nature can hardly make one part perform two actions with advantage."

282. "Thus, we hear of pocky itch and of scurvy and the venereal disease combined; but this supposition appears to me to be founded in error. I have never seen any such cases, *nor do they seem to be consistent with the principles of morbid action* in the animal œconomy. It appears to me beyond a doubt that no two actions can take place in the same constitution, or in the same part, at one and the same time." *Hunter's Works*, vol. ii. p. 132. "As I reckon every operation in the body an action, whether universal or partial, *it appears to me beyond a doubt* that no two actions can take place in the same constitution, nor in the same part, at one and the same time; the operations of the body are similar in this respect to actions or motions in common matter. *It naturally results from this principle,* that no two different fevers can exist in the same constitution, nor two local diseases in the same part, at the same time. There are many local diseases which have dispositions totally different, but having very similar appearances, have been supposed by some to be one sort of disease, by others to be a different kind, and by others again a compound of two diseases." . . . . "These, therefore, are often supposed to be mixed, and to exist in the same part. Thus we hear of a pocky-scurvy, a pocky-itch, rheumatic-gout, &c. &c., which names, *according to my principle,* imply a union that cannot possibly exist." *Ibid.*, vol. iii. pp. 3, 4.

283. Dr. Robert Williams (*Encyclopædia of the Medical Sciences*, London, 1847, 4to, p. 688) says, "The diagnosis between gout and rheumatism is often exceedingly difficult, so much so that nosologists have given a mixed class, or rheumatic gout. Mr. Hunter warmly opposed this compound appellation, for, in his opinion, no two distinct diseases, or even distinct diatheses, can co-exist in the same constitution; a law, it must be admitted, to have many exceptions." Compare *Watson's Principles and Practice of Physic*, London, 1857, vol. i. p. 312; "acting upon the aphorism of John Hunter (an aphorism, however,

Whether or not this be the case, it is equally interesting to notice the process of thought which led Hunter to bestow infinitely more pains in arguing from the general theory, than in arguing to it. Indeed, he can hardly be said to have argued to it at all, since he obtained it by a rough and hasty generalization from what seemed to be the obvious properties of inorganic matter. Having thus obtained it, he applied it to the pathological phenomena of the organic world, and especially of the animal world. That he should have adopted this course, is a curious proof of the energy of his deductive habits, and of the force of mind which enabled him so to set at naught the traditions of his English contemporaries, as to follow a method which, in the opinion of everyone who surrounded him, was not only full of danger, but could never lead to truth.

Other parts of his pathology abound with similar instances, which show how anxious he was to assume principles on which he could build arguments. Of this kind, were his ideas respecting sympathy, as connected with action. He suggested, that the simplest forms of sympathy would probably be found in the vegetable world, because there, the general arrangements are less intricate than in the animal world.[284] On this supposition, he constructed a series of curious and refined speculations, of which, however, I must confine myself to giving a very short summary. As animals sympathize more than vegetables, this helps us to understand why it is that their movements are more numerous. For, sympathy, being a susceptibility to impression, is also a prin-

---

which requires some qualification), that two diseases or actions cannot go on in a part at the same time." According to another authority, "There can be little doubt that two or more zymotic processes do often go on simultaneously in the blood and body; a fact of profound interest to the pathologist, and worthy of attentive investigation." *Report on the Public Health for* 1847, in *Journal of the Statistical Society,* vol. xi. p. 168, London, 1848. See also, on the co-existence of specific poisons, *Erichsen's Surgery,* 2d edit. London, 1857, p. 430. Mr. Paget, in his striking, and eminently suggestive *Lectures on Pathology,* London, 1853, vol. ii. pp. 537, 538, has made some interesting remarks on one part of the theory of co-existence; and his observations, so far as they go, tend to corroborate Hunter's view. He has put very forcibly the antagonism between cancer and other specific diseases; and especially between the cancerous diathesis and the tuberculous.

284. "The most simple sympathy is perhaps to be found in vegetables, these being much more simple than the most simple animal." *Principles of Surgery,* in *Hunter's Works,* vol. i. p. 327.

ciple of action.[285] Like other principles of action, it may be either natural or diseased.[286] But, whichever it be, it can, in plants, have only one mode of development, because, in them, it can only be influenced by stimulus; while in animals, which have sensation, it has necessarily three modes, one from stimulus, one from sensation, and a third compounded of the other two.[287] These are the largest divisions of sympathy, if we consider the organic world as a whole. In single cases, however, sympathy admits of still further subdivision. We may reason from it, in reference to the age of the individual;[288] we may also reason from it in reference to temperament, since, in point of fact, temperament is nothing but susceptibility to action.[289] And when sympathy is in action, we may, by analyzing our idea of it, reduce it to five different heads, and may classify it as continued, or contiguous, or remote, or similar, or dissimilar.[290] All these supplied Hunter with principles from which, by reasoning deductively, he attempted to explain the facts of disease; for, according to him, disease merely consists in a want of combination of actions.[291] By this process of thought,

285. "This principle of action, called sympathy," &c. *Ibid.*, vol. i. p. 318.

286. "Sympathy may be divided into two kinds, the natural and the diseased." *Principles of Surgery*, in *Hunter's Works*, vol. i. p. 320; see also *A Treatise on the Blood, Inflammation, &c.*, in *Works*, vol. iii. p. 6.

287. *Croonian Lectures on Muscular Motion*, in *Hunter's Works*, vol. iv. p. 207; and exactly the same words in his *Phytology*, in *Hunter's Essays*, London, 1861, vol. i. p. 361.

288. "Local or partial sympathy is found more in old than in young; whereas universal sympathy is more in young than in old. Sympathy is less determined in young persons, every part being then ready to sympathize with other parts under disease." . . . . "As the child advances, the power of sympathy becomes partial, there not being now, in the constitution, that universal consent of parts, but some part, which has greater sympathy than the rest, falls into the whole irritation; therefore the whole disposition to sympathy is directed to some particular part. The different organs acquire more and more of their own independent actions, as the child grows older." *Hunter's Works*, vol. i. pp. 322, 323.

289. "Susceptibilities for dispositions and actions appear to me to be the same with what are understood by temperament. Temperament is the state of the body fitting it for the disposition or action it is then in." *Hunter's Works*, vol. i. p. 307.

290. *Hunter's Works*, vol. iii. p. 393.

291. "As every natural action of the body depends, for its perfection, on a number of circumstances, we are led to conclude, that all the various combining actions are established while the body is in health, and well disposed; but this does not take place in diseased actions, for disease, on the contrary, consists in the want of this very combination." *Hunter's Works*, vol. iii. p. 10. Compare vol. i. p. 310: "I have explained that a disease is a disposition for a wrong ac-

he was induced to neglect those predisposing causes, to which inductive pathologists pay great attention, and with which the works of his English contemporaries were much occupied. Such causes could only be generalized from observation, and Hunter made no account of them. Indeed, he even denies their real existence, and asserts that a predisposing cause, is simply an increased susceptibility to form disposition to action.[292]

By reasoning from the twofold ideas of action and of sympathy, Hunter constructed the deductive or synthetic part of his pathology. This he did as a Scotchman, and to this, had he always lived in Scotland, he would probably have confined himself. But being for forty years surrounded by Englishmen, and having his mind impregnated by English habits, he contracted something of their mode of thought. We, accordingly, find that a considerable portion of his pathology is as inductive as the most eager disciple of Bacon could desire; forming, in this respect, a striking contrast to the purely synthetic method of Cullen, the other great pathologist of Scotland. In the attempt, however, which Hunter made to mix these two methods, he perplexed both himself and his readers. Hence that obscurity, which even his warmest admirers have noticed, though they have not perceived its cause. Vast as his powers were, he was unable to effect a complete union between induction and deduction. That this should have happened, will not surprise any one, who considers how some of the greatest thinkers have failed in this, the most difficult of all enterprises. Among the ancients, Plato failed in induction, and all his followers failed with him; since none of them have placed sufficient confidence in

---

tion, and that the action is the immediate effect of the disposition, and that either the actions, or the effects of those actions, *produce the symptoms which are generally called the disease;* such as sensations, which are commonly pain of all kinds, sickness, alteration visible or invisible in the structure of the part or parts that act, and sympathy."

292. "There is no such thing, strictly speaking, as a predisposing cause. What is commonly understood by a predisposing cause is an increased susceptibility to form disposition to action. When I say I am predisposed for such and such actions, it is only that I am very susceptible of such and such impressions." *Hunter's Works,* vol. i. p. 303. See also p. 301: "The most simple idea I can form of an animal being capable of disease is, that every animal is endued with a power of action, and a susceptibility of impression, which impression forms a disposition, which disposition may produce action, which action becomes the immediate sign of the disease; all of which will be according to the nature of the impression and of the part impressed."

facts, and in the process of reasoning from particulars to generals. Among the moderns, Bacon was deficient in deduction, and every Baconian has been similarly deficient; it being the essential vice of that school to despise reasoning from general propositions, and to underrate the value of the syllogism. It may, indeed, be doubted if the history of the world supplies more than two instances of physical philosophers being as great in one form of investigation as in the other. They are Aristotle and Newton, who wielded each method with equal ease, combining the skill and boldness of deduction with the caution and perseverance of induction, masters alike of synthesis and of analysis, as capable of proceeding from generals to particulars, as from particulars to generals, sometimes making ideas precede facts, and sometimes making facts precede ideas, but never faltering, never doubting which course to take, and never allowing either scheme unduly to encroach on its opposite. That Hunter should be unable to perform this, merely proves that he was inferior to these two men, whose almost incredible achievements entitle them to be termed the prodigies of the human race. But what he did was wonderful, and, in his own department, has never been rivalled. Of the character and extent of his inquiries, I have given a sketch, which, notwithstanding its imperfections, may serve to illustrate the antagonism of the Scotch and English intellects, by showing how the methods peculiar to each nation struggled for mastery in that great mind, which was exposed to the action of both. Which method predominated in Hunter it would be hard to say. But it is certain, that his understanding was troubled by their conflict. It is also certain, that, owing to his love of deduction, or of reasoning from general ideas, he exercised much less sway over his English contemporaries, than he would have done if he had exclusively followed their favourite method of reasoning from particular facts. Hence, the disproportion between his influence and his merits. As to his merits, it is now admitted, that, in addition to his physiological discoveries, and the great pathological views which he propounded, we may trace to him nearly all the surgical improvements which were introduced within about forty years after his death.[293] He was the first who explained, and, indeed, the first

293. Hunter died in 1793. In 1835, Mr. Palmer writes: "Those who have traced the progress of modern surgery to its true source, will not fail to have

who recognized, the disease of inflammation of the veins, which is of frequent occurrence, and, under the name of phlebitis, has latterly been much studied, but which, before his time, had been ascribed to the most erroneous causes.[294] On general inflammation, he threw so much light, that the doctrines which he advocated, and which were then ridiculed as whimsical novelties, are now taught in the schools, and have become part of the common traditions of the medical profession.[295] He, moreover, introduced

---

discerned, in the principles which Hunter established, the germs of almost all the improvements which have been since introduced." *Hunter's Works,* vol. i. p. vii. Eighteen years later, Mr. Paget says of Hunter's views respecting the healing of injuries: "In these sentences, Mr. Hunter has embodied the principle on which is founded the whole practice of subcutaneous surgery; a principle of which, indeed, it seems hardly possible to exaggerate the importance." *Paget's Lectures on Surgical Pathology,* London, 1853, vol. i. p. 170. At pp. 197, 198: "After what I have said respecting the process of immediate union, it may appear that Mr. Hunter was more nearly right than his successors."

294. "Inflammation of the veins, originally studied by Hunter, has of late years attracted the attention of many distinguished Continental and British pathologists." *Erichsen's Surgery,* London, 1857, p. 475. "No subject more amply illustrates the essential services which the science and art of medicine have derived from pathological anatomy than that of phlebitis. By this study many a dark point in the phenomena of disease has been either thoroughly elucidated, or, at all events, rendered more comprehensible. We need only refer to the so-termed malignant intermittents, consequent upon wounds and surgical operations,—to certain typhoid conditions, puerperal diseases, and the like. John Hunter, the elder Meckel, and Peter Frank, were the first to commence the investigation." *Hasse's Anatomical Description of the Diseases of the Organs of Circulation and Respiration,* London, 1846, p. 10. "Hunter was the first to open the way, and since that period the scalpel has shown that many previously unintelligible malignant conditions are attributable to phlebitis." *Jones and Sieveking's Pathological Anatomy,* London, 1854, p. 362. On the application of this discovery to the theory of inflammation of the spleen, see *Rokitansky's Pathological Anatomy,* vol. ii. p. 173, London, 1849; compare vol. iv. p. 335.

295. Sir Benjamin Brodie says: "It is true that the essential parts of John Hunter's doctrines as to inflammation and its consequences are now so incorporated with what is taught in the schools, that to be acquainted with them you need not seek them in his works; but I recommend you, nevertheless, to make these your especial study, for the sake of the other valuable information which they contain, and the important views in physiology and pathology which, in almost every page, are offered to your contemplation." *Brodie's Lectures on Pathology and Surgery,* London, 1846, p. 25. "John Hunter, whose treatise on Inflammation is a mine in which all succeeding writers have dug." *Watson's Principles and Practice of Physic,* London, 1857, vol. i. p. 146. "The appeal to philosophical principles in Hunter's works was, indeed, the cause of their being a closed volume to his less enlightened contemporaries; but, though the principles implied or expressed, subjected them to the scorn and neglect of those

what is probably the most capital improvement in surgery ever effected by a single man; namely, the practice in aneurism of tying the artery at a distance from the seat of disease. This one suggestion, and the first successful execution of it, are entirely owing to John Hunter, who, if he had done nothing else, would, on this account alone, have a right to be classed among the principal benefactors of mankind.[296]

---

less imbued with the spirit of philosophy, the results of those principles, verified as they were by facts, have gradually and insensibly forced themselves on the conviction of the profession; and though adopted silently, and without acknowledgment, as if the authors themselves had forgotten or were ignorant from whence they were derived, they now form the very groundwork of all books, treatises, and lectures on professional subjects." *Green's Vital Dynamics,* London, 1840, p. 81. Finally, I will quote the very recent testimony of Mr. Simon, who, in his masterly, and singularly beautiful, essay on Inflammation, has not only brought together nearly every thing which is known on that interesting subject, but has shown himself to be possessed of powers of generalization rare in the medical profession, or, indeed, in any other profession. "Without undue partiality, an Englishman may be glad to say that the special study of Inflammation dates from the labours of John Hunter. An indefatigable observer of nature, untrammelled by educational forms, and thoroughly a sceptic in his method of study, this large-minded surgeon of ours went to work at inflammation with a full estimate of the physiological vastness of his subject. He saw that, in order to understand inflammation, he must regard it, not as one solitary fact of disease, but in connexion with kindred phenomena—some of them truly morbid in their nature, but many of them within the limits of health. He saw that, for any one who would explain inflammation, all inequalities of blood-supply, all periodicities of growth, all actions of sympathy, were part of the problem to be solved." . . . . "He cannot be understood without more reflection than average readers will give; and only they who are content to struggle through a veil of obscure language, up to the very reality of his intent, can learn with how great a master they are communing." . . . . "Doubtless, he was a great discoverer. But it is for the spirit of his labours, even more than for the establishment of new doctrine, that English surgery is for even indebted to him. Of facts in pathology, he may, perhaps, be no permanent teacher; but to the student of medicine he must always be a noble pattern. Emphatically, it may be said of him, that he was the physiological surgeon. Others, before him (Galen, for instance, eminently), had been at once physiologists and practitioners; but science, in their case, had come little into contact with practice. Never had physiology been so incorporated with surgery, never been so applied to the investigation of disease and the suggestion of treatment, as it was by this masterworkman of ours. And to him, so far as such obligations can be personal, we assuredly owe it that, for the last half-century, the foundations of English surgery have, at least professedly, been changing from a basis of empiricism to a basis of science." *Simon on Inflammation,* in *A System of Surgery,* edited by T. Holmes, London, 1860, vol. i. pp. 134–136.

296. Mr. Bowman, in his *Principles of Surgery (Encyclopædia of the Medical Sciences,* London, 4to, 1847) says (p. 831): "Before the time of Hunter, the operation was performed by cutting into the sac of the aneurism, and tying the

But, so far as his own immediate reputation was concerned, all was in vain. He was in the midst of a people who had no sympathy with that mode of thought which was most natural to him. They cared nothing for ideas, except with a view to direct and tangible results; he valued ideas for themselves, and for the sake of their truth, independently of all other considerations. His English contemporaries, prudent, sagacious, but short-sighted, seeing few things at a time, but seeing those things with admirable clearness, were unable to appreciate his comprehensive speculations. Hence, in their opinion, he was little else than an innovator and an enthusiast.[297] Hence, too, even the practical improvements which he introduced were coldly received, because they proceeded from so suspicious a source. The great Scotchman, thrown among a nation whose habits of mind were uncongenial to his own, stood, says one of the most celebrated of his disciples, in a position of solitary and comfortless superiority.[298] Indeed, so little was he regarded

---

vessel above and below. So formidable was this proceeding in its consequences, that amputation of the limb was frequently preferred, as a less dangerous and fatal measure. The genius of Hunter led him to tie the femoral artery, in a case of popliteal aneurism, leaving the tumour untouched. The safety and efficacy of this mode of operating have now been fully established, and the principle has been extended to all operations for the cure of this formidable disease." See also p. 873: *Paget's Surgical Pathology,* vol. i. pp. 36, 37; and *Erichsen's Surgery,* pp. 141, 142, 508, 509.

297. The majority of Hunter's contemporaries considered his pursuits to have little connexion with practice, charged him with attending to physiology more than surgery, and looked on him as little better than an innovator and an enthusiast." *Ottley's Life of Hunter,* p. 126. In a work, which was written by a surgeon only the year after Hunter died, the reader is told, in regard to his remarkable inquiries respecting animal heat, that "his experiments, if they be true, carry with them no manner of information:—if they be true, no effect for the benefit of man can possibly be derived from them." *Foot's Life of Hunter,* London, 1794, p. 116. At p. 225, the same practitioner reproaches the great philosopher with propounding "purely a piece of theory, without any practical purpose whatever." Foot, indeed, wrote under the influence of personal feelings, but he rightly judged that these were the sort of charges which would be most likely to prejudice the English public against Hunter. It never occurred to Foot, any more than it would occur to his readers, that the quest of truth, as truth, is a magnificent object, even if its practical benefit is imperceptible. One other testimony is worth quoting. Sir Astley Cooper writes of Cline: "His high opinion of Mr. Hunter shows his judgment; for almost all others of Mr. Hunter's contemporaries, although they praise him now, abused him while he lived." *The Life of Sir Astley Cooper, by Bransby Blake Cooper,* London, 1843, vol. ii. p. 337.

298. "Those who far precede others, must necessarily remain alone; and their actions often appear unaccountable, nay, even extravagant, to their distant followers, who know not the causes that give rise to them, nor the effects which

by that very profession of which he was the chiefest ornament, that, during the many years in which he delivered lectures in London on anatomy and on surgery, his audience never amounted to twenty persons.[299]

I have now completed my examination of the Scotch intellect as it unfolded itself in the seventeenth and eighteenth centuries. The difference between those two periods must strike every reader. In the seventeenth century, the ablest Scotchmen wasted their energies on theological subjects, respecting which we have no trustworthy information, and no means of obtaining any. On these topics, different persons and different nations, equally honest, equally enlightened, and equally competent, have entertained, and still entertain, the most different opinions, which they advocate with the greatest confidence, and support by arguments, perfectly satisfactory to themselves, but contemptuously rejected by their opponents. Each side deeming itself in possession of the truth, the impartial inquirer, that is, he who really loves truth, and knows how difficult it is to obtain it, seeks for some means by which he may fairly adjudicate between these conflicting pretensions, and determine which is right and which is wrong. The further he searches, the more he becomes convinced that no such means are to be found, and that these questions, if they do not transcend the limits of the human understanding, do, certainly, transcend its present resources, and have no chance of being answered, while other and much simpler problems are still unsolved. It would be strange, indeed, if we, ignorant of so many lower and subordinate matters, should be able to reach and penetrate these remote and complicated mysteries. It would be strange if we, who, notwithstanding the advances we have made, are still in the infancy of our career, and who, like infants, can only walk with unsteady gait, and are scarce able to move without stumbling, even on plain and level ground, should, naithless, succeed in scaling those dizzy heights, which, overhanging our path, lure us on

---

they are designed to produce. In such a situation stood Mr. Hunter, with relation to his contemporaries. It was a comfortless precedence, for it deprived him of sympathy and social co-operation." *Abernethy's Hunterian Oration*, p. 49.

299. "These he continued for several years; but so far were his talents, and his enlightened views, from exciting the attention they merited, that his hearers never amounted to twenty." *Ottley's Life of Hunter*, p. 28.

where we are sure to fall. Unfortunately, however, men are, in every age, so little conscious of their deficiencies, that they not only attempt this impossible task, but believe they have achieved it. Of those who are a prey to this delusion, there are always a certain number, who, seated on their imaginary eminence, are so inflated by the fancied superiority, as to undertake to instruct, to warn, and to rebuke the rest of mankind. Giving themselves out as spiritual advisers, and professing to teach what they have not yet learned, they exhibit in their own persons that most consistent of all combinations, a combination of great ignorance with great arrogance. From this, other evils inevitably follow. The ignorance produces superstition; the arrogance produces tyranny. Hence it is, that, in a country like Scotland, where the pressure of long-continued and adverse circumstances has consolidated the power of these pretenders to wisdom, such sad results become conspicuous in every direction. Not only the national character, but also the national literature, feel their influence, and are coloured by them. It was, therefore, natural that, in Scotland, in the seventeenth century, when the authority of the clergy was most uncontrolled, the consequences of that authority should be most apparent. It was natural that a literature should be created such as that of which I have given some account; a literature which encouraged superstition, intolerance, and bigotry; a literature full of dark misgivings, and of still darker threats; a literature which taught men that it was wrong to enjoy the present, and that it was right to tremble at the future; a literature, in a word, which, spreading gloom on every side, soured the temper, corrupted the affections, numbed the intellect, and brought into complete discredit those bold and original inquiries, without which there can be no advance in human knowledge, and consequently no increase of human happiness.

To this, the literature of the eighteenth century offered a striking and most exhilarating contrast. It seemed as if, in a moment, all was changed. The Baillies, the Binnings, the Dicksons, the Durhams, the Flemings, the Frasers, the Gillespies, the Guthries, the Halyburtons, the Hendersons, the Rutherfords, and the rest of that monkish rabble, were succeeded by eminent and enterprising thinkers, whose genius lighted up every department of knowledge, and whose minds, fresh and vigorous as the morning, opened for themselves a new career, and secured for their country a high place in the annals of European intellect. Something of what they effected, I have endeavoured to narrate; much, however, has been left untold. But I have brought forward sufficient evidence to convince even the most sceptical reader of the splendour of their achievements, and of the difference between the noble literature which they produced, and those wretched compositions which disfigured the preceding century.

Still, great as the difference was, the two literatures had, as I have shown, one important point in common. Both were essentially deductive; and the proof of this, I have given at considerable length, because, though it has, so far as I am aware, escaped the attention of all previous inquirers, its consequences were of the utmost moment to the fortunes of Scotland, and are, moreover, full of interest to those who, in their investigations of human affairs, desire to penetrate below the mere surface and symptoms of things.

If we take a general view of those countries where science has been cultivated, we shall find that, wherever the deductive method of inquiry has predominated, knowledge, though often increased and accumulated, has never been widely diffused. On the other hand, we shall find that, when the inductive method has predominated, the diffusion of knowledge has always been considerable, or, at all events, has been beyond comparison greater than when deduction was prevalent. This holds good, not only of different countries, but also of different periods in the same country. It even holds good of different individuals in the same period, and in the same country. If, in any civilized nation, two men, equally gifted, were to propound some new and startling conclusion, and one of these men were to defend his conclusion by reasoning from ideas or general principles, while the other man were to defend his by reasoning from particular and visible facts, there can be no doubt that supposing all other things the same, the latter man would gain most adherents. His conclusion would be more easily diffused, simply because a direct appeal, in the first instance, to palpable facts, strikes the vulgar with immediate effect; while an appeal to principles is beyond their ken, and as they do not sympathize with it, they are apt to ridicule it. Facts seem to come home to every one, and are undeniable. Principles are not so obvious, and, being often disputed, they have, to those who do not grasp them, an unreal and illusory appearance, which weakens their influence. Hence it is that inductive science, which always gives the first place to facts, is essentially popular, and has on its side those innumerable persons who will not listen to the more refined and subtle teachings of deductive science. Hence, too, we find historically that the establishment of the modern inductive philosophy, with its varied and attractive experiments, its material appliances, and its constant appeal to the senses, has been intimately connected with the awakening of the public mind, and coincides with that spirit of inquiry, and with that love of liberty, which have been constantly advancing since the sixteenth century. We may assuredly say, that scepticism and democracy are the two leading features of this great scientific movement. The seventeenth century, which ushered in the Baconian philosophy, was remarkable for its insubordinate spirit, especially in the country where that philosophy originated, and where it most flourished. In the next age, it was transplanted into France, and there, too, it worked upon the popular mind, and was, as I have already pointed out, one of the principal causes of the French Revolution.

If we look still closer into this interesting question, we shall find further corroboration of the view, that the inferences of an inductive philosophy are more likely to be diffused than those of a deductive one. Inductive science rests immediately upon experience, or, at all events, upon experiment, which is merely experience artificially modified. Now, an immense majority of mankind, even in the most advanced countries, are, by the constitution of their minds, incapable of seizing general principles and applying them to daily affairs, without doing serious mischief, either to themselves, or to others. Such an application requires not only great dexterity, but also a knowledge of those disturbing causes which affect the operation of all general theorems. The task, being so difficult to perform, is rarely attempted; and average men, possessed of a tolerably sound judgment, do, with good reason, rely mainly on experience, which is to them a safer and more useful guide than any principle, however accurate and scientific it might be. This begets in their minds a prejudice on behalf of experimental inquiries, and a corresponding dislike of the opposite and more speculative method. And it can, I think, hardly be doubted, that one of the causes of the triumph of the Baconian philosophy, is the growth of the industrious classes, whose business-like and methodical habits are eminently favourable to empirical observations of the uniformities of sequence, since, indeed, on the accuracy of such observations the success of all practical affairs depends. Certainly, we find that the overthrow of the purely deductive scholasticism of the Middle Ages has been every where accompanied by the spread of trade; and whoever will carefully study the history of Europe, will discern many traces of a connexion between the two movements, both of which are marked by an increasing respect for material and empirical interests, and a disregard of ideal and speculative pursuits.

The relation between all this and the popular tendency of induction, is obvious. For one person who can think, there are at least a hundred persons who can observe. An accurate observer is, no doubt, rare; but an accurate thinker is far rarer. Of this, the proofs are too abundant to be disputed. Indeed, no one can mix with his fellow-creatures, without seeing how much more natural it is for them to notice, than to reflect; and how extremely unusual it is to meet with any one, whose conversation, or whose writings, bear marks of patient and original thought. And, inasmuch as thinkers are more prone to accumulate ideas, while observers are more prone to accumulate facts, the overwhelming predominance of the observing class is a decisive reason why induction, which begins with facts, is always more popular than deduction, which begins with ideas. It is often said, and probably with truth, that all deduction is preceded by induction; so that, in every syllogism, the major premiss, however obvious and necessary it may appear, is merely a generalization of facts, or a record of what the senses had already observed. But this opinion, whether true or false, does not affect what I have just stated, because it concerns the origin of our knowledge, and not its subsequent treatment; that is to say, it is a metaphysical opinion, rather than a logical one. For, even supposing that all deduction rests ultimately on induction, it is, nevertheless, certain that there are innumerable cases in which the induction takes place at so early a period of life that we are unconscious of it, and can by no effort recall the process. The axioms of geometry afford a good specimen of this. No one can tell when or how he first believed that the whole is greater than its part, or that things which are equal to the same thing are equal to one another. All these preliminary steps are concealed from us, and the strength and dexterity of deduction are displayed in the subsequent steps by which the major premiss is adjusted, and, as it were, fitted to the minor. This often requires great subtlety of thought, and, in every instance, the external world is put aside, and lost sight of. The process, being ideal, has no concern, either with observations or experiments. The suggestions of the senses are shut out, while the mind passes through a long train of successive syllogisms, in which each conclusion is turned into the premiss of a new argument, until, at length, an inference is deductively obtained, which, to those who merely hear it enunciated, seems to have no connexion with the first premisses, though, in reality, it is the necessary consequence of them.

A method, so recondite, and so hidden from the public gaze, can never command the public sympathy. Unless, therefore, the human mind should undergo some remarkable change in its nature as well as in its resources, the sensuous process of working upwards from particular facts to general principles, will always be more attractive than the ideal process of working downwards from principles to facts. In both cases, there is no doubt a line of argument essentially ideal; just as, in both cases, there is an assemblage of facts essentially sensuous. No method is pure, or stands entirely by itself. But, inasmuch as, in induction, the facts are more prominent than the ideas, while, in deduction, the ideas are more prominent than the facts, it is evident that conclusions arrived at by the former plan, will, as a general rule, obtain a wider assent than conclusions arrived at by the latter plan. Obtaining a wider assent, they will produce more decisive results, and will be more likely to shape the national character and influence the course of national affairs.

The only exception to this, is theology. There, the inductive method, as I have already observed, is inapplicable, and nothing remains but deduction, which is quite sufficient for the purposes of the theologian. For, he has a peculiar resource which supplies him with general principles, from which he can argue; and the possession of this resource forms the fundamental difference between him and the man of science. Science is the result of inquiry;

theology is the result of faith. In the one, the spirit of doubt; in the other, the spirit of belief. In science, originality is the parent of discovery, and is, therefore, a merit; in theology, it is the parent of heresy, and is, therefore, a crime. Every system of religion the world has yet seen, recognizes faith as an indispensable duty; but to every system of science it is a hindrance, instead of a duty, inasmuch as it discourages those inquisitive and innovating habits on which all intellectual progress depends. The theologian, thus turning credulity into an honour, and valuing men in proportion as they are simple-minded and easy of belief, has little need to trouble himself with facts, which, indeed, he sets at open defiance, in his eagerness to narrate portentous, and often miraculous, events. To the inductive philosopher, such a license is forbidden. He is obliged to ground his inferences on facts which no one disputes, or which, at all events, any one can either verify for himself, or see verified by others. And if he does not adopt this course, his inferences, be they ever so true, will have the greatest difficulty in working themselves into the popular mind, because they will savour of subtlety and refinement of thought, which, more than any thing else, predisposes common understandings to reject the conclusions at which philosophers arrive.

From the facts and arguments contained in this and the preceding chapter, the reader will, I trust, be able to see why it was that the Scotch intellect, during the seventeenth and eighteenth centuries, was preëminently deductive; and also why it was that, in the eighteenth century, the Scotch literature, notwithstanding its brilliancy, its power, and the splendid discoveries of which it was the vehicle, produced little or no effect on the nation at large. That literature, by its bold and innovating character, seemed peculiarly fitted to disturb ancient prejudices, and to rouse up a spirit of inquiry. But its method, both of investigation and of proof, was too refined to suit ordinary understandings. Therefore, upon ordinary understandings it was inoperative. In Scotland, as in ancient Greece, and in modern Germany, the intellectual classes, being essentially deductive, have been unable to influence the main body of the people. They have considered things at too great an altitude, and at too great a remove. In Greece, Aristotle alone had a true idea of what induction really was. But even he knew nothing of crucial instances and the theory of averages, the two capital resources of that inductive philosophy which we now possess. Neither did he, nor any of the great German philosophers, nor any of the great Scotch philosophers, attach sufficient importance to the slow and cautious method of gradually rising from each generalization to the one immediately above it, without omitting any intermediate generalization. On this method, Bacon, indeed, insists too strongly, since many most important discoveries have been made independently of it, or, I should rather say, in contradiction to it. But it is a wonderful weapon, and none except men of real genius can dispense with its use. And when they do dispense with it, they cut themselves off from the general sympathies of their age and country. For, these small and proximate generalizations, which they neglect, are precisely those parts of philosophy which, being least removed from the region of visible facts, are best understood by the people, and, therefore, form the only common ground between thinkers and practitioners. They are a sort of middle term, which, being comprehended by both classes, is accessible to either. In all deductive reasoning, this intermediate, and, if I may so say, neutral, territory disappears, and the two classes have no meeting-place. Hence it is, that the Scotch philosophy, like the German philosophy, and like the Greek philosophy, has had no national influence. But in England, since the seventeenth century, and in France, since the eighteenth century, the prevailing philosophy has been inductive, and has, therefore, not only affected the intellectual classes, but also moved the public mind. The German philosophers are far superior, both in depth and in comprehensiveness, to the philosophers either of France or of England. Their profound researches have, however, done so little for their country, that the German people are every way inferior to the French and English people. So, too, in the philosophy of ancient Greece, we find a vast body of massive and original thought, and, what is infinitely better, we find a boldness of inquiry and a passionate love of truth, such as no modern nation has surpassed, and few modern nations have equalled. But the method of that philosophy was an insuperable barrier to its propagation. The people were untouched, and went grovelling on in their old folly, a prey to superstitions, most of which the great thinkers despised, and often attacked, but could by no means root out. Bad, however, as those superstitions were, we may confidently say that they were less noxious, that is, less detrimental to the happiness of man, than the repulsive and horrible notions advocated by the Scotch clergy, and sanctioned by the Scotch people. And on those notions the Scotch philosophy could make no impression. In Scotland, during the eighteenth century, superstition and science, the most irreconcilable of all enemies, flourished side by side, unable to weaken each other, and unable, indeed, to come into collision with each other. There was co-existence without contact. The two forces kept apart, and the result was, that, while the Scotch thinkers were creating a noble and most enlightened literature, the Scotch people, refusing to listen to those great masters of wisdom which their country possessed, remained in darkness, leaving the blind to follow the blind, and no one there to help them.

It is, indeed, curious to observe how little effect was produced by the many great works written by Scotchmen in the eighteenth century. If we except the *Wealth of Nations,* I can hardly call to mind one which has perceptibly influenced public opinion. The reason of this exception may be easily explained. The *Wealth of Nations* restricted the action of government within narrower limits than had ever been assigned to it by any other book of great merit. No previous political writer of admitted genius, had left so much to the people, and had demanded for them so much liberty in managing their own affairs, as Adam Smith did. The *Wealth of Nations,* being thus eminently a democratic book, was sure to find favour in Scotland, which was eminently a democratic country. Directly men heard its conclusions, they were prejudiced in favour of its arguments. So, too, in England, that love of liberty, which for many centuries has been our leading characteristic, and which does us more real honour than all our conquests, all our literature, and all our philosophy put together, invariably causes a popular bias on behalf of any claim to freedom. We, therefore, notwithstanding the activity of interested parties, were predisposed to the side of free trade, as one of the means of letting each man do what he liked with his own. But to imagine that ordinary minds are capable of mastering such a work as the *Wealth of Nations,* and of following without confusion its long and intricate arguments, is simply absurd. It has been read by tens of thousands of persons, who accept its conclusions because they like them; which is merely saying, because the movement of the age tends that way. The other great work of Adam Smith, namely the *Theory of Moral Sentiments,* has had no influence except on a very small class of metaphysicians, although its style is, as some think, superior to the *Wealth of Nations,* and it is certainly easier to understand. It is, moreover, much shorter, which, to most readers, is no small recommendation; and it deals with subjects of great interest, which come home to the feelings of all. But the age, not caring for its conclusions, neglected its arguments. On the other hand, the *Wealth of Nations* harmonized with the general tendency, and its success was supreme. It quickly moved, not only philosophers, but even statesmen and politicians, who eventually put into force its leading recommendations, though, as their laws and their speeches abundantly prove, they have never succeeded in mastering those great principles which underlie it, and of which the freedom of trade is but a minor accessory.

Putting aside the *Wealth of Nations,* we shall find that the Scotch literature of the eighteenth century did scarcely any thing for Scotland, considered as a whole. How it has failed in its great aim of weakening superstition, is but too apparent to whoever has travelled in that country, and observed the habits and turn of mind still predominant. Many able and enlightened men who live there, are so cowed by the general spirit, that, for their own comfort, and for the peace of their families, they make no resistance, but tacitly comply with what they heartily despise. That they err in doing so, I, at least, firmly believe; though I know that many honest, and in every respect competent, judges are of opinion, that no man is bound to be a martyr, or to jeopardize his personal interests, unless he clearly sees his way to some immediate public good. To me, however, it appears that it is a narrow view, and that the first duty of every one is to set his face in direct opposition to what he believes to be false, and, having done that, leave the results of his conduct to take care of themselves. Still, the temptation to a contrary course is always very strong, and, in a country like Scotland, is by many deemed irresistible. In no other Protestant nation, and, indeed, in no Catholic nation except Spain, will a man who is known to hold unorthodox opinions, find his life equally uncomfortable. In a few of the large towns, he may possibly escape animadversion, if his sentiments are not too bold, and are not too openly expressed. If he is timid and taciturn, his heresy may, perchance, be overlooked. But even in large towns, impunity is the exception, and not the rule. Even in the capital of Scotland, in the centre of intelligence which once boasted of being the Modern Athens, a whisper will quickly circulate that such an one is to be avoided, for that he is a free-thinker; as if free-thinking were a crime, or as if it were not better to be a free-thinker than a slavish thinker. In other parts, that is, in Scotland generally, the state of things is far worse. I speak, not on vague rumour, but from what I know as existing at the present time, and for the accuracy of which I vouch and hold myself responsible. I challenge any one to contradict my assertion, when I say that, at this moment, nearly all over Scotland, the finger of scorn is pointed at every man, who, in the exercise of his sacred and inalienable right of free judgment, refuses to acquiesce in those religious notions, and to practise those religious customs, which time, indeed, has consecrated, but many of which are repulsive to the eye of reason, though to all of them, however irrational they may be, the people adhere with sullen and inflexible obstinacy. Knowing that these words will be widely read and circulated in Scotland, and averse as I naturally am to bring on myself the hostility of a nation, for whose many sterling and valuable qualities I entertain sincere respect, I do, nevertheless, deliberately affirm, that in no civilized country is toleration so little understood, and that in none is the spirit of bigotry and of persecution so extensively diffused. Nor can any one wonder that such should be the case, who observes what is going on there. The churches are as crowded as they were in the Middle Ages, and are filled with devout and ignorant worshippers, who flock together to listen to opinions of which the Middle Ages alone were worthy. Those opinions, they treasure up, and, when they return to their homes, or enter into the daily business of life, they put them in force. And the result is, that there runs through the entire country a sour and fanatical spirit, an aversion to innocent gaiety, a disposition to limit the enjoyments of others, and a love of inquiring into the opinions of others, and of interfering with them, such as is hardly any where else to be found; while, in the midst of all this, there flourishes a national creed, gloomy and austere to the last degree, a creed which is full of forebodings and threats and horrors of every sort, and which rejoices in proclaiming to mankind how wretched and miserable they are, how small a portion of them can be saved, and what an overwhelming majority is necessarily reserved for excruciating, unspeakable, and eternal agony.

Before bringing this volume to a close, it may be fitting that I should narrate an event, which, notwithstanding its recent occurrence, and the great attention it excited at the time, has, amid the pressure of weightier matters, fallen into comparative oblivion, although it is full of interest to those who study the various forms of national character, while it, moreover, supplies an admirable illustration of the essential antagonism which still exists between the Scotch and English minds; an antagonism extremely remarkable, when found among nations, both of whom, besides being contiguous, and constantly mixing together, speak the same language, read the same books, belong to the same empire, and possess the same interests, and yet are, in many important respects, as different, as if there had never been any means of their influencing each other, and as if they had never had anything in common.

In the year 1853, the cholera, after having committed serious ravages in many parts of Europe, visited Scotland. There, it was sure to find numerous victims among a badly fed, badly housed, and not over-cleanly people. For, if there is one thing better established than another respecting this disease, it is that it invariably attacks, with the greatest effect, those classes who, from poverty or from sloth, are imperfectly nourished, neglect their persons, and live in dirty, ill-drained, or ill-ventilated dwellings. In Scotland, such classes are very numerous. In Scotland, therefore, the cholera must needs be very fatal. In this, there was nothing mysterious. On the contrary, the mystery would have been if an epidemic, like the Asiatic cholera, had spared a country like Scotland, where all the materials were collected on which pestilence feeds, and where filth, penury, and disorder, abound on every side.

Under these circumstances, it must have been evident, not merely to men of science, but to all men of plain, sound understanding, who would apply their minds to the matter without prejudice, that the Scotch had only one way of successfully grappling with their terrible enemy. It behoved them to feed their poor, to cleanse their cesspools, and to ventilate their houses. If they had done this, and done it quickly, thousands of lives would have been spared. But they neglected it, and the country was thrown into mourning. Nay, they not only neglected it, but, moved by that dire superstition which sits like an incubus upon them, they adopted a course which, if it had been carried into full operation, would have aggravated the calamity to a frightful extent. It is well known that, whenever an epidemic is raging, physical exhaustion and mental depression, make the human frame more liable to it, and are, therefore, especially to be guarded against. But, though this is a matter of common notoriety, the Scotch clergy, backed, sad to say, by the general voice of the Scotch people, wished the public authorities to take a step which was certain to cause physical exhaustion, and to encourage mental depression. In the name of religion, whose offices they thus abused and perverted to the detriment of man, instead of employing them for his benefit, they insisted on the propriety of ordering a national fast, which, in so superstitious a country, was sure to be rigidly kept, and, being rigidly kept, was equally sure to enfeeble thousands of delicate persons, and, before twenty-four hours were passed, prepare them to receive that deadly poison which was already lurking around them, and which, hitherto, they had just strength enough to resist. The public fast was also to be accompanied by a public humiliation, in order that nothing might be wanting to appal the mind and fill it with terror. On the same occasion, the preachers were to thunder from their pulpits and proclaim aloud the sins of the land; while the poor benighted people, panic-struck, were to sit in awe, were to remain the whole day without proper nourishment, and retire to their beds, weeping and starved. Then it was hoped that the Deity would be propitiated, and the plague be stayed. As soon as the entire nation had taken the course, which, of all others, was most certain to increase the mortality, it was believed that man having done his worst, the Almighty would interpose, would violate the laws of nature, and, by working a miracle, would preserve his creatures from what, without a miracle, would be the inevitable consequence of their own deliberate act.

This was the scheme projected by the Scotch clergy, and they were determined to put it into execution. To give greater effect to it, they called upon England to help them, and in the autumn of 1853, the Presbytery of Edinburgh, thinking that from their position they were bound to take the lead, caused their Moderator to address a letter, ostensibly to the English Minister, but in reality to the English nation. In this choice production, a copy of which is now lying before me, the Home Secretary is assured that the members of the Presbytery had delayed appointing a day for fasting and humiliation on their own ecclasiastical authority, because they thought it likely that one would be appointed by the royal authority. But as this had not been done, the Presbytery respectfully requested to be informed if it was intended to be done. They apologized for the liberty they were taking; they had no desire unduly to intrude themselves; neither did they wish the Home Secretary to answer their question unless he felt himself justified in doing so. Still, if he were able to answer it, they would be glad. For, there was no doubt that Asiatic cholera was in the country; and such being the case, the Presbytery of Edinburgh were interested in knowing if the appointment by the Queen of a national fast was in contemplation.[300]

This letter, which, through the medium of the press, was sure to become well known and to be widely read, was evidently intended to act on public opinion in England. It was, in fact, a covert reproach on the English Government for having neglected its spiritual duties, and for not having perceived that fasting was the most effectual way of stopping an epidemic. In Scotland, generally, it received great praise, and was regarded as a dignified rebuke addressed to the irreligious habits of the English people, who, seeing the cholera at their doors, merely occupied themselves with sanatory measures, and carnal devices to improve the public health, showing thereby that they trusted too much to the arms of the flesh. In England, on the other hand, this manifesto of the Scotch Church was met with almost universal ridicule, and,

300. "The members were of opinion," writest the Moderator, "The members were of opinion that it was likely, in the circumstances, that a national fast would be appointed on royal authority. For this reason, they delayed making an appointment for this locality, and directed me, in the mean time, respectfully to request that you would be pleased to say—if you feel yourself at liberty to do so—whether the appointment of a national fast by the Queen is in contemplation. The Presbytery hope to be excused for the liberty they use in preferring this request."

indeed, found no favourers except among the most ignorant and credulous part of the nation. The minister to whom it was addressed, was Lord Palmerston, a man of vast experience, and perhaps better acquainted with public opinion than any politician of his time. He, being well aware of the difference between Scotland and England, knew that what was suitable for one country was not suitable for the other, and that notions which the Scotch deemed religious, the English deemed fanatical. On a former occasion, the imperial government, yielding to the clamour which a few active and interested men succeeded in raising, had been foolish enough to set themselves in this matter in opposition to the temper of the age, and to enjoin public observances which, happily, were not strictly obeyed, but which, in so far as they were obeyed, heightened the general terror by reinforcing natural fears with supernatural ones, and thus, depressing the nervous system, increased the chance of mortality from the pestilence. To have the plague in our country is bad enough, since, do what we may, many victims will be struck down by it. But a fearful responsibility is entailed upon those who, at such a period, instead of exerting themselves to check its ravages, either by precautionary measures, or by soothing and re-assuring the people, do every thing in their power to aggravate the calamity, by encouraging that superstitious dread which weakens the popular energy at the very moment when energy is most requisite, and troubles the coolness, the self-reliance, and self-possession, without which no crisis of national danger can ever be averted.

This time, however, there was no risk of the government committing so serious a blunder. Lord Palmerston, who knew that the sound sense of the English people would support him in what he was doing, directed a letter to be sent to the Presbytery of Edinburgh, which, unless I am greatly mistaken, will, in future ages, be quoted as an interesting document for illustrating the history of the progress of public opinion. A century ago, any statesman who had written such a letter, would have been driven from office by a storm of general indignation. Two centuries ago, the consequences to him would have been still more disastrous, and would, indeed, have ruined him socially, as well as politically. For, in it, he sets at defiance those superstitious fancies respecting the origin of disease, which were once universally cherished as an essential part of every religious creed. Traditions, the memory of which is preserved in the theological literature of all Pagan countries, of all Catholic countries, and of all Protestant countries, are quietly put aside, as if they were matters of no moment, and as if it were not worth while to discuss them. The Scotch clergy, occupying the old ground on which the members of their profession had always been accustomed to stand, took for granted that the cholera was the result of the Divine anger, and was intended to chastize our sins. In the reply which they now received from the English Government, a doctrine was enunciated, which to Englishmen seems right enough, but which to Scotchmen sounded very profane. The Presbytery were informed, that the affairs of this world are regulated by natural laws, on the observance or neglect of which the weal or woe of mankind depends.[301] One of those laws connects disease with the exhalations of bodies; and it is by virtue of this law that contagion spreads, either in crowded cities, or in places where vegetable decomposition is going on. Man, by exerting himself, can disperse or neutralize these noxious influences. The appearance of the cholera proves that he has not exerted himself. The towns have not been purified; hence the root of the evil. The Home Secretary, therefore, advised the Presbytery of Edinburgh, that it was better to cleanse than to fast. He thought that the plague being upon them, activity was preferable to humiliation. It was now autumn, and before the hot weather would return, a considerable period must elapse. That period should be employed in destroying the causes of disease, by improving the abodes of the poor. If this were done, all would go well. Otherwise, pestilence would be sure to revisit them, "in spite"—I quote the words of the English minister—"in spite of all the prayers and fastings of a united, but inactive nation."[302]

This correspondence between the Scotch clergy and the English

301. "The weal or woe of mankind depends upon the observance or neglect of those laws."

302. "Lord Palmerston would, therefore, suggest that the best course which the people of this country can pursue to deserve that the further progress of the cholera should be stayed, will be to employ the interval that will elapse between the present time and the beginning of next spring in planning and executing measures by which those portions of their towns and cities which are inhabited by the poorest classes, and which, from the nature of things, must most need purification and improvement, may be freed from those causes and sources of contagion which, if allowed to remain, will infallibly breed pestilence, and be fruitful in death, in spite of all the prayers and fastings of a united, but inactive nation."

statesman, is not to be regarded as a mere passing episode of light or temporary interest. On the contrary, it represents that terrible struggle between theology and science, which, having begun in the persecution of science and in the martyrdom of scientific men, has, in these later days, taken a happier turn, and is now manifestly destroying that old theological spirit, which has brought so much misery and ruin upon the world. The ancient superstition, which was once universal, but is now slowly though surely dying away, represented the Deity as being constantly moved to anger, delighting in seeing His creatures abase and mortify themselves, taking pleasure in their sacrifices and their austerities, and, notwithstanding all they could do, constantly inflicting on them the most grievous punishments, among which the different forms of pestilence were conspicuous. It is by science, and by science alone, that these horrible delusions are being dissipated. Events, which formerly were deemed supernatural visitations, are now shown to depend upon natural causes, and to be amenable to natural remedies. Man can predict them, and man can deal with them. Being the inevitable result of their own antecedents, no room is left for the notion of their being special inflictions. This great change in our opinions is fatal to theology, but is serviceable to religion. For, by it, science, instead of being the enemy of religion becomes its ally. Religion is to each individual according to the inward light with which he is endowed. In different characters, therefore, it assumes different forms, and can never be reduced to one common and arbitrary rule. Theology, on the other hand, claiming authority over all minds, and refusing to recognize their essential divergence, seeks to compel them to a single creed, and sets up one standard of absolute truth, by which it tests every one's opinions; presumptuously condemning those who disagree with that standard. Such arrogant pretensions need means of support. Those means are threats, which, in ignorant times, are universally believed, and which, by causing fear, produce submission. Hence it is, that the books of every theological system narrate acts of the grossest cruelty, which, without the least hesitation, are ascribed to the direct interposition of God. Humane and gentle natures revolt at such cruelties, even while they try to believe them. It is the business of science to purify theology, by showing that there has been no cruelty, because there has been no interposition. Science ascribes to natural causes, what theology ascribes to supernatural ones. According to this view, the calamities with which the world is afflicted, are the result of the ignorance of man, and not of the interference of God. We must not, therefore, ascribe to Him what is due to our own folly, or to our own vice. We must not calumniate an all-wise and all-merciful Being, by imputing to Him those little passions which move ourselves, as if He were capable of rage, of jealousy, and of revenge, and as if He, with outstretched arm, were constantly employed in aggravating the sufferings of mankind, and making the miseries of the human race more poignant than they would otherwise be.

That this remarkable improvement in religious ideas is due to the progress of physical science, is apparent, not only from general arguments which would lead us to anticipate that such must be the case, but also from the historical fact, that the gradual destruction of the old theology is every where preceded by the growth and diffusion of physical truths. The more we know of the laws of nature, the more clearly do we understand that every thing which happens in the material world, pestilence, earthquake, famine, or whatever it may be, is the necessary result of something which had previously happened. Cause produces effect, and the effect becomes, in its turn, a cause of other effects. In that operation we see no gap, and we admit of no pause. To us, the chain is unbroken; the constancy of nature is unviolated. Our minds become habituated to contemplate all physical phenomena as presenting an orderly, uniform, and spontaneous march, and running on in one regular and uninterrupted sequence. This is the scientific view. It is also the religious view. Against it, we have the theological view; but that which has already lost its hold over the intellect of men is now losing its hold over their affections, and is so manifestly perishing, that at present no educated person ventures to defend it, without so limiting and guarding his meaning, as to concede to its opponents nearly every point which is really at issue.

While, however, in regard to the material world, the narrow notions formerly entertained, are, in the most enlightened countries, almost extinct, it must be confessed that, in regard to the moral world, the progress of opinion is less rapid. The same men who believe that Nature is undisturbed by miraculous interposition, refuse to believe that Man is equally undisturbed. In the one case, they assert the scientific doctrine of regularity; in the other, they assert the theological doctrine of irregularity. The reason of this difference of opinion is, that the movements of nature are less complex than the movements of man. Being less complex, they are more easily studied, and more quickly understood. Hence we find, that while natural science has long been cultivated, historical science hardly yet exists. Our knowledge of the circumstances which determine the course of mankind, is still so imperfect, and has been so badly digested, that it has produced scarcely any effect on popular ideas. Philosophers, indeed, are aware, that here, as elsewhere, there must be a necessary connexion between even the most remote and dissimilar events. They know that every discrepancy is capable of being reconciled, though we, in the present state of knowledge, may be unequal to the task. This is their faith, and nothing can wean them from it. But the great majority of people have a different faith. They believe that what is unexplained is inexplicable, and that what is inexplicable is supernatural. Science has explained an immense number of physical phenomena, and therefore, even to the vulgar, those phenomena no longer seem supernatural, but are ascribed to natural causes. On the other hand, science has not yet explained the phenomena of history; consequently, the theological spirit lays hold of them, and presses them into its own service. In this way, there has arisen that famous and ancient theory, which has received the name of the moral government of the world. It is a high-sounding title and imposes on many, who, if they examined its pretensions, would never be duped by them. For, like that other notion which we have just considered, it is not only unscientific, but it is eminently irreligious. It is, in fact, an impeachment of one of the noblest attributes of the Deity. It is a slur on the Omniscience of God. It assumes that the fate of nations, instead of being the result of preceding and surrounding events, is specially subject to the control and interference of Providence. It assumes, that there are great public emergencies, in which such interference is needed. It assumes, that, without the interference, the course of affairs, could not run smoothly; that they would be jangled and out of tune; that the play and harmony of the whole would be incomplete. And thus it is, that the very men who, at one moment, proclaim the Divine Omniscience, do, at the next moment, advocate a theory which reduces that Omniscience to nothing, since it imputes to an All-Wise Being, that the scheme of human affairs, of which He must, from the beginning, have foreseen every issue and every consequence, is so weakly contrived as to be liable to be frustrated; that it has not turned out as He could have wished; that it has been baffled by His own creatures, and that, to preserve its integrity, its operations must be tampered with, and its disorders redressed. The great Architect of the universe, the Creator and Designer of all existing things, is likened to some clumsy mechanic, who knows his trade so ill, that he has to be called in to alter the working of his own machine, to supply its deficiencies, to fill up its flaws, and to rectify its errors.

It is time that such unworthy notions should come to an end. It is time that what has long been known to philosophers, should also be known to historians, and that the history of mankind should cease to be troubled by what, to those who are imbued with the scientific spirit, must seem little better than arrant trifling. Of two things, choose one. Either deny the Omniscience of the Creator, or else admit it. If you deny it, you deny what, to my mind at least, is a fundamental truth, and, on these matters, there can be no sympathy between us. But if you admit the Omniscience of God, beware of libelling what you profess to defend. For when you assert what is termed the moral government of the world, you slander Omniscience, inasmuch as you declare that the mechanism of the entire universe, including the actions both of Nature and of Man, planned as it is by Infinite Wisdom, is unequal to its duties, unless that same Wisdom does from time to time interfere with it. You assert, in fact, either that Omniscience has been deceived, or that Omnipotence has been defeated. Surely, they who believe, and whose pride and happiness it is to believe, that there is a Power above all and before all, knowing all and creating all, ought not to fall into such a snare as this. They who, dissatisfied with this little world of sense, seek to raise their minds to something which the senses are unable to grasp, can hardly fail, on deeper reflection, to perceive how coarse and material is that theological prejudice, which ascribes to such a Power the vulgar functions of a temporal ruler, arrays him in the garb of an earthly potentate, and represents him as meddling here and meddling there, uttering threats, inflicting punishments, bestowing rewards. These are base and grovelling conceptions, the offspring of ignorance and of darkness. Such gross and sordid notions are but one remove from actual idolatry. They are the draff and offal of a by-gone age, and we will not have them obtruded here. Well suited they were to those old barbarous times, when men, being unable to refine their ideas, were, therefore, unable to purify their creed. Now, however, they jar upon us; they do not assimilate with other parts of our knowledge; they are incongruous; their concord is gone. Every thing is against them. They stand alone; there is nothing left with which they harmonize. The whole scope and tendency of modern thought force upon our minds conceptions of regularity and of law, to which they are diametrically opposed. Even those who cling to them, do so from the influence of tradition, rather than from complete and unswerving belief. That child-like and unhesitating faith, with which the doctrine of interposition was once received, is succeeded by a cold and lifeless assent, very different from the enthusiasm of former times. Soon, too, this will vanish, and men will cease to be terrified by phantoms which their own ignorance has reared. This age, haply, may not witness the emancipation; but, so surely as the human mind advances, so surely will that emancipation come. It may come quicker than any one expects. For, we are stepping on far and fast. The signs of the time are all around, and they who list may read. The handwriting is on the wall; the fiat has gone forth; the ancient empire shall be subverted; the dominion of superstition, already decaying, shall break away, and crumble into dust; and new life being breathed into the confused and chaotic mass, it shall be clearly seen, that, from the beginning there has been no discrepancy, no incongruity, no disorder, no interruption, no interference; but that all the events which surround us, even to the furthest limits of the material creation, are but different parts of a single scheme, which is permeated by one glorious principle of universal and undeviating regularity.

Index